POWER
WITHOUT
RESPONSIBILITY

Power Without Responsibility is a classic, authoritative and engaged introduction to the history, sociology, theory and politics of media and communication studies. Written in a lively and accessible style, it is regarded as the standard book on the British media, and has become required reading for students and teachers of media and communication studies. Previous editions have been translated into Arabic, Chinese, Korean and Portuguese.

This new edition has been substantially revised to bring it up to date with new developments in the media industry. Its three new chapters describe the battle for the soul of the internet, the impact of the internet on society, and the rise of new media in Britain. In addition, it examines the recuperation of the BBC, how international and European regulation is changing the British media, and why Britain has the least trusted press in Europe.

James Curran is Professor of Communications at Goldsmiths College, University of London. **Jean Seaton** is Professor of Media History at the University of Westminster.

POWER
WITHOUT
RESPONSIBILITY

Some reviews of previous editions:

'. . . the best guide to the British Media.'
Nick Cohen, *New Statesman*

'This is a useful and timely book.'
Richard Hoggart, *Times Educational Supplement*

'Many students and young people in and around the British media will make *Power Without Responsibility* into a new orthodoxy.'
Jeremy Tunstall, *Encounter*

'Excellent new study.'
Tribune

'A classic text.'
Stage and Television Today

'An invaluable general textbook for the specialist student of communications as well as a guide into a complex area for social scientists.'
Teaching Politics

'Curran and Seaton's writing, scholarly but not academicist, manages that rare and difficult task of rendering complex information and different theoretical approaches in a style open to teachers and post-16 students alike. No reading list for courses in media or the social sciences should be without *Power Without Responsibility*. It not only fuels the mind, it liberates it.'
Journal of Educational Television

POWER
WITHOUT
RESPONSIBILITY

The press,
broadcasting, and new media
in Britain

Sixth edition

James Curran and *Jean Seaton*

Routledge
Taylor & Francis Group

LONDON AND NEW YORK

First edition published 1981
by Fontana
Second edition published 1985
by Methuen & Co. Ltd

Third edition published 1988
Fourth edition published 1991
Fifth edition published 1997
Reprinted 1998, 2000, 2002
all by Routledge

Sixth edition published 2003
by Routledge
11 New Fetter Lane, London EC4P 4EE

Simultaneously published in the USA and Canada
by Routledge
29 West 35th Street, New York, NY 10001

Routledge is an imprint of the Taylor & Francis Group

© 1981, 1985, 1988, 1991, 1997, 2003
James Curran and Jean Seaton

Typeset in Times by M Rules
Printed and bound in Great Britain by MPG Books Ltd, Bodmin

British Library Cataloguing in Publication Data
A catalogue record for this book is available from the British Library

Library of Congress Cataloging in Publication Data
A catalog record for this book has been requested

ISBN 0-415-24389-0 (hbk)
ISBN 0-415-24390-4 (pbk)

To Joan Seaton and the memory of
Albert Seaton, Nancie and Geoffrey Curran

Contents

About the authors

James Curran is Professor of Communications at Goldsmiths College, University of London. He is the author or editor (some jointly) of *Mass Communication and Society*; *The British Press*; *Newspaper History*; *Culture, Society and the Media*; *British Cinema History*; *Media, Culture and Society: A Critical Reader*; *Bending Reality*; *Impacts and Influences*; *Mass Media and Society*; *Cultural Studies and Communications*; *Media, Ritual and Identity*; *Media Organisations In Society*; *De-Westernizing Media Studies*; *Media and Power*; *Contesting Media Power* (forthcoming). He has been an amateur journalist, as a weekly columnist for *The Times* and editor of *New Socialist*, and a Visiting Professor at the Universities of California, Oslo and Stockholm.

Jean Seaton is Professor of Media History at the University of Westminster. She is editor (with Ben Pimlott) of *The Media in British Politics*, (with Tim Allen) *The Media of Conflict*, and *Politics and the Media at the Turn of the Millennium*. Her next book is called *Carnage and the Media*. She has been commissioned by the BBC to write the volume of the official history of the Corporation during the 1980s.

Acknowledgements

Although this book is very much a joint effort there has been some division of labour. Thus Jean Seaton has concentrated on broadcasting and the sociology of the mass media (chapters 8–15, 19, 20 and 22), and James Curran on the history and political theory of the press, and on new media (chapters 1–7, 16–18, 21, 23–4). However, in some parts of the book it is impossible to say where the work of one author ends and that of the other begins.

We would like to thank the BBC Written Archive Centre for the help of its staff and the use of copyright material, the IBA for information on audiences, and the British Library of Economic and Political Science for permission to quote from the unpublished diary of Hugh Dalton. We are also obliged to J. Walter Thompson Ltd, Leo Burnett Ltd (incorporating the London Press Exchange), the Mirror Group, Associated Newspapers, the Thomson Organization, Express Newspapers, the *Daily Telegraph,* and the *Guardian* for access to company archives and research reports.

We are very grateful to Nick Garnham, Anthony Smith, Colin Seymour-Ure, Malory Wober, Simon Clarke, Simon Frith, Keith McLelland, Nick Hartley, Alan Lovell and Angela Smith for making many useful comments on draft chapters. James Curran would also like to thank Andrew Goodwin for his invaluable contribution to Chapter 6, as well as Angus Douglas and Garry Whannel for skilfully preparing the content analysis summarized in Chapter 7, and Brendon Wall and Gill Bucknall for help in compiling Table 3 (in the fourth edition).

We owe a great debt to Mies Rule, Janet Sandell and Angela Smith for typing successive drafts of past editions of this book with their usual speed, accuracy and congeniality.

In relation to this edition, James Curran would like in particular to thank Korinna Patelis for first educating him about the internet, and Jonathan Hardy for continuing his education. His thanks go to Nick Couldry and Colin Lusk for reading three chapters at short notice, and for making helpful comments. Finally, he would like to express very great appreciation to his colleague Richard Smith, who fed him with invaluable information for chapters 7, 18, 21 and 24.

Jean Seaton would like to thank the long succession of nannies who have helped look after her sons while various editions of this book were written. For the sixth edition, Timea Gorkova provided support and interest.

James Curran would like to thank his wife, Margaret Hung, for urging him to write his part of the book and for sustaining him – with her laughter, zaniness, intelligence and good sense – in the writing of it.

Finally, we are especially grateful for the great care with which Ben Pimlott read the manuscript. His detailed criticisms and suggestions immensely improved the final version of the book. We are also particularly indebted to him for giving us the title.

Preface to the sixth edition

This edition contains for the first time a section on the rise of new media (Part III). Chapter 16 describes the battle for control of the internet, while Chapter 17 assesses the net's influence on contemporary society. Chapter 18 examines the growth of new media in Britain, and assesses how much it has really changed the media system.

The history of the press and broadcasting has been recast to take account of the conversion of much of the national press to New Labour, and the revival of the BBC. In addition, Chapter 24 has been rewritten in order to register the increased influence of European and international politics on British media policy and development. Other parts of the book have been revised to take account of new trends and scholarship.

Part I

Press history

1

Whig press history as political mythology

The orthodox interpretation of the development of the British press has remained unchanged for over a century. 'The British press,' writes David Chaney, 'is generally agreed to have attained its freedom around the middle of the nineteenth century.'[1] This view, first advanced in the pioneering Victorian histories of journalism, has been repeated uncritically ever since in standard histories both of the press and of modern Britain.

The winning of press freedom is attributed partly to a heroic struggle against the state. The key events in this struggle are generally said to be the abolition of the Court of Star Chamber in 1641, the ending of press licensing in 1694, Fox's Libel Act, 1792, and the repeal of press taxation – the so-called 'taxes on knowledge' – in the period 1853 to 1861. Only with the last of these reforms, it is claimed, did the press finally become free.

This landmark in the history of Britain is also held to be the product of the capitalist development of the press. Indeed, some researchers place greater emphasis on the market evolution of the press than on its legal emancipation. 'The true censorship,' Professor Roach writes of the late Georgian press, 'lay in the fact that the newspaper had not yet reached financial independence, and consequently depended on the administration or the parties.' The growth of newspaper profits, largely from advertising, supposedly rescued the press from economic dependence on the state. This view has been restated succinctly by Ivon Asquith in a scholarly study of the early nineteenth-century press. 'Since sales were inadequate to cover the costs of producing a paper,' he writes,

> it was the growing income from advertising which provided the material base for the change of attitude from subservience to independence. . . . It is perhaps no exaggeration to say that the growth of advertising revenue was the most important single factor in enabling the press to emerge as the Fourth Estate of the realm.

Orthodox histories of the press, with their stress on the free market and legal emancipation as the foundation of press freedom, provide a powerful, mythological account with a contemporary moral. Thus, the historical account of the advertiser as the midwife of press freedom is invoked by journalists on the left as well as on the right to justify the role of advertising in the press. 'The dangerous dependence of newspapers on advertising,' wrote Francis Williams, a former editor of the Labour *Daily Herald*,

> has often been the theme of newspaper reformers – usually from outside its ranks. But the daily press would never have come into existence as a force in public and social life if it had not been for the need of men of commerce to advertise. Only through the growth of advertising did the press achieve independence.

Similarly, journalists sometimes cite the historic struggle against state control as grounds for opposing any state-sponsored reform of the press. For instance, John Whale concludes a brief historical account of state censorship with the warning that politicians are still seeking 'indirect ways of bringing state power to bear on unsympathetic journalism'. The principal way this is being manifested, he cautions, is in proposals to curb concentration of press ownership.

However, while Whig history is invoked to oppose change in the press, it is summoned as an ally to justify the fundamental reorganization of broadcasting. For instance, the Peacock Committee – appointed by the Thatcher government to investigate the funding of the BBC – retold the history of the dismantling of press censorship[2] as a prelude to arguing for the eventual removal of all broadcasting regulation (which it equated with 'censorship'). In effect, it deployed a particular view of newspaper history to advocate the reconstruction of television along the free market lines of the press.

Orthodox accounts of press history thus have policy implications for the present day. Part of the ideological resonance of these accounts stems also from their powerful evocation of the part played by the free press in empowering the people during the nineteenth century. According to the *New Cambridge Modern History*, financially independent newspapers became 'great organs of the public mind' which expressed public opinion and made governments accountable. The emergent, free press, it is also argued, made a vital contribution to the maturing of Britain's democracy by becoming more responsible and less partisan. Even a Marxist such as Raymond Williams noted with approval that after 1855 'most newspapers were able to drop their frantic pamphleteering',[3] while the radical historian Alan Lee portrayed the late Victorian period as a 'golden age' of British journalism.

Agreement among historians is not total. There is a continuing debate about when newspapers became independent of political parties. A number of historians also express misgivings about the growing 'commercialization' of the press, and are sharply critical of the first generation of press lords. But few contest the conventional wisdom, embalmed in a much acclaimed two-volume study by Stephen Koss, that there was 'a transition from official to popular control' of the press. Fewer still contest the central thesis of Whig press history that this 'progress of the press' was central to 'the broadening of political liberty'.

What follows is a long overdue attempt to reappraise the standard inter-pretation of press history.[4] It will indicate the need not merely to re-examine critically the accepted view of the historical emergence of a 'free' press but to stand it on its head. The period around the mid-nineteenth century, it will be argued, did not inaugurate a new era of press freedom and liberty; it estab-lished instead a new system of press censorship more effective than anything that had gone before. Market forces succeeded where legal repression had failed in conscripting the press to the social order.

Notes

1. Notes for each chapter have been limited, although their number has tended to grow with each new edition. An extensive bibliography is provided at the end of the book.
2. The Peacock Committee's historical account is extremely simplistic, and ignores the revisionist interpretations advanced by historians of the seventeenth- and eighteenth-century press.
3. R. Williams, *The Long Revolution* (Harmondsworth, Pelican, 1965), p. 218. He later modified his view in R. Williams, 'The press and popular culture: an his-torical perspective' in G. Boyce, J. Curran and P. Wingate (eds), *Newspaper History* (London, Constable, 1978).
4. A number of important studies of early nineteenth-century working-class poli-tics – notably by the Thompsons, Hollis, Wiener and Epstein – provide evidence that, by implication at least, casts doubt on the conventional Whig thesis of the triumphant rise of a free press in mid-Victorian Britain. The wider implications of these studies for reinterpreting press history have been buried, however, because their focus is on early working-class struggles rather than on the long-term development of journalism.

2

The struggle for a free press

The remarkably resilient Whig interpretation of press history is sustained by focusing attention upon mainstream commercial newspapers, while ignoring or downplaying the development of the radical press. Only if this selective perspective is maintained does the conventional view of the rise of a free press appear plausible.

During the second half of the eighteenth century and in the early nineteenth century, a section of the commercial press did indeed become more politically independent partly as a consequence of the growth of advertising. This additional revenue reduced dependence on political subsidies; encouraged papers to reject covert secret service grants (the last English newspaper to receive a clandestine government grant was the *Observer* in 1840); improved the wages and security of employment of journalists so that they became less biddable; and, above all, financed greater expenditure on newsgathering so that newspapers became less reliant on official sources and more reluctant to trade their independence in return for obtaining 'prior intelligence' from the government. This shift was symbolized by *The Times*'s magisterial declaration on Boxing Day, 1834 that it would no longer accept early information from government offices since this was inconsistent with 'the pride and independence of our journal', and anyway its 'own information was earlier and surer'.

However, the growth of advertising did not transform the commercial press into an 'independent fourth estate'. On the contrary, the development of modern political parties from the 1860s onward encouraged a closer interpenetration of party politics and commercial journalism. A number of leading proprietors in Victorian and Edwardian Britain were Members of Parliament, while some national newspapers were subsidized by party loyalists or from party funds until well into the twentieth century. This continuing involvement with government or opposition parties belied the often repeated claim that the press was an *independent* check on Parliament and the executive; in reality, newspapers long remained an extension of the party system.[1]

The conventional portrayal of advertising as the midwife of press independence is also directly contradicted by the emergence of the radical press as a political force in the early nineteenth century. As we shall see, pioneer radical papers did not obtain significant advertising support; yet they were independent both of government and of political groupings in Parliament. Their rise demonstrated plainly that newspapers could – and did – become autonomous from the state through financial support other than advertising.

The rise of the radical press as an extra-parliamentary force also revealed the limitations of official censorship. Successive governments sought to curb the radical press through the lawcourts. But although seditious and blasphemous libel law was framed in a catch-all form that made any kind of fundamental criticism of the social order a legal offence, it was not always easy to enforce. Juries, empowered by Fox's Libel Act (1792) to determine guilt or innocence, were often reluctant to convict. This was brought home to the authorities by the sensational acquittals of Eaton, Hardy and Tooke in the 1790s, Wooler and Hone in 1817, and Cobbett in 1831. The sharp edge of the law was further blunted in 1843 when Lord Campbell's Libel Act made the statement of truth in the public interest a legitimate defence against the charge of seditious libel.

Even before the 1843 Act was passed, the authorities had come round reluctantly to the view that libel prosecutions were often counter-productive. When the editor of *The Republican* was prosecuted in 1819, the paper's circulation rose by over 50 per cent. Similarly disillusioning experiences prompted the Attorney-General to conclude in 1843 that 'a libeller thirsted for nothing more than the valuable advertisement of a public trial in a Court of Justice'. This disenchantment was reflected in a shift of government policy: there were only sixteen prosecutions for seditious and blasphemous libel in the period 1825 to 1834, compared with 167 prosecutions during the preceding eight years.

Instead the authorities came to rely increasingly on the newspaper stamp duty and taxes on paper and advertisements as a way of curbing the radical press. The intention of these press taxes was twofold: to restrict the readership of newspapers to the well-to-do by raising cover prices; and to limit the ownership of newspapers to the propertied class by increasing publishing costs. The belief was that substantial stakeholders in society would conduct newspapers 'in a more responsible manner than was likely to be the result of pauper management',[2] and that it was potentially dangerous to social order to allow the lower ranks to read newspapers at all.

The stamp duty was increased by 266 per cent between 1789 and 1815. Publications subject to the stamp duty were redefined in 1819 to include political periodicals. In addition, a security system was introduced which required publishers of weeklies to register their papers and place financial bonds of between £200 and £300 with the authorities. Although the ostensible purpose of this requirement was to guarantee payment of libel fines, its real objective was to force up further the cost of publishing and thus ensure, as Lord Castlereagh explained to the Commons, that 'persons exercising the power of the press should be men of some respectability and property'.[3] Ironically in view of the way in which newspaper costs were to soar subsequently in an unfettered capitalist market, the government was persuaded by the parliamentary opposition that its original intention of insisting on a bond of £500 represented an unacceptable limitation on the freedom to publish.

The government's reliance on taxes and securities as a way of containing the radical press worked for a time. The upsurge of radical journalism that occurred in the wake of the Napoleonic War weakened in the 1820s. But with the revival of radical agitation in the early 1830s, the authorities faced a more formidable challenge – the systematic evasion of the stamp duty by an underground press supported by a well-organized distribution network and able to finance 'victims' funds' for the families of people imprisoned for selling unstamped newspapers.

The government responded initially by seeking to enforce the law more effectively. Printers of unstamped newspapers were rounded up; supplies of paper were intercepted; sellers of underground papers were gaoled. At least 1130 cases of selling unstamped newspapers were prosecuted in London alone during the period 1830 to 1836, but, despite these measures, the radical press continued to flourish. 'Prosecutions, fines and imprisonments were alike failures', the minister in charge of the fight against the unstamped press later recalled.[4] By the summer of 1836 the government was forced to concede defeat. The Commons was informed on 20 June that the government 'had resorted to all means afforded by the existing law' but that it 'was altogether ineffectual to the purpose of putting an end to the unstamped papers'.

A crisis had been reached. By 1836 the unstamped press published in London had an aggregate readership of at least two million. According to government estimates, its circulation even exceeded that of the respectable, stamped press. The whole system of press control seemed on the point of final collapse, since leading publishers of stamped papers warned the government that they would also evade the stamp duty unless more effective steps were taken to enforce it.

The Whig government responded to the crisis with a well-planned counteroffensive. New measures were passed which strengthened the government's search and confiscation powers. Penalties were also increased for being found in possession of an unstamped newspaper, and the stamp duty was reduced by 75 per cent in order to make 'smuggling' less attractive. Thus what has been seen as a landmark in the advance of press freedom was manifestly repressive both in intention and effect. As Spring Rice, the Chancellor of the Exchequer, explained to the Commons, a strategic concession, combined with increased coercive powers, was necessary in order to enforce a system that had broken down. The aim of these new measures, he stated candidly, was to 'put down the unstamped papers'.[5]

The government's new strategy succeeded in its immediate objective. 'No unstamped papers can be attempted with success,' declared Hetherington, a leading radical publisher, shortly after being released from prison, unless 'some means can be devised either to print the newspaper without types and presses, or render the premises . . . inaccessible to armed force.'[6] By 1837 the clandestine radical press had disappeared.

Compliance with the law forced radical newspapers to raise their prices, even though the stamp duty was much reduced. Whereas most unstamped papers had sold at 1d in the early 1830s, most of their successors in the 1840s sold at 4d or 5d – a sum that was well beyond the means of individual workers. However, the government's aim of destroying the radical press was frustrated by organized consumer resistance. Informal groups of working people pooled their resources each week to purchase a radical paper. Union branches, clubs and political associations financed the collective purchase of newspapers. Even taverns were threatened with the withdrawal of custom unless they bought radical papers. Partly as a consequence of this concerted action, new radical papers emerged which gained even larger circulations than those reached by their best-selling unstamped predecessors.

Admittedly, after 1836, the radical press was not as strong in relation to the respectable press as it had been before. Between 1836 and 1855 there was a substantial growth in the number and circulation of commercial local weekly papers as well as in the readership of religious publications and of family and 'useful knowledge' magazines. However, since much of this expansion appears to have taken place among the middle and lower-middle classes,[7] it did not greatly diminish the radical press's influence within the working class.

The principal rivals to the radical press within the working class (of whom well over half were literate or semi-literate by the 1830s) were almanacs, printed ballads, gallowsheets and chapbooks. However, radical newspapers far outstripped rival *political* publications read by the working class.

Indeed, the radical press was the circulation pace-setter for the nation's press throughout much of the period 1815 to 1855. Cobbett's radical *Twopenny Trash* broke all circulation records in 1816 to 1817. This record was probably beaten by the left-wing *Weekly Police Gazette* which, to judge from a government raid on its premises, had a circulation of over 40,000 in 1836 – well over double that of leading conservative weeklies such as the *Sunday Times* and *Bell's Life in London*. In 1838 the militant *Northern Star* gained the largest circulation of any newspaper published in the provinces and, in 1839, the largest national circulation of any paper apart from the liberal radical *Weekly Dispatch*. Its success was followed by the still larger circulation secured by the radical *Reynolds News,* the paper with the second-largest circulation in Britain after the liberal radical *Lloyds Weekly* in the early 1850s. Both publications were the first newspapers to break through the 100,000 circulation barrier in 1856.[8]

Newspaper circulations during the first half of the nineteenth century seem very small by modern standards, but circulation statistics provide a misleading historical index of newspaper consumption, because the average number of readers per copy has declined markedly since the mid-nineteenth century. A copy of a leading radical paper such as the *Northern Star,* selling at 4½d in 1840, cost approximately the equivalent of almost £3 today. Sharing of high-cost papers, together with the widespread practice of reading papers aloud for the benefit of the semi-literate and illiterate, resulted in a very high number of 'readers' for each newspaper sold. Hollis and Epstein estimate, for instance, that radical papers in the 1830s and 1840s reached upward of twenty readers per copy. This compares with an average of only two to three readers per copy of contemporary daily papers. Yet even if a cautious estimate of ten readers per copy is taken as the norm for radical papers in the early Victorian period, it still means that leading militant papers such as the *Northern Star* and its successor, *Reynolds News,* each reached at their peak, before the repeal of the stamp duty, half a million readers. This was at a time when the population of England and Wales over the age of 14 was little over ten million. The emergent radical press was thus a genuinely popular force, reaching a mass public.

The economic structure of the radical press

The circulation success of the radical press was a direct consequence of the growth of a radical trade union and political movement. However, this success was also facilitated by the prevailing economic structure of the press industry. Since this is an important aspect of the central argument that follows, it is worth examining in some detail the finances of the early radical press.

The initial capital required to set up a radical paper in the early part of the nineteenth century was extremely small. Most radical unstamped papers were printed not on a steam press, but on hand presses, which cost as little as £10 to acquire. Metal type was often hired by the hour and print workers paid on a piecework basis.

After 1836 leading stamped radical papers were printed on more sophisticated machinery. The *London Dispatch,* for instance, was printed on a Napier machine, bought with the help of a wealthy well-wisher and the profits from Hetherington's other publications. The *Northern Star* had a printing press specially constructed for it in London. Even so, launch costs were extremely small in comparison with the subsequent period. The *Northern Star,* for instance, was launched in 1837 with a total capital of £690, mostly raised by public subscription.

Financing a paper during its initial establishment period could often cost more than setting it up. Even so, early trading losses were minimized by low operating costs. Radical unstamped papers paid no tax, relied heavily upon news reports filed by their readers on a voluntary basis, and had small newsprint costs because of their high readership per copy. Consequently radical unstamped newspapers needed to attain only small circulations in order to be economically viable. For instance, the *Poor Man's Guardian,* a leading newspaper of the early 1830s, broke even as soon as its circulation reached 2500.

Even after 1836, when a penny stamp duty had to be paid on each copy, the running costs of the radical press remained relatively low. The influential *London Dispatch* reported, for example (17 September 1836), that 'the whole expense allowed for editing, reporting, reviewing, literary contributions etc., in fact, the entire cost of what is technically called "making up" the paper, is only six pounds per week'. In the same issue it reported that, at its selling price of 3½d, it could break even with a circulation of 16,000. Similarly the *Northern Star* which, unlike its predecessors, developed a substantial network of paid correspondents, claimed to be spending little more than £9 10s a week on its reporting establishment in 1841. Selling at 4½d, it was able to break even with a weekly circulation of about 6200. This low break-even point meant that its run-in costs were very small. Indeed the *Northern Star* almost certainly moved into profit within its first month of publication.

Because publishing costs were low the ownership and control of newspapers could be in the hands of people committed, in the words of Joshua Hobson, an ex-handloom weaver and publisher of the *Voice of West Riding,* 'to support the rights and interests of the order and class to which it is my pride to belong'. Some newspapers, such as the *Voice of the People,* the *Liberator* and the *Trades Newspaper*, were owned by political or trade union organizations. Others were owned by individual proprietors such as Cleave, Watson and Hetherington, many of them people of humble origins who had risen to prominence through the working-class movement. While not lacking in ruthlessness or business acumen, the people they entrusted with the editing of their newspapers were all former manual workers like William Hill and Joshua Hobson, or middle-class activists like O'Brien and Lorymer, whose attitudes had been shaped by long involvement in working-class politics. A substantial section of the popular newspaper press reaching a working-class audience was thus controlled by those who were committed to the working-class movement.

This influenced the way in which journalists working for the radical press perceived their role. Unlike the institutionalized journalists of the later period, they tended to see themselves as activists rather than as professionals. Indeed many of the paid correspondents of the *Poor Man's Guardian, Northern Star* and the early *Reynolds News* were also political organizers for the National Union of the Working Classes or the Chartist Movement. They sought to describe and expose the dynamics of power and inequality rather than to report 'hard news' as a series of disconnected events. They saw themselves as class representatives rather than as disinterested intermediaries and attempted to establish a relationship of real reciprocity with their readers. As the editor of the *Northern Star* wrote in its fifth anniversary issue,

I have ever sought to make it [the paper] rather a reflex of your minds than a medium through which to exhibit any supposed talent or intelligence of my own. This is precisely my conception of what a people's organ should be.

The second important feature of the economic structure of the radical press in the first half of the nineteenth century was that it was self-sufficient on the proceeds of sales alone. The radical unstamped press carried very little commercial advertising and the stamped radical press fared little better. The *London Dispatch* (17 September 1836) complained bitterly, for instance, of the 'prosecutions, fines and the like et ceteras with which a paper of our principles is sure to be more largely honoured than by the lucrative patronage of advertisers'. The grudge held against advertisers by the *London Dispatch* and other radical newspapers was fully justified. An examination of the official advertisement duty returns reveals a marked disparity in the amount of advertising duty per 1000 copies (an index that takes account of circulation difference) paid by the radical press compared with its more respectable rivals. For example, in 1840 two middle-class papers published in Leeds (the *Leeds Mercury* and *Leeds Intelligence*) and the four leading national daily papers (*The Times, Morning Post, Morning Chronicle* and *Morning Advertiser*) all paid over fifty times more advertisement duty per 1000 copies than the radical *Northern Star,* a Leeds-based paper with a national circulation.

A similar pattern emerges in the case of the other leading radical papers for which returns are available. In 1817, for instance, Cobbett's *Political Register* received only three advertisements: its advertisement duty per 1000 copies was less than one-hundredth of that of respectable rival periodicals, although this disparity was somewhat reduced by the 1830s. The *London Dispatch* in 1837 was only marginally better off: it paid per 1000 copies less than one twenty-fifth of the advertisement duty collected from each of its main respectable rivals in London, also with a national circulation.

This lack of advertising support meant that radical papers had limited money at their disposal for editorial development. Some were even forced to close down, even though they had larger circulations than respectable rivals better endowed with advertising. The radical press was thus put in a position of competitive disadvantage at a time when the high price of newspapers, inflated by the stamp duty, was already a major deterrent against buying papers among the working class.

Yet despite these substantial disadvantages, the absence of advertising did not prevent the radical press from flourishing. While fortunes were not easily made, radical newspapers – both stamped and unstamped – could be highly profitable. Hetherington, the publisher of the stamped *London Dispatch,* was reported to be making £1000 a year from his business in 1837. Similarly the stamped *Northern Star* was estimated to have produced a remarkable profit of £13,000 in 1839 and £6500 in 1840, which was generated very largely from sales revenue.

This independence from advertising was itself a liberating force. Radical papers were, by the 1830s, increasingly oriented towards a working-class audience, and became more uncompromising in their attacks on capitalism. They were not forced to temper their radicalism or to seek a more affluent readership by the need to attract advertising. Instead they were free to respond to the radicalization of the working-class movement because they relied on their readers rather than advertisers for their economic viability.

The impact of the radical press

The radical press did not merely reflect the growth of the working-class organizations; it also deepened and extended radical consciousness, helping to build support for the working-class movement.

One of the most important, and least remarked on, aspects of the development of the radical press in the first half of the nineteenth century was that its leading publications developed a nationwide circulation. Even as early as the second decade, leading radical papers such as the *Twopenny Trash, Political Register* and *Republican* were read as far afield as Yorkshire, Lancashire, the Midlands and East Anglia, as well as in the south of England. By the early 1830s the principal circulation newspapers like the *Weekly Police Gazette,* the *Poor Man's Guardian* and *Dispatch* had a distribution network extending on a north–south axis from Glasgow to Truro, and on an east–west axis from Norwich to Carmarthen. Part of the impact of the radical press stemmed from this central fact – the extent of its geographical distribution.

The radical press was effective in reinforcing a growing consciousness of class and in unifying disparate elements of the working community, partly because its leading publications provided national coverage and reached a national working-class audience. It helped to extend the often highly exclusive occupational solidarity of early trade unionism to other sectors of the labour community by demonstrating the common predicament of union members in different trades throughout the country. Workers attempting to set up an extra-legal union read in the radical press in 1833 to 1834, for instance, of similar struggles by glove workers in Yeovil, cabinet-makers and joiners in Glasgow and Carlisle, shoemakers and smiths in Northampton, and brick-layers and masons in London, as well as of working-class struggles in Belgium and Germany. Similarly the radical press helped to reduce geographical isolation by showing that local agitation – whether against Poor Law Commissioners, new machinery, long working hours or wage reductions – conformed to a common pattern throughout the country. The radical press further expanded its readers' field of social vision by publishing, particularly in the later phase from the 1830s onward, news that none of the respectable papers carried, and by interpreting this news within a radical framework of analysis. It was, in the words of the Chartist leader Feargus O'Connor, 'the link that binds the industrious classes together'.[9]

The radical press also helped to promote working-class organizations. Movements ranging from early trade unions to political organizations, such as the National Union of the Working Classes and the Chartist Movement, partly depended for their success on the publicity they obtained from the radical press. O'Connor recalled that before the emergence of Chartist newspapers, 'I found that the press was entirely mute, while I was working myself to death, and that a meeting in one town did nothing for another'. Press publicity stimulated people to attend meetings and to become involved in political and industrial organizations; it also brought the activist vanguard of the working-class movement into national prominence, helping, for example, to transform unknown farm workers victimized for joining a trade union in the remote village of Tolpuddle into national working-class heroes. No less important, it also contributed to the morale of activists in the working-class movement who were confronted by what must have seemed, at times, insuperable odds. Without the *Northern Star,* declared one speaker at a local Chartist meeting, 'their own sounds might echo through the wilderness'.[10]

Above all, the radical press was a major mobilizing force in its own right. We have become so accustomed to the individualized pattern of newspaper consumption amidst a steady flow of information from a variety of media that it is difficult to understand the political significance of newspapers in the early nineteenth century. Newspapers were often the only readily available source of information about what was happening outside the local community and, in some cases, generated passionate loyalty among their readers. Fielden recalls, for instance, 'on the day the newspaper, the *Northern Star,* O'Connor's paper, was due, the people used to line the roadside waiting for its arrival, which was paramount to everything else for the time being'. The impact of the radical press was reinforced further by the discussions that followed the reading out loud of articles from newspapers in taverns, workshops, homes and public meetings, vividly described in numerous memoirs and reminiscences.[11] This social pattern of consumption (which continued on a diminished scale late into the nineteenth century) resulted in political newspapers having a much greater agitational effect than those of today.

The first wave of radical papers from the 1790s through to the late 1820s played an important part in the general reorientation that preceded the political mobilization of a section of the working class. They raised expectations both by invoking a mythical past in which plenty and natural justice had prevailed, and by proclaiming the possibility of a future in which poverty could be relieved through political means. It was this raising of hopes, combined with a direct assault on the Anglican 'morality' which sanctioned the social order, that most alarmed parliamentarians at the time. As Dr Philimore, MP, warned the Commons following official reports that servants and common soldiers had been seen reading radical newspapers,

> Those infamous publications . . . inflame [working people's] passions and awaken their selfishness, contrasting their present conditions with what they contend to be their future condition – a condition incompatible with human nature, and with those immutable laws which Providence has established for the regulation of civil society.[12]

The radical press not only helped to erode political passivity, based on fatalistic acceptance of the social system as 'natural' and 'providential', but also began to dispel the collective lack of confidence that had inhibited working-class resistance. The least valued section of the community was able to obtain a new understanding of its role in society through its own press. 'The real strength and all the resources of the country,' characteristically proclaimed Cobbett's *Political Register*, 'ever have sprung from the *labour* of its people.' This novel view of the world, popularized through the more radical journals, provided a means of reordering the entire ranking of status and moral worth in society. The highest in the land were degraded to the lowest place as unproductive parasites: working people, in contrast, were elevated to the top as the productive and useful section of the community. The early militant press thus fostered an alternative value system that symbolically turned the world upside down. It also repeatedly emphasized the potential power of working people to effect social change through the force of 'combination' and organized action.

The radical press played a part in radicalizing the emergent working-class movement by developing a more sophisticated political analysis. The first generation of radical papers was trapped inside the intellectual categories of the eighteenth-century liberal attack on the aristocratic constitution. Conflict was generally portrayed in political terms as a struggle between the aristocracy and the 'productive classes' (usually defined to include working capitalists as well as the working classes), while criticism was focused mainly upon corruption in high places and repressive taxation that was said to impoverish the productive community. By implication, this critique left the economic reward structure of society fundamentally unchanged.

By the 1830s the more militant papers had shifted their focus of attack from 'old corruption' to the economic process which enabled the capitalist class to appropriate in profits the wealth created by labour. Conflict was redefined as a class struggle between labour and capital, between the working classes and a coalition of aristocrats, 'millocrats' and 'shopocrats'. This more militant analysis signposted the way forward towards a far-reaching programme of social reconstruction in which, in the words of the *Poor Man's Guardian* (19 October 1833), workers will 'be at the top instead of at the bottom of society – or rather that there should be no bottom or top at all'.

This new analysis was often conflated with the old liberal analysis in an uncertain synthesis. There was, moreover, a basic continuity in the perspectives offered by the less militant wing of the radical press, which gained in influence during the 1840s. But such continuity should come as no surprise. It was only natural that the political complexion of the broad left press should reflect the ebb and flow of militancy within the radical movement. Nor is it at all surprising that traditional political beliefs should have persisted in view of what we now know about the resilience of belief systems. But so long as the activist working class controlled its own popular press, it possessed the institutional means to explore more radical understandings of society. It also had a collective resource for defining, expressing and maintaining a radical public opinion different from that proclaimed by the capitalist press, as well as a defence against the ideological assault mounted on the working class through schools, churches, mechanics' institutes and useful knowledge magazines.

The militant press sustained a radical subculture, which represented a potential threat to the undemocratic social order. Indeed in 1842, a General Strike was called to secure universal suffrage through the force of industrial action. It received extensive support in industrial Lancashire, much of Yorkshire and parts of the Midlands. While the strike was crushed, and some 1500 labour leaders were imprisoned, it was a sign of an increasingly unsettled society in which the radical press had become a powerful force.

In short, the control system administered by the state had failed. Neither prosecutions for seditious libel nor a tax system designed to restrict newspaper readership had succeeded in preventing the rise of the radical press. As we shall see, this prompted thoughtful parliamentarians to consider whether there might be a better way of containing insurgent journalism.

Notes

1. In the past twenty years, six researchers – George Boyce, Alan Lee, Stephen Koss, Colin Seymour-Ure, Lucy Brown and Hannah Barker – have documented the press's continuing involvement in party politics long after the press is supposed to have blossomed as an 'independent fourth estate'. Their studies have thus modified one aspect of the traditional Whig interpretation of press history. For more about this, see Chapter 5.
2. Pelham, *Parliamentary Debates,* 11 (1832), cols 491–2.
3. Castlereagh, *Parliamentary Debates*, 91 (1819), cols 1177ff.
4. Spring Rice, *Parliamentary Debates,* 138 (1855), col. 966.
5. Spring Rice, *Parliamentary Debates,* 34 (1836), cols 627–34; 37 (1837), col. 1165.
6. *London Dispatch* (17 September 1836).
7. Report of the Select Committee on Newspaper Stamps (SCNS), *Parliamentary Papers,* 17 (1851); Milner-Gibson, *Parliamentary Debates*, 135 (1853), col. 1136, among others.
8. P. Hollis, *The Pauper Press* (London, Oxford University Press, 1970), p. 95; *Parliamentary Debates,* 34 (1836), col. 627; SCNS Appendix 4; V. Berridge, 'Popular Sunday papers and mid-Victorian society' in G. Boyce, J. Curran and P. Wingate (eds), *Newspaper History* (London, Constable, 1978), p. 249.

9. *Northern Star* (16 January 1841).
10. *Northern Star* (26 August 1848).
11. For instance, W. E. Adams, *Memoirs of a Social Atom*, vol. 1 (London, Hutchinson, 1903), pp. 164–6; interview with Wesley Perrins, *Bulletin of the Society for the Study of Labour History* (1970), pp. 16–24.
12. Dr Philimore, *Parliamentary Debates*, 91 (1819), col. 1363.

3

The ugly face of reform

The parliamentary campaign against 'the taxes on knowledge' is generally portrayed as a triumphant campaign for a free press, sustained by an amalgam of special interests but motivated largely by libertarian ideals in opposition to the authoritarian legacy of the past.[1] The only discordant note in this inspiring account comes from the parliamentary campaigners celebrated in this historical legend. Their aims and, indeed, their public utterances are difficult to reconcile with the historic role assigned to them in liberal ideology.

Widespread evasion of the stamp duty in the early 1830s caused press regulation to become a major political issue. Traditionalists argued that the government should enforce the stamp duty with tougher measures, while a relatively small group of reformers in Parliament argued that the stamp duty had become unenforceable in the face of mass resistance and should be repealed. The two sides in the debate did not disagree over objectives so much as over tactics. As the Lord Chancellor succinctly put it in 1834,

> the only question to answer, and the only problem to solve, is how they [the people] shall read in the best manner; how they shall be instructed politically, and have political habits formed the most safe for the constitution of the country.

Traditionalists alleged that abolition of the stamp duty would result in the country being flooded with 'atrocious publications'. Reformers countered by arguing that the stamp duty merely suppressed 'the cheap reply' to seditious publications from responsible quarters. Radical publishers were not being stopped by inefficient controls; instead they were being given a clear field in which to indoctrinate the people with 'the most pernicious doctrines' without encountering effective competition.[2]

Underlying this difference over tactics were divergent approaches to social control. Supporters of press regulation tended to favour coercion. Reformers, on the other hand, generally stressed the importance of engineering social

consent. As Bulwer Lytton argued when proposing the repeal of the stamp
duty in 1832:

> At this moment when throughout so many nations we see the people at war
> with their institutions, the world presents to us two great, may they be
> impressive examples. In Denmark, a despotism without discontent – in
> America, a republic without change. The cause is the same in both: in both
> the people are universally educated.

The parliamentary repeal lobby argued that the lifting of the stamp duty
would encourage men of capital to invest in an expanding market and consequently enrol 'more temperate and disinterested friends of the people who
would lend themselves to their real instruction'. In particular, many of the
parliamentary campaigners of the 1830s believed that cheap newspapers,
owned by business people, would become an educational weapon in the fight
against trade unionism. Francis Place, the organizing secretary of the repeal
campaign, even told a Parliamentary Select Committee in 1832 that 'there
would not have been a single trades union either in England or Scotland' if
the stamp duty had been repealed some years earlier. Similarly Roebuck
informed the Commons that if the stamp duty had been lifted agricultural
workers at Tolpuddle would probably not have been so ignorant as to have
joined a trade union. Another leading campaigner, Grote, was even more
sanguine about the benefits of an expanded, capitalist press: 'a great deal of
the bad feeling that was at present abroad amongst the labouring classes on
the subject of wages' was due, he believed, to 'the want of proper instruction
and correct information as to their real interests' caused by taxes on the
press.[3]
   What these parliamentary campaigners for a 'free press' emphasized was
not libertarian principle but the need for a more active approach to political
socialization. However, their speeches occasionally betrayed anxiety that the
time might not be right to lift controls on the press. This ambivalence perhaps
explains why so few among the repeal lobby of MPs voted consistently
against the government's counter-offensive in 1836 designed, as we have seen,
to restore the stamp duty and destroy the radical press. In the revealing words
of Collet, who was later to co-ordinate the campaign for a free press in
Westminster, the government's attack on radical journalism was 'not a liberal,
but it was in some respects, a statesman-like measure'.[4]

The new campaign

A new parliamentary lobby against 'the taxes on knowledge' was organized in
1848. Although it claimed to be a broadly based group, it had a narrow social
base. As Cobden confided privately, 'exclusively almost, we comprise steady,
sober middle-class reformers'. The driving force behind the campaign were

Liberal industrialist MPs who saw in the repeal of press taxation a means of propagating the principles of free trade and competitive capitalism. In particular, they hoped that a reduction in newspaper prices, following the abolition of press taxes, would assist the growth of the local commercial press with which many of them were closely associated, and would undermine the dominant position of the 'unreliable' *Times* by exposing it to increased competition.

The campaign won the backing of politicians of all persuasions, as well as a variety of groups such as temperance campaigners, educationalists and publishers (though the latter were deeply divided over the stamp duty). While supporters of the campaign had different reasons for wanting to reach a wider public, they were united in believing that the social order would be rendered more secure if it was based on consent fostered by an expanded, capitalist press. 'The larger we open the field of general instruction,' declared Palmerston when speaking for the repeal of the stamp duty in the Commons, 'the firmer the foundations on which the order, the loyalty and good conduct of the lower classes will rest.' Repeal the taxes on knowledge, proclaimed the Irish politician Maguire, and 'you render the people better citizens, more obedient to the laws, more faithful and loyal subjects, and more determined to stand up for the honour of the country'. 'The freedom of the press,' argued Gladstone, 'was not merely to be permitted and tolerated, but to be highly prized, for it tended to bring closer together all the national interests and preserve the institutions of the country.' The new market-based press, in their view, would be a stabilising force.[5]

However, while the fundamental objectives of the campaign against press taxes were the same as before, its rhetoric was modified. Whig history was invoked more often to stigmatize supporters of press taxes as enemies of liberty and the heirs of court censorship. Opposition to press taxation was voiced more frequently in the form of abstract and elevated principle. Freedom of expression should not be taxed; truth will confound error in open debate; good publications will drive out the bad in fair competition; and truth will triumph in the free marketplace of ideas.

However, reformers sometimes combined libertarian and authoritarian arguments in ways that now seem incongruous. They seemed often to be unaware of any tension between the objectives of freedom and social control. Thus Alexander Andrews, editor of the first journalists' trade journal, argued that the great mission of a free press was to 'educate and enlighten those classes whose political knowledge has been hitherto so little, and by consequence so dangerous'. This theme of political indoctrination fused naturally and unselfconsciously with that of liberty. 'The list of our public journals,' Andrews continued, 'is a proud and noble list – the roll call of an army of liberty, with a rallying point in every town. It is a police of safety, and a sentinel of public morals.'[6] The very facility with which these dissonant themes could be conflated reveals the ideological universe within which the press freedom campaign was constructed. A tacit model of society which acknowledged no conflict of class interest, only a conflict between ignorance and enlightenment and between the individual and the state, provided the intellectual framework in which a free press could be perceived both as a watch-dog of government and a guard-dog of the people.

Indeed, the respectable campaign for press freedom was never simply about press freedom; it was also motivated by a desire to stabilize the social order in Britain at a time when mainland Europe was rocked by the 1848 revolutions and their aftermath. The campaign may also be viewed as being part of a reformist drive to restructure that social order. Commitment to the principle of free competition, and its extension to new spheres of economic and public life, was the central goal of middle-class reform. The material blessings of the free market had been extensively invoked in the 1830s and 1840s in the campaign against the corn laws which restricted grain imports into Britain. The virtues of free competition were also widely aired in the 1850s in attacks on public appointments through social connection. This culminated in the 1870s in the overhaul of the civil service and armed forces, which widened middle-class access to influential and remunerative employment. The campaign against the 'taxes on knowledge' was thus part of a wider discourse deployed against protection of the landed interest and the unreformed, aristocratic state. It also reflected growing confidence among middle-class reformers (some of whom were involved in a parallel campaign to set up public libraries) that their version of enlightenment would prevail through the enlargement of 'public knowledge'.

The key members of the press freedom campaign were also under no illusion that a free market would be neutral. More sophisticated than their predecessors in the 1830s, they had a better understanding of how the press industry worked. The repeal of press taxes, declared Milner-Gibson, President of the Association for the Promotion of the Repeal of the Taxes on Knowledge, would create 'a cheap press in the hands of men of good moral character, of respectability, and of capital'. Fully aware of the rising capitalization of popular newspaper publishing in the USA, he believed that free market processes would favour entrepreneurs with large financial resources. Free trade, he stressed, in common with other leading campaigners, would 'give to men of capital and respectability the power of gaining access by newspapers, by faithful record of the facts, to the minds of the working classes'. The free market, argued Sir George Lewis, the Liberal Chancellor of the Exchequer, would promote papers 'enjoying the preference of the advertising public'. Furthermore, reformers argued, responsible control over a cheap press would educate public demand. As one campaigner put it, 'The appetite grows by what it feeds on.'[7]

Some reformers also believed that an expanding capitalist press would raise the pay, status and quality of journalists, with the clear implication that this would promote moderation and good sense. The establishment of a cheap press, explained Hickson, a leading campaigner, would create a new hierarchical system of communication in which journalists 'two or three degrees' above the labouring classes would enlighten them. To Gladstone, the principal attraction of repeal was that it would lead to more men of 'quality' working in the press, and consequently educating the people. 'A perfectly free press,' wryly commented the journalist J. F. Stephen, 'is one of the greatest safeguards of peace and order' since successful journalists belong to 'the comfortable part of society' and will 'err rather on the side of making too much of their interests than on that of neglecting them.'[8]

Reinforcing this commitment to creating a cheap, unrestricted press was a growing conviction that it was now safe to lift controls. The radical working-class movement was on the retreat in the 1850s. There was, proclaimed reformers, 'a great increase of intelligence among the people.'[9] Even those who were uncertain whether the working class would 'become the glory, or might prove greatly dangerous to the peace, of the country' agreed that it was a good time to attempt an experiment. Significantly, only those who were convinced that the lower classes were wedded to radical prejudices (and this group included not only entrenched traditionalists but also some distinguished liberals committed to free market competition in other spheres)[10] remained resolutely opposed to the repeal of the stamp duty.

The campaign against press taxes was conducted with remarkable skill and tenacity. Reformers packed the Parliamentary Select Committee on the stamp duty and largely determined the contents of its report. They attacked poorly briefed ministers and won the support of officials in the Board of Inland Revenue. They harassed the government through the law courts, exposed the inconsistencies in the way the stamp duty was enforced, organized public meetings, petitions and deputations, and attacked press taxes in sympathetic newspapers. Their political virtuosity was finally rewarded with the abolition of the advertisement duty in 1853, the stamp duty in 1855, the paper duty in 1861 and the security system in 1869.

However, the parliamentary campaign for a free press was never inspired by a modern libertarian commitment to diversity of expression. Indeed, the ruthless repression of the unstamped press in the mid-1830s had much the same objective as the campaign which set the press 'free' twenty years later: the subordination of the press to the social order. All that had changed was a growing commitment to positive indoctrination of the lower orders through a cheap press, and a growing conviction that free trade and normative controls were a morally preferable and more efficient control system than direct controls administered by the state. Underlying this shift was the growing power and confidence of the Victorian middle class, which dominated the parliamentary campaign for repeal of press taxes and recognized in the expanding press a powerful agency for the advancement of their interests.

The confidence of reformers in the outcome of free market competition proved to be justified. The radical press was eclipsed in the period after the repeal of press taxes. The reasons for this have never been adequately explained.

Notes

1. For instance, G. A. Cranfield, *The Press and Society* (Harlow, Longman, 1978), p. 205. This view is contested in relation to the 1830s by P. Hollis, *The Pauper Press* (London, Oxford University Press, 1970) and J. H. Wiener, *The War of the Unstamped* (New York, Cornell University Press, 1969).

2. *Parliamentary Debates,* 13 (1832), cols 619–48; 23 (1834), cols 1193–1222; 30 (1835), cols 835–62; 34 (1836), cols 627ff.; 35 (1836), cols 566ff., 46 (1837), cols 1164–84. In actual fact the radical unstamped press did not have a 'clear field'. The authorities harassed radical unstamped papers, while regularly turning a blind eye to 'moderate' unstamped papers in the early 1830s.

3. Place, Select Committee on Drunkenness, *Parliamentary Papers,* 8 (1834), question 2054; Roebuck, *Parliamentary Debates,* 23 (1834) cols 1208–9; Grote, *ibid.,* col. 1221.

4. C. D. Collet, *History of the Taxes on Knowledge: Their Origin and Repeal,* vol. 1 (London, T. Fisher Unwin, 1899).

5. Palmerston, *Parliamentary Debates,* 127 (1854), col. 459; Maguire, *Parliamentary Debates,* 157 (1860), col. 383; Gladstone, cit. J. Grant, *The Newspaper Press: Its Origins, Progress and Present Position* (London, Tinsley Brothers, 1871–2).

6. A. Andrews, *The History of British Journalism to 1855* (London, Richard Bentley, 1859), vol. ii, p. 347.

7. Milner-Gibson, *Parliamentary Debates,* 137 (1855), col. 434, and *Parliamentary Debates,* 110 (1850), col. 378; Lewis, *Parliamentary Debates,* 137 (1855), col. 786; Whitty, Report of the Select Committee on Newspaper Stamps (SCNS), *Parliamentary Papers,* 17 (1851), para. 600.

8. Hickson, SCNS (1851), para. 3, 169; Gladstone, *Parliamentary Debates,* 137 (1855), col. 794: J. F. Stephen, 'Journalism', *Cornhill Magazine,* 6 (1862).

9. Bulwer Lytton, *Parliamentary Debates,* 137 (1855), col. 1118; Ingram, *Parliamentary Debates,* 151 (1858), col. 112; Digby Seymour, *Parliamentary Debates,* 125 (1853), col. 1166.

10. For instance, J. R. McCulloch, *Dictionary of Commerce and Commercial Navigation* (London, Longman, Brown & Green, 1854), p. 893.

4

The industrialization of the press

During the half-century following the repeal of the 'taxes on knowledge', a number of radical newspapers closed down or were eventually incorporated, such as the *Reynolds News,* into the mainstream of popular Liberal journalism. Militant journalism survived only in the etiolated form of small circulation national periodicals and struggling local weeklies. Yet this decline occurred during a period of rapid press expansion, when local daily papers were established in all the major urban centres of Britain and a new generation of predominantly right-wing national newspapers came into being. These included newspapers such as the *People* (1881), *Daily Mail* (1896), *Daily Express* (1900) and *Daily Mirror* (1903), which have played a prominent role in British journalism ever since.

Most historians, on the left as well as on the right, attribute the decline of radical journalism to a change in the climate of public opinion. The collapse of Chartism in the early 1850s produced a wave of disillusion. Some radical activists were absorbed into the Liberal Party, particularly after the upper strata of the working class gained the vote in 1867. Trade unions also became more inward-looking, seeking to improve wages and working conditions rather than to restructure society. These changes were reinforced by the winning of significant social reforms and, above all, by the relative success of the British economy: most workers in employment became substantially better off during the second half of the nineteenth century. Intensive proselytization of the working class through schools, churches, youth clubs, and other socializing agencies such as the Volunteer Force also contributed to the spread of anti-socialist views.

These developments diminished the potential market for radical journalism. They also had another consequence which has tended to be overlooked. The reduction of support for the left made it more difficult to raise money within the working-class movement for new publishing ventures. As the TUC Congress debates in the early part of the twentieth century make clear, many Liberal and Lib–Lab trade unionists were reluctant to invest their members' money in setting up new socialist publications because they had become reconciled to the commercial press.

However, while this *Zeitgeist* interpretation partly accounts for the fall of the radical press it is an incomplete explanation. It is generally based on the over-simplistic assumption that journalists are influenced by prevailing ideas of the time, and are forced to respond in a competitive market to the demands of the sovereign consumer. Consequently the press ventriloquizes, it is claimed, the views of the public.

In fact the evidence clearly shows that there was no close correspondence between the climate of opinion in the country and the political character of the press. What may be broadly defined as the radical press was still a powerful force in popular journalism in 1860 when the working-class movement was divided and defeated. In sharp contrast, the radical press was dwarfed by its rivals fifty years later, when the radical movement was gathering momentum.[1] The steady growth of general trade unionism, the radicalization of skilled workers, the spread of socialist and Labourist ideas, the rise of the suffragette movement and the revival of industrial militancy did not give rise to an efflorescence of radical journalism in the decade before the First World War, although it produced a few notable publications. The absence of a close correlation between press and public opinion is underlined further by voting figures. In the 1918 general election, for instance, the Labour Party gained 22 per cent of the vote but did not win the unreserved support of a single national daily or Sunday newspaper.

Lucy Brown has advanced a supplementary explanation for the decline of 'critical vigour' in the Victorian press. She shows that the political élite devoted more time and skill to cultivating the press, and became increasingly dominant as sources and definers of news. However, while this helps to explain the rightward drift of part of the commercial press, it still does not account for the eclipse of radical journalism. The militant press's adversarial style effectively inoculated it against the gentler arts of press management described by Brown. The defeat of the radical press was more fundamental: it was eclipsed rather than seduced.

Virginia Berridge has advanced a more compelling, if flawed, explanation of the decline of committed journalism.[2] This was due, she argues, to the 'commercialization' of the popular press. New popular papers came into being which were primarily business ventures, relying on sensationalist manipulation of popular sentiment rather than what she calls the 'genuine arousal' of militant journalism. In other words, they concentrated on entertainment rather than taxing political analysis, and consequently secured a much larger audience than politically committed papers.

Berridge's pioneering analysis focuses attention upon a significant change within part of the radical press. Its circulation during the 1840s was swollen by the emergence of the *News of the World* and *Lloyds Weekly,* both commercial papers whose initial radicalism was the product more of commercial expediency than of political commitment. As the *News of the World* frankly stated in its first issue (1 October 1843), 'It is only by a very extensive circulation that the proprietors can be compensated for the outlay of a large capital in this novel and original undertaking.' Although the same issue contained an impassioned attack upon conditions in some poor-houses, where inmates were forced to wear prison clothes, the paper also made clear that its general orientation was to please as many people as possible by serving 'the general utility of all classes'. This led to the adoption of consensual views, and the growth of entertainment at the expense of political news. Yet, not very surprisingly, Sunday papers in the *News of the World* mould, with a professionally processed combination of news, sport, human interest stories and political commentary, proved more appealing than the didactic journals that were the principal organs of the left in late Victorian Britain.

This explanation is persuasive as far as it goes. But it glosses over one striking feature of the development of the radical press. During the first half of the nineteenth century left-wing papers evolved from being journals of opinion, based on a quarto format, into broadsheet newspapers carrying news as well as commentary. This change was particularly marked during the 1830s, and was accompanied by a significant broadening of news content. Some of these radical papers began to develop a wide audience appeal by drawing upon the popular street literature tradition of chapbooks, broadsheets, gallowsheets and almanacs. Indeed, Cleave's *Weekly Police Gazette*, the *London Dispatch* and the early militant *Reynolds News* were important partly because they started to rework this popular tradition in ways that projected a radical ideology through human interest news and entertainment as well as through political coverage.

Why, then, did the committed radical press retreat increasingly in the second half of the nineteenth century into the ghetto of narrowly politicized journalism? Why did it leave the field of popular news coverage and entertainment to the commercial press? Thus the question that needs to be asked is not why Victorian working people should have preferred the *News of the World* to rather arid socialist journals such as *Justice* and *Commonweal,* but why the radical press should have failed to live up to its early promise (or, in Berridge's terms, to its early indications of superficiality).

Her analysis is an historical version of a standard critique of mass culture. This assumes that communication processed commercially as a commodity for the mass market is inevitably 'debased' because it relies on the manipulation of public tastes and attitudes for profit. This is based on assumptions that are open to question. In the context of Victorian Britain, it also obscures under the general heading of 'commercialization' the complex system of controls institutionalized by the industrialization of the Victorian press.

The freedom of capital

One of the central objectives of state economic controls on the press – to exclude pauper management – was attained only by its repeal. This was partly because a craft system of production was replaced by an industrial one. The lifting of press taxes set up a chain reaction: lower prices, increased sales and the development of new print technology to service an expanding market. Rotary presses, fed by hand, were introduced in the 1860s and 1870s and were gradually replaced by web rotary machines of increasing size and sophistication in late Victorian and Edwardian England. 'Craft' composing was mechanized by Hattersley's machine in the 1860s, and this was replaced by the linotype machine in the 1880s and 1890s. Numerous innovations were also made in graphic reproduction. These developments led to a sharp rise in fixed capital costs. For example, Northcliffe estimated half a million pounds as 'the initial cost of machinery, buildings, ink factories and the like, and this was altogether apart from the capital required for daily working expenses' in setting up the *Daily Mail* in 1896.[3]

The rise in fixed costs made it more difficult for people with limited funds to break into mass publishing. It also generated a relationship of economic inequality since leading publishers were able to obtain large economies of scale (through spreading their 'first copy' costs over a large print run). In addition, major publishers such as Edward Lloyd gained significant economies of scope by diversifying into paper manufacture in the 1870s and 1880s. However, while new technology raised the level of investment needed to start a paper, and tended to strengthen the position of major publishers, it did not in fact constitute an insuperable obstacle to the launch of new publications with limited capital even in the national market. Newspapers such as the *Daily Herald,* launched in 1912, could be started with only a limited outlay by being printed on a contract basis by an independent printer.

A more important financial consequence of the repeal of press taxes was to force up the running costs of newspaper publishing. National newspapers became substantial enterprises, with growing newsprint bills and staff costs. They also cut their cover prices. The combination of rising expenditure and lower cover prices forced up the circulation levels that newspapers needed to achieve in order to be profitable. This raised, in turn, the run-in costs of new papers before they built their circulations to break-even point. New newspapers could be launched with limited funds and derelict newspapers could be bought relatively cheaply. It was increasingly the establishment of newspapers that required large financial resources.

Thus in 1855 Disraeli was advised by D. C. Coulton that a capital of about £20,000 was needed to start a London daily paper. In 1867 W. H. Smith estimated that about £50,000 was needed to fund a new London morning paper. By the 1870s Edward Lloyd needed to spend £150,000 to establish the *Daily Chronicle* (after buying it for £30,000). During the period 1906 to 1908

Thomasson spent about £300,000 attempting to establish the liberal daily, *Tribune.* By the 1920s, however, Lord Cowdray spent about £750,000 attempting to convert the *Westminster Gazette* into a quality daily. Even more was spent on developing mass-circulation papers during the same period.

Indeed, the full extent of the material transformation of the press is perhaps most clearly revealed by comparing the launch and establishment costs of newspapers before and after the industrialization of the press. As we have seen, the total cost of establishing the *Northern Star,* a national weekly newspaper, on a profitable basis in 1837 was little more than £690. It was able to break even with a circulation of about 6200 copies, which was probably achieved in its first month. In contrast the *Sunday Express,* launched in 1918, had over £2 million spent on it before it broke even, with a circulation of well over 250,000. Thus while a public subscription in northern towns was sufficient to launch a national weekly in the 1830s, it required the resources of an international conglomerate controlled by Beaverbrook to do the same thing nearly a century later.[4]

These statistics illustrate the privileged position of capital in the creation of the modern press. Even when the costs of launching and establishing a popular paper were relatively low in the 1850s and 1860s, they still exceeded the resources readily available to the organized working class. The *Beehive,* for instance, was started in 1862 with capital of less than £250 raised by trade union organizations and a well-to-do sympathizer. Its inadequate funding crippled it. Although it set out to carry both news and features and to reach a wide audience, it lacked the finances to be anything other than a weekly journal of opinion. Despite a small amount of additional capital put up by unions and other contributors, it was also forced to sell at double the price of the large-circulation weeklies it had been intended to compete against. In effect, its undercapitalization condemned it to the margins of national publishing as a specialist, if influential, weekly paper.

As the resources of organized labour increased, so did the costs of establishing a national paper. It was not until 1912 that papers financed and controlled from within the working class made their first appearance in national daily journalism – long after most national daily papers had become well established. The brief career of the *Daily Citizen,* and the early history of the *Daily Herald,* illustrate the economic obstacles to setting up papers under working-class control. The *Daily Citizen,* launched in 1912 with a capital of only £30,000 (subscribed mainly by trade unions), reached a circulation of 250,000 at its peak within two years and was only 50,000 short of overhauling the *Daily Express.* But although the *Daily Citizen* almost certainly acquired more working-class readers than any other daily, it still closed three years after its launch.

The more left-wing *Daily Herald,* started with only £300 and sustained by public donations, lurched from one crisis to another despite reaching a circulation of over 250,000 at its meridian before 1914. On one occasion it came out in pages of different sizes and shapes because someone 'found' old discarded paper supplies when the *Daily Herald* could no longer afford to pay for new paper. On another occasion it bought small quantities of paper under fictitious names from suppliers all over the country. Later it secured paper supplies without a guarantee by threatening to organize, through its trade union connections, industrial action against paper manufacturers. While the *Daily Citizen* closed, the *Daily Herald* survived by switching from being a daily to becoming a weekly during the period 1914 to 1919. Lack of sufficient capital prevented its continuation in any other form.

The rise in publishing costs helps to explain why the committed left press in the late nineteenth century existed only as undercapitalized, low-budget, high-price specialist periodicals and as local community papers, an important but as yet relatively undocumented aspect of the residual survival of the radical press. The operation of the free market had raised the cost of press ownership beyond the readily available resources of the working class.

Market forces thus accomplished more than the most repressive measures of an aristocratic state. The security system introduced in 1819 to ensure that the press was controlled by 'men of some respectability and capital' had fixed the financial qualifications of press ownership at a mere £200 to £300. This financial hurdle was raised over a hundredfold by the market system between 1850 and 1920.[5]

However, although the heavy capitalization of the British press was an important factor inhibiting the launch of new radical papers, it still does not explain the ideological absorption of radical papers already in existence before the repeal of the press taxes. Nor does it fully explain why small-circulation radical papers could not develop into profitable mass-circulation papers and accumulate enough capital, through retained profits, to finance new publications. For an answer to these questions we need to look elsewhere.

The new licensing system: advertising

The crucial element of the new control system was the strategic role acquired by advertisers after the repeal of the advertisement duty in 1853. Before then, the advertisement tax had made certain forms of advertising uneconomic. As John Cassell, the publisher of popular useful knowledge publications, argued before the Parliamentary Select Committee on Newspaper Stamps, 'It [the advertisement duty] entirely prevents a certain class of advertisements from appearing: it is only such as costly books and property sales by auction that really afford an opportunity of advertising and for paying the duty.'

Cassell exaggerated the impact of the advertisement duty for political reasons. The growth of trade, and the halving of the advertisement duty in 1833, had led to a substantial increase in press advertising in the 1830s and 1840s. Even before that, most commercial newspapers – but not the radical press –

had been reliant on advertising, but it was only with the abolition of the advertisement duty in 1853 that popular press advertising came fully into its own. Between 1854 and 1858, for instance, *Reynolds News* increased its advertising volume by over 50 per cent. This surge in advertising expenditure, combined with the repeal of the stamp and paper duties, transformed the economic structure of the popular press. The modal price of popular papers was halved in the 1850s and halved again in the 1860s. At the new prevailing price structure, nearly all newspapers – including those with very large circulations such as *Reynolds News* – depended on advertising for their profits since their reduced net cover prices no longer met their costs. Advertisers thus acquired a *de facto* licensing power because, without their support, newspapers ceased to be economically viable.

Rising circulations, decreasing print unit costs and, between 1875 and 1895, the sharp fall in the price of newsprint did not diminish the central role of advertising in the press. Advertising expenditure increased steadily in the Victorian and Edwardian period, rising to an estimated £20 million in 1907. This financed bigger papers, more staff and the introduction of sale-or-return arrangements with distributors. It also helped to underwrite a further halving of the price of most popular papers to ½d in the late Victorian period.

The political implications of newspapers' economic dependence on advertising have been ignored largely because it is assumed that advertisers bought space in newspapers on the basis of market rather than political criteria. But political considerations played a significant part in some advertisers' calculations during the Victorian period. In 1856 the principal advertising handbook detailed the political views of most London and local newspapers with the proud boast that 'till this Directory was published, the advertiser had no means of accurately determining which journal *might be best adapted to his views,* and most likely to forward his interests' (emphasis added).[6] Even non-socialist newspapers found that controversial editorial policies led to the loss of commercial advertising. The *Pall Mall Gazette*'s advertising revenue dropped sharply in response to its 'Maiden Tribute' crusade in 1885 in which the editor 'procured' a 15-year-old girl as part of his paper's campaign to raise the legal age of consent to sex. The *Daily News* was boycotted by some advertisers in 1886 when it campaigned for Home Rule. Government advertising long continued to be allocated on a partisan basis. As late as 1893 the incoming Home Secretary, Herbert Asquith, was told that generally 'it is the custom to transfer advertisements according to the politics of governments'.

Political prejudice in advertising selection almost certainly declined during the latter part of the nineteenth and early twentieth centuries. The rise of advertising agencies, the emergence of major, national advertisers and the increasing availability of circulation statistics encouraged the adoption of a more professional approach. Even so, the frequent remonstrations against 'mixing business and politics' in advertising manuals published between 1850 and 1930 suggest that political prejudice continued to influence some advertisers.

However, even when political partisanship played no part in advertising selection, left-wing publications still faced discrimination on commercial grounds. As the head of a well-known advertising agency wrote in 1856, 'Some of the most widely circulated journals in the Empire are the worst possible to advertise in. Their readers are not purchasers, and any money thrown upon them is so much thrown away.' Newspapers read by the well-to-do were assessed differently. 'Character is of more importance than number,' advised an advertising handbook in 1851, adding that 'A journal that circulates a thousand among the upper or middle classes is a better medium than would be one circulating a hundred thousand among the lower classes.' Similar, though usually more qualified, advice continued to be given for some time. For example, Sir Charles Higham, the head of a large advertising agency, wrote in 1925, 'A very limited circulation, but entirely among the wealthy . . . may be more valuable than if the circulation were quadrupled.'[7]

Some advertisers also made a key distinction between the skilled and poor working class. Indeed, the latter were often excluded from the early market research surveys in the 1920s on the grounds that they were not worth bothering about. Once newspapers became identified with the poor, they found it difficult to attract advertising. As an advertising handbook cautioned in 1921, 'You cannot afford to place your advertisements in a paper which is read by the down-at-heels who buy it to see the "Situations Vacant" column.'[8]

This combination of economic and political discrimination by advertisers crucially influenced the development of left-wing journalism. In the first place, it exerted pressure on the radical press to move upmarket in order to survive. A number of radical newspapers redefined their target audience, and moderated their radicalism, in an attempt to attract the more affluent readers whom advertisers wanted to reach.

This process is well illustrated by the career of *Reynolds News*. It was founded in 1850 by George Reynolds, a member of the left-wing faction of the Chartist National Executive. Reynolds had urged a 'physical force' strategy in 1848 and opposed middle-class collaboration in the early 1850s. His paper was initially in the *Northern Star* tradition of class-conscious radicalism, and had close links with the working-class movement.

Yet despite its radical origins, *Reynolds News* changed under the impact of the new economic imperatives of newspaper publishing. The fact that it never provided, even at the outset, a consistent theoretical perspective doubtless made it vulnerable to ideological incorporation. Inevitably it was influenced by the decline of radicalism in the country during the 1850s and early 1860s, but an important factor in its absorption was the need to attract advertising revenue. The change was symbolized by the inclusion of regular features on friendly societies in the year after the repeal of the advertisement duty, as a ploy to attract advertising. Thus enterprises which had been attacked in militant newspapers as 'a hoax' to persuade working-class people to identify with capitalism became a much-needed source of revenue for *Reynolds News.*

The paper continued to take a radical stand on most major events of the day, but it expressed increasingly the individualistic values of the more affluent readers whom it needed to attract. It adopted some of the tenets of liberal political economy that it had attacked during the 1850s, including the palliatives of 'prudent marriage' (i.e. sexual restraint) and emigration as solutions to unemployment. It became still more populist, focusing on the vices of the aristocracy, corruption in high places, and poverty as a source of melodrama (rather than as a condition to be overcome through socialist advance). Its early assault on the workings of industrial capital was modulated to criticism of monopoly and speculators, while criticism of shopkeepers as the exploitive agents of capital gave way to articles that tacitly accepted the market economy. *Reynolds News* became a paper that catered for the coalition of lower-middle-class and working-class readers necessary for its survival. Acquired by the Dicks family in 1879 and later by J. H. Dalziel, it gradually evolved into a conventional Liberal paper.

Reynolds was accused of commercial opportunism by contemporary critics (including Karl Marx); yet it is difficult to see what else he could have done if the paper was to survive the transition to an advertising-based system. Even the radical *People's Paper* boasted in 1857 of its appeal to 'high paid trades and shopkeepers' in its promotion to advertisers. Failing to attract affluent readers in sufficient numbers, the *People's Paper* was forced to close down with a circulation far larger than middle-class weeklies such as the *Spectator* and *John Bull.*

Radical newspapers could survive in the new economic environment only if they moved upmarket to attract an audience desired by advertisers or remained in a small working-class ghetto, with manageable losses that could be offset by donations. Once they moved out of that ghetto and sought a large working-class audience, they courted disaster. If they sold at the competitive prices charged by their rivals, they made a loss on each copy due to lack of advertising. If they increased their sales, they merely incurred greater losses and moved more heavily into debt.

This fate befell the London *Evening Echo,* which was taken over by wealthy radicals in 1901 and relaunched as a socialist paper. A special number was issued, firmly committing the paper to 'the interests of labour as against the tyranny of organized capital'. In the period 1902 to 1904 its circulation rose by a remarkable 60 per cent, leading to its abrupt closure in 1905. The *Evening Echo*'s advertising had failed to keep pace with its growth of circulation, making its continuation impossible.[9]

The same thing almost happened to the *Daily Herald* when it was relaunched as a daily in 1919. It spent £10,000 on promotion – a small amount by comparison with its main rivals, but sufficient to ensure that it sharply increased its circulation. 'Our success in circulation,' recalled George Lansbury, 'was our undoing. The more copies we sold, the more money we lost.' The situation became increasingly desperate when, aided partly by the unexpected publicity of attacks on the *Daily Herald* by leading members of the government alleging that it was financed from Moscow, the *Daily Herald*'s circulation continued to rise in 1920. 'Every copy we sold was sold at a loss,' mourned Lansbury. 'The rise in circulation, following the government's attacks, brought us nearer and nearer to disaster.'[10] The money raised from whist drives, dances, draws and collections was not enough to offset the short-fall of advertising. The desperate expedient of doubling the paper's price in 1920 was not enough to secure its future. Money from the miners and the rail-waymen prevented the paper from closing. But the only way the paper could be saved, in the long term, was by being taken over as the official organ of the Labour Party and TUC in 1922. A paper that had been a freewheeling vehi-cle of the left, an important channel for the dissemination of syndicalist and socialist ideas in the early part of the twentieth century, became the official mouthpiece of the moderate leadership of the labour movement.[11] Lack of advertising forced it to become subservient to a new form of control.

In short, one of four things happened to national radical papers that failed to meet the requirements of advertisers. They either closed down; accommo-dated to advertising pressure by moving upmarket; stayed in a small audience ghetto with manageable losses; or accepted an alternative source of institu-tional patronage.

Yet publications which conformed to the marketing requirements of adver-tisers obtained what were, in effect, large external subsidies which they could spend on increased editorial outlay and promotion in order to attract new readers. Rising advertising expenditure also provided a powerful inducement to entrepreneurs to launch publications directed at markets that advertisers particularly wanted to reach. Between 1866 and 1896 the number of maga-zines increased from an estimated 557 to 2097, many of which were trade, technical and professional journals aimed at specialized groups attractive to advertisers. The number of local dailies grew from only two in 1850 to 196 in 1900, falling to 169 by 1920 due mainly to the casualties caused by intense competition. There was also a substantial expansion in the number of local weekly papers from fewer than 400 in 1856 to an estimated 2072 in 1900, declining to an estimated 1700 by 1921. Above all, there was a substantial increase in the number of national daily and Sunday papers, mostly founded between 1880 and 1918, which catered for either mass, middle-market audi-ences or small élite audiences.[12]

This growth in the number of publications was accompanied by an enor-mous expansion in newspaper consumption. Annual newspaper sales rose from 85 million in 1851 to 5604 million in 1920. Only part of this increase was due to rapid population growth: the number of newspapers purchased *per capita* over the age of 14 rose from six copies in 1850 to 182 copies in 1920.

Even allowing for a reduction in the number of readers per copy, due to a marked decline in the collective purchase and reading aloud from newspapers, this still constitutes a remarkable increase in the audience reached by the press. Sunday and local daily papers achieved aggregate circulations of 13.5 million and 9.2 million respectively by 1920. In contrast the national daily press with a predominantly middle-class public had a circulation of only 5.4 million in 1920, while the local weekly press (which was particularly strong in rural areas) had 6.8 million circulation.[13]

This growth was facilitated by new print technology, rising advertising subsidy and lower cover prices. The rise of mass consumption was also a product of cumulative social and economic change. Adult literacy (as measured very imperfectly by the ability to sign one's name) rose from 69 per cent in 1850 to 97 per cent in 1900. The normal number of hours worked in many industries fell from sixty hours a week to fifty-four hours or fewer between 1850 and 1890, and average real wages rose by an estimated 84 per cent between 1850 and 1900. The resulting expansion of the capitalist press had important consequences for the political development of Britain.

Impact of the industrialized press

At the turn of the nineteenth century, traditional educationalists such as Hannah More taught working-class children to read but not to write. The industrialization of the press led to a similar division of function. Workers became consumers but not the producers of meaning, save in the subjective sense of critically reading 'between the lines'.

Many of the new local dailies were started or bought by leading local industrialists. Both the *Northern Daily Express* and the *Northern Leader* were bought by colliery owners; the *South Shields Gazette* was acquired by Stevenson, a member of a local chemical manufacturing family; the *Bolton Evening News* belonged to local industrialists, the Tillotsons; the *Yorkshire Post*'s principal shareholder was the Leeds banker Beckett-Denison; the *Ipswich Express* was owned by Colman, the mustard manufacturer, and so on. These papers offered a very different view of the world from that of the early radical press they supplanted. Papers such as the *Northern Star* had amplified class conflicts in the local community ('to talk of reconciliation between the middle and working classes in Leicester will, henceforth, be a farce'[14] was a typical lead-in to one of its news reports). In contrast the new local commercial press tended to block out conflict, minimize differences, and encourage positive identification with the local community and its middle-class leadership. Characteristic of this style of consensual journalism was a report in the *Leeds Mercury* (printed in the same city as the *Northern Star*) of a local dignitary addressing the annual public soirée of the Leeds Mechanics Institute on the subject of 'these popular institutions, sustained by the united efforts of all classes . . . thereby to promote the virtue, happiness and peace of the community'.[15]

The early militant press had fuelled suspicion of middle-class reformists with a barrage of criticism against 'sham-radical humbugs' and 'the merciful middle-class converts to half Chartism at half past the eleventh hour'.[16] In contrast the new local daily press encouraged its readers to identify with the political parties controlled by the dominant classes. Ten of the new local dailies that emerged between 1855 and 1860 were affiliated to the Liberal Party; eighteen created between 1860 and 1870 were affiliated to the Tory or Liberal Party, and forty-one of the local dailies created in the following decade were similarly linked to the two great parties. The new party press built support for the modern party system, helping to transform aristocratic factions in Parliament into mass political movements. This reinforced the division of the working class by entrenching opposed partisan commitments within it. It also led to the assimilation of some working-class activists into a parliamentary system that throughout the nineteenth century was still only quasi-democratic.

The new Liberal press, in particular, played a significant role in rerouting radical politics. It frequently diluted or adapted radical themes to such a degree that they acquired a new meaning. The co-operative ethos that would prevail in a radically transformed society, proclaimed as an objective by some militant papers in the 1830s and 1840s, was transmuted into the spirit of partnership between masters and men that would make the British economy prosper. The early radical stress on moral regeneration through social reconstruction became a celebration of moral improvement through the spread of middle-class enlightenment. In addition, the value formerly attached to self-education as a means of ideological resistance to class domination gave way to a stress on the undifferentiated acquisition of 'knowledge' as the route to individual self-advancement and economic progress. Admittedly these transformations drew upon a radical tradition that contained contradictory elements within it. However, by emphasizing the liberal rather than more radical lineaments of this tradition, the new press contributed to the restabilization of the social order.

There were of course important differences between individual newspapers, not least in their reporting of trade unions and the emergent women's movement. But notwithstanding these differences, all national newspapers launched between 1855 and 1910, and the overwhelming majority of new local daily papers, encouraged positive identification with the social system. The shift that this represented is perhaps best illustrated by the way in which Queen Victoria was portrayed. Most radical papers in the period 1837 to 1855 were aggressively republican: the Queen was vilified as politically partisan and reactionary, the head of a system of organized corruption, the mother of a brood of royal cadgers, and the friend and relative of European tyrants. In contrast the new press portrayed the Queen particularly from the mid-1870s onward as a dutiful and benign matriarch, who symbolized in an almost talismanic way the moral and material progress of her reign. Projecting her as a living embodiment of national unity, they also played a key role in converting the jubilee celebrations of 1887 and 1897 into popular, mobilizing rites of national communion.

Above all, the new popular press fostered the wave of imperialism that swept through all levels of society. Popular newspapers tended to portray Britain's colonial role as a civilizing mission to the heathen, underdeveloped world, and as an extended adventure story in which military triumphs were achieved through individual acts of courage rather than through superior technology. Common to both themes was pride in Britain's ascendancy: as the *Daily Mail* (23 June 1897), the most popular daily of late Victorian Britain, enthused:

> We send out a boy here and a boy there, and the boy takes hold of the sav-
> ages of the part he comes to and teaches them to march and shoot as he
> tells them, to obey him and believe in him and die for him and the Queen.
> A plain, stupid, uninspired people they call us, and yet we are doing this
> with every kind of savage man there is.

This celebration of Britain's dominion sometimes struck a more atavistic note, as in this report of the 1898 Sudan expedition in the *Westminster Gazette*:

> A large number of the Tommies had never been under fire before . . . and
> there was a curious look of suppressed excitement in some of the faces. . . .
> Now and then I caught in a man's eye the curious gleam which, despite all
> the veneer of civilization, still holds its own in man's nature, whether he is
> killing rats with a terrier, rejoicing in a prize fight, playing a salmon or pot-
> ting Dervishes. It was a fine day and we were out to kill something. Call it
> what you like, the experience is a big factor in the joy of living.

The paper which celebrated 'potting Dervishes' was, in terms of the political spectrum represented by the contemporary national press, on 'the left'. It was, for example, one of the few papers not to join the press campaign for vengeance during the Boer War. However, it joined all other daily papers of note in providing Hun-hating support for Britain's involvement in the First World War.

Conclusion

The radical press was defeated decisively after the abolition of the 'taxes on knowledge'. Its defeat cannot be attributed solely to the changed climate of opinion, following the collapse of the Chartist Movement. This *Zeitgeist* or 'sovereign consumer' interpretation, though often invoked, fails to explain why the press, taken as a whole, moved further to the right than public opinion; nor does it explain why the subsequent revival of the radical movement did not give rise to a stronger revival of radical journalism. Both the extent and permanence of the eclipse of the radical press as the dominant force in national popular journalism was due to structural changes in the press industry. The industrialization of the press, with its accompanying rise in publishing costs, led to a progressive transfer of ownership and control of the popular press from the working class to wealthy businessmen, while dependence on advertising encouraged the absorption or elimination of the early radical press and stunted its subsequent development before the First World War.

Notes

1. For the relative weakness of the radical press in 1910, see A. J. Lee, 'The radical press' in A. Morris (ed.), *Edwardian Radicalism, 1900–1914* (London, Routledge & Kegan Paul, 1974).
2. V. Berridge, 'Popular Sunday papers and mid-Victorian society' in G. Boyce, J. Curran and P. Wingate (eds), *Newspaper History* (London, Constable, 1978). This interpretation has since been developed by J. Chalaby in *The Invention of Journalism* (London, Macmillan, 1998) and M. Conboy in *The Press and Popular Culture* (London, Sage, 2002).
3. R. Pound and G. Harmsworth, *Northcliffe* (London, Cassell, 1959), p. 206.
4. A. J. P. Taylor, *Beaverbrook* (London, Hamish Hamilton, 1972), p. 175.
5. The costs of market entry for mass publishing were particularly high in Britain due to the dominant role of the national press. This explains partly why the radical press in Britain was much weaker than in some other European countries, where the press remained decentralized and entry costs were lower.
6. *Mitchell's Newspaper Press Directory* (Mitchell, 1856). It should be noted, however, that Mitchell himself cautioned advertisers against political bias.
7. *Mitchell's Newspaper Press Directory* (Mitchell, 1856); Anon., *Guide to Advertisers* (1851); C. Higham, *Advertising* (London, Williams & Norgate, 1925), p. 166.
8. C. Freer, *The Inner Side of Advertising: A Practical Handbook for Advertisers* (London, Library Press, 1921), p. 203.
9. F. W. Pethick-Lawrence, *Fate Has Been Kind* (London, Hutchinson, 1943), pp. 65ff.
10. G. Lansbury, *The Miracle of Fleet Street* (London, Victoria House, 1925), pp. 160ff.
11. H. Richards, *The Bloody Circus: The Daily Herald and the Left* (London, Pluto, 1997).
12. The figures for regional dailies relate to Britain and for other categories of publications to the UK, as reported in *Mitchell's Newspaper Press Directory*.
13. N. Kaldor and R. Silverman, *A Statistical Analysis of Advertising Expenditure and of the Revenue of the Press* (Cambridge, Cambridge University Press, 1948), p. 84.
14. *Northern Star,* 7 May 1842.
15. *Leeds Mercury,* 14 June 1851.
16. *Northern Star,* 26 February and 11 June 1842.

5

The era of the press barons

The era of the press barons is often seen as a maverick interlude in the development of the press when newspapers became subject to the whims and caprices of their owners. According to this view, the press barons built vast press empires and ruled them like personal fiefdoms. In the hands of men like Beaverbrook and Rothermere, newspapers became mere 'engines of propaganda', manipulated in order to further their political ambitions. As Stanley Baldwin declared in a memorable sentence (suggested to him by his cousin, Rudyard Kipling), 'What proprietorship of these papers is aiming at is power, and power without responsibility – the prerogative of the harlot throughout the ages.'

The despotic rule of the press barons is usually compared unfavourably with a preceding 'golden age' when proprietors played an inactive role and 'sovereign' editors conducted their papers in a responsible manner. In some accounts, too, the era of Northcliffe and Rothermere is contrasted with the period after the Second World War when journalists became more educated, independent and professional. The press barons have thus become favourite bogeymen: their indictment has become a way of celebrating the editorial integrity of newspapers, both past and present.

But in reality the reign of the press barons did not constitute an exceptional pathology in the evolution of the press, but merely a continuation of tendencies already present before. Indeed, insofar as the barons may be said to have been innovators, it is not for the reasons that are generally given. They did not break with tradition by using their papers for political propaganda; their distinctive contribution was rather that they downgraded propaganda in favour of entertainment. Nor did they subvert the role of the press as a fourth estate; on the contrary it was they who detached the commercial press from the political parties and, consequently, from the state. What actually happened is, in some ways, the exact opposite of historical mythology.[1]

The creation of press empires

The newspaper chains built by the press barons were not a new phenomenon. Multiple ownership of weekly newspapers had developed as early as the eighteenth century. Local daily chains had also emerged shortly after the regional daily press was established in the mid-nineteenth century. By 1884, for instance, a syndicate headed by the Scots-American steel magnate Carnegie controlled eight dailies and ten weeklies.

Although some papers controlled by the press barons gained a dominant market position, this too had happened before. *The Times*, for example, had dominated the respectable daily press during the early Victorian period. This recurring pattern arose from the unequal competitive relationship that developed between strong and weak papers. As soon as one paper gained a market lead, it was in a strong position to move further ahead because it had more money than its rivals from both sales and scale economies to invest in editorial development.

While the press barons reached a growing audience as a consequence of a rapid increase in circulation, this was also not new. There had been a sustained growth of newspaper consumption ever since the seventeenth century, and this growth was already accelerating before the press barons made their mark.

The large empires created by the press barons may thus be viewed as a continuation of three well-established trends – chain ownership, an expanding market and a tendency for a few papers to become dominant. All that happened was that some of these trends became more pronounced during the period of their ascendancy. In the first place there was, between 1890 and 1920, a rapid growth of newspaper chains which incorporated national as well as regional papers. By 1921 the three Harmsworth brothers (Lords Northcliffe, Rothermere and Sir Lester Harmsworth) controlled newspapers with an aggregate circulation of over six million – probably the largest press group in the western world at the time.[2]

Between the wars, concentration of press ownership entered a new phase, with the spectacular consolidation of the regional chains. The percentage of provincial evening titles controlled by the five big chains rose from 8 to 40 per cent between 1921 and 1939; their ownership of the provincial morning titles also increased, from 12 to 44 per cent during the same period. The power of the chains was extended further by the elimination of local competition. Between 1921 and 1937, the number of towns with a choice of evening paper fell from twenty-four to ten, while towns with a choice of local morning paper declined from fifteen to seven.

The principal pace-setters in the expansion of the regional chains were the Berry brothers, Lords Camrose and Kemsley. Their group grew from four daily and Sunday papers in 1921 to twenty daily and Sunday papers in 1939. This was achieved only after a long-drawn-out and costly 'war' with Lord

Rothermere, which was eventually resolved in a series of local treaties in which the three lords divided up different parts of the country between them.

There was also, during the inter-war period, an enormous increase in the sales of national dailies which for the first time overtook that of local dailies. Between 1920 and 1939 the combined circulation of the national daily press rose from 5.4 million to 10.6 million, while that of the local daily and weekly press remained relatively static. This major expansion of the London-based press meant that some proprietors gained enormous audiences even when they owned relatively few papers. This applied in particular to Lord Beaverbrook, controller of the *Daily Express*, the leading popular daily of the late 1930s.

These changes meant that, after the death of Lord Northcliffe in 1922, four men – Lords Beaverbrook, Rothermere, Camrose and Kemsley – became the dominant figures in the inter-war press. In 1937, for instance, they owned nearly one in every two national and local daily papers sold in Britain, as well as one in every three Sunday papers that were sold. The combined circulation of all their newspapers amounted to over thirteen million.

However, their pre-eminence was not in fact as great as that of their less well-known predecessors. In 1937 the three leading Sunday papers' owners (Kemsley, Beaverbrook and Camrose) controlled 59 per cent of national Sunday newspaper circulation – significantly less than the 69 per cent share of national Sunday circulation controlled by three less power-hungry proprietors (Dalziel, Riddell and Lloyd) in 1910. Similarly in 1937 Rothermere, Beaverbrook and Cadbury controlled 50 per cent of national daily circulation – again, much less than the 67 per cent share controlled by Pearson, Cadbury and Northcliffe in 1910.

This relative decline was due partly to the re-emergence of a significant labour press. The Co-operative Movement bought *Reynolds News* in 1929: the TUC formed a partnership with Odhams to relaunch the *Daily Herald* in 1929; and the Communist Party established the *Daily Worker* in 1930. The rising capitalization of the press led also to an increased dispersal of share-holdings. Two important papers, the *Daily Mirror* and *Sunday Pictorial*, ceased to have a controlling shareholder in the mid-1930s. The press magnates' hegemony over the press was, in fact, waning during the period celebrated for their ascendancy.

Press barons and proprietorial control

Not all press proprietors were interventionist. For instance, Astor, joint owner of *The Times* after 1922, was teased by his friends for not reading his own paper. Even the quintessential press barons – Northcliffe, Rothermere, Beaverbrook and Kemsley – did not exercise a uniform degree of control. They tended to lavish attention on their favourite papers, while taking a lesser interest in others they controlled.

Thus in the late 1930s Beaverbrook deluged the *Daily Express* with instructions to support appeasement ('No War Talk. NO WAR TALK' read one telegram of that period), but did not seem to mind that its sister paper, the *Sunday Express,* expressed growing disquiet about Germany's remilitarization, or that another of his papers, the *Evening Standard,* under the socialist editor Percy Cudlipp, urged a popular front against fascism. Similarly Northcliffe was mainly concerned in his later years with the *Daily Mail,* a preoccupation that his brother Rothermere later shared.

The two archetypal press barons, Northcliffe and Beaverbrook, had very different personal styles. While Northcliffe was notorious for personally harassing his staff, Beaverbrook's remoteness was legendary. In *Scoop,* Evelyn Waugh satirized a visit to him:

> The carpets were thicker [as one approached Lord Copper's private office], the lights softer, the expressions of the inhabitants more careworn. The typewriters were of a special kind: their keys made no more sound than the drumming of a bishop's finger-tips on an upholstered prie-dieu. The telephone buzzers were muffled and purred like warm cats. The personal private secretaries padded through the ante-chambers and led them nearer and nearer to the presence.

Yet despite their differences of personality, both men exercised detailed control over their favourite papers through a constant barrage of instructions. Beaverbrook sent 147 separate instructions to the *Daily Express* in one day. Northcliffe would sometimes phone his staff at 6 in the morning: 'Wake up! Have you seen the papers yet?' he would demand. One editor, who replied that you could not get the *Mail* in Northlake at 6 a.m., was woken at 5 the next morning by a copy delivered to his door by a pantechnicon.

The press barons maintained their personal domination with extreme ruthlessness. Northcliffe, in particular, had a brisk way of dismissing employees. 'Who is that?' Northcliffe said on the phone. 'Editor, *Weekly Dispatch,* Chief,' came the reply. 'You were the editor,' responded Northcliffe. When a luckless subeditor filled a lull in conversation over lunch with the information that he had been shipwrecked three times, Northcliffe said abruptly, 'Four times.' Beaverbrook also had a fearsome reputation. 'Fleet Street,' recalled one of his employees, 'was strewn with the corpses of *Express* editors.'[3]

The barons combined terror with generosity. Journalists' memoirs and official histories are full of anecdotes about the sudden gifts, holidays and salary rises which were showered on staff. As a genre these stories could be called 'courageous underling gets his reward'. They usually take the form of the plucky journalist standing up for himself (or, more rarely, for what he believes) in the face of the baron's fury. They are clearly intended to enhance both the baron, who is revealed as discriminating and fundamentally right-minded in his judgements, and the journalist, whose independence is

demonstrated by his courage. But what they actually reveal is an almost continuous process of humiliation. Bernard Falk, usually rewarded with a cigar
when he took down Northcliffe's dictated social column for the *Mail*, was
once allowed to choose the one he wanted. 'What!' said Northcliffe, 'You have
the nerve to pick on those cigars! Don't you know, young man, that they cost
3/6 each?' 'Yes,' said the fearless reporter, 'but they're worth every penny.'
Another editor who dared to disagree with Northcliffe recorded gratefully the
telegram he received: 'My dear Blackwood, you are grossly impertinent to
your affectionate Chief.'

   Losing a battle with a press baron hardly made such a good story. Buckle,
the editor of *The Times* (whose editorial independence Northcliffe had
promised to uphold), was eased out of the editorship when he failed to adapt
to the political views and managerial strategy of the Chief. Lewis Macleod,
literary editor of the *Daily Mail,* received a communiqué from Northcliffe:
'This is the last occasion on which I can tolerate Macleod's gross neglect and
carelessness. He will read this message out to the editorial conference on
Monday.' When Northcliffe was angered by what he thought were defects on
the *Daily Mail*'s picture page, he lined up all those involved in its production
and put the tallest man in charge. Feeling dissatisfied with the *Mail*'s advertising department, he appointed the commissionaire to vet advertisements.
Beaverbrook was also unpredictable, though not on the scale of Northcliffe.[4]
Yet behind both men's seemingly random acts of ferocity and generosity,
there was often a careful regard for their self-interest. Beaverbrook insisted,
for instance, that some of his best journalists write under pseudonyms so that,
if they left the *Express,* they could not take with them the goodwill generated
by their copy.

   Northcliffe and Beaverbrook shaped the entire content of their favourite
papers, including their layout. Thus Northcliffe raged at an employee at *The
Times,* 'What have you done with the moon? I said the moon – the *Moon.*
Someone has moved the moon! . . . Well, if it's moved again, whoever does it
is fired!' (The position of the weather report had been changed.) Beaverbrook
and Northcliffe constantly pestered journalists about the language and phras-
ing of their reports. 'To Eastbourne's balding, myopic, Edinburgh-trained
physiotherapist, William John Snooks, 53, came the news that . . .' parodied
Tom Driberg, a former *Express* journalist, in the approved Beaverbrook style.
Both press barons also interfered in the choice of pictures. 'Alfonso' (King of
Spain), complained Northcliffe, 'is always smiling. This smile is not news. If
you get a picture of Alfonso weeping, *that* would be news!'

   The barons' personal foibles influenced the selection of news stories,
thereby helping to shape the news values of the national press. Northcliffe
had a lifelong obsession with torture and death: he even kept an aquarium
containing goldfish and a pike, with a dividing partition, which he would lift
up when he was in need of diversion. His obsession was reflected in his first
magazine, *Answers,* which dealt with such enquiries as: 'How long is a severed

head conscious after decapitation?' The first feature article Northcliffe wrote for his first evening newspaper described the day he spent with a condemned murderer in Chelmsford Prison. He later briefed *Daily Mail* staff to find 'one murder a day'. Similarly Beaverbrook, a hypochondriac, told the editor of the *Daily Express* that 'the public like to know . . . what diseases men die of – and women too'.

Proprietors' perceptions of their readers set the tone of their papers. The *Daily Express* aimed, in Beaverbrook's words, at 'the character and tempera-ment which was bent on moving upwards and outward', reflecting Beaverbrook's North American admiration for self-made success. The *Daily Mail*, on the other hand, projected a more static, hierarchical world appeal-ing, as Northcliffe put it patronizingly, to 'people who would like to think they earned £1,000 a year'.

The proprietorial control exercised by the press magnates did not represent, however, a decisive break with the past. Indeed, Lucy Brown's revisionist account of the Victorian commercial press even argues that 'what is an important and unvarying generalization is that the sovereign powers of deci-sion were exercised by the proprietors and not by the editors'. Many of the Victorian editors celebrated for their independence, such as C. P. Scott of the *Manchester Guardian* (1877 to 1929), were either owner-editors or members of the proprietorial family. Other leading editors prove, on close examination, to have been less autonomous than has usually been claimed. Even Delane of *The Times,* often seen as a model of the sovereign editor, was repeatedly excluded from key planning decisions affecting the development of his paper. Indeed, he was so convinced that he was going to be sacked at one stage that he started 'taking dinners' in order to become eligible to practise as a barris-ter. Others were less fortunate: Cook, Gardiner, Massingham, Greenwood, Annand, Watson and Donald were only some of the distinguished editors who were compelled to resign between 1880 and 1918 as a result of political disagreements with their proprietors.

The tradition of editorial sovereignty which the press magnates allegedly destroyed was, to a large extent, a myth. The press barons were no different from their immediate predecessors in involving themselves in the editorial conduct of their papers. What made them innovators, to some degree, was that they were heavily involved in the business side of their papers. Yet even this difference should not be overstated since some of the earlier pioneers of 'popular' journalism, notably Edward Lawson and Edward Lloyd, were also active business managers.

Profits and politics

However, the press barons are usually portrayed as journalist-politicians – a view of themselves which they publicly cultivated. Beaverbrook, for instance, told the first Royal Commission on the Press that he ran the *Daily Express* 'merely for the purpose of making propaganda and with no other motive'. Yet this simple image of propagandist has tended to obscure another, more important aspect of their dominion over the press – their demotion of politics.

Intense competition resulted in rising levels of paging, bigger editorial staffs and, above all, massive promotion. Northcliffe and Rothermere led the way by spending, up to 1928, approximately £1 million on the *Daily Mail*'s readers' insurance scheme in order to attract more readers. Rival press magnates fought back with competitions offering lavish prizes and their own readers' insurance schemes. After a legal judgment in 1928 outlawed newspaper competitions as lotteries, promotion shifted towards free gifts. Teams of canvassers moved through the countryside offering housewives anything from cameras and wristwatches to silk stockings and tea-kettles, in return for taking out a newspaper subscription. The promotion for the *Daily Herald* alone is estimated to have amounted to £1 per new reader between 1930 and 1932. Even in 1937, when the 'circulation war' had abated, a typical national daily newspaper employed five times as many canvassers as editorial staff.[5] The effect of this heavy promotion and rising editorial outlay was to force up costs, and therefore the circulations that popular newspapers needed to achieve in order to stay profitable.

Publishers were consequently under increasing pressure to give more space to material with a general appeal to less differentiated audiences. The editorial implications of this were spelt out in market research, which most leading publishers commissioned during the 1930s, into what people read in newspapers. A major survey, based on a national quota sample of over 20,000 people and commissioned by the *News Chronicle* in 1933, revealed, for instance, that the most-read news in popular daily papers were stories about accidents, crime, divorce and human interest. They had a near-universal appeal. In contrast most categories of public affairs news had only an average or below-average readership rating. This was because, although some aspects of public affairs had an above-average readership among men and people over the age of 35, they had a weak appeal among women and the young. Public affairs content was thus, in marketing terms, a commodity with a sectional appeal. It lacked, moreover, the passionate following among a large minority commanded by sport, and it also lacked the appeal to advertisers possessed by some minority consumer features.

Pressure to maximize audiences consequently resulted in the cumulative downgrading of political coverage. By 1936 six out of our sample of seven papers devoted more space to human interest content than to public affairs – indeed, in some cases three or four times as much.[6] Among popular papers, the one exception to this trend towards depoliticization was the *Daily Herald,* which allocated 33 per cent of its editorial content to public affairs in 1936. This reflected the socialist priorities of the paper's TUC-nominated directors. To the press barons, by contrast, profits mattered ultimately more than politics.

This shift away from the traditional concept of a *news*paper was part of a long-term trend dating back to the mid-nineteenth century. It accelerated, however, during the inter-war period. Thus between 1927 and 1937 home political, social and economic news almost halved as a proportion of total news in the *Daily Mail*.[7]

The quality press remained more faithful to the traditional concept of the newspaper, despite the fact that market research showed that the most-read news items in quality dailies were very similar to those in popular papers.[8] However, quality newspapers continued to give high priority to public affairs as a consequence of a felicitous conjunction between professional and commercial concerns. By the mid-1930s, over two-thirds of quality newspaper income came from advertising. This was generated by charging high rates to reach small but affluent audiences: diluting this select readership with working-class readers, attracted by a popular editorial strategy, would have been economically counter-productive.

The rise of the 'fourth estate'

The press barons are usually accused of using their papers as instruments of political power, but they were hardly unique in this. What actually made the more notorious press magnates fundamentally different from their immediate predecessors was that they sought to use their papers not as levers of power within the political parties, but as instruments of power against the political parties. The basis of the establishment's objection to men like Rothermere and Beaverbrook was not that they were politically ambitious, but that they were politically independent.

In the early twentieth century the majority of London-based daily papers were owned by wealthy individuals, families or syndicates closely linked to a political party. Between 1911 and 1915, for instance, funds from the Unionist Central Office were secretly paid through respectable nominees to the *Standard, Globe, Observer* and *Pall Mall Gazette.* A wealthy Conservative syndicate, headed by the Duke of Northumberland, bought the Tory *Morning Post* in 1924. Similarly, Lloyd George engineered the purchase of the *Daily News* in 1901 by the Cadbury family in the Liberal interest, and arranged the purchase of the *Daily Chronicle* in 1918 through a syndicate headed by Dalziel with money accumulated through the sale of honours and laundered through the Lloyd George Fund.

This pattern of political control was undermined by the growth of advertising expenditure (mostly on the press) which nearly trebled from £20 million in 1907 to £59 million in 1938. This funded an escalating rise in editorial and promotional spending, and increasingly made papers too expensive for political parties and their supporters to sustain. Pearson refused to dig deeper into his pocket to keep the *Westminster Gazette* going in the Liberal cause after 1928; Lloyd George and his associates were forced to sell the *Daily Chronicle* in 1928; the TUC gave up financial control of the *Daily Herald* to the Odhams Group in 1929; no Tory syndicate could be found to prevent the *Daily Graphic* from closing in 1926 or the *Morning Post* from disappearing in 1937.

The enormous expansion of advertising weaned the national press from dependence on the political parties. Although most major press barons were Tories, they were first and foremost newspapermen. With the exception of papers controlled by Beaverbrook in his early days, all their publications were subsidized solely by advertising, and consequently were free to operate entirely independently of political patronage. An independent 'fourth estate', prematurely announced in the mid-nineteenth century, came much closer to reality under the press barons.

Beaverbrook and Northcliffe played an important role in the political revolt that unseated Asquith as premier in 1916, and established Lloyd George in his place. After the war they adopted a more unconventional, outsider role. Between 1919 and 1922 Rothermere, aided by Northcliffe, launched a virulent campaign against 'squandermania', urging extensive cuts in public spending, the abandonment of wartime planning controls and the sale of publicly owned enterprises. When the Coalition government partially rejected these policies, Rothermere appealed directly to the country by backing the Anti-Waste League in parliamentary by-elections in 1921. Three Anti-Waste League candidates succeeded in winning at Dover, Westminster St George's and Hertford. Although these victories were not matched by by-election gains elsewhere, Rothermere had demonstrated the strength of grass-roots Conservative opposition to government policies. Partly in response to this pressure, the Ministries of Shipping, Munitions and Food were abolished, a wide range of public controls was lifted, and publicly owned factories and shipyards were sold off.

The Anti-Waste Campaign petered out with the breakup of the Coalition government in 1922, and its replacement by a Conservative administration. However, Beaverbrook and Rothermere later became persuaded that Britain's economic problems could be solved by converting the Empire into a free trade zone protected by a high tariff wall. Unable to convince the Conservative Party leadership, they again made an independent foray into politics by backing the United Empire Party (UEP). In 1930 its candidate, Vice-Admiral Turner, won unexpectedly in the safe Tory seat of Paddington. His success was followed by another by-election upset at East Islington where Labour won and the official Conservative candidate was beaten by the UEP into third place. This precipitated a revolt within the Conservative Party. Sir Robert Topping, the chief Conservative agent, wrote a memorandum saying that the party leader, Stanley Baldwin, should go. His view was endorsed by most leading Conservatives consulted by Neville Chamberlain, the party chairman. Baldwin agreed to go quietly, telling the chairman bitterly that 'the sooner, the better' suited him.

After further reflection, Stanley Baldwin decided to stay and fight, staking his political career on the outcome of the parliamentary by-election at Westminster St George's. Mounting a brilliant political campaign in which he shifted attention from empire free trade to the unaccountable power of the press barons, he helped the official Conservative candidate Duff Cooper to win with a comfortable majority. Thereafter Baldwin's personal position was safe, though he was sufficiently shaken to make what was, in effect, a private peace treaty with Beaverbrook shortly after the by-election.

The political impetus behind the empire free trade campaign was broken by the 1931 crisis, the collapse of the Labour government and the landslide election victory won by the Coalition administration headed by Ramsay MacDonald. It was also weakened by lack of enthusiasm in the Dominions for the press barons' grand design. Nevertheless, Beaverbrook and Rothermere succeeded in strengthening the imperialist wing within the Conservative Party and some imperial preference policies were implemented during the 1930s. This was more than Joseph Chamberlain, the great apostle of empire free trade, achieved during the nineteenth century despite his explosive impact on late Victorian politics.

Rothermere subsequently came out in support of the British Union of Fascists (BUF) in 1934. His papers pumped out stirring calls such as 'Give the Blackshirts a Helping Hand' (*Daily Mirror,* 22 January 1934) and 'Hurrah for the Blackshirts' (*Daily Mail,* 15 January 1934). The *Evening News,* under his control, even ran a competition for the best letter on the theme of 'Why I like the Blackshirts'. This support from a mass-circulation press thrust a relatively obscure organization into the limelight and contributed to an increase in its membership. However, Rothermere withdrew his support after little more than five months, thereby helping to deny the BUF the legitimacy it needed in order to attract 'respectable' support.

Press barons and social order

Some historians have interpreted the relative failure of the press barons to persuade people to vote for their right-wing political projects as evidence that they exercised no significant political power. However, this implies mistakenly that the influence of the press barons can be assessed only in terms of winning support for a change in public policy, as if they were merely the equivalent of a pressure group. In reality, their main impact lay in the way in which their papers selectively represented the world. This tended to strengthen the mainly conservative prejudices of their readers, and reinforce opposition, particularly within the middle class, to progressive change.

Their papers projected imaginary folk devils, the most threatening and prominent of which were Marxists whose secret allegiance was to a foreign power. Even the moderate and ineffectual administration, headed by Britain's first Labour Prime Minister, Ramsay MacDonald, was branded in 1924 as being subject to Marxist influence. In the subsequent general election battle, the 'red peril' campaign reached new heights. 'Civil War plot by Socialists' Masters' screamed the *Daily Mail*'s (25 October 1924) front-page banner headline, heading a report of a letter supposedly sent by Zinoviev (President of the Third Communist International in Moscow) to the British Communist Party. Although the letter was patently a forgery, it was given massive, largely uncritical publicity by all the press barons' papers, and was shamelessly exploited to define the choice before the electorate as a simple one between moderation and Marxism, British civilization or alien domination. 'Vote British, not Bolshie' urged the *Daily Mirror* (29 October) in its front-page headline. Underneath it printed the question in heavy type: 'Do You Wish to Vote for the Leaders of Law, Order, Peace and Prosperity?' (with reassuring pictures of Lloyd George, Baldwin, Asquith and Austen Chamberlain), 'or to Vote for the Overthrow of Society and Pave the Way to Bolshevism?' (with sinister pictures of Russian leaders).

It is doubtful whether such crude propaganda deterred many would-be Labour voters – not least because the majority of working people did not read a daily paper in 1924 (unlike ten years later). Although the Labour Party lost forty seats, its share of the vote increased by 3.2 per cent largely because it fielded sixty-four more candidates. But the effect of the sustained red scare in the press was to polarize the election between left and right. The centre vote collapsed, with the Liberal Party being reduced from 158 to forty seats. The hysteria whipped up by the press also contributed to a massive increase in turn-out, which rose by over two million compared with the previous general election called only eleven months before. The combined effect of Liberal defections and higher turn-out increased the Conservative vote and resulted in a landslide Tory victory.

The press also tended to interpret conflict within a conservative framework. Most national newspapers portrayed retrospectively the 1926 General Strike, called by the TUC in support of coal-miners, as a contest between a minority and the majority. This majority–minority paradigm detached workers from their class backgrounds, and obscured the causes of the conflict. It also enabled trade unionists to be portrayed as being opposed to the democratically elected government and the 'rule of the majority'. This, in turn, justified retribution as an act of self-defence. 'Trade unionists in this country,' declared the *Observer* (16 May 1926), 'are and always will be a minority, and if they seriously try to break the majority, they make it quite certain that the majority, if further provoked, will break them.' The portrayal of trade unionists as an unrepresentative minority also facilitated their identification with communist subversion. 'The defeat of the General Strike,' thundered the *Daily Mail* (14 May 1926), 'will end the danger of communist tyranny in Europe.' A similarly persuasive and traditionalist framework was deployed in explaining the deepening Depression. It was portrayed widely as a 'natural catastrophe', comparable to a hurricane or flood. In this way, the appropriate response was defined as national unity in the face of a common calamity.

The press controlled by the barons helped to sustain the social order by stigmatizing its radical opponents. Thus, the communist-dominated Unemployed Workers' Movement received hostile coverage when it organized marches of unemployed workers from Scotland, Wales and the north of England, all converging on London early in 1929. The *Daily Mail* (24 February 1929) called it 'a weary tramp to advertise Reds', while *The Times* (11 January 1929) called it 'heartless, cruel and unnecessary'. In common with most other papers, they deflected attention from the issue of unemployment by defining the protest mainly in terms of the threat it posed to law and order. Significantly, the press provided much more sympathetic coverage of the 1936 Jarrow March, which had the support of both Conservative and Labour councillors and a much more limited political agenda. The press thus helped to police the boundaries of legitimate dissent.

However, the central core of the conservatism expressed by papers under the barons' control was a deep and emotional attachment to Britain and her empire. This intense patriotism sometimes shaded off into open racism and, particularly in the case of the papers controlled by Rothermere, aggressive anti-semitism. The *Daily Mail* (10 July 1933) interpreted Hitler's rise as a response to 'Israelite' provocation. As it patiently explained:

> The German nation was rapidly falling under the control of its alien elements. In the last days of the pre-Hitler regime there were twenty times as many Jewish government officials in Germany as had existed before the war. Israelites of international attachments were insinuating themselves into key positions in the German administrative machine.

Such interpretations fanned anti-semitism in Britain, and were linked to a campaign against Jewish asylum seekers. 'The way that stateless Jews from Germany are pouring in from every port of this country is becoming an outrage', *Daily Mail* 30 August 1938. This campaign exerted pressure, in turn, on the authorities to deny refuge to people later slaughtered in the death camps. As many as ten times the number of European Jews were blocked as were granted asylum in Britain during the later 1930s.[9]

Modification of economic controls

Although the press became more independent of political parties and of government, it still operated within an economic framework which limited the range of opinion that could be heard. The rise in publishing costs during the inter-war period, funded largely by advertising, sealed off entry into the national newspaper market. With one exception, no new national daily or Sunday newspaper was successfully established between 1919 and 1939, largely because of the prohibitive cost of starting new papers. The one exception – the communist *Sunday Worker,* launched in 1925 and converted into the *Daily Worker* in 1930 – was boycotted by distributors, and was so underfinanced that it existed only on the margins of publishing with a small circulation.

The easiest way to break into national newspaper publishing was to buy an established newspaper. However, a substantial outlay was still necessary if the acquired title was to be developed and promoted. This was beyond the readily available resources of the Co-op when it took over *Reynolds News.* Indeed, the triumphant rise of the *Daily Herald* would never have happened on such a spectacular scale if Odhams had not acquired a 51 per cent interest in the paper in 1929 and spent £3 million on its relaunch. Carrying twice as many pages as before, equipped with a northern as well as a London printing plant, and very heavily promoted, the *Daily Herald* increased its circulation from a little over 300,000 in 1929 to two million in 1933. Without this backing by one of the country's largest publishing corporations, Labour's official voice would have been muzzled by underinvestment.

The persistence of advertising discrimination against left publications still acted as a further brake upon their development. *Reynolds News,* for instance, received only 0.82d per copy in gross advertising revenue in 1936, less than half that obtained by the *Sunday Express* (1.9d per copy) and less than one-eighth of that bestowed on the *Sunday Times* (6.4d per copy).[10] Left publications were also forced to close down with circulations far higher than some of their more right-wing rivals. Thus the *Clarion* closed in 1933 with a circulation of over 80,000 copies – more than four times that of the *Spectator* and ten times that of the *Economist.* Even massive circulations were not enough to attract some mass-market advertisers. In 1936 the *Daily Herald* obtained less than half the gross advertising revenue per copy of the smaller-circulation *Daily Mail.*

However, advertising hostility to the radical press was not as great during the inter-war period as it had been before. The standard advertising textbook of the 1930s advised that 'the first test that must always be applied to a press advertising medium is the cost of placing an advertisement of a given size before a given number of suitable readers'. This precept could be followed because the information became available on which to make such a calculation. Circulation figures became more reliable during the 1920s and this trend was consolidated by the establishment of the Audit Bureau of Circulation in 1931. More importantly, survey research into the size and social composition of newspaper readership was introduced on a commercial basis in 1924 and obtained official endorsement from the advertising industry in 1930.

This encouraged a more impersonal approach to advertising selection, based on quantifiable cost criteria, in which political value judgements played a less important role. Readership research also caused advertisers to reassess stereotypical images of left publications as being read by the 'down at heel'. For instance, the 1934 official readership survey showed that the *Daily Herald* was read by more middle-class people than *The Times* (largely because the *Herald*'s readership, though predominantly working class, was so much bigger).

The development of market research in the 1920s also helped radical publications by underlining the economic importance of the working-class market. Typical of the shift of orientation among some advertisers during this period was Sun-Maid Raisins, which changed its advertising from high-class women's magazines to mass-market media in 1929 because research 'shows that 91.2 per cent of the families of Great Britain have incomes of under £400'.[11] The adoption of more sophisticated methods of analysis reinforced this more positive valorization of the working-class market. 'Inequalities of consumption', concluded the principal marketing manual of the mid-1930s, 'are less than inequalities of income, and inequalities of income are less than inequalities of wealth.'[12] A similar message was put rather less abstractly in the trade promotion of Odhams, the publisher of the *Daily Herald, John Bull* and other working-class publications. As one of their advertisements proclaimed, 'If the housewives who read *John Bull* put their purses together next year, they could buy the Giaconda diamond or Da Vinci's "Mona Lisa" hundreds of times over, then they could spend the change on the richest treasures of Bond Street or the Rue de la Paix.'

Selling the working class to advertisers was made easier by the growth of working-class purchasing power, and the related growth of consumption of mass-market goods. *Per capita* annual consumer expenditure at constant (1913) prices rose from £42 in 1921 to £54 in 1938, a large increase that reflected the rise of real wages among working people in employment during the Depression. This contributed to an enormous increase in the purchase of heavily advertised, branded products such as cosmetics, medicines, bicycles and electrical appliances.

These cumulative changes were of crucial importance in enabling the *Daily Herald* to survive as a successful daily. Even in 1933, when the *Daily Herald* became the largest circulation daily in the western world, it was still trading at a loss, but by 1936 it had picked up over £1.5 million in gross advertising receipts. Its rise was not stalled, as before, by a precipitous, unilateral price increase. This was because the paper had ceased to be an advertising pariah.

Changes in the orientation of advertisers contributed to another important development in the press – the relaunch of the *Daily Mirror* and *Sunday Pictorial*. In the early 1930s the *Daily Mirror* seemed to be a dying paper. Although it had a disproportionately middle-class readership, it was denied the usual benefits of reaching an affluent audience because, as a tabloid, it was mistakenly believed by many advertising agencies to be read only sketchily. In addition, its circulation was declining by about 70,000 a year and had dropped below 800,000 by 1933. In anticipation of the paper closing. Rothermere sold most of his shares in the *Daily Mirror*.

Rothermere's disengagement enabled the paper to change direction. Bartholomew was created editorial director in 1933, and skilfully reoriented the paper towards the lower end of the market. This had been neglected by dailies due to advertising pressure, and was waiting to be exploited. Moreover, downscale media were no longer shunned by the advertising industry due to its growing recognition of the importance of working-class consumers. The inspiration behind the paper's relaunch was essentially a marketing one, and this was reflected in the close involvement of a leading advertising agency, J. Walter Thompson (JWT), in every stage of the paper's rebirth. JWT carried out market research into readers' preferences; advised on layout; supplied staff to become key members of the new *Mirror* team; and, most important of all, advised clients to advertise in the rejuvenated paper.

A change in market direction for the *Daily Mirror* required a corresponding shift in the paper's politics. As Cecil King, the paper's advertising director, put it:

> Our best hope was, therefore, to appeal to young, working-class men and women. . . . If this was the aim, the politics had to be made to match. In the depression of the thirties, there was no future in preaching right-wing politics to young people in the lowest income bracket.

However, the *Daily Mirror*'s make-over was more cautious and gradual than legend suggests. The paper in fact backed Baldwin as Prime Minister in the 1935 general election, gradually adopted an anti-appeasement policy, but drew back from anything as extreme as support for the Labour Party. It also developed an ambivalent social identity that mirrored its political uncertainty. It published simultaneously features about the aristocracy and 'show business' stars aimed seemingly at very different readerships.

This caution was dictated partly by a desire to recruit new readers without alienating old ones. It also reflected a concern about not being typecast as a working-class daily in the eyes of advertisers. The *Daily Mirror* constantly emphasized its continuing appeal to middle-class readers in its self-presentation to the advertising industry. Indeed, in 1938 it even mounted a promotion campaign in the advertising trade press boasting of its upper-class 'A' readership (the top 5 per cent of the country). 'Only one of the six popular national papers,' the *Daily Mirror* proclaimed, 'can claim more "A" class readers.'

The really important change represented by the *Daily Mirror*'s make-over, however, was not its anxious flirtation with social democracy, but its relegation of politics in favour of content with a wide appeal to women and young readers. Between 1927 and 1937 the *Daily Mirror* cut by half the proportion of its news devoted to political, social, economic and industrial issues.[13] The shift meant that, in 1936, the *Daily Mirror*'s coverage of domestic public affairs was less than half that of its sports coverage, and little over one-third of its coverage of crime, sex and other human interest content. Even more striking, its analysis of public affairs, whether in the form of editorials or feature articles, accounted for a mere 2 per cent of its editorial content.[14] The *Daily Mirror*'s relaunch constituted a key moment in the incorporation of the press by the entertainment industry.

The *Daily Mirror*'s circulation rose to 1.5 million by 1939 and, after an initial period of difficulty, its advertising revenue also increased substantially. The *Mirror*'s success inspired a similar marketing operation on its sister paper, the *Sunday Pictorial,* in 1937, under the aegis of Cecil King and Hugh Cudlipp. The *Sunday Pictorial* also moved away from right-wing politics and a middle-class social identity without becoming left wing or working class.

In short, advertising patronage still inhibited the development of radical journalism. Yet the rise of working-class living standards, and changes in the way in which advertisers selected media, had encouraged part of the popular press to drift from its conservative moorings. The foundation had been laid for the development of a powerful social democratic press that would push for reform in the different social and economic context of the Second World War.

Notes

1. A useful, recent assessment of the press barons, not mired in mythology, is provided in P. Catterall, C. Seymour-Ure and A. Smith (eds), *Northcliffe's Legacy* (Basingstoke, Macmillan, 2000).
2. Circulation figures for the inter-war period are not entirely reliable. The principal sources for circulations used in this chapter have been T. B. Browne's annual *Advertisers' ABC*; Royal Commission on the Press 1947–9 Report (London, HMSO, 1949); N. Kaldor and R. Silverman, *A Statistical Analysis of Advertising Expenditure and of the Revenue of the Press* (Cambridge, Cambridge University Press, 1948); W. Belson, *The British Press* (London, London Press Exchange, 1959); the Audit Bureau of Circulations; and individual publishers.
3. In fact most of Beaverbrook's senior editors kept their jobs for exceptionally long periods of time, though this was less true of his more junior employees.
4. Northcliffe's unpredictability increased to the point of insanity, possibly induced by syphilis.
5. *Report on the British Press* (London, Political & Economic Planning, 1938), p. 132.
6. The relative proportion of space devoted to different categories of article is what is significant in discussing the evolution of the newspaper as a genre. For a different view, see Ralph Negrine, *Politics and the Mass Media in Britain* (2nd edn) (London, Routledge, 1994). Our content analysis was based on a sample of twelve issues of daily, and six issues of Sunday papers, in 1936. Public affairs is defined as political, social, economic, industrial, scientific and medical affairs. For a summary of the results, see Chapter 7, this volume.

7. *Royal Commission on the Press 1947–9 Report,* Appendix 7, p. 250.
8. *A Survey of Reader Interest* (*News Chronicle,* 1934).
9. L. London, *Whitehall and the Jews, 1933–48* (Cambridge, Cambridge University Press, 2000).
10. 'A statistical survey of press advertising during 1936' (London Press Exchange Ltd records). The figures exclude certain forms of classified advertising.
11. 'The Sun-Maid plan 1929–30' (J. Walter Thompson Ltd records).
12. G. Harrison and F. C. Mitchell, *The Home Market: A Handbook of Statistics* (London, Allen & Unwin, 1936), p. 6.
13. *Royal Commission on the Press 1947–9 Report,* Appendix 7, pp. 257–8.
14. See n. 5. This represented a reduction in real terms during the period 1927 to 1937, notwithstanding the increase in the size of the *Daily Mirror* and the rise in the proportion of its editorial content devoted to news.

6

The press under public regulation

Nostalgia has encouraged the belief that the British people closed ranks with bulldog determination under the unchallenged leadership of Churchill during the Second World War. This mythical view obscures the political and social crisis of the early war years, which led to a major confrontation between the government and the left press.

Many senior politicians and officials doubted the commitment of the British people to winning the war. A significantly named Home Morale Emergency Committee of the Ministry of Information reported in June 1940 on 'fear, confusion, suspicion, class feeling and defeatism'. Even the Ministry's parliamentary secretary, Harold Nicolson, confided in his diary during this period, 'It will now be almost impossible to beat the Germans.'[1] For at least the first two and a half years of the war, the relationship between the authorities and the press was dominated by a constant and probably misplaced concern about the state of public morale.

This anxiety was combined with growing concern among conservative politicians and civil servants about the growth of radicalism in Britain. In February 1942 the Home Intelligence Division reported a wave of admiration for Soviet Russia and a growing suspicion among sections of the working class that financial vested interests were hampering the war effort. A month later it commented on what was to become a familiar theme – the flowering of 'home-made Socialism' of which important elements were 'a revulsion against "vested interests", "privilege", and what is referred to as "the old gang"' and 'a general agreement that things were going to be different after the war'.[2] Left-wing press criticism, in these circumstances, appeared to some to be especially damaging. It was strengthening political division at home when the country needed to be united against a common enemy, as well as undermining military discipline and impeding efficient production. Indeed, the maintenance of public morale came close to being equated by some ministers and officials with suppressing radical criticism of any kind.

Yet a succession of military defeats provoked mounting attacks on 'the old gang'. In 1940 Neville Chamberlain was forced to resign as Prime Minister.

The new Coalition government under Churchill also came under growing attack as the military situation deteriorated. A cumulative political crisis developed which was only partly defused by changes in the Cabinet and leadership of the armed forces in 1940, 1941 and 1942. Press censorship thus became part of a beleaguered administration's battle for survival.

The Second World War was also different from previous wars in that the British people were in the front line for the first time. The strategic objective of the blitz was to both physically impede war production and destroy psychologically the will of the civilian population to service the war effort. Extensive censorship controls were needed, it was claimed, in order to combat the new, deadly technology of aerial warfare.

Censorship and resistance

Amid mounting fears of invasion in the summer of 1940, the government issued regulations which gave the Home Secretary sweeping powers to control the press. The most important of these was Regulation 2D, conferring on the Home Secretary the personal power to ban any publication which published material 'calculated to foment opposition to the prosecution to a successful issue of any war in which His Majesty is engaged'. The regulation also denied the offending publication any automatic right of appeal or recourse to the law courts. As one angry MP declared, 'Its effect will be to put the Ministry of Home Security in a position by no means inferior, as regards the scope of its powers over newspapers, to that occupied by the distinguished Dr Goebbels in Germany.'[3]

A major campaign was organized against these new measures. Leading members of the old political establishment, including Lloyd George, were mobilized, and much of the press joined in the protest. Concerted opposition was mounted in the Commons with the result that the government secured ratification of the regulations by only thirty-eight votes – the smallest majority on any issue gained by the new government. This opposition was important because it secured two vital concessions that limited the way in which the regulations were subsequently implemented. First, Sir John Anderson, the Home Secretary, gave an undertaking that the regulations would not be amended without parliamentary consultation. Cabinet memoranda show that three months later this pledge was effective in blocking moves to ban publications which were deemed to 'disrupt the unity of effort' in the country.[4] Second, Sir John Anderson indicated in the Commons that the regulations would apply only to papers opposed to the continuance of the war. When government ministers later wanted to close down a pro-war paper, they felt it necessary to reinterpret the scope and purpose of the regulations. This created a delay which enabled effective opposition to be organized.

Silencing the communist press

The communist *Daily Worker* and the *Week* were closed on 21 January 1941. The *Daily Worker* had modified its anti-fascist editorial policy following the signing of the Nazi–Soviet pact in 1939, and attacked the war as a struggle between imperialist powers. The ostensible ground for banning the two publications was that they were impeding the war effort by setting people against the war. This was not borne out by research undertaken by the Ministry of Information, which indicated that they had little influence on public attitudes. The *Daily Worker* accounted for less than 1 per cent of total national daily circulation, while the *Week* had even smaller sales.

But if the two papers did not damage public morale, they disturbed the peace of mind of some government ministers. The *Daily Worker* campaigned against a number of shortcomings, such as the lack of deep shelters, which the government was not in a position to rectify in the short term. The *Daily Worker* also published vituperative attacks – including a cartoon portraying Bevin, the Minister of Production, as being in the pay of capitalist bosses – which caused deep personal offence.

The ban on the two papers was also part of a wider government campaign against communism in Britain which was being organized by the interdepartmental Committee on Communist Activities, including representatives from the Foreign Office and MI5, strongly supported by leading right-wing ministers. That the ban was motivated, in part, by political prejudice – and not simply by a concern about the papers' impact on public morale – is confirmed by the unwillingness of the authorities to allow the *Daily Worker* to begin republication when the British Communist Party came round to full-hearted support of the war.

The government chose to close down the two communist papers by ministerial decree rather than prosecute them through the law courts. Summary execution was preferred, partly because the government feared that it might lose the case and partly because, as a private memorandum from the Home Secretary explained, a law suit would provide the *Worker* with 'a good opportunity for propaganda against what it would describe as the government's effort to "gag" the press'.[5] Although the government's actions clearly amounted to an attack on press freedom, public 'watchdogs' were mostly silent or approving. When the Home Secretary informed the Newspaper Proprietors Association of the ban, only one person objected. In Parliament the more successful of the two motions opposing the government's actions attracted eleven votes.

Harassment of the left press

The assault on the communist press was part of a wider move to curb criticism from left papers. The *Daily Herald,* which had been outspokenly critical during the early stages of the war, moderated its tone when the Labour Party joined the coalition. Pressure was brought to bear upon the paper through its TUC-nominated directors. Appeals to loyalty also helped to subdue criticism of the government in *Reynolds News,* the paper of the Co-operative Movement, but the *Daily Mirror* and *Sunday Pictorial,* which moved sharply to the left during the war, were much more difficult to deal with. They were not controlled by the labour movement, nor were they answerable to a dominant shareholder (as the Cabinet discovered after authorizing an investigation into the shareholders of the two papers).

At first, pressure was exerted informally through a series of meetings between senior members of the government and directors of the two papers. When this failed, Churchill urged a more direct approach. Both papers, he argued in a Cabinet meeting on 7 October 1940, published articles that were subversive. He went on to suggest that a conspiracy lay behind this criticism. 'There was far more behind these articles,' Churchill warned, 'than disgruntlement or frayed nerves. They stood for something most dangerous and sinister, namely an attempt to bring about a situation in which the country would be ready for a surrender peace.'[6]

The new Home Secretary, Herbert Morrison, asked for time to consider the issue. The next day he circulated a sharply worded memorandum to his Cabinet colleagues in which he suggested that 'there is much in the papers [*Daily Mirror* and *Sunday Pictorial*] which is calculated to promote a war spirit. They seem to be clearly anxious for the defeat of Hitlerism.' After arguing that government action would be counterproductive, he concluded: 'It is a tradition of the British people that they still remain obedient to the constituted authorities while retaining their liberty to ridicule and denounce the individuals who are actually in authority.'[7]

An unlikely struggle developed in which Morrison, the archetypal machine politician, vigorously defended press freedom against Churchill, a former journalist famous for his eloquent speeches in defence of liberty. In the next Cabinet meeting, Churchill accused the *Daily Mirror* and *Sunday Pictorial* of 'trying to rock the boat' and demanded 'firm action to deal with this menace'. He was strongly supported by, among others, Sir John Anderson who was in favour of issuing a warning to the two papers and then closing them down if they did not change. Morrison opposed this, arguing that such action would divide the Commons on party lines and amount to 'interference with the liberty of the press'.

In the end the Cabinet agreed, at Beaverbrook's suggestion, to exert pressure on the two papers through the Newspaper Proprietors Association (NPA). A meeting was arranged between Beaverbrook and Attlee, representing the government, and the NPA. The proprietors were warned that compulsory censorship might be introduced if the *Daily Mirror* and *Sunday Pictorial* were not more restrained. The proprietors protested strongly at the meeting, but subsequently urged the senior management of the *Daily Mirror* and *Sunday Pictorial* to exert a moderating influence on their staff. The effect of this intervention was limited. 'We shall pipe down for a few weeks,' Cecil King, a director of both papers, commented in his diary.

Churchill's allegations that the two papers were motivated by a desire to secure 'a surrender peace' was unjustified. Both papers were totally committed to winning the war. Indeed, they had opposed appeasement with Germany before anti-appeasement had become government policy; they had also backed Churchill for the leadership on the grounds that he would push for a more vigorous prosecution of the war. Indeed, at times, the *Daily Mirror* assumed almost the John Bull style of the Prime Minister: 'We appeal to every worker and every employer to play the man . . . stick to your job unless it is foolhardy to do so' (30 September 1940). The *Sunday Pictorial* was no different. Pillorying Lloyd George as 'the Marshal of the weak and the terrorized' when he proposed a negotiated settlement, it had even less time for pacifists. 'Put the lot behind barbed wire,' it urged.

The real reason for the attack on the two papers was that they had become increasingly critical of the government. The *Sunday Pictorial* (29 September) called the reverse at Dakar 'another blunder' while the *Daily Mirror* referred pointedly to 'futile dashes at remote strategic points'. Both papers began also to urge for social reform at home. But they left no doubt in the minds of their readers that victory against Hilter was what mattered most. 'However bad the "pluto-democratic" world may be,' declared a *Daily Mirror* columnist, 'it is at least better than the depravity that would suppress all independent action and thought under the devilish way of life commended by Nazi fanatics.'

Clashes between the government and the *Mirror* and *Pictorial* recurred throughout 1941 and early 1942, largely because both sides had irreconcilable understandings of the national interest.[8] Leading Conservative ministers believed that criticism of officers in the *Daily Mirror* – including a reference to them as 'brassbuttoned boneheads, socially prejudiced, arrogant and fussy' – served to undermine the respect for rank that was the basis of good discipline in the army. They also felt that the *Daily Mirror*'s calls for post-war reconstruction were needlessly introducing political controversy and dividing the nation at a time of national emergency. The *Daily Mirror*, with an average circulation of 1,900,000, had become in their view a serious obstacle to winning the war.

Daily Mirror journalists, on the other hand, saw themselves as contributing to the war effort. They argued that Britain, in its hour of need, could not afford the incompetence that arose from snobbery and privilege: responsible jobs should go to those selected on the basis of ability rather than of birth. And plans for a new deal after the war were not divisive in a society already divided by class inequalities; on the contrary, a programme for 'winning the peace' would help win the war by motivating people to contribute even more to the war effort.

These differences flared up into a full-scale confrontation in March 1942. The occasion, though not the cause, of the confrontation was a cartoon published in the *Daily Mirror* by Zec which showed a torpedoed sailor adrift on a raft in the open sea with the caption: 'The price of petrol has been increased by one penny – official.' This was interpreted by Churchill and many of his Cabinet colleagues as an irresponsible attack upon the government for sanctioning oil company profiteering at the expense of people's lives. Its real intention was quite different: Zec meant it as an attack upon the needless waste of petrol by dramatizing the human sacrifice involved in shipping oil to Britain. This was how it was understood by most people, according to a Home Intelligence Report, as well as by most MPs who commented on it in a subsequent Commons debate.[9]

Ministers' misunderstanding of the Zec cartoon was a symptom of their growing demoralization. In the three months preceding the confrontation with the *Daily Mirror,* the allies had suffered defeats at Guam, Wake, Hong Kong, Manila, the Dutch East Indies, Rangoon, Benghazi and Singapore. In the embattled atmosphere of Cabinet discussions, the press came to be blamed by ministers on the left as well as the right for some of the things that were going wrong. Bevin, the Labour Minister, demanded in a highly emotional state, 'How was he to "press" people almost into the Merchant Navy if they were then to see the suggestion [in the Zec cartoon] that they were being "pressed" in order to put the price of petrol up for the owners?' The *Daily Mirror*'s staff had become scapegoats for failure. 'We will flatten them', Churchill told his Information Minister, Brendan Bracken.[10]

The assault on the *Daily Mirror* was part of the government's struggle for political survival. A *Daily Mirror* editorial on 16 February 1942 came very close to demanding a new administration:

> The assumption that whatever blunders are committed, and whatever faults are plainly visible in organization, we must still go on applauding men who muddle our lives away, is a travesty of history and a rhetorical defiance of all the bitter lessons of past wars.

This indictment was published at a time when a number of insiders believed that the government could be forced to resign. Churchill himself believed that he might be ousted. 'My diary for 1942,' writes a member of Churchill's personal entourage, 'has the same backcloth to every scene: Winston's conviction that his life as Prime Minister could be saved only by victory in the field.' Even the general public, previously more loyal to the premier and his administration than the political élite, showed signs of turning against Churchill in early 1942.[11]

The attack on the *Daily Mirror* was thus a pre-emptive strike against the government's principal critic. Its purpose, as discussion among Cabinet ministers made clear, was not only to silence the *Daily Mirror* but also to intimidate the rest of the press into being less critical. Churchill demanded the immediate closure of the *Daily Mirror* in a full Cabinet meeting on 9 March 1942. The matter was referred to a Special Committee under the chairmanship of Sir John Anderson. The committee was advised by the law officers (rather surprisingly in view of the terms in which censorship regulations had been introduced) that it was legal to close down the *Daily Mirror* because, although it supported the war, it impeded its 'successful prosecution'. Indeed, the Lord Chancellor urged immediate suspension of the paper since the experience of the last war suggested, in his view, that quick, decisive action would be effective. 'When the then Home Secretary quite illegally suppressed the *Globe* newspaper,' he recalled inaccurately, 'there was a row in the House in one debate in which the government received overwhelming support, and nothing was ever heard of the *Globe* newspaper again.'[12]

The committee did not, however, endorse this proposal although it agreed that 'it would be helpful if an example could be made' to curb press criticism. Those opposed to an immediate ban stressed that 'it was clear from the debates in parliament at the time when Regulation 2D had been enacted that it would be used to deal with Communist, Fascist or Pacifist Anti-War agitators' – but not, they pointed out, 'for the purposes now suggested'. There had to be a public redefinition of the government's censorship powers before anything could be done.[13]

At this stage a near consensus had been reached in favour of banning the *Daily Mirror*. The hawks, who wanted immediate suspension, had been strengthened by the recruitment of Bevin, the only trade union leader in the Cabinet. The opposition of the doves, on the other hand, had weakened. They stood out for giving the *Daily Mirror* one last chance in which to reform itself, while at the same time seemingly consenting to the paper's suppression if it did not 'improve'. Even Morrison, the principal dove and the minister who would be responsible for carrying out Cabinet policy, apparently agreed that if the *Daily Mirror* people 'did not amend I would suppress them'.[14]

Morrison announced that Defence Regulation 2D empowered the government to ban pro-war papers which undermined the war effort, even if the offence was not intentional but merely arose from a 'reckless and unpatriotic indifference' to the interests of the nation. He added that the *Daily Mirror* would be banned without further notice unless 'those concerned recognized their public responsibilities'. The same warning was given personally to the *Daily Mirror*'s senior management, and a report of the meeting was released to the press.

Most members of the government clearly did not anticipate the storm of protest that followed. A large group of MPs demanded a special debate in the Commons. In a packed House a Liberal MP, Wilfred Roberts, aptly quoted an article published in the USA by the Minister of Information, Brendan

Bracken. In this Bracken had argued that 'the savage censorship imposed on the French press played no small part in the fall of France. It encouraged defeatism, and bred complacency. A blindfolded democracy is more likely to fall than to fight.' A Labour MP, Frederick Bellenger, then cited an article written by Herbert Morrison during the First World War in which he had urged all soldiers not to fight 'your German brother' in an imperialist struggle. Morrison was pointedly asked why he was not now extending the same freedom of expression to others.

As the debate progressed, the government rather than the *Daily Mirror* was placed in the dock. While loyal Conservative MPs rallied to Morrison's defence, the great majority of Labour and Liberal MPs who spoke were sharply critical. The Coalition administration was confronted, as Morrison had feared, with an issue that divided the Commons along party political lines.

Newspaper proprietors and editors were also not as compliant as they had been over the closure of the *Daily Worker*. While many Sunday and local papers supported the government, the majority of national daily papers sided with the *Mirror*. It thus became clear that closing down the *Daily Mirror* would lead to a major confrontation with a powerful section of the press.

The strength of opposition was such that the *Daily Mirror* was never really in any danger of being closed down after March 1942. Thereafter official displeasure took the form of harassment, such as Churchill's personal request that Cecil King be conscripted into the armed forces.[15] The victory was not, however, entirely one-sided. The *Daily Mirror*'s outspoken radicalism became more subdued and the paper's most controversial columnist, Cassandra (Connor), decided it was time to join the army.

The defence of the *Daily Mirror* overlapped with a major campaign to lift the ban on the *Daily Worker*. Mass rallies were organized in Trafalgar Square and in London's Central Hall. The Labour Party Annual Conference voted down its national executive's recommendation by backing the ending of the ban. The Cooperative Congress and the Scottish TUC followed suit. In the face of this escalating pressure from the organized working class, the government relented. The ban on the *Daily Worker* was lifted on 26 August 1942 – more than a year after the USSR had become one of Britain's closest allies.

The defeat of censorship

The *Daily Mirror* and *Daily Worker* campaigns were part of a wider victory. The government rejected general schemes for compulsory censorship of the press. It also turned down an insidious proposal for allocating rationed newsprint to publications according to their contribution to the war effort. The notorious Regulation 2D was never invoked again after the closure of the *Daily Worker*.

Admittedly, the government drew back from taking full advantage of its censorship powers partly because the press proved, on the whole, to be co-operative. The Chairman of the Newspaper Emergency Council, for instance, wrote to the Ministry of Information in 1939 that 'our respective tasks and duties are complementary'.[16] Some editors even took the Ministry of Information to task for being too permissive in its advisory guidelines. The press, including critical and independent-minded papers such as the *Daily Mirror*, consciously sought to bolster public morale at the expense of objective reporting. Coercive censorship was made, to some extent, unnecessary by self-censorship.

The authorities also refrained from exercising greater control over the press for purely pragmatic reasons. Military censorship of dispatches sent by war correspondents accompanying the armed forces provided a discreet means of filleting uncomfortable news. A number of senior Ministry of Information officials also became convinced that compulsory censorship was unnecessary, once they came round to the view that public morale was holding up. Some also believed that the credibility of a largely co-operative press would be undermined if it was seen to be directly controlled by the government. These arguments from the Ministry of Information helped to deflect more authoritarian attempts to censor newspapers. When the military situation improved after the summer of 1942, and the position of Churchill's administration became secure, ministers also became notably less sensitive to criticism.

However, widespread commitment to the ideal of a free press also played an important role in preventing illiberal politicians such as Churchill and Anderson from silencing their press critics. Press freedom was one of the symbols of democracy that Britain was defending against Nazi Germany. Indeed, this was the central theme of anti-censorship campaigns, and was not something that the government could readily ignore. When a senior official in the Ministry of Information wrote that 'it would be improper to propose in this country either a moral or a political censorship of opinion, for that would be contrary to the last 300 years of English history', he added a significant postscript: 'It would also be perilous in view of the recent events surrounding the *Daily Mirror* and *Daily Worker* and the parliamentary and public attention that has been paid to them.'[17] In resisting the abuse of arbitrary censorship powers, relatively obscure politicians such as Bellenger and Roberts, along with a large number of now-forgotten labour movement activists, kept alive the tradition of an independent press. The political processes of a democratic society saved the government from itself.

Freedom from commercial controls

Ironically it was partly the government's economic intervention in the press industry that caused leading politicians to be subject to such critical scrutiny.

Newsprint was rationed, on a statutory basis, in 1940 in order to husband a scarce resource and ensure its equitable distribution. Its unintended effect was to liberate the press from some of the economic pressures that had previously inhibited radical journalism.

Newspaper managements voluntarily curtailed in 1940 the amount of advertising they took because newsprint rationing reduced papers to less than one-third of their pre-war size. This self-imposed rationing was formalized in 1942 by new regulations which restricted the proportion of newspaper space that could be allocated to advertising. As a consequence, the money that people paid for their papers once again made a substantial contribution to the finances of the press. London-based dailies, for instance, derived 69 per cent of their revenue from sales in 1943, compared with only 30 per cent in 1938.

Newsprint rationing also redistributed advertising expenditure. Newspapers which had difficulty attracting advertising before the war found agencies begging them to take their placements due to the general shortage of advertising space. This meant that radical editorial policies and low-paid readerships no longer carried a financial penalty.

These changes did not in themselves account for the sharp move to the left made by some papers during the war. The experience of the war changed the outlook of some journalists and expanded consumer demand for radical journalism. As A. C. H. Smith has shown, a radicalizing rapport developed between the *Daily Mirror* and its audience. Readers' letters and documentary-style reporting influenced the tone and orientation of the whole paper, helping it to acquire a distinctively working-class voice. However, while economic controls did not cause the wartime transformation of the *Daily Mirror* and *Sunday Pictorial,* they provided the economic environment that made it possible.

Economic pressures had restrained both papers from moving further to the left in the late 1930s. But the wartime liberation from advertisers meant that they could aim exclusively at a working-class public. They could also develop clear political identities in keeping with the greater social homogeneity of their readers. Survey research shows that the *Sunday Pictorial* entered the war with a disproportionately middle-class readership and re-emerged after the war with a mainly working-class one. Similarly the *Daily Mirror* had the most cross-sectional readership of all national dailies in 1939, but its readers were solidly proletarian by 1947. The readers of both papers were overwhelmingly Labour immediately after the war.

Newsprint rationing also reduced the polarization between quality and popular papers. Popular papers were no longer under intense pressure to seek ever larger audiences because circulation levels were 'pegged' during much of the war. By reducing costs and redistributing advertising, newsprint controls also increased the profitability of many newspapers. These changes coincided with a new interest not only in war news, but also in public affairs in general. As a consequence the proportion of space devoted to public affairs doubled in all wartime popular national dailies, save in the already news-oriented *Daily Herald*.

Wartime controls thus contributed to the development of a radical, repoliticized press. The aggregate circulation of the *Daily Mirror* and *Sunday Pictorial*, combined with that of the *Daily Herald, Reynolds News* and *Daily Worker,* amounted to nearly nine million copies in 1945. This formidable grouping of papers was supplemented by the progressive *Picture Post,* an illustrated weekly with a readership (as distinct from circulation) of well over four million people. Not since the mid-Victorian period had the left enjoyed so much press support.

These publications provided a strong impetus behind social democratic change in wartime Britain. This can be illustrated by the reception given to the Beveridge Report, published in 1942, which provided the basis of many of the reforms later implemented by the Attlee government. The report was hailed by the left press with banner headlines, congratulatory editorials and detailed summaries of its recommendations. It 'will so much break the old order', proclaimed the *Sunday Pictorial* (6 December 1942), 'that it will rank as little short of a Magna Carta for the toiling masses in Britain'. According to the *Daily Herald* (2 December 1942) the report was a 'massive achievement'. The *Daily Mirror* (2 December 1942) was equally lyrical. Shrewdly anticipating counter-arguments, it also published a sober article by Beveridge entitled, 'Britain Can Afford It'. The report also received sympathetic coverage from liberal papers such as the *News Chronicle* and *Manchester Guardian,* and even from the conservative *Daily Mail.* As Cecil King noted at the time, 'The volume of press support is so great that it seems to be assumed in the House that it will be politically impossible to drop the Report.'

What might have been a relatively obscure official document, which the Tory Minister of Information had initially wanted to be published quietly, was transformed with the help of press publicity into a cornerstone of the new consensus. Indeed, a British Institute of Public Opinion survey in 1943 found that no fewer than 86 per cent of people wanted the Beveridge Report to be adopted. Radical newspapers were thus helping to lay the foundation for Labour's 1945 landslide victory more than two years before Labour's election campaign even began.

In short, public regulation during the Second World War helped rather than hindered the growth of radical journalism. Government attempts to silence the radical press were eventually stopped by public protests, while official economic controls had the effect of making the press more responsive to changes in the public mood. State intervention proved to be, on balance, a liberating rather than a repressive influence.

Notes

1. Ministry of Information (INF) 1/250, Report to Policy Committee (June 1940); H. Nicolson, *Diaries and Letters 1930–45* (London, Collins, 1967), p. 96
2. INF 1/292, Home Intelligence Weekly Report 73 (16–23 March 1942), Appendix.
3. *Parliamentary Debates*, 363 (1940), col. 1307.
4. CAB 66/12, WP 402 (40) (8 October 1940).
5. CAB 66/14 (23 December 1940).
6. CAB 65/9, WM 267 (40) (7 October 1940).
7. CAB 66/12, WP 402 (40) (8 October 1940).
8. See, for instance, W. Armstrong (ed.), C. King, *With Malice Toward None* (London, Sidgwick & Jackson, 1970), pp. 94–9 and 103–7.
9. H. Cudlipp, *Walking on the Water* (London, Bodley Head, 1976), pp. 134–6; INF 1/282 Home Intelligence Weekly Report 78 (23–30 March 1942); *Parliamentary Debates*, 378 (1942), cols 2233–308.
10. Simon, CAB 66/23, WP 124 (42) (17 March 1942); Bevin and Churchill cited in A. J. P. Taylor (ed.), *Off the Record: W. P. Crozier, Political Interviews 1933–43* (London, Hutchinson, 1973), pp. 311 and 325.
11. Eden cited in J. Harvey (ed.), *The War Diaries of Oliver Harvey 1941–5* (London, Collins, 1978), p. 94; Churchill cited in Lord Moran, *Winston Churchill* (London, Sphere, 1968); INF 1/292 Home Intelligence Weekly Report 72 (February 1942).
12. In fact the *Globe* was suspended only briefly.
13. CAB 65/25, WM 35 (42) (18 March 1942).
14. A. J. P. Taylor (ed.), *Off the Record: W. P. Crozier, Political Interviews 1933–43* (London, Hutchinson, 1973), p. 325.
15. Cecil King was medically unfit for the armed forces. This was the reason why he had not joined up in the first place.
16. INF 1/187, Letter to Censorship Bureau (10 September 1939).
17. INF 1/238, Memorandum from R. H. Parker (15 April 1942).

7

The press in the age of globalization

The leading historian of the British press, Stephen Koss, portrays the post-war period as the apotheosis of political journalism. 'By 1947,' writes Koss, 'the party attachments of papers – as they had been understood to operate over the preceding hundred years – were effectively abandoned.' The press became fully independent of political parties and hence government, thus completing the 'halting transition from official to popular control'.[1]

This supposedly resulted in a marked improvement in the quality of political reporting and analysis. According to Koss:

> Newspapers grew steadily more catholic and less partisan in their ordinary news coverage. When confronted by a general election, they usually expressed a party preference, but always with at least a gesture of pragmatism and often for a different party from the one they had previously endorsed.

This more open-minded style of journalism is attributed by Koss to the emergence of a new type of proprietor who was 'a businessman first and foremost', oriented towards what sold rather than what furthered a party interest or ideological viewpoint. The man who 'personified' this pragmatic, undoctrinaire approach, in Koss's judgement, is Rupert Murdoch, whose 'papers, both in Britain and elsewhere, lurched from one party persuasion to another for reasons that were seldom articulated and manifestly more commercial than ideological'.

This analysis is broadly echoed by many other accounts of the post-war press. Their common theme is that newspapers were emancipated not only from party tutelage but also from the personal dominion of press magnates. According to John Whale, for instance, 'the newspaper's staff is left to get on with the job' in the modern press because many of the new proprietors 'have global problems of trade and investment to occupy their minds'. Like Koss, he sees control of the contemporary press as residing increasingly in the marketplace.

Like all persuasive mythologies, these portrayals connect to an element of truth. But their overall assessment is misleading because they inflate short-lived trends into permanent transformations, and ignore developments which run counter to their conclusions. The post-war press was not transformed, in reality, by the arrival of 'market democracy'.

Growth of press autonomy (1951 to 1974)

During the immediate post-war period a substantial section of the press remained subject to the personal control of interventionist proprietors: the second Viscount Rothermere, Beaverbrook, Camrose, Kemsley and, after 1948, David Astor. The labour movement papers, the *Daily Herald* and *Reynolds News,* were also tethered to the editorial line laid down by their political masters.

However, this hierarchical pattern of control gave way to a greater delegation of editorial authority in the regional press and in a growing section of the national press. The person who typified this change was Lord Thomson, who acquired the Kemsley empire in 1959 and *The Times* in 1967. Within the framework of an agreed budget, his editors enjoyed a high degree of autonomy. Publicly he declared, 'I do not believe that a newspaper can be run properly unless its editorial columns are run freely and independently by a highly skilled and dedicated professional journalist.' His British editors have broadly corroborated this statement. Harold Evans, for instance, could recollect only one occasion in his fourteen years as editor of the *Sunday Times* when he received political guidance from Lord Thomson: the proprietor, he was told in 1974, would be unhappy if the *Sunday Times* supported the Labour Party in the forthcoming general election.

Fleet Street became less hierarchical in the 1960s and early 1970s. The *Daily Herald* was freed from following the Labour Party line; Sir Max Aitken proved to be less dictatorial than his father, Lord Beaverbrook; Astor's proprietor-editor regime at the *Observer* came to an end; and, perhaps, most important of all, Cecil King was ousted in 1968 after authorizing a front-page article in the *Daily Mirror* calling for the removal of the Prime Minister and the establishment of a national government without discussing the matter with the paper's editor. King's lordly action was in the seigneurial tradition of his uncle, Lord Northcliffe: his dismissal by his fellow directors in response to what they called his 'increasing preoccupation with politics' seemed, at the time, to signify the end of an era.

These changes in the control of the press coincided with the rise of specialist correspondents. Their number increased and they acquired a greater degree of autonomy than general reporters. As Jeremy Tunstall's research in the late 1960s showed, specialist correspondents tended to hunt in packs and to regularly exchange information and ideas with each other. This fostered the development of a group consensus and encouraged journalists to resist pressure from their news desks.

The devolution of authority within newspaper organizations, at a time of broad political consensus, encouraged a more bipartisan approach to political reporting and commentary. This was reflected, for instance, in the growing number of newspapers which invited politicians to write articles opposing the editorial line of their leaders during general election campaigns. However, although the interventionist tradition of proprietorship waned during the 1960s, it did not disappear. This was highlighted by a private management inquiry commissioned by publishers, which concluded in 1966:

> When all allowances have been made for variations within the industry, its most striking feature, and possibly its greatest problem, is its dominance by a small number of highly individualistic proprietors with their own personal interests and philosophy of management.

This was clearly a reference to the proprietorial regimes at the *Telegraph, Express*, and *Mail* groups.

The extent to which political partisanship declined has also been overstated. Thus Stephen Koss's sweeping claim that national newspapers 'often' supported 'a different party from one they had previously endorsed' was not in fact true of the period under consideration. Between 1945 and February 1974, the *Daily Express, Daily Mail, Daily Mirror, Daily Telegraph, Daily Sketch* and *Daily Herald/Sun* supported with unwavering loyalty the same political party in every general election (as did the *News Chronicle* and *Daily Graphic/Sketch* before their closures). Only the pre-Murdoch *Times* and the *Guardian* approximated to Koss's mythical norm.

Increased partisanship and centralized control (1974 to 1992)

Moreover, national newspapers became markedly more partisan between 1974 and 1992. This was partly in response to the growing polarization of British politics, but it also reflected the cumulative impact of a new generation of partisan, interventionist proprietors. The extent of their editorial involvement has perhaps been exaggerated by a succession of journalists' memoirs and reminiscences which have tended to focus on untypical periods of conflict between proprietors and editors caused by changes of ownership and editorial strategy. However, they leave no doubt that Koss's portrayal of Murdoch, and other proprietors, during this period as market-led pragmatists is deeply misleading.

Indeed, Koss's claim that the political orientation of Murdoch's papers fluctuated in response to the shifting currents of public opinion is, for this period, wrong. Murdoch's British papers moved to the right because their proprietor became increasingly right-wing, and this shift was imposed regardless of the views of their readers. The *Sun* switched from Labour to support for an all-party coalition in October 1974, and became strongly Conservative

thereafter despite the fact that over half of its readers were Labour supporters. Indeed, it evolved into a partisan Thatcherite paper *in opposition* to its
readership (only 40 per cent of whom supported the Conservatives even in the
landslide 1987 general election).[2] Similarly, *The Times* and the *Sunday Times*
became Thatcherite papers under his control at a time when political partisanship was weakening and the political centre was gaining in support. Only
Today, acquired by Murdoch in July 1987, exhibited some independence,
though within strict bounds. It developed a green tinge, returned to the
Conservative fold in time for the 1992 general election, strayed briefly to the
left and was then closed down.

Murdoch imposed an editorial reorientation of his papers in Britain
through a personalized style of management reminiscent of the earlier press
barons. 'I did not come all this way,' he declared at the *News of the World,* 'not
to interfere.' Stafford Summerfield, its long-serving editor, found to his
dismay that the new proprietor 'wanted to read proofs, write a leader if he felt
like it, change the paper about and give instructions to his staff'. A series of
clashes with Murdoch, partly over the issue of whether the editor should be
accountable to the paper's board or to Murdoch personally, hastened
Summerfield's departure.

A subsequent editor of the *News of the World,* Barry Askew, also records
Murdoch's extensive editorial interventions when he was in London. 'He
would come into the office,' Askew recalls, 'and literally rewrite leaders which
were not supporting the hard Thatcherite line.' Askew, who was not a
Thatcherite enthusiast, lasted for only nine months.

Murdoch reconstructed the *Sun* by working closely with a talented but
compliant editor, Sir Larry Lamb, whom he had handpicked for the job.
However, he adopted a more circumspect approach towards *The Times* and
Sunday Times. During his bid for Times Newspapers in 1981, he was asked
whether he would change their character. 'Oh no, no, I would not dream of
changing them at all', he had replied. But to assuage sceptical critics, Articles
of Association and independent directors were imposed at Times Newspapers
with the intention of preserving their editorial independence.

Although Murdoch never issued a direct editorial instruction to the editor
of the *Sunday Times*, Frank Giles, he made his views forcibly known.
'Murdoch, the paper spread out before him,' Giles recollects, 'would jab his
fingers at some article or contribution and snarl, "What do you want to print
rubbish like that for?" or pointing to the by-line of a correspondent, assert
that "that man's a Commie".' Further pressure was funnelled through Gerald
Long, the new managing director appointed by Murdoch, prompting the
editor to establish a dossier called the 'Long Insult File'. Undermined by a
series of calculated humiliations (on one occasion, Murdoch entertained
guests by firing an imaginary pistol at his editor's back), Frank Giles retired
early. His replacement was a more reliably Conservative journalist, Andrew
Neil, who moved the paper further to the right. According to Neil, 'Rupert

expects his papers to stand broadly for what he believes: a combination of right-wing republicanism from America mixed with undiluted Thatcherism from Britain.'

The editor of *The Times,* Harold Evans, recalls similar pressure from his proprietor. Murdoch 'creates an aura', recollects Evans:

> The aura he created in 1981–2 was one of bleak hostility to Edward Heath and the Tory rebels, and contempt for the Social Democrats. He did this by persistent derision of them at our press meetings and on the telephone, by sending me articles marked worth reading which espoused right-wing views, by jabbing a finger at headlines which he thought could have been more supportive of Mrs. Thatcher – 'You're always getting at her' – and through the agency of his managing director, Long.

Long bombarded the editor with memos containing reprimands such as 'the Chancellor of the Exchequer says the recession has ended. Why are you having the effrontery in *The Times* to say that it is not?' Evans was also kept in a dependent position by not being given a fixed editorial budget. Consequently, he was compelled to seek permission for editorial decisions involving significant spending. As relationships soured due to the centrist political orientation of the paper, and its slow growth of circulation against a background of heavy losses, Murdoch actively fomented opposition among a group of journalists personally hostile to the editor. In an atmosphere thick with intrigue, in which Evans's personal aide was secretly reporting to the opposition group, Evans resigned in 1983 rather than 'be subjected to a thousand humiliations, challenged on every paperclip'. He was followed by a succession of editors, all of whom were right-wing. However, the launch of the *Independent* in 1986 forced *The Times* to respond to new competition by being less predictably Conservative and, later, by slashing its price. Peter Stothard, who became a successful editor (1992–2002), restored some of *The Times*'s tarnished authority, and greatly increased its circulation.

Another active interventionist, Victor (later Lord) Matthews, was head of the Express Group between 1977 and 1985. 'By and large editors will have complete freedom,' he promised, 'as long as they agree with the policy I have laid down.' During his first flush of enthusiasm as proprietor, he forced his editors to endure lengthy discourses of homespun political philosophy, which then had to be recreated as editorials. Only the most outrageous *ex cathedra* judgements seem to have been resisted. 'I had to plead against the *Evening Standard*,' remembers Simon Jenkins, its former editor, 'being expected to call for a nuclear first strike on Moscow, to rid the world of communism, just like that.' Lord Matthews's staff were also a little taken aback by his novel sense of news values. 'I would find myself in a dilemma,' he publicly declared, 'about whether to report a British Watergate affair because of the national harm. I believe in batting for Britain.'

However, what perhaps most clearly reveals how little Matthews conformed to Koss's idealized view of the new generation of proprietors was Matthews's troubled relationship with his new paper, the *Daily Star,* launched in 1978. Ironically this paper owed its existence to commercial considerations, since it was conceived primarily as a way of making better use of underemployed printing plant and staff. Matthews was persuaded initially that it had to be relatively radical since it was aimed at a 'downmarket', mostly Labour-voting audience. But when the *Daily Star*'s editor, Peter Grimsditch, argued that the paper should actually support the Labour Party in the 1979 general election, Matthews vetoed this on explicitly political grounds. Even after the election, he responded to the paper more as a partisan reader than as a market-oriented publisher. For example, on reading the proofs of a *Daily Star* leader critical of the Thatcher government's first budget, he angrily phoned the editor, 'There aren't any poor. You can take my word for it. There are no poor in this country.' The leader was duly modified to accommodate this insight.

In the end, Grimsditch was sacked and the paper became another Tory tabloid. It vigorously supported the Conservative Party in the 1983 election, even though only 21 per cent of its readers voted for Mrs Thatcher. Even when Lord Matthews was ousted by Lord Stevens in a corporate take-over in 1985, the *Star* continued to be a right-wing paper that reflected the Conservative views of its new proprietor rather than the predominantly centre-left views of its readership. As Lord Stevens explained, 'I would not be happy to be associated with a left-wing paper. I suppose the papers echo my political views. . . . I do interfere and say enough is enough.'

The third dominant personality to emerge in the national press was Robert Maxwell, a former right-wing Labour MP who acquired the Mirror Group in 1984. He brought to an end the relatively autonomous regime that had existed when the group was owned by Reed International during the 1970s and early 1980s. In the early days of his proprietorship he was in the office almost every night phoning, according to Alastair Hetherington, as often as six times in the evening staff who were working on political reports. 'I certainly have a major say,' he declared, 'in the political line of the paper [*Daily Mirror*].' Running newspapers, he added on another occasion, 'gives me the power to raise issues effectively. In simple terms, it's a megaphone.'

However, his control over the megaphone slackened when he became involved in ever more desperate attempts to save his heavily indebted media empire, including stealing from his employees' pension fund. Facing imminent ruin in 1991, he slipped overboard from his private yacht in what appears to have been a suicide.

The other dominant publisher to emerge was the right-wing Canadian businessman Conrad Black, who acquired the Telegraph Group in 1987. He adopted initially a hands-off strategy after appointing senior executives who were, as he put it, 'in general sympathy ideologically and philosophically' with his outlook. However, in 1989 he established a base in England, and expressed concern about the *Daily Telegraph*'s 'flirtation with incorrect thinking about Ulster and about South Africa'. The editor, Max Hastings, who had been appointed as a new broom editor and had presided over a major purge of journalistic staff, found himself the butt of increasing pressure. Eventually, he made way in 1996 for a more reliably right-wing editor, Charles Moore.

The rise of personal proprietorship was paralleled by the rise of authoritarian editorship. Thus Sir David English, editor of the *Daily Mail* (1971 to 1992), was a domineering force who reshaped the paper. Outside his office in the old Mail building, there was an iron post known sardonically to staff as the laughing column. It propped up sycophants helpless with laughter when the editor popped out to tell another of his triumphant anecdotes. English was unusual in that he acted relatively independently of his tax exile proprietor, the third Viscount Rothermere. Although Rothermere claimed to map 'the overall strategy my papers will take', he was probably less of a back-seat driver than he professed. More representative of the new style of assertive editor, albeit in an extreme form, was Kelvin MacKenzie, editor of the *Sun* (1981 to 1994). MacKenzie had a licence to bully and intimidate within the news-room providing he performed satisfactorily as his proprietor's *alter ego*, pushing up sales and giving vent to Murdoch's right-wing, anti-Establishment views. However, when the *Sun*'s circulation declined and its excesses became a political liability, MacKenzie was squeezed out.

The two notable exceptions to this general pattern of resurgent proprietors and assertive editors in the national press, during this period, was the liberal regime at the *Guardian*, controlled by the Scott Trust, and the turbulent years of the *Observer*, under Lonrho's control (1981 to 1993). Lonrho's head, Tiny Rowland, never succeeded in dominating the *Observer*, though, as we shall see, this was not from want of trying.

Palace revolution, 1992 to 2003

In the period after 1992, there was both continuity and change at the top. The two dominant right-wing publishers, Murdock and Black, remained, while Paul Dacre assumed the mantle of his mentor, Sir David English, in perpetuating his authoritarian right-wing regime at the Mail group. The Mirror group passed into the control of Trinity Mirror without a controlling shareholder, and reverted to something approaching its pre-Maxwell mould. However, the ailing Express group passed into the hands of Richard Desmond, publisher of 'adult' and gossip magazines. The *Observer* was swallowed by the Scott Trust, while a newcomer – Independent Newspapers – came to be controlled by the Irish entrepreneur, Tony O'Reilly.

While editorial management remained largely centralized, something happened in this period that requires an explanation. The press – including the Conservative Mail and Telegraph groups – harried mercilessly the

Conservative administration headed by John Major (1992 to 1997). This was not entirely without precedent in the post-1945 period. Conservative newspapers had attacked the Conservative Macmillan administration in 1961 to 1963. Even the largely cheer-leading Conservative press during the Thatcher era had moments of difference with the government. What was new was that virulent attacks on a Conservative government in the 1990s was followed subsequently by the defection of a sizeable section of the Conservative press to the New Labour camp. Never before had Labour had the backing of the majority of the press, but in the 1997 and 2001 general elections it received respectively 61 and 70 per cent of national daily circulation,[3] even though in these elections it obtained no more than 43 per cent of the vote.

This defection partly reflected a growing crisis within the Conservative Party. The Major government lost authority, following Britain's forced exit out of the Exchange Rate Mechanism in 1992. It also became embroiled in conflict over Europe, and was caught up in sexual and financial scandals. Its travails were followed by a sustained collapse of the Conservative vote. This fell from 42 per cent in 1992 to 31 and 32 per cent in 1997 and 2001, respectively. A failing, unconfident party thus contrasted with New Labour – a party relaunched under a new name, combining a significant part of the Thatcherite legacy with a commitment to public services, united and electorally successful.

It is tempting therefore to explain the change in the press as a market-oriented response to a political shift in the country, but what actually happened was a good deal more complicated than this. The key defector was Rupert Murdoch, who transferred one-third of the national press's circulation from Conservative to New Labour, and thus transformed at one stroke the political affiliation of the British press. However, his papers did not change their underlying editorial orientation in response to a perceived change in the country; their argument was rather that Blair was the only credible Conservative worth supporting intentional in 1997. In addition, while continuing to support New Labour in principle, Murdoch's papers still pursued a right-wing agenda in the early 2000s. The Murdoch press thus changed its political loyalty, but not its politics.

This adjustment began with an elaborate courtship in the mid-1990s. Tony Blair was invited to address the massed ranks of New Corporation executives in Hayman Island, Australia in July 1995. In an eloquent speech, he made clear his commitment to an open and free economy. The meaning of this was spelt out when New Labour shifted its position on monopoly controls. It had supported, in a Lords debate, the then Conservative government's intention of blocking large press groups from buying ITV or Channel 5. It then attacked this policy in the Commons in April 1996 on the grounds that it 'treat[s] newspaper groups unfairly in their access to broadcasting markets'.[4] New Labour in effect proposed itself as Murdoch's champion. Further political flirtation followed, culminating in Murdoch's support for Blair in the 1997 general election.

In March 1998, Tony Blair returned the favour by phoning on Murdoch's behalf his Italian counterpart Romano Prodi, asking him whether the Italian government would block Murdoch's proposed £4 billion bid for Berlusconi's Italian TV network. When information about the call leaked out, the Cabinet press office first denied it, then proclaimed that Blair was backing Britain.[5] However, Murdoch's bid for the football club Manchester United, was referred in 1998 to the Monopolies and Mergers Commission, and subsequently rejected. There then developed an outwardly warm but wary relationship between Blair and Murdoch in which both sides sheathed their swords. Blair's government never exerted pressure on Murdoch's BSkyB to reduce its large import of cheap American programmes in accordance with the Television Without Frontiers Directive, despite nudges from the Independent Television Commission. New Labour also redeemed its 1996 pro-monopoly stand by making it possible for Murdoch, through the 2003 Communications Act, to buy Channel 5 (but not ITV). Murdoch's papers, in turn, occasionally snarled at but did not maul the New Labour government.

In effect a tacit deal was forged between two power-holders – one a market-friendly politician and the other a pragmatic businessman – in a form that sidelined the public. This was consistent with Murdoch's record over the past thirty years. He has at every opportunity promoted right-wing views and causes, yet has always been willing – when his economic interests were significantly involved – to draw back and make compromises. An Australian who became an American citizen, he showed no emotional attachment to the British Conservative Party when it fell on hard times. His conservatism was global rather than local: he was not a member of the Westminister village. In this he differed from the previous generation of Conservative press magnates such as Lords Camrose, Kemsley, Hartwell and, by adoption, Beaverbrook. A similar sense of critical distance seems also to have influenced the Canadian Conrad Black (at least in the early 1990s) and the tax-exile Viscount Harmsworth, who allowed their papers to undermine the Major government. Globalizing influences on the British press appear to have weakened local tribal loyalty.

The other architect of the press's realignment behind New Labour, though a much less significant one, was Richard Desmond. Attacked as a 'pornographer' whose vital assets included the adult Fantasy Channel and *Asian Babes*, he was the target of a 'stop Desmond' campaign when he gained control of the Express group in 2000. A number of MPs pressed for the take-over to be referred to the Competition Commission on the grounds that another soft-porn publisher, David Sullivan, had previously been declared 'unfit' to acquire the *Bristol Evening News*. Desmond's instinct, in this situation, was to gravitate towards official power. Bearing a gift (a large donation to the Labour Party), he was received warmly at the New Labour court. The

Express, though a Conservative paper in the 1997 election, rooted for New Labour in 2001.

Concentration of press ownership

The reason why the decision of just two men changed the nature of the British press was because so many titles were bundled together in a small number of newspaper groups. There was a rapid surge of national press concentration in the early post-war period as a consequence of closures and mergers. This was followed by the development of increased joint ownership of daily and Sunday papers in the more recent period. By 2002, just three publishers controlled two out of three national papers sold in Britain (see Table 7.1).

Table 7.1 *Concentration of ownership of daily and Sunday newspapers, 1947 to 2002*

	The three leading corporations' shares of:		
	Total daily and Sunday paper circulation	National daily circulation	National Sunday circulation
	%	%	%
1947	42	62	60
1961	65	88	82
1976	53	72	86
1989	57	73	80
1995	N/A	74	81
2002	N/A	70	79

Sources: derived from *Royal Commission on the Press* 1947–9 *Report* (1949), Appendices 3 and 5; *Royal Commission on the Press 1961–2 Report* (1962), Appendices 2, 3 and 4; *Royal Commission on the Press* 1974–7 *Final Report* (1977), Annex 3; *Annual Report of the Press Council* 1989 (1990), Table 4 and Audit Bureau of Circulation (1989, 1995 and 2002).

Note: The three leading publishing corporations have been defined in terms of their market share of *each* of the categories of publication listed in this table. Total daily and Sunday paper circulation has been calculated by multiplying daily paper circulation six times to obtain a weekly circulation of daily and Sunday papers. This gives lower but more adequate figures than those calculated by the Press Council, which treated Sunday and daily circulation as equivalent and merely add the two together.

What is less often noticed is that there was simultaneously a spectacular increase of regional press ownership. The top five publishers increased their proportion of regional evening paper circulation by over half between 1947 and 2002. Their share of local weekly newspaper circulation more than doubled between 1989 and 2002 – a trend given minimal attention in the mainstream press (see Table 7.2).[6] The biggest of these all-devouring regional chains, Trinity Mirror, also expanded by acquiring the second biggest national newspaper publishing group in 1999.

Table 7.2 *Concentration of ownership in the regional press, 1947 to 2002*

| | The five leading chains' share of: | | | |
	Regional evening newspaper circulation	Regional morning newspaper circulation	Local weekly circulation	Local weekly freesheet circulation
	%	%	%	%
1947	44	65	8	–
1961	53	70	13	–
1976	58	69	25	NA
1989	54	73	27	38
2002	69	85	70	75

Sources: derived from *Royal Commission on the Press 1947–9 Report* (1949), Appendices 4 and 5; *Royal Commission on the Press 1961–2 Report* (1962), Appendices 2, 3 and 4; *Royal Commission on the Press 1974–7 Final Report* (1977), Annex 3; and N. Hartley, P. Gudgeon, and R. Crafts, *Concentration of Ownership in the Provincial Press* (Royal Commission on the Press 1974–7, Research Series 5); *Annual Report of the Press Council 1989* (1990), Tables 4 and 5; Newspaper Society Intelligence Unit, 1 July 2002.
Note: The five leading chains are not all the same in each category of publication.

This consolidation of press ownership was part of a more general trend in which concentration occurred in a number of media industries including television, commercial radio, music, book publishing and video rentals.[7] Some newspapers are linked through cross-ownership to other UK media, or are part of international media empires (see Table 7.3). The most notable example of this latter trend is the Murdoch press. Its four leading British newspapers are merely a northern outpost of a worldwide group that includes newspapers around the world (such as the *New York Post*), a major publishing house (HarperCollins), a major film company (Twentieth Century Fox), and, above all, Fox TV in the USA, BSkyB in Europe and Star TV in Asia. Rupert Murdoch is, in Bagdikian's phrase, a 'lord of the global village'.

Dependence and corruption

This trend towards concentration was accompanied for a time by the growing integration of the press into businesses such as engineering, transport, oil and banking. In some cases, corporations outside the press (such as Atlantic Richfield, Lonrho, Trafalgar House and Reed) acquired major publications; in others, established press groups moved extensively into other activities. This trend became particularly pronounced in the period between 1969 and 1986, causing the third Royal Commission on the Press to conclude (in 1977) that 'the press has become a subsidiary of other industries'.[8]

This change in the status of the press was partly a response to its financial difficulties between the ending of newsprint rationing in 1956 and the

Table 7.3 *The conglomeration of the British press*

	Main British press interests	Selected other media interests	Selected non-media interests
Daily Mail & General Trust (Rothermere)	*Daily Mail* *Mail on Sunday* Northcliffe Newspapers	Teletext IntoFrance British Pathé DMG Radio (Australia)	Risk Management Solutions (US) Bouverie Holdings Landmark Information Group property information
Guardian Media Group (Scott Trust)	*Guardian* *Observer* *Manchester Evening News* Trader Media Group	Real Radio Jazz FM *Mail & Guardian* (S. Africa) workthing.com	
Hollinger International (Black)	*Daily Telegraph* *Sunday Telegraph* *Spectator*	*Jerusalem Post* *Sun-Times* (Chicago) Hollinger Digital (US)	
Independent News & Media (O'Reilly)	*Independent* *Independent on Sunday* *Belfast Telegraph* *Islington Gazette*	*Irish Independent* PeopleNewspapers (Ireland) APN News & Media (Australia) Wilson & Horton (New Zealand) Lusomundo Media (Portugal)	
News Corporation (Murdoch)	*Sun* *News of the World* *The Times* *Sunday Times* *TES* *THES* *TLS*	BSkyB Fox Broadcasting (US) STAR Asian TV and radio network Twentieth Century Fox *New York Post* *The Australian* HarperCollins publishers	Australian Indoor Tennis Championship National Rugby League (Australia) Broadsystem telemarketing

Northern & Shell (Desmond)	*Daily Express* *Sunday Express* *Daily Star* United Provincial Newspapers United Magazines	*OK* magazine *Forum* *Liverpool FC* official magazine	Lakeside Trading Estate Ensign Oil & Gas (US)
Pearson	*Financial Times* *Economist*	Channel 5 TV Thames TV Euston Films Grundy Productions Penguin Books Dorling Kindersley Recoletos media and publishing group (Spain)	
Reed-Elsevier	Reed Regional Newspapers Reed Business Publishing IPC Magazines	Butterworth Hamlyn Reed Elsevier Nederland Reed Elsevier France Reed Elsevier US	Reed Travel Group
Trinity Mirror	*Daily Mirror* *Sunday Mirror* *People* *Daily Record* *Sunday Mail* *Racing Post* Scottish & Universal Newspapers Ltd Western Mail & Echo Ltd Liverpool Daily Post & Echo Ltd Birmingham Post & Mail Ltd	Trinity Publications Ltd Inside Communications Ltd	

Source: Who Owns Whom 2001–2002, London: Dun & Bradstreet, 2001; Trinity Mirror corporate website http://www.trinitymirror.com; Independent News and Media plc corporate website http://www.independentnewsmedia.com

introduction of cost-cutting technology in the mid-1980s. Thus in 1966 five out of eight national newspapers made losses totalling £4.3 million. By 1975 four national dailies and six out of seven national Sunday papers made an even larger loss. In 1982 the national press was reported to have made a net loss of £29 million. These financial problems encouraged publishers to diversify into more profitable areas. Loss-making papers also became relatively cheap to buy (though not to support).

However, when conglomerate controllers bought up the rotten boroughs of the fourth estate, they were seeking more than just an immediate return on their investment. Their motives were mixed. Some were lured by the social prestige that newspaper ownership brought or the excitement induced by what Leonard Woolf described as the 'magnetic field of highly charged importance, influence . . . and vocational delusions'. For other business leaders, newspaper ownership was little more than an investment in corporate public relations. It extended their range of business and political connections, increased their corporation's prestige, and, through judicious editorial appointments, contributed to the maintenance of public opinion favourable to private enterprise. As the Chairman of Atlantic Richfield (which spent approximately $20 million subsidizing the *Observer* before selling it to Lonrho) explained to his shareholders in 1978:

> Despite the social upheaval of the last few years, Atlantic Richfield's primary task remains what it has always been – to conduct its business within accepted rules to generate profits, thereby protecting and enhancing the investment of its owners. But . . . senior management recognise that the Company cannot expect to operate freely or advantageously without public approval.

The winning of 'public approval' tended to be linked to support for the Conservative Party during this period. A number of major press groups – Trafalgar House (which controlled for a time the Express group), United Newspapers and Pearson – gave substantial donations to the Conservative Party in the 1970s and 1980s. Owning (and subsidizing) newspapers and making political donations to the pro-business party were part of the same project.

However, while journalists on right-wing papers tended to accept that their proprietors' support for business interests *in general* was legitimate, they opposed any attempt to promote a particular company owned by their employer. This said, there developed 'grey areas' where journalists stepped gingerly for fear of treading on corporate toes. As *The Times*, then owned by the conglomerate Thomson Organization, candidly told the third Royal Commission on the Press: 'Coverage of Thomson organization activities [including oil and travel] in Thomson newspapers tends, certainly, to be drily factual.'

This period of conglomerate control contained seedy, unheroic moments when compromises were made and resented. However, one of the beneficial consequences of new technology introduced in the mid-1980s was that it restored the profitability of the press. This coincided with a general trend towards the de-conglomeration of industry, and led to the refocusing of the press around its core business, and related media and leisure activities.

But while conflicts of interest became less extensive, they did not go away. One form in which they resurfaced was in relation to cross-media promotion within the same organization. For example, when Murdoch's newspapers gave disproportionate coverage to the British launch of its sister company Sky Television in 1989, only journalists on one of his newspapers – *The Times* – made a formal protest. *The Times*'s independent directors declined, much to their discredit, to investigate the protest beyond speaking to the editor.

Another source of pressure came in the area of international news, and related to the regulatory politics of global media expansion. Thus Rupert Murdoch was threatened by the Malaysian government in 1994 with reprisals against his business empire, at a critical moment in the development of his Asian satellite TV business, following prominent reports in the *Sunday Times* that senior officials and ministers had received backhanders in the building of the Pergau dam, funded with British aid. Murdoch remonstrated with the *Sunday Times* editor Andrew Neil: 'You're boring people. You are doing too much on Malaysia. . . . They're all corrupt in that part of the world.' This contributed to a souring in the relationship between the two men, culminating in Neil's transfer to the United States. Murdoch is reported to have assured Malaysia's Prime Minister Mahathir that his 'rogue editor' had been 'sorted out'.

Yet right-wing newspapers never became, even in the era of conglomerate compromise, mere mouthpieces of big business. The desire of some press controllers to promote pro-market views was constrained by the need to win over readers with different viewpoints, or who wanted primarily to be entertained. The commitments of press controllers were also offset to some extent by the professional concerns of journalists.

Compliance and resistance

If the trend after the 1960s was for more centralized systems of editorial control to be established in the national press, this did not go unchallenged. Strongest resistance occurred in the broadsheet press where journalists had become accustomed to a higher degree of autonomy than their tabloid counterparts, and where the new regimes represented a greater rupture with the past. Yet there was only one occasion when journalists actually succeeded in decisively defeating their proprietor.

When Tiny Rowland acquired the *Observer* in 1981, he intended to make substantial changes. The paper's liberal coverage of Africa, he warned, was abetting the advance of communism. In traditional proprietorial style, he appointed a new roving Africa correspondent without consulting the editor.

However, he had been forced, like Murdoch, to accept new Articles of Association and independent directors at the *Observer*, designed to prevent him from taking editorial control. The independent directors at the *Observer*, unlike those at Times Newspapers, had been chosen by staff which made them more of an obstacle. And whereas Murdoch moved with consummate skill at Times Newspapers, first appointing caretaker editors and encircling them with people he could trust, Rowland blundered in with an ill-judged ultimatum that undermined his authority.

Donald Trelford, the *Observer*'s editor, wrote an article in April 1984 reporting that Zimbabwe's armed forces were torturing and killing their own citizens in the dissident Matabeleland province. This put Rowland in a difficult position since his corporation, Lonrho, derived £15 million of its profit from investments in Zimbabwe. Rowland also had an uneasy relationship with the Zimbabwe Prime Minister Robert Mugabe, since he had backed his principal rival Joshua Nkomo in a recent election. Seeking to protect his commercial interests, Rowland told Trelford to withdraw the article.

Trelford refused and was backed in his stand by all his editorial staff and independent directors. In the highly publicized row that followed (in which Lonrho reportedly cancelled advertising in its own paper), Rowland had little real choice but to back off. Lonrho's corporate image had already been tarnished by the Conservative leader Edward Heath's celebrated attack on it as 'the unacceptable face of capitalism'. It would have been seriously undermined if Rowland had agreed, in these circumstances, to Trelford's offer of resignation.

Even so, this only proved to be the opening skirmish in a long-running battle. The *Observer* again came under pressure from its parent company, this time to attack the way in which the Al Fayed brothers had worsted Lonrho in a take-over battle for the House of Fraser group. 'In summary,' read one internal note, 'Mr Rowland [Lonrho's chief executive] would greatly appreciate any assistance in persuading Mrs Thatcher to publish the report of the inspectors into House of Fraser' that was strongly critical of the Al Fayeds. Between 1985 and 1989, the paper responded by publishing a series of articles criticizing the Fraser take-over, and calling for it to be quashed. This culminated in the publication of an unprecedented midweek issue, dedicated to attacking the 'Phoney Pharaoh' Mohamed Al Fayed, to coincide with Lonrho's AGM. *Observer* journalists protested to their independent directors who, after a formal enquiry, concluded that the paper's reputation had been 'tarnished'.

The same pattern of pressure and resistance was repeated on other occasions. David Leigh, head of the *Oberver*'s investigative team, refused to return in 1989 to a story about British Aerospace malpractice in selling Tornado aircraft, on the grounds that it had been planted by Lonrho executives and was being inflated for reasons of corporate rivalry. He eventually resigned over the issue, declaring that the *Observer* 'had become a sick paper'. His verdict was echoed by the paper's former deputy editor Anthony Howard, who declared that 'without any overt pressure being applied, there has developed a tendency to anticipate Mr Rowland's wishes and to cater for his interests'.

But perhaps the key point was that corporate self-censorship was actively opposed. In the event, Trelford survived as editor until 1993. He trod a difficult tightrope, balancing the demands of his proprietor with those of his suspicious and increasingly critical staff. An easier life beckoned as a media professor to which he 'retired' gracefully.

The partial success of journalists' resistance on the *Observer* was in marked contrast to what happened on the *Sunday Times*. This is worth reporting briefly because it draws attention to something that the academic literature tends to ignore: the pressures and sanctions that a determined new management can bring to bear in order to change the culture and ethos of a news organization.

The *Sunday Times* evolved into a neo-Thatcherite paper in the early 1980s partly in response to the increasing influence of new right ideas in the early phase of the Thatcherite era. However the principal cause of change was a management-imposed shift of editorial direction. Murdoch's appointment of Andrew Neil as editor in 1983 was part of a general shake-up in the editorial hierarchy of the *Sunday Times* in which section editors from the pre-Murdoch regime were gradually weeded out. This removed the buffer that had partly insulated reporters and feature writers from the full impact of the change in the paper's ownership. Neil's regime inaugurated, according to Claire Tomalin, the paper's former literary editor, 'a reign of terror'. 'I was extremely aware of a great deal of misery and bullying,' she recalls. Her recollection of this period is echoed by other journalists whom we interviewed. For example, Peter Wilby, the paper's former education correspondent, recalls: 'There was a tone of fear . . . a horrible, "totalitarian" atmosphere.'[9]

Certain sorts of story – what Neil called 'wet' or 'lefty' stories – were discouraged or downplayed. Thus Donald McIntyre, the paper's labour correspondent, had a running battle over his reporting of the miners' strike (1984 to 1985) in which he was regularly pressed by the editor to adopt a less critical attitude towards the National Coal Board and the government. Sometimes McIntyre felt that the editor's criticism was justified; sometimes he argued back; but at other times, he admitted, he censored himself 'to some extent'. The trouble with arguing back, McIntyre explained, is that it 'starts to become counter-productive and you get to the point where you either had to leave or you just become a sort of joke'. McIntyre chose to leave.

At times the pressure on journalists from the old regime was extremely abrasive. On one occasion, John Shirley, the paper's chief reporter (and right-wing Labour supporter), was denounced by Neil as a 'left-winger' and

'Trotskyist' in a voice so loud that the news-room fell into a hushed silence. Shirley became so enraged by changes on the paper that he cancelled its delivery to his home. 'A lot of people were being bullied,' according to the *Sunday Times*'s former features editor, Don Berry. 'Life was deliberately made unpleasant for them in the hope that they would go.' Thus Joan Smith, who had complained about the way in which her report of the Greenham Common anti-nuclear protest had been altered, was told by the news editor, Anthony Bambridge, on 25 January 1984: 'The editor feels you have got in a rut on nuclear matters. He would like to see you broaden your range. He would like to see you in the paper more often.' Smith asked how often and was told every week, ideally. She then pointed out that she had had forty-six stories published in the past forty-four weeks. Bambridge replied, 'You are to be congratulated. I am having a terrible time. You are not the only one who is thinking of leaving.' Two months later, Smith left the *Sunday Times*.

But the principal way in which the paper was propelled editorially to the right was through a cumulative process of attrition. This is graphically described by Isabel Hilton, the Latin American specialist at the *Sunday Times* until July 1986:

> What would happen is that you would write a story and it would disappear. The copy would vanish around the building and people would write little things into it and take out other things. It would eventually appear in a very truncated form with the emphases changed. It had all been done at stages along the way. To try and make a fuss about this on a Saturday when everything was very busy was very difficult.

The accumulation of pressures led some journalists to internalize controls. 'The sense of intimidation,' according to Hilton,

> was so strong that people actually started censoring themselves because it is very unpleasant to get into this kind of argument all the time. It is not just a collection of incidents, it's a collection of incidents *and* the atmosphere, which in the end is so depressing. You stop functioning as a journalist. There are things you just don't bother to pursue because you know you just won't get them into the paper.

Hilton eventually left. Her example was followed by many others, although not all went for the same reasons. In early 1981, there were some 170 journalists on the *Sunday Times*. At least a hundred journalists left the paper between February 1981 and March 1986. This exodus included most of the best-known *Sunday Times* journalists from the pre-Murdoch era.

The changes in the *Sunday Times* during the period 1981 to 1986 were part of a more generalized assertion of hierarchical control in the national press. However, the level of overt conflict at the *Sunday Times* was atypical.

A number of factors generally minimize clashes. Proprietors usually influence the ethos of an organization in a cumulative way. They choose the editors they want, and get rid of them if they 'fail'. Editors' freedom of action is curtailed by the house tradition of the paper, budgetary controls, management guidelines, and an implicit framework of understanding about how the paper should develop. Increasingly editors in the changed managerial environment of the 1980s also came to accept proprietorial intervention as legitimate. As Max Hastings, then editor of the *Daily Telegraph*, put it: 'I've never really believed in the notion of editorial independence as such. I would never imagine saying to Conrad [his proprietor], "you have no right to ask me to do this, I must observe my independence."' Additional considerations perhaps came into it. When Hastings was woken up late at night by his proprietor and expected to converse fluently for an hour or more, his new wife would whisper to him: 'Think of the money, think of the money.'[10]

A variety of other influences cushion conflict in a newspaper. Journalists tend to be selected in the first place partly on the grounds that they will 'fit' in. Conforming to hierarchical requirements brings rewards in terms of good assignments, high exposure, promotion and peer group esteem. Resistance invites escalating sanctions. As Anthony Bevins, the late distinguished political journalist, wrote (with an element of overstatement):

> It is daft to suggest that individuals can buck the system, ignore the pre-set 'taste' of their newspapers, use their own news-sense in reporting the truth of any event, and survive. Dissident reporters who do not deliver the goods suffer professional death. They are ridden by news desks and backbench executives, they have their stories spiked on a systematic basis, they face the worst form of newspaper punishment – by-line deprivation. . . . It is much easier to pander to what the editors want.

Accommodation was facilitated by other factors. While newspapers were exposed to contradictory influences, these were not evenly balanced. News-gathering continued to be based on routines organized around powerful groups and institutions adept at meeting the press's needs – most notably various branches of the state which were under the political authority of Conservative administrations throughout the 1980s and early 1990s. Prevailing news values accorded particular weight to these accredited sources, thereby legitimizing heavy reliance on them. Single party rule was accompanied by a shift to the right in the political climate of opinion (though not to the extent that the Conservatives' political hegemony based on the first-past-the-post electoral system suggested). The structures of news-gathering and a shift in the political culture tended to reinforce the predominantly centre-right orientation of the national press. Most journalists were adjusted without difficulty to managerial shifts. While there are no recent data about journalists' political attitudes, Tunstall's pioneering survey of specialist correspondents in 1968 affords an indication of their outlook. He found that only 2 per cent of those working for right-wing Labour or centrist papers said that they were 'well to the left' of their publications.

Changes in the structure of journalism as an occupation during the 1980s and 1990s also seem to have exerted a 'moderating' influence. The national press came to make increased use of freelancers, stringers and those on temporary contracts who often found themselves competing against a growing reserve army of underemployed or aspirant journalists. At the same time, national newspapers offered well-rewarded berths for 'staff' journalists. This combination of economic privilege and a widening abyss of economic insecurity nurtured a more compliant workforce.

Restoration of market controls

While market pressure to please consumers constrained proprietors, it did not automatically override their political commitments. This was because the market did not function in the idealized way imagined by neo-liberals. Market distortions caused consumer power to be curtailed.

A key change in the functioning of the market occurred in the late 1940s and early 1950s when newsprint rationing was greatly reduced, culminating in its abolition in 1956. This restored the press's heavy dependence on advertising. It also led to a more unequal distribution of advertising since advertisers were no longer restricted in their choice by lack of space, and were free to respond to differences in the purchasing power of newspaper readerships.

Political prejudice played only a small part in this reallocation. A small number of advertising agencies admitted to the second Royal Commission on the Press (1962) that their clients sometimes vetoed left-wing publications. The ill-fated *Scottish Daily News*, founded as a radical co-operative in 1975, was told by an irate advertiser: 'I'm not going to keep a newspaper which, the first time I get a strike, will back the strikers.' A pre-launch feasibility study for another failed left newspaper, the *News on Sunday*, also concluded on the basis of interviews with agency executives that its politics would deter some advertisers.

However, political considerations played an even smaller part in advertising selection in the post-1945 period than they had before. Precise calculations of the cost of opportunities to see advertisements in rival publications, analysed in terms of the social characteristics and, later, buying behaviour of readers, became the main basis for drawing up press advertising schedules. Intuitive assessments of editorial influence, in which ideological judgements sometimes crept in, became less significant. This was reflected, for example, in the first two handbooks on advertising media planning published under the auspices of the Institute of Practitioners in Advertising. The first, issued in 1955, included a whole chapter on the 'character and atmosphere' of advertising media containing speculation about 'the intangible effects of accompanying editorial and advertising'. Its successor, published in 1971, was openly disparaging about this approach.[11]

However, if, after newsprint rationing, the increasing inequality of advertising allocations was caused primarily by economic disparities in society, it still had political consequences. During the 1950s, advertising income was redistributed in favour of upscale and midscale publications. This operated against the left press because, generally speaking, its readers were less affluent than those of the right-wing press. Certain contingent factors exaggerated this distortion. The rapid growth of employment and financial advertising benefited primarily upscale papers, while downscale papers suffered more than others from the rise of television as an advertising medium because their readers tended to be heavy viewers of commercial television. Income inequalities also began to increase in the 1980s and 1990s, after a thirty-year period of little change.

The death of radical papers

The redistribution of advertising in the 1950s coincided with a fall in national circulations. These reached a peak in 1951, dropped and then rallied, only to fall sharply after 1957. This induced, in turn, a rapid escalation of expenditure as newspapers desperately tried to escape the general circulation decline by spending more on larger papers no longer subject to strict newsprint controls. Detailed evidence shows that there was a marked deterioration in the financial position of the national press between 1957 and 1965 because its costs rose much faster than income.

Popular social democratic papers thus found themselves in a double bind. They were exposed like the rest of the press to the general deterioration in the cost and revenue structure of the industry. They tended also to be particularly badly hit by the redistribution of advertising, following deregulation. This was especially true of the *Daily Herald* which had three drawbacks in advertising terms: its readership was disproportionately working class, male and ageing. In the advertising space famine of 1945, its advertising per copy sold had been more than that of either the *Daily Express* or *Daily Mail*. By 1964 it was less than half of either paper.

The *Daily Herald* also lost readers partly as a consequence of its continuing commitment to the Labour Party during the Conservative ascendancy of the 1950s. But its loss of advertising far exceeded its loss of sales, and was a more important cause of its downfall. In 1955 the *Daily Herald* had an 11 per cent share of both national daily circulation and advertising revenue. By 1964 its share of circulation had declined modestly to 8 per cent but its share of advertising had slumped to 3.5 per cent.

Indeed, despite its loss of sales, the *Daily Herald* still retained a substantial following. It was not true, as Sir Dennis Hamilton suggested, that the *Daily Herald* 'was beset by the problem which has dogged nearly every newspaper vowed to a political idea: not enough people wanted to read it'. When it closed in 1964, it had a circulation of 1,265,000. This was more than five times the circulation of *The Times* of which Sir Dennis Hamilton was then editor-in-chief.

The *News Chronicle,* a long-established Liberal daily, succumbed in 1960 with a substantial circulation of 1,162,000. This was roughly on a par with the highly profitable *Daily Telegraph* buoyed up by upmarket advertising. Similarly the *Sunday Citizen* (formerly *Reynolds News*) folded in 1967. This was a quality paper in terms of the relatively extensive coverage it gave to public affairs, but by 1965 it obtained per copy sold one-tenth of the advertising revenue of the *Sunday Times* because it did not appeal to an élite audience.

The closure of these three social democratic papers was part of an epidemic that also killed off the *Empire News, Sunday Dispatch, Sunday Graphic* and *Daily Sketch* between 1960 and 1972. All these papers succumbed to similar pressures to those that decimated the centre-left press. They all had a predominantly working-class readership and, in terms of mass marketing, relatively 'small' circulations. They thus fell between two stools: they had neither the quantity nor the social 'quality' of readership needed to attract sufficient advertising for them to survive in a deregulated economy.

Adjusting to the advertising system

One response of downscale papers to the economic realities of post-war publishing was to try to break out of the working-class market. The editorial implications of this are graphically illustrated by the troubled post-war history of the *Daily Herald.*

The *Daily Herald*'s management responded initially to the paper's growing shortfall in advertising not by modifying its editorial policy but by seeking new and more imaginative ways of selling the paper to the advertising industry. In particular, it sought to combat the negative image of the paper's readers as poor by initiating research which showed that they were heavy spenders on certain products such as canned meat, desserts, cereals and beer.

The diminishing success of this promotion encouraged the *Daily Herald*'s management to undertake in 1955 a fundamental review of the paper's editorial strategy and market position. Two clear options emerged from this review. One, inspired partly by market research into what people read in popular papers, was to devote less space to political and industrial coverage and more to human interest stories, photographs and strip cartoons. This was identified as the most promising way to rebuild a mass circulation and, in particular, to 'bring in women – vital to the advertising department'.[12]

The second option, and the one that was eventually adopted, was to attract more advertising by seeking to upgrade the paper's readership both socially and educationally. This strategy led to the appointment of John Beavan as editor in 1960 with the remit to lure former *News Chronicle* readers and, above all, to attract 'the intelligent grammar school boy'. The paper moved upmarket, and included features about books, classical music and even ballet. It also loosened its ties with the Labour Party and the TUC, and moved politically to the right.

Yet despite these changes, the *Daily Herald*'s readership remained obstinately proletarian. Indeed, even by 1963 to 1964, only 13 per cent of its readers were middle class. Yet its owners were conscious that the traditional, loyalist union subculture from which the *Daily Herald* sprang was in decline. The paper's management, influenced by the Gaitskellite revisionism of the early 1960s, concluded that the cloth-cap, traditional Labour Party identity of the paper was putting off potential readers and that the only way to blast the paper successfully into the middle market was to relaunch it under a new name, the *Sun*. As a prelude to this, the TUC was persuaded to sell its share of the paper in 1964 to the International Publishing Corporation (IPC) which had acquired Odhams' shares in the paper three years earlier.

The intention behind the relaunch was to construct a new coalition of readers composed of working-class, 'political radicals' (the old *Herald* readership) and young, upwardly mobile 'social radicals'. 'The new paper,' according to an internal memorandum, 'is to have the more representative make-up essential to advertisers.'[13] But the difficulties inherent in this strategy were dauntingly revealed in prelaunch research which showed the enormous gulf that separated the two wings of the coalition. 'Social radicals', defined largely in terms of their attitudes towards race, hanging and issues such as increasing access to (but not abolishing) public schools, turned out to be only marginally more inclined to vote Labour than Conservative or Liberal, and to be not greatly more likely to read the *Daily Herald* than the *Daily Telegraph*. Ranking high among the favourite reading of 'social radicals' were the society gossip columns of the *Daily Express* and *Daily Mail* expressing social values fundamentally at odds with the class-conscious, often resentful attitudes of many *Herald* readers recorded by Odhams's previous surveys.

These findings suggest that it would have been more sensible for the *Daily Herald* to have been relaunched as a more popular, working-class daily. But this strategy was rejected by IPC because it would have meant spending money attacking another paper in the same group, namely the *Daily Mirror*. Instead the launch proceeded along its preconceived lines, seemingly unaffected by the corporation's own research.

In the event, the editorial staff of the *Sun* never succeeded in finding an editorial formula which reconciled the two very dissimilar groups that they were seeking to attract. IPC's market research showed that the paper failed both to please old *Herald* readers and to attract young, affluent, social radicals.[14] The paper struggled on as an underfinanced, deradicalized hybrid until it was sold to Murdoch at a low price in 1969.

The *Sun* was then reoriented towards a mass working-class market. The recasting was done with consummate skill, making the *Sun* Britain's best-selling daily. It greatly increased its entertainment coverage, in particular human interest reporting of show business and TV stars, developed a more explicit style of soft porn, and shrank its coverage of public affairs. It evolved a complex editorial formula – mistakenly dismissed by some critics as simple-minded – which was both hedonistic and moralistic, iconoclastic and authoritarian, generally Conservative in its opinions and radical in its rhetoric. It also anticipated the Thatcherite era by expressing new right argu-ments before Margaret Thatcher herself.

It was an ironic ending for a daily that had been the only consistent sup-porter of the Labour Party for over half a century. Revealed by market research to have had the most devoted readership of any popular daily as late as 1958,[15] it was first enfeebled and then converted into a paper which stood for everything that the old *Daily Herald* had opposed.

Consensual pull of the mass market

Other reformist papers adjusted to post-war market conditions by muting their radical commitment in a bid to maximize sales. This pattern of accom-modation is illustrated by the post-war history of the *Daily Mirror*. It emerged triumphant from the radical wartime and immediate post-war period to become the top circulation daily paper in 1949. But the 1951 general election inaugurated a long period of Conservative ascendancy. Other indi-cators registered a change in the market environment. The *Daily Mirror's* growth of circulation slowed down in the early 1950s, and began to fall after 1955. The paper also failed to maintain the substantial share of advertising it had won in the 1940s. Its management became increasingly aware that the tide of radicalism which had helped to sweep the paper to the top was receding, and began to worry about whether the paper was moving out of step with the times. It responded by steering the *Daily Mirror* more towards the centre of gravity in the mass market – the political centre. The class divisiveness of the paper's 'us and them' rhetoric of the 1940s softened in the 1950s and early 1960s into the more inclusive and acceptable rhetoric of 'the young at heart' against 'the old', the modern against the traditional, 'new ideas' instead of 'tired men'. The *Daily Mirror's* commitment to the Labour Party remained but it changed in character. Increasingly it took the form of opposition to the Conservative Party rather than positive advocacy of a socialist alternative.

In the late 1950s, the paper also pursued, for a mixture of motives, young and upwardly mobile readers. They brought in additional advertising because they were particularly sought after by advertisers; they seemed to embody important, new social trends; and they were an accessible part of the market because their newspaper-reading habits were relatively unfixed. The effect of this redirection was to make the paper's readership more socially and politically heterogeneous. By 1964 one-third of the paper's readership opposed the Labour Party and its readership profile was considerably more upmarket than it had been in the 1940s. This was perceived by the *Mirror*'s management to impose a limitation on the paper's radicalism. As Cecil King, then Chairman of the Mirror Group, explained in 1967:

> Today newspaper circulations are vast assemblies of people of all social classes and all varieties of political view. A controller who tried to campaign for causes profoundly distasteful, even to large minorities of his readers, would . . . put his business at risk.

However, Cecil King's market fears, and those of his senior colleagues, perhaps rationalized their own personal inclinations. King's youthful radicalism had waned as he grew older. Hugh Cudlipp, his close colleague and successor as chairman of the Mirror Group, subsequently left the Labour Party to join the SDP. Their centrism was reflected in the choice of political advisers to the Mirror Group in the 1950s and 1960s – Alfred Robens, George Brown and Richard Marsh, all right-wing Labour politicians who subsequently defected to the Conservatives or Liberal–SDP Alliance (later Liberal Democrats).

The *Daily Mirror* succeeded in recouping the circulation it had lost in the late 1950s, and displayed flashes of its old radicalism during the 1960s until it was challenged by the renascent *Sun*. Between 1969 and 1985, its sales fell into almost continuous decline and this free-fall was resumed again in the early 1990s. The paper's successive managements responded defensively by cutting back on the *Daily Mirror*'s campaigning journalism. The paper also experimented with different populist registers in an attempt to find a new voice that would appeal to a younger readership. Its inner uncertainty and waning radical commitment were symbolized by its changes of masthead. Under the Maxwell regime, its old campaigning masthead slogan 'Forward with the People' was resuscitated in a patriotic form, 'Forward with Britain'. This was replaced in turn with a slogan defining the paper's identity exclusively in market terms: 'Colour Newspaper of the Year'.

By the mid-1990s, the *Daily Mirror* had in some ways more in common with its rival the *Sun* than with its former incarnation in the 1940s as one of Britain's greatest radical papers. In the late 1990s, a brave attempt was made to recapture some of the *Mirror*'s former radicalism under the editorship of Piers Morgan. However, this adjustment was contained within a package that was overwhelmingly entertainment-centred. This reflected another key change that took place in the press after 1945.

Depoliticization of the popular press

The commercial pressures reshaping the *Daily Herald* and the *Daily Mirror* affected popular papers more generally. These emerged from their cocooned existence in the 1940s and early 1950s into an intensely competitive environment where the mounting pile of dead titles was a constant reminder to publishers of the consequences of failing to adjust to change. The decline of circulation that began in the 1950s continued in a seemingly remorseless way, with a temporary recovery of popular newspaper sales only in the late 1970s and early 1980s. Underlying this slide were three key trends: a reduction in the number of households buying more than one paper in response to newspapers' increased size and cost, a steady decline in the proportion of adults reading national papers after 1967, and the modest growth of quality papers at the expense of the popular press. Editors of popular papers became acutely aware that they were swimming against the market tide.

Although advertising expenditure on the national press steadily increased, popular nationals' share of advertising declined gradually after 1953. More important, their advertising profit margins were seriously eroded during the 1960s and 1970s because most popular papers failed to increase their advertising rates in line with rising costs in an attempt to fend off competition from ITV. Popular newspapers responded to their mounting economic problems by doubling cover prices in real terms between 1962 and 1985, but this policy merely fuelled publishers' anxiety about losing readers.

However, the principal driving force behind the pressure to maximize sales was a sustained rise in costs. National newspapers more than quadrupled their paging between 1945 and 1975 and almost doubled them again in the subsequent period up to 1996. Their staff numbers also increased and were paid substantially more in real terms. Between 1946 and 1974, the annual costs of the average national and London daily increased fourteen-fold.[16] The circulation war that began in 1981 and led to the largest ever give-away prizes of £1 million in 1985, before switching to lavish advertising promotion in the late 1980s, further fuelled the rise in costs. Soaring expenditure intensified the need to stay ahead in the circulation battle.

How this could be achieved was spelt out in extensive market research commissioned by increasingly anxious publishers. This revealed a remarkable constancy in what people read in national newspapers over four decades. The most read items were found to be human interest stories and certain entertainment features because their appeal transcended differences of age, class and gender. Sport was popular among men, as were women's features among women. However, public affairs coverage attracted generally low average readership scores because it appealed less to women than to men and less to the young than to the over-35s.

The managements of popular newspapers responded by giving more space to content with a common denominator appeal. They expanded human interest content, entertainment features, sports and women's articles (see Table 7.4).[17] This growth took place at the expense of public affairs coverage which declined, as a percentage of editorial space, by at least half in all our sample popular papers between 1946 and 1976. Indeed, public affairs took up less space than sport in all these papers by 1976.

In effect the make-up of popular papers reverted to their pre-war character in response to similar market pressures. However, the downgrading of political coverage was carried to even more extreme lengths in three sample papers – *The People/Sunday People,* the *Sunday Pictorial/Mirror* and the *Daily Herald/Sun.* In the latter case, public affairs as a proportion of editorial space was down by almost two-thirds in 1976 compared with thirty years earlier. A supplementary content analysis also reveals that public affairs stories were chosen less often as lead, front-page articles in popular newspapers in 1976 compared with 1936. Evidence for the subsequent period is contradictory.[18] What seems to have happened is that the depoliticization of the popular press deepened in the 1980s, but was at least partly reversed between 1987 and 1997.[19]

The increasingly frenetic pursuit of readers also led to a general lowering of journalistic standards, especially during the periods of most intense competition. This gave rise to a number of well-publicized excesses in the 1970s and 1980s: inventing an overnight love tryst between Prince Charles and Lady Diana Spencer on a lonely railway siding in the royal train (*Sunday Mirror*); fabricating a fictitious interview with Mrs Marica McKay, the widow of the Falklands VC hero (*Sun*); touching up a photograph of 'Lady Di' to give a hint of nipples in a low-cut dress (*Sun*); offering 'blood money' to relatives and friends of the 'Yorkshire Ripper', Peter Sutcliffe (*Daily Mail, Daily Express, Daily Star* and *News of the World*); pillorying a child as the 'Worst Brat in Britain' without mentioning that he was ill due to contracting meningitis (*Sun*); and, most notoriously of all, reporting as 'The Truth' misleading claims that football hooligans had urinated on police officers, attacked rescue workers and stolen from injured fans in the Hillsborough football stadium disaster (*Sun*).

Gap between quality and popular newspapers

To a much greater degree than the popular press, broadsheet papers maintained a commitment to serious political coverage. Between 1936 and 1976, both the *Daily Telegraph* and the *Observer*, for example, actually increased their relative coverage of public affairs, while reducing or merely maintaining their human interest content (see Table 7.4). The very rapid growth in the size of broadsheets after 1985 contributed to a large *absolute* increase in entertainment content. However, as a percentage of the total, political stories only declined markedly in the early and mid-1980s, and rose again subsequently to a level that was higher in 1997 than in 1957.[20] A significant difference thus remained between a politicized élite press, and a relatively depoliticized mass press.

This difference is rooted in the historical development of the press, and is attributed usually to the chasm that supposedly separates the sophisticated preferences of educated élites and the more basic interests of the masses. In

Table 7.4 *The editorial contents of selected national daily and Sunday newspapers, 1936 to 1976*[a]

Percentage of editorial space	Daily Express			Daily Herald		Sun	Daily Mail		
	1936	1946	1976	1936	1946	1976	1936	1946	1976
Advertising (proportion of total space)	43	18	44	42	17	40	46	18	36
Editorial (proportion of total space)	57	82	56	58	83	60	54	82	64
Photographs[b]	13	7	13	9	5	16	15	7	14
Illustrations[b]	4	4	5	2	4	6	5	4	5
Public affairs news[c]	14	29	12	23	34	8	15	27	12
Public affairs features[c]	4	10	6	10	11	6	4	12	8
Finance	10	4	7	6	1	1	9	3	10
Sport	22	18	27	19	20	30	20	19	23
Human interest news	20	20	16	14	14	14	14	19	17
Human interest features	10	6	12	8	4	20	15	3	10
Consumer and women's features	7	2	4	5	3	2	8	2	5
Horoscopes, cartoon strips, quizzes and competitions	4	3	6	3	3	8	3	4	5
Arts and entertainments	6	4	7	6	4	7	5	5	9
Other features	5	5	4	6	4	7	7	6	3

	Daily Mirror			Daily Telegraph			Sunday Express			People / Sunday People			Sunday Pictorial / Sunday Mirror			Observer		
	1936	1946	1976	1936	1946	1976	1936	1946	1976	1936	1946	1976	1936	1946	1976	1936	1946	1976
	29	16	42	47	35	48	51	16	56	38	22	44	24	25	46	46	36	49
	71	84	58	53	64	52	49	84	44	62	78	56	76	75	54	54	64	51
	21	8	18	8	2	9	14	4	13	11	4	21	26	25	20	3	3	12
	7	15	8	1	1	1	4	6	9	2	2	2	6	6	6	1	–	3
	10	18	9	19	40	26	8	20	5	10	15	2	7	10	5	20	28	16
	2	7	4	3	9	4	10	19	12	4	11	6	10	16	6	6	19	14
	4	–	1	20	8	20	5	2	2	1	1	1	2	–	2	7	2	10
	15	9	28	14	11	18	21	20	25	25	28	30	18	20	27	17	12	16
	21	29	17	14	12	13	15	11	12	18	15	13	11	14	13	7	5	5
	27	5	16	10	10	2	23	9	17	23	17	22	15	26	28	6	7	8
	6	4	2	3	1	5	4	2	10	3	3	5	8	5	5	4	2	11
	6	16	10	1	1	1	4	6	6	8	8	6	14	3	5	3	5	1
	4	1	8	6	3	10	3	4	6	3	2	6	7	3	6	25	20	15
	7	10	5	9	7	3	8	7	4	7	2	10	9	3	4	5	4	5

Notes: ᵃSample 252 issues.   ᵇThese are also tabulated in terms of their content.
ᶜDefined as political, social, economic, industrial, scientific and medical affairs.
All figures have been rounded off to the nearest whole number.

fact, studies commissioned by publishers over a period of sixty years regularly revealed that quality and popular paper readers were rather similar in their likes and dislikes. Thus to take but one example, the most read stories in Sunday quality papers during the period between 1969 and 1971 were human interest stories about ordinary people, followed by human interest stories about celebrities – precisely the most read stories in the *Sunday People* and *Sunday Mirror* during the same period.[21]

The polarization between the two sectors arose primarily from the divergent ways in which they were funded. The quality press generally derived over two-thirds of its revenue from advertising, secured through appealing to high-spending, niche audiences. The popular press, on the other hand, obtained over half of its revenue from sales and its value to advertisers was rooted in its circulation success. Thus one sector needed to 'select' its readers as a way of safeguarding its advertising income, while the other needed to build and retain a mass circulation.

These divergent economic pressures affected the way in which each sector related to the market. Popular papers catered for the lowest common denominator of mass demand, in the process ignoring the preferences of a significant minority of the readers who would have liked more public affairs coverage. By contrast, quality papers privileged the politicized minority among their readers as a way of avoiding the indiscriminate expansion of circulation. This often coincided with the concerns of senior journalists in the quality press.

Failure to respect these different market rules could produce bizarre consequences, as was demonstrated when *The Times*, under a new owner, Lord Thomson, went for promiscuous growth. Between 1966 and 1969 the paper increased its circulation by 60 per cent through heavy promotion and a more popular editorial approach. However, a significant number of its new readers were indigent students, lower-middle class or even working class. Advertisers objected to paying premium rates for the privilege of attracting readers from outside their advertising target group, many of whom could be reached more cheaply through other publications. Consequently, advertising failed to keep up with the rise in circulation, and the paper incurred steeply increasing losses. Thoroughly chastened, *The Times* reversed its policy by raising its price, adopting a more austere editorial policy and changing its promotional message in a successful bid to lose 96,000 unwanted circulation between 1969 and 1971. When *The Times* went for growth almost a quarter of a century later, it targeted its appeal very deliberately to affluent readers of papers such as the *Daily Telegraph* and *Daily Mail*. Even so, its spectacular rise in circulation between 1993 and 1996 also produced heavy losses.

More far-reaching than advertisers' indirect influence on the market orientation of newspapers was their direct impact on the structure of the press. By 2002, five out of ten national dailies served the top end of the market, and accounted for 20 per cent of circulation.[22] The other 80 per cent of the market had to settle for what remained. Under this bifurcated system, the only significant minority papers to survive were those that served advertising-rich audiences. For example, *Today* closed down in 1995 with a circulation of 573,000, significantly more than that of the upscale *Guardian* or *Financial Times* but not enough to keep it alive.

Representation was unequal in terms of weight as well as numbers. The only papers offering detailed coverage of public affairs reflected the concerns and interests of élite publics. This tended to reinforce élite domination of politics.

Economic power was thus converted into ideological power. Yet this came about not through blackmailing pressure exerted by advertisers on editorial content – the usual concern of radical critics – but through an impersonal process in which influence was largely unsought. Economic inequalities in society gave rise to unequal advertising outlays on the press. This influenced, in turn, the structure of the press, its balance of contents and definition of desired readership.

Curtailment of choice

The escalating costs of publishing in the first four decades after the Second World War imposed a further limitation on the ideological spectrum of the press. The rise in staffing, paging and promotional expenditure had the effect of stifling competition. Only established national newspaper enterprises, able to economize by making use of existing print capacity and services, were able to incur the enormous cost of launching a new national paper. Others were excluded or were deterred by the high cost involved. During the 1970s and early 1980s the trade union movement discussed the possibility of starting a new national daily, and even commissioned a detailed feasibility study through the TUC. Reluctantly it concluded in 1984 that it lacked the funds to go ahead with the project despite the fact that its privately commissioned consumer research indicated that there was a substantial market demand for a new left daily.

The only new voices to be heard in Fleet Street before the advent of new technology merely amplified the existing chorus. In the half century before 1986, just four new national papers were established: the *Sun, Daily Star, Sunday Telegraph* and *Mail on Sunday*. All these papers originated from leading press groups, and consolidated their oligopoly. Politically, they were all on the right and strengthened Conservative domination of the national press.

Mythologizing of new technology

Between 1986 and 1989 a technical revolution took place in the national press. Digital typesetting with direct input by journalists and advertising staff was introduced, and photocomposition fully replaced the manual casting of copy in hot metal type. Pages were designed and made up on computer terminals linked to plate-making rather than being pasted up on a board. Powerful, new web-offset machines, requiring fewer production staff, were installed and colour printing was introduced. Facsimile transmission was adopted, enabling the physical separation of editorial and production processes and the simultaneous printing of newspapers at different sites. This reduced distribution costs and facilitated the more intensive use of printing presses.

These technical innovations were accompanied by a revolution in the social organization of production. Thousands of printers were made redundant between 1986 and 1988. The old system of production, in which shop-floor control was effectively subcontracted to trade unions, was streamlined into a low-cost, mass-production process controlled by management. After 1989, a number of national publishers also enforced individual contracts with journalists, and derecognized the National Union of Journalists.

The introduction of new technology was funded principally in two ways. Reuters, owned jointly by leading press groups, was floated in 1984 and produced a windfall sale of shares. Most national publishers also sold their historic properties in the centre of London, and moved to cheaper sites. In 1989 the last national newspaper rolled off the last printing press, in Fleet Street, marking the end of a historic tradition that went back almost to the beginning of British journalism.

A skilled public relations campaign prepared the way for this transformation. Press managements argued that computerized technology would transform the national press by reducing costs. New papers would be easy to set up, and minority journalism would flourish with the aid of low-cost technology. These arguments were echoed by distinguished journalists and politicians on the centre-left as well as the right in a general mobilization of public opinion against Fleet Street's printers. 'Murdoch may have done more for the freedom of the press than a dozen Royal Commissions,' enthused Bill Rodgers, Vice-President of the SDP, after the press tycoon shed his Fleet Street production workers. Only the intransigence of some in the print unions, argued Ian Aitken, political editor of the *Guardian,* prevented the emergence of 'entirely new newspapers representing all points of view'. His counterpart at the *Observer,* Robert Taylor, also wrote enthusiastically about how new technology would undermine 'the tyranny of the mass circulation press, with its mindless formula journalism appealing to the lowest common denominator'.

The man who initially embodied all these hopes for the future was Eddy Shah, a publisher of freesheets in the north-west and the victor of a famous confrontation with the National Graphical Association. He announced in 1985 to general acclaim that he was setting up a new national daily and Sunday paper in a green field site, miles from Fleet Street, using the latest in print technology. He was widely hailed as the harbinger of a new era.

But it was in fact Rupert Murdoch who made the first, decisive move by building a new printing plant in Wapping, East London. Although he told the print unions that he intended merely to print a new local daily there, he secretly established a large, new plant, costing over £66 million, capable of printing all his national newspapers. An alternative production workforce was recruited with the help of the maverick electricians' union and trained to operate the new technology. An alternative distribution system was also established through an Australian transport company, Thomas Nationwide Transport, to prevent effective sympathy action by organized labour. As a final precaution, Murdoch reconstituted his Wapping plant as a separate company so that picketing by his Fleet Street employees outside Wapping would be technically illegal.

Murdoch then issued an ultimatum to the print unions requiring them to accept a legally binding, no-strike agreement in which 'new technology may be adopted at any time with consequent reductions in manning levels' and in which anyone involved in industrial action during the term of the contract would be dismissed without appeal. The print unions, although agreeing belatedly to new technology and voluntary redundancy, refused to sign an agreement which effectively removed union protection. A strike was called and Murdoch's Fleet Street production workers mounted a forlorn, nightly vigil outside the coils of razor wire surrounding the Wapping plant. Their frustration flared into occasional violence during ritualized mass pickets, which resulted in some print workers being gaoled and their unions heavily fined. After more than a year, the strike was called off amid bitter recriminations.

Murdoch's success was followed by a wave of redundancies in Fleet Street as rival press groups introduced new technology. New papers were also launched in the period 1986 to 1989, seemingly fulfilling optimistic predictions about the impact of new technology. But these predictions were based, as it turned out, on a myth: the widespread belief that overpaid and underworked print workers accounted for the major part of newspaper costs. In fact, production wages comprised only an estimated 21 per cent of Fleet Street costs before new technology was introduced.[23]

'Downsizing' the production force thus did not change fundamentally the economics of publishing. The launch and establishment of new national newspapers still required large resources. *Today* and *Sunday Today* were launched with an initial outlay of £22.5 million; the *Independent* with an establishment fund of £21 million; the *News on Sunday* with around £6 million; the *Sunday Correspondent* with £18 million; and the *London Daily News* with an outlay of well over £30 million in its first year.

Outlays remained high because new technology was relatively expensive and had only a limited impact in lowering non-wage costs. Newspapers still had to attain relatively high circulations in order to break even. The run-in period when new papers were building circulation, and trading at a loss, added to the effective establishment cost.

Just how little things had changed was revealed by Shah's supposedly mould-breaking launch of *Today* and *Sunday Today*. Shah's central problem – apart from lack of editorial insight – was shortage of money. A substantial part of his launch fund was spent on setting up a modern plant. This led him to economize on prelaunch preparations which contributed to the production problems and indifferent editorial quality of the early issues of his papers. He then ran out of money after only ten weeks and found it impossible to secure further credit, largely because the equity proportion of his capital amounted to only £8.5 million. As a consequence the first national newspapers to be launched by an outsider in half a century were taken over by a leading press conglomerate, Lonrho. Along with other subsidiary backers, Lonrho injected a further £24 million into the Today group in 1986 to 1987, effectively doubling the establishment outlay. *Sunday Today* was closed down and *Today* was acquired by the leading monopolist Rupert Murdoch, who attempted to resuscitate it as a commercial proposition and failed.

One problem Shah shared with other would-be publishers was that he had to leap over the publishing equivalent of a high jump from a very short run-up. The length of the run-up was affected by how much money the publisher was able to spend on getting the paper right, and building a following. The height of the jump depended on the advertising bounty that readers brought with them. A paper aimed at the working class, such as the *News on Sunday*, needed in 1987, using the latest technology, around 800,000 circulation to break even. A paper aimed at the affluent, such as the *Independent*, required approximately half this amount in 1988.

The net impact of new technology was modest because it did not lower entry costs substantially or change the distorting role of advertising. Of the small shoal of minnows that swam for a time near the hulks of the established press, only two survived. Casualties included two left papers, *News on Sunday* (1987) and *Sunday Correspondent* (1989 to 1990), the first of which was editorially dismal and both of which were undercapitalized. Shah again attempted with too little money to launch a new national paper, *The Post* (1988), which lasted for only thirty-three issues. The *London Daily News* (1987) was killed off with the help of a short-lived, spoiling paper launched by the monopoly *London Evening Standard*. The only mainstream newspapers to stay the course were the *Independent* and *Independent on Sunday*. However, they only avoided closure by surrendering their independence. Initially, the *Independent* attracted talented journalists, breathed new life into a bi-partisan tradition of journalism, and made great headway in building circulation. It then depleted its limited resources by launching a Sunday paper during a recession, lost momentum, and was finally torpedoed by Murdoch and Black who slashed the prices of rival papers. The *Independent* and *Independent on Sunday* limped into harbour, and were taken over ultimately by an international media group based in Ireland.

The only partial exception to this record of relative failure was the launch of *Sunday Sport* in 1986, and its expansion into a weekday title, *Sport*. These caricatured the excesses of tabloid journalism, with invented stories such as 'World War II Bomber Found on the Moon', and its predictable follow-up 'World War II Bomber Found on the Moon Vanished'. However, their diet of sport, crime and pornography, without public affairs coverage, make them specialist publications rather than national newspapers. They are also not very popular: their survival has been due to their paring down of costs, with skeletal staffs, no general news service, and a heavy reliance on cheap, bought-in material.

The expansionary period of the national press is now probably over. The major press groups forestalled the threat of further challenges by forcing up costs. They multiplied newspaper sections, held down prices and in the late 1980s poured money into promotion. No new national newspaper has been launched since 1989, apart from the specialist *Sunday Business* started in 1996, and the Sunday stablemate of the *Star*, launched in 2002. The latter – the product of a powerful press group – probably typifies what at best we may expect in the future.

In short, the technical transformation of the press never produced a corresponding editorial revolution. It led to a cleaner, cheaper system of production; it gave rise to fatter newspapers with new sections; and it added two centrist titles to the already crowded top end of the market. But what it did not do was enrich popular journalism through the proliferation of viable, minority newspapers, or by significantly extending the ideological range of the press. The Fleet Street 'revolution' was a rainbow that came and went, though not before dazzling gullible and impressionable journalists.

Retrospect

The shift towards a delegated pattern of control in part of the national press during the 1960s and early 1970s was reversed during the later 1970s and 1980s. A new generation of predominantly right-wing proprietors emerged who adopted a more interventionist and personalized style of management. Yet even in those papers where proprietors were relatively inactive, control was still exercised through the selection of senior management and mediated through traditional structures of news-gathering and the influence of dominant political values.

The impact of managerial change was reinforced by the impersonal operation of market forces. Rising costs and the redistribution of advertising, following deregulation, helped to decimate the social democratic press, and contributed to the taming and depoliticization of the popular radical papers that survived.

The rightward shift of the press during the 1970s and 1980s was also a response to a sea-change of opinion. However, the changing complexion of the press overstated the public shift to the right. This was demonstrated by the yawning gap that developed between editorial and electoral opinion, particularly after 1970. In the 1983, 1987 and 1992 general elections, the Conservative Party never secured more than 43 per cent of the vote, yet the Conservative press's share of national daily circulation fluctuated between 64 and 78 per cent. When a large part of the press subsequently realigned itself to New Labour, the shift represented a change of political affiliation rather than of orientation. The press still remained predominantly right-wing.

Partly as a consequence of increasing concentration of ownership, the press failed also to reflect the growing diversity of public opinion. Indeed, the national press – although numbering seventeen or more titles during the period 1969 to 2003 – had unanimous editorial opinions on a surprising number of issues. For example, every national daily and Sunday paper supported the aborted union 'reforms' proposed by the government in 1969. During the 1975 referendum every national newspaper supported Britain's entry into the EEC. In 1980 every national daily opposed the TUC's 'day of action'. In 1981 every national paper which expressed an editorial opinion supported the more right-wing candidate Denis Healey in the Labour Party's deputy leadership contest. In 1985 all national papers applauded Neil Kinnock's attack on the 'hard left' of his party.

Between 1974 and 1993, only two national papers (the *Daily Mirror* and *Sunday Times*) supported briefly the withdrawal of British troops from Northern Ireland, even though this was favoured by the majority in most polls conducted during this period. The Campaign for Nuclear Disarmament won significant minority support, yet lacked the backing of a single national newspaper. Only one national (the *Independent on Sunday*) in 1996 was explicitly republican, despite the fact that one in five at that time favoured the abolition of the monarchy. However, the press did diverge to some extent in relation to the 2003 Gulf War.

The rightward drift of the press had significant political consequences. In particular, the closure of large-circulation, centre-left papers removed key institutional props that had helped to sustain a popular radical tradition in early post-war Britain. The *Daily Herald* had provided reinforcement for a Labourist, trade union subculture; *Reynolds News* had celebrated the collectivist self-help tradition of the Co-operative Movement; the *News Chronicle,* a paper which had periodically upset its post-war owners by being too radical, belonged to an older, ethical Liberal tradition. Together, these three papers reached, on their deathbed, an average issue readership of 9.3 million people.

The trade union movement was also weakened by a sustained press campaign against it during the 1970s and early 1980s. Reporting of industrial relations tended to focus on conflict, framed in terms of its harmful consequences rather than its causes. Thus Denis McQuail found that the three most frequently recurring themes in national daily reports of industrial disputes in 1975 were loss of output, loss of work by those not involved, and inconvenience or danger to the public. Implicitly, strikers were portrayed as being in conflict primarily with the public rather than with their employers. This selective definition was sustained further by under-reporting the role of management. Indeed, actions or statements by employers and their organizations accounted in 1975 for only 2 per cent of the main items of industrial relations reports in national dailies. McQuail found little difference in the pattern of reporting of industrial relations between right-wing Labour and Conservative papers.[24]

The press also mounted a sustained and effective attack on the Labour left. This culminated in the tabloid campaign against 'loony left' councils in 1996 to 1997, the impact of which stemmed from a series of seemingly factual reports featuring left-wing councillors doing manifestly dotty things. Thus individual 'loony left' councils in London were alleged to have banned black bin liners as racist, proscribed the nursery rhyme 'Baa Baa Black Sheep', spent almost £0.5 million on 'twenty-four super-loos for gypsies', and insisted that gays should go to the top of the council house waiting list. All these reports proved, on investigation, to be misleading.[25]

The national press generally endorsed the basic tenets of the capitalist system – private enterprise, profit, the 'free market' and the rights of property ownership. By frequently invoking the consensual framework of the national interest and by projecting positive symbols of nationhood (such as sporting heroes), the press fostered a national identity at the expense of class solidarity. The press also reinforced dominant political and social norms by mobilizing public indignation against a succession of public enemies portrayed in stereotypical ways – youth gangs, squatters, student radicals, muggers, football hooligans, union militants, urban rioters, gay carriers of the 'killer plague', asylum seekers and terrorists.

The press built support for the social system in less direct and obvious ways. Its focus on political and state office as the seat of power tended to mask the central influence of economic élites and global markets in shaping public policy. By regularly reporting political and economic news as disconnected events, it encouraged acceptance of the power structure as natural, part of the way things are. Embedded also in its entertainment features were values and assumptions that were not quite as apolitical as they appeared to be at first sight. Its expanding consumer and lifestyle sections concerned with music, travel, motoring, fashion, homes, health and personal finance tacitly promoted a seductive view that consumption is a way of expressing self in a real world far removed from, and transcending, structures of power. Above all, its greatly enlarged human interest and entertainment content tended to portray tacitly society as a structure of individuals, explain events in individual terms, and to offer individual-moral rather than collective solutions to problems. The press's support for a conservative, 'common-sense' view of the world may have contributed more towards maintaining an inegalitarian social order than its explicitly political content.

Notes

1. S. Koss, *The Rise and Fall of the Political Press in Britain*, vol. 2 (London, Hamish Hamilton, 1984) p. 4.
2. MORI, June 1987. This excludes those who were undecided or intended to abstain.
3. D. Butler and G. Butler, *Twentieth-Century British Political Facts, 1900–2000* (Basingstoke, Macmillan, 8th edn, 2000), p. 536; T. Austin and T. Haines (eds), *The Times Guide to the House of Commons June 2001* (London, Times Books, 2001), p. 46.
4. Amendment to Broadcasting Bill moved by Dr John Cunningham, *Parliamentary Debates*, 275 (84), col. 551, 16 April 1996.
5. N. Chenoweth, *Virtual Murdoch* (London, Secker & Warburg, London), p. 201.
6. Data are available in different forms. In 2001, the top five publishers' share of regional daily and Sunday, free or paid for 'sales' in 2001 was 72 per cent and of total paid for and free local weekly 'sales' 68 per cent, as computed in *Johnson Press plc and Trinity Mirror plc: A Report into the Proposed Merger* (London, Stationery Office, 2002), Table 3.1. Since the report, Johnston (ranked four) has acquired RIM (ranked five) in a process that seems to have attracted no public comment.
7. This is explored further in Chapter 18.
8. *Royal Commission on the Press 1974–7 Final Report* (London, HMSO, 1997), p. 149.
9. My thanks to Brendan Wall for help in conducting interviews.
10. M. Hastings, *Editor* (Basingstoke, Macmillan, 2002), p. 235.
11. J. W. Hobson, *The Selection of Advertising Media* (London, Business Publications, 1955); J. R. Adams, *Media Planning* (London, Business Books, 1971). There was, however, a reaction against overdependence on quantitative approaches in media planning during the late 1970s.
12. *'Daily Herald* reader interest surveys recommendations', p. 8 (London, Odhams Ltd records, 1955).
13. 'Attitudes to newspapers and newspaper reading' (London, International Publishing Corporation (IPC) records, 1964), p. 3.
14. 'Report of an investigation into the transition from the *Daily Herald* to the *Sun*' (London, IPC records, 1968).
15. 'Report of a survey to study attitudes to daily newspapers' (London, Odhams Ltd records, 1958).
16. Estimated from *Royal Commission on the Press 1947–9 Report* (London, HMSO, 1949), Table 4, p. 82, and *Royal Commission on the Press Interim Report* (London, HMSO, 1976), Table E5, p. 96.
17. A representative sample (twelve issues of dailies and six of Sundays per year) was selected in a way that gave appropriate weight to each quarter of the year, each week in the month and each day in the week. A code–recode comparison of a representative sample of 1491 items yielded 83 per cent agreement in their classification.
18. Two essays provide evidence that is partly contradictory. See D. Rooney, 'Thirty years of competition in the British tabloid press: the *Mirror* and the *Sun* 1968–1998', and S. McLachlan and P. Golding, 'Tabloidization in the British press: a quantitative investigation into changes in British newspapers, 1952–1997', both in C. Sparks and J. Tulloch, *Tabloid Tales* (Lanham, Rowman & Littlefield, 2000).

19. S. McLachlan and P. Golding, *ibid.*, p. 86, figure 3.11.
20. *Ibid.*, p. 87, Figure 3.12.
21. *Sunday Times,* Marketing Research Studies, 1969 to 1971; Sunday Paper Readership Surveys, International Publishing Corporation Marketing and Research Department, 1969–71.
22. This does not include the *Morning Star* since it is usually unobtainable in newsagents.
23. The latest available figure for the national newspaper press in the pre-new technology period, as reported in *Royal Commission on the Press Interim Report* (London, HMSO, 1976), Table E11, p. 101.
24. D. McQuail, *Analysis of Newspaper Content*, Royal Commission on the Press Research Series 4 (London, HMSO, 1977). The impact of this press coverage was reinforced by that of television. See Glasgow University Media Group, *Bad News* (London, Routledge & Kegan Paul, 1976) and *More Bad News* (London, Routledge & Kegan Paul, 1980).
25. Goldsmiths Media Research Group, *Media Coverage of London Councils* (London, Goldsmiths College, University of London, 1987).

Part II

Broadcasting history

8

Reith and the denial of politics

There are two accounts of the origins of the BBC. The first is that the Corporation was the personal achievement of John Reith. The second is that its emergence was accidental. According to the first view the BBC's monopoly of broadcasting was an inevitable consequence of the Corporation's cultural mission, while for the second, as R. H. Coase has written, 'The problem, to which the monopoly was seen as a solution by the Post Office, was one of Civil Service administration. The view that a monopoly in broadcasting was better for the listener was only to come later.'

These theories appear to conflict. According to one view Reith made history fit his vision. According to the other, a great institution took a particular form because no one appreciated its future importance. Both, however, have a central flaw in common: they disregard political and social change in the world outside broadcasting.

Discovering an audience, a director, and the money

Broadcasting – the transmitting of programmes to be heard simultaneously by an indefinitely large number of people – is a social invention, not a technical one. The capacity to broadcast existed long before it was recognized. 'Wireless telegraphy' was developed during the First World War for military purposes. It was used as a substitute for the telephone, but one with the disadvantage that it was impossible to specify the audience which heard the message. An American engineer, David Sarnoff, first saw the possibilities of radio in 1916. 'I have in mind a plan of development which would make radio a "household utility" like the piano or electricity,' he wrote. 'The idea is to bring music into the house by wireless.'

Yet for some time after popular broadcasting had started in the 1920s, wireless was regarded as little more than an experimental toy. It took Northcliffe, a pioneer in the commercialization of leisure, to demonstrate the potential audience for the new invention. He arranged a promotion stunt for the *Daily Mail*. Dame Nellie Melba was to be broadcast singing from

Chelmsford. This event which began 'with a long silvery trill' and ended with *God Save the King* attracted a much larger audience than had been expected. It made the wireless manufacturers aware for the first time of a potentially huge market for them to supply.

In 1922 there were nearly a hundred applications to the Post Office from manufacturers who wanted to set up broadcasting stations. This demand created the need for control. As Peter Eckersley, one of the company's first employees, wrote later, 'The BBC was formed as an expedient solution to a technical problem. It owes its existence to the scarcity of air waves.' The Postmaster General solved the problems of radio interference by persuading rival manufacturers to invest jointly in one small and initially speculative broadcasting station: The British Broadcasting Company. John Reith was made its Managing Director.

How would the BBC have developed if its first director had been a career civil servant, a banker, or a Bloomsbury intellectual? Many of the features of broadcasting which are taken for granted today would certainly be absent. Reith's domination of the Corporation in its early days was massive, totalitarian, and idiosyncratic, and for many decades the traditions of the BBC seemed to flow directly from his personality. The British Broadcasting Company was set up as a business. Reith turned it into a crusade. 'Scotch engineer, Calvinist by upbringing, harsh and ruthless in character', as A. J. P. Taylor has described him, Reith used 'the brute force of monopoly to stamp Christian morality on the British people'. While waiting to find out whether his application for the directorship had been successful Reith wrote in his memoirs, 'I kept my faith alive night and morning and encouraged myself with the text "Commit thy way unto the Lord, trust also Him and He shall bring it to pass".' Later he was to exhort his staff to dedicate themselves to 'humility in the service of higher pursuits. The desire for notoriety and recognition', he warned, 'sterilizes the seeds from which greatness might spring.'

This ability to impose his will on staff was helped by his size. Churchill nicknamed him 'Wuthering Heights' and senior staff would stand on stairs to argue with him, 'so that I can see you eye to eye, Sir'. His administrative style, and indeed his private diary, were characterized by abuse. Memoranda sent to Reith would return peppered with 'rubbish', 'stupid', 'soft minded idiocy', 'he lies'. Frequently he saw his life in nautical terms: the Corporation was a ship and he was at the helm. He was pompous, humourless, arrogant, and, like most megalomaniacs, paranoid and self-pitying. Yet the near absurdity of his vision enabled him to foresee the power of the new service.

Broadcasting was to be financed partly by a tariff on wireless sets, and partly by a licence fee. These sources soon proved inadequate for the rapidly expanding station. Listeners evaded the tariff by building their own sets with cheap foreign components. They then evaded the full licence fee by applying for experimental licences. The BBC complained, and the manufacturers were angry that the monopoly of wireless production was not proving as profitable as they had hoped. Hence in 1923 the Sykes Committee was set up by the Post Office to inquire into the Company's finances. This rejected advertising as a source of revenue because 'The time devoted to it . . . would be very small and therefore exceedingly valuable.' Radio advertising would interfere with market competition by favouring large firms. Instead the report recommended that a simple licence fee should be raised to finance the service.

The Crawford Committee, two and a half years later, unquestioningly accepted the necessity of a broadcasting monopoly, and recommended that the private company be replaced by a 'Public Commission operating in the National Interest'. The service was felt to have outgrown the petty limits of a business enterprise. 'Formed at a moment when broadcasting was still embryonic – regarded by many as a toy, a fantasy, even a joke,' the report argued, 'the company by strenuous application to its duties aided by the loyalty of its staff has raised the service to a degree which reflects high credit on British efficiency and enterprise.'

In 1926 the British Broadcasting Company closed, and the new British Broadcasting Corporation opened. Reith was delighted that the unique status of his organization was recognized. 'The Royal Academy and the Bank of England function under Royal Charter,' proclaimed the 1927 *Handbook*. 'So does the BBC. It is no Department of State.'

The BBC as a public corporation

The BBC came to be seen, in the words of William Robson, as a 'sociological invention of immense significance', and a 'breathtaking administrative innovation'. Hilda Matheson, the first head of the Talks Department, wrote in 1933 that the Corporation was 'wholly in keeping with the British constitution, and it is more and more common to find it quoted as a possible model for the management of other national services for which private control and direct state management are equally unsuitable'. What, then, was the novelty of the BBC's organization and to what extent was Reith responsible for it?

Reith did not invent the notion of a public corporation. Neither did the Corporation simply emerge accidentally. Reith exploited a theory because it was convenient to do so. The Post Office, which played a critical role in the BBC's development, was itself an early example of a nationally run business. William Beveridge had commented in 1905 that the GPO was the 'one socialist experiment . . . that now works well'. Forestry, water, and electricity were all important public corporations set up in the years before the BBC was even thought of. Lincoln Gorden, the economist, wrote that by the 1920s, 'Public boards had become all the rage, politicians of every creed when confronted with an industry or a social service which was giving trouble or failing to operate efficiently – create a board.'

The First World War had been critical in establishing the conditions for the acceptance of a 'Public Service Utility'. Despite bitter opposition the centralized control of health, insurance, coal, and ultimately the rationing of food had been introduced. These were seen as exceptional wartime measures. By the 1920s, however, a generation of reformers who had been civil servants during the war were experienced in organizing the centralized distribution of resources. Indeed for a brief period after the war even the government accepted a more interventionist role. The BBC was formed in this period.

The development of the public corporation depended on the rejection of both market forces and politics in favour of efficiency and planned growth controlled by experts. Briggs has pointed out that the acceptance of the BBC and its monopoly was a consequence of the 'substantial and influential support' the Company received between 1924 and 1925. The monopoly remained in Reith's keeping because 'a large number of important people and a large section of the interested public felt that it was right that this should be so'. These influential people were those who were personally impressed by Reith: the Post Office officials; the director of the wireless manufacturers' association; even the Prime Minister, Baldwin.

However, the idea of the BBC also had more general support. There was a widespread dissatisfaction with the *ad hoc* nature of industrial competition. Even in the 1920s, during the first post-war slump, there was a sense that there must be alternative ways to manage the distribution of resources. Men like Beveridge, who had demonstrated the justice of centralized control in the arrangements for social security and in the rationing of food during the First World War, were opposed to the social consequences of industrial competition. In 1934 Beveridge was to argue:

> In a free market economy consumers can buy only that which is offered to them, and that which is offered is not necessarily that which is most advantageous. It is that which appears to give the best prospect of profit to the producer.

This kind of attitude, which Beveridge later developed and popularized in his broadcasts, was surprisingly widely held in the early 1920s. For example Sir Stephen Tallents, who was to play a prominent role in the BBC as well as in the British documentary movement, had worked on rationing with Beveridge, and held very similar opinions. Reith's view that capitalist competition was not wrong but could be inefficient was therefore hardly original.

The BBC was to be used repeatedly as a prototype of the public corporation, especially by Herbert Morrison. Perhaps the feature which particularly attracted socialist writers was the BBC's distance from the world of capitalist industry. The Corporation made no profits. But in addition the goods it made, programmes, were in theory accessible to an infinite number of consumers. It was also a completely new enterprise with no capitalist inheritance to weigh it down. As Robson wrote, 'The BBC is an engine of the mind . . . it represents socialized control not encumbered with compensation.'

It was this aspect of broadcasting which Reith grasped. He argued that it was in the very nature of the medium that it should be available for all, for it 'ran as a reversal of the natural law that the more one takes, the less there is left for others'. In broadcasting, he wrote, 'There is no limit to the amount which may be drawn off. It does not matter how many thousands there may be listening; there is always enough for others.'[1] In order to exploit broadcasting fully, Reith had argued, it must be governed by social and not financial priorities.

Thus considerations of profit would have restricted the service to the populous urban areas. Reith was determined that the BBC must serve the whole nation. However, Reith also saw that a national service was vital for the defence of the Corporation's monopoly. 'About a week ago', he wrote in 1923, 'we got wind of a projected attack.' This was to be 'based on the grounds that under the present system we had already reached the limits of our expansion. The deduction to be drawn was that the British people would never be supplied with adequate services unless the principle of competitive commercialism were admitted.' Reith rejected commerce because it would have diminished his empire and lowered its status. But he also believed it to be inefficient in the management of national resources. Many shared this view.

Even the government had come to see some kinds of goods as exceptional. In 1927 the film industry, suffering from foreign competition, was protected by import controls, because films were of 'outstanding national importance'. The BBC had been established because the government was anxious not to exercise unfair patronage by granting a monopoly to any one commercial company. But it had also been considerably affected by the report of a Post Office official, F. J. Brown, on a visit to the USA where 'an epidemic of broadcasting was raging'. Thousands of American companies had started broadcasting and President Hoover had demanded central control over the new technology, claiming that it was as if '10,000 telephone subscribers were crying through the air for their mates'. As a result of interference, Hoover declared, 'the ether will be filled with frantic chaos'.[2] The British government realized on the basis of the American experience that broadcasting was a new kind of resource whose management demanded a new form of administration.

The BBC was founded on a rejection of politics. From the start of broadcasting there had been anxieties that the service would become an agency of government propaganda. Sir Charles Trevelyan, a Labour representative on the Sykes Committee, asked the Company's lawyer whether 'for public reasons a government could intervene to prevent anything it regarded as undesirable being broadcast'. He was told that there might be control of the news, but that a government was unlikely to bother with concerts, lectures, speeches, or the weather.

While Reith believed that the BBC should be above politics, politicians at first believed the BBC to be beneath them. Direct public ownership was rejected because it was felt 'A Member might well shrink from the prospect of having to defend in Parliament the various items in a government concert.'

Reith despised politicians and disliked party politics. Although at various times he had political ambitions, he hated the 'toadying, the cringing pursuit of popularity' which he believed characterized politics. 'It is pathetic', he wrote, 'how apprehensive Labour leaders are of their followers and how little control they seem to have over them.' Reith often misjudged the significance of political events (he felt that the split and collapse of the Labour government in 1931 was unimportant, 'Silly, over money'). 'The whole horrid technique of politics should be abolished,' he wrote in his diary. 'Government of a country is a matter of proper administration, in other words efficiency. It need not be different in nature from the government of a business – only in degree' (29 November 1936). Perhaps the most significant feature of Reith's distaste was the sense that politics led to vacillation and compromise when firm government was needed. Reith was not alone in this view. Indeed an interest developed during the late 1920s and early 1930s, from the extreme right to the fellow travelling left – and including the Keynesian centre – in the benefit of planning.

'The Next Five Years Group' and Political and Economic Planning (known then as PEP!) were groups involving members with different political allegiances but who were agreed on the need for more social planning. 'It may be', wrote one reformer in *The New Outlook,* 'that the Party structures will act for some time as an obstacle in the way of new developments.' Macmillan summed up this position:

> Most of us recognize that the old system of free unplanned Capitalism has passed away. Most of us agree that a leap forward to complete state planning is politically impossible. But . . . our search is for some practical scheme of social organization . . . which is neither.[3]

On the left, the XYZ club and the New Fabian Research Bureau soon became the natural home for planners and economists.

It has been argued by Scannell and Cardiff that the BBC legitimized its model of broadcasting, not by the huge audience the service soon attracted, but by reference to the élite of 'the great and the good who trooped into studios to educate and inform on every subject from unemployment to the Origin of the Species: Shaw, Wells, the Webbs, Beveridge, Keynes and Huxley – the roll call is endless'. Broadcasting, they argue, was dominated by a specific, reforming, fraction of the middle class. 'They saw themselves as superior to the aristocracy, for they were efficient and uncorrupt, and claiming to act for the general good, they presumed (naturally) to speak and act on behalf of the working classes.' Robert Skidelsky has argued that Keynes's economic theories provided the basis for a new liberal politics in the 1940s, which avoided class struggle and yet implied 'Keynes's most characteristic belief: that public affairs should and could be managed by an elite of clever and disinterested public servants' (*Encounter,* April 1979). The BBC provided a cultural institution which performed the same function. Indeed the economic and political structure of the BBC was also a product of the experience and beliefs of this reforming intelligentsia. Reith's view of what he intended the BBC to be, those pressures he perceived as threatening, and the alternatives he rejected, were typical of what has been seen as a 'middle opinion'. Indeed it might be claimed that the success of the BBC vindicated the view that a strong middle-class consensus lay beneath the dissent and turmoil of the 1930s.

However, this view should perhaps be modified. Marwick has admitted in an article called 'Middle opinion in the thirties' that 'They did not in their own day achieve much, these advocates of political agreement, the "soft centre" as they were not unjustly called.' Indeed, the 'great and the good' were, as Hugh Dalton wrote in 1936, 'more or less eminent persons who are disinclined to join any existing political party, but who are prepared to collaborate with others in writing joint letters to the Press, and in such organizations as the Next Five Years Group'. They were a band of leaders – but they had no followers. As Pimlott has argued in *Labour and the Left in the 1930s,* their policies might have developed 'into the basis of a powerful campaign for a British New Deal as a frontal assault on mass unemployment'.[4] But in fact the supporters of middle opinion were politically isolated. Keynes and Beveridge had to wait until the Second World War to see their ideas implemented. Yet the BBC was not merely a dream or a plan for reform. It was a rapidly growing institution. By the middle of the 1930s it had become an established and central component of British culture.

Perhaps pressures other than those of the liberal intelligentsia were at work in the making of the BBC? Certainly, unlike Beveridge's plans for insurance, the BBC cost the government no money. The personal connections of the BBC producers were with Bloomsbury literati rather than with liberal reformers. Reith was more an evangelist than a liberal. 'Anything in the nature of a dictatorship is the subject of much resentment these days,' he wrote in 1924. 'Well somebody has to give decisions.' While liberals planned, Reith bullied, wheedled, and built an empire. 'It is occasionally indicated to us that we are apparently setting out to give the public what we think they need and not what they want – but few know what they want, and very few what they need.'

Reith was authoritarian and successful. In the 1930s the new liberals were neither. Moreover, although they dominated broadcast talks, this category hardly dominated the BBC's output. Despite Reith's preoccupation with culture, contemporary critics most frequently accused the Corporation of philistinism. 'The company undoubtedly saw itself as a cultural force', wrote R. S. Lambert, 'by which it meant something constituted to avoid the postures of vulgarity.' Perhaps the BBC was less dominated by the concerns of the liberal intelligentsia and more successful in the 1930s because it was paternalist. Perhaps, also, it gave the public what it wanted rather more than Reith was prepared to admit. For, as the BBC *Handbook* shows, by 1934 the BBC was broadcasting more light music, comedy, and vaudeville than any other European station. It was hardly the stuff of social revolution.

The BBC and political independence

How was the BBC's independence from partisan political pressure to be achieved? The directors of the private company were replaced by publicly appointed Governors in 1926. These were to be the trustees of the public interest. At first the Governors and Reith disagreed about how the responsibility should be divided between them.

Thus Philip Snowden's wife Ethel – described in Beatrice Webb's diaries as having 'caricatured social climbing' (19 March 1932) – arrived at the BBC expecting an office, a secretariat, and a full-time job. Appointed a Governor as a 'convenient representative of both Labour and Women', she believed the Director General should play an administrative role, and that the Governors should make all policy decisions. Reith detested her, and commented that she thought that 'there ought to be a board meeting every day . . . an abominable exhibition by her. A truly terrible creature, ignorant, stupid and horrid.' He saw her as a threat to his own position. Indeed he was quite correct to do so. Hugh Dalton, the Labour politician, recorded in his diary (3 August 1930) that Ethel Snowden had asked G. D. H. Cole – another Governor – to help her get rid of Reith. 'Who would she suggest as his successor?' Cole had asked. 'I would gladly take it on myself,' Ethel had replied.

Herbert Morrison wrote in his important work on nationalization, *Socialization and Transport*, 'It is a matter of argument whether the Director General of Broadcasting should, or should not, be a strong personality.' Reith's views were quite straightforward: he wanted to be in control, and he wanted the Governors to back up his decisions.

The Corporation was supposed to be independent and non-partisan: in practice it was not even indirectly accountable to Parliament. In a Report on the Machinery of Government written in 1918, the Webbs had opposed the increased use of public corporations because

> when a board is set up without explicit status provided for ministerial responsibility to parliament – the situation is obviously unsatisfactory. Only ministerial responsibility provides safeguard for the citizen . . . and consumer.

However, these objections were not understood. The government had felt in 1925 that 'The progress of science and the harmony of art would be hampered by too rigid rules and too constant supervision by the state.' So, between Reith, anxious to avoid having the content of broadcasting politically manipulated, and therefore determined to evade political control, and the government, anxious to avoid responsibility for trivia, the BBC was left with no effective accountability. This omission came to be treated as though it were a principle. Herbert Morrison later claimed to have invented it. Robson wrote in 1935 that it was

> in strict conformity with the English tradition . . . derived as a practical expedient to perform a particular function, without any concern for general principles – or indeed any awareness that questions of principle were involved.

It is perhaps better seen as the elevation of an uneasy compromise into an ideal type.

The BBC and the General Strike

The BBC's practical interpretation of impartiality was soon tested during the General Strike in 1926. Reith knew that the survival of the Corporation (whose constitution had not yet been formally accepted) depended on its conduct during the crisis.

One effect of the strike was to create a national audience for broadcasting. At the end of 1926 Hilda Matheson was able to write, 'The public and wireless listeners are now nearly synonymous terms.' Beatrice Webb noted in her diary that 'The sensation of the General Strike centres around the headphones of the wireless set.' Although there were only 2 million licence holders these represented a far greater number of listeners, and 'communal listening' was a feature of the crisis as people gathered in halls and outside shops to hear the news.

The BBC seemed more important because of the absence of all other sources of information. An old age pensioner in the 1950s told Julian Symons that he still had 'the little homemade crystal set which worked lovely with the iron bedstead for an aerial . . . and which told me what was *really happening*'. Despite the inadequacy of its news the Corporation emerged from the strike with a national audience and increased authority.

Another effect of the General Strike was that the BBC invented modern propaganda in its British form. During the First World War persuasive techniques had been crude. All Germans were characterized as vicious beasts intent on murdering children and raping nuns. Anthony Smith has argued that a rejection of the

> propagandists of the First World War, and the ensuing reaction against the black-out that they had perfected were among the profoundest influences on the men who came to lay the foundations of broadcasting in the early nineteen twenties.

The First World War view of propaganda was still accepted by many during the strike. Its main proponent was Churchill and its main instrument the *British Gazette*. This was a daily news-sheet that few took seriously, so evidently biased were its contents. Churchill wanted to commandeer the BBC, as the government had the right to do. Reith argued that if the BBC was taken over the strikers would merely close the service down. Apart from destroying 'the pioneer work of +3g years', by shattering public confidence in broadcasting, 'It was no time for dope, even if the people could have been doped.' He argued that to suppress information was likely to exacerbate the crisis. His most telling point was that by gaining the trust of both strikers and the government the BBC could positively facilitate a resolution of the crisis:

> In the end conciliations of some kind must supervene and . . . the BBC could act as a link to draw together the contending parties by creating an atmosphere of good will towards its service on both sides.

Reith argued that the trust gained by 'authentic impartial news' could then be used. It was not necessarily an end in itself.

He stated, however, that 'Since the BBC was a national institution and since the Government in this crisis was acting for the people . . . *the BBC was for the Government in the Crisis too.*'

Indeed it was Reith's own political judgement which controlled policy throughout the strike. Briggs has pointed out:

> He preferred mediation to showdown. If his views had coincided with those of the sponsors of the *British Gazette* he would have had fewer qualms about allowing the BBC to fall directly into the hands of the government. As it was, his personal conviction gave strength to his resistance on constitutional principles.

Reith, as another writer, Patrick Renshaw, has argued, 'would have supported the union against the owners. But he was certainly not prepared to support the TUC against the Government.' However, Reith's 'distinct' view seems very close to that of the most implacable opponent of the strike, Churchill. Martin Gilbert argues that Churchill was quite prepared to accept a conciliatory policy towards the resolution of the coal-miners' dispute with the owners; it was only the general and political strike he was opposed to.

Until 1926 the press had prohibited the BBC from collecting any news. The strike allowed the Company to develop a news service of its own. This reported statements by the strikers as well as the strike-breakers. One of the bulletins on 4 May started with the TUC statement, 'We have from Land's End to John O'Groats reports of support that have surpassed our expectations.'

During the strike no representative of organized labour was allowed to broadcast, and the Leader of the Opposition, Ramsay MacDonald, was also banned. These restrictions were imposed by the government. Reith thought them wrong, but said he could do nothing about them. Willie Graham, one of the strike leaders, wrote angrily to him:

> The Government emphatically deny that they interfere with the BBC in any way. On the other hand the company states that it was not a free agent. I am sure that you will agree that it is impossible to make any sense of these two statements.

Called by some workers the 'British Falsehood Corporation', the BBC learnt how to censor itself during the strike in order to forestall government intervention. Nevertheless the General Strike marks the end of the propaganda based on lies and the start of a more subtle tradition of selection and presentation.

Throughout the strike the government had emphasized that the strikers were politically motivated and hence unconstitutional. The BBC emerged from the crisis with an ethic of political neutrality, which was expressed as much in the tone of its broadcasts as in any formal regulations. This was to have profound consequences for politics.

Governments and the BBC in the 1930s

The General Strike initiated a pattern that was to recur throughout the 1930s: the BBC was forced to pass off government intervention as its own decision. In 1935 it was proposed to include talks by a communist and a fascist – Harry Pollitt and Sir Oswald Mosley, respectively – in a series on the British constitution. The Foreign Office protested, arguing that Pollitt could not be allowed to broadcast as he had recently made a speech supporting armed revolution. The BBC responded by referring the matter to the Governors, who declared that, 'More harm than good could be done if a policy were adopted of muzzling speeches.' A BBC official told the Foreign Office, 'We can't chuck Pollitt unless, under our charter, we are given instruction from government that he is not to broadcast.'

The Foreign Office remained adamant that Pollitt should not broadcast. They suggested, however, that the question could resolve itself into the undesirability of *Mosley* speaking.[5] The matter was finally brought to an end when the Postmaster General wrote to Reith pointing out that as the Corporation licence was due for renewal, it would be wiser to comply with government demands. The BBC then asked for permission to say why the programmes had been banned.

The government reacted sharply. According to a Cabinet minute:

> It would be neither true nor desirable to state publicly that the talks would be an 'embarrassment to the Government' at the present time. But it would be true to say that 'they would not be in the national interest'.

Despite the feeling of Corporation officials like Tallents and Graves that the BBC's chances of survival were better if it were seen to be acting in strict accordance with the Charter, the series was dropped and no mention made of government pressure.

An even more remarkable example of the BBC's relationship with the government occurred in the period immediately before the outbreak of the Second World War. On 25 August 1939 the Labour leaders Hugh Dalton and Harold Laski, together with the General Secretary of the TUC, Walter Citrine, wanted to broadcast a direct personal message and warning to the German people. In an interview with them, the Director General of the BBC, Ogilvie (who had replaced Reith in 1938), refused to tell them whether their request would be granted. In the event, news that a 'statement' had been made was broadcast, but nothing whatsoever was mentioned about its contents.

Ogilvie, Dalton pointed out, clearly wanted to consult the Foreign Office but refused to admit this. The next day the Labour leaders complained to the Foreign Secretary, Halifax, of the way in which the BBC had treated them. By this time Ogilvie apparently claimed that he had told Dalton and Citrine that he was going to consult the Foreign Office.

Walter Citrine complained to Halifax that 'Our people are getting pretty fed up with being expected to shout with the government one day and being treated like a lot of children or nobodies the next.' He went on to say that Ogilvie (who had been a Conservative MP) 'might be good enough to help them [the Tories] collect material to rag Lloyd George with – but that doesn't satisfy me that he is fit to be Director General of the BBC'.[6] This incident demonstrates the continuous and insidious dependence of the Corporation on the government. It is not merely that the decision whether to broadcast the message was referred to the Foreign Office. In addition, Ogilvie was predicting Foreign Office policy, and indeed covering for it. Earlier, the BBC had been concerned to make government pressure on its decisions public. In 1939 it was protecting the Foreign Office, and passing off Foreign Office demands as its own policy.

Since 1927 the BBC had been strenuously courting government departments in an attempt to evade press restrictions on its reporting. 'We ought to be the arbiters of what Government news goes out,' wrote a Corporation official, 'not a commercial company like Reuters.'[7] A close relationship with civil servants grew up and government pressure was often exercised informally and personally. 'Vansittart would like the BBC to get pro-France in our news and stop using words like insurgent,' Reith wrote in his diary in 1937. The Corporation was most concerned that disputes with governments should not be resolved by the emergence of any official regulations.

This cautious self-protection was shrewd, and may have been the only strategy available. However, it made the BBC vulnerable to bullying. At various times it was implied that the licence fee might not be allowed to rise, or even that the Corporation's licence to broadcast might be terminated. As a result the most important constraint came to be the Corporation's anxiety to pre-empt the threats.

The BBC, society, and programmes

During a decade of depression and industrial decline, the BBC grew, quadrupled its staff, raised salaries, and acquired vast buildings. One writer, D. G. Bridson, recalled his shock at being asked to work for the BBC. 'In 1935 I mentally bracketed it with Parliament, the Monarch, the Church and the Holy Ghost,' he wrote.

However, the Corporation also intended to become part of the Establishment. Its development into an authoritative institution was a complex process. This was expressed in the choice of outside broadcasters, and what they were allowed to say. It was also expressed in how the Corporation treated them, and its own staff. It was expressed in the distance between what it claimed to do and what it did.

In a decade of hunger marches and 'red united fighting fronts', the BBC regarded a succession of royal broadcasts as the triumph of outside broadcasting and actuality reporting. Broadcasting in the 1930s was dominated by state openings, royal anniversaries, visits, deaths and births, and by the Coronation. 'The floral decorations for His Majesty's broadcast', ran one press release, 'will be one bowl of hiskura (mauve) and a small vase of grape hyacinths.'

In 1923 Reith had exercised a servile cunning in his attempt to persuade the Dean of Westminster to allow the Duke of York's wedding to be broadcast. It would, he suggested, even have advantages 'from the devotional point of view'. Many who 'by sheer force of circumstance, or negligence had little to do with the Church' would hear the 'measured cadence of the sacred words'.[8] The experience, Reith implied, might change their hearts.

Reith's greatest coup was the annual Christmas message delivered by the Monarch. These events were usually preceded by an 'Empire programme', making contact with far-flung colonial stations. 'Goodbye Wilmington', ran one, 'and a Happy Christmas to you all . . . behind us the mountains which encircle Vancouver are still lost in darkness . . . though a faint radiance announces that dawn is on its way.'[9] George V's funeral resulted in an eighty-page BBC policy document, 'Procedures on the death of a sovereign'.

Reith and the Corporation did not merely present traditional pageantry to a wider audience. They established a new manner for royalty which was more appropriate to the twentieth century. Reith made suggestions for what royalty should say, and how they should say it. He recognized what kinds of occasion a royal presence would grace – and benefit from. One of the bitterest complaints of Reith's old age was his omission from royal Garden Party invitation lists. He felt he had 'done much to serve the House'. Indeed the BBC was responsible, at least in part, for moulding a new domestic and populist image for the Monarchy.

The BBC was a little less sensitive to the needs of trade unionists. One of the clearest aspects of what came to be known as the 'William Ferrie incident', was the incomprehension of the Corporation's bourgeois but liberal-minded staff, when confronted with a worker.[10] Ferrie, a communist trade unionist, was invited to reply to a talk given by Sir Herbert Austin, who had spoken on the immense improvement of working-class conditions during the twentieth century. This was in 1932. Ferrie committed the Corporation equivalent of original sin by departing from his written script when he reached the microphone. He began to tell the public how the BBC had censored him, and horrified Corporation officials rushed to fade out the programme. Ferrie later wrote:

> I was particularly incensed at their demand that I should put across that the slogan 'Workers of the World Unite' is not a revolutionary slogan. I also refused to drop my h's and talk as they imagine a worker does.

His talk had quite clearly been altered to make it more politically acceptable. But the way in which it was done is even more revealing. The BBC censored him in ways that the officials would hardly have recognized as such. 'Your language', commented Mary Adams, 'was too literary and impersonal.' Ferrie, to her surprise, came 'in an agitated state', to see her at her Chelsea home. He arrived at the studio with three colleagues 'for support'. All of this seemed odd to middle-class BBC producers, even though Mary Adams was sympathetic to the union case. It seems in retrospect a perfectly regular way for a working-class trade unionist to deal with an institution that seemed bent on intimidating him.

The BBC was more intentionally autocratic in its treatment of its own staff. Reith would banish rebels from the centre of the empire to the periphery. 'You're a very dangerous man Harding,' Bridson recalls Reith telling one, 'I think you'd better go up North where you can't do so much damage.' Indeed by 1937 the only doubts about the Corporation's monopoly were centred on the rights of its staff. There were several symptomatic scandals during the 1930s. The first was the forced resignation of P. P. Eckersley, an engineer and programme innovator of enormous talent who had worked for the Corporation since 1926. Eckersley wrote his own epitaph, 'He had ideas: We stopped them.' He was obliged to resign because he was cited in a divorce case.

The second was over the pressure brought to bear on the editor of the *Listener,* R. S. Lambert, to discourage him from continuing with a libel action. Lambert was warned that he had no future career in the Corporation if he pursued the case. Later he argued that 'This opinion crystallized the dangerous doctrine that the individual owes more loyalty to his employer, than to his fellow employees.'

Reith's view was succinct. 'It's a mug's game', he wrote in a book called *Personality and Career,* 'to pull contrary to your boss.' In 1937 the Ullswater Report recommended, under pressure from Attlee, that a Staff Association should be set up, and for the first time the BBC's workers had organized representation.

The BBC saw itself as a humane and enlightened employer, which had always pursued strictly egalitarian and meritocratic appointment procedures. In 1934 an internal report commented complacently that there was 'a good proportion of women to men on the staff'. This was true, but most of the women were secretaries.

Hilda Matheson and Mary Somerville had set up the key Talks Department and the Education Service when the Company started. It was a woman's initiative which had started the Sound Archive. Women, however, were never announcers, rarely presenters, and the proportion of women in administrative and creative posts declined. Between 1926 and 1936 the Corporation's staff had increased fourfold yet, as the BBC's annual reports show, the number of women in creative jobs had risen by little more than one-third, and in senior administrative positions by barely one-quarter.

Nevertheless, the atmosphere in the BBC, a new exciting glamorous place where it was better, as Peter Eckersley remarked, 'to have discreet affairs than to remarry', is summed up by Maurice Gorham:

> The BBC secretaries were beginning to bloom though they reached full flower later. By that time many of them were pin money girls. It was a great sight to see them going out at lunch, high heeled, sheer stockinged, beautifully made up, talking disdainfully in high clear voices.

By the 1930s the BBC had become an august institution. It was not a crude agent of the status quo, rather it advocated acceptable change, in some areas, in certain circumstances, sometimes.

The BBC and journalism

Indeed, by the end of the decade the sheer amount of news that broadcasting and the press were flooded with was so large that, had it wished to, a government could hardly have pre-censored it all. However, a new tradition in reporting imposed new criteria of selection on the news. Journalists stopped being passionate advocates, saw themselves rather as independent professionals, and their writing as a negotiated product of conflict between partisan views. This self-image and its practical consequences were most fully developed in the BBC. Reith was not opposed to conflict. On the contrary, he fought the press for the right to broadcast on contentious issues. But the BBC and the new 'professional journalist' retained a monopoly over deciding its limits.

The BBC and appeasement

The BBC's brokerage was subject to pressure. In the eyes of the BBC's programme-makers, politics was an activity which only happened between major
political parties. Two kinds of political dispute never reached the air waves:
divisions within parties and the expressive politics of the streets. Winston
Churchill, repeatedly excluded from broadcasting because his views were seen
as eccentric, wrote to Reith saying he wished he could buy broadcasting time.
He preferred the American commercial system 'to the present British method
of debarring public men from access to a public who wish to hear'. In 1933
Churchill and Austen Chamberlain complained that the BBC 'had introduced an entirely new principle of discrimination into British public life,
namely the elimination from broadcasting of any Members of Parliament
who were not nominated by the Party leaders or the Party Whip'. Such a crucial innovation, they protested, should be decided by parliament, not
arbitrarily imposed by the BBC.[11]

The most important dispute the BBC ignored, and one which cut across
party loyalties, was that of the government's policy of appeasing German
territorial ambitions. Churchill claimed that the BBC conspired with the
press to exclude all opponents of this policy from any access to the public.
Gilbert and Gott have suggested that appeasers were effective for so long
mainly because of their success in keeping the opponents of German rearmament out of public office. However, the control of public knowledge
and opinion was also crucial. An early reference to Polish rearmament lost
a producer his job in 1932. Speakers were banned because of their hostility
to the fascist states. Later, the BBC was to apologize for its attitude during
the 1930s by explaining that, while mistaken, it was merely following the
trend of opinion of the times. Yet the BBC's silence is extraordinary as it was
itself making extensive plans for the Corporation's conduct and survival
during a possible war.

Reith's diary first mentions preparations for war in 1933: plans for the
physical protection of transmitters and broadcasting stations were in hand by
1935; Reith was involved in discussions over the organization of a Ministry of
Information in the event of war by 1936; details of trains in which to send
personnel from London were established by 1937. Thus the BBC was secretly
preparing for a war which it did not officially expect, while the public were
kept in ignorance of these cautious foresights.

The BBC at the end of the decade

Reith resigned in 1937, restless and dissatisfied. The BBC no longer stretched
him, and he hoped for something better which never came. Increasingly, as
the prospect of high office receded, he regarded the Corporation which he
had created with resentment. It had not, he came to feel, treated him well.

By the end of the 1930s the BBC seemed a natural and inevitable solution to the problem of administering a national broadcasting system. It had won the right to discuss controversial politics against the determined opposition of suspicious governments and a jealous press. But it developed unnecessary conventions, and had become too defensive. The real test of the Corporation's independence was to come during the Second World War.

Notes

1. J. W. C. Reith, *Broadcast Over Britain* (London, Hodder & Stoughton, 1924), p. 52.
2. F. J. Brown, 'Broadcasting in Britain', *London Quarterly Review*, 145, 3 (January 1926).
3. H. Macmillan, 'Looking forward' in the Next Five Years Group, *The New Outlook,* 1 (8 May 1937).
4. See B. Pimlott, *Labour and the Left in the 1930s* (Cambridge, Cambridge University Press, 1977).
5. 'The citizen and his government' (1935–6), *BBC Written Archives.*
6. The unpublished diary of Hugh Dalton (25–29 August 1939). For a further development of this affair, see J. Seaton and B. Pimlott, 'The struggle for balance: the BBC and the Labour Movement 1920–45' in J. Seaton and B. Pimlott (eds), *Politics and the Media in Britain* (Aldershot, Gower, 1987).
7. 'Relationship between the government and the BBC: the Foreign Office', *BBC Written Archives.*
8. Duke of York's wedding, *BBC Written Archives* (Royalty).
9. Christmas broadcasts, *BBC Written Archives* (Royalty).
10. The William Ferrie incident, *BBC Written Archives.*
11. The Churchill and Chamberlain complaint, *BBC Written Archives* (Churchill).

9

Broadcasting and the blitz

The 'Dunkirk spirit' and the comradeship of the air-raid shelter during the blitz have long been part of our national self-image. How much was this myth and how much reality? Officials concerned with civilian morale in the Ministry of Information and the Home Office who had seen ordinary people as unintelligent and weak during the phoney war in 1939 came to see them as dependable, shrewd, and courageous by 1940. What was the cause of this change?

It is clear that the BBC, almost certainly the most important instrument of domestic propaganda during the war, conducted a campaign intended to convince the public of its own endurance and solidarity. The BBC emerged from the war as both a symbol and an agent of the victory. More than at any other time, the BBC was part of, and seen to be part of, the history of the nation.

'The people will break'

When war was declared in 1939 most people expected a cataclysm. Pre-war pessimism about popular morale had largely been forgotten, yet it had been common to many groups who were otherwise opposed to each other.

During the 1930s another war was felt to be imminent. The main aim of many politicians was to avert the repetition of a disaster like that of the First World War. Even pacifists organizing peace pledges came to feel, like Vera Brittain, that they were trying 'Canute-like to reverse the inexorable'. Indeed memories of the First World War dominated the British as they entered the Second.

The success of the fascist dictatorships had led to a growing distrust and fatalism about the political will of the 'masses'. J. A. Hobson argued in the left-wing *Political Quarterly:*

> No one could have predicted the possibility of the collapse of all codes of
> decent conduct, all standards of justice, truth, and honour, not only in

international affairs but in the revealed nationalism of the brutalitarian state, the facile acquiescence of whole peoples in the absolute domination of self-appointed masters, and the amazing credulity of the educated classes under the spells of the crudest propaganda. (January 1938)

Many on the left believed that the organization of the resistance to fascism would lead to totalitarianism at home. 'If you go to war to save democracy', Kingsley Martin wrote in the *New Statesman* (1 September 1939), 'you will give up democracy in doing so, and find that you are fighting for the overseas investment of your own capitalist classes.' Even after the outbreak of war Sir Charles Trevelyan, a former Labour Minister of Education, wrote privately, 'I have a deep-seated feeling that none of the people want to fight, and that the war will collapse.' It was thus felt by some on the left either that the workers would refuse to fight a war against fascism abroad, because it would only lead to fascism at home, or that they would not fight anyway, because of the iniquitous lack of justice in Britain.

The marches and demonstrations of the 1930s had led the right to believe that British workers were too anarchistic and socialist to be trusted to fight. Those in authority were also anxious about the effects of class division on morale. As early as 1926 a pioneering social scientist, Lasswell, had written, 'Governments of Western Europe can never be perfectly certain that a class-conscious proletariat will rally to the clarion of war.'

Indeed the whole concept of 'public morale', which so preoccupied the government during the war, originated in the 1930s. It was a concept based on naïve psychological and sociological assumptions; in particular, that individuals' attitudes and behaviour were peculiarly susceptible to manipulation in the conditions of modern 'mass' society. 'Morale' was seen as single and malleable. The success of the fascist dictators had confirmed these views, and demonstrated that the urban masses acted in response to crowd psychology and not according to rational political calculation. One reason for this view of the masses, as Bruntz indicated, was the widespread belief that superior allied propaganda had helped to shorten the First World War. *The Times* in 1918 had argued that effective propaganda had hastened victory by a year, and consequently saved a million lives. Indeed, as Shils pointed out, the Nazis may have overestimated the effect of propaganda because they concluded that 'If Germans failed to be tricked by propaganda this time, success was assured.' In addition, the decades between the two wars had seen the dramatic success of commercial propaganda in advertising. The people, then, were thought to be persuadable.

Parallel to this anxiety was the belief that the new technology of destruction, the bombing attack on cities, would lead to a collapse of civilian society. These fears were based on exaggerated projections of the number of deaths which could be expected for each ton of explosives dropped, and on the biased intuitions of military 'experts' about how civilian populations would respond to bombing. 'In simple terms', Titmuss wrote, 'the experts foretold a mass outbreak of hysterical neurosis among the civilian population.' Psychoanalysts argued that under the strain of bombing, people would 'regress', and behave like frightened and unsatisfied children. A group of eminent psychologists reported to the government that 'The utter helplessness of the urban civilian today when confronted with the simplest task outside his ordinary work is likely to be a potent factor . . . in the war effort.' Experts confidently predicted that for every survivor injured by bombs at least three others would be driven mad.

It was therefore widely believed that the British worker would be devastated by an attack from the air. Perhaps this fear explains the curious official ambivalence about the approaching war during the late 1930s. Detailed preparations were made for war, yet rearmers were still banned from the microphone. An atmosphere of dignity, gloom, and appeasement dominated broadcasting even after the declaration of war. Harmon Grisewood recalled that at the end of September 1939 the new Director General, Ogilvie, suggested that a lady cellist, playing a duet with a nightingale in a wood, should be broadcast to Germany. Ogilvie believed that the sound would induce peaceful and harmonious thoughts in the belligerent fascists.

The first months of war

When the war started normal programmes were replaced by news bulletins interspersed with serious and appropriate music. 'Almost everything is obscured at present,' the *New Statesman* commented on 9 September. 'For the first days of the war the BBC monotonously repeated news which was in the morning papers and which it had itself repeated an hour earlier. While each edition of the papers repeated what had already been heard on the wireless.' The news black-out was as complete as the black-out of the streets. During the phoney war the BBC paid for nominal independence by doing exactly what the government wanted. Jack Payne noted that the music department was 'deep in memos', one of which listed the eighty banned German and Italian composers, including Monteverdi, who had died in 1643. Another BBC employee claimed that the only explanation for the failure of the Germans to devastate Bush House was that 'no BBC administrator had remembered to send Hitler the memo reminding him to have it done'.[1]

When more varied programmes started from new provincial centres in unlikely country houses, they were rather less well-organised versions of what had gone on before. Basil Deane, who ran the Entertainment National Service Association (ENSA), the organization responsible for the entertainment of the troops, wrote, 'Public anxiety was not lessened by the forced gaiety of variety artists whose personal jokes and excessive use of each other's Christian names – syndicated familiarity – savoured of self-advancement and was out of key with the national mood.' Many early propaganda broadcasts had a peevish, hectoring tone. A month after the outbreak of war a British Institute of Public Opinion poll showed that 35 per cent of the public were dissatisfied with the BBC and 10 per cent did not listen to it. In the winter of 1939 to 1940 Mass Observation reported that rumours were rife; the people apparently did not believe the newspapers, the Ministry of Information, or the BBC. They trusted only their friends.

The 'phoney war' forced the BBC to regionalize and extemporize. The most important change was the Corporation's dramatic growth in size. In 1939 the BBC had 4000 staff, by the beginning of 1940 6000, and by November of that year nearly 11,000. Roger Eckersley, the staid brother of Peter Eckersley, wrote, 'I knew directly or indirectly most of the senior staff up to the outbreak of war. Now, I shared lifts with complete strangers.' It became increasingly difficult to control the hordes of new staff and this in itself led to a period of anarchy and change. The new employees were quite different from the regular Corporation men. George Orwell broadcast to the colonies and India, William Empson to China, Herbert Read organized poetry readings, Edward Blunden arranged talks, and Basil Wright and Humphrey Jennings made programmes on the principles of documentary. According to Orwell:

> The British Government started the present war with the more or less openly declared intention of keeping the literary intelligentsia out of it, yet after three years almost every writer, however undesirable his political history or opinions, had been sucked into the various ministries or the BBC. . . . No one acquainted with Government pamphlets, the Army Bureau of Current Affairs lectures, documentary films and broadcasts to occupied countries . . . can believe that our rulers would sponsor this kind of thing if they could help it.

The notion of a Corporation converted from philistine reaction to progressive culture became part of the fable of the BBC at war. It was a particularly public example of a common tension that characterized much war work. Conservative administrative authorities were forced to work with creative intellectuals. Scientific 'boffins' invented curious bombs for the military; literary and artistic 'boffins' did intelligence work. The Ministry of Information was notorious for the strange collection of dilettantes, anthropologists, and advertising copy writers which it employed. Duff Cooper, who directed the ministry, wrote that a monster had been created, 'so large, so voluminous, so amorphous, that no single man could cope with it'.[2] 'Frustrated' was the word he came to hate most: the plaintive cry of brilliant amateurs thwarted by bureaucracy. Yet the intellectuals were more prepared to take risks as they had no careers to jeopardize. The *Radio Times* became filled with pictures of distinguished chemists putting bicycle power to strange purposes, and professors of literature 'thinking' about future programmes; the image of 'boffin' at least provided an accommodation and role for experts. For a brief period it was respectable, and even useful, to be serious. Nevertheless the BBC, wrote Orwell, felt 'halfway between a girls' school and a lunatic asylum'.

Programme changes

The first radio personality of the war was not a patriotic politician or a staunch common man, but Lord Haw Haw. By 1940 William Joyce dominated German propaganda to England. His voice was rich, apparently upper class, 'Cholmondely-Plantagenet out of Christ Church',[3] and caused much speculation. It was difficult to avoid Joyce's wavelength when tuning into British stations, as Rebecca West recalled. 'There was an arresting quality about his voice which made it a sacrifice not to go on listening.'

Everyone in Gosport knew that Haw Haw knew that their town hall clock was two minutes slow. In Oxford everyone knew when the Germans were going to bomb the Morris works; Lord Haw Haw had told them. The myth of the English aristocrat with inside knowledge of the German High Command – a kind of diabolical Peter Wimsey – was powerful. What Lord Haw Haw said was less important than what the British came to believe he had said.

It has been argued that Haw Haw was ineptly used by the Germans, who failed to keep him adequately informed about military developments. However, both the government and the BBC were seriously worried about the broadcasts. Robert Silvey of the Audience Research Department was commissioned to conduct a survey of Joyce listeners for the BBC. 'It produced highly reassuring results,' he wrote in the BBC *Handbook*. 'It showed that the British welcomed the new guest to the fireside as a diverting entertainment in the first bleak wartime winter.' But the survey included some less comfortable findings: by the end of 1939 over 30 per cent of the population was listening to Joyce regularly. The BBC's Home Broadcasting Board had sneered that only 'adolescents, and middle-aged women' listened to him. Silvey's work revealed that every kind of person heard the programmes. The reassuring feature of the audience, little understood at the time, was that Haw Haw's listeners were particularly discriminating ones. Most read one or more newspapers; 34 per cent of the listeners were *Times* readers. Those most exposed to enemy propaganda were those least likely to be taken in by it. Yet Joyce's ability to hold an audience demonstrated either that the BBC was failing to entertain or that its news was distrusted.

The fall of France in 1940 demonstrated the potential power of enemy propaganda. It was widely believed that German broadcasts were responsible for the failure of the French civilians to resist the German invasion, and for the strength of the French 'fifth column' of collaborators. British officials felt that radio was crucial, yet the BBC was too solemn, aloof, and boring. The problem was urgent.

1940 and cheerful patriotism

Dunkirk has been seen by most historians as a key turning point in the war. A massive defeat was turned into triumph, and the British, curiously relieved to be without allies, found a new determination to win the war. Calder sees Dunkirk as the point at which the 'old gang' of pre-war reactionaries was finally exposed. Found to be guilty they were thrown aside. After Dunkirk, he argues, people were concerned with winning the war, and ensuring a 'New Deal' for the peace. Mass Observation noted a steady growth of left-wing opinion from this period.

What is remarkable is the absence of any evidence of popular pressure for a negotiated peace. Rationally invasion seemed certain, and defeat, accompanied by appalling devastation, seemed likely. Yet where, during the 'phoney war' period, there had been a degree of indifference, now there was a closing of ranks. It was not that morale was high, nor that anybody believed Britain was likely to win the war: rather the war was accepted. The public decided to try and survive it as best it could.

Broadcasting contributed to this shift in mood. It ceased to be merely exhortative. It became more sensitive to popular feeling and, in consequence, more successful in moulding or at least channelling public opinion.

Dunkirk meant that the war changed from being an affair of soldiers abroad to one of civilians at home. It was quickly followed by the Battle of Britain and then the blitz. The kind of war that people had expected had arrived. Yet, though devastating, the catastrophic effects widely predicted in the 1930s did not occur. Survivors went on with what Churchill called 'their job of living through the blitz'. Even Mass Observation, which documented the panic and virtual disintegration of civilian life in the worst hit towns at some times during the winter, noted the remarkable capacity of the public to adapt to new conditions. In London, Tom Harrisson wrote, 'the unfailing regularity' of German attacks 'greatly raised the ability to adjust, and created the best organized centre in the country'.

The First World War was traumatic partly because the horror of a large-scale modern conflict had been far greater than anybody had ever imagined. The Second World War – especially on the civilian front – was bearable precisely because literature, memory, and rhetoric had led everybody to expect a repetition. Yet civilians in cities, like men in trenches, were prisoners. In the First World War the troops called trenches on the Western front by familiar names, Piccadilly, Liverpool Street, Elephant and Castle, Penny Lane. In 1940 it was the real places in Britain which suffered. They could not escape. There were civilian front and relief lines. In the First World War men would be regularly moved back from the front to security behind the lines. In the Second World War (as Titmuss argued) the underprivileged survived the stress of attack partly because there was a variety of 'safety valves' they could use. The government never stopped the nightly 'trekking' out of the city centres, nor did it resist the take-over of tube stations as deep shelters. On any one night of the blitz seven out of ten Londoners slept in their beds. But in any single week during the blitz nearly everyone spent at least a night in the shelters or the equivalent. Civilians thus survived the stress partly because – like the soldiers in the First World War – they took some relief from the front.

The prevailing atmosphere in 1940 among the civilian ranks was, as in the 1914 army, one of 'us' against 'them'. The opposition was as much to the unbelievable bureaucracy of British administration, as to the Nazis themselves. Strachey expressed this mood when he wrote:

> There is no public record of the labour of the interdepartmental committee, of the co-ordinating committee, the Board of Enquiry, or of the Treasury minute, or indeed of the final Cabinet minute which settled upon the word 'incident' as the designation of what takes place when a bomb falls on a street.

One way of dealing with the Second World War was to refer firmly to the First. Like many of his listeners the broadcaster J. B. Priestley's own image of fighting was based on memories of 1914–18, and he particularly liked to draw parallels between trench life in the First World War and civilian mores in this one.

In his memoirs, Priestley referred to a folksong of the Great War:

> 'It's hanging on the old barbed wire
> I've seen 'em, I've seen 'em.'
> ... [E]ven the devilish enemy, that death-trap the wire, has somehow been accepted, recognized, acknowledged, almost with affection.

A similar point about public attitudes in the Second World War was made by John Strachey:

> No the people didn't call Germans Huns ... or dirty bastards. No one knows in what region of the unconscious the English people decided that their formidable enemy were best called Jerry. .... There is in it an acceptance of destiny; of a destiny to resist. There is a refusal to take the panoply of the German might at its own evaluation.

Both writers are pointing to an attitude of familiarity, though not of contempt, for the enemy. This had first developed among soldiers in the proximity of the trenches. In the First World War it had separated them both from those who lived in the security of high commands, and from everyone in the safety of home. In the Second, such irony was an appropriate attitude for civilians' nightly encounters with bombers.

To what extent did the BBC lead, follow, or play a part in the creation of a new rhetoric to handle the experience of being bombed nightly?

The war brought the blue joke and an anarchistic, almost surreal, assault on authority to the radio. Shows like ITMA (It's That Man Again) never challenged the basis of authority; rather they consolidated it by making a joke of its misuse. In the 1930s radio comics had been warned that there were to be 'no gags on Scotsmen, Welshmen, clergymen, drink or medical matters'. ITMA thrived on innuendo, and on a skilful nudging at the previously taboo.

The programme was based on a formula. It had a repertoire of characters with stock phrases. Funf, 'the enemy agent with the feet of sauerkraut', made a joke of the spy panic of 1940. 'This is Funf speaking', he would intone muffled by a glass. 'After you Claude – No, after you Cyril', RAF pilots would quip as they queued to begin the attack, using another ITMA catchphrase. Each programme had eighteen-and-a-half minutes of talk into which an attempt was made to pack 'at least one hundred laughs'.[4]

A great strength of the show was its topicality. The writers visited factories and army camps to pick up current slang. The programme would be rewritten up to the hour before it was broadcast in order to include jokes on the latest news. ITMA summed up public frustration and gave it vent. In an early show transmitted from Bush House, itself next door to the Ministry of Works, Tommy Handley issued a memo. 'To all concerned in the Office of Twerps. Take notice that from today, September the twenty-fourth, I the Minister of Aggravation, have power to confiscate, complicate and commandeer.' In 1940 there was a period of remorseless exhortation of the public by the government. Frank Owen noted in the literary magazine, *Horizon,* that he was obliged to pass thirty-seven government posters on the way from his house to the Post Office. The Ministry of Food was particularly active in impressing on the public the virtues of the carrot. An ITMA sketch took note:

Door opens. Voice: Do you know what you can do with a carrot?
Tommy Handley: Yer.
Door closes.

Frank Worsley, the producer, thought that the humour of ITMA was 'the closest radio had come to the everyday jokes that ordinary people have always made. . . . The characters were not trying to be funny in themselves, they were only funny in relation to the situation.'

One of the show's most popular characters was 'Mrs Mopp, the vamping vassal with the tousled tassel', a charlady who worked for a pompous civic dignitary. 'Can I do you now sir?' she would ask. Mrs Mopp was perhaps the most famous version of a familiar figure of the period. She glares at German bombers during an attack in an *Express* cartoon by Giles (20 November 1940). 'Never mind about it not being arf wot we're giving them – let's git 'ome,' demands her husband. The same figure – phlegmatic and grumpily imperturbable – was dug out of ruins. She was a mythical figure, and real people were frequently credited with her well-known characteristics. 'Mrs Wells is an obstinate woman,' John Strachey wrote about one lady who survived an air raid. 'You may drop big bombs on her, you may kill her dearly loved husband before her eyes, you may bury herself and her daughter under her home: but you do not alter her.' People who signed themselves 'Mrs Mopp' sent letters to the *Listener* and the *Radio Times*; she was discussed in the *New Statesman* and she asked the Brains Trust questions.

Mrs Mopp was an image of the working-class woman at war. Her characteristics were an indefatigable appetite for work, and stubbornness. She did not mean to be heroic, but simply to get on with things. Titmuss saw her in 'a certain Mrs B., a beetrootseller by trade', who brings order and comfort to a shelter in Islington but who returns daily to her stall.

When 'charladies' had first been mentioned in a broadcast in 1938 by John Hilton, the programme received hundreds of letters correcting his language. He should have called them 'charwomen' for, wrote the aggrieved listeners, they were hardly ladies.[5] By 1942 charladies were featuring regularly in BBC programmes – recognition of a kind of the importance and power of working-class women. 'Kitchen front' programmes were broadcast 'for the busy working woman – the charlady'. 'Mrs Mopp', said Priestley on the radio, 'could easily believe there weren't any women in Germany . . . just tramping, bragging, swaggering males, silly little boys.' 'When I think of the country now,' said another speaker on the Home Service at the height of the blitz (*Listener*, 9 September 1941), 'I see representing the country an embattled Mrs Mopp shaking her fist at the sky. "I'll do yer," she says, "I'll do yer".'

The other woman the BBC gave the nation was 'the girl next door', Vera Lynn. She sang sweet but not sexy songs. The typical 'crooning' style implied an intimate relationship between the singer and her listener. This was hardly appropriate, and possibly embarrassing, to the communal listeners of the Forces Programme. Vera Lynn was the solution. A Vera Lynn song was a cross between a hymn and a pub song.

Yet nostalgia and sentiment were not thought by the BBC to be proper fare for fighting men. 'Why should we hear so much from Vera Lynn?' Deputy Director Graves wrote angrily. 'How can men fit themselves for battle with these debilitating tunes in their ears?' The BBC Board of Governors remarked testily, 'Sincerely Yours deplored – but popularity noted'.[6] Military authorities demanded something more martial, yet the show survived, simply because it had such a vast and enthusiastic audience. 'The girl next door' was loyal, sincere, faithful, ordinary, and unsophisticated. She was 'the mainstay of most war fiction', Tom Harrisson noted in a review of war literature written in *Horizon* (December 1941) and was the heroine of a number of films.

'The people are changing'

According to contemporary commentators, the war made the public more serious-minded. This view has been accepted by later historians. Perhaps it should be qualified. Robert Silvey certainly felt in 1946 that there was no evidence that public taste had 'deepened'. Val Gielgud, Director of Drama during the war, recalls that when a 1940 production of *Hamlet* was interrupted at the grave scene, the BBC was inundated with letters from people who wanted to know what happened next. Yet there was undoubtedly a shift in interest. The public appetite for news broadcasts became insatiable. Less predictably, the audiences for serious music increased sharply, and drama ratings doubled between 1939 and 1941. At the start of hostilities the BBC had assumed that the people would be 'too tired for much heavy stuff', and in too sombre a mood to appreciate variety. Both assumptions were revealing – and both proved wrong.

It was generally believed that the masses were becoming more informed, and the success of programmes like the Brains Trust was seen as evidence of this. 'One of the surprises of wartime radio', wrote Howard Thomas, the programme's producer, 'is that five men discussing philosophy, art and science, should have a regular audience of ten million listeners.' As many people listened to the Brains Trust as to the most popular variety shows. Such was the influence of current affairs and discussion broadcasting that the Brains Trust formula replaced orthodox debating in innumerable social clubs and societies. It was particularly popular with local Conservative Associations.

The Brains Trust panel consisted of three regular members and two visiting guests. The original trio were Julian Huxley, the scientist, the philosopher Joad, and Commander Campbell, a retired soldier. In retrospect Campbell seems like a character from Evelyn Waugh, or perhaps Captain W. E. Johns – an enjoyable overdrawn caricature with a background of exotic experience: he claimed to be able to sleep with his eyes open, to have solved the mystery of the *Marie Celeste,* to have seen and smelt sea serpents, and to have 'married' a South Sea Island girl by eating some fish with her.

Brains Trust questions were wide-ranging. 'Why should we learn algebra?' asked a class of Manchester schoolgirls. 'Why can you tickle other people but not yourself?' asked a bus conductor. 'What is hate?' enquired a schoolmistress. A group of RAF pilots who asked why flies could land on ceilings started a dispute which lasted months. To be mentioned on the Brains Trust was fame indeed. A week after *War and Peace* had been recommended by the panel it had gone out of print. This kind of impact was hard to ignore. In 1941 the Ministry of Food was exhorting women to make the new, economical, soya 'Joad in the Hole'.

The importance of the show was recognized by Whitehall in other ways. There was concern about the programme straying into delicate political areas, highlighted by the fact that Joad and Huxley were socialists. In 1942 questions on religion were banned because the churches complained that the programme had an agnostic bias. In 1943 the government banned the discussion of politics, and MPs were excluded from the panel. When Huxley attacked patent medicines and called for a National Health Service the Tories complained. After a period of increasing restriction the original panel were forbidden to appear together. From 1943 each was allowed to broadcast only one programme in three.

The Brains Trust was somewhere between a culture and an institution. Like other programmes it provided a new currency of conversation. Women in shelters discussed Campbell's views on hypnosis. (He claimed it could be beneficial: 'I knew a man who put his wife to sleep with it at weekends.') In 1940 the *Listener* reported that Gilbert Murray's jokes were swapped in bus queues. 'Veni, Vidi, Vichy,' he had said. 'I came, I saw, I concurred.'

The success of the Brains Trust was the basis for many theories about public opinion during the war: left-wingers felt that a population interested in the panel's views on social justice would also be susceptible to socialism. Whether or not this was right, the programme presented to the listener an image of himself as engaged, participant, and capable of confounding experts. Perhaps the real significance of the Brains Trust was that it represented a shift not just in public attitudes, but in the Corporation's willingness to cater for them. Despite restrictions and political interference the Trust provided for and encouraged an immense public curiosity about the natural world, the world of affairs, and about questions of ethics, philosophy, and psychology, and in so doing it began to foster a less aloof and distant image of the Corporation.

Yet the most dramatic image of the radio at war is of families clustered around their sets listening with reverence to speeches by Churchill, the news, or J. B. Priestley's Sunday night talks. These commanded some of the largest audiences ever known. 'By 1941 over 50 per cent of the adult population listened to them,' reported Silvey. It is therefore worth considering them closely.

Before the war the BBC had rarely allowed Churchill to broadcast. The Corporation even censored him after the war had begun. He was considered too anti-German. Churchill had come to hate the BBC. Yet his speeches as Prime Minister, always delivered first to parliament, were perhaps the most dramatic events of wartime broadcasting. He claimed that he merely gave words to what people felt: 'The people's will was resolute and remorseless, I only expressed it, I had the luck to be called upon to give the roar.' Churchill believed that military success, rather than propaganda, was the only way to win a war. 'If words could kill,' he broadcast in 1939, 'we would all be dead already.' Despite his claim to the contrary, Churchill was of course an expert propagandist, and the government, whatever it said in public, remained desperately concerned with the public mood throughout the war.

If Churchill expressed confidence in the people, J. B. Priestley claimed to represent them. His first series of 'Postscripts' started after Dunkirk at the peak listening time after the Sunday evening news. The series turned him into a household name. 'I found myself', he wrote, 'tied like a man to a gigantic balloon – to one of those bogus reputations that only the media know how to inflate.'

Churchill combined an appreciation of practical problems with a deep, almost metaphysical romanticism, based on an appeal to honour, national pride, and a sense of history. Priestley was just as practical but looked to the future. He helped to give the war an aim beyond military victory by focusing attention on the world to be built in the aftermath. Priestley talked about a level of society with which Churchill had had little contact and of which he understood less. While Churchill talked of Henry V and quoted Macaulay, Priestley's examples were Falstaff and Sam Weller.

Priestley's success, however, had essentially the same foundation as that of Churchill. It was based on an appeal to traditional values; indeed, on an appeal to a traditional social order. Priestley's Postscripts make a virtue of getting on with the job in hand, even when there were no alternatives. Like Churchill, Priestley linked current events with the past. He reminded listeners after Dunkirk of Hardy's descriptions of the Napoleonic wars, and described it as another English epic. 'So typical of us, so absurd, yet so grand and gallant that you hardly know whether to laugh or cry.' Official propaganda, Priestley claimed, encouraged people to see the war as an interruption. It was, he said, rather 'a chapter in a tremendous history'.

Postscripts continually emphasized the rural nature of Britain. In the First World War officers read *The Field* and *Country Life* in the trenches, and war poets contrasted the seasons and images of nature with the war. Priestley, broadcasting to the most urbanized population in the world, referred in ten out of his seventeen talks to the country and nature. 'I don't think that there has ever been a lovelier English spring than this last one', he said at the start of the Battle of Britain, 'now melting into full summer.' Later, after the news that the British had been obliged to sink the French fleet, he started the broadcast by saying that he had seen two heartening things that week. 'The first was a duck and the second was a dig in the ribs.' The duck swimming with her ducklings, 'triumphant little parcels of light', was in a country pond; the dig in the ribs was given by Churchill to Bevin in Parliament before the grim announcement. Priestley talked about factories and the blitz, British restaurants and London humour, but the village or the Welsh hills were more frequently the setting for his talks. Priestley provided his listeners with a way of handling their experiences. 'I don't like danger', he said in November 1940, when Londoners were facing their twenty-eighth consecutive night of bombing, 'but the fact that we are all at least within reach of danger seems to me a better, not a worse, feature of the war.' In the First World War men in the trenches, and the writers who recorded their lives, had survived its horrors by rejecting romantic heroism. In the Second, Priestley made the everyday and commonplace heroic.

Priestley demanded 'more flags and less red tape, hard work and high jinks'. He challenged the old order and called for more social justice. Like Ed Murrow later, he praised the courage of individuals and criticized their leaders for ineptitude. In his second series of Postscripts he proposed to talk about money, class, and equality. 'I received', he wrote, 'two letters.' One was from the Ministry of Information, telling him 'that the BBC was responsible for the decision to take me off the air'. The other was from the BBC saying 'that a directive had come from the Ministry of Information to end my broadcasting'. They were both anxious to make it clear that 'the order to shut me up had come from elsewhere'. The Minister of Information, Brendan Bracken, had seen Priestley earlier and warned him to say more about Dickens and less about the government. As with the Brains Trust there had been complaints in Parliament about Priestley's socialism. Churchill felt it intolerable that the BBC should broadcast criticism of the government, and ordered Priestley to be gagged. Already, within the Corporation, the Controller of Talks had written to Ryan, the Controller of News:

> Priestley has definite social and political views which he puts over in his broadcasts. . . . The question which I want to raise is one of principle, whether any single person should be given the opportunity of acquiring such influence . . . merely on the grounds of his merits as a broadcaster, which are, of course, very great.[7]

Priestley's removal was widely greeted as a sign of government censorship. The *New Statesman* printed a selection of the letters of protest, 'representative of the many others we have received'. Even the *Radio Times* printed letters of complaint for several weeks.

The removal of Priestley showed how limited was the official concern for reform. Priestley's programmes proposed different priorities from the war aims laid down by Churchill. To talk of new orders and redistribution was, in the view of the government, merely to distract the public from the urgent business of winning the war. Yet it was at precisely this point in the war that even the officials in the Ministry of Information were beginning to urge the government to plan post-war reconstruction. The public, they argued, needed the prospect of a better future to enable them to cope with the rigorous present. Priestley had merely started the shift in propaganda a little early. Later it was to be taken up with growing enthusiasm by the government itself.

Harold Nicolson dismissed the talks as 'sentimental banalities'. Priestley himself was puzzled by their success. Subsequently they have been seen as a major contribution to a change in public mood. Yet the most notable feature of Priestley's talks was that a concern for ordinary people and their future emerged and was expressed by very traditional images of rural England, village communities, and nature. This was hardly the rhetoric of a revolutionary.

The news

The most important wartime programme was the news. Information about the conduct of the war was the main determinant of morale on the Home Front. Indeed the BBC's claim to accuracy and objectivity was, in itself, a propaganda weapon – a demonstration of the superiority of democracy over totalitarianism. This was particularly true because the BBC – much more than the press – was the 'voice of Britain'. Unlike newspapers, its messages reached a wide foreign audience in neutral and occupied countries. Broadcast news also seemed to be an authoritative reflection of official policy and opinion. There were allegations on the left that the real facts of the situation were kept from the people; these were particularly relevant during the period of the 'phoney war' when many on the left expected imminent defeat. The Service Ministries, on the other hand, viewed radio news with suspicion for a different reason: they saw it as a threat to morale.

News, like everything else for the duration, was determined by the necessity of winning the war. The Corporation's sense of priorities was often very close to that of the government. There was narrow-minded and bigoted censorship. But some of the omissions which the BBC was later blamed for were more a result of the contemporary understanding of what could be done in the war, than of deliberate suppression. Thus, for example, the BBC did not so much fail to inform the public about the holocaust – indeed what it knew it told – rather this news was not given a prominent position, and there was little consideration of what might be done to save the remaining Jews. This was largely because the BBC accepted the government's views that the allied victory was the only 'realistic' condition for effective action.[8]

However, such was the demand for news that when little of the real thing was available because of military inactivity, the public created its own. Rumours acquired a special influence. The Ministry of Information waged a relentless and unsuccessful campaign against them. Mass Observation divided them into three categories: impressive, informative, and inhibited.[9] The first were a compensation for non-involvement in the war; the second were based on an attempt to improve the teller's prestige, and the third kind, the inquiry claimed, were based on fear. Mass Observation argued that rumours arose from a general distrust of published and broadcast sources, and so were a product of official censorship. But they may also have been a simple reflection of anxiety, a context in which to talk about the war. The BBC always argued that rumours could be stopped only by more comprehensive news.

Several departments contended for the right to control the BBC. Even more believed that they deserved it. The Ministry of Information was concerned to encourage morale at home; the Political Intelligence Department to scavenge information from abroad; the Foreign Office to maintain friendly relations with allies and neutral countries; while the Ministry of Economic

Warfare was interested in the immediate effects on the enemy's industry and morale, even if this involved ignoring the interests of the neutrals.

At the start of the war an official wrote that the Ministry of Information 'recognized that for the purpose of war activities the BBC is to be regarded as a Government Department'. (He added: 'I wouldn't put it quite like this in any public statement.'[10]) This implies a rather different relationship between broadcasting and the government than that which the BBC claimed. Yet the control by the ministries was often irregular and contradictory. For a time even the BBC's Director Generalship was divided: one Director to say yes to the ministry (broadcasters joked) and the other to say no to the staff.[11]

The Ministry of Information, which had most direct control over broadcasts, had been the butt of much humour when it was formed: the inefficiency of its organization seemed to be surpassed only by the scale of its notional operation. It was believed to be staffed by brilliant but dotty amateurs. Nigel Riley (who resigned from the ministry) pointed out that in 1940 of 999 ministry employees only forty-seven were journalists. The ministry was supposed to build morale, yet until 1941 it based its judgements on little except hunches and intuition. Stories about the department's gentlemanly eccentricities were legion. One incident involved a ministry official dispatched to lecture in the provinces on the wickedness of gossip. Complaints came back that his speech had been almost entirely composed of long quotations in Latin. 'Oh', replied the department, 'Latin? It's usually Greek with him.'

Reith, who was appointed Minister of the Department in 1940, was deeply depressed by its pointlessness and disorganization. Nevertheless, before Churchill dismissed him later in the same year, he had begun to define the work of the ministry and to discipline its staff. Reith believed that it was essential to have news and propaganda controlled by the same authority. By the end of the war, Ian Maclaine has argued, the ministry was actively defending the press and broadcasting from the Service Ministries.

Broadcasting and the press

Which did people believe more, the newspapers or broadcasting? Intellectuals certainly did not trust the Corporation. They recalled its role during the General Strike. 'What could possibly take the place of newspapers?' wrote the editor of the *Picture Post* (18 December 1940). 'There surely cannot be any sane man or woman who would argue that the Ministry of Information, or its near relation the BBC, have so far offered a serious alternative to the newspapers in conveying information?' Yet there were also grounds for distrusting the press. Newspapers had deceived the public in the interest of the Establishment over the abdication crisis.

The war heightened a long-standing rivalry between press and radio. The *Listener* was voicing a widely held BBC view in 1941 when it claimed that while radio was concerned to report events as they occurred, news in the press was regarded as entertainment. A Home Service talk in March 1941 maintained that newspaper stories might have come 'from a report from a Mexican correspondent of a Portuguese journal quoted in a Roman paper'. The public had little idea of the tricks employed by the press in presenting events.

Mass Observation reported that radio was the most important medium of information in 1941, and that by the end of the war it had replaced the newspapers for some kinds of news, particularly immediate accounts of battles.[12] When more systematic surveys asked people to rank the media on which they based their opinions, radio came far below personal experience and several points below newspapers. Yet between January 1940 and the end of the war in Europe the authority of the press fell steadily, from third to sixth place in people's ranking. In contrast the position of broadcasting remained constant throughout this period between fifth and sixth place.[13] By the end of the war people had come to trust broadcasting more – at least in comparison with other sources of information.

Topicality and the BBC

The Second World War made topicality the dominant news value. German scoops had shocked the public and done much to discredit the Corporation at the start of the war. Topicality then became the key weapon in the BBC's defence against the expansionist censorship of the Service Ministries. The Ministry of Information recognized the importance of getting news on the air as quickly as possible. A memorandum ordered 'Action to strengthen confidence in BBC news. Confirmed items to be included in earliest available bulletins, even at the expense of friction with the Press.'[14]

From 1939 the BBC's news section grew rapidly, gathering material from an increasingly wide range of sources, including monitoring foreign broadcast sections. The BBC also developed the ultimately 'topical' news, the 'on the spot' or 'outside' broadcast. By late 1944 teams of broadcasters were regularly accompanying British units both in France and the Far East. Commentators developed a way of reporting conditions at the front which related the soldiers' experience more closely to their families at home. 'If you've got a brother or a husband or a sweetheart in Normandy today,' started one famous report from the war zone in 1944, 'there's a fair chance you might see your name riding along the dusty roads, your name on a truck, on a lorry, on a bulldozer, on a tank, somewhere in France.' The style of war reporting was also closely modelled on an earlier form of outside broadcasting: sports programmes. A reporter describing a bombing raid on Hamburg was angrily compared by a *Radio Times* correspondent (30 September 1944) to 'someone at a Welsh Rugby International – not a person watching death and destruction'.

The war led to a victory for those who believed in the superiority of the scientific assessment of public opinion. At the start of the war the government believed that this could be tested by consulting pressure groups and opinion leaders. By the end of the war the public was being polled, probed, and tested by a multitude of official surveys. These new sources of information made it clear that in everyday matters of which the public had experience, it was essential that news should be given quickly and accurately. If people had been bombed out of their homes and their towns devastated, it was imperative that the BBC should be able to say so. Knowledge of the extent of destruction was an important factor in coming to terms with it. At the start of the blitz Maurice Gorham had written, 'The news sounded all the more alarming for being so vague.' But by November 1940, although scrupulously censored for information which might be useful to the Germans, it had become more precise. In Britain, at least, 'topicality' became the dominant news value as a consequence of the war.

The 'manner' of the news

Before the war the BBC's announcers had been anonymous: this was felt to be more dignified. However, from the start of the war they were named, and this innovation excited considerable comment at the time. The change was introduced in order that, in the case of invasion, the public would not be taken in by orders issued by the enemy. After the war it was discovered that the Germans had carefully trained substitute announcers to sound like Alvar Lidell and Stuart Hibberd to be used during the proposed invasion of England. However, the BBC maintained some pre-war standards. The announcers, despite sleeping in a lavatory adjoining the studio, and living for days underground, continued to present the news in dress suits. When the BBC received a direct hit which made an audible thump in the middle of a bulletin, the announcer paused, a whispered 'Are you all right?' was heard, and then he continued, with Corporation-bred aplomb, to read the news without comment.

Before 1939 style had often seemed more important than comprehensibility in BBC news broadcasting; during the war ease of understanding became paramount. There was a new anxiety about syntax and vocabulary, and scripts were scrutinized for difficult words and constructions. The Corporation also became more sensitive about the voices of its news-readers. Clement Attlee, Deputy Prime Minister as well as leader of the Labour Party, complained that the monopoly of upper-class voices was likely to offend workers. Indeed this anxiety was shared, and a Home Morale Emergency Committee in the Ministry of Information suggested that 'something might be done to diminish the present predominance of the cultured voice upon the wireless. Every effort should be made to bring working-class people to the microphone.'

The Corporation responded by employing Wilfred Pickles, whose voice combined the properties of being both working class and northern.

Broadcasting had developed a unique pitch of speech in the 1930s and 1940s, a high and hard voice. One news-reader, Joseph Macleod, wrote that he had two voices. One was low, gruff, and Scottish. The other, which he always used when broadcasting, was 'young, suave, rather pedantic and intolerant, a voice in a higher register'. The war also made the tone of voice a more sensitive matter than before. Macleod lost his job, ostensibly because his style of announcing was too 'tendentious'. He was accused of putting too much emphasis on certain words, and apparently sneering at the government. He was dismissed, according to Harold Nicolson, soon after Bracken had 'spoken openly about the left-wing fanaticism of certain members of the BBC, especially in the news room'. Clearly the tone of an announcement could establish the public attitude towards the news. One news-reader wrote of the problems posed, for example, by announcing the suicide of the Commander of the *Graf Spee* after the ship had been lost. If the announcer sounded pleased the item 'would sound gloating. While if he sounded sympathetic it would sound fifth column.' The BBC's solution to this problem was that announcers should sound as 'official, neutral, and unaffected as possible'. The BBC announcer, it had been decided, should sound like a civil servant.

Another, more urgent, reason why announcers became so careful of their words and their timing was the problem of the sarcastic comments which German broadcasters had at first managed to slip in during pauses in bulletins. The only way to stop this was to read the news smoothly and unhesitatingly. By the last months of 1940 the only comment a German commentator managed to intrude was an exasperated, 'Oh that's not fair!'

The news, enemies, allies, and neutrals

Another, more romantic image of the Corporation at war was of the BBC as provocateur, spy, and supporter of resistance movements. The Corporation recruited many refugees to staff the foreign broadcasts, and these formed a new and exotic element within the Corporation's staid departments. 'The Hungarian Unit,' read a dry memo of the period, 'a duel averted by Duckworth.' A recurring tension in all of these sections was between the demands of the centrally controlled news service, and the interests of individual nations. The Danish section complained that they were not allowed to deal with events in Denmark itself in sufficient detail. According to Bennett, the correspondents who supplied the service with its information from neutral Sweden even organized a news strike in an attempt to change the BBC's policy.

Other countries complained that the broadcasts implicitly criticized the occupied countries. Listeners who took risks to hear the BBC felt that they should be complimented on their resilience, rather than condemned for their failure to do more. Indeed, like home broadcasting, the Foreign Service suffered from a tendency to exhort rather than inform or support in the first year of the war. Richard Crossman argued that too many of those employed in directing propaganda had come from the advertising world. 'Do you suffer from National Socialism?' was their line. 'Then buy British Democracy!'

Another tension was the extent to which the broadcasts should encourage (as one BBC administrator put it) 'listeners to *do* something rather than *feel* something'. It seemed presumptuous to instruct foreigners in sabotage when the British had little experience of it, and were themselves safe. More significantly, the dramatic success of the 'V' campaign, when in 1941 Dutch, French, Belgians, and Scandinavians in occupied Europe were asked to use the letter 'V' as a rallying sign, revealed the dangers of such a strategy. In one Vichy town, Moulins, graffiti Vs for 'Victoire' were so numerous that the Germans imposed fines and penalties on the whole town. In Prague 'multitudes of little Vs had appeared on all sides'. From Belgium it was reported that 'never had so much chalk been sold so quickly'. The campaign, initiated almost accidentally, was evidently a success. Its effects, however, were disastrous. It merely exposed those who were prepared to be active resisters to the Germans at a time when there was no possibility of any allied invasion. Men lost their lives in a campaign with no practical goal. In addition, the BBC was in effect making foreign policy. The campaign was stopped. Crossman later argued that it was a great mistake for those involved in psychological warfare to suggest that they have 'a mystical substitute for military action'. Broadcasting had to be as concerned with preventing resisters from acting unwisely as with prompting them to action when the right moment came.

It is not easy to assess the effect of the BBC's foreign broadcasts. Indeed it is difficult enough to decide what the overall impact of resistance was on the German war effort. Every clandestine listener, however, had already committed an act of resistance, and the BBC's service provided information – even if of a selective kind – to populations who were starved of news. The BBC's bulletins provided most of the material for the underground press in occupied Europe. M. R. D. Foot has concluded that the role of broadcasting was to 'keep the mechanism of the canal gates of freedom oiled and in decent order, till the water levels of fluctuating public opinion could move up and down again'.

This image of the heroic BBC was not, however, shared in the USA. 'To Americans, not very enthusiastic about British cooking, the warmed up remnants of the original meal were not very palatable. News bulletins – one half an hour long – often contained items from yesterday's American press,' wrote an academic, Emmanuel Katz, in 1944. The constant stress on the collapse of social barriers in Britain only emphasized how tenacious they had been, and to what extent they still survived. However, American public opinion was never wholly pro-British, and the attitudes towards broadcasting were part of a wider feeling about the war.

In matters concerning the allies the BBC's policy was dictated by government. When the Russians started to fight the Nazis, the cover of the *Listener* was devoted to a pageant in honour of Russia, while the *Radio Times* was packed with tributes to Russian workers. This was a period of extraordinary enthusiasm for Russia and all things Russian. As Elizabeth Bowen wrote of a character in her wartime novel, *The Heat of the Day*, 'The effect of her was, at first glance, that of a predominating number of London girls this summer when the idealization of Russia was at its height – that of a flying try at the Soviet comrade type.' However, the BBC was told not to include the *Internationale* in the popular Sunday evening concert of allied national anthems. The Corporation abandoned the series rather than be embarrassed by the sound of the communist song.

Conclusion: 'my country true or false?'

In 1939 the Home News Service editor had said that in the event of war the BBC would 'tell the truth and nothing but the truth, even if the news was horrid'. By the end of the war the Corporation was arguing that the pursuit of truth had been victorious. 'Today', the 1946 *Handbook* proclaimed, 'we can point to the history of broadcasting in Europe and say that certain good principles in broadcasting have defeated the worst possible principles.' During the war the BBC seldom lied if it could avoid doing so. Indeed as the war began with a series of devastating defeats for the allies it might have been difficult to disguise the situation. However, that the BBC could claim independence was at least partly because it suited the government that it should do so. For the government continually intervened in the conduct of the Corporation, and merely chose not to control it directly.

Veracity, however, was perhaps the only acceptable aim for a democratic news policy. More practically, telling the truth was probably the most effective propaganda with which to face a sustained war. 'You must hate propaganda to do it well,' Richard Crossman wrote, 'and we British did hate it and therefore took more trouble to conceal what we were doing.'

The contemporary judgement of the BBC's performance was enthusiastic. 'In a world of poison the BBC became the great antiseptic,' said Léon Blum, the French socialist leader. Recently the claims of broadcasters that they have independence have been challenged. 'Bias' and opinion are fundamental conditions of the production of news, not accidental pathologies. Hence the work of the BBC during the war has been viewed with greater scepticism. A belief in its independence is little more than a self-adulatory part of the British myth.

The BBC cannot simply be distinguished from its totalitarian opponents in terms of its intentions. In both Britain and Germany broadcasting was seen as a crucial instrument in the war effort. Indeed both countries even shared practical concerns: hopes should never be raised unless they could be met;

controversy between enemy allies was, as Goebbels claimed, 'a small plant which thrives best when it is left to its natural growth'. He continued that 'News policy is a weapon of war. Its purpose is to wage war and not to give out information.' The BBC also viewed news as part of propaganda. However, the use of the 'news' weapon was determined by quite different constraints and pressures in a democratic society.

British home propaganda depended on an informed public. The BBC remained a civilian institution, whose employees saw themselves primarily as broadcasters. Once committed to a policy of informing the public, the war acted as an incentive within the Corporation for an improvement in the news services. Although the BBC broadcast optimistic official figures for enemy fighters shot down in the Battle of Britain, tended to treat raids on Germany as victories, cut, edited, and censored news, its main purpose remained that of telling people what was happening.

If the Service Ministries and the government were concerned to limit the amount and kind of information broadcast, the main pressure within the Corporation was to tell the people as much as possible. This did not mean telling them everything, but the heritage of obligations imposed by the Corporation's public service monopoly meant that the public knew more than might have been expected.

In Britain, Asa Briggs has observed, the mystique of radio meant little. In Germany, the new medium had been credited with almost magical powers of suggestion. These views affected the way in which broadcasting was used in both countries. The dominating image of the BBC during the war (indeed the dominating image of the war in Britain) was one of relentless domesticity. 'Every time I listen to these programmes I cry,' a factory worker told Mass Observation about a radio link-up between soldiers and their families. 'You hear the women giving the men their messages . . . they can hardly get through sometimes.' Another describes her day. She gets back from work 'about nine o'clock, and they've got the wireless on. Dad's asleep in the chair – the kiddies are in bed.' Families were united around the radio; 52 per cent of respondents to one survey always listened to the news with their families, 76 per cent preferred to do so if possible. In Titmuss's classic account of the development of welfare policy during the war, he saw the security of the family as the crucial guarantor of good morale. By 1945 the radio had become an essential element of the image of the family in its home.

Before the war the BBC had regarded the regular expectation of particular kinds of programmes as 'lazy listening'. In contrast, during the war the BBC made considerable efforts to develop such habits. Regular programmes produced predictable audiences. The knowledge of these could be used in propaganda appeals and information campaigns. Indeed the predictability of the daily broadcasts was a kind of security in itself. 'At the moment, all similes for safety are slipping,' wrote C. A. Hodson in 1941. 'How can one say as safe as houses?' But the BBC at least seemed dependable. Modern programme planning, a matter of inducing habit, was at least in part a consequence of the war.

By 1945 the Corporation had apparently become less aloof. Programmes like ITMA, Hi Gang, and Worker's Playtime introduced a more vigorous tradition of speech and humour to broadcasting, one that was closer to the music hall tradition than the well-mannered 'variety' of pre-war programmes. They were part of a feeling that the British war, unlike that of the prudish Germans, was taken seriously, but never solemnly. Even government propaganda came to appreciate the 'common man's sense of humour':

> Those who have the will to win
> Eat potatoes in their skin,
> Knowing that the sight of peelings
> Deeply hurts Lord Woolton's feelings

exhorted the Ministry of Food. Humour was part of the protective self-image with which the British faced air attacks and the possibility of invasion. It was an image that the BBC helped to create, and was determined to encourage. Harold Nicolson even broadcast talks on the subtle superiority of British humour to that of the status-conscious Germans (*Listener,* December 1942).

There was, of course, another war which did not get much broadcasting time. This was one of apathy, and dingy making-do rather than cheerful resilience. Life in shelters was not always a protracted East End party; it was squalid, with inadequate sanitary arrangements, little food, and chaotic overcrowding. Novels of the period document the dreariness and austerity of life in Britain after several years of war, and newspapers campaigned against the petty-mindedness of official regulations and bureaucracy. The BBC did not campaign for the public on any of these issues.

However, the Corporation succeeded in producing a dignified but humorous image of what kind of people the British were. It was not that the BBC 'came closer to the people'. Rather it represented them as a liberal, compassionate, reforming administrator might have seen them. The BBC innovated within a repertoire of very traditional ideas. Subsequently it has been argued that there was a significant change in public mood during the war. The people became determined that there would be greater social justice after it. Certainly the war changed the BBC, and it changed public taste.

Yet the day after the war in Europe ended, the public changed again. The audience for the news dropped by half, and never returned to wartime levels.

Notes

1. D. G. Bridson, *Prospero and Ariel: The Rise and Fall of Radio* (London, Gollancz, 1971), p. 269.

2. D. Cooper, *Old Men Forget* (London, Hart-Davis, 1953), p. 79.

3. Harold Hobson, *Daily Express* (14 January 1940).

4. T. Kavanagh, *Tommy Handley* (London, Hodder & Stoughton, 1949), p. 73.

5. *Listener* correspondence, *BBC Written Archives* (John Hilton).

6. Board of Governors' Minutes (5 July 1941), *BBC Written Archives.*

7. Maconachie to Ryan (6 September 1940), *BBC Written Archives.*

8. See for further development of this example, J. Seaton, 'The BBC and the Holocaust', *European Journal of Communication*, vol. 2, 1, 1987.

9. Mass Observation (October 1940), File 473, 'What the people are talking about today'.

10. A. P. Waterfield to W. Palmer, *Ministry of Information Files*, INF 1/238.

11. A. S. Hibberd, *This is London* (London, Macdonald & Evans, 1950), p. 307.

12. Mass Observation, *The Press and Its Readers* (London, Art & Technics, 1949), p. 41.

13. 'The British Institute of Public Opinion Survey, the attitudes towards the press and broadcasting and other sources of information (1940–5)' in H. Cantril (ed.), *Public Opinion 1935–46* (New Jersey, Princeton University Press, 1951).

14. *Ministry of Information*, INF 1/250, Home Morale Emergency Committee, Item 13 (22 May 1940).

10

Social revolution?

It is a commonplace of twentieth-century social history that world war has been the agent, or at least the catalyst, of major change. What has been less noticed is the extent to which wartime forms of organization – born of the unusual conditions and needs of the moment – have created structural fossils in important areas of policy, surviving immutably in peacetime, but with no particular relevance to the post-war world.

Broadcasting and education provide interesting examples of this process. Both were drastically reorganized at the end of the Second World War. In each case the most striking feature of the reforms was the imposition of a 'tripartite' division, based on a supposed hierarchy of talent. The changes represented a sharp move away from a view of society as an aggregate of individuals towards an official concept of particular groups with separate needs.

Broadcasting

Reith's programme policy depended on an assumption of cultural homogeneity: not that everybody was the same, but that culture was single and undifferentiated. He had been determined to avoid the mediocrity which he believed would accompany freedom of choice. 'It is occasionally indicated to us that we are apparently setting out to give the public what we think they need and not what they want,' he wrote in 1924. '[B]ut few know what they want, and very few what they need.' Advisory panels of 'experts' were established to lay down canons of taste in music, and to adjudicate correct pronunciation. Their purpose was to give authority to cultural values, not to represent listeners' interests.

Reith believed that the function of broadcasting was primarily educative: its purpose was to train 'character'. According to this view, your class of origin and what you learnt mattered less than how you lived and how you learnt. This principle was the basis for his programming policy. Men might be unequal, but they could all try equally. Hence the Corporation defended a policy of mixed programming, in which talks, light music, chamber music, quizzes, vaudeville and plays succeeded each other. The service was not planned to provide appropriate listening for different interests, or to allow people to avoid what was serious in favour of the trivial. Reith was determined that the audience should encounter everything that broadcasting could offer.

Mixed programming determined many aspects of the Corporation's policy between the wars. In 1934 a BBC administrator wrote that 'the most advantageous single extension or change in programme policy'[1] would be to stop broadcasting programmes at regular times and so break the audience's conservative listening habits. This was part of the Corporation's campaign against what was contemptuously known as the 'tap' listener 'who wants to have one or more very light programmes available at all hours between breakfast and bedtime'.[2] 'The BBC', the 1932 *Yearbook* claimed, 'definitely aims at having an interval of four or five minutes between programmes . . . it is obviously irritating for a listener who, switching on his set to hear, say, the news, finds himself listening to the last minute of an opera or vaudeville turn.' Listening was a serious business.

The BBC's belief in cultural homogeneity was a useful weapon in the defence of its broadcasting monopoly, particularly against the commercial wireless exchanges. These retransmitted a selection of BBC and continental programmes to simple home 'speakers', improving reception and making it cheaper. The number of such stations had risen from 34 in 1929 to 343 by 1935. The BBC argued, in the 1931 *Handbook,* that the relay system

> contains within it forces which uncontrolled might be disruptive of the spirit and intention of the BBC charter. The persons in charge of wireless exchanges have power, by replacing selected items of the Corporation's programmes with transmission from abroad, to alter entirely the general drift of the BBC's programme policy.

The BBC was defending its own position, and what it assumed was a generally recognizable set of cultural values. Reith's objection to audience research was also based on the principle of cultural homogeneity. He did not want to know popular preference, because of the danger that programme organizers would pander to it.

The BBC had a distinctive model of the listener. 'Broadcasting is not mass projection, though it seems to be so, it is an individual intimate business,' wrote Hilda Matheson, the first head of the Talks Department in the *Sociological Review* (no. 3, 1935). The personal relationship between listener and programme was elevated into a principle. The class and tastes of groups of listeners were irrelevant. Any variety in programmes was justified by the changing moods of the average listener and not by reference to the interests of different groups. In this way, 'entertainment' had its appropriate place: it was meant to provide periods of relaxation in the broadcasting diet of the Reithian 'average' listener.

The Reithian approach was paralleled during the 1920s and 1930s by similarly 'unitary' assumptions in state education. The content of state education between the wars was common to all schools: children merely received more or less of it. At the top of the ladder children had access to 'the whole world of learning', while at the bottom they had 'the hems of learning only'.[3] The curriculum was governed by notions of a 'general liberal education', a direct legacy of Matthew Arnold's philosophy of education.

Educational policy reflected the traditional psychology of the nineteenth century, argued the Spens Report on secondary education in 1938:

> with its emphasis on faculties and its belief in the doctrine of formal education and mental transfer which played an important part in perpetuating a curriculum common to all pupils.

It was assumed that most boys and girls were equipped with the same mental endowments, that most of them developed the same way, and at almost the same rate of progress. Although some scholarships were available to the academic secondary grammar schools, these were very scarce, and most pupils paid fees. University scholarships were even more rare. Yet all the children in grammar schools followed a pattern of education which was designed to secure university places which only 3 per cent of them actually attained. Even in non-academic secondary schools, the curriculum was merely a weaker version of the university-dominated teaching of the grammar schools.

State education, like state broadcasting, was (in theory) designed to enable the hard-working and able to develop those faculties which were regarded as common to all. In education there was also emphasis on the development of 'character', a nebulous and undefined moral concept, taken undiluted from the 'muscular Christian' ethos of leadership training which governed public schools. Until Cyril Burt's ideas on scientific intelligence testing were accepted during the 1940s and 1950s, the ideology of 'character' pervaded educational policy as well as broadcasting.

In many ways, of course, education and broadcasting are not comparable: for one thing, state education hardly grew at all during the 1930s while broadcasting developed very quickly. For another, broadcasting was centrally controlled with a national monopoly, while education was administered locally, and alongside (rather than in competition with) a prestigious private sector. Nevertheless, broadcasting and schooling as communicators of accepted values have enough in common for the similarity to be striking. The similarities in the organizational changes, which occurred as a result of the impulse for reform created by the Second World War, are more remarkable still.

Reform, the war, and education

The needs of war radically altered education and broadcasting. The Education Act, 1944, which introduced compulsory secondary education for all, has been seen by many as the finest achievement of a great reforming minister, R. A. Butler, who based it on what he described to his biographer, Ralph Harris, as a 'sensationally ingenious report'. More recent assessments have been less enthusiastic. According to Brian Simon,

> Through the late 1940s and 1950s when so much might have been accomplished, the development of secondary education for all was restricted and distorted by the dead hand of a doctrine brought to a point during the depressed 1930s – the doctrine that in effect secondary education is not for all.

The Education Act recommended that schools be reorganized 'firstly to provide opportunities for a special cast of mind to manifest itself . . . indeed to develop specialized interests and aptitudes'.[4] The Act was not the result of radical political pressure, but of official initiatives within the Board of Education itself. In 1938 the Spens Report had suggested that 'It is becoming more and more evident that a simple liberal education for all is impractical.' It drew a distinction between those children 'who work with hands, work with tongue, or work with pen' and suggested that 'one child differs from another far more than is generally supposed'. The Norwood Report and the 1944 Act went further and argued that these differences were held in common by groups of children. They distinguished between three kinds, the child 'who is interested in learning for its own sake, who is interested in causes and who can grasp an argument. . . . [He] is sensitive . . . he is interested in the relatedness of related things . . . he will have some capacity to enjoy from an aesthetic point of view.' A child of this kind was to go to a grammar school, the distinct feature of which 'lies in the intellectual ideal which it upholds'. This category of school was to retain the values which had been intended for all schools before the war, and was to produce the new professional and managerial élite.

The second kind of child 'often has an uncanny insight into the intricacies of mechanisms, whereas the subtleties of language construction are too delicate for him. To justify itself to his mind, knowledge must be capable of immediate application.' These children would 'go into industry' and were to attend the new technical schools.

The third kind of child 'may have much ability but it will be in the realm of facts. He is interested in things as they are . . . he must have immediate return for his effort.' These residual children were to attend the new secondary modern schools. These schools were to be separate but equal and were, according to the report (incredibly) to have 'parity of prestige'. The purpose of the modern schools was distinct because these children would need education for their leisure: 'This homely aspect of education is often the basis of future happiness, and is as vitally necessary as it can be interesting.' It was implicit in the Norwood Report and the Act that there were children who could think, children who could do, and the rest.

This division of schools and children was not consciously based on any scientific evidence, but was justified on the grounds that 'these rough groupings have in fact established themselves in general educational experience'. Immediately the Act was published Cyril Burt attacked its underlying psychological assumptions. He argued that his own work had long since demolished the myth of separate 'mental types', and that the proposed reforms had overlooked the fundamental discovery of his work on intelligence: that anyone who was above average in any one aspect of intellectual performance was likely to be above average in all of them. 'It is difficult to see', he wrote, 'how even administrative necessity can lead us to discern the indistinguishable and to find three types of mind when they do not exist.' However, Burt's attitude was surprising, for the process of selection and division was to be carried out with his own 'scientific' intelligence testing. More strikingly, the proportions of children which it was projected would attend each kind of school closely approximated to Burt's 'normal curve' of the distribution of intelligence within the population. Indeed, in an article devoted to 'The psychology of listeners', Burt wrote: 'Politically no doubt all men are born equal. Mentally however, as the results of surveys incontestably show, the range of individual differences is far wider than had ever been suspected.'[5]

The classification of children proposed by the Act depended on the war experience of Burt's followers in training and assigning members of the armed services to appropriate jobs. Psychologists used increasingly detailed tests developed from Burt's work, not only to guarantee that the various services had equal shares of intelligent personnel, but also to distinguish between 'skill' and 'character', and to identify a whole range of special mechanical, logical, and clerical abilities. 'The value of vocational or educational classification', wrote Vernon and Barry about their work as psychologists during the war, 'lies not merely in the closer co-ordination of human capacity with job . . . but also with their effects on morale.' Workers, they argued, were happier if they were not disturbed by association with those with abilities far beyond, or behind, their own. Thus during the war 'streaming' was developed and rationalized.

The effect of the war is also revealed in the provision of the new 'technical' schools. During the war there had been a shift in the subjects in which children were examined towards the sciences, in response to the increased need for technical skills. Lord Hankey wrote in 1941 that 'Technical colleges, although ill housed, ill equipped and understaffed had responded without hesitation to the needs of the services and industry and had magnificently reorganized themselves to train men and women for the war effort.' It was these experiences, a dramatic increase in the need for technical and scientific workers, and the reorganization of schools and training to produce them, which had led to the creation of the new 'technical schools' and the perception of the 'practically able' child.

In the Act it was expected that these new schools would take some of the children who would previously have gone to grammar schools, and direct them into more technical and industrial work. These schools simply failed to appear. This was partly because money was not available. Also during the war the government had been able to direct the allocation of the entire workforce; in a post-war world this was far more difficult. Moreover, hopes that private industry would seek technically educated school-leavers for training did not materialize; employers continued to prefer young people with a 'general' academic education where they could get them.

R. A. Butler had written in 1942 that

> Education cannot by itself create the social structure of a country. I have to take the world as I find it and the world I find is one in which there is a very diversified range of types. Educational progress must be along the grain of human nature.[6]

Yet arguably the Act and its implementation was precisely an attempt at massive social engineering. It was not, as Simon has argued, merely a rationalization of the status quo, but marked a major change in the official perception of the child. It also represented a new recognition of class, and the fragmentation of culture. The old, liberal culture survived, but was confined to the curricula of the 'professionals' in their grammar schools; while in modern schools children for whom exams were inappropriate were to be taught how to entertain themselves.

Reform, the war, and the BBC

The war also revolutionized the BBC. During the war Reith's 'cultural unity' was abandoned. After a visit to the troops in France, Ogilvie, Reith's successor as Director General, had come back convinced that the morale of the forces would be improved by knowing that their families at home were listening to the same programmes with them, but also that the Corporation's whole programming would have to change. Ian Hay, a BBC comptroller, had written in 1939, 'We shall need a lot of entertainment before this business is over.' It was recognized that the new forces service would have to be quite different from a 'watered-down version of our peacetime programmes', for 'if we give them serious music, long plays, or peacetime programme talks they will not listen'.[7] The lure of the continental stations could not be ignored during the war and programme changes would inevitably have more long-term consequences. An official wrote ominously, 'We shall not be able to return to our Sunday policy when the war ends.'

More light music, comedy, crooning, and jazz were justified not only by the immediacy of wartime demands, but also, crucially, by a new model of the psychology of the listener. The first step argued that the service had to be changed because troops were listening to it communally in the mess or in camps. Then it was suggested that different programmes were appropriate to different occupations. Very quickly the audience research department was trying to establish which kinds of music had the best effect on factory production.

Modern wars change the status of entertainment: leisure is seen as an aspect of 'public morale'. This was particularly true in Britain after 1940. Nevertheless, the Corporation was anxious not to be accused of producing 'programmes fit for morons', and the *Listener* printed many letters on this subject. 'I think you will find this army more highbrow than you suppose,' wrote one officer (15 February 1941).

What had first been seen as a temporary expedient became a permanent feature when the General Forces Programme was changed to the Light Programme in 1946. Grace Wyndham Goldie commented on the consequences of this innovation for the internal structure of the Corporation. 'It is not only that this is lighter, more gay, fresher in its approach; but for good or evil it is more closely related to the box office than any broadcasting in England has ever been before' (*Listener*, 26 December 1940). Competition was introduced between various parts of the Corporation. It meant the recognition of distinct groups whose tastes the BBC was obliged to identify rather than to change. This internal reform was of more fundamental importance than the competition later offered by commercial television. An editorial in the *Listener* claimed that 'the position is that the Forces Programme is carefully planned and not a casual proliferation of high jinks for low brows' (13 March 1941). Yet providing the public with what it wanted had become central to the Corporation's plans.

The introduction of a 'Light' Programme inevitably had implications for the Home Service. As early as 1940 the Home Service Board had decided that the 'barometer of listeners' preferences' should be a regular item on its agenda. However, the Home Service also broadcast the main news bulletins, and came to be seen as the part of the BBC which was most concerned with 'citizenship, family and home'.

The final and most revealing innovation was the introduction of the Third Programme. An internal memorandum in 1944 had suggested that the BBC should provide three competing services. Programme A 'should be of the highest possible cultural level, devoted to artistic endeavour, serious documentary, educational broadcasting, and the deeper investigation of the news, corresponding in outlook to a *Times* of the air'. Programme B, 'the real home programme of the people of the United Kingdom', would 'give talks which would inform the whole democracy rather than an already informed section, and be generally so designed that it will steadily, but imperceptibly, raise the standard of taste, entertainment, outlook and citizenship'.[8] Programme C was to divert, and needed little detailing.

The Third Programme was a survival of the Reithian ethic of 'mixed' programming. It emphasized that it should be judged by the whole programming of the service rather than individual items.

> The daily broadcasting schedules rush by the listener like the scenery past the windows of an express train. . . . The Third Programme from the beginning has arrived at a standard which has brought it into conflict with this ephemeral characteristic of broadcasting.[9]

Elsewhere, Harold Nicolson wrote, 'Every cultural pill is coated with sugar; and an item which it is felt might be unpalatable is tendered with a tone of apology, or with the horrid cheeriness of the scoutmaster, the padre, or the matron.' The Third regarded broadcasting as an art.

The 1950 White Paper on the future of broadcasting argued that 'listeners will now normally have a wider choice of contrasting programmes', while Nicolson, who had been involved in the creation of the Third, was at pains to point out that 'at no time, I am glad to say, did we entertain the doctrine that the listening public should be segregated between sheep or goats'. Sir William Haley, the Director General who had originally thought of the Third, put the classification clearly in a lecture given in 1948:

> Before the war the system was to confront [the listener] with pendulum-like leaps. The devotees of [Irving] Berlin were suddenly confronted with Bach. . . . Since the war we have been feeling our way along a more indirect approach. It rests on the conception of the community as a broadly based cultural pyramid, slowly aspiring upwards.

This concept resembled the hierarchy of ability.

Progress or rationalization?

By the end of the war British broadcasting and education had been radically reformed. Is it a coincidence that the two most important vehicles of national culture were reorganized almost simultaneously and in each case along very similar lines?

The reforms may have been made possible by the new weight given to public opinion by the war. However, in both areas of policy the form which the changes took depended on a new official way of looking at children on the one hand, and at listeners on the other. In this, distinctions were in effect being made between the tastes, abilities, and interests of different social groupings.

Listeners and children are not obviously analogous. Yet what is striking is the similarity in proportions of people assigned, quite independently, by education and broadcasting authorities to three categories. It is as though in the natural order of things there were three types of children and three types of listeners reflecting a three-way divide in society as a whole. It was expected that the population would divide as follows:[10]

Grammar schools 5%	Third Programme 6%
Technical schools 15%	Home Service 20%
Modern schools 80%	Light Programme 74%

In both cases the figures were based more on a hunch than statistics, and in both cases they proved wholly unrealistic. In education the technical schools barely got off the ground and completely failed to produce the technical administrators that had been expected; instead the grammar school section expanded. The estimate of the Third Programme audience of serious listeners was wildly optimistic; it never attracted more than 1–2 per cent of listeners. Neither projection was officially justified in terms of social class; yet in both cases what seems to have occurred is the imposition on social policy of official assumptions based on military and administrative experience.

There has been much discussion about the social effects of the war. Calder and Marwick have pointed to a major upheaval; Addison has suggested the culmination of a long, slow revolution in attitudes; Pelling argued that there was not much fundamental change at all. What is clear is that there was a dramatic and permanent increase in the power and scope of government. Whitehall's view of society and human nature, essentially meritocratic and hierarchical, pervaded policies which in normal times would have been fought out in the political arena. The reforms in both broadcasting and education reflected an approach to organization which had more to do with a civil service conception of the world as itself writ large, than with the reality of the world as it existed. Thus in Whitehall there were administrative, executive, and clerical grades (and in the services there were officers, NCOs, and privates). Officials found their own tripartite system natural and efficient. In creating new structures for the public they assumed a similar pattern of talent and need. In broadcasting, as in education, reforms contained a contradiction. On the one hand they were progressive in that they sought to cater for the whole society; but on the other they reinforced class divisions by giving new life to old hierarchical assumptions.

Notes

1. Filson Young to Dawney, BBC Internal Memorandum, 'Programme policy', *BBC Written Archives* (3 March 1934).
2. 'Programme revision committee', *BBC Written Archives* (June 1934).

3. Board of Education, *Inspectors' Report* (1932), p. 12, para 7 [Cmd 4068].
4. *The Nation's Schools: Their Plans and Purposes*, Ministry of Education Pamphlet 1 (London, HMSO, 1945).
5. Sir Cyril Burt, 'The psychology of listeners', *BBC Quarterly*, IV, 1 (April 1949), p. 7.
6. Lord Butler, *The Education Act of 1944 and After*, The First Noel Buxton Lecture, University of Essex (Harlow, Longman, 1965), p. 21.
7. Ryan to Nicolson, BBC Internal Memorandum, *BBC Written Archives* (17 January 1940).
8. 'Programme development', BBC Internal Memorandum, *BBC Written Archives* (14 February 1944).
9. BBC, *The Third Programme: Plans for October–December 1944.*
10. Sources for education figures, Ministry of Education circular 731 (1944), quoted in P. H. J. H. Gosdon, *Education in the Second World War* (London, Methuen, 1976); and for broadcasting, *Listener* (February 1946), and BBC Internal Memorandum, 'Projection for the Third Programme', *BBC Written Archives* (14 May 1946).

11

The fall of the BBC

In 1946, when television broadcasting was resumed, the BBC's popularity at home and prestige abroad were even greater than before, largely because of the wartime experience. Yet barely a decade later, the BBC's monopoly of the air waves was destroyed. Television and subsequently radio were placed on a new competitive footing. More than anything else, this has shaped the aims, structure, and output of all television programming over the last quarter of a century.

The change was not brought about by public pressure, but by a small group within the ruling Conservative Party. It was opposed by bishops, vice-chancellors, peers, trade unions, the Labour Party, and most national newspapers. Reith compared the introduction of commercial broadcasting into Britain with that of dog racing, smallpox, and bubonic plague.[1] The objections to commercial broadcasting were diverse, but most were anti-American, and opposed the encouragement of crude materialist desires. Criticisms of this kind were particularly vehement on the left. More recently, however, some socialist writers have taken a different view, arguing that commercial television was, in fact, a cultural liberator, taking the control of broadcasting out of the hands of a patronizing and paternalist establishment, and increasing the scope of genuinely popular influences.

Austerity, monopoly, and the Beveridge Report

The BBC's prestige contributed to its undoing. The Corporation had assumed that it was invulnerable and so had the 1945 Labour government which consequently did not hurry to renew its licence. In 1947 Beveridge was asked to conduct an inquiry into the BBC's affairs. He might have been expected to sympathize with Reith's legacy of benevolent, high-minded despotism at the BBC, for Beveridge had once claimed that his ideal society would be run by neither Parliament nor dictators, but by professional administrators – 'social doctors' – who would organize society 'to adapt the social and economic relations of clients so as to produce the maximum economic health'.[2] However, as a liberal, Beveridge was highly critical of the Corporation.

He distrusted the tone and character of the BBC, which 'beginning with Londonization, going on to secretiveness and self-satisfaction, and ending up with a dangerous sense of mission became a sense of divine right'. He was constantly on the watch for 'the four scandals of monopoly: bureaucracy, complacency, favouritism and inefficiency'. Written in Beveridge's inimitable style, the report nevertheless finally recommended that the Corporation's licence be renewed, because the alternative, American-style commercial television, seemed far worse.

The recommendations of the Beveridge Report were ignored by the Conservatives after they beat the Labour Party in the 1951 general election. Instead, Selwyn Lloyd's dissenting minority report, which was in favour of commercial broadcasting, became the basis for the commercial lobby. Nevertheless, Beveridge's findings influenced the form of British commercial broadcasting. First, the report preferred spot adverts to sponsored programmes because they gave advertisers less control over programme content. 'A public broadcasting service', the report commented, 'might have its controlled and limited advertisement hour, as every newspaper had in its advertising columns, without sacrificing the independence of standards of broadcasting.' Second, the report advocated the regionalization of broadcasting and the decentralization of the BBC. These arguments affected the organization of the commercial system when it was introduced.

The commercial television lobby has been seen by some writers as a tiny group of back-bench MPs, 'who worked night and day on the project'. However, they were supported by the immense power of the great entertainment industries. Pye Radio, the largest West End theatre management, and J. Walter Thompson, the advertising agency, were all involved in the campaign. Although a member of the group declared in the House of Commons that 'Any suggestion that the Bill was fostered by commercial interests is a complete figment of the imagination of the Party opposite', the speaker at the time was a director of various electronics firms who expected to profit out of an increase in the market for televisions.[3] 'At what point', H. H. Wilson asked, 'were the members speaking as MPs representing their constituencies, and when were they speaking as directors, managers or employees of advertising agencies, market research organizations or radio and television manufacturers?'

However, the most important organizer of the lobby was a broadcaster, Norman Collins. He had been director of the Light Programme, and controller of BBC Television. When he was not appointed Chief Executive of Television, Collins resigned from the BBC. He told *The Times* that he had left

because of a clash of principle . . . whether the new medium of TV shall be allowed to develop at this, the most crucial stage of its existence, along its own lines and by its own methods, or whether it shall be merged into the colossus of sound broadcasting.

The commercial lobby fought a hard and frequently unscrupulous battle. It was successful because important members of the government, including the Prime Minister, Churchill, were not prepared to defend the BBC. Significantly the campaign also had the active support of Lord Woolton. He had modernized the Conservative Party organization before the 1951 election and brought a new kind of candidate into parliament. This group represented industry and advertising rather than law or hereditary wealth.

Woolton wanted free enterprise to dominate the 'new age of post-war prosperity'. 'Our individual lives today', he complained in a broadcast, 'are hemmed in by no less than 25,000 controls.' He wanted to associate the party with the long-term material aspirations of the people, and believed that commercial television would help to do this.

The opposition to commercial television was organized by the National Television Council with Christopher Mayhew as its secretary. Support came from surprising quarters. 'The Establishment', wrote Henry Fairlie, 'came as near as it has ever done to organizing a conspiracy against the government of the day – a Conservative Government.'[4] This group objected to the cultural consequences of commercial television: it would 'vulgarize, bowdlerize, and coarsen', wrote one critic.

The argument became more fierce when it was learnt that in the USA the Coronation had been shown interspersed with NBC's television chimp, J. Fred Muggs, selling tea. A deodorant had been advertised just before the ritual anointment. Horrified MPs suggested that if a commercial system were started here, royal tours would be interrupted by commercial breaks extolling the makers of the Queen's chairs and carpets.

Nevertheless the Act introducing commercial television was passed in 1954 because most Tories believed that in some way it would promote industry, commerce, and the free market. The new service was named, by some genius of euphemism, 'Independent Television'.

Commercial television and the new world

'A whole new world has come,' proclaimed the first commercial television *Yearbook* in 1955. 'We've won, and now we can really get going,' said Norman Collins. 'The importance of the introduction of commercial TV goes far beyond any question of the merits of commercial versus public service broadcasting,' wrote Wilson, 'for it may also seem to symbolize a change within the Conservative Party, and give expression to an accumulation of influences which are securing the future of British society.' ITV brought about a revolution, it has been claimed, because it challenged the complacent pre-war conservatism of the BBC. The Corporation was staffed by narrow-minded, middle-class professional bureaucrats who had little sympathy for working-class interests. Norman Collins complained of the 'apathy, disinterest and often open hostility towards the new medium' that existed within the BBC. Lord Simon of Wythenshawe, chairman of the BBC Governors, claimed that during the early 1950s only about one-fifth of the business the Director General presented to the board was concerned with television. Indeed in 1946 when Haley was shown a television demonstration he had remarked that he would not have one in his house.

The BBC, one producer wrote, regarded radio as 'the father figure, established and responsible', while television was seen as a 'spendthrift tiresome adolescent'.[5] The BBC bureaucrats, secure in the imperial comforts of Broadcasting House, deluged television producers in the unheated wastes of north London with memos. These detailed the proper procedures for the purchase of books and why it was outrageous to suggest that book covers should be cut up, even to be shown on the screen. The tensions were exacerbated by the influx into television of cameramen, technicians, and directors who were used to the high living which characterized the precarious film world. 'Disorder has been repeatedly reported from the television studios . . . new employees do not seem to have become one with the Corporation,' read one ominous memo of the period. 'Perhaps', another memo replied, 'a brief course on the history of the Corporation might be of assistance?'[6]

Indeed during the 1950s the Corporation appointments policy was apparently designed to keep the new service in order, rather than accelerate its development. Gerald Beadle was an amicable BBC administrator, quietly approaching retirement in the Western Region, when the call came. 'About 1953', he remarked, 'every BBC directorship in London was filled by younger men than me . . . but then in 1956 something quite unexpected happened . . . at the age of fifty-seven I was appointed Director of TV.' Beadle was to hold this post during the critical early years of commercial television.

Beadle was a typical example of the BBC administrator of this period. The Corporation man, as Burns has argued, did not work for the BBC, he worked *in* it – as a secular church of professional excellence. One writer noted that a Corporation producer 'breathes the BBC ritual welcome to eminent persons as they arrive' (to have their personalities 'brought out', rather than be put on the spot), 'How good of you to come!' (*Encounter,* October 1960). The Corporation saw itself as a particularly dedicated branch of the civil service, and this image affected its approach to television.

However, the BBC's performance during the 1950s needs scrutiny. Despite the overwhelming bureaucracy, a remarkable generation of television producers and directors started work during this period. They were to dominate the entire output of British television, on both channels, for the next twenty years. Even the Corporation's lack of interest in television had benefits. Because it was seen as relatively unimportant it was left alone. Goldie claims this allowed programme-makers far greater initiative.

The most serious charge against the BBC was that it starved the new service of funds. In 1950 the BBC's television budget was only one-half of that allocated to the Home Service. However, in the period of experimental broadcasts during the 1930s, television had been able to develop only because the BBC had been willing to subsidize it out of wireless revenues. (In the USA, where it depended on advertising funds, the service was forced to close because the pictures and reception were inadequate to attract a commercially useful audience.) The BBC also pursued a policy of national coverage and by 1956 98 per cent of the country was able to receive television. This was achieved only by a massive redistribution of resources away from the rich south-east, where there were many television owners, to the more remote regions. A national service was an investment which could not at first have been made by the commercial companies.

Competition new and old

It has been argued that commercial competition changed the BBC. Competition forced the Corporation to consider public wants more seriously. 'The BBC will have to abandon the ivory towers for the beaches! People prefer fun,' wrote one critic (*Daily Mail*, 15 February 1957). Peter Black comments that a kind of myth developed, based on an image of 'the energetic thrusting showbiz visionaries elbowing aside the complacent bureaucrats of the BBC, by presenting a series of audacious novelties that blew the stale air of monopoly out of television and sent the invigorating breezes of free enterprise whistling through it'.[7] Others have argued that subsequently broadcasting has been dominated by the need to maximize the audience.

Yet competition came to the BBC long before Independent Television was thought of. The decisive break with Reithian paternalism occurred during the war, when the General Forces Network was established. Similarly the BBC had always been obliged to prove that the size of its audience legitimized its receipt of the licence fee. Indeed the BBC had been subject to competition from foreign commercial stations since the 1930s. It was the challenge of Luxembourg which had broken the dismal Reithian Sunday on the radio. However unctuously it was defended, the BBC had abandoned the concept of planned programming considerably before the introduction of Independent Television, while programme-makers have always been most sensitive to the competition offered by colleagues. Anthony Smith has argued in *British Broadcasting* that 'Producers within the BBC were more often conscious of an internal competition within the different sections of the BBC.' This, he claimed, led in the 1960s to 'an enormous flowering of talent and inventiveness'. Such internal pressure had the greatest effect on standards and innovation within both authorities.

In addition the threat posed by commercial competition was more limited than its advocates have suggested. At first the two authorities fought a bitter ratings war. They soon discovered that the public would watch anything in preference to a party political programme. (The parties reacted swiftly and ensured that these broadcasts were shown simultaneously on both channels.) When ITV offered the audience the Hallé Orchestra, the BBC's share of the audience rose. When the BBC offered the people *La Bohème,* the numbers watching fell to 2 per cent. However, both soon discovered the comforts of competition and the security provided by the dependability of the enemy's programming. It was found that documentaries and current events programmes achieved their maximum audience only if they were shown at the same time. As Burns commented, 'Competition now seems to be accepted as a fact of life for both the BBC and ITV, and is defended by both. There is one obvious reason for this; it makes life easier for them.' A rigidly conventional use of time and categories of programmes was reinforced by competition.

Commerce and the audience

It is often assumed that ITV changed television because it won the battle for the audience. This is not the case. Indeed commercial television had little effect on the growth of the television audience, nor did it decimate the numbers watching BBC.

Between 1955 and 1956 the commercial companies struggled to acquire an audience. Howard Thomas wrote that by January 1956, 'The situation was very grim. The costs of running commercial television were enormous for the audience was simply not large enough to attract advertising revenue.'

However, the situation improved. In a well-publicized campaign in 1957 Sir Kenneth Clark was claiming a 79:21 preference for the commercial channel. In December of the same year, out of 539 programmes listed by TAM in the top ten ratings, 536 were from ITV and only 3 produced by the BBC. 'Once they had a choice', Black wrote, 'the working-class audience left the BBC at a pace that suggested ill will was more deeply entrenched than good.' The first *ATV Showbook* put the point more jubilantly: 'We've got the audience,' it proclaimed. Norman Collins said that the BBC would soon 'grind to a halt'.

Certainly the BBC panicked. *Ariel,* the staff magazine, became full of warlike metaphors about 'beating back the enemy' and getting into 'fighting formation'. As large numbers of staff left the Corporation for the higher salaries and more makeshift offices of the commercial companies, Sir Ian Jacob wrote, 'I doubt whether any organization in peacetime has been subject to comparable strain' (*Ariel,* 3, 1956).

Corporation officials became obsessed with maintaining a 30 per cent share of the audience. Television was typically being interpreted in terms of the audience distribution of radio. Furthermore its audience was being seen in terms of an obsolete distribution of the population between classes. According to this view, the commercial companies would concentrate on entertainment (like the Light Programme, which drew 68 per cent of the audience), leaving more serious programming to the BBC (like the combined Home and Third services which drew 32 per cent of the audience).

The apparent collapse of the audience posed a dilemma. The BBC might be destroyed because its share of the audience would no longer justify the collection of a licence fee from all viewers. Or the BBC might be destroyed because it would be forced to emulate the commercial programmes.

However, the argument about which service had won the largest audience was confused, in the first place because the two authorities counted their audience in different ways. 'For us,' wrote Robert Silvey, the head of the BBC's audience research, 'it meant people, and for ITV it meant TV sets. Our method was based on questioning samples of the population about their previous day's viewing; ITV's on metered records of when TV sets in a sample of homes had been switched on.' Although both methods showed trends in viewing behaviour, they could not be directly compared.

Indeed the commercial companies had not 'won' a 70 per cent share of the total viewing audience as Clark had implied. Rather this was the proportion of those viewers who had purchased a new television set which could receive both channels. At first this was a tiny fraction of the total audience. Even as late as 1960 the ITA estimated in its annual report that fewer than 60 per cent of licence holders had two-channel sets. Given their considerable financial investment, it was hardly surprising that viewers with new sets at first preferred the novelty of commercial television. Nevertheless, throughout the 60s. period the BBC's total audience was over twice that of ITV.

Indeed the introduction of commercial television had no independent effect on the overall growth of the television audience.

As Table 11.1 shows this was fast but steady. The pattern of gradual growth was interrupted only once, when two years before the start of ITV the Coronation produced a dramatic rise in viewers. The BBC did not 'lose' an audience, nor did commercial choice increase the speed of audience growth.

Public service: private enterprise

Commercial television in Britain was hardly revolutionary. Indeed it was carefully modelled on the BBC. The traditions of public service were inherited by the new authority.

The ITA was responsible for regulating the commercial stations and made no programmes. Like the BBC, ITV was licensed only for a limited period, a system which ensured that the whole of British broadcasting came under periodic review. Like the BBC it had a publicly appointed controlling board. 'The BBC triumphed', Peter Black wrote, 'because all of those chosen as members of the IBA might equally well have been BBC Governors.'

The new service was more limited than the BBC. It was banned from broadcasting its own opinions, and the injunction that it should observe 'impartiality in the treatment of all controversial issues' has been interpreted

Table 11.1 *Growth of television audience*

Year	No. of new TV licence holders
1946–7	14,560
1947–8	57,000
1948–9	112,000
1949–50	344,000
1950–1	420,000
1951–2	685,319
1952–3	693,192
1953–4	1,110,439
1954–5	1,254,879
1955–6	1,235,827
1956–7	1,226,663
1957–8	1,123,747
1958–9	1,165,419

Source: BBC Handbooks (1946–59)

narrowly to imply a balance of views within each programme. As Smith points out, the prohibitions 'listed in the 1954 Act are broadly consistent with the general editorial policy of the BBC, but they have been used over the years to oblige independent TV not to do certain types of programme'. Hence ITV has been given less political independence than the BBC.

Thus Independent Television was made in the image of the BBC. Introduced after a controversy which *The Economist* called 'a soufflé of high principles and politics' (15 June 1954), which disguised a simple profit motive, commercial television was nevertheless formed as a public service.

Commerce, finance, and television

Indeed television was so expensive it had always seemed likely that it would have to be financed commercially. 'Had there been no war in 1939', Briggs remarks, 'it is conceivable that commercial TV would have come to Britain fifteen years before it did.' Even in the limited experimental stage, television was an exorbitantly expensive medium. In 1937 a BBC *Handbook* had estimated that an hour of television cost twelve times as much to produce as the most expensive programme on the radio. Even Reith, in his evidence to the Selsdon Committee in 1934, claimed that he had 'no objection in principle to the sponsor system and we do in fact do something which is near to that and might do it in the future'. Sir William Haley wrote in 1945, 'Television will cost more than the Corporation's usual sources of funds can easily provide.' Beveridge had rejected sponsorship, but was not hostile in principle to some commercial involvement in television.

The BBC itself had been pressing for some kind of commercial financing of television since the 1930s, partly because it was felt that business interests could have little serious effect on what was seen as a trivial means of entertainment. Within the BBC, television was regarded as an extension of the Light Programme. As such it might be expensive, but it could hardly be important. 'In terms of the ethos which had been cultivated within the BBC during the fifties', wrote Burns, 'Light Entertainment remained an unfortunate necessity, its marginal character inescapably perpetuated in the adjective tagged to it.' Commerce, television, and programme policy had been closely linked since the 1930s.

New programmes and the new style

Perhaps the most important innovation which ITV introduced was the change of mood which it brought to broadcasting. The atmosphere of the new companies, owned and run by showmen like Val Parnell and the Grade brothers, was quite different from the stifling solemnity of the BBC bureaucracy. 'It was more like Klondyke than Maida Vale,' wrote Howard Thomas. When Thomas went to see Lew Grade at ATV about new programme ideas he would be met by a cloud of cigar smoke, and Grade would throw open a drawer bulging with receipts and bills. The haggling would then begin. Describing Parnell and Grade negotiating a new contract for ATV Thomas wrote, 'They sat like boxers pausing between the rounds of a heavyweight championship.'

Once ITV had begun broadcasting, it no longer had to fight the moral scruples of the establishment and its first priority was to capture an audience. 'Variety,' claimed the first *ATV Showbook*, 'although accumulating the largest number of viewers, has been taken to task by critics of commercial television who have asked for "more cultural programmes and less airy frolics".' The article continued, 'Many will agree with ATV chief executive Val Parnell when he says there is a lot of culture to be gained from watching a great clown performing.' However, it was not the big top or the *Commedia Dell'Arte* which drew the ATV audience, but rather the giveaway shows, Double your Money, Take your Pick, and Beat the Clock. The Labour MP, Tom Driberg, compared the audience's howl of laughter at one of these shows to that of the circus crowd in ancient Rome (*New Statesman,* 25 December 1959).

Independent Television did not, however, 'soundly beat the BBC at its own game', as a *Daily Mail* critic claimed in 1956. BBC drama, serials, and documentaries were consistently preferred to those of ITV. Consequently in 1956 news, documentaries, classical music, current events, and drama on ITV were cut by one-third. 'A craven definition of "serious"', Black claims, 'killed off promising programmes whose only offence was that though entertainment, they were a novelty.'

ITV's most important contribution to television was to develop a format for the news. The BBC bulletin had been read by an unseen newscaster accompanied by still photographs. Cardiff and Scannell argue that this failure

> left a gaping hole in the very centre of television programme output. The function of a daily news service is not simply the continuous up to the minute monitoring, processing and defining of immediate national and international news events. It also serves to define the currency and top-icality of events and issues for current affairs programmes.[8]

Independent Television News attracted an immense audience. It used jour-nalists as news-readers, allowed them to write their own scripts, and showed them on the screen.

Robin Day, one of ITN's first newscasters, commented in his memoirs that 'The man on the screen had a further task, to win the professional confidence of his colleagues.' ITN developed television journalism in new directions, despite the limitations imposed upon it by the Television Act. The obligation to exercise balance proved particularly difficult. 'Any problems?' Day once asked the news director. 'Yes,' Cox replied bitterly, 'a call from a chap called Pontius Pilate who says his case has not been properly put.' The success of the ITN approach in turn provoked the BBC into improving its own news ser-vices.

However, ITV also inherited many traditions from the BBC. One disgrun-tled critic claimed, 'The BBC has precedents for everything, for handling a monarch's abdication, a State Opening of Parliament or a boy scouts' jam-boree.'[9] The opening years of television seem little more than an extension of the wireless, where history was relentlessly marked by a succession of royal events (with outside coverage).

More significantly the BBC solved many of the political and social dilem-mas that confronted television. The BBC showed the first televised election, and established the rules governing politicians' access to television, while the practical consequences of 'neutrality' and 'balance' in a visual medium were developed by a new generation of BBC producers and presenters. Goldie employed several young Labour ex-MPs defeated in the 1951 general election to make current events programmes. Later she claimed her choice was vindi-cated because Mayhew, Taverne, and Wyatt moved from the left to the middle and right of the political spectrum. These shifts in attitude might also demon-strate the power of the ethic of consensus which came to dominate television journalism. The commercial companies simply took over the conventions developed within the BBC. Both, wrote Stuart Hood, 'interpreted impartial-ity as the acceptance of that segment of opinion which constitutes parliamentary consensus. Opinion that falls outside that consensus has diffi-culty in finding expression.' Hood suggests that the median of acceptable opinion may shift, but the consensus, once arrived at, is always shared by both companies.

The BBC had also set precedents for the solution of technical dilemmas in television journalism before ITV started. New rhetorics of documentary and current affairs coverage were established. At first most cameramen had been trained in the cinema, and had little experience of journalism. 'In those early days', one producer wrote, 'I often discarded glamorous pictures of cherry orchards, or flocks of bleating lambs, or children dancing in playgrounds because, though improbably useful in a travelogue, they did nothing to a study of, say, the relationship of Yugoslavia to the USSR.'[10] She concluded that as pictures would always override words a style had to be found which ensured that they would reinforce rather than distract from the meaning of a piece. It was also recognized that the use of film raised problems of authenticity. Viewers could easily be led to believe that a film taken in the past actually portrayed events happening in the present. One solution was to use someone who had helped to make the film as the programme presenter. Reviewing the BBC magazine series Foreign Correspondent in the *Listener* (May 1959), Goldie had written that they

> were using film but we were not trying to make films. We wanted the programmes to be dominated by the personality of the commentator. . . . We were all feeling our way but when the series finished we felt that we had hit on a new form that had come to stay in television. The key to the new form is the use of film to illustrate a personal experience.

This form was quite opposed to the style of the British documentary movement, in which the film purported to represent an authoritative reality, rather than any personal view.

These innovations and cautious explorations of the specific properties and opportunities of televised politics and current affairs were made well before ITV started. They solved dilemmas that were common to any television service. ITV did not challenge or alter the rules established by the BBC; it merely helped to develop them further.

End of a monopoly: vulgar new world

The introduction of Independent Television did not mark such a decisive break with the BBC. Rather the brash new companies owed more to the Corporation than has usually been recognized. The BBC had already begun to change in fundamental ways before ITV was started. The commercial station provided a stimulus for the maturing of a national television service. Sir Hugh Greene claimed that dramatic changes were to come later in the 1960s, and these were as much to do with a shift in the political climate as with any administrative innovations.

This is not to deny that the BBC had a radically different manner and organization from Independent Television. Like the British Raj, the BBC combined privilege and moral purpose. It was a world in which 'unsoundness' was a major crime. Independent Television provided an alternative source of employment for dissidents and had no deadweight of custom or dignity. Personnel moved continually and freely between the two authorities by the 1960s.

However, commercial television was also modelled on and limited by the BBC. Originally intended as a political counterweight to what was seen as the BBC's 'red' bias, ITV was as vulnerable to political pressure. The BBC depended on public support for the legitimacy of its licence fee, as ITV depended on it for advertising revenue.

It has often been claimed that ITV was a vulgar debaucher of cultural standards. In the pursuit of profit it merely pandered to the lowest common denominator of public taste. More recently a far more subtle case has been advanced which is not so crudely anti-commercial. This claims that ITV was rather an energizing, populist force which gave expression to working-class culture.

Notes

1. J. C. W. Reith, *House of Lords* (22 May 1952), H. L.176: 1293–451.
2. Quoted in J. Harris, *William Beveridge* (Oxford, Clarendon, 1977), p. 311.
3. Captain L. P. S. Orr MP, *House of Commons Debates* (22 June 1951), 529:327.
4. H. Fairlie, 'The BBC' in H. Swynnerton Thomas (ed.), *The Establishment: A Symposium* (London, New English Library, 1962).
5. G. Wyndham Goldie, *Facing the Nation: Television and Politics 1936–1976* (London, Bodley Head, 1977), p. 45.
6. 'Television staff policy', *BBC Written Archives* (1955).
7. P. Black, *The Mirror in the Corner* (London, Hutchinson, 1972), p. 115.
8. P. Scannell, 'The social eye of television', *Media, Culture and Society*, 1, 1 (1979).
9. H. Fairlie, 'TV: idiot box', *Encounter* (August 1959).
10. G. Wyndham Goldie, 'TV report', *Listener* (23 October 1968).

12

Class, taste, and profit

Post-war affluence was measured in consumer durables. Cars, refrigerators, and washing machines made it easier to do what had always been done. Television changed people's social life and habits. Commercial television was believed to alter their aspirations and values as well.

In the late 1950s and early 1960s television was central to a debate about supposed changes in the British class structure. The growth of a mass television audience and the setting-up of a commercial service were seen as agents of a revolution that was eroding class distinction and increasing social mobility. Television has more often been seen as a destructive than as a creative force. In the 1950s many regarded it as a threat to traditional ways of life, and hence to the basis of traditional political loyalties.

In 1962 the Pilkington Report summed up this debate. The Director General, Sir Hugh Greene, later called the report 'the most important piece of work on the purposes of broadcasting which has appeared in this or any other country'.[1] Pilkington attempted to establish the criteria for producing – and judging – good broadcasting. In fact the report was very much a product of its time, and was constrained by current sociological fashions.

The myth of the disappearing working class

During the 1950s it was argued that affluence was destroying the working class. The general elections of 1955 and 1959 seemed to support the view that there were no longer two nations: fewer and fewer people were prepared even to support the Labour Party. Two complementary explanations were put forward. According to the first, as the working class had become richer it was actually disappearing through assimilation into the middle class. According to the second, a working class had continued to exist but prosperity had undermined an awareness of its own interests: capitalism was successfully eradicating the consciousness (though not the reality) of class.

The first view was particularly popular among right-wing Labour politicians (who used it to justify an attempt to remove socialism from the party's constitution). 'The steady upgrading of the working class,' wrote Anthony Crosland in his book *The Future of Socialism,* 'both occupationally and still more in terms of political and social aspirations, renders Labour's one-class image increasingly inappropriate.' It was also widely held by social scientists who invented the inelegant term 'embourgeoisement' to describe the alleged process. As Butler and Rose wrote after the 1959 general election, 'It is more than ever possible to speak of the Conservatives as the country's usual majority party . . . the Labour Party has to face the fact that its support is being eroded by the impact of age and social change.'

Between 1951 and 1958 real wages rose by 20 per cent. The proportion of manual workers who owned their own homes rose from 32 per cent to 39 per cent in the four years before 1962.[2] Between 1951 and 1964 the number of television sets rose from 1 million to 13 million. Indeed as televisions were clearly not useful, the widespread ownership of sets merely appeared to confirm what Crosland called the 'pubs, pools and prostitutes' view of the working class which was seen to 'waste all its higher income on alcohol, tobacco, gambling and fun . . . if not actually women'.[3]

During the same period working-class habits also changed. People went on more holidays, went to the cinema less frequently, began drinking more at home and less at pubs. As these goods and habits had previously been the prerogative of higher social classes, it was assumed that their use also entailed middle- and upper-class views and beliefs.

The second explanation of the decay of the working class depended on the centrality of culture. The rituals which were a source of strength to working-class life were disappearing, partly (so it was argued) because of the homogenizing influence of television. Paradoxically working-class culture was celebrated just as it seemed to be about to vanish. Indeed its condition was detailed by a generation of academics whose origins were working-class, but all of whom had been upwardly mobile.

'To live in the working class', wrote Richard Hoggart, 'is to belong to an all-pervading culture, one in some ways as formalized and stylized as any that is attributed to the upper classes.'[4] Jackson and Marsden in their book on working-class life argued that two and a half centuries of urban life 'have established distinct working-class styles of living with very real values of their own. Values which are perhaps essential to society and which do not flourish that strongly in other reaches of society.'[5] In a chapter headed ' An acceptance of the working-class life', they remarked that obliterating these values and way of life 'can be so quick in a technological society . . . the mass media, the central planning office, the bulldozers are all characteristic instruments of change'. In a related series of studies Wilmott and Young compared the warm closeness of a Bethnal Green working-class community with the more isolated life of a new suburb. In the East End the emphasis was on the informal collective life and the extended family, the pubs and the open air market. 'There is a sort of bantering warmth in public,' they claimed, which in the new suburb, Woodford, was reserved for the family home. There seemed to be more uniformity in gardens, attitudes, and behaviour in Woodford than in the East End. 'Maybe uniformity is one of the prices we have to pay for sociability in a more mobile society,' they concluded.[6]

Television was important because it was seen as replacing old communal forms of leisure with isolated and standardized entertainment. 'In many parts of life', Hoggart argued, 'mass production has brought good: culturally the mass produced makes it harder for the good to be recognized.' Indeed for writers like Hoggart culture was the most important aspect of a society's achievement.

Hoggart applied F. R. Leavis's concern with the moral quality of élite literary culture to a broader problem of working-class life. For Leavis, Annan wrote, 'The analysis of the text is only important in so far as it reveals the profundity or morality of the writer's moral consciousness.'[7] Leavis was concerned to evaluate the purpose of literature. 'Where there is not in the literary critical sense a significant contemporary culture', he wrote, '*the mind* is not fully alive.'[8] Hoggart was concerned to judge modern working-class culture. He concluded that 'Most mass entertainments are in the end what D. H. Lawrence described as "anti-life". They are full of corrupt brightness and improper appeals and moral evasions.' Progress had been reduced to material improvement: 'It only offered an infinite perspective of increasingly good times. Technicolour TV, all smelling, all touching, all tasting TV.'

Thus the Pilkington Report was the product of two contemporary concerns: that the working class was being absorbed into the middle class, and that working-class culture was decaying because of the industrialization of leisure. Raymond Williams wrote that 'From 1956 to 1962 there was an intense development of ideas in the field of culture and communication, and by the time of the Pilkington Report this had reached the level of open and conventional politics.'[9] The committee had been asked to review the development of television. In fact they did much more, producing a report which judged the nation's culture. Television, the report argued, was 'one of the major long-term factors that would shape the moral and mental attitudes, and the values of our society'.

Yet the working class did not disappear, and neither did working-class culture. There is little evidence that people lose a sense of their social identity simply because they become comparatively better off. Indeed the really remarkable feature of the period was not affluence – the rise in living standards looks far less impressive when it is compared with the growth in other European countries – but full employment. For the first time there was work for everyone, and it gave working-class culture, taste, and life a confidence which it had rarely had before.

The Pilkington Report depended on a sentimentalization of an earlier 'golden age', just as Hoggart and Wilmott and Young had before it. Indeed it demonstrates a puritanical distaste for the effects of improved material conditions. Although its concern with the influence of television on social and cultural behaviour is important, the standards by which it judged the mass media were based on false premises about the nature of working-class life.

The power of the media

The Pilkington Report also depended on a crude view of the power of the media to influence individual behaviour. Advertising, and in particular its newest and most dramatic form, the television commercial, was regarded as immensely persuasive. The effect of advertising was dramatized by the contrast with the war, when advertising had not only been limited, but also pursued rather novel goals. A cartoon by Fougasse in 1942 wryly made the point: it compared the huge pre-war billboard extolling the public to 'Eat more and more Meatio' with the tiny wartime poster which read, 'Save Meatio, don't use more than you need!'[10] In this context the post-austerity explosion of advertising amazed the public, and academics and politicians became very sensitive to its effects .

Television advertising in particular was regarded as sinister. It was often equated with 'brain-washing' techniques which had been exposed during the Korean war. 'It may well be', wrote Daniel Bell in the *Listener* (December 1956), 'that our fears are excessive, that the pliability of the consumer, like that of the "indoctrinated" communist youth, is an exaggerated fact.' The fashion for 'motivation research' seemed to suggest that advertisements relied on an appeal to people's irrational and subconscious feelings in order to sell goods. The model of the consumer as a rational hedonist was replaced by another in which many goods were purchased not for their intrinsic worth or usefulness, but in an attempt to assuage anxieties. Marketing, dependent on the 'eight hidden needs' (most of which could be reduced to one – sex), was claimed to have dramatic effects. 'The ability of advertisers to contact millions of us simultaneously through television has given them the power to do good or evil on a scale never before possible,' one persuader put it.[11] Leavis wrote that 'a new brand of applied psychology . . . and a highly specialized profession' had been developed. 'Years of carefully recorded and tabulated experiment [led advertisers] to develop their appeal in the confidence that the average member of the public will respond like an automaton.'[12] Television advertising, which reached people in the defenceless privacy of their own homes, seemed to assume that consumers were unable to introspect sufficiently to understand their own motives.

The working class were felt to be the group most vulnerable to the ambitions of advertisers. 'There is one kind of person who seems particularly responsive to advertising: the man or woman who is moving up from one class to another,' Mark Abrams argued in a broadcast in 1956. 'These people – and there are an incredible number in Britain – have to shed their old buying habits and acquire new ones. The class-destroying function of modern advertising is cumulative,' he suggested:

> The initial effect is to encourage people to want to buy consumer goods formerly enjoyed by their social betters. As they achieve this and become more socially mobile, advertising and television provide them with knowledge that enables them to fill their new role.[13]

Indeed the first television commercials seemed to confirm this view of the direct impact of the media on behaviour. Shops almost immediately sold out of the advertised goods, and jubilant market researchers discovered that the public recalled the commercials long after they had first been shown. But this was only a temporary effect.

Indeed later research has shown how complex the relationship between media message and audience behaviour is. The public is not a passive empty box merely waiting to be filled with the injunctions of advertisers. How people react to what they see is determined by their class, age, and the beliefs they already hold. Nor is the public subconscious so easily manipulated as many assumed. As one contemporary market researcher pointed out, surveys which concluded that housewives did not like macaroni which cooked to a wet sticky mass because wet sticky masses aroused sexual guilt in them were not treated with the scepticism they deserved.[14] Some critics reacted cautiously to the power of advertisements: 'I cannot think so poorly of British Fathers', wrote Tom Driberg in the *New Statesman* (20 December 1958), 'as to accept the diagnosis proclaimed by one ITV advertiser last week, "Every daddy *deserves* a Brylcreem home dispenser for Christmas".' However, most critics believed it to be overwhelming. Advertising executives were credited with a power they would have been delighted to exercise, but which was far in excess of their rather unpredictable performance.

This overestimation of the manipulative power of the media influenced the Pilkington Report. It led to a crude view of the public – particularly the working-class audience – as passive, gullible, and misled.

Real and false wants

The Pilkington Report dismissed expressed public preferences as unreal and the product of commercial manipulation. A Labour Party report on advertising written in 1962 developed some of these arguments. Advertising, it claimed, could not be defended by the assertion that it merely reflected the times. For, in order to make advertisements, individuals were obliged to make decisions. In so far as advertisers determined what was shown they were responsible for their choices. Some people, the report argued, had claimed that advertising 'reinforces attitudes of materialism, only too prevalent in society'. In the committee's opinion,

This charge is probably the opposite of the truth: for it seems more likely that what advertising does is to interfere with the appreciation of material goods to the extent that it substitutes for a genuine assessment or perception of their qualities, vague sentiments and fantasies.

The choices that were expressed under these conditions were consequently not 'real'.

The Pilkington Report's assessment of commercial television depended on a similar view of the exploitation of working-class false consciousness for profit. The argument was based on two premises. First, that the public's expressed choice was not a real one because it had not been offered the entire range of possible options from which to choose. It made its choice of television programmes from a culture already limited by the imperatives of profit. Second, the public was in itself limited: the choices it made were deformed by the inadequacies of its education, wealth, and leisure. The working class has, of course, been particularly damaged in these ways.

The report's attitude towards cultural choice was particularly clear in its discussion of entertainment. ITV defended itself by arguing that its programmes were popular. Pilkington replied that

> to give the public what it wants is a misleading phrase . . . it has the appearance of an appeal to democratic principle, but the appearance is deceptive. It is in fact patronizing and arrogant, in that it claims to know what the public is but defines it as no more than the mass audience, and it claims to know what it wants, but limits its choice to the average of experience.

The commercial companies suggested that there was no need to consider entertainment as it was so unimportant. However, for Pilkington, the individual programme was analogous to the text for the literary critic. As such it was as essential to judge 'trivial entertainment' as more serious programmes. Pilkington found most entertainment programmes unsatisfactory.

However, as Crosland pointed out, it was patronizing and perhaps unwise to dismiss expressed public wants as irrelevant. He argued that the range of newspapers and television programmes was 'still considerable, certainly wide enough to offer genuine comparison'. Indeed most people, for most of the time, chose the escapist, the diverting, or the trivial. Policy should not ignore these needs, but should also seek to encourage minority interests.

The Pilkington Committee's fears that the public was passive led it to consider audience preferences as little more than the expression of commercial manipulation. Consequently the report became insensitive to public taste. Indeed it endorsed the BBC's popular music policy when this was clearly out of touch with what people wanted to hear, as the success of the pirate stations soon demonstrated.

Entertainment, politics, and advertising

The Pilkington Committee was romantically committed to a concept of folk culture. Its emphasis on the importance of the 'authenticity' of cultural products meant that many other considerations were ignored. For instance, television entertainment programmes often implicitly supported particular political values. Yet the report's emphasis on the cultural purposes of programmes has meant that long-term political consequences have rarely been discussed. In addition the report depended on a series of misleading images about the nature of working-class life and culture which affected its tone and distorted its recommendations. Often Pilkington seemed perilously close to despising what was popular and entertaining, and approving only that which was rigorous and demanding.

This was unfortunate, because the report's identification of programmes as the central focus for any assessment of broadcasting is crucial. Moreover, its recognition of the structural effects of advertising on the quality of programmes is original and shrewd, and still pertinent a generation later. In addition, attempts by Pilkington to mitigate the impact of advertising by giving the third channel to the BBC, and by strengthening the power of the ITA over the companies were important factors in improving the commercial service. In particular, the report, which had been wonderfully orchestrated by Sir Hugh Greene, also gave the BBC the *élan* and confidence which were the basis for its most exciting expansion in the 1960s.[15] For the first time, the Corporation attempted to make broadcasting something like a quality popular newspaper. This is perhaps the most challenging model for a national broadcasting service.

Notes

1. Sir Hugh Greene, 'The future of broadcasting in Britain', Granada Guildhall Lecture (1972), p. 24.
2. M. Pinto Duschinsky, 'Bread and circuses: the Conservatives in office 1951–64' in V. Bogdanor and R. Skidelsky (eds), *The Age of Affluence* (Harmondsworth, Penguin, 1970), p. 55.
3. C. A. R. Crosland, 'The mass media', *Encounter* (November 1962).
4. R. Hoggart, *The Uses of Literacy* (London, Chatto & Windus, 1957), p. 16.
5. B. Jackson and D. Marsden, *Education and the Working Class* (London, Routledge & Kegan Paul, 1962), p. 223.
6. P. Wilmott and M. D. Young, *Family and Class in a London Suburb* (London, Routledge & Kegan Paul, 1960), p. 129.
7. N. Annan, 'Love among the moralists', *Encounter* (February 1960), p. 37.
8. F. R. Leavis, *The Common Pursuit* (London, Chatto & Windus, 1952), p. 192.
9. R. Williams, *Communications*, revised edn (London, Chatto & Windus, 1966), p. 10.
10. Fougasse (pseud. C. K. Bird), *The Changing Face of Britain* (London, Methuen, 1950), p. 15.

11. V. Packard, *The Hidden Persuaders* (Harlow, Longman, 1957), p. 259.
12. F. R. Leavis and D. Thompson, *Culture and Environment* (London, Chatto & Windus, 1953), p. 48.
13. M. Abrams, 'Advertising', *Listener* (15 December 1956), p. 1089.
14. M. Abrams, 'Motivation research', *Advertising Quarterly* (November 1959), p. 311.
15. See M. Tracey, *A Variety of Lives: The Biography of Sir Hugh Greene* (London, Bodley Head, 1983).

13

How the audience is made

Commercial television produces audiences not programmes. Advertisers, in purchasing a few seconds of television time, are actually buying viewers by the thousand. The price they pay is determined by the number of people who can be expected to be watching when their advert is shown. Hence advertisers regard programmes merely as the means by which audiences are delivered to them. The sequence of programmes in any evening, week, or season reflects the quest of commercial customers to get the largest or most appropriate public they can. 'The spot is the packaging,' wrote a market researcher in *Advertising Quarterly,* 'the product inside the package is an audience.' These are the realities which help to determine what kinds of programmes are made, when they are shown, and who sees them.

Commercial television was introduced in the 1950s because it was claimed that it would bring competition into broadcasting, and make the service more responsive to popular demands. The Independent Television channel was supposed to break the narrow élitism of the BBC's cultural policy. Indeed once it had been given a regional structure, it was also supposed to promote provincial culture and oppose the BBC's metropolitan bias. Finally, commercial television, its advocates claimed, would be less vulnerable to political pressure. Unlike the BBC, its finances would be independent of official control.

Few of these hopes were fully realized. The allocation of the franchise areas in which commercial companies were given the right to broadcast was designed to produce a system in which four (later five) of the largest and wealthiest regions made most of the programmes for the national network. The smaller companies made most of their programmes for local consumption; only a few of their products were to be shown nationally.

The first commitment of the commercial companies was to make a profit. Hence they were concerned to minimize the financial risks involved in making programmes. The smaller regions, whose audiences were not so attractive to advertisers, could not afford to invest in expensive programmes unless they were guaranteed a national showing. Similarly the large networking companies needed to be able to show their programmes in every region in order to cover their costs. Consequently decisions about which programmes were to be networked became centralized.

This centralization was formally established when the Independent Television Companies Association (ITCA) was set up in 1971. This decided which programmes were to be shown on the national network, and how much the smaller companies had to pay towards the costs of the major programme producers. The smaller companies, however, complained that the ITCA was dominated by the five major programme networking companies.

The Independent Broadcasting Authority

Yet British 'commercial' television was not merely a product of market forces. If financial pressures were the only influence, the programme-makers' aim would always be simply to reach the largest possible audience for the smallest amount of money.

In practice this would have meant a diet of American soap opera, variety shows, filmed series, quizzes, and chat shows, based on proven formulae, endlessly repeated. 'Minority' programming would cater only for groups defined primarily in terms of their consumption patterns. Current affairs would have been confined to news bulletins, and advertising spots would have been longer, more frequent, and more intrusive. In addition, even more programmes would have been bought from abroad – particularly the USA – and fewer programmes made in Britain or directed at a British audience. Commercial broadcasting did not develop all of these features in Britain, because of the framework of public regulations within which it was obliged to operate. Nevertheless, these pressures remain the dominant features of a commercial service.

The Independent Broadcasting Authority (IBA) exerted a major influence on commercial television. The powers of the authority were widened following the report of the Pilkington Committee (1962), but the most public job of the IBA was to license television franchises, and to reallocate these periodically. The authority was also required to ensure 'balanced programming', 'due impartiality' in the treatment of controversial issues, and a high quality in programme production as a whole. To enforce its recommendations the IBA could determine the broadcasting schedule, prohibit the transmission of particular programmes, or even revoke the franchises of offending companies. In addition, the IBA monitored and controlled the amount, timing, quality, and content of advertisements shown on commercial television.

When commercial television started in Britain in 1956, there was little idea of what form it would take. 'All we had in the beginning', recalled Sir Robert Fraser, the first Director General of the ITA, 'was an Act of Parliament, an untested authority, a little prefab in a mews by Marble Arch, and a bit of money we had to pay back.'[1] Nevertheless, the new controlling authority quickly developed a commitment to public service. Thus in the first months of broadcasting, as Sir Kenneth Clark recalled, the IBA threatened to make current affairs programmes itself to counter a proposal to abandon such programmes by the commercial companies. The determination of the authority to maintain minority programming in peak viewing time was similarly demonstrated when it came to reallocate franchises. In 1967 some of the original commercial franchises were not renewed. As a result, programme scheduling on ITV had an important though secondary goal, that of securing the reallocation of franchises. 'Advertisers understand that current affairs and news programming is a condition of the survival of the commercial television companies,' wrote one advertising executive recently. 'It is no good complaining about them.'[2]

The IBA also intervened in the construction of the programme schedules, requiring that one-third of all material broadcast by commercial TV companies should be 'serious non-fiction, sensibly distributed over the week as a whole in appropriate times'.[3] Without this intervention, a service which many people relied on as their primary source of news might have carried very little current affairs coverage.

The IBA's intervention also helped to maintain a wider range of cultural output than would otherwise have been the case. In 1956 'serious programming' accounted for 19 per cent of the companies' schedules. This rose to 26 per cent in 1959, and 36 per cent in 1965, a proportion which was maintained. However, official figures were inflated by the growing number of programmes which were classed as serious documentaries, but which were on entertainment topics (such as Alan Whicker's series). In addition, there were an increasing number of consumer-oriented programmes (on cars, holidays, and gardening, for example), some of which scarcely qualified for their official classification as 'serious and informative'. Nevertheless, programming on commercial television undoubtedly included more serious material because of the IBA's influence, and many of these programmes gained large audiences. The most striking example was ITN's News at Ten, which was enormously innovative in its presentation of news and which regularly featured in the IBA's yearly 'Top Twenty' popularity ratings.

The Authority was also important in maintaining the standards of entertainment on commercial television. It limited the number of cheap American imports and the frequency with which programmes were repeated. The IBA also assisted the smaller regional companies by charging the more profitable regions a higher rent for the use of the television transmitter which it owned, and thus made them subsidize the rental of the poorer companies. In addition, through its position on the committee which decided which programmes were shown on the central network, it ensured that some of the regional programmes were shown nationally.

Regions and audiences

The Television Act, 1954, had not specified how commercial television was to be organized. It had laid down no principles to guide the allocation of contracts. When commercial companies began to submit proposals to the ITA they suggested many different ways of dividing commercial broadcasting between competitors. Thus some contractors offered to provide particular kinds of programmes, all the light entertainment, or all the music; others proposed to make the programmes for particular times of day, 6–9 pm or 3–7 pm. However, Sir Robert Fraser decided that the system should be based on regional companies. In this way, he intended to prohibit the growth of a centralized monopoly based on London, and to 'give real creative power to the regions'.

Yet the principle of the federal structure seemed threatened from the very start. During the first two years commercial television was so expensive to run, reached such a small audience, and was so unprofitable that there was little interest in the smaller regions. It was during this disastrous period that Roy Thomson acquired Scottish Television at a very low cost. It was only when this company overcame its initial difficulties that the other regional services began to develop. Thomson, famous for having said that owning a commercial station was like having a licence to print money, soon made Scottish Television profitable. 'I like monopolies', he said, 'when I operate them.'[4]

Regional commercial broadcasting has survived, but in a form that makes sense in economic rather than cultural terms. Thus Tyneside and Teesside have little in common apart from geographical proximity. Yet they were given a combined television station because only the joint purchasing power of their audience was sufficient to make up a marketing unit. A more serious case was that of Harlech Television, supposedly a Welsh station, but actually required, for commercial reasons, to cater for a large English audience as well. It has been argued that some regional television stations, for example Border Television, may have strengthened, or even created, a sense of local identity. However, most of the regions have no real justification except in marketing terms. Apart from London, television regions have not even approximately coincided with local authority areas. This has at least inhibited the discussions of local political issues.

The regionalism of commercial television appears less firmly rooted in popular needs than in the convenience of the market.

Indeed the most important response by the commercial companies to regional differences within Britain was to identify and sell distinctive characteristics in marketing terms. 'Granada has the skilled workers: surveys prove it!' read an advertisement in a 1959 trade magazine. 'Westward where women cook,' read another in *Campaign* in 1962. In 1979 Southern Television was pointing out that its A, B, and C1 housewives cook, and have time to be *femmes fatales* afterwards (*Campaign,* 5 July 1979). The differences between the habits and tastes of the various regional audiences became an essential feature of sales campaigns. In 1962 one writer claimed that 'The television regions made scientific selling more possible than ever before.'[5] New products could be launched in regions where they were most likely to be successful, and advertising campaigns could be tested by pilot surveys in a particular region. In the same way regional television meant that additional advertising pressure could be applied in any area where sales were slumping. The most important effect of the regional structure of commercial television was to change the marketing map of Britain.

Franchises and owners

The cost of developing commercial television was at first so great that franchises had to be given to syndicates which had the resources to undertake the necessary capital investment. This brought an important change in the kind of people who controlled broadcasting. Hitherto in the BBC responsibility had been vested in professional administrators whose social origins, training, and attitudes reflected the 'public service' philosophy of the Corporation. Independent television introduced a new type of executive, business-oriented and entrepreneurial, geared to the commercial criteria of the sponsors. Thus while the BBC was directed by Sir William Haley, who had started his career as a journalist on the *Manchester Guardian,* and who became editor of *The Times,* Associated Television's first director was Lew Grade, a show business and theatre impresario.

By the time that the franchises were reallocated in 1967, commercial television had become highly profitable, and consequently the justification for allowing it to be controlled by speculative capital no longer held good. Indeed such vast profits had been made from a publicly owned asset, the air waves, that the prospect of their reallocation created a flood of applications. There was an atmosphere reminiscent of Klondyke gold fever. Many of Britain's major corporations financed 'prospecting' companies composed of theatre managers and entertainment moguls spiced with a few peers or eminent members of the BBC. Although changes were made in the new franchises, instead of widening control, the redistribution, in practice, merely consolidated the power of the great media empires.

This pattern continued until the 1980s; the government encouraged the oligopolistic tendencies of the broadcasting industry itself – in the name, of course, of freedom. If one contradiction of this period was that free market rhetoric was accompanied by interventionist practice, another was that talk about a media market-place was accompanied by its virtual eradication. Technological change, with its requirement of long-term investment and large-scale capitalization, produced a bureaucratic jungle of profit-taking conglomerates which now own huge shares in all the media which the public consumes.

By 1990 the small number of corporate owners were not competitive in a sense that could be conceivably expected to produce an improved product: but their financial rivalry undoubtedly imposed pressure to produce a cheaper one. That meant an almost inevitable lowering of standards: it is cheaper to buy in agency news than to send a reporter to the scene, it is cheaper to buy in internationalized soap opera than to make your own drama, and so on.

The victims of media concentration are variety, creativity, and quality: while the future proliferation of broadcasting channels in the hands of a shrinking band of operators is certain to make matters worse.

Ownership and control of television

However, the control of commercial television companies could not simply be equated with ownership. Those who actually produced commercial television programmes enjoyed a significant degree of autonomy. But, most important of all, the pressure of market forces imposed powerful constraints on what could and could not be broadcast. These operated irrespective of the formal ownership of commercial television. In a study of the way in which programming is determined in the USA, Wolf argued that ownership does not explain the differences in programming between stations. 'It may be', he suggested,

> that those who saw such influences labored under a false analogy between the small town newspaper editor who may have shaped every word in his paper, and the television corporate executive, who according to the analogy controlled what was shown on the air.[6]

Indeed he concluded that in the USA the more diversely owned companies were less likely to take the networked programmes, particularly the news, current affairs, and documentaries, and more likely to replace them with old movies, old quiz shows, or old operas. They did this simply because of the pressure to attract the largest possible audience.

The economic and social organization of broadcasting is very different in Britain from that which Wolf describes in the USA. There, the more diversely owned companies were the smaller and less successful ones, which were more vulnerable to market pressures. Nevertheless, the inevitable pursuit of profit within a commercial system must have some similar consequences for the programming decisions which can be made in any country. Market forces operate as a continual limiting pressure on any commercial broadcasting system. Yet it is also clear that more socially diverse patterns of ownership could be an important factor in creating the conditions for more adventurous and varied programming.

The audience that advertisers want

The most important pressure on television scheduling and programme-making is that of advertising expenditure. If television companies sell audiences, what kinds of audiences do advertisers want, and how are they packaged to attract sales? Indeed how does the real purpose of producing audiences for advertisers affect the apparent purpose of producing programmes for audience consumption?

The American system of programme sponsorship, in which advertisers pay for individual programmes, was rejected when commercial television started in Britain on the grounds that it gave advertisers direct power over programme content. Instead only 'spot advertising' was permitted. Advertisers could buy time slots only between or within programmes. At first, advertisements were limited to an average of six minutes per hour. Later, when it was seen that this led to an accumulation of advertisements in peak viewing times, which had above average amounts of advertising, it was decided to limit advertisements to no more than seven minutes in any one hour.

The decision to adopt restricted spot advertising had been hailed as a victory for public service broadcasting. 'The prohibition of sponsorship was an inspiration of the Television Act', declared Fraser, 'since it established the supremacy of the editorial principle.'[7] Spot advertisements were compared with newspaper advertising. They were seen as guaranteeing the independence of programme-making from the influence of advertisers: no rational person, it was argued, supposes that what newspapers publish in their editorial columns is determined by advertisers. Spot advertising would protect the editorial integrity of commercial television. 'Advertising will be an asset worn as a bright feather in the cap of free TV,' Sir Robert Fraser wrote, 'not as a soiled choker around the throat.'

Sponsorship of all programmes except news and current events was finally permitted in 1988. However, on the ITV channels there continued to be a fierce battle about who could sponsor what – and considerable anxiety about potential commercial abuses of the authority of some programmes. Such niceties, of course, were not part of the satellite broadcasting regime. Here there were few restrictions on sponsorship and far more advertising was allowed. Indeed, one of the oddities of the intense political campaigns of the period was the BBC's failure to point out, in its own defence, that while the British public enjoys some adverts, repeated research has shown how irritating they find too many. Historically, the British public has enjoyed and endured less advertising per hour of viewing than any American or European viewer. They may be appalled when the full commercial diet of adverts reaches them.

However, during the 1980s, powerful interests complained to a sympathetic government that the ITV companies and the IBA were using their monopoly too effectively. Between 1981 and 1989, the advertising revenue of commercial television doubled in real terms, fierce competition for air time raised the price of advertising, and increased the discretionary power of companies. Thus there was great commercial pressure to create alternative sources of air time: cable, satellite, and a competing commercial terrestrial Channel 5 were proposed, in order to bring down advertising costs. Advertisers believed they had a strong interest in breaking the economic basis of the existing ITV companies' cultural power.

Hostile critics argued that the IBA had become too closely identified with the ITV companies. A new body, the Independent Television Commission, was set up to preside over the 'deregulated' commercial system, but with far more limited powers than its predecessor. Thus franchises for ITV (which after 1993 became known as Channel 3) were to be auctioned. Auction winners will then hold franchises for ten years. The ITC will have little authority to demand changes in programme performance. Thus while the Commission is obliged to ensure that public sensibilities about images of sex or violence are not offended, it has limited authority with which to perform the more critical task of ensuring that good programmes continue to be made and shown by companies desperately trying to recoup the huge capital expense of their franchise bid.

The IBA's powers, however imperfectly exercised, stemmed from its economic sanctions within the ITV system. Since its inception, the ITC has developed imperialist ambitions. Clearly it would like to use its controls to bring traditional public service criteria to bear on the enlarged commercial sector. Indeed, the ITC is probably responsible for a profound metaphorical change in ministers' language. In 1986 guarantees of programme quality were to be a 'factor' in allowing applicants to enter the auction for Channel 3 franchises; by 1987 they were being discussed as a 'hurdle'; they rose during 1988 to a 'fence'; and by 1990 they were confidently described as 'a barrier to the inferior'. But metaphors alone will not control commercial pressures to maximize profits, and it remains to be seen how far the ITC can realize its ambitions.

Yet many of the pressures exercised by advertisers on the content of programmes have remained remarkably consistent since the start of commercial broadcasting. The extent to which they affect programmes and schedules depends on the ways in which they are balanced and regulated.

Thus it is clear that even spot advertising does not preclude advertisers from calculating how the editorial content of programmes affects the impact of their advertising message. 'After all', as an advertiser wrote as early as the 1950s, 'an advert is seen as part of a programme' (*Campaign,* 14 March 1956). Advertisers have prior knowledge of programme schedules which are published each quarter in advance of their transmission. They thus know the general character, if not the precise content, of the programmes with which their advertisements will be shown. There have been cases in which advertisers have avoided certain programmes on the grounds that their content is unlikely to dispose viewers to respond favourably to their advertisements. This is most common when the content of the programme clashes directly with the appeal of the advertisement (for example, airlines have withdrawn advertisements from appearing in documentaries about air disasters). However, it has also occurred when a programme is thought to have associations that detract from the broad image of the product.

In contrast, some programmes may be preferred because they provide an editorial environment conducive to a favourable response to particular advertisements, or because their prestige is thought likely to enhance that of the product or service advertised within them. Thus advertisements for newspapers appear near the news, and those for beer are often placed close to programmes on sport. The very fact that such intuitive judgements associated with programme content can influence how advertising time is bought must affect the decisions made by the companies about scheduling.

This pressure is, however, marginal. The main consideration of advertisers is not the programme environment of their advertisements, but the size and composition of the audience that the programmes will attract. Advertisers buy television time in two ways. Sometimes they buy a 'guaranteed audience', that is a fixed number of viewers. This may be made up of many small sections of the audience and spread over a whole range of programmes with low ratings. Alternatively it may be composed of a few large audiences during peak viewing times. In either case, what is bought is viewers. However, advertisers may also purchase particular advertising slots. The television companies may oblige advertisers to buy a 'package' of slots, composed of some of the peak viewing times the advertisers want, but combining other less attractive slots. Nevertheless, advertisers are more in control of the kinds of audiences their campaign will reach if they buy specific slots.

Commercial television rapidly became the leading advertising medium for mass consumer products and so was under pressure to put on programmes with an appeal to a mass audience. However, many patrons of commercial television have sought to reach particular constituents within the mass market, in particular women (who are the key decision-makers in many consumer purchases) and young people. Since commercial television derives its revenue from advertisers and not from viewers, the commercial system is thus led towards catering for these groups. Thus the success of commercial breakfast television depends almost entirely on its capacity to attract an audience rich in consuming housewives.

Market research can provide a detailed breakdown of the audience profile for particular programmes. A massive investment is made in monitoring how many and what categories of people watch each programme. This research assists the television companies to produce programmes that will deliver the required audiences, and provides them with an accurate measurement of the audiences which they have sold.

Research also helps advertisers predict from advance programme schedules what audiences they can expect to buy. This research takes the form of continuous monitoring of a representative sample of viewers, providing detailed figures for programme viewing analysed in terms of the size and class of audience. It is supplemented by additional surveys that analyse other more specialized characteristics of viewers. This research has established that certain types of programmes – soap operas, situation comedies, the main news bulletin, and variety programmes – have a generalized appeal that transcends differences in social class, age, and sex. It also reveals that other types of programmes – most notably political documentary programmes and serious drama – are not watched as much by women and young people. The results have shown a remarkable stability of viewing preferences since the introduction of commercial television. There has been little change in the pattern of mass viewing, apart from a small shift away from variety and sport.

The way in which commercial television time is sold generates pressure for quantity of audience, rather than quality of audience appreciation. It has even been suggested that some advertisers prefer television programmes not to be too involving, for fear of detracting from the impact of their advertisements. This has been called the 'Let's-give-the-public-the-shows-they-*least*-like-so-they'll-watch-the-ads' theory.[8] The widespread use of video-recording machines has made research into the effects of advertising even more complex. Little is yet known about the extent to which the public uses this technology to avoid adverts. But it is assumed that 'spooling on' is a common habit.

The IBA attempted to offset the pressure for quantity of audience by circulating the companies with a weekly Audience Appreciation Index, which monitors the quality of audience response to individual programmes. This index has consistently shown that information programmes are more highly appreciated than those concerned with entertainment. There seems to be an inverse relationship between audience size and audience enjoyment.

However, it is doubtful whether this intervention had much influence on the time-buying decisions of advertisers, as no connection has yet been established between the audience's enjoyment or involvement in programmes, and their responsiveness to advertisements shown at the same time. The implications of audience appreciation research have only lately begun to be developed. It has been argued that within the two categories of information and entertainment programmes, those with large audiences tend to have higher appreciation scores than those with small audiences. Indeed some market researchers have come up with the less than remarkable finding that the more demanding a programme is, the better it has to be before people will watch it.[9]

The pressure on commercial television to maximize audiences naturally leads to a preference for 'entertainment' as opposed to 'serious' programmes. Within the broad category of entertainment there is a preference for programmes which have previously demonstrated their appeal to women and young people. Hence there is a bias against showing sport at some times of the day, as it mainly appeals to men. Commercial pressures have also led programme-makers to emphasize the personal and human interest aspects of documentary stories. Thus structural social problems are treated in the form of individual case studies. This kind of programme reaches a wider audience, particularly among women, than other documentary styles. The prominence given to certain types of programmes on commercial television is a direct consequence of the pressures generated by advertising for the production of certain types of audiences.

Advertising also generates a strong pressure for the television companies to produce predictable and regular audiences, as well as to maximize them. While the ratings for any particular programme may be hard to predict, because they depend so much on factors outside the control of any commercial company (in particular what the BBC is showing), viewing patterns over a year, as well as the categories and sequences of programmes, have been easy to predict.

Advertisers rely on programme schedules to produce the audiences which they pay for. This has encouraged attempts to use the sequence of programmes in order to manipulate the size of an audience over an evening. Consequently programmes with a broad audience appeal are shown early in the evening, in an attempt to capture viewing families for a particular channel for the rest of the night's programmes. Scheduling attempts to expand and consolidate the mass audience throughout the evening. It is this pressure which leads to the screening of 'minority' information programmes outside peak viewing times, and to the 'twinning' of BBC and ITV schedules for current affairs programmes. By doing this the companies may minimize choice, but they also minimize the loss of audience from programmes that get low ratings. In addition, current events programmes are thus seen by a far larger general audience than would otherwise be the case.

The proliferation of broadcasting channels which was so enthusiastically advocated by advertisers will, however, make many of these calculations increasingly insecure. Already the use of videos makes the assessment of impact of adverts more difficult. Accelerating fragmentation of the great national audiences previously enjoyed by the duopoly may provide, as some have argued, many new specialized concentrations of consumers, or it may provide nothing more than smaller, more unpredictable audiences. Indeed, the most enthusiastic advocates of 'deregulation', the advertisers, have begun to be anxious about the future effectiveness of advertising on TV at all.

Whatever happens, there is evidence that these commercial attempts to manipulate the audience are only partly successful. Goodhardt has argued that most families watch television sporadically. The 'inheritance factor' (or the likelihood of watching the programme that comes next) seems effective for only one programme, not the whole evening's viewing. Nor would it seem that people become loyal to a channel because they are addicts of particular series. Out of forty serials screened in the spring of one year only 54 per cent of people who saw one episode of any serial also saw the next. Most of the people watching the second half of the story were different from those who had seen its beginning.[10]

Nevertheless, the commercial companies necessarily continue to try and maximize their audiences. The pursuit of the largest possible audience is not in itself harmful. But if it is narrowly interpreted, it may lead to schedules that are cautious, conservative, and very rarely break established patterns.

The needs of all advertisers using commercial television are not the same. Some have sought more specialized groups within the mass audience, and the financial significance of this kind of advertising is growing. This is indicated by the growth of corporate advertising, in which giant companies are merely concerned to project an image of their activities rather than any specific product. In addition, there has been an increase in consumer durables and motor advertising. These categories have risen as a proportion of total tele-vision advertising expenditure from 7 per cent in 1968 to 30 per cent in 1988.[11] This has been accompanied by a fall in food, drink, and household advertis-ing directed at the mass market. Furthermore, there has been a growing tendency even among mass-market-oriented advertisers towards directing their campaigns at particular segments of the market.

The impact of this shift, however, has been muted by the difficulties involved in translating the aims of marketing strategies into buying television time. There have been fashions in market research which determine how the audience is offered to the advertiser. In the 1950s and 1960s motivational research was dominant. 'Beecham's buyers are a little more likely to strive, and are a little more neurotic,' stressed an Associated Rediffusion survey in 1962. 'Compared, that is with Aspro, Anadin and Disprin buyers, however, they are noticeably more extrovert.' Increasingly, though, there was a trend towards pilot studies of particular products and towards attempts to segment target markets with a fine precision.

However, despite attempts (by Leo Burnett and the British Bureau of Market Research in particular) to develop 'psychographic' profiles of televi-sion viewers, such methods remain impressionistic. No satisfactory method has been developed that enables advertising men or women to select time slots in a way that allows them to reach the types of personalities believed to be particularly susceptible to their advertising campaigns. Consequently com-mercial television companies have not been obliged to cater for particular groups (at least those defined by psychological categories) to any great extent.

Advertisers have been most interested in reaching 'light viewers', who are like the 'floating' voters in election studies. The success of a campaign may depend on the proportion of light viewers, who might not otherwise know about the product, that it can reach. For a time, light viewers were regarded as being particularly selective in their television watching habits. This was partly because a large proportion of light viewers were middle class, and were believed to be discriminating.

However, this view has now been challenged. Goodhardt has suggested that light viewers tend not to watch particular types of programmes, nor do they prefer low-rating minority programmes. They tend to be as unselective as heavy viewers, but merely watch less television. Hence support of minority programmes does not seem to be a means of reaching the light viewer. On the contrary, it appears that advertising on high-rating programmes represents the most efficient way of reaching light viewers. Another study suggests, furthermore, that the pursuit of light viewers is in itself misguided. What matters is not how many advertisements of a particular product are seen, but how many in relation to the number of advertisements of a competing product.[12] The light viewer sees less than the heavy viewer of *all* the competing products on television. It may, therefore, be better to reach him or her through other advertising media.

A further problem for the advertiser is that neither minority programmes nor particular *genres* of programmes can be relied on to deliver specialized audiences. Goodhardt's analysis of the housewife audience for twenty different categories of programme showed that only Westerns are positively sought out by any viewers. Westerns were the only kind of programme with a slightly higher level of 'duplication viewing' – that is the likelihood of a viewer seeing more than one programme within this category – than could be explained by channel loyalty or overall rating figures. Most people, Goodhardt's work suggests, see further programmes of any particular *genre* only because they prefer one channel, or because the programme has a high rating, not because they are specifically interested in its content. 'People who watched one arts programme', according to Goodhardt, 'had no more tendency to see another arts programme than to see, say, a Western or a religious programme, or a sports programme with a comparable weighting.'

This characterization of television audiences as indiscriminate and promiscuous in their viewing habits has been challenged. Sue Stoessel argued that the results of Goodhardt's research were misleading because they aggregated behaviour over several weeks. This obscured major changes in viewing behaviour from week to week. It is only by examining these detailed changes in viewing behaviour, she suggested, that preferences for individual programmes could be revealed. An analysis of changes in viewing figures over successive weeks reveals the effects of positive choice and preference, as does an analysis that distinguishes between audience behaviour in the different regions. In London, she argued, light viewers are more heavily concentrated among the audiences of some specific programme types. There are significant groups of viewers, at least in the London area, who do choose to watch programmes because of their content.[13]

This debate is likely to continue. The apparent failure of different categories of programmes to divide audiences into conveniently specialized groups has important implications. It may reduce the potential for commercial television to create new patterns of programmes. A low-rating current affairs programme has little to offer advertisers if it delivers, not a dis-criminating élite (like a 'quality' national newspaper), but large numbers of heavy viewers so hypnotized that they cannot even summon the energy to switch off the ballet or Third World poverty programme offered at the mar-gins of peak viewing times.

Indeed the audiences for specialized programmes do not necessarily share other characteristics which would make them marketable packages for sale to advertisers. A shared interest in Westerns does not imply, for instance, a propensity to trade in a new car each year or a tendency to be a young couple setting up home for the first time. On the other hand, if Stoessel is correct, there is a market for élite and quality advertising in television, but it may not be most efficiently reached through this medium.

Indeed in so far as advertising has promoted minority programming hith-erto, it has tended to be in a form that produces groups of viewers which are marketable. Travel programmes, and those about cars and cooking, have all developed partly because they cater for audiences with a shared interest in buying certain sorts of products. The advertising for cable and satellite television depends on the development of this commodity-based 'narrow-casting'. The greater choice of channels will, it is suggested, offer advertisers more refined groups of audience interest. However, those with less material interests in common have been, and will continue to be, less favoured.[14]

Public regulation and the public interest

In its time the IBA played an important role in mitigating the adverse effects of advertising on broadcasting. Nevertheless, at times the Authority was pas-sive. For example it was reluctant to ensure that companies adhered to the programme policies on which they won franchises. It was difficult for the Authority to be more active in its surveillance, partly because its statutory obligations were imprecise in many areas. However, political realities limited its power more fundamentally. The commercial television lobby is highly organized and politically effective. It employs public relations officers and cul-tivates an able group of MPs. In addition, many newspapers are sympathetic to the commercial television lobby. Its interests are also protected by an extensive network of contacts based on the interlocking directorships linking commercial television companies to other banking and industrial organiza-tions. In contrast, the IBA was less effectively organized as a political lobby, and its powers of supervision – which were inevitably the product of political negotiation – were consequently constrained. Finally, the IBA would be 'pun-ished' for its interventions into schedules or programme decisions. Thus, having been required to present more balanced programming over Christmas, the companies could retaliate by showing programmes which got only very low ratings.

However, the aims of the IBA were furthered by the presence of the BBC as a 'public service' institution, committed to broad social and political objectives rather than to the maximization of profit. There was in Britain a great convergence between public and commercial broadcasting in which the two systems influenced each other.

In addition, for much of its history commercial television was in a strong bargaining position in relation to advertisers. ITV was able in the past to resist some advertising pressure precisely because it was in a seller's market. Companies sold advertising time in ways which reduced the pressures to maximize audiences. The high profits and monopolistic position of commercial television created an environment in which the IBA could be more effective.

Swinging sixties and sober seventies

In the 1960s and 1970s television came of age. Since 1970 there has been a remarkable revolution not in the technology but in the content of broadcasting. In this period, television rapidly developed its own forms – in the treatment of politics, interviews, documentaries, and plays – which were quite different from the earlier styles of radio or film. During the 1960s television humour began to take the form of satirizing itself – an indication of how widely the conventions of the new medium had been publicly absorbed.

This was partly a product of a more generally liberal mood, which made a wider range of possibilities available for broadcasters. After Pilkington, the BBC became a more adventurous organization. At the same time, the independent television companies became more secure, because more profitable. By the 1960s, moreover, television had taken over from the cinema a mass working-class audience.

In many ways the vast size of the television audience has posed problems for the medium. There is a continual pressure to screen programmes that will attract the largest audiences and cause offence to the smallest numbers of viewers. Yet the attempt to reach a big audience while meeting 'public service' criteria has been a creative tension.

Some commentators, like Stuart Hood, Michael Tracey, Anthony Smith, and even Sir Hugh Greene, have seen the period since the early 1970s as one of increasing caution in television. Not only has the reporting of the troubles in Northern Ireland provided many problems for the broadcasting institutions, but also the BBC and ITV have become more vulnerable to government threats over a broad range of issues.

Channel 4, minorities, and money

Yet it was a reinterpretation of the public service principle which produced Channel 4. The ideas behind the creation of this new channel were a product of the tensions identified during television's most creative and expansionist years. But it was also influenced by the political problems of the period. However, by the time the station opened there had been a change not only in the general economic climate but also, more damagingly, in the conditions of competition for television audiences.

Channel 4 'publishes' programmes made by independent production companies. It does not make any programmes of its own, although it does commission them. Originally it was financed by the existing commercial companies who supplied much of its material. As it did not sell its own advertising time it was somewhat removed from the direct pressures experienced by the rest of the commercial sector. The 1990 Broadcasting Act changed this: the channel is now to be made more vulnerable to advertisers' interests. However, it is still obliged to screen programmes for the various 'minority' interests that are not well served elsewhere in the television system.

The minority-based rationale of Channel 4 had a number of origins. Perhaps the most important was the experience of even the most distinguished and 'marketable' producers and directors that it was impossible to work, in Britain, outside the BBC or ITV companies.[15] Those who wanted to make programmes that did not conveniently fit into the patterns of viewing developed by the duopoly, or those who simply wanted a greater control over their own material, found it difficult to raise the necessary finance or find buyers for what they made. It was argued that there evidently were audiences within the mass of viewers with more distinctive tastes and needs, but the existing channels allowed these consumers little opportunity to demonstrate their preferences. A new pattern of differently organized production companies, liberated from the limitations of the ITV or BBC systems, would be able to find and develop these more specialized audiences. Therefore any innovation in the television service ought to make it possible for 'independent' producers to explore the interests of these minorities.

It was also strongly argued that television had failed to reflect Britain's contemporary cultural diversity. Reformers emphasized the needs of the various Black and Asian communities, as well as those of minorities like the young and the old, for programmes which dealt with their concerns and ways of life. Any new service, it was suggested, should produce material for these social and ethnic minorities.

Finally, some market researchers believed that the blunt instrument of television advertising could, by the 1980s, be refined. A new channel could offer programme incentives that attracted discriminating 'minorities' of selective television viewers and could sell them the things they had particular interests in. For the first time television would be able to deliver higher concentrations of the more affluent consumers that advertisers wanted.

The logic of Channel 4 looked appealingly neat. It would offer greater freedom of choice, and serve minorities neglected elsewhere. Unfortunately the minorities that producers, social reformers, and advertisers were interested in were somewhat different.

Channel 4 represents an important (and perhaps the last) reinterpretation of the public service role of broadcasting. In this version, the freedom of creative individuals to risk making the programmes they want to make is seen as the guarantor of public good. It was a Labour government which decided to back the new channel (although a Conservative one presided over its birth). Labour support was based on a feeling that the political consensus developed by the existing broadcasting services was too restrictive. Consequently the channel was given the opportunity to create new conventions for dealing with controversial and political issues. It is not obliged to balance views within a programme, but only over the whole schedule and over time. It can, therefore, broadcast more clearly partisan material.

However, the channel's capacity to innovate depends on the politics of money. The only ultimate defence Channel 4 has for its new style and new programmes is their ability to attract advertising revenue. By the 1980s the Conservative government was using the success of Channel 4 to attack public service broadcasting, by demanding that greater numbers of programmes should be produced by 'independent' companies. Yet Channel 4's innovations had been completely dependent on the development of public service ideals.

In the late 1980s both the BBC and ITV companies were obliged to take an increasing proportion of their programmes from the 'independent' sector; by 1993 this is expected to account for 25 per cent of their output. This has led to the emergence of some culturally important and commercially successful companies – and of innovative programmes. 'The Media Show', the astutely topical series on Stalin, and many others were made by production companies outside the duopoly. However, whether such companies are actually independent, except in the formal sense, is dubious. A recent survey by the London Business School showed that they were all financially precarious with low profit margins.[16] People set up independent television companies because they want to make programmes – not because they want to make money. The study also showed how completely dependent these companies were on the patronage of the established channels. The new satellite companies were, as yet, hardly interested in their quality products.

The limitations of commercial broadcasting are largely the result of the economic pressures to which it is exposed. That British commercial television has been in some ways superior to others is due to the public service traditions and institutions that have so far determined its development. Nevertheless, the implications of a comment by Sidney Bernstein, the television industrialist, should always be borne in mind. 'Commercial television is a very unusual business,' he said, '. . . you don't necessarily make more money if you provide a better product.'

Yet the market and the audience for television programmes is altering dramatically under the impact of a whole series of technological changes. Whether the advantage of increased variety will be enough to offset the dilution of resources remains to be seen. Indeed this period may yet be regarded, in television terms, as a lost golden age.

Notes

1. Sir Robert Fraser, *ITA Notes* (October 1970).
2. P. Todd, 'Scarcity of TV time!', *Campaign* (26 January 1979).
3. *IBA Annual Report* (1978).
4. R. Thomson, *Contrast: Television Quarterly* (winter 1961), p. 107.
5. Associated Rediffusion, 'Cold and flu remedies', *Market Profiles*, 6 (1962).
6. F. Wolf, *Television Programming for News and Current Affairs* (New York, Praeger, 1972).
7. Sir Robert Fraser, *ITA Notes* (January 1970).
8. C.E. Setlow, 'TV Rating, there just might be a better way', *New York Times* (31 December 1978).
9. T. P. Barwise, A. S. C. Ehrenberg, and G. J. Goodhardt, 'Audience appreciation and audience size', *Journal of the Market Research Society*, 21, 4 (October 1979), p. 269.
10. G. J. Goodhardt, A. S. C. Ehrenberg, and M. A. Collins, *The Television Audience: Patterns of Viewing* (Farnborough, Saxon House, 1975).
11. Tables of advertising expenditure in *Admap*, No. 2, 1988.
12. A. Roberts and S. Prentice, 'Reaching light TV viewers', *Admap* (March 1979).
13. S. Stoessel, reply to Roberts and Price, 'The real weight of light viewers', *Admap* (June 1979), p. 277.
14. M. Johnson, 'Narrow-casting – problems and opportunities', *Admap* (June 1983).
15. See S. Lambert, *Channel 4* (London, British Film Institute, 1982).
16. *Independent Television Production: Finance and Dependency*, London Business School Report (Dec. 1989).

14

Video, cable, and satellite

Video, cable, and satellite technologies, and their attendant communication novelties – ways of transmitting entertainment, words, pictures, data, voices, and other services in huge variety, over vast distances, at ferocious speeds – have been discussed in such extravagant terms, and introduced with such little debate, that their wider social and economic implications have often been ignored. We are in danger of seeing emerging patterns as necessary, or even more dangerously as technologically determined, and accepting the consequences fatalistically.

Seventy-year-old audience habits have changed. The impact of these developments will go far beyond what people do with their leisure. There is also the likelihood of direct impact on political behaviour and institutions. Every previous innovation in communications, from the emergence of the mass circulation press through the development of radio and television, has profoundly altered not only how politics is understood in societies, but the nature of political negotiation itself. Such an immense set of changes as are now occurring will inevitably revolutionize political expectations, behaviour, and institutions. We, as yet, can only speculate about the likely effects: but they will clearly influence the future of democracy. Yet we have seen thirty years of speculation driving policy. Audience behaviour has proved more stable.

Experts have been divided between the neophiliacs and the cultural pessimists. Neophiliacs write of the disappearance of class (by which they mean that traditional types of work will be replaced), the disappearance of workplaces (as the work-bench is supplanted by the home computer terminal), and the eventual relocation of the production process to the developing world as the management of information (about production and consumption) becomes the key commodity in the technologically advanced economies.

Such predictions seem premature. Neophiliac arguments bring to mind an earlier debate about the arrival of the 'post-industrial' society. Comments by Anthony Smith and John Howkins belong to the same tradition as Daniel Bell and Alain Touraine,[1] who argued that the expansion of the service sector, increasing expenditure on the production of knowledge, and ever larger investment in research, together with changes in the technologies of production and leisure, were creating a new social order. *Plus ça change:* as Krishan Kumar has argued, similar developments become apparent early in the history of industrialization, and do not represent any qualitative change.[2] Many of the neophiliac predictions of future patterns are based on naïve extrapolation from current trends, and ignore the idiosyncrasies of historical development.

The pessimists, on the other hand, see changes in mass commercial culture as a subversion of 'standards'. In the discussion of broadcasting technologies, the new 'cultural' pessimists, such as Nick Garnham and Richard Collins, joined hands with the 'industrial' pessimists like Henry Braverman,[3] who shared concern over the impact of computer and information technology on employment. Thus broadcasting becomes the fulcrum of a wider social and economic upheaval. The pessimists see little evidence for the emergence of new cultural patterns and much evidence for the irreparable damage to old ones.

In practice this 'revolution' represents the continued industrialization of the service sector. New technology performs old tasks more efficiently: in particular the sorting, correlating, and ordering of information in bureaucracies. Many of the current problems in broadcasting policy concern the next stage: the domestication of the computer.

Indeed from both sides of the British political spectrum great, and perhaps unrealistic, hopes of industrial revival have been pinned on the exploitation of new communications technologies. On the one hand those on the left have argued that the provision of a national cable network is similar to the laying down of the other great service infrastructures of industrial society: water, rail, and road. It has been persuasively suggested that markets for goods and products increasingly exist not in physical space, but between those who are in contact via the networks of cable communication. Goods and services can be produced anywhere and to any specification with the complex exchange of data provided by cable facilities. It has thus been argued that the state should invest in a massive programme of cable provision in order to provoke a dramatic new regional and national economic revival. Advocates of this strategy point to the success of French governments' attempts to modernize communications. Using the notion of 'informatics', the French argued that access to, and understanding of, the most modern means of communication is part of being a contemporary citizen. Consequently, French policy makers have suggested that the state must educate the people and provide the means for the fullest possible public participation in this technology. The French government has also based its policy on the belief that the industrial possibilities of cable systems can only be developed if the technology is in the widest possible use. Thus in France there has been a typically 'dirigiste' development of cable and telephone services by the state, according to a clearly laid-down plan, with little room for liberal 'free market' principles.

However, those on the right have also been concerned to develop cable and computer services. Indeed, much recent broadcasting policy, as we shall see, has been directed at encouraging private, individual investment in cable and when this failed, it hoped to substitute satellite service. There has been no commitment in Britain to an extension of citizenship rights or knowledge. Indeed, the direction of broadcasting policy which it might be argued should always be considered along with education, has been to exaggerate the divisions between groups of people. British broadcasting policy was previously based on the concept that it had to make the same rights available to all audiences, citizens, voters. This is no longer the case. Increasingly policy is based on one right only: the 'right' to pay for extra services. Thus Conservative policy makers, while also emphasizing the importance of cable communication, have been prepared to reduce the access to information and services of most citizens in the belief that development could most efficiently be led by those who can pay for it.

There is also a key economic problem (a reflection of distinct patterns within the British economy) which influences policy decision within this area. The Conservative government during the 1980s, although it wished to encourage the private acquisition of cable television (so that the public would at least become a potential market for the other goods and services cable might offer), was also concerned, rather belatedly, with the provision of advanced communications to the financial and banking sector. So dominating was this interest in the British economy, that fulfilling its urgent needs for greatly expanded new information services became an overriding but unstated priority within government policy. Many of the decisions in this area were thus, covertly, determined by the perceived interests – or by the pressure exerted – by this sector of the economy.

The effects of the development of increasingly interdependent technologies of telephone, data, and broadcasting services have all, in England, been used to diminish the democratic access to these services. Thus, traditionally, heavy (business) telephone users subsidized lighter (domestic) subscribers' long-distance calls, which tended to be shorter and less frequent. As the costs of communication became an ever-more important item in commercial budgets, the pressure to reduce costs and to influence policy increased. Broadcasting policy too has been determined more by concerns to protect, for instance, the domestic electronics industry, than by an interest in the political and cultural obligations of broadcasting.

The problems posed by this kind of development are common to all countries. Few countries, however, have such strong broadcasting traditions as Britain, or have had such determined neophiliacs at the helm. When the Conservative government came to power in 1979 an official ideology of non-interference in the market was buttressed by a vigorously neophiliac view of information technology. A key Cabinet Information Technology Advisory Panel (ITAP), including experts in electronics and industrialists but nobody with any broadcasting experience, concluded that industrial revival was to be stimulated by 'cabling up' the nation. The necessary conditions for this economic miracle (a large proportion of homes linked to high-quality cable networks), it was argued, would best be created by providing an alluring range of television channels for the eager public. That these would inevitably offer a consistent diet of old films, sport, American soap opera, and light entertainment was regarded as incidental.

In 1982 the committee urged the adoption not of North American models, but of the most sophisticated cabling system that would permit households to receive and use several hundred different channels. Thus the nation would be lured into the new infrastructure by stealth: having paid for cabling in order to receive more entertainment, television users would find themselves linked conveniently to a variety of multipurpose networks with opportunities for computerized shopping, working, and learning. 'It is as if', one commentator suggested, 'the Roman Senate had sanctioned, without debate, the proposition that improvements to the supply system of the Roman legions should first be introduced by speeding up the chariots in the hippodrome.'[4]

So solid was the expectation of a virtually insatiable appetite for television, that official calculations have been based on the assumption that the technological leap forward could be accomplished without support from public funds. Britain was the only country in Europe which expected the entire capital cost of laying a cable system to be paid for by the sellers and consumers of the recycled programmes and films. In West Germany, France, and Japan, state investment in a comprehensive cable system has become a major, and expanding, element in the annual budgets.

Apart from the problem of initial finance, there are other grounds for wondering whether neophiliac hopes are not premature. Thus in the USA – where the success of cable had been seen as providing a model for Britain – the cable revolution seems to be failing, or at least stabilizing. In the last half of the 1980s more cable stations closed in the USA than opened.

Indeed, popular programmes aimed at mass audiences, supposedly the basis of cable expansion, have failed to find adequate markets. So far where cable has succeeded commercially there has been a price. In 1995 the most profitable American cable network offered its viewers a 'choice' of twenty movies repeated on a monthly basis.[5] The pressure of real or supposed mass taste has been inexorable: even in Manhattan, with its sophisticated viewers, CBS was forced to end the brief experiment of providing one quality station. Multi-channel television has since then taken off. In America pornography has been defined an issue of freedom of speech – and consequently given the protection of the Constitution in New York. One quarter of cable stations now offer pornography.

Indeed, in Britain there is an additional factor, more powerful than in the USA: video. The proportion of video-owning homes is already twice as great in Britain as in the USA and, despite the recession, video ownership continues to grow faster in Britain than in any other European countries. By 1995 most families possessed a video: a development not taken into account by official calculations earlier. Satellite television services, launched with immense publicity, have still to attract large audiences or make big profits. Unconstrained by the public service obligations, the first, Sky Television, owned by Rupert Murdoch, provided four channels pitched relentlessly at the supposedly popular tabloid market: a children's channel which offered nothing but cartoons, a film channel (for which, in addition to a dish, you have to buy a decoder), and two other channels showing replicas of exhausted formula programmes, mostly presented by familiar formula faces. This service so far has hardly added to the 'choice' the sovereign consumer could indulge in. Indeed, by buying up sports events it clearly diminishes public choice. So far, cable and satellite services have yet to be really successful here. In addition to these satellite services Channel 5 was launched with radically simplified programme formats in 1997. These changes mean that the behaviour of the television audience as well as television production values and finance are bound to alter. Nevertheless, there is evidence that in the battle for public viewing hours, these new 'viewing' opportunities face a more formidable task than had been expected. Certainly in Britain there had been no cable 'revolution' by the start of the 1990s,[6] nor was a post-industrial society much in evidence.

The end of public service broadcasting?

Certainly satellite, cable, and video in combination will accelerate the decline in audiences for existing networks: more viewing opportunities will mean fewer viewing hours. One change is a move away from 'family viewing'. Evidence from satellite television showed that rather than arguing about what to watch together, family members were separating to watch different programmes. Thus apparently while fathers watch sport (in the sitting room), mothers are now relegated to viewing soap operas in the kitchen, while teenagers consume pop video channels in their bedrooms.[7] The take-up of satellite and video demonstrates that the public is willing to spend a higher proportion of its disposable income on entertainment, but this fragmentation of the audience has barely been explored by advertisers and its wider social implications have, as yet, hardly been considered. As ratings fall financing programme content becomes more difficult. The range of quality programmes and perhaps even the possibility of innovative broadcasting may still be a victim. The public service ideal depends for its realization on funding. In the new hyper-competitive climate, even advertisers, who had been so clamorous in their demands for more advertising time, were becoming anxious about the likely *over-supply* of time. As the White Paper on the Development of Cable Systems and Services pointed out, one hour of home-grown documentary could cost £20,000. By contrast, an hour of American soap opera could be bought for as little as £2000. One possibility therefore is a trend similar to that in the cinema of the 1940s and 1950s: fewer programmes made in Britain, and an ever-expanding proportion of imports.

Here Thatcherite market liberalism had particularly disastrous effects. With the abolition of quotas for foreign programmes, there was little to restrain cable and satellite stations from importing much and commissioning little. With no rules to enforce a balanced diet of programming, the new stations naturally turned, like their American counterparts, to the lowest common denominator of pop, chat, soap, and sport. Perhaps the wider range of viewing which satellite, cable, and video provide will lead to an imaginative exercise by viewers of 'freedom of choice'. Existing evidence, however, suggests the opposite: audiences will not have the freedom to consume anything other than an even greater concentration of pop, chat, soap, and sport than now.

If this analysis is correct, a shift of power within the networks is likely to follow. Where broadcasting is protected through subsidy, monopoly, or legislative requirements, producers can be given their head; where commercial pressures necessitate a heavy reliance on imported package deals and low-budget formula programming, producers will be reduced, in effect, to corporation men: executives carrying out company policy. With less money available, making fewer 'original' programmes, initiative will be at a low premium. In particular, there may be less incentive to make programmes about British subjects, political, social, or cultural, purely for domestic consumption. Indeed, it is ironic that much of the privately commissioned research for the satellite stations has shown just how wise the consumer is, and how badly served by neo-liberal belief in market forces. The public have found the existing satellite services repetitive, limited, and based on all too familiar styles and formats. They also recognize that the BBC, ITV, and Channel 4 offer a greater variety of programmes, and of course they still continue to watch far more of these than the satellite stations, albeit increasingly to their own schedules on video. Even in homes with high satellite or cable use, terrestrial television programmes are still key.

Some people do, of course, have specialist interests which satellite channels may serve. Nevertheless, so far the public remain more discriminating as a body of viewers than as newspaper readers. Yet, it seems oblivious to the likely disappearance of the services it values most. Under the current regime, market forces, not consumer interests, will come to determine programme making.

There is a further danger or at least an area of uncertainty. Until recently the economics of television was determined by an invariable: people bought television sets to watch programmes put out by the networks. The relationship between programme-maker and viewer, through the medium of a single-purpose instrument, and the role of public policy in regulating programme content, were based on this simple truth. The old relationship is rapidly weakening and soon will hold no more. Watching 'live' programmes ('live' in the sense of received from the ether) is already only one of the purposes of a television set. When it becomes increasingly common to use television not only for video, but also to make hotel reservations, monitor electricity consumption, and place bets, 'live' viewing may become a comparatively minor factor in the calculations of those who buy, sell, and produce television sets, with inevitable consequences for those who make programmes as well. At the same time, computers now offer broadcasting. The internet offers many services – the mix is altering. At the same time, the obligations of public policy become more difficult to define when the 'content' of television is no longer so evidently a single 'cultural' product.

Politics and new technology

There will also be consequences for politicians and political parties. Broadcasting, and especially television, has been a vehicle of political integration, establishing what Denis McQuail has called the 'common coin of values, ideas, information and cultural expression'. Arguably television has set the political agenda: ordering public priorities and arousing public concern for good or ill.

Key to this process has been the national audience. The power of television has been based to a considerable degree on lack of choice: almost any nationally networked programme is certain to count its viewers in millions. Cable, video, and satellite have increased the range of 'choice' without necessarily increasing variety or quality of subject matter (perhaps, as has been argued, reducing it). It was argued in the 1990s that a larger number of highly competitive commercial stations would fragment: the national audience would vanish. In fact, broadcasting still assembles national audiences around great events, and 'terrestrial' or national broadcasting has held on to much larger audiences than predicted. Indeed, we still need to avoid premature judgement. Such changes might have beneficial results or bad ones. Given the centrality of broadcasting to modern politics, however, it is virtually certain to alter the nature of the political game. Already some effects of increased 'choice' on political culture can be seen. The recent proliferation of quality newspapers has nevertheless lessened the impact of each. In the long run, this diminished authority will undoubtedly influence both the role and the standard of these newspapers. A similar process is taking place with television: the fragmentation of the national audience means that the significance of any one programme or channel may be greatly reduced in the future. It is important not to be confused here. It is not being suggested that the media will have less effect: just that their effects will be different.

These effects, however, remain speculative. Will national coverage be reduced in importance relative to local issues? Such a development might be positive. It might provide citizens with greater awareness of what affects them directly, and give more scope to local campaigns and pressure groups. On the other hand, the example of the existing local press gives little ground for optimism. Lack of initiative, cost, and the fear of writs have discouraged the vast majority of newspapers, including the big-circulation regional dailies, from acting as anything more than publishing houses for politicians' handouts.

If, therefore, a diversity of local television stations produces an increase in local political reporting, the benefits remain uncertain. What does seem likely is that the present 'privileged' status of news and documentary, which has been a prominent feature of public service television, will be eroded even further. Political coverage at least held its own as inter-channel competition increased: between 1956 and 1976 the time devoted to politics quadrupled on average. Channel 4 increased the variety and range of political programmes. But this trend began to be reversed in the late 1980s. During the 1992 general election, campaign coverage on the two major channels (BBC1 and ITV) was restricted to little more than a series of interviews with leading personalities: examination of campaign issues was relegated to BBC2 and Channel 4. Cable stations with small budgets and instant commercial targets are scarcely likely to widen the range or deepen the level of discussion. Indeed, for all its failings, television coverage of politics in Britain has been serious and sustained. As Scannell has argued, broadcast politics has widened access to political processes. Indeed, it may be argued that political programmes with the depth of reporting of the quality press (though with its definition of the limits of political discussion) are served out, for largely historical reasons to do with the public service origins of the BBC, to a *Sun-* and *Star*-buying public. Much recent research in the UK and the USA has shown the decline in time given to news, a fall in public interest in it – and especially, a marked decline in the provision of foreign news.[8] It seems likely that the commercial pressures of cable and video may ensure that, instead of deriving political information from television, large numbers of people will, in effect, be deprived of any reliable political information at all.

Even if there is no reduction in the time allotted to current affairs and documentary programmes, cuts in budgeting are bound to have a deleterious effect on quality and, in particular, originality. National and international reporting all too easily becomes a collaborative exposure of the viewpoint of the spokesman for a particular interest, provided that the interest in question has Establishment approval. The reason is cost as much as bias: investigative journalism, digging beneath the surface and asking uncomfortable questions, involves more time, resources, and financial risk. Here competitive pressures are likely to be the enemy of imagination, professionalism, and above all, that which is controversial and radical.

Censorship

Some political effects of the new technology are speculative. Others are already frighteningly apparent. One development in the second category is the closing of doors which many had regarded as permanently unlocked: the reimposition of censorship in a new form, made the more dangerous because it is occurring in response to a public mood that owes much to fear of the new technology itself.

While dismantling 'public service' standards in broadcasting, and claiming to liberalize and free the system, the Thatcher government in fact presided over the introduction of an accumulation of supervisory quangos to control videos, satellite, cable, and terrestrial broadcasting. All are concerned primarily with the exclusion of 'offensive' imagery. The movement started with the video recording bill. This introduced a system of bureaucratic pre-censorship of a kind unprecedented since Oliver Cromwell's 'licences of the press'. Ostensibly it was concerned with pornographic and violent home videos dubbed by the press as 'video nasties'. In practice the implications have been wider. The legislation set aside the earlier 'interpretative' view of screen images, held by the British Board of Film Censors (BBFC). This view was concerned with evaluating the meaning and intention of scenes, and emphasized that it was in context that any given act had to be judged. This view was replaced, in effect, with an index of prohibited acts. All videos have to be submitted to the board, and may be liable for censorship if they contain any material which deals with 'human sexual activity', 'images of human sexual organs' (potentially even if the films are made as part of training programmes for medical staff), or 'mutilation, torture, or other acts of gross violence' (like scenes of war and sporting events). Defence on the grounds of artistic or literary merit has been increasingly set aside.

Film censorship has a long and in some respects a hilarious history. The BBFC, however, had come to see its role as one of 'leading public taste as much as curbing it'. More recently, its board of nominees, for the first time directly appointed by the Home Office, have tended to apply specific standards of permissible and non-permissible sexual or violent acts. This style of regulation has come increasingly to determine considerations in all the other regulatory bodies. Thus there has been a decisive shift in public policy towards the media: away from the encouragement of the good towards the deletion of what government-appointed committees regard with distaste.

Perhaps the availability of unpleasant material to the public, especially young people, will be reduced by all these supervisory bodies. However, the history of censorship in general reveals little evidence of a beneficial effect on public morality or mental health. But whatever the possible benefits, the dangers of illiberalism are manifest: thus, for example, coverage of wars, deliberately and rightly intended to shock, may well be restricted.

Conclusion

Should we, therefore, side firmly with the cultural pessimists against the neophiliacs? The answer is that much depends on the behaviour of broadcasters and programme-makers and, more particularly, governments, in the face of technological advance. Both neophiliacs and cultural pessimists emphasize the *power* of new technologies. Machines and inventions are not inherently powerful, nor is the use to which they are put inevitable. While the new technology brings with it many dangers, as well as many opportunities, its impact will depend crucially on how it is managed. We have now been through two episodes of technological brinkmanship, in which serious discussion has been stiffled. All too often policy has been driven more by phantasy than realism. It has led to over-hyped and then over-extended telecommunications and IT industries.

Notes

1. See, for example, A. Smith 'The fading of an industrial age', in J. Curran, H. Smith, and P. Wingate (eds) *Impacts and Influences* (London, Routledge, 1987).
2. K. Kumar, *Prophecy and Progress* (Harmondsworth, Penguin, 1978).
3. See, for example, R. Collins, N. Garnham and G. Locksley, *The Economics of Television* (London, Croom Helm, 1987).
4. *Parliamentary Information Review*, No. 2, Cable and Services (June 1988).
5. New York Cable Stations, 'Cable Digest: the Future of Film Channels', No. 3, (November 1995).
6. In societies where the state was prepared to take a more 'dirigiste' role, like France and West Germany, the revolution was more advanced. See, for instance, G. Nowell Smith, *The European Experience* (London, British Film Institute, 1989); or Nick Costello, 'Telecommunication and cable in France, America and the UK', *European Commission Special Paper*, No. 3 (Jan. 1990).
7. MORI/NOP survey, *Satellite Television and Family Viewing* (Jan. 1990).
8. See Steven Barnett, 'A small iceberg travelling south', report for the ITC, on Broadcast news, 2001.

15

Broadcasting roller-coaster

For most of the BBC's existence, the principle of 'public service' embodied in the 1926 Charter had not been the special preserve of the Corporation. Indeed, the idea that some organizations should operate for the public good and at the public expense was shared by all political parties, as well as the leaders of private industry and commerce, and ordinary voters. In the 1980s, however, the idea was strongly challenged for the first time. For broadcasters who had taken 'public service' for granted, life suddenly became uncomfortable.

One problem was the issue of political independence. Institutions like the BBC, whose *raison d'être* included the principle of impartiality, are never at ease with very ideological governments. Their distress becomes acute when there is only one party in office for a protracted period. In the case of public service broadcasting it needs the threat of potential opposition power, as a sabre to rattle warningly at governments. Yet, as the Conservative Party won one election after another from 1979 onwards, British politics became increasingly one-party rule. Indeed, the emergence of a coherent, highly ideological project for the transformation of British politics and society after 1982 put the BBC even more under threat.

The new Thatcherite project was highly individualistic: it argued that public interest could only be secured by maximizing the capacity of individuals to choose; and that government should seek to abandon controls, not exercise them. 'Deregulating', however, often had an ironic effect: a policy supposed to get government off people's backs often turned out, in practice, to be highly centralizing. Frequently, fiercely *dirigiste* measures of deregulation became instruments for delegitimizing, eradicating, and diminishing any institution or organization that had alternative views. In addition, the project could be a politicizing one. The fashionable neo-liberal creed often ignored cultural constraints: like scientific socialism in a different era, it was over-rational.

'The New Right', as John Gray points out, 'failed to perceive the dependence of individualistic civil society on a dwindling but real patrimony of common ideas, beliefs and values.' In other words, the possibility of extreme individualism depended on the cultural, educational structures that formed active, independently minded individuals. Public service broadcasting had been founded precisely to shore up and improve the common store of ideas, values, and knowledge. Thus, the story of public service broadcasting in the 1980s and 1990s had a far wider resonance than the question of whether people watch one chat show or another. It is a story of whether a plurality of voices can survive – and at what cost – in monolithic times.

Of course, the BBC and all responsible broadcasters always are, always have been, and always will be, worried about how to deal with politicians. The problem is that recently, handling politicians has become more important than making programmes, thinking of new programmes, relating creatively to audiences, or expressing what is going on within the nation. On the other hand, only if broadcasters abandon trying to provide a comprehensive and objective schedule, and opt instead for entertainment, will the pressures cease.

In turn, all politicians seek to influence, cajole, bully, manipulate, and prejudice, if they can, how broadcasters deal with their affairs. Broadcasting is far too important to them for seemly good manners. Indeed, consideration of how the media will react is playing a larger part in political calculation than before. Policy, not just its presentation, is increasingly tuned to media reaction – despite, or perhaps because of, the declining capacity of media news organizations to interpret and process sophisticated news. In a sense, nobbling the media, however you do it, is just politics.

However, what marked out the 1980s was that political pressure assumed a new form. For the very first time since British broadcasting started in 1926, the issue became not merely what the BBC did, but whether it would survive at all. Indeed, to some members of the Conservative government, the BBC as an institution, and public service as an ideal, began to be seen as key obstacles to its attempt to revolutionize how Britain was run, and its ways of thinking. Public service was seen as the inefficient self-serving camouflage of groups who wanted to protect their own interests from the correcting force of competition. Mrs Thatcher put the case inimitably in her memoirs: 'Broadcasting was one of those areas – the professions, such as teaching, medicine and the law were others – in which special pleading by powerful interest groups was disguised as high minded commitment to some common good.'[1]

Regarding the BBC as an irritatingly arrogant, cosily protected establishment dinosaur, Thatcherites marked it down for eradication in the radical right cultural revolution. At first, Mrs Thatcher merely sought to harness two quite contradictory pressures to cure the BBC of the tendencies she objected to. The first consisted of the self-appointed moral regulators, such as Mrs Whitehouse's Viewers' and Listeners' Association, with vociferous support in the middlebrow press, who argued that television was to blame for a decline in morals in the country. Public service broadcasters, the Prime Minister put it, rephrasing the words of Adam Smith, 'were claiming the rights of poetry, but providing us with a push pin'. The second consisted of the commercial interests of her most influential supporters in the press, particularly those of Rupert Murdoch (whose name and organization significantly received no mention in her memoirs). Murdoch was interested in the profits that could be made if British television was 'deregulated'. This would make it easier for his present or future chances to succeed. As his deal with Tony Blair and the Labour party showed in the run-up to the 1997 election Murdoch liked to extract maximum commercial interest from his newspapers' political power. Mrs Thatcher, however, argued that increasing competition would lead to an improvement, 'raising' standards of taste and decency. This was an odd position, because everywhere else unregulated competition had tabloidized, coarsened, and vulgarized broadcasting. Indeed, the Premiere showed a touching faith in Murdoch's capacity to raise standards – his previous contribution to halting moral decline having been the relaunch of the *Sun*.

Mrs Thatcher never saw much television, except when she was on it. However, her husband, who watched a lot, was widely reported to have given her daily resumés of its iniquities. But broadcasting happens to be almost the only industry which politicians ever see much of at work, as they slip in and out of studios. During Mrs Thatcher's premiership, College Green, a windswept triangle of grass with good shots of the Houses of Parliament behind it, virtually became part of the British, as yet unwritten constitution. College Green, and Millbank next to it, where the television stations broadcast much of their political reporting, increasingly took over from Parliament itself as the most critical area of public life, especially at times of crisis, the place where politicians hunt for attention, and journalists hunt for someone with an angle. Mrs Thatcher's observation of the television industry at work, 'too many men, too much waste!' fuelled her conviction that television embodied the hydra-headed enemy of British laxity: archaic union practices that preserved unnecessary jobs, and smug management. In contrast, print journalism caused the Conservative government few problems in the 1980s. In her first term of office, the Prime Minister gave knighthoods to the editors of the *Sun*, *Sunday Express*, and *Daily Mail*. In return, these and other newspapers softened their criticism of the government and concentrated their attacks on its enemies – a novel interpretation of the duties of the Fourth Estate. One minister asked Mrs Thatcher about her favourable press, and she replied guilelessly, 'That's because I've been so kind to them.'[2] She did not think broadcasters treated her fairly, nor did she set out to be nice to them.

However, there were many other aspects of broadcasting that increased tension between broadcasters and politicians during the 1980s. The Prime Minister was angered by the sceptical ways in which some broadcasters dealt with her, and she believed they were promoting an out-of-date view of the contemporary world. Bernard Ingham, her abrasive No. 10 Press Secretary, called them (the broadcasters) – the Dimblebys and Elsteins – the unelected princelings of broadcasting. Less personally, but more provocatively, in practice, public service broadcasting was not merely any one organization – it was the product of a regulated market. In the regulated market the worst economic pressures to produce the cheapest programmes for the most viewers can be counterbalanced by the requirements to be impartial, to inform, to entertain and to educate, to match the audience share of the competition, and to secure licences to broadcast. Yet the guiding idea of the 1980s, and one that has survived Mrs Thatcher's departure, was that any market regulation impeded the proper outcome of market choice. The more sophisticated interpretation of choice, according to which regulation provides a wider variety of programmes for a wider variety of audiences, was anathema to governments for whom deregulation, privatization, and the efficacy of market choice were the main instruments of reform and which had become, by the 1990s, ends in themselves. Thus the very basis of public service broadcasting made it peculiarly vulnerable to government attention.

However, it was inevitably politics that most inflamed the relationship. Sweeping government denunciations of the BBC's left-wing bias, and of alleged misreporting, and allegations against journalists, became routine. Individual presenters, television executives, journalists, particular items, and whole strands of coverage were targeted. The cumulative effects of such intimidation were profound. 'If the television of the western world uses its freedom continually to show all that is worst in our society', said Mrs Thatcher after the reporting of the riots of 1981, 'How can the uncommitted judge?'[3] As Hugo Young, in his biography of Mrs Thatcher, *One of Us*, argued: 'The less formal, but no less purposeful attacks, led by Mrs. Thatcher herself, on the BBC and other television broadcasters who threatened to loosen ministers' control over the agenda of the nation were ferocious.'

The Prime Minister's determination to reform broadcasting was given an added twist by the political challenges her government faced. First, she regard much of the BBC's reporting of the Falklands War (particularly the use, on news broadcasts, of the term 'the British troops', rather than 'our troops') as almost treasonable. She was incensed by a 1983 election phone-in which included tough questions by members of the public – as she wrote 'put up, not properly edited out' – about the conduct of the war, especially the sinking of the *Belgrano* (an Argentinian cruiser, sunk controversially, within the exclusion zone around the Falklands, while it was apparently attempting to leave the area). Above all there was the reporting of Northern Ireland.

Brian Wenham, an influential BBC programme maker and bureaucrat, contemplating the evidence about one programme, *Real Lives*, which caused an early prime-ministerial explosion, later observed that 'It was usually Ireland, it was usually the BBC, it was usually a row bigger, with more heads rolling, than you'd ever think possible.'[4] Eddie Mirzeoff, a senior BBC producer, talked about the pervasive self-censorship to which the rows led: 'the cost was always in programmes we did not make, ideas we dare not have.'

Certainly, the government's reaction to the BBC's handling of Northern

Ireland was a major factor in the growing sense of panic within the BBC during the 1980s. It was in part a battle about unspecified constitutional rights. The BBC claimed, on the basis of its obligation to be impartial and to inform, the right to include Sinn Fein, the protestant extremists, and sometimes the IRA, as voices that needed to be heard, while the government claimed the political right to exclude from the BBC voices which they thought had to change in order to win a right to a voice. The government always interpreted exposure as endorsement. 'Publicity', said Mrs Thatcher famously, 'is the oxygen of terrorism.'

Mrs Thatcher often gave the impression that broadcasters existed to support her, correct, views. If they gave airtime to other points of view they were, in effect, opposing her. As she had been elected and they had not, her views were legitimate, those of others were not. Impartiality – even over as intractable and complex an issue as Northern Ireland – was seen as a mischievous disguise for disloyalty. Time and again, broadcasters offended her over their handling of the issue: indeed, they were bound to. Mrs Thatcher's feelings on this issue need exploring, for they ran high. That they did so was understandable. Shortly after she was elected, the MP Airey Neave, a close friend and confidant since Mrs Thatcher had been an aspiring, unmarried young lawyer in the 1940s, was blown up by the INLA, a splinter faction of the IRA. The BBC screened an interview with an INLA representative, who triumphantly boasted of the achievement. Many found the interview offensive, but revealing. Mrs Thatcher, mistakenly, saw it as support for INLA views. Later, in 1984, she and her husband survived an IRA bomb in the hotel in Brighton where she was staying for the Conservative Party Conference. Perhaps not surprisingly, an intolerance of argument over Northern Ireland ossified into a narrow-minded zeal. Many observed that the bombing had profoundly changed her.

Thereafter, almost any television reporting in this area seemed to add to her fury. A number of incidents were interpreted as further evidence of subversion. There was the initial refusal of the BBC to hand over its film of the terrible mob lynching of two plain clothes policemen; there were interviews with members of the IRA; there were attempts to include IRA and protestant community political representatives in studio discussions; there were conflicts over a series of programmes – *Real Lives*, *A Question of Ulster*, *Death on the Rock* – which increased tension between broadcasters and politicians. After the Prime Minister had seen, and been enraged by, *Real Lives*, a programme which showed the 'everyday' lives and families of a Protestant and a Sinn Fein extremist, the Broadcasting Ban was imposed. This meant that when members of terrorist groups appeared on television, their voices could not be heard and actors had to read their words. This ban did nothing to reduce public interest in paramilitary personalities. It did, however, constitute a humiliation to the public service broadcasters, as it was little more than a visible badge of government power. It also meant that television executives did not make programmes about Northern Ireland if they could help it. However, the long-running Ulster saga did not go away, and its existence meant that government hostility to public service broadcasting continued to be underpinned by the Prime Minister's fierce passion about the issue.

In addition to this, the war on the 'complacent' public service tradition was ardently supported by a range of newspapers. The *News of the World* called the BBC 'The Boring Bonkers Corporation', The *Mail* said it was '(utterly) Biased (morally) Bankrupt and (politically) Corrupt'. The lead, however, in BBC bashing was provided by the *Sun, The Times* and the *Sunday Times,* shock troops of Thatcherism in its Maoist phase. The *Sun* described the BBC on one day as being 'Boring Old Auntie', and on the very next day accused it of 'Sleaze and Sluttery'. Broadcasting was attacked for loose morals, extravagance, fifth columnism and offending against public taste. *The Times,* for the first time since the Abdication crisis, ran editorials on three consecutive days to the same theme: the inadequacy of the BBC. However, as newspapers, unlike MPs, are not required to declare an interest, none of these scions of Murdoch's News International felt called upon to mention that their proprietor happened to have growing ambitions for his satellite television stations. In every sphere, from the domestic British to the international market, the BBC and the BBC's World Service, and more gen-erally the constraints of public service programming, with its emphasis on programme diversity and impartiality, stood in the way of News International. And indeed, anyone who stood in the way of the party most likely to deliver policies friendly to News International was also an enemy. As William Shawcross shows in his biography, Rupert Murdoch has little or no interest in news or programming, and while he routinely 'asset strips' news rooms, he has seldom invested in media content. His interest in politics tended to reflect the needs of his businesses: beyond that he was apolitical. Thus the News International campaigns against the existing broadcasting arrangements increased in parallel with the Corporation's interest in satellite. The *Sun's* shrill demand that 'Aunty Must Go' was a pragmatic piece of commercial lobbying.

As if this fetid brew of political and economic hostility were not enough to seal the fate of the BBC, technological and social developments in satellite and cable broadcasting would have meant that any administration would have had to consider how to handle changes to what had been a relatively stable competition which had developed between ITV and the BBC over thirty years. Whatever happened, the 'du-opoly' of public service broadcast-ers would have been bound to face considerable competitive challenge for audiences by the end of the decade. The adjustment, the possibilities, the role of 'public service' advantages in these changes were not inevitable. Different policies would have different outcomes, but a period of rapid and potentially difficult change was unavoidable.

Moreover, the era of public service broadcasting also seemed to have passed throughout the world. In many countries it appeared that 'public ser-vice' channels, of varying strengths and success, were being obliged to take on advertising, faced rapidly declining audience shares, and suffered a loss of authority. Even in sympathetic political climates, like those of Scandinavia and the old Commonwealth, public service broadcasters found it difficult to maintain distinctive broadcasting values. The sense of a regulated diet of programmes, even the sense of a scheduled progression of programmes and predictable audiences, looked as if it might fray or even disappear once the public had a larger choice of channels to choose from, and more things to do with their television sets.

All over the world in the 1980s, public service channels were being deregulated and as a result saw their audiences collapse. Some even began to suggest that in any case the heyday of television had passed. The very peculiar capacity of the medium to assemble, address, and touch the emotions of huge national audiences simultaneously seemed to be disappearing. Television had become one component of a huge entertainment industry that now included music, films, videos, and the rapidly expanding computer market. Commentators began to suggest that television had lost its dominating cultural role. However, most people continued to watch television regularly. It was perhaps more accurate to say it was the power of the television corporations, the programmes, and schedules which were changing.

Thus the alliance of political and commercial interests, arraigned against public service broadcasting in the mid-1980s, looked overwhelming. The radical ideas of right-wing think-tanks such as the Institute of Economic Affairs and the Adam Smith Institute, criticized for their extremism and impracticability in the early part of the decade, seemed positively mainstream and cautious later. In particular, they advocated the break-up of the BBC, the superiority of advertising revenue over licensing revenue, and the benefit of consumer 'choice' through increased channel availability. They argued that regulation was unnecessary, and praised the role of auctions in allocating commercial broadcasting licences. It was not just that the political climate had changed; everything that had previously been a source of protection for public service broadcasting suddenly made it vulnerable. The BBC was, as the decade progressed, under sustained commercial and political threat as never before.

Government attacks

How did the government go about 'dealing with the problem of the BBC' – the issue that Mrs Thatcher was so determined to address? The first line of attack was political. Part of the 'consensus' that Mrs Thatcher's administration set out to change was the idea that appointments to public bodies, such as the BBC's Board of Governors, should be more or less bipartisan. Prime ministers and home secretaries had, of course, liked to exercise choice in these appointments in the past. Thus, Harold Wilson had appointed the ITV Chairman, Charles Hill, as BBC Chairman in 1971 to bring the Corporation to heel. However, even Hill could not be regarded as a party political placement; he had been a Conservative, not a Labour minister.

The Conservative government believed that such delicacy on such a point was unnecessary, and indeed inefficient. If the BBC was to be encouraged to be friendly towards the government's project, you needed to be sure of the loyalty of those who ran it. Hence, during the 1980s, appointments to the BBC's Board of Governors became increasingly politicized. Qualified but unsympathetic candidates were not appointed, while ill qualified ones were – a process of committee management which indeed applied to many other public bodies as well. Hugo Young in his biography of Mrs Thatcher quotes a colleague: 'Margaret usually asked "Is he one of us?" before approving an appointment.' It was the appointment of sympathetic chairmen of the Governors that gave the government its real power over the BBC. The first Chairman appointed by the new administration was Stuart Young who happened to be the brother of a Conservative government minister. However, he showed signs of going native on the BBC. His successor, Marmaduke Hussey, was made of sterner stuff. Hussey, an ebullient Second World War veteran, had no background in broadcasting, had come straight from being the Chairman of Times Newspapers, where his confrontation with the unions had helped to change Fleet Street, but had also led to the paper being closed for a year. One of his qualifications may have been that he had worked for Murdoch and, in a sense, was unlikely therefore to cause Murdoch problems. A charming, forceful man, he saw his Chairmanship as a full-time job to 'sort out the BBC'. Over the next decade, he oversaw all the major changes in the Corporation, brutally dismissed one director general, shabbily pushed aside the next, and appointed the third, John Birt, without even advertising the job, or considering other candidates. Coming from newspapers, he treated the BBC, one critic remarked, 'rather as if he had owned it'. He was treated with a fearful deference by the Corporation until the end of his reign.

Hussey's influence was supposedly balanced by that of his deputy Lord Joel Barnet, a former Labour Treasury Minister who also chose to work at the BBC on a full-time basis. Barnet, however, accepted much of the Hussey diagnosis, and once even acknowledged that he did not, in practice, represent any difference in view from Hussey. Meanwhile, the Board of Governors, one critic commented, came to represent 'an unfortunate combination of low calibre and high prejudice'.

Of course, the 'packing' of boards, and in turn the administration of increasingly large tracts of contemporary life by committees and quangos rather than by elected government had been an article of faith of the Conservative reforms. One argument was that there should be a move from 'representative' boards of directors, chosen because, however loosely, they stood for specific interests (in the BBC this might mean the regions, or writers, or women or educators) to so-called 'corporate boards', where individuals were selected on their merits. Well managed, this could be a useful development. In practice, however, it was taken to mean that members should be chosen for their adherence to an agenda. Indeed, against a background of mounting unease about the impact of some of these ideas on the quality of services, in 1994 the Nolan Committee on Standards in Public Life was asked to address the problem of whether the perceived bias in public appointments was a media-induced mirage – or a real issue. Nolan concluded that there was clear evidence of a political bias in those who had been appointed: '[I]ndividuals who are Conservative Party supporters, or whose companies donate to the Conservative Party, are more likely to be found on appointed boards, than those who support Labour or the Liberal Democrats.'[5] The report also recommended that when 'individuals had political interests they ought always to be declared'. The Committee recommended that an independent commissioner should oversee all such appointments. Nolan's 'public service' ethic incorporated the values of selflessness, integrity, objectivity, accountability, openness, honesty, and leadership. In the case of the BBC there was evidence of direct interference in appointments to the Board of Governors and, perhaps more importantly than Nolan's virtuous criteria, individuals were nearly always selected for their compliance, and never for their independence.

With the Chairmanship in a safe pair of hands, and a politically packed Board of Governors, the government had a Trojan horse to take their policies right to the centre of the Corporation. There was a dramatic shift of power inside the BBC, with the Chairmen and the Board of Governors extending their power and interfering over an increasingly wide area. The Board of Governors is, constitutionally, the BBC, and as such has an immense authority within the Corporation: to have a Board that was hostile to everything the Corporation had done was deeply demoralizing. The first casualty was the independent-minded representative of an Olympian BBC tradition and elegant draughtsman of memoranda, the Director General, Alisdair Milne. In his memoirs Milne laid down his battle credits: a succession of brilliant, innovative programmes, whose object had been first, in *Tonight*, a hugely successfull news magazine, to get on a level of conversation with viewers, and famously, in *TW3*, the pioneering satire show, 'to address, late on a Saturday night, people who are more aware of being persons and more aware of being citizens than at any other time of the week'. He had defined the job of Director General as being to engineer a harmonious relationship with the Chairman and, above all, 'to provide a climate of confidence in which programme makers can do their best work'.[6] Milne was certainly not able to achieve harmony with Hussey, nor was he able to control a sense of mounting hysteria in the BBC. Personality always plays a part in appointments and dismissals, and Milne and Hussey did not get on, partly for the good reason that Hussey regarded Milne as part of 'the problem' he had been sent in to sort out. Milne was peremptorily sacked. The first he knew of his departure was when, in a lunch break between meetings, Patricia Hodgson, the BBC's Secretary ('carved from deep frozen Oil of Ulay', according to one wit) used his Christian name – not the usual DG – in asking him to see Hussey, who disposed of him and told him to leave the building, in which he had worked for over thirty years, by tea-time. Milne was succeeded as Director General by Michael Checkland – an accountant who had never made a programme but who had nevertheless worked for the BBC for many years, and who was known for his prudent capacity to save money, and more interestingly, to save it to spend wisely on important projects. Checkland was finally replaced by John Birt, first as Deputy Director General, and then as his replacement. Mrs Thatcher's memoirs icily assert that 'the appointment of Duke Hussey, and later of John Birt, as Director General represented an improvement in every respect'. At last she apparently had her men in place.

During the late 1980s and 1990s it was widely believed that the governors of the BBC were working behind the scenes to make programme makers not so much yield to government pressure as to make it unnecessary. In many ways this was part of the new managerialism: managers and boards were not merely required to take hard decisions, but there was a macho-pride to be taken in making these decisions as unpleasant as possible. In part, of course, this was merely an attempt to browbeat groups of people with values, or indeed the social capital of respect, into compliance. It was part of a far wider plan to limit the authority of professionals. However, it was also, in itself, an expression of the new orthodoxy: to manage properly it had to hurt.

The second line of Conservative attack on the BBC was, of course, the licence fee. When there are periods of 'natural' revenue expansion, when television ownership was increasing, or there was a switch to colour licences, when the BBC's funds increase because of a change in demand for its services, the Corporation has greater independence. There was no such natural increase in the 1980s, and television production costs were rising faster than general inflation. Thus, simply by not raising the licence fee, the government could impose savage cuts on the Corporation. Most prime ministers have probably warned the BBC's director generals that the licence fee would be cut. Most have not, in the end, meant it. During the 1980s and 1990s, the fee was eroded by a government that was intent on changing the nature of the BBC. Having abandoned their original ambition simply to abolish the Corporation, the government determined to exert their power, not only by interfering with the licence fee, but also by changing expectations, and radically altering the ecology of broadcasting institutions within which the BBC works. The aim was to change the kind of institution that the BBC aspired to be. Death by beheading was to be replaced by death by salami cuts. There had been no doubt, among politicians on both sides and in pressure groups, that the object of the 1990 Broadcasting Act had been intended to be the destruction of the BBC. Peacock had not put advertisements on the screen and although, by the late 1980s, as the next recession hit, the last thing any commercial station or indeed even any advertiser wanted, was more broadcast advertising time;

nevertheless, having been thwarted once, 'this time the feeling was', commented one politician, 'we'll get them'. The likelihood that the Corporation would disappear, its dominance undermined, and its capacity to think, create and win audiences, was high.

Survival or sea change?

Yet the BBC, despite the most determined onslaught it has ever faced, survived. The BBC was understandably reluctant to point out that it had won. It would not have been tactful. Yet, as Anthony Smith, one architect of Channel 4, remarked afterwards: 'It was a miracle. All the fire was deflected from the BBC on to ITV – the opposition got it.' And when the Broadcasting Act was finally passed it was indeed commercial television – the partner in a public service duopoly – that undoubtedly took the brunt of assault. Lord Thompson – a previous Chairman of the IBA – ruefully pointed out: 'When the BBC needed help, we gave it. But they kept their head down when we were under attack.' The campaign had been started by Brian Wenham's masterly organization of the BBC's evidence to the Peacock Committee. It developed through Extending Choice (that characteristic product of managerialism, the BBC's mission statement), through Producer Choice (the introduction of internal markets) and a continued process of management reorganization. The BBC ducked and weaved in every way it could. Using reform both as an expedient political face-saver, and sometimes as a real agent of necessary change. Thus, despite the strong pro-government bias on the Board of Governors (who seemed to dislike much of what the Corporation did, and who beguilingly claimed to be 'often too busy actually to watch television'), despite the animus of a very directed Prime Minister, and despite the pressure on revenue, the BBC survived.¹In this light, Hussey, Birt, and all the rest are not villains but, on the contrary, heroes, doing what had to be done, or doing what had to be seen to be done, and radically propelling the BBC along the road to a real future.

But what BBC, for what purposes, and at what cost, survived? Most popular accounts of the reforms emphasize their costs and consequences. In two powerfully argued and sharply contrasting books, Chris Horrie and S. Clarke's *Fear and Loathing at the BBC*, and Steve Barnett and Andrew Curry's *The Battle for the BBC*,[7] it is suggested that at the very least the process of reform in the BBC was awkward, ruthless, inefficient, unhappy, and self-destructive – and that, in the end, the Corporation only survived by voluntarily and lavishly doing to itself almost everything a hostile government wanted. Indeed, the debate is similar to one that recently raged among art historians, discussing the fate of much great medieval painting and sculpture during the Reformation, when previously sacred images were seen as idolatrous and attacked. It has been suggested that many great works were saved from the image breakers by being *slightly* defaced. A nose or an eye were sacrificed, say some, to save the whole. Others argue that on the contrary, the sense and purpose of the whole was lost by the defacement and that afterwards the images simply decayed and fell apart. Is that what has happened at the BBC?

Another version of this account is that the quite horrible means by which the BBC secured change, the ruthless exclusion of alternative voices in the process, the application of management and production targets, the process by which, far from becoming less bureaucratic it has become (like many other institutions) it was asserted far more top-heavy, were all instituted, not to make better programmes but to deal with politics. Dissent, argument, creativity, such an account suggests, are the source of vigorous and creative programmes. Most people who have left the BBC now have little good to say for it. But then, on the other hand, their accounts may be biased.

Managers and the media

There is, first of all, no doubt that the organization needed an overhaul. A British Steel manager invited to talk to the BBC in the early 1980s said that he came away convinced that something had to change. The Corporation was over-bureaucratic, too large, too cumbersome. It did not, he added, feel like a modern, slim, confident organization.[8] Management was the big 1980s idea, and institutions, businesses, and services throughout the nation were adjured to 'manage' themselves better.

However, the BBC had, in the past, been rather good at 'management'; indeed, when the Corporation was first set up, 'public service management' had itself been a huge innovation and was much praised and copied as a valuable new way of running an enterprise. Indeed, Ian MacIntyre in his biography points out that the first Director General, Reith, came to the BBC precisely as a manager, one with the highly relevant experience acquired on active service in World War One, where his job had been to improve the quality of the hugely increased productivity of mass-produced American armaments factories. The BBC had grown fast and gone on growing, because it was always an organization that took management seriously. On the other hand, 'management' within the Corporation was originally carefully separated from 'programmes'. 'Good Management', wrote Reith, 'is what is necessary to provide the conditions in which good programmes – far more important – can be made.'

During the early post-World War Two period, the BBC's response, both to staff shortages and to production problems, had been increasingly to assimilate wider aspects of the production process into the organization. The BBC had grown. Of course, the trend had been present since the BBC began, when, in order to have sound engineers or to build adequate transmitters, the Corporation had found that it had to train them itself: its problems were too specialized for the general level of technical training provided by the market.

However, with the emergence of television, the process accelerated. The BBC instigated make-up and make-up training, set-building, lighting, costume design, studio design, studio space, and more and more engineering within the Corporation as it found it needed them. In so doing the BBC both established production standards and became the main provider of training for the entire broadcasting industry. Although it could be argued that this had been an important infrastructure for broadcasting in Britain and that the industry was a vital one, nevertheless, as money got tighter, it became harder for the BBC to continue to be such a generous patron. The sense of an over-staffed, over-protected, over-bureaucratic corporation made the BBC vulnerable to calls for reform. But something had to change, it had become increasingly difficult to innovate – resources and money were used efficiently – but inflexibly.

However, one of the difficulties in analysing the impact of 1980s managerialism on the purpose and function of institutions like the BBC is that quite separate problems and solutions were deliberately confused in the project 'to manage better'. The first aim was to make sure that resources were used efficiently: this was often genuinely urgent. However, the second aim was to reduce dissent within organizations, while the third was to demonstrate that organizations were willing to be 'managed' better. In a rite of passage, it became a ritual of the Thatcherite cultural revolution that organizations like the BBC should admit their guilt, and perform acts of contrition and expiation before finally emerging, to use the fashionable managerial jargon, 're-tooled'. It was not merely that the BBC required direction and change, but that it was necessary that these should be seen to be difficult and that the end result should be a 'new' BBC.

The real problem, of course, is how you measure improvement in management in an organization like the BBC. As John Harvey Jones, the former Chairman of ICI and a prominent management 'guru' of the 1980s pointed out, organizations have to change continually, and better management should mean greater scope for entrepreneurial innovation. But who are the 'entrepreneurs' in a broadcasting empire – the managers or the programme makers? Moreover, the BBC, like any large and old organization, has been perpetually reorganized ever since it was founded. In the early 1970s it had already undergone four major organizational changes in forty years. In the beginning, 'administration' had been firmly separated from programme making and output, and indeed the separation had become 'an article of faith', remaining as a convenient fiction as late as the 1970s. When Tom Burns talked to the top levels of the BBC hierarchy in the late 1960s for his book, several complained that 'Managers were seen by everyone else as lepers'. Managers and administration were still far less important than programmes. It was still the roll-call of good, innovative, successful programmes that really ambitious broadcasting careers were made from. Burns reported one respondent as saying, 'Everybody in the Corporation, I suspect, sneakingly wants to get nearer and nearer to programmes, and I think, too, that one is always frightened as an administrator of stopping something.'[9] For the ambitious and driven, the pull, the gravitas in broadcasting was through making programmes, and remained so until the late 1980s. Yet the reality was changing. By then, the people who made programmes were far less important than the people who did the accounting for programmes.

Running a modern broadcasting organization almost inevitably develops a tension between industrialization and craft production. A great deal of television is in effect mass produced, falling into a narrow range of categories, sit-coms, game shows, chat shows, soap operas, and so on. There are also other more idiosyncratic kinds of programme. However, there is always pressure to reduce costs and standardize production. As we have seen, this became more acute during the 1980s. Nevertheless, within these constraints the challenge is to produce novel, intriguing, stimulating, fun, serious, enlightening programmes. Such creative products will always in part be a product of a culture, ways of thinking, a rewards system – what actually gets you on, and ultimately the kinds of personality that survive best in a system. Thus the question of creativity is never simply one of resources – although television is costly, both in terms of money and organizational needs. Nevertheless, the difference between good and indifferent programmes is one of giving permission and receiving encouragement.

However, one mounting pressure as the 1980s moved on was a sense not so much of permanent revolution as of permanent hysteria within the BBC. One young current affairs journalist, just down from Oxford, described it as 'a very volatile panicky place', where crises were always breaking out. Birt and Hussey calmed everything down.[10]

The BBC entered the process of being reformed with a naturally articulate and vociferous staff. The journalist recalled meetings in the BBC canteen at Lime Grove, an old labyrinthine building where news and current events were produced, ripe with corners for conspiracies, 'where producers screamed and management cowered'. Indeed, John Birt's initiation into the Lime Grove experience, confronting angry producers assembled to hear his plans, is said to have rocked him by its unrestrained hostility. He returned from the meeting determined to change the culture, no doubt to change the people, and while he was about it to pull down the building – and to call in the management consultants.

Managers and management

The BBC called in four different firms of management consultants to oversee its reform during the late 1980s and 1990s. Such advice is not cheap. Such people do not make programmes. What do management consultants do? Ideally, they enable an organization to do what it does better, or they may help it to change what it does. This may be all very desirable and, as we have seen, the BBC may have needed something like it. However, management consultants tend, on the whole, to accentuate the role of managers. In a widget industry, managers, not workers, may be the people who create new opportunities for the firm. This is only partly true in broadcasting, where the people who make things make the opportunities. There was a radical shift in power within the BBC: what had been a producers' programme-led hierarchy became a management-led power structure.

Titles and salaries illustrate this trend. Thus, when an outstanding head of radio drama resigned, his job was replaced by that of a drama business unit manager. The change in title reflected a change in priorities, and a shift in the kinds of talents apparently required. Another indicator was that the salaries paid to the exhausting front line current event and news personnel, who in a real sense are the BBC 'face to the world', between 1980 and 1995 fell from having been equal to those of comparable managers to being less than one-third. Inevitably, management-led organizations recruit people who want to be managers.

The consultants, apart from harassing liberal-minded producers into line for the government, were also widely believed to be there less 'to make the organization run more efficiently', and more to increase the Director General's control over unruly troops. Certainly, one of the things management consultants can do is describe in apparently uncontestable, neutral, and pseudo-technocratic terms, the apparently inevitable necessity of doing what those who call on them want. Yet, in order to meet the government's onslaught greater discipline was necessary.

Management became increasingly fashionable and important during the 1980s. Many believed that better management was an instrument which could reform ailing British institutions and habits. Those in apparently radical think-tanks – such as Demos – endorsed the desirability of wholesale changes to the organization of institutions, and a steady stream of political pamphlets discussed efficiency, and how to measure outcomes. Indeed, for those organizations that were wealthy enough to measure what their impact was, it was a useful tool. 'Modernization' became synonymous with change brought in from outside an organization. The emphasis in whole rafts of social thinking moved from what kind of services were desirable to how they were to be delivered. Under this there was also – as is usual – a political change in emphasis. The 'new managerialism' substituted a legitimate concern for the efficiency of the process of production for an older and perhaps also legitimate question about distribution.

One of the problems in assessing the effect of these ideas was that there was an element of genuine utopianism in some of the thinking. Thus Charles Handy, a humane and liberal management guru, produced a series of ideas for the reform of organization which he saw as both desirable for management and liberating for individuals. Later he was to ruefully acknowledge that their outcome – in practice – was often disastrous.

Some new principles of management were enthusiastically applied to enterprises everywhere. The first was the 'death of organization'. Handy had written that 'the telephone makes it possible for people to work together without being in the same place'.[11] He went on to consider the impact of communication changes and said that organizations, institutions, offices, careers, were all fast becoming irrelevant. It was not merely that commerce would become leaner – a new radical division of labour should be developed. You could be liberated from the inflexible institution because its work would change more rapidly. Businesses should become increasingly 'federal', buying in and commissioning specialized work as they needed it: 'Life in more and more organizations is going to resemble a consultancy firm' he claimed. Handy's optimistic utopian vision of a new social order, with individuals freed from jobs and companies, and in charge of their own work destiny as never before, included a claim that in future hierarchies would be old hat, organizations would be 'flat'; workers, he claimed, would 'have a right to do their own things in their own way as long as it is in the common interest, that people need to be well informed, well intentioned, and well educated in order to interpret their common interest.'

Handy's ideas suited the BBC well. The Corporation faced savage financial cuts, and the consequences of the 1990 Broadcasting Act – that it eventually commission 25 per cent of its programmes from outside the Corporation in the independent producers' sector. A plan for forcing through some drastic reorganization was needed and the new managerialism looked one way forward. Such reform was also, no doubt, seductive, because despite Handy's vision, delayering, federalist, re-tooled organization also happened to provide the upper of the hierarchies that survived with hugely increased powers.

Why did the BBC bother with all the management hoo-ha, and not just cut bits off? The benign interpretation is that management wanted to make sure it got rid of the right – that is the worst – bits. The more sceptical view is that they wanted to legitimate what they did. The least attractive view is that, although there were endless meetings, guidelines, mission statements, and flow charts, they had no clear vision of what a streamlined 'better' BBC would be like – except that it should be more docile and smaller; but perhaps they were trying to find out.

The process began slowly but gathered speed. Indeed, when Mrs Thatcher was replaced by decent Mr Major, the BBC juggernaut of reform went right on rolling. Part of the incentive for reform came from the need to cut production costs, and to use plant and people more efficiently. This led to the 'TV Resource Study', which started from the assumption that regional BBC plant was under-used and should be 'reorganized', i.e. that some of it should be shut down and that expensive London plant ought to be better used or disposed of. More to the point, perhaps, the management consultants suggested that 'plant', television studios, and the resources and people should be utilized on a twenty-four hour-a-day, seven-day-a-week schedule. This plan, jauntily entitled 'The Twenty Four Hour Rolling News Day' claimed to be about a 'new concept in news readiness'. In fact, one critic claimed that its primary target was the rewriting of staff contracts. In the past, long hours had meant overtime payment; in the future they meant just that, long hours.

The structural supports now seen as 'irrelevant' or surplus were lopped wholesale. However, the problem was whether the way in which cuts were made was rational or even cost-effective. Expensive new Manchester studios were 'disposed' of before they even opened. Elstree Studios, tatty but fertile in programmes, were deemed to have the wrong image, and sold. But the 'TV Resource Study' was the place where the real motor of BBC reforms was invented. At first it was called the 'internal market', but a public relations alarm bell rang, and a special brainstorming session was set up to think of something better. It came up with 'Producers' Choice'.

This title, instantly recognizable as another example of 'Newspeak', sounded positive, programme centred, something you'd like to have. It did not sound like lots of meetings, lots of invoices, and the 'wholesale transformation of perfectly good programme makers into second rate accountants', which is how one producer described it.[12]

'Producers' Choice' was intended, like the other artificial internal markets of the 1990s, to make costs transparent. In the past, not only had there been a good deal of cross-subsidization within budgets, but also many of the resources used in making programmes – studios, training, and so on – had been paid for centrally. The new stern philosophy in public affairs argued that this led to waste and extravagance because the true costs of using any resource were disguised. 'Producers' Choice' was supposed to make the real costs of making programmes apparent. However, it was also intended as a mechanism that would discreetly dispose of parts of the organization. So producers, having been allocated budgets, had to buy in the services they needed as cheaply as they could. That the real purpose of the exercise was to shut departments was made clear by the simple diktat that, while producers were encouraged to look outside the BBC for services, production departments were prohibited from trying to sell their services beyond the Corporation.

The trouble with artificially constructed internal markets – in all institutions – is that while they may drive down the costs of the central activity of the institution (replacing hips, teaching students, making programmes), they also require much of their resources to be spent on accounting and monitoring financial systems. They redistribute resources away from the central activity. Producers (like teachers, nurses, doctors, and so on) spent more of their time than was congenial, possibly a great deal more than was efficient, filling in forms and sending out invoices. Power usually flows from where the money is used – and so there was a further shift in power within the organization. In the early 1990s the staff magazine and the national press were full of BBC job advertisements: 'financial assistants', 'accountants', 'financial controllers' were much in demand. Many of the management consultants brought in from outside jumped ship and became BBC managers instead, not programme makers. Nevertheless, the reforms did deliver far greater resources back to programme makers in the end.

The second part of the agenda was to make the BBC more orderly. Was this a necessity in order to bring the Corporation into line with Conservative ideology so that it might survive, or did it, as some have claimed, bring about a collapse of traditional BBC values? John Harvey-Jones, the great industrialist, in his gospel of management, *Making It Happen,* comments:

> 'our forebears have given our companies a tradition of open speaking and respect for differences of opinion which is, in my view, the most precious single inheritance we have. There is no way in which a vision of the future can be developed among a group of people unless they have a very high degree of toleration, and indeed enthusiasm for argument.'[13]

Toleration was not a word that many felt characterized discussions in the BBC in the 1990s.

A guiding tenet of the new managerialism was that long-term careers within organizations are bad: not so much for people, but for organizations. Anyone who actually stays with an organization must be a dullard. People were supposed to hop from job to job. Indeed, there is now almost a cult of the 'outsider'. In the late 1960s, when Tom Burns was writing his book, most people within the BBC could think of their own long-term interests and those of the Corporation together. Although competition with ITV, and then Channel 4, gave individuals real freedom and flexibility, nevertheless they could focus ambition, groom experience, have expectations, and calculate.

During the 1990s, the BBC became a rich source of baroque fables about the impact of 'managerialism' on an articulate and competitive group of people and, moreover, a group well able to mobilize publicity on their own behalf. The conflict between the managers and staff often represented a battle about words. Language and the problems of its use had always taken a concrete form in broadcasting. Indeed, the early history of the medium was of the slow, cautious licensing of spoken ad-libbed speech, as opposed to scripted language. The use of scripts had been both a means of social and political control, ensuring that dangerous, untoward, or offensive things did not get said, and it had also been a way of refining and attending to the impact of speech. Only very gradually were people's own voices and words permitted on air, legitimizing new points of view in public debate. Today, there is more unscripted broadcasting than ever. Nevertheless, the meaning and impact of language remains a vital and delicate part of broadcasting culture. Words matter to journalists, and are what their work depends upon. As BBC journalists are not yet at the tabloid end of the market, they use words to describe, identify, and discriminate.

Yet, one of the consequences of the new managerialism is the use of words for obfuscation rather than clarification. The use of words to disguise intention rather than to reveal it. It seemed to many that everything had to be translated into a new vocabulary: long-winded, tedious, pompous, technocratic. Journalists loathed the corrosion of words. A disgruntled wit called the new language 'Birtspeak'. It was easy to assume it had a purpose.

The management revolution at the BBC, as everywhere else, meant interminable meetings. It also created many examples of that newly fashionable ritual – the management 'away day'. This was accompanied by enforced 'joie d'esprit' involving strange settings (once in a marquee, disconcertingly like a big top), which disguised the reality that real jobs, futures, the nature of the BBC, were all on the line. What gave rise to bitter jokes was the perverse distance between the ostensible intent and the manner of these events – the supposed 'open' discussion, 'exchange of views', jolly team spirit-building, and what was seen to be their real purpose, the identification and exclusion of opponents. Indeed, what journalists felt they reacted to was the undermining of language as a means of describing. Nevertheless, attention reality was refocused. If the first part of the project had been to save the Corporation from the government, the second was to make it work better within the Corporation.

History and managers

Another aspect of 1980s managerialism was a contempt for history, and a cavalier rewriting of it. Of course, this may, in part, be necessary. The world changes: concern for how things were done may be an impediment to how they must now be done. On the other hand, institutions only really function at their best if people working in them want to do more rather than less than is necessary. Tradition and history – values even – and a pride in what has been done well can be invaluable stimulants to ambition. Institutions also have to remember their history so that they do not repeat their mistakes. The past can be a resource for the future, not just a hindrance to it.

Yet, within the BBC, 'looking back' was seen as being a characteristic of the 'old guard', the people who had run the Corporation in the inefficient past. To say why things had been done as they had, or to query the logic of innovation (for example, of spending a lot of time and money attempting to create a 'price' for studio time, when there was in no real sense a market for it) was to 'mark you down as a doomed, old-speak person', recalled one veteran. 'The past was a very dangerous place to mention', maintained another.[14]

But perhaps all the hostility to change was just part of a recurring romanticism about the past? Or perhaps the myth of a golden history is necessary to organizations like the BBC, where, unlike many industries, people ought not to be consensus-minded. Being difficult (up to a point) may indeed be a very important part of good journalism.

Indeed, an organization like the BBC that has endured, and developed, always at the very edge of rapidly evolving technology, has a peculiar relationship with its own past. It is made all the more strange by the way in which it can *use* its past. Old programmes are continually reshown, readapted. The 'past' of the BBC is more visible than that of most firms, and the BBC's involvement in its audience's past is also complex. People remember events and themselves through what they saw or heard broadcast. Elaborating conservative tradition has been one way of handling dramatic technological change. Indeed, the fatigued sense that there has recently been too much change which seems to characterize people working for the BBC, is a product not only of change – which the Corporation has always had to do – but of having to produce rationales as well as action.

The BBC shared this sense of 'too much change' with several other institutions. Indeed, those working in the Health Service, for example, just like those in the BBC naturally have to deal with constant change because treatment is altering all the time. On the other hand, the core activity of other institutions, like education, that also complain of 'too much change' remain remarkably constant over time. But perhaps what all these services share is that they provide goods which cannot easily, and perhaps ought not to, be assessed by profitability. 'Good' broadcasting, and 'good' education are not easy to measure – though we may feel quite secure about identifying them when we see them.

Nevertheless, the past's superiority is a recurring theme in the BBC's self-perception. When the Corporation moved out of its original, cramped offices on Savoy Hill in 1926, one broadcaster asserted that the old offices 'had been quite the most pleasant club in London'; before, he went on, 'all was intimacy and harmony. After, all was bureaucracy and conflict.' During the Second World War, one broadcasting official recalled 'the old, intimate, close days of pre-war broadcasting'; after it, others repined 'the urgent, close sense of purpose the war produced in the BBC'. Grace Wyndham Goldie, a doyenne of a whole generation of broadcasters and a stern innovator in political broadcasting, nevertheless said that 'the smaller BBC of the early 1950s meant that ideas flowed more freely'. Tom Burns pointed out that by the mid-1970s everyone he talked to in the BBC complained that it had recently become 'too big', yet in fact the Corporation had grown far less quickly than in the previous decade. By the 1990s, BBC employees were still saying that it was far too big, even though it had recently got much smaller. But above all they said that, in the past, working for the BBC had felt like a vocation; people were sometimes infuriated by it, but also proud of it as an idea and as a standard. Argument, they also claimed, had been allowed, encouraged, and was not stoppable.

In the early 1990s, some distinguished voices expressed deep anxiety about the kind of place the Corporation was becoming. They were all the more impressive because none of them were under any threat: they mattered too much. Indeed, in different ways, they summed up, in the programmes they had made, the independence of their views, the accumulated concessions and stands they had taken and, in a creative authority, why public service broadcasting had been an important and exciting part of public and private life. David Attenborough, a great programme maker, and in his time a very distinguished BBC administrator, and Mark Tully, a legend in India on which he had reported for years, argued that the BBC had become a hostile, demoralized, over-managed and secretive place. The dramatist, Dennis Potter, in a scathing attack on Rupert Murdoch and the BBC at the Edinburgh Television Festival (1987), lamented the retreat of all television from innovative programme making.

Of course, the BBC culture is wordy, sarcastic, urbane, discontented, sometimes fashionable – and perhaps, properly, always likely to be disgruntled. Sniping, gossiping, and griping are part of the atmosphere. Yet, in this period, the BBC, like many other managerialized institutions, became a feverish place, with the political pressure from outside transmuted into intense internal pressure. Perhaps again because, ultimately, the BBC makes ideas, trades in images, the impact of managers and their 'correct' and 'incorrect' ideas is felt more personally. 'I don't mind being told what to do by some chap in a suit who's never edited a programme', complained one BBC producer, 'but I'm buggered if I'm going to be told what to think.'[15]

Leaders

Part of the new managerialism of the 1980s was an importing of a kind of posturing ruthlessness. Everywhere, passengers, patients, and those out on parole were renamed 'clients' in the public services. If Hussey was sent into the BBC by the Conservative government to bring it into line, John Birt was widely seen as his agent in the new tough mode.

Birt had been a very successful and innovative programme maker in the smaller but hugely fertile LWT. Trained as a scientist, one observer claimed that he thought in structures, and then tried to make the organization fit the ideas. He was, commented another, 'a facts and figures man'. Asked to speak about quality drama, he wanted evidence about numbers of plays shown, hours broadcast, percentages of viewers. Those who worked with him also commented that he was 'a rules man – his plan was always to decide on a "rule" and keep to it'. Privately energetic and charming, in public meetings, although always well prepared, he could, in the early days, be wooden, an odd mixture of shyness and bombast. He became more relaxed and confident as his tenure moved on. Yet arguably, the two previous, indisputably great Director Generals – John Reith and Hugh Greene in the 1960s – had both also often been accused of being overbearing and dictatorial. Greene was also a mischievous person. Both men combined aggressive style with a widely recognized – if not always approved of – image of what the BBC should do. Birt began his career at the BBC in the most difficult times the Corporation had ever experienced, but he did have a vision. He was subjected to a furious, unrestrained barrage of press opposition. At first, some sensed that he didn't particularly like the BBC. Roger Bolton, a former BBC producer and respected programme maker, wrote in the *Guardian*: 'The BBC has a deep and abiding hold on those who have worked for the Corporation'; he went on, 'The overwhelming impression given by those who now run the BBC is that they have no affection for it and for its past achievements, and no respect for its programme makers.' But then some saw Bolton as a critic, in turn, with an axe to grind. Birt was, he would argue, focused on the future.

Simmering internal resentment, combined with a hawkish press, meant that Birt's every action was under media scrutiny. It didn't help that the twelfth Director General of the BBC got his job almost by fiat, and that able, respected competitors, like John Tusa, who had recently successfully reformed the prestigious World Service (and carried an enthusiastic staff with him), were told by Hussey that there was no point in applying. How he was appointed was not Birt's fault, but it made him look like the product of the kowtowing politics of the 1980s. What became known as 'Armani-Gate' also did damage. The title came from the Director General's preference for stylish designer suits. However, it shocked BBC employees (many of whom were now on short-term contracts and had recently been sternly warned by the rectitudinous Corporation that they must pay their taxes properly) when they discovered that the Director General himself apparently did not actually work for the Corporation. Instead, he was paid his salary through a holding company which permitted him to make a small – and indeed in the rest of broadcasting, routine – tax advantage. At the time it was as if a great British institution had been so undermined by the Conservative onslaught that those who were supposed to hold its future dearest were not committed to it.

Birt was saved as influential and objective commentators rallied to support him. Particularly important was a letter sent by senior journalists to the *Independent*, publicly backing him. 'Old axes are grinding' Polly Toynbee, Peter Jay, and others wrote, and 'old scores are being settled in the attack on the Director General'. He was certainly helped by distinguished and, on the whole, left-wing members of the general committee. It was a delicate moment; Michael Checkland, the previous Director General, reduced a meeting to roars of appreciative laughter when he began a speech by quoting his BBC employee number. The problem was not whether Birt was or was not venal, but what people thought it meant for the BBC. Indeed, the incident may have been a turning point in showing that the public still cared quite passionately about the Corporation.

As the 1990s progressed the BBC calmed down. Perhaps this was because all the opposing voices had been shunted off, retired, or were too busy. Perhaps it was because political pressure from government and opposition had changed from volatile hysteria to a steady pressure of objections, attempts to arrange favourable news running order, lunches, and telephone calls. Or perhaps it was because the BBC had been reformed and was more in control of its own agenda of change than in the volatile 1980s.

There was also a shift of power within the Corporation; Birt was even prepared to humiliate Hussey – soon to retire anyway. The Chairman, married to a Lady-in-Waiting to the Queen, was given no prior warning and was hugely embarrassed that the BBC had conducted a secret, and constitutionally damaging, deal with the Princess of Wales for a revenge interview to put her case against Prince Charles. It was seen by the BBC as a scoop – and it netted the Corporation a huge world audience. Whether it was proper, or properly conducted or not, seemed to matter little. Certainly Hussey was ruthlessly sidelined as his influence waned.

By the 1990s, the BBC was undoubtedly more disciplined. Most important of all it was producing some outstanding programmes. However, above all, under John Birt, the BBC had, against all the odds, survived.

Who saved the BBC?

How was Mrs Thatcher thwarted? Part of the answer was just politics. There was an important element in her Cabinet who were determined to protect the BBC. Of these William Whitelaw was undoubtedly the most influential: no one could have been closer to her, making his determined opposition all the more effective. Whitelaw pointed out that when the Conservatives were in opposition in 1965 the BBC's Director General had been very determined to protect Conservative opposition interests against the then Labour Government. It was a debt that was amply repaid. Whitelaw saw it as important evidence of the benefits of independent, impartial public service broadcasting.

'In a difficult field', he was to write. 'We should be most careful not to endanger what we have achieved.' Early on in government Whitelaw oversaw the implementation of a Labour plan, and introduced Channel 4. He remained a resourceful Cabinet player. Whitelaw had said, 'It's committee work and behind the door work, and respect that gets you what you want' and, almost in direct contradiction to his leader, concluded that 'I am always disturbed by talk of achieving higher standards in programmes at the same time as proposals are introduced leading to deregulation, and financial competition because I do not believe that they are basically compatible.'[16] Whitelaw knew what he didn't want, and traded his indispensability to the Prime Minister for it. After the early, lunatic faith that the Prime Minister held, that a technological transformation of Britain could be carried out on the backs of people's appetites for old movies, and after Rupert Murdoch had got everything he could wish for in terms of favourable policies for his new satellite station, Mrs Thatcher's attention also turned elsewhere.

The second factor was that, despite growing competition, people still liked watching BBC programmes. Popularity – and a sense that programmes reflect and shape viewers' and listeners' interests, that there are some programmes at the edge of public opinion and pleasure – proves the most solid defence for broadcasters. Yet in the beginning, programmes seemed very removed from the heart of the new regime – and the fertile argument, and sense of ideas flowing that encourage creativity, seemed so alien to the new, neatly managed structure – that there was a fear that the Corporation had been saved, but that quality broadcasting had not. There were continuous and growing anxieties about radio, which worsened with the departure of one of Birt's most respected appointees, Liz Forgan, from the post of Head of Radio. She had left because the next stage in rationalization was to be the creation of 'bi-medial departments', serving both radio and television. It was feared that the specialized culture of, for example, children's television, or the alternative news agenda of the World Service, would be lost. However, at least by the mid-1990s, the argument was again about programmes.

One effect of the Broadcasting Act had been to create new opportunities for all the people who could not bear the old broadcasting sector any more – in the independent sector. Indeed, for at least one generation public service broadcasting values (that you made programmes because they were important and interesting and necessary) survived in the best of the independent companies. So the BBC exported values – and could import back programmes made by its own kind of broadcaster.

The third factor was that the reforms cut costs at the BBC. However, huge sums were wasted on the way. Early on, the producer's choice system was discovered to be paying some costs twice, and money was 'lost' in the system (malcontents grumbled that at least under the old scheme transferred funds were spent on programmes not 'lost'). Money was also mishandled in setting up BBC Enterprises. This was a typical 1990s venture. The idea was that it earned the BBC 'extra' revenue by exploiting BBC programmes. It cost more than it ever brought in. Nevertheless, however ramshackle the process, a leaner, more cost-conscious BBC did emerge.

Perhaps Birt was more in debt to all the dissidents than he realized. So vociferous was the campaign, as successive waves of reorganization cut swathes through what journalists saw as central BBC ways of doing things, it certainly seemed that the process was very painful. Loud complaints may, ironically, have served to placate the government that the BBC was being reformed as it would wish.

Birt, and his team, managed to steer the Corporation through the greatest ever challenge to its existence. By the mid-1990s the BBC felt as if it were, slightly grimly, on a course it understood. It is a story which may show how flexible British establishment institutions can be. The BBC remained a national and international institution; it had not, in the end, been fatally politically compromised. It made good programmes. The public also actually cared about it. It was Birt's particular capacity, in a way, to look forward, and the Corporation began to prepare for how it might give a 'public service' interpretation to the opportunities of digital television.

Public service can perhaps only be measured by what it is institutions agonize over. If you are only there to make a profit, everything is far simpler. Questions like: What do children need? How ought the public to be informed about the election? What new dramatists should be developed? How do we reflect the debate about contemporary society? and many others, are simply not relevant in a commercial system. But they continue to be relevant in the BBC.[17]

Broadcasting in the twenty-first century

Indeed, by the beginning of the new millennium, the unthinkable had happened. The BBC emerged from two decades of political and technological (if not creative) turmoil as the strongest player on the British broadcasting scene and with an enhanced international presence.

At the start of the 1990s the BBC it had seemed possible that the Corporation was doomed to a twilight life of decreasing revenue, declining and fragmented audiences, and enfeebled performance. The best it might expect a reduced role making programmes for elite minorities or worthy causes that commercial broadcasters would not touch because of their narrow appeal. The BBC whose whole history has been one of combining popular and quality programming would fade into insignificant mediocrity.

That this was its likely fate was all the clearer when what was happening elsewhere was taken into account. Other public service broadcasters all over the world had become pale shadows of their former selves. They had lost finance and clout. Even great national broadcasters like NBC in America had been eviscerated by a combination of de-regulation, and a collapse in the will to protect information as a public good. Canadian public service broadcasting had lost monopoly rights, finance and swiftly lost audience share: it was reduced to appealing for charitable funds from viewers to continue to make programmes. Australian public service broadcasting suffered a similar fate. A previously robust element of a broader commercial programme making culture, public service barely survived either as an institution or as a set of values. Similarly RAE in Italy was reduced to a small, apologetic organisation. Almost everywhere the story was the same. These precipitous declines were not inevitable but the predictable outcomes of broadcasting policy. On a more positive note novel news services like CNN swiftly gained authority and reach in their reporting – yet CNN was more widely watched in the rest of the world than it was in America. All over the world, traditional public service broadcasters were in trouble – how could it survive here?

Meanwhile, throughout the 1990s, it was argued that 'broadcasting' or terrestrial broadcasting at least, was doomed by inexorable technological change (actually this was always talked about as if it were good; technology would promote progress). Experts confidently predicted that people would stop watching old-fashioned steam-television, and that if they did watch it they would customize their programme choice from the huge range of new channels available. In any case they would not be watching television or listening to the radio because they would be too busy buying products and services off the net – or 'interacting' with it. The theorists of interactivity were very clear that this was absolutely novel, engrossing – and very superior to old, passive spectatorship. They dismissed any idea that when you look at a picture and are delighted by it, or read a novel and find yourself transported into the mind and understanding of characters within it, watch a drama and feel involved in the outcome of the story, or contemplate news with apprehension, you are altered by the experience. 'Interactivity' was, it was claimed, revolutionary.

Indeed, the main concern throughout the 1990s was the means of delivery of new services and not their content. Indeed, content delivery was changing; by 2002 nearly 40 per cent of British homes had access to cable or satellite television. Meanwhile sports, especially football, had been transformed as money was pumped into them in order, at least in part, to develop exclusive access to attract viewers to the new services. Of course there were profound changes in audiences' behaviour. People spent time in the new sociabilities of the net, they spent time on video-games and watched videos. Indeed, many movies began to look increasingly like video games, and were often made as much for the home video market as for public display. Evidence from the Independent Television Commission showed that multi-channel households watched a variety of offers, and browsed through entertainment opportunities more freely. There was some evidence that the multi-channel homes (that might soon be in the majority) did not watch television collectively, and watched television slightly less overall than previous generations. Younger people in a period of great affluence went to the cinema more.

Yet people went on watching television in far greater numbers and for far more of the time than had been predicted at the start of the new technological revolution. Moreover, the majority of them continued to watch terrestrial channels (however they received them) more than any other channels. Channel 5 – originally given very light regulation because it was not expected to last more than a few years – grew into a serious competitor for ITV. (The light touch regulation made it attractive to buyers who saw it as a way to tabloidize the television market.) Channel 4 went from strength to strength in the 1990s. ITV, saddled with huge auction bids to pay off, lacking the regional tension that had once made it so creative, and having made many mistakes on its way to the new digital channels, began to have more acute problems. When the long boom of the 1990s stuttered to a halt, all the commercial broadcasters faced severe adjustments as advertising revenues collapsed. But these problems were trivial in comparison to a stark and unexpected reality: people still liked watching television for the same kinds of reasons that they had liked watching it in the past. Most startling of all, the BBC survived, flourished and became – (for the moment at least) the dominant player. It was a remarkable outcome.

Partly it was the product of a frequently ignored problem – that of content. Despite the huge attractions of sports channels which soon bought up all sorts of events and privatised them (and outpriced the terrestrial stations), and children's channels that offered a reliable diet of cartoons, steam-television still made new programmes that people wanted to see – and imported the best of foreign production. In the case of the BBC the outcome was largely a vindication of the Birt–Hussey reforms. Together with an astute, well-prepared move into digital, the BBC offered new services that lead people into a new era of broadcasting and information. BBC World, from a shaky and unconvincing start, improved and began to grow into an authoritative new international presence. The BBC website received more hits than any other in the UK: the BBC was again a persuasive representative of the nation all over the world. Ultimately broadcasting services confounded the pessimists because they were still able to touch audience tastes, pleasures and hopes.

Yet broadcasters were also able to exploit a political and regulatory regime which – in the end – supported them. The public takes its leisure for granted, yet even fans enjoying their passion depend on structures of broadcasting that are politically determined. This is as true of wholly commercial systems of broadcasting as of those with a public service component. These political realities cannot alter the terms of international broadcasting trade – but they can modify their impact if there is the will to do so.

Nevertheless, the ideals of public service broadcasting were under powerful new strains. News especially suffered from many challenges. Rolling 'live' news is more vulnerable to unsubstantiated rumour than the old, slower kind. 'Representing' the nation is more complex, for you must find, for example, the 'representative' Muslim voices (not just the excitingly newsworthy extremist ones) – and broadcasters have to be acutely aware across a whole landscape of political interest. Audiences, through the long comfortable boom years perhaps felt little to threaten them and were less interested in threats to other people's safety, in the new complicated international disorder of the post-cold war world. As the press reacted to the dominance of broadcasting and became more campaigning and opinionated (and less concerned with news as such which the broadcasters could do better) this in turn reflected back on broadcasters – who despite their dominance still seem to find it hard to establish independent news agendas. In America broadcast news has become more like the press: more partisan, less impartial. It is rather disturbing to watch – but many argue that it is the way forward for news. In addition, much political coverage seems to operate in a simple – and misleading – moral universe of rights and wrongs. As successful political negotiation always deals with making painful concession about strongly felt interests, the very basis of democratic politics is all too often traduced. In particular, the idea of politics as a discussion about genuinely difficult-to-resolve issues is being lost.

Legislation, technological change and evolving audience habits could swiftly alter the broadcasting landscape again. There is no divine right to broadcast. Yet, despite the threats and the problems – and the alternatives – we still seem to like it. Perhaps, grudgingly and almost unconsciously, we value broadcasting as part of a national conversation: it still remains a mirror we hold up to our increasingly diverse selves.

Notes

1. Margaret Thatcher, *The Downing Street Years* (London, HarperCollins, 1995), p. 210.
2. Hugo Young, *One of Us* (London, Cape, 1992), p. 510.
3. Mrs Thatcher, speech to the Parliamentary Press Gallery, 11 July 1981.
4. Institute of Contemporary British History, 'Witness Seminar', *Real Lives* (February 1995).
5. *The Nolan Report on Standards in Public Life*, Cmnd. 2850, 1995, 1. para 70.
6. Alisdair Milne, *Director General: The Memoirs of a British Broadcaster* (London, Hodder & Stoughton, 1988), p. 74.
7. Steve Barnett and Andrew Curry, *The Battle for the BBC: A British Broadcasting Conspiracy* (London, The Aurum Press, 1994); Chris Horrie and S. Clarke, *Fuzzy Monsters: Fear and Loathing at the BBC* (London, Heinemann, 1994).
8. Interview with Chris Beauman.
9. Tom Burns, *The BBC: Public Institution and Private World* (Basingstoke, Macmillan, 1977), p. 43.
10. Author interview.
11. C. Handy, 'Balancing corporate power: a new Federalist paper, *Harvard Business Review*, 1992, p. 572.
12. Author interview.
13. J. Harvey-Jones, *Making it Happen* (London, HarperCollins, 1991).
14. Author interview.
15. Quoted in Steve Barnett and Andrew Curry (op. cit.), p. 219.
16. William Whitelaw, *The Whitelaw Memoirs* (London, The Aurum Press, 1989), p. 285.
17. This chapter is based on a number of confidential interviews with policy makers, broadcasters, and politicians.

Part III

Rise of new media

16

Scientists, capitalists, and cyberchartists

Introduction

In the nineteenth century, people were so filled with awe by the mighty power of the newspaper and periodical that it became the convention to refer to the press with an upper case 'P', befitting its status (and also differentiating it from the printing press). When this awe gave way to familiarity, the press was demoted to a lower case 'p', and commentary about the press became more rational.

We are still in the awestruck stage as far as the internet is concerned. Convention requires that the internet be designated with an upper case 'I', and the world wide web with upper case 'Ws' (though we have resisted this here). The wonderment this convention expresses goes some way towards explaining why so much current discussion of the net is naive and credulous.

There are two leading schools of thought. One sees the internet as a technology of freedom that is empowering humankind, making accessible the world's knowledge, building 'emancipated subjectivities', promoting a new, progressive global politics, and laying the foundation of the 'new economy'.[1] The other sees the internet as an over-hyped technology whose potential value has been undermined by 'digital capitalism' and social inequality.[2] Which view is right?

We will attempt to reach a conclusion by means of a circuitous route that takes us through the history of the internet (this chapter) and its sociology (Chapter 17). When combined together, this body of research points to a clear verdict: neither view is correct.

Historical overview

The internet has gone through four main phases. In its first phase, during the 1970s, it was used by scientists as a way of sharing expensive computer resources, exchanging research data and corresponding through email. It was the research tool of a techno-élite.

During the early and mid-1980s, the internet (broadly defined) entered its subcultural and proto-commercial phase. Its use widened as a consequence of the proliferation of computer networks, and became more varied. Usenet groups (specialist discussion groups) were formed; 'virtual communities', forged through the net, took shape; and some early internauts played identity games. Knowledge of a new argot, often derived from science fiction, became part of the grass-roots net subculture, introducing new acronyms such as MOO (a chat room represented as a physical place) and MUD (multi-user dungeon or, more soberly, multi-user domain). This was the period when a number of digerati enthusiasts proclaimed to the uninitiated that the internet was a life-changing, world-redeeming invention. However, the rise of grass-roots networks in the early 1980s coincided with the emergence of commercial online services, and a sustained growth of business networks – and these were to prove a more significant development in the long run.

The third phase, from the later 1980s to the mid-1990s, was a period of transition when the deployment of the net as a research tool and subcultural playground gave way increasingly to commercial use. In 1991, prohibitions on the commercial use of the core internet were lifted. In 1993, commercial software was introduced which made the web (created in 1990) more accessible. In 1995, the American core internet backbone was privatized. This transitional period closed, with the sleeping giant of Microsoft awakening to the success of the internet, and assessing how best to profit from its growing popularity.

The fourth phase, from the mid-1990s to the present day, marked the commercialization of cyberspace. Net companies, selling directly to the public, mushroomed. Net advertising became widespread, and new ways were devised to monitor users for commercial purposes. General portals sought to simplify the internet experience for the public in profitable ways. Commercial content became more prominent, and civic discourse less so.

However, this commercial take-over was incomplete. The net's culture and uses, shaped by its early pre-market development, did not disappear. The new commercial regime encountered strong resistance both from within the computer world and from the public at large. The net was pulled by opposed forces in different directions.

As a consequence, the net contains contradictory features, and can develop potentially in different ways. To make sense of the present, and glimpse into the future, it is necessary to examine more closely the past.

Underlying science

One way of viewing the history of the net and the web is to see it as the culmination of scientific innovation. It is an important perspective that tends to be neglected by non-scientists.[3]

One strand of innovation that led to the internet was the development of the computer. In the 1940s the first operational electronic digital computers were built – the British 'Collossus' in 1943 and the more advanced American ENIAC in 1946. These and subsequent 'first generation' computers were massive machines, costing vast sums, attended by a white-coated priesthood, and dependent on thousands of notoriously unreliable valves. Three key developments subsequently transformed the computer, enabling it to become smaller and more powerful. In 1947, transistors were invented, and gradually replaced computer valves. In 1958, integrated circuits were introduced in the form of silicon chips incorporating thousands of miniaturized transistors. In the early 1960s, this led to the introduction in research and business organizations of so-called 'minicomputers' – though these were enormous by today's standards. This led to the final decisive breakthrough: the microprocessor invented by Ted Hoff in 1969. This is the integrated circuit that incorporates the functions of the central processing unit of a computer, its 'heart'. Its invention led to the development of microprocessor-based personal computers, the first of which was manufactured in 1975 in the form of a do-it-yourself kit for hobbyists. The late 1970s marked the beginning of the personal computer boom that has continued to this day.

A second strand of innovation, the development of computer networking, may also be seen as a cumulative process. During the 1950s, a computer language evolved that drew on the pioneer work of a number of scientists, most notably Konrad Zuse. This still left unresolved how computers, using different systems, could communicate with each other. The first step was the building of an intermediary computer (IMP) in the late 1960s that functioned as a processing link between the computer 'host' and the network. This was followed in the early 1970s by the development of conventions (*protocols*) governing the dialogue between machines. This began with formulating shared codes for transporting communications (Transmission Control Protocol, shortened to TCP), and for addressing computers (Internet Protocol, shortened to IP). These were adopted eventually both in the United States and globally, though only after much difficulty. The other, linked breakthrough was the development of packet-switching during the 1960s and 1970s. This was an ingenious system whereby messages were disaggregated into units (*packets*) before dispatch; sent through different routes, depending on the flow of communications traffic; and reassembled on arrival. Each packet was wrapped in a kind of digital envelope containing transport and content specifications.

Protocols governing computer interaction and packet-switching technology made possible the development of the internet. This began in 1969 as a computer network (ARPANET) established by the US Defence Department, with nodes in four American universities. It grew rapidly in the 1970s and 1980s to become the backbone of a larger system that encompassed a number of networks. Its rise was paralleled by the development of a second major network started in 1982 by the US National Science Foundation. This second network became linked to the first; built links with national networks around the world in the late 1980s; and took over ARPANET's backbone role in 1990. In the United States, a cumulative process of convergence also took place, in which a variety of outsider networks – business, commercial and grass-roots services – developed closer links to the American public system during the period between 1983 and 1995. The modern internet, in the sense of a publicly accessible, worldwide network of computer networks, came of age in the late 1980s, and took off in the 1990s.

An ancillary development that facilitated the building of this global network was the improvement of modern communications infrastructure. Initially, computer networking was conducted through telephone wires, but later came to use routinely both satellite and advanced cable. Satellite communication dates from the launch of Telstar in 1962, but developed fully only from the 1970s onward. The first, local *broadband* cable systems were laid in the early 1980s, while transcontinental systems were extended across the Atlantic and Pacific Oceans in the late 1980s. Between 1996 and 1999, there was a tenfold increase in transatlantic cable capacity, underlining the point that the sea still matters as well as the sky in coping with the growing volume of communications traffic.[4]

The third strand of innovation took the form of advances in computer software. The revered pioneer of software design is Vannevar Bush. He argued in the 1930s and 1940s that computers should be viewed not as giant calculating machines but as a technology that can assist human beings to store, retrieve and analyse creatively all kinds of information. Some claim to discern in his 1945 outline of a hypothetical 'memex' machine the essential elements of what became scroll bars, home pages, computer displays and scanning. However, it was not until 1963 that Douglas Engelbart and his team developed in a concrete form recognizably modern software, including graphics-based interfaces, and the now ubiquitous 'mouse', the pointing device used to roam the computer screen. This was followed by the emergence of *hypertext* software, first developed in a simple form by Ted Nelson in 1965 and greatly refined subsequently. The key benefit of hypertext is that it enables computer users to move from one part of a text to another, linked text by clicking on an icon or symbol. In this way, it offers flexible and lateral intellectual pathways.

In 1990, Tim Berners-Lee and his associates at CERN, Geneva, invented the world wide web. This took the form of a software program that enabled people to access, link and create communications in a single global 'web' of information. This was achieved through the development of new conventions governing the interaction between machines. One convention specified the location of the information (URI, later revised usually to URL); a second specified the form of information transaction (HTTP); and the third a uniform way of structuring documents (HTML). Before their general adoption, people experienced enormous difficulties in finding information on the net, and also in releasing information that others could find. Various protocols that had evolved for exchanging information were not compatible, and there was no generally accepted way of linking information in different documents.

While the web proved to be a momentous development, it built upon advances that had preceded it. The web was superimposed on the internet, and incorporated its protocols. Without the prior existence of global computer internetworking, and the development of communications infrastructure underpinning it, the web would not have been possible. The popularization of personal computers was also a pre-condition of the web. It provided the dispersed computer power that enabled users to put their own content on the web, as well as the technical means to run web software. Finally, Berners-Lee's invention incorporated past software innovations, not least hypertext links that were a key feature of his project. Indeed, the world wide web may be viewed, in one sense, as part of a continuum of software development: subsequent innovations made the web easier to navigate, and introduced an audio and video dimension.

The web thus marked the coming together of three different strands of innovation. *It joined personal computing to networking through connective software.* This gave rise to a technological development with the potential to change the world. The internet and the web provide a global medium of communication in a context where the world's media system is overwhelmingly national and local. It allows individuals and groups to send as well receive communications, in contrast to the one-way communication flows of conventional media. It is highly versatile, lending itself to different uses. Above all, the internet began as the least controlled part of the media system, subject neither to state nor market domination.

Birth pangs of the web

A central theme of the 'history of ideas' approach to scientific discovery is that most important inventions have a clear intellectual bloodline. They are usually the product not of a flash of insight coming from nowhere, but of an incremental progression of thought and practice. The invention of packet-switching, central to the birth of the internet, provides a case in point. It was conceptualized by Paul Baran in 1964; developed and implemented by Donald Davies and Lawrence Roberts in the later 1960s; revised significantly by Vinton Cerf and Robert Kahn in 1974; and refined thereafter. The 'auteur' theory of the creative process, to be found in some versions of film theory, gets short shrift in the academic history of science.

While this fastidious approach is broadly correct, it tends to downplay the excitement of discovery at least as it is experienced in the low-key register of academic life. Yet the birth pangs of the web were not entirely free of drama. Its inventor, Tim Berners-Lee, was low down in the food chain of academic grants when he began work on the web. He was a scientist, without a Ph.D., on a temporary fellowship in the European physics laboratory, CERN. His repeated requests for additional resources all met with polite refusals. Indeed, he began to fear that his web project – justified on the less than straightforward grounds that it would facilitate information-sharing between scientists *within* the laboratory, rather than around the world – might be cancelled. When he first unveiled his visionary work it met with a lukewarm response from his CERN colleagues, with the exception of Robert Cailliau.

The future of the web thus seemed to depend upon winning external recognition. Berners-Lee was convinced that the way to achieve this was to present his project at a key conference, due to be held in 1991 in San Antonio, USA, where all the people who mattered in the computer world would be present. He and his colleague, Robert Cailliau, submitted to the conference what was arguably one of the most important scientific papers of the last quarter of a century, only for it to be rejected on the pedantic grounds that it failed to situate its arguments adequately within the relevant literature. However, they were given permission to present the web in the second division form of a demonstration.

The two young scientists flew to San Antonio, only to discover to their horror that the hotel where the conference was to be held had no direct internet access. They persuaded the hotel to extend a phone line to the demonstration room, and the neighbouring university (identified by a local taxi driver) to allow use of its dial-in service to their home computer. Their final hurdle involved locating a soldering iron in order to bypass an American plug that did not fit their Swiss modem. The demonstration was a triumph. 'At the same conference two years later,' Tim Berners-Lee recalls with a trace of smugness, 'every project on display would have something to do with the Web'.[5]

Political economy of invention

If scientific advance often takes the form of a logical or associative progression of thought, it is also crucially shaped by the wider context of society. A number of societal factors affect *when* and also *where* scientific progress takes place. One of these – patronage – was especially important in the case of the development of the internet.

The internet is an offspring of the Pentagon. When the USSR launched the first space satellite in 1957, the US Defence Department responded by establishing the Advanced Research Projects Agency (ARPA) with the aim of mobilizing more fully American universities and research laboratories behind the country's Cold War effort. Among the new agency's many projects was a scheme to promote interactive computing, through the creation of ARPANET, the world's first advanced computer network. Although the network was conceived originally as a way of sharing expensive computer time, it acquired subsequently a more important rationale. Computer networking would facilitate, it was argued, the development of a sophisticated military command and control system. It also provided a means of sustaining communications channels in the event of a nuclear attack from the Soviet Union.

When ARPANET was identified as part of America's last line of defence against the 'evil empire', it became a spending priority. The development of packet-switching technology and the creation of a rapidly expanding computer network – both central to the birth of the internet – received major funding from the US Defence Department.

Military spending also assisted indirectly the internet by fostering external conditions favourable to its development. The army funded the first American computer in 1946. So great was the armed forces' subsequent support of 'the nascent computer industry' that it became, in the words of a distinguished analyst, 'virtually a military subsidiary'.[6] This financial backing helped to establish the USA as the world's leading computer manufacturer, and producer of computer software. The American state also sponsored the American space programme, whose by-product – satellite communications – facilitated the functioning of the global internet.

In effect, the American state underwrote a major part of the research and development process that gave birth to the modern internet. This was not something that the private sector would have undertaken readily because it was not apparent, in the early days, that computer networking between academics, linked to the defence programme, had any commercial future. Indeed, the commercial giant, AT&T, was actually invited in 1972 to take over ARPANET, the forerunner of the internet, and declined on the grounds that it lacked profit potential. It was the American state that picked up the bills in a context of limited commercial interest. Yet, after underwriting the cost of technology development, and the creation of a significant user base, the American state then proceeded to shepherd the internet to market. During the 1980s, the government financed manufacturers to modify the design of new computers in order to lay the foundation for commercial internetworking.[7] The lifting of the prohibition of commercial use of the public internet in 1991 was followed by privatization of the public backbone of the internet in 1995. In effect, the internet became a state-sponsored commercial system.

The developmental role of the American state in funding, managing and then commercially floating the internet sits uneasily with the minimalist, 'night-watchman' role assigned to government in American neo-liberal ideology. It actually corresponds more closely to the social market conception of the state as 'capitalist entrepreneur' that was once strongly advocated by European social democrats.[8] One reason why American political reality deviated from political rhetoric was the significant influence exerted by business on American telecommunications policy. However, the very much more important reason was that the American state allocated enormous resources to establishing military and technological superiority over the Soviet Union during the height of the Cold War. The internet was a Dr Strangelove project.

Similar levels of public investment were not available elsewhere, even in countries where the conditions for early internet development were promising. Britain built the first modern computer in the 1940s; developed a significant computer industry in the 1950s; and was the first country to develop, in prototype, packet-switching in 1968. But this auspicious start did not gain extensive state financial support, especially in relation to computer projects that offered only a long-term return.[9] It was not until 1981 that the Post Office launched a full-scale packet-switching service – using, after this long delay, expensively licensed American hardware.

Cultures of invention

The internet was the product not only of human ingenuity and state patronage, but also of the values of the people who first developed it. Data-processing systems do not have a fixed form determined by some inner technological logic but are influenced by the concerns and goals of their inventors, and of the contexts in which they operate. For example, IBM developed a highly centralized communication system for business organizations, in which the main computer had a master–slave position to terminals, and the relationship of users to the production and consumption of the data system depended on their position within the corporation. The IBM system both reflected and reproduced, Patrice Flichy argues, the hierarchical culture of the firm.[10]

By contrast, the internet came out of a very different world, though its supposed Edenic character has become the subject of much mythologizing. According to conventional accounts, the early internet reflected the freedom-loving values of the American scientists who designed it, and of the grass-roots activists who took it up. This love of freedom was then secured by the freedom of the marketplace, ensuring that the internet became a great engine of human enlightenment.

There is just enough truth in this account to ensure its longevity. However, it greatly simplifies by editing out or downplaying features of the net's development which do not accord with its story-line. It also grossly distorts by failing to acknowledge the central conflict that developed between the freedom of the net and the assertion of market control. What actually happened is different from the legend.

Jane Abbate's pioneering history shows that the American military was not a benign, self-effacing 'sugar-daddy' of the net whose role was confined to paying the bills. On the contrary, she concludes, 'networking techniques were shaped in many ways by military priorities and concerns'.[11] One overwhelming military priority was 'survivability'; in other words, a communication system that would be invulnerable to devastating attack. This led the military to sponsor a decentralized system, without a vulnerable command centre that could be destroyed by the enemy. It also led to the development of network technology that would enable the system to function if parts of it were destroyed – a key attraction of packet-switching that dispensed with dedicated, open lines between sender and receiver. Another military priority was to secure a diverse networking system since this was best suited to different, specialized military tasks. This gave rise to the net's modular structure in which different networks could be added on easily, once minimum requirements were met. It also resulted in the addition of satellite and wireless for internetworking since these were well adapted to communications with jeeps, ships and aeroplanes.

However, if the military strongly influenced design objectives, academic computer scientists actually conceived and implemented the net's design. Indeed, academics working for ARPA had a significant degree of autonomy, helped by the fact that military objectives largely coincided with scientific ones. Thus the military concern for survivability dovetailed with the desire of the different university departments, which constituted the early internet, to retain their freedom and independence. Similarly, military endorsement of network diversity accorded with the academic goal of making the internet a better research tool by incorporating more networks. When there was a serious clash between paymasters and scientists over the issue of security, it was resolved amicably through the division of the internet into military and civilian networks in 1983.

Partly as a consequence of this harmonious relationship (sustained, seemingly, even during the Vietnam War), scientists were in a position to impose their values on the general development of the net. The ideology of science is committed strongly to the open disclosure of information and, in principle, to intellectual co-operation in order to further the shared goal of scientific advance. This was manifested in the co-operative way in which internet protocols were developed. It was also reflected in the open release of these protocols since the internet's builders were seeking to promote good science, not to make money through proprietary exclusion. The culture of science also fosters interaction and discussion, and this influenced the way in which the early internet came to be used. Emailing soon eclipsed remote computing as the early internet's principal function.

However, the culture of academic life is, in largely unconscious ways, exclusionary. Academic work is seldom addressed to people outside the relevant knowledge community, which is why so much of it is buried in obscure publications and self-referential vocabulary. This exclusionary tradition was also a feature of the early internet. Considerable computer expertise was needed for people to go online, and academic computer scientists showed little interest in changing this.

The third cultural influence shaping the early internet was the American counter-culture of the 1980s. This was constituted primarily by three overlapping (and not always mutually harmonious) subcultures. A hippy subculture sought individual self-realization through the development of self-knowledge and freedom from repressive convention; a communitarian subculture aimed to promote togetherness through a change of social attitudes, and experiments such as the commune; and a radical subculture hoped to achieve collective emancipation from patriarchal capitalism or, in a more populist mode, to 'give power to the people'. While this counter-culture was very much in decline by the 1980s, it directed considerable energy towards redefining the online world – perhaps from disappointment about how things had turned out offline.

The counter-cultural movement redefined the meaning and purpose of the internet. Even in the early days of ARPANET, computer use was not confined solely to work since some of its users had emailed each other about science fiction. Commercial online services in the early 1980s also offered chat rooms and the opportunity to shop online. But the counter-culture helped to develop new uses for the net: as a campaign organizer, virtual community and subcultural playground.

These were pioneered partly by local area networks, run usually as co-operatives heavily dependent on volunteer labour. This localized approach was typified by the WELL (Whole Earth Lectronic Link), set up in the San Francisco area in 1985.[12] It was the brainchild of Stewart Brand, then a radical rock concert impresario, and Larry Brilliant, a left-wing doctor and Third World campaigner. Brilliant enrolled numerous fellow former members of Hog Farm, a large, self-sufficient agricultural commune in Tennessee (once supposedly boasting over a thousand members). They created an electronic commune that grew into 300 computer-mediated 'conferences' which brought together social and political activists, as well as enthusiasts of all kinds. One of its largest subgroups was composed of followers of the radical rock group the Grateful Dead. Deadheads (as they were disrespectfully called) spent hours online discussing the Grateful Dead's enigmatic lyrics and exchanging music recorded at live gigs – something the group supported as part of its public stand in favour of the 'pirating' of its music.

There also developed geographically dispersed grass-roots networks, usually set up by students in university campuses. These included Usenet (1979), BITNET (1981), FidoNet (1983) and PeaceNet (1985). The most important of these were Usenet news groups built around the UNIX system. They were set up initially to discuss issues to do with UNIX software and trouble-shooting. They proliferated to cover a wide range of issues, growing from three sites in 1979 to 11,000 by 1988. During these early years, Usenet created a significant space for the expression of minority views, and exploited the global potential of the internet by building extensive international links.

The counter-culture also contributed to the emergence of radical computer capitalism. Thus Steve Jobs and Steve Wozniak, who launched Apple in 1980, came out of the alternative movement. Jobs had travelled to India in a quest for personal enlightenment, while Wozniak was heavily involved in the radical rock scene. In 1982, Wozniak personally funded the organization of a rock festival dedicated to the Information Age. At the festival, which attracted more people than Woodstock, there was a giant videoscreen on which was projected a simple message:

> There is an explosion of information dispersal in the technology and we think this information has to be shared. All great thinkers about democracy said that the key to democracy is access to information. And now we have a chance to get information into people's hands like never before.[13]

In addition, the counter-culture influenced a number of postgraduate students in computer science departments during the 1970s and 1980s. This gave a sharper edge to the stress on freedom, open disclosure and interaction as formative influences on the technical evolution of the net. Crucially, the counter-culture also created a milieu that sustained a determined defence of the pre-market internet when it came under attack (about which more below).

The fourth cultural influence shaping cyberspace was a tradition of public service. If the internet was incubated primarily in the United States, the world wide web was a European invention and came out of a legacy which bequeathed great parks, public libraries, art galleries, public television and radio systems and subsidized art house film industries dispersed throughout Europe. The web's principal architect, Tim Berners-Lee, was inspired by two key ideas that are leitmotifs of the public service tradition: the idea of opening up access to a public good (in this case, the storehouse of knowledge contained in the world's computer system), and of bringing people into communion with each other (in this instance, through the connective potential of the computer). Underpinning Berners-Lee's approach was a set of attitudes that has a distinctive public service trademark. Although not anti-market in a fundamentalist sense, it finds fulfilment in service to others, and resents the exaltation of market values above all else. This resentment is expressed by Berners-Lee in response to a question which, he says, he is often asked in the United States (though less frequently in Europe): Does he regret not making money out of the world wide web?

> What is maddening is the terrible notion [implied in this question] that a person's value depends on how important and financially successful they are, and that this is measured in terms of money . . . Core in my upbringing was a value system that put monetary gain well in its place.[14]

Berners-Lee's decision not to promote the web through a private company was prompted mainly by a concern that it could trigger competition, and lead to the subdivision of the web into private domains. This would have subverted his conception of 'a universal medium for sharing information'. Instead, he persuaded CERN to release in 1991 the world wide web code as a free gift to the community. He became subsequently the head of a public service agency regulating the web (World Wide Web Consortium (W3C)), since this enabled him to 'think about what was best for the world, as opposed to what would be best for one commercial internet'.[15]

The fifth cultural influence shaping the net was the values of the market. At first, these seemed benign and progressive. Their initial effect was to counter the exclusionary norms of academic life by democratizing the web. In 1993, a commercial web browser (Netscape) was launched that used colour images, and made the web more accessible. Indeed, it played a key role in popularizing use of the web. It was followed by the creation of commercial websites that were fun to visit.

In the mid-1990s, all aspects of the internet seemed enormously positive. Even if the internet was a product of a superpower war-machine, its military legacy was terminated in 1990 when ARPANET handed over control of the public internet backbone to the National Science Foundation. A combination of academic, counter-cultural and public service values had created an open public space which was decentralized and largely uncontrolled. It had established a tradition of co-operation in which software codes were freely disclosed, and it had greatly extended the uses made of the net, not least through the creation of the world wide web. The growing influence of commerce seemed merely to be extending the benefits of this new medium to more people, without detracting from its fundamental nature.

Commercialization of the internet

The largely uncritical reception given to the increasing commercialization of the net during the mid-1990s accorded with the ethos of the period. This was a time when deregulated capitalism was trumpeted as the only way to organize an efficient economy, and when capitalism's victory over communism was hailed as the 'end of history'. The mood music of the time was reinforced by the outpourings of net experts. The MIT guru, Nicholas Negroponte, set the tone in a celebrated book, published in 1995, which portrayed the internet as the centrepiece of a democratizing digital revolution. 'The information industry,' he declared, 'will become more of a boutique business . . . the customers will be people and their computers agents.' The public, he predicted, will *pull* what it wants from the internet and digital media, rather than accept what is *pushed* at it by media giants. Fundamental change was already upon us. Media consumption, he claimed, is becoming 'customized' according to individual taste, and 'the monolithic empires of mass media are dissolving into an army of cottage industries', making obsolete 'industrial-age cross-ownership laws'.[16] Similarly Mark Poster, another revered net expert, also concluded in 1995 that we are entering the 'second media age' in which monopoly is being replaced by choice, the distinction between senders and receivers is coming to an end, and the ruled are being transformed into rulers.[17] In these, and most other commentaries, the market was not viewed as a limitation on the emancipatory power of the net.

The coalition that had created the pre-market internet fractured during the mid-1990s. Some academic computer scientists set up internet companies and became millionaires. Others quietly acquiesced to software licensing restrictions. University administrators looked for ways to make money out of their computer science departments. A new generation of computer industry managers emerged, whose informality and populism seemed to set them apart from the stuffy corporate culture of their predecessors. In this changed environment, capitalism seemed hip: the way to make money, express individuality and prevent the state from taking control. The language used to discuss new media changed. The metaphor of the 'information superhighway', with its 1950s association of statist modernism, gave way to the romantic image of 'cyberspace', derived from science fiction.[18] Everything seemed wondrous, transformative, positive.

However, the accelerating force of commercialization began to change the internet in ways that had not been anticipated. The open disclosure of information in pursuit of scientific advance that had shaped the net began to be superseded by the imposition of intellectual property rights in pursuit of profit. Software codes were no longer disclosed openly on an automatic basis, but were often restricted by licensing arrangements. Still more potentially undermining of the traditions of the early net was the transparent desire of some leading net companies to charge website fees. They intended to make free visits only a temporary measure, in order to foster a 'habit' that users would be willing to pay for once they were hooked. This threatened to change the internet out of all recognition, transforming an open electronic commons into fees-only, private enclosures.

The belief that 'peripheral voices' would move centre-stage in the digital era – central to a naive mid-1990s view of the internet – became increasingly implausible. This was partly because some search engines evolved into general portals which 'mainstreamed' the internet experience.[19] Their central objective was to retain users for as long as possible in order to sell their 'eyeballs' to advertisers and, also subsequently, to sell information about their net behaviour. This led general portals to construct 'hub and spoke' websites, in which users were encouraged to follow defined pathways, and return to the home base before venturing out again. These pathways led to 'channels' which structured the internet experience. For example, in 2002, Yahoo! UK offered a basic choice between shopping, information, fun, business, personal and connect channels, while its main rivals offered variations of the same. Within content 'channels', prominence was given to what was popular (since the aim was to retain users) and also to what was sponsored. Thus, in 2002, AOL UK had a tie-in with Blockbusters for entertainment; MSN UK with Encarta for 'learning'; and Freeserve with Barclays Bank for business information. In short, the rise of general portals encouraged a middle-of-the road, convergent use of the internet, strongly dependent on established sources.

The beguiling vision of boutiques, cottage industries and consumer-sovereigns, conjured into being by Californian net academics, proved to be wide of the mark. A small number of companies, most notably Microsoft and America Online (AOL), gained pole position in the early commercial development of the net. The net's growing popularity then prompted leading media corporations – Time Warner, Vivendi, Disney, Bertelsmann, News Corporation, among others – to launch sophisticated websites or to form joint ventures with major telecommunications or software companies in order to establish a significant online presence. These media superpowers had enormous assets: back catalogues of content, large reserves of cash and expertise, close links with the advertising industry, brand visibility and cross-promotional resources. Although their start-ups sometimes floundered, enough succeeded for them to dominate cyberspace in a remarkably short period of time. In 1998, over three-quarters of the thirty-one most visited news and entertainment websites were affiliated with large media firms.[20] In 1999, the websites of broadcast TV networks and MSNBC were the most visited sites by 'news users'.[21] The effect of the media majors' incursions into cyberspace was also to raise the prevailing level of costs. Creating and maintaining a multi-media, audience-pulling website became an expensive business, offering few openings to those with limited resources.

A side effect of commercialization was to promote net advertising. The advertising industry introduced first of all the banner advertisement (a horizontal strip, reminiscent of early press display advertisements). This was followed by advertisements of different shapes such as 'button', 'skyscraper' and pop-up 'interstitials', and by new types of advertisements that contain audio-visual or dynamic elements (more like television commercials). Online selling to the public also became a more prominent feature, especially after the adoption in 1997 of a standard protocol for credit card transactions.

In this new commercial world, professional conventions – such as maintaining a 'fire-wall' between editorial and advertising – were weakened. In particular, the emergence of stand-alone, promotion websites converted advertisers into controllers of editorial content, rather than buyers of space, designated as advertising, in environments controlled by professional media staff – the offline norm. Typifying this new net phenomenon was the Pepsi website which offered, in 2002, a Britney Spears mini-site, games, music, and an opportunity to learn about the 'Joy of Pepsi'. This 'ad-free ad' approach can lead to abuse. Naomi Klein cites as an example of lowered standards a website called Parent Soup, paid for by Fisher-Price, Starbucks, Procter & Gamble and Polaroid. It calls itself a 'parent's community', and imitates a user-driven newsgroup. However, when parents go to Parent Soup, they receive such 'branded wisdom' as the way to improve your child's self-esteem is to take Polaroids of her.[22]

New layer of control

A central feature of the early net, its absence of central control, was weakened as a consequence of commercialization. Net entrepreneurs developed 'cookies' – markers deposited by websites on computer hard drives – in order to log and transmit information about user behaviour. They also introduced authentication procedures for identifying users, and the status of communications (for example, by developing a digital watermark registering whether a communication has been paid for). A whole new technology of commercial surveillance came into being during the 1990s.

This surveillance was deployed very extensively. In the United States, an estimated 92 per cent of commercial websites aggregate, sort and use for commercial purposes data about people's use of the net, wherever they are.[23] Most people make themselves vulnerable to this monitoring by waiving their rights to privacy in order to gain website access. Overriding 'human rights' protection of privacy is minimal in the United States, though there is more protection in Europe. In addition, people's use of the net is often monitored at work. According to a study released in 2000, 73 per cent of US firms routinely check on their workforce's use of the net.[24]

The internet has thus ceased to be an anonymous place and instead has become a glasshouse (although many people appear not to be aware of this when they go online in the privacy of their homes). Moreover, while surveillance technology was developed for purely commercial purposes (to sell data about users, protect financial transactions and prevent piracy) it began to be used in other ways. In the late 1990s, government agencies used surveillance technology to identify net users, share information about them, and prosecute them (as in the case of international paedophile rings). While there is nothing wrong in governments intervening to protect the vulnerable, such as abused children, it underlines the point that the internet is no longer 'uncontrolled'. Indeed, authoritarian governments have become adept at using the vulnerable point in the internet system – internet service providers – in order to snoop and censor.[25]

Corporate pressure was also brought to bear in the United States (and elsewhere) for the net to become subject to stronger property protection. In 1976, the United States passed a Copyright Act, which extended copyright to software. This was buttressed in 1998 by the Digital Millennium Act, which greatly strengthened legal provision against 'circumvention'. Its effect was to overprotect intellectual property rights in cyberspace at the expense of 'fair use'.[26] The likelihood is that increased pressure will be exerted in the future to strengthen still further intellectual property rights, both in national and international jurisdictions, since the music majors are currently losing their battle against music piracy.

Cyberchartist revolt

In short, the internet changed profoundly as a consequence of the establishment of a market system, the successful incursion of media majors into cyberspace, and the imposition of a new layer of technological control. However, these trends did not go unopposed.

When the progressive coalition which shaped the early internet fell apart, one group stood firm. This was an informal community of hackers who set about opposing 'proprietary software' – programs whose use was restricted by private patent or copyright. They may be likened to nineteenth-century Chartists on several counts, even if their central objectives were different. Hackers played a significant part, as did the Chartists, in keeping open channels of free expression;[27] they were inspired, like many Chartists, by an ethic of co-operation; and, like numerous Chartists, some sought to defend a nostalgically remembered past against the new market order. But, above all – and this is perhaps the key point – they participated in the *same*, continuing battle for media freedom.

The cyberchartist revolt began in 1984 when Richard Stallman, a radical programmer at MIT, set up the Free Software Foundation. He had been outraged when a colleague had refused to pass on a printer code on the grounds that it was now restricted by licence. This seemed to Stallman something new and alien, an enforced form of selfishness that violated the norm of co-operation on which his professional life had been based. His outrage turned to anger when AT&T announced its intention to license the widely used and previously unrestricted UNIX operating system. In his view, this amounted to the corporate capture, with the full authority of the law, of a program that had been communally produced.

Richard Stallman, a bearded, romantic figure with the appearance of an Apostle, gave up his secure job and set about building almost single-handedly a free alternative to the UNIX operating system. It was called GNU (standing for 'GNU is not UNIX'). Between 1984 and 1988, Stallman designed an editor and compiler, which were hailed by the cyberchartist community as masterpieces of skill and ingenuity. Subsequently, his hands became damaged from overwork, and he slowed down. The GNU project was still some way from completion. However, a then unknown Finnish student, Linus Torvalds, who had heard Stallman give a charismatic talk in Helsinki, filled the gap. With the help of his friends, Torvalds developed in 1990 the missing kernel of the GNU system. The hacker community collectively improved the resulting GNU/Linux system, making it one of the most reliable in the world. Such was its sustained success that IBM decided in 1998 to hitch its wagon to the hacker star. It officially backed the Linux system, agreeing to invest money in its further development without seeking to exercise any form of proprietary control.

IBM also embraced, on the same terms, the Apache server. This derived from a program released free by a publicly funded agency, the National Center for Supercomputing Applications (NCSA) at the University of Illinois. Initially full of bugs, it was transformed by the hacker community through cumulative improvements ('patches'), and renamed Apache. It became a widely used free server – its success again accounting for its open source adoption by IBM.

What partly underpinned the effectiveness of this concerted protest was that it enlisted the protection of the state (something that libertarian hackers tend to ignore). The Free Software Foundation set up by Stallman released its projects under a General Public License (GPL). This contained a 'copyleft' clause (the wordplay is typical hacker humour) requiring any subsequent improvement in free software to be made available to the community under the GPL. Contract and copyright law was thus deployed to prevent companies from modifying free software and then claiming the resulting version as their property. It was also used to ensure that future refinements in free software were 'gifted' back to the community. A similar legal formula was adopted by the less radical, 'open' (as distinct from 'free') source movement, though in a more permissive form.

The cyberchartist revolt kept alive the tradition of the open disclosure of information. It perpetuated the co-operative norms of the scientific community in which people make improvements, or develop new applications (such as the world wide web), on the basis of open access to information, and then return the favour by making the basis of their discoveries freely available. In this way, cyberchartists perpetuated the moral economy of academic science, with its belief in co-operation, freedom and open debate in pursuit of scientific advance. They also undermined attempts to impose a market regime on the net by making available free or open source alternatives.

Who were these remarkable people, and what inspired them to challenge corporate power in cyberspace? They were a relatively homogeneous group, consisting mainly of highly trained computer workers employed by universities, research laboratories and the computer industry, as well as university students and knowledgeable computer enthusiasts. Their first, and best, chronicler, Steven Levy, argues that they tended to subscribe to a shared set of beliefs.[28] These can be summarized as five precepts: information should be free; respect should be earned through constructive achievement, not position or credential; never trust authority; computers have the power to improve the world; for this reason, they should be put to work for the benefit of humanity. While Cyberchartists' motives were philanthropic, it is also clear that many enjoyed hacking enormously. They gained satisfaction from the thrill of creativity in building or improving new programs. They were gratified by the recognition they received from their peers. Many also derived a sense of purpose from working for the good of society, and living by a set of values superior to those of conformist corporate culture. The hacker tradition combined pleasure with service to others, and drew upon a hybrid culture that married individualism to collectivism. This conjunction is expressed succinctly in a stanza quoted admiringly by Richard Stallman:

> If I am not for myself, who will be for me?
> If I am only for myself, what am I?
> If not now, when?[29]

As the cyberchartist revolt developed, splits emerged on generational lines. Older cyberchartists, like Stallman, were intent upon preserving the values of the pre-market internet, while younger ones, like Torvalds, tended to be less anti-market. The computer industry boom also winnowed the ranks of cyberchartists, separating the dedicated from the dilettantes. As Eric Raymond, another chronicler of the hackers' revolt, comments:

> commercial demand for programmers has been so intense for so long that anyone who can be seriously distracted by money is already gone. Our community has been self-selected for other things – accomplishment, pride, artistic passion, and each other.[30]

Yet, in media legend, hackers are destructive and threatening: they spread viruses, break into computer systems in ways that imperil lives, and engage in online theft. This demonization obscures a crucial distinction between 'hackers' and 'crackers', 'white' and 'black' hats, those who work for the good of society and those who are antisocial, which is widely understood within the hacker community. To lump the two together is to seek to delegitimate cyberchartists in much the same way that an attempt was made to stigmatize Chartists as law-breakers in the 1840s.

Consumer resistance

The cyberchartist revolt was effective mainly because it was backed up by recalcitrant consumers. The pre-market internet had accustomed people to expect internet software to be free. Net companies found it difficult to re-educate them into paying.

This is illustrated by early attempts to commercialize the web. In 1993, the publicly funded agency, NCSA, released free its pioneer browser, Mosaic, on the net. Within six months, a million or more copies were downloaded. Members of the Mosaic team then set up a private company and offered an improved, commercial version, Netscape, on a three-month, free trial basis. However, demands for payment after the free trial were widely ignored. Netscape's management then had to decide whether to insist on payment or change tack. It opted to make its service free because it feared – probably rightly – that continued attempts to charge would cause people to migrate to a free alternative. Netscape turned instead to advertising and consultancy as its main source of revenue.[31]

Companies which tried to charge website fees also ran into trouble. A large number failed.[32] The only type of web content for which a significant number of people seemed willing to pay was either pornography or financial information. This also had the effect of propelling pioneering net companies towards advertising as their main source of revenue.

The virtues of net advertising were widely trumpeted. The net reached a mainly young and affluent audience. Its technology enabled advertising to be targeted towards specialist groups with almost surgical precision. Above all, the net offered a unique selling point: consumers could click on an advertisement, be taken direct to the advertiser's site, obtain more information and buy the product or service in question.

The only problem was that there appeared to be built-in resistance to net advertising because it was viewed from the start as intrusive. An early warning signal came in 1994 when the US law firm, Canter and Siegel, posted an advertisement for its immigration law advice service to thousands of news groups. The following day, it was so inundated with abusive replies ('flames') that its internet service provider crashed repeatedly.[33] In 1995, a survey found that two-thirds of Americans did not want any net advertising.[34] People became adept at avoiding ads by clicking the delete button. New ways of engaging user interest ran into problems: audio-visual ads were expensive, and took time to download. In the UK, crude banner ads still accounted for 52 per cent of net advertising expenditure in 2001. Worst still, the extent of net user resistance to advertising became embarrassingly transparent. In 2001, the percentage of users 'clicking through' to advertising sites was generally less than 1 per cent.[35] For all of these reasons, net advertising grew at a much slower pace than had been anticipated. In 2002, it still amounted to only 1 per cent of the UK's total media advertising expenditure.[36]

Direct selling on the net also proved to be much more difficult than anticipated. It tended to be confined to a limited range of products such as music, live events, books and holidays. Many people, it transpired, liked to shop in person, and were doubtful about the security of online credit card purchases. The dawning realization that net retailing was going to take a long time to establish successfully, and would require a heavy investment with a deferred and speculative return, was the main cause of the dotcom crash of 2000 to 2001.

The online Klondike rush was over almost before it had begun. It was not only small net companies that ran into trouble. Even market leaders such as Yahoo! were forced to issue profit warnings, and major conglomerates such as AOL Times Warner and Vivendi had to restructure, partly as a consequence of failed net investments. Venture capital which had poured money into the internet economy lost confidence and withdrew support.

In short, commercialization did not take hold fully because the economy of the internet proved to be precarious. Underlying this fragility was the unwill-ingness of the public to buy heavily online, respond to net advertising and pay website fees. A revolt within the computer world, and unobtrusive resistance from the public, stalled – at least for a time – the market take-over of the net.

Contested space

The history of the internet is thus a chronicle of contradiction. In its mainly pre-market phase, the internet was powerfully influenced by the values of academic science, American counter-culture and European public service. It began as a research tool. It blossomed into a subcultural playground and medium of grass-roots concerns, and it developed the world wide web as a public space open to all.

However, this early formation of the web was overlaid by a new commer-cial regime. Major media organizations established popular websites, while general portals organized the internet into a convergent, 'mainstream' expe-rience. Net entertainment shifted minority views to the margins.

Yet the old order refused to surrender without a struggle. Dissenting computer workers resisted the new regime of enforced intellectual property rights by making available free or open source software. Users, conditioned by the pre-market norms of the net, declined to be re-educated into consumers.

As a result, the internet came to exhibit incongruent features. It is still a decentralized system in which information is transmitted via independent, variable pathways through dispersed computer power. But on top of this is imposed a new technology of commercial surveillance which enables com-mercial operators – and potentially governments – to monitor what people do online. In a similarly contradictory way, the internet is managed by public ser-vice trusts, a legacy from its pre-market past, but nearly all the net's major players are now private companies. Likewise, the web remains an open space in which to roam, but most of its most visited sites are privately owned. Yet these websites are mostly loss-making because they dare not charge visitors for fear they go elsewhere – where it is free.

The balance struck between the old and the new is inherently unstable, and may well change quite rapidly; but, as of now, the two leading understandings of the net both seem simplistic. The net is not an uncontrolled agency of enlightenment where the 'push' culture associated with powerful media cor-porations has been vanquished in favour of the 'pull' culture of the sovereign user; yet, equally, the internet is not a featureless mall of digital capitalism. It remains a contested space, exposed to the opposed influences of pre-market and market regimes.

So far, we have offered a history of the internet which foregrounds its tech-nology and American origins, and contrasts a period of professional and grass-roots influence with the subsequent attempt to impose a new order of market control. This largely leaves out wider questions about the consequences of the net, and its relationship to the structures of global society. These issues are best addressed by sociologists to whose work we now turn.

Notes

1. Leading exponents of this position are N. Negroponte, *Being Digital* (London, Hodder & Stoughton, 1996 [1995]); and M. Poster, 'Cyberdemocracy: internet and the public sphere', in D. Porter (ed.) *Internet Culture* (New York, Routledge, 1997), and, in a more circumspect form, H. Rheingold, *The Virtual Community* (Cambridge, MA, MIT Press, 2000, rev. edn).
2. D. Schiller, *Digital Capitalism* (Cambridge, MA, MIT Press, 2000), a bold and innovative attack on internet orthodoxy. See also a more guarded exposition of a similar position in R. McChesney, *Rich Media, Poor Democracy* (Urbana, University of Illinois Press, 1999).
3. The best introductory accounts of the underlying science involved in the development of the internet are J. Naughton, *A Brief History of the Future* (London, Phoenix, 2000), a book that makes internet science exciting; and J. Gillies and R. Cailliau, *How the Web Was Born* (Oxford, Oxford University Press, 2000).
4. A. Briggs and P. Burke, *A Social History of the Media* (Cambridge, Polity Press, 2002) p. 291.
5. T. Berners-Lee, *Weaving the Web* (London, Orion, 2000), p. 56.
6. B. Winston, *Media Technology and Society* (London, Routledge, 1998), p. 218.
7. M. Cassells, *The Internet Galaxy* (Oxford, Oxford University Press, 2001).
8. S. Holland (ed.), *The State as Entrepreneur* (London, Weidenfeld & Nicolson, 1972). This position now has more support in Scandinavia and mainland Europe than it does in Britain.
9. J. Abbate, *Inventing the Internet* (Cambridge, MA, MIT Press, 2000); J. Gillies and R. Cailliau, *How the Web Was Born*, Oxford, Oxford University Press, 2000).
10. P. Flichy, 'New media history', in L. Lievrouw and S. Livingstone (eds) *The Handbook of New Media* (London, Sage, 2002).
11. J. Abate, *Inventing the Internet* (Cambridge, MA, MIT Press, 2000), p. 144. Although this is the best relevant history, it mistakenly portrays the commercialization of the net as extending the freedom and diversity traditions of the early internet.
12. H. Rheingold, *The Virtual Community* (Cambridge, MA, MIT Press, 2000, rev. edn).
13. P. Flichy, 'The construction of new digital media', *New Media and Society*, 1 (1), 1999, p. 37.
14. T. Berners-Lee, *Weaving the Web* (London, Orion, 2000), p. 116.
15. Ibid., p. 91.
16. N. Negroponte, *Being Digital* (London, Hodder & Stoughton, 1996 [1995]), pp. 57–8 and 85.
17. M. Poster, *The Second Media Age* (Cambridge, Polity Press, 1995).
18. T. Streeter, 'Romanticism in business culture: the Internet, the 1990s and the origins of irrational exuberance', in A. Calabrese and C. Sparks (eds) *Toward a Political Economy of Culture* (Boulder, CO, Rowman & Littlefield, 2003, forthcoming).

19. V. Miller, 'Search engines, portals and global capitalism', in D. Gauntlett (ed.) *Web Studies* (London, Arnold, 2000).
20. R. McChesney, *Rich Media, Poor Democracy* (Urbana, University of Illinois Press, 1999), p. 163.
21. C. Sparks, 'From dead trees to live wires: the Internet's challenge to the traditional newspaper', in J. Curran and M. Gurevitch (eds) *Mass Media and Society* (London, Arnold, 2000, 3rd edn), p. 283, Figure 13.8.
22. N. Klein, *No Logo* (London, Flamingo, 2001), pp. 42–3.
23. L. Lessig, *Code and Other Laws of Cyberspace* (New York, Basic Books, 1999, p. 153.
24. M. Castells, *The Internet Galaxy* (Oxford, Oxford University Press, 2001), p. 74.
25. M. Price, *Media and Sovereignty* (Cambridge, MIT Press, 2002); L. Stein and N. Sinha, 'New global media and communication policy: the role of the state in the twenty-first century', in L. Lievrouw and S. Livingstone (eds) *The Handbook of New Media* (London, Sage, 2001).
26. L. Lessig, *The Future of Ideas* (New York, Random House, 2001).
27. See Chapter 2.
28. S. Levy, *Hackers* (London, Penguin, 1994).
29. Cited S. Williams, *Free as in Freedom* (Sebastopol, CA, O'Reilly, 2002), p. 102.
30. *Ibid.*, p. 167.
31. T. Berners-Lee, *Weaving the Web* (London, Orion, 2000), pp. 107–8.
32. D. Schiller, *Digital Capitalism* (Cambridge, MA, MIT Press, 2000); C. Sparks, '*From dead trees to live wires: the Internet's challenge to the traditional newspaper*', in J. Curran and M. Gurevitch (eds) *Mass Media and Society* (London, Arnold, 2000, 3rd edn).
33. G. Goggin, 'Pay per browse? The Web's commercial future', in D. Gauntlett (ed.) *Web Studies* (London, Arnold, 2000), p. 106.
34. R. McChesney, *Rich Media, Poor Democracy* (Urbana, University of Illinois Press, 1999), p. 132.
35. L. Cheshire, 'What influence has advertising had upon the development of the Internet?' (Unpublished BA dissertation, Goldsmiths College, University of London, 2002).
36. *Advertising Statistics Yearbook 2002* (London, Advertising Association, 2002).

17

Sociology of the internet

Introduction

There is a very large literature, dubbed 'internetphilia' by Korinna Patelis,[1] which argues that the internet offers a solution to a series of intractable problems. It is represented to be a patent medicine for our social ills: the decline of social community, political apathy, national prejudice, social discrimination, public disempowerment, and much else besides.

This tradition extols the virtues of internet technology which, it claims, has brought into being a self-expressive, interactive, egalitarian, global, virtual space world. This virtual world is redeeming the real world, and correcting its shortcomings.

The counter-argument to this is that cyberspace is shaped not so much by its wondrous technology as by the structures and processes of the real world. The online world, in this view, is defined by the offline world, not the other way round.

This is a central debate in net sociology. It also provides a good starting point for assessing the role and influence of the net.

Global understanding

It is often argued that the internet is shrinking the universe and promoting international understanding.[2] This view focuses on the potential of internet technology to enable free and equal exchange between people around the globe. What it ignores is the way in which this global interchange is distorted by unequal relations between rich and poor.[3]

At the end of the twentieth century, 20 per cent of the world's population disposed of 86 per cent of its wealth. This affluent fifth is in general the best educated, most technologically advanced section of the globe: it also has the highest density of computers per head, and accounts for most of the world's full-time online workers. These advantages structure the opportunity to communicate in cyberspace. Thus, in 2000, London had more internet websites than the whole of Africa.[4] More generally, the United States and western Europe generate much of the content of the web, while whole areas of the world contribute very little.

The capacity to win attention is even more unequal than the opportunity to communicate in cyberspace. We have already seen how media conglomerates account for a high proportion of the most visited websites because they have back catalogues of content, large resources and high visibility. These advantages help to create privileged centres of online communication. In 2000, the USA produced almost two-thirds of the top thousand most visited websites. Still more remarkable, it accounted for 83 per cent of the total pageviews of internet users.[5]

This dominance is facilitated by language. Less than 10 per cent of the world speak English as their first language. But English is becoming intelligible to a growing number of people, and has begun to assume the function once occupied by Latin in medieval Europe as the shared language of a transnational élite. In the late 1990s, an estimated 85 per cent of the web was written in English.[6]

There are thus strong pressures that act like a magnetic force of attraction pulling people towards the USA and northern centres of the world wide web. The converse is also true. Communications, not written in English and not positioned at the top of search engines' hierarchies, obtain scant attention. For example, anything written in Marathi is likely to be ignored in the global dialogue of the web, even though the population of Mahrashtra and adjacent Marathi-speaking areas, in India, exceeds that of Britain.

If the opportunity to gain attention is distributed unevenly, so too is consumption. In 2000, a mere 0.16 per cent of the Indian population were internet users, compared with 41 per cent in the United States. This disparity is replicated around the world, and gives rise to a global community of internet users which bears little relationship to the distribution of the world's population. North America and western Europe accounted for 66 per cent of internet users in 2000, while the whole of Latin America and Africa accounted for only 5 per cent.[7]

In short, the imbalance of power and resources in the offline world structure the online world. The 6 per cent of the world who use the net are recruited primarily from the affluent; they consume content generated mainly by the rich centres of the world; and they communicate usually in a language that most of the world does not understand. Yet, if the stock fantasy of the net utopians is to be believed, this provides the basis of the global dialogue that is nurturing global understanding, and defining the world's priorities. This fantasy is not simply wrong. It is also pernicious because it encourages the privileged to delude themselves that their concerns are globally representative.

Freedom from place

Another frequently invoked claim is that the internet is transforming our relationship to the physical world.[8] This is based primarily on inferences derived from the nature of internet technology. Because the net is global, its use is thought to be weakening identification with place ('deterritorialization'), and in particular with the nation. And since the net enables the formation of virtual communities of like-minded people, unconnected to where they live or work, it is also said to be loosening ties to specific contexts ('disembedding'). Physical and virtual geographies are allegedly de-merging in a form that is weakening national prejudice, and eroding the link between social interaction and locality.

As theoretical formulations, these arguments seem plausible. However, they appear rather less commanding when they are assessed in the light of actual evidence about internet use. Empirical research shows time and again that the virtual world is best viewed as an extension of the structures and processes of the real world, rather than as a technologically determined space that is reconfiguring society.

To illustrate this, we will turn to perhaps the best ethnography of the net – Daniel Miller and Don Slater's engaging study centred on Trinidad. They show that the net is absorbed into the everyday life and social practices of its users. They also reveal that the net promotes, rather than detracts from, a sense of place. A number of Trinidadian websites parade symbols of national identity, or express pride in national achievements. Chat rooms celebrate a strong sense of being 'Trini' by enacting through 'ole talk' and 'liming' what is widely perceived to be national traits – the ability to communicate, entertain, be warm and expressive. Encounters with people of other nations in virtual space heighten rather than diminish a sense of national belonging. Many Trinidadians view themselves as 'virtual' envoys, seek to convey a favourable impression of their country, and are sometimes taken aback by how little other people seem to know about their culture and traditions. Indeed, Miller and Slater conclude (with perhaps an element of debunking overstatement) that '"being Trini" and "representing Trinidad" were not always the central or most conscious aspect of internet activities, but we rarely found an internet experience in which they did not feature'.[9] The net also facilitates an idealization of Trinidad among Trinidadians living in Britain, and provides a concrete way of staying in touch with relatives in Trinidad.

It may be that this case study is untypical. There is, argue Miller and Slater, a widespread desire among Trinidadians to identify with a stable, national community, partly as a consequence of the dislocations caused by slavery, migration and colonial subordination. In some other countries with a less traumatic past, where the tug of national identity is weaker, the net may promote a different relationship to place.

Yet at the heart of Miller and Slater's account is a core theme that does seem to provide a secure basis for generalization. The virtual world emerges in their analysis not as a featureless space determined by its technology, but as a field of interaction shaped by local contexts. People relate to the net in terms of attitudes, cultural references and concerns derived from diverse, *real-world* locations, and this strongly influences in turn what they get out of the net. This insight accords with all that we know about media consumption in general, accumulated through two generations of audience research.[10]

This stress on the socially situated basis of net consumption also accords with other studies. The net is generally used as an extension of everyday relationships: it provides a way of staying in touch with friends and relatives, much like the phone, and – in the past – the mailed letter.[11] Whether it also supports an identification with place depends upon the particular orientations and social contexts of net users. Thus, Larry Gross reveals the growing importance of the net in providing a source of identity and moral support for isolated, gay teenagers, without links to local gay subcultures, and for gay men in countries where gay sex is illegal.[12] In this case, the net seemingly provides an escape from an oppressive local context to a placeless, global gay village.

By contrast, Madhavi Mallapragada argues that the net helps to sustain an imperilled 'Indian' identity among diasporic Indians living in the United States. The net offers them a channel of communication with friends and relations in India. It disseminates symbols of Indian identity and culture, and provides a forum of discussion on identity themes (such as how to persuade Indian-American teenagers to identify with their Indian heritage). The net also offers a socially acceptable way of searching for eligible Indian life partners.[13] In this case, then, the net fosters identification with a national homeland.

These two case studies point in opposite directions. Yet they have one thing in common: they both show that the meanings derived from the net are shaped by users' concerns and terms of reference. Their overarching implication is thus that different user inputs and contexts give rise to different symbolic uses of the net.

Given the current stock of knowledge about the net, it is not possible to say whether the net promotes 'freedom' from a sense of place; but what we do know is that this is certainly not true in relation to some users. Confident generalizations about how the net is promoting deterritorialization and disembedding, inferred from its technology, are simplistic and misleading.

Social emancipation

This insistence on the need to contextualize the use of the net in its social setting in order to assess the net's wider influence on society runs counter to another widely canvassed view of the net. This sees the virtual world as a vanguard social space in which a more tolerant, egalitarian and emancipated universe is being forged. This virtual realm of the imagination is promoting social emancipation in the real world.

The progressive nature of the online world is derived, allegedly, from its 'postmodern technology'.[14] This enables anonymous interaction, in which people are able to escape from the visible markers which proclaim their gender, age and ethnicity, and position them in ascribed social roles. People can assume online whatever identity they want, and also talk about themselves with unaccustomed frankness, in this way exploring fundamental questions about who they are and whom they want to be. Role-playing (as in pretending to be a member of the opposite sex) can also be liberating, it is argued, because it enables people to experience at first hand conditioned social responses and to acquire new insight about others.

'Virtual disembodiment' – being taken out of one's physical self in the virtual world – is thus said in cybercultural studies to assist the building of emancipated subjectivities, and the gaining of enlightenment. This claim is invested with added significance as a consequence of theoretical developments in poststructuralist theory. These stress that there is no fixed and essential self, defined by biology, nature or reason, but rather identities that are always 'performances' enacted in relation to others. Seen in this light, the virtual world is a place for working out, the equivalent of a health club in which the purposive self can be exercised into a desired shape. It is also, in some accounts, a prefigurative space in which the patterns of the future – in particular fluid, mobile identities freed from the constraints of tradition – can be discerned and cultivated.[15]

However, there are good grounds for thinking that the significance of online role-playing has been exaggerated. While identity games received much attention during the early, experimental phase of the internet in the 1980s, their popularity has since declined. When net use became more widespread, it also became more mundane. A major American survey found in 2000 that 91 per cent of users regularly use email, compared with 28 per cent who participate regularly in chat rooms or online discussions.[16] Online role-playing is concentrated increasingly among teenagers.

Some academic analysts overstate the empowerment of online fantasy games by examining what happens in these games in a form that is abstracted from the social context of reception. Consider, for example, Mizuko Ito's admired account of the 'virtually embodied' in which he describes how Melissa assumes the identity of Tenar when she goes into Multi User Dungeons (MUDs). Tenar is apparently 'a powerful and well-liked figure' who has had virtual sex with, and married, a number of other MUDders. This, we are told, is very strengthening because Melissa is able to import aspects of her dynamic Tenar personality into her everyday world, and her fantasy life 'animates her real life'.[17] Since we are told almost nothing about Melissa's real life, we are forced to take this claim on trust. However, there is one aspect of Melissa 's online identity that seeds doubts. Melissa describes her body online, as it used to be when she was a svelte 18-year-old. What, one wonders, are the social pressures and personal anxieties that cause Melissa to present herself as younger and, by implication, sexier than she is now? Does Melissa's wish fulfilment really make her stronger, or does it increase her sense of loss and reluctance to come to terms with increasing age? It is an entirely characteristic weakness of this celebratory account – and others like it – that such questions are never even addressed.

This 'cyberculture' tradition of research has one even more fundamental flaw. Its underlying notion of empowerment is based on 'self-constitutive strategies of being' – put simply, on individuals taking control through redefining who they are. The virtual world is celebrated because it assists imaginative forms of redefinition and re-enactment. However, this approach tends to discount the compelling ways in which social roles and identities are imposed through early socialization and peer group pressure, and tends to ignore the structures of power that underpin these forms of social regulation. It exaggerates therefore the ease with which significant change can be effected through mind games. Yet, in reality, it requires collective action and political power to engineer fundamental change. The history of the women's movement is instructive in this respect. In Britain, it required large-scale social and political organization, sustained over 140 years, to effect the legislative reforms, institutional changes and cultural shifts needed to achieve even a limited and incomplete social revolution.[18]

Political emancipation

If the internet is not delivering effortless social emancipation through online fun, perhaps it is advancing a progressive politics. After all, it is argued with undeniable eloquence that internet technology converts the desk into a printing press, broadcasting station and place of assembly.[19] This enables 'many-to-many communication' which allegedly is changing the way we do politics. In this view the net is rejuvenating civil society, generating political activism and launching exciting experiments of popular participation in government. Established centres of power, and monopolies of communication, are being bypassed ('disintermediated'); counter-public spheres are being created through net-mediated conferences and chat rooms; and a process of progressive mobilization is under way that will empower the people.

Again, this infectious optimism follows a now familiar pattern. It extrapolates from the technological potential of the net the view that a powerful engine of change is at work, and then fastens on to a few hopeful straws of evidence to confirm the advent of a brave new world. What this approach fails repeatedly to grasp is that the virtual world is not 'determined' by its technology, and 'programmed' to promote progressive change. Rather, the online world is shaped powerfully by the dynamics of the offline world. This limits the power of the net to effect progressive change.

Thus in most advanced liberal democracies, political activism is a minority activity and many people's interest in politics, in ordinary circumstances, is limited. For example, tracking surveys in the USA show that, between 1980 and 2000, less than one in ten Americans attended a political meeting, gave to political funds or helped a political organization.[20] Indeed, the indications are that, for a variety of reasons, the level of political engagement in long-established democracies is falling. In Britain, membership of political parties is in long-term decline, a trend experienced in a number of other European countries.[21] Voting turnout in the 1997 British general election (71 per cent) was the lowest since 1935.[22] Turnout (of under-registered voters) in the 2000 American presidential election was just 50 per cent, dramatically down by comparison with the 1950s and 1960s but consistent with the recent run of US elections.[23]

This low, and probably declining, level of political involvement in the real world influences the content of the virtual world. This is borne out by the content analysis of net content undertaken by Kevin Hill and John Hughes.[24] They found only 6 per cent of web pages in 1997, and only 12 per cent of Usenet news group messages between 1995 and 1996, to be 'political'. The net is no different from most other media in that it marginalizes politics.

However, political communication on the net – even if it is only a tiny part of total net content – is still voluminous. This enables, it has been suggested, politically 'homeless' dissidents to seek out alternative information on the net, and 'reconnect' to the political system through participation in the politics of protest. However, in what is still the best political study of the net, Hill and Hughes skewer this argument in merciless detail. They found that political users of the net in the United States are more inclined than the average citizen to vote for the major two political parties. Political net users are also better informed, more liable to vote in elections, and, in this sense, more fully integrated into the American political system. Above all, they do not tend to seek out information that is unavailable in the normal news environment, but turn instead to mainstream sources such as the CNN and MSNBC websites. In short, large numbers of Amercian political users of the net are news junkies, who routinely turn to the citadels of establishment journalism for more rather than 'different' information.

Hill and Hughes also challenge the view that cyberspace is oriented towards the left or to alternative opinion. Their content analysis of political web pages suggested that 78 per cent fell within the mainstream of American political culture. The exceptions, on both left and right, were in general less sophisticated, smaller and less visible through internet search indices than mainstream content. In the self-organized sections of the net – Usenet news groups and America Online's chat rooms – heterodox views got more (though only a little more) space. However, the right was found to be more vocal, initiating and active than the left.

When the net was a marginal, experimental sphere in which counter-cultural movements were especially active, the net had a different significance, but those halcyon days are over. As the net became more mainstream, and major media conglomerates moved in, the net ceased to be the alternative space that it had been. Indeed, all the indications are that in Europe we are already moving into a new phase in which the state and political parties are mobilizing their large public relations resources to spin messages in cyberspace. In the next general election, the net will be used by the main political parties on a scale never attempted before in Britain.

E-government

However, it is often claimed that the interactive technology of the net enables people to engage in public decision-making in new, more direct and meaningful ways. This may become true in the future, although the evidence so far is not very encouraging.

The best-known public participation project in Europe is Amsterdam's Digital City (called DDS in the Netherlands). It began in 1994 as a ten-week experiment to improve communication between the council and local people. Proving to be unexpectedly popular, it was then reconstituted the following year under a publicly funded Foundation as a virtual city structured around the metaphor of the square. Different squares were given over to particular topics (such as film, art or politics), and, in each of these, cybercafés were established as meeting places. The net was then still a relative novelty, and the experiment brought together diverse groups in the city – hackers linked to the university, artists and musicians, radical activists drawn from the squatters' movement, among others. At its height, the project involved thousands of people; facilitated popular access to computers and online services; and organized votes on a range of issues. It became celebrated in radical circles (as did a similar experiment in Bologna, Italy). However, the level of public involvement fell away after the initial excitement wore off. Acute conflicts undermined the project from within, and adequate long-term, public funding proved not to be forthcoming. By 2001, DDS was in deep trouble and its future seemed uncertain.

Other more modest but, in the long term, probably more significant experiments have been attempted. One approach involves using the net to extend existing procedures of consultation, typified by the work of Citizens Online Democracy (UKCOD) founded in Britain in 1995. For example, in 1997, it co-ordinated and published submissions to the Cabinet Office in response to publication of the Freedom of Information White Paper. What made this first online scrutiny of proposed government legislation noteworthy was that 30 per cent of submissions came from individuals – very much higher than the norm.[25] The net offers, seemingly, a channel in which the unorganized can become more easily involved in democratic consultation.

However, in general, five recurrent problems have bedevilled online participation in government.[26] The first is that citizens' inputs can be divorced from policy outputs: they are mere simulations of open government, unconnected to the real structures of policy-making. The second, linked problem is that some online innovations are really public service promotions: they are about improving consumption of services rather than participation in policy. The third problem is linked to the first two: some people are reluctant to take part in online participation experiments because they think that they will not be taken seriously. The fourth problem has to do with the status of online participation: instant judgements based on pressing a button are open to the republican objection that democracy needs to be accompanied by debate and deliberation. The fifth difficulty is still more fundamental, and at present undermines all attempts to use the net as an agency of direct democracy. Quite simply, cyberdemocracy is not representative.

In most countries, there are large disparities of internet access between rich and poor, young and old, the ethnic majority and some minorities. In the United States, for example, 70 per cent of those earning more than $75,000 used the internet in 2000, compared with 19 per cent among those earning under $15,000.[27] This is very similar to the situation in Britain (see Chapter 18).

E-commerce

The internet is said to being transforming the way business is done. According to Philip Evans and Thomas Wurster, the internet is redefining the relationship between businesses and three groups of people – customers, suppliers and employees – by changing the mode of communicate between them. 'In a deconstructing world', they conclude, the foundations of traditional business strategy are 'blown to bits'.[28] The internet is also said to be the driving force in the creation of a mysterious new entity – the 'new economy'.

What substance do these claims have? Certain industries sometimes lumped together under the heading of the 'information and knowledge economy' – electronics, computing, telecommunications, media and information content producers – are among the fastest growing sectors of advanced economies. They have generated new streams of wealth without changing the goals and dynamics of the market system.[29] They have also displaced unskilled work with skilled work, creating increased rewards for the highly educated and already affluent but shrinking opportunities for lower socio-economic groups. However, the internet is a relatively late and small-scale entrant to the information economy. While it has given birth to prosperous internet service providers, it has failed to sustain a stable, profitable net content-producing industry.

Nor has the advent of online selling to the public brought into being an important 'new economy' retail sector. Net marketing expert Crispin Jameson points to seven factors limiting its growth.[30] The internet, he points out, does not eliminate the need in many sectors to invest heavily in stock, promotion, delivery and service: for example, Amazon made a massive outlay in creating the world's largest bookshop before becoming a successful online bookseller. Many people are nervous about credit card security online, especially in relation to small, unknown companies. In addition, numerous consumers enjoy (often unconsciously) the experience of shopping; want to see the product before buying it; expect the immediate gratification of possession; lack ready access to a personal computer; and are sometimes intimidated by the technical requirements of buying online. It is only in some markets – such as books, music products, video games, computer software, travel, insurance and live events – that the net has made major inroads.

Online shopping is eclipsed by online business-to-business sales. The latter represents, it is claimed, an area of innovation which has changed the dynamics of business.[31] Computer mediation has diminished administration and transport costs in a way that has probably helped the small company. It has enabled a greater number of buyers and sellers to connect to each other. It has extended the geographical reach of their interactions (with European, American and Asian companies regularly competing against each other in open tenders for major contracts). It has also enabled some companies to bypass 'old economy' intermediaries to sell directly to business customers.

However, even this thesis is not quite as straightforward as it seems. Some of the changes wrought by the internet were first set in motion by the electronic data interchange (EDI) systems initiated in the 1960s. Indeed, one reason why new information technology has significantly influenced business-to-business commerce is precisely because it is the culmination of long-term change that preceded the internet and extranet.

The internet, or rather computer networking linked to the net, has also facilitated the development of globally interdependent financial markets operating in real time. These markets have greatly increased capital flows across national boundaries, added to the instability of the global economy, and exerted a powerful cumulative pressure on national governments to converge around market-friendly policies. This said, modern communications technology is only one facilitating factor in the rise and growing political influence of financial markets (and is much less important than the dismantlement of the Bretton Woods system of economic regulation, for mainly political reasons).[32] Once again, the argument that the net has effected a major transformation is not as strong as it at first appears.

The claim that the net is changing the economic order now centres on the argument that the modern firm is 'adapting to the internet as its organisational form'.[33] This takes the form of a decentralized network enterprise, guided by a flat hierarchy, making extensive use of casual labour, able to respond quickly and flexibly to market feedback, with the capacity to deploy customized production strategies in response to specialized demand. This 'new economy' model, it is claimed, takes full advantage of new communications technology to secure productivity gains, to innovate and adapt to the requirements of the global economy. It is the way of the future.

The only problem with this argument is that it relies very heavily on a small number of examples of success (usually featuring Dell and Cisco Systems), some of which have proved to be transient. Giant corporations, able to reap economies of scale and scope, dominate most sectors from bio-chemicals and car manufacture to oil and food retailing. It may be that the 'network enterprise' (formerly called the 'cluster model') will prove triumphant in some markets, particularly those that are fragmented or subject to rapid change. But the case has yet to be made convincingly that it is the business template of the new global order.

In the relevant literature, there is one significant absence. The internet offers an interactive, many-to-many channel of communication ideally suited to promoting deliberative and inclusive forms of democracy in the workplace. But this aspect of the internet's potential is rarely discussed because it does not fit the profit agenda of the e-commerce debate. In its own way, this is a telling reflection of the way in which online communication is shaped by offline power-holders.

Wonders of the net

The limitations of the view that the virtual world is determined by its technology have been highlighted for two reasons. It has a prominent place in the internet literature, and warrants critical scrutiny in its own right. It also offers misleading solutions to problems for which the real remedy lies elsewhere. For this reason its emptiness needs to be exposed.

Yet if the technological determinist argument is recast as a question – Does internet technology make any difference? – it prompts an immediately affirmative response. Internet technology opens up new possibilities and hopes, and new forms of fulfilment. It makes available a treasure trove of information, over a thousand million unique pages of internet content, most of which is freely accessible.[34] It offers new forms of pleasure, not least the 'file sharing' of music and films. It provides a convenient way of staying connected, through email, with an extended network of people. However, of its many functions, we will focus in conclusion on just three which could make a significant difference to the future organization and direction of political life.

First, the internet makes it easier to transmit alternative views to a wider audience. Its email, conferencing and chat room functions facilitate expression of minority views. Software – now freely available – makes it *relatively* easy to establish and develop a website. The cost of 'publishing' online is lower than it is offline because costs are partly laid off on readers, who pay for reproduction and distribution through their personal computer and connection charges.

However, the evolving online distribution system is a serious obstacle to gaining attention on the web. Search engines are the key mechanism for determining which sites are visited. Only a quarter of websites are listed by directory-based search engines such as Yahoo![35] In the case of spider-based search engines (which use software to content analyse websites), only 16 per cent of sites are included on individual engines, and only 42 per cent in total on all the major engines. Yet inclusion is only the first hurdle. The next is to be listed in the top ten or twenty in a search engine's rankings since most people do not persevere beyond this point. This is where most websites drop from sight. While their originators can buy prominence through payment to search engines, this becomes expensive for more than a very short burst of promotion.

In effect, alternative voices tend not to be heard in the main square of the electronic public sphere, but they still get heard in some online back streets. This is because market censorship remains less developed and effective in the online world than it is in the offline world.

The other source of censorship is the state. Although the internet is no longer 'uncontrolled', its decentralized global structure makes it more difficult for authoritarian governments to censor than is the case with offline media. For example, the net provides a space for dissenting voices in Indonesia and Malaysia, which find difficulty in obtaining a hearing in the press and television.[36] Because the net is international, dissidents can also win support or sympathy outside their country. A good contemporary example of this is the way in which the dissenting (and pre-modern) Falun Gong sect has used the net to mobilize international protest against its repression by the Chinese government.[37]

Second, the net provides a means of expression that is well adapted to collective forms of organization. The net played a significant part, for example, in the planning and mobilization of the anti-globalization protests in 1999 to 2002. However, it was only one of a number of means of agitprop communication, including leaflets, posters, mail-outs, phone calls, mainstream media publicity, graffiti, and, increasingly crucial, cheap air travel.[38]

Third, the global, interactive nature of the internet makes it an important democratic tool at a strategic moment. The power of the nation state is waning, with its authority especially in the economic sphere shifting towards international agencies, global financial markets and transnational businesses. These growing centres of power are not held adequately to account because participatory democratic politics is still organized mainly around nation states. This problem is exacerbated by the fact that news media around the world (save for a tiny number of broadcasting channels) are overwhelmingly national and local. Their news values tend to be inward-looking; their scrutiny of global agencies consequently inadequate; and their linking of groups in political debate organized within national polities.[39]

A democratic void is thus opening up as a consequence of a general failure to supervise adequately global power-holders, and the failure of nation-based news media to maintain adequate oversight of their activities. However, the rise of the net offers an opportunity for organized groups to communicate their concerns, and engage in reciprocal debate, in an international context. Already new internet ventures – such as the international net magazine, OpenDemocracy, launched in 2001 – are facilitating international dialogue over a wide range of issues.[40] They are fostering the development of a global civil society, currently the best hope of holding to account the new, global structure of power (including the military hyperpower of the United States).

A key limitation on the internet as a democratizing force remains its enormously unrepresentative social base. However, this is likely to be partly corrected over time. The development of the global television market brought into being major exporting production centres, from Hong Kong to Brazil, catering for different socio-linguistic markets, which weakened American dominance.[41] As the internet develops a similar process will occur, with computer hosts growing rapidly outside the USA–European bloc and communicating in languages other than English. The continued diffusion of computers is also likely to reduce social disparities of net access within affluent countries. This said, the composition of the internet community is likely to remain skewed in favour of privilege for a very long time to come.

Conclusion

The wide-eyed, internetphiliac approach is deeply flawed. The net has changed out of all recognition from its pioneering days when the vision of the net as the redeemer of social ills was first promulgated. The civic discourse and subcultural experiment that so excited early net commentators has given way to an increased emphasis on entertainment, business and electronic mail. The second defect of this approach is more fundamental than merely being out of date. It failed to grasp that inequalities in the real world distort cyberspace, and limit its potential for improving society.

Yet the position squarely opposed to this tradition is also open to criticism. It mistakenly argues that the whirlwind force of digital capitalism has overtaken the internet, and converted it into another consumer media service. In actual fact, a formidable combination of radical hackers and recalcitrant consumers has staged a highly effective rearguard action that has prevented the commercial balkanization of the web, and rendered the commercial internet economy precarious rather than all-conquering. The internet is still a contested space, its future unresolved.

There is also an alertness to the wonders of net technology, at the centre of the internetphiliac approach, that is worth defending in a critical way. The global reach of net technology, the way it facilitates self-expression and interaction, the avenue it opens up to the world's knowledge and entertainment, all make the net and the web life-enhancing inventions. The net also offers an opportunity for progressive groups to connect and organize beyond national frontiers, and coalesce in a global context. In a world where national sovereignty is eroding in favour of global agencies, the net has emerged at a strategic moment as a key tool of global communication in defence of popular democracy.

Indeed, further thought needs to be given to how to develop, through new public policies, the potential of the internet. The forces of commerce will overwhelm in the long term the tradition of public service on the net, unless the latter is given a helping hand. In the twentieth century, the liberal state expanded the public sphere and empowered the public through the development of public service broadcasting. This entailed public funding of radio and television in a national context. Perhaps the next step is to consider how this process can be extended through state support of a global public service form of net journalism, directed towards a global civil society.[42]

Notes

1. K. Patelis, 'The political economy of the Internet', in J. Curran (ed.) *Media Organisations in Society* (London, Arnold, 2000).
2. H. Rheingold, *The Virtual Community* (Cambridge, MA, MIT Press, rev. edn, 2000).
3. This is now part of a standard (but valid) left critique of the internet, to be found, for example, in C. Sparks, 'The internet and the global public sphere', in W. Lance Bennett and R. Entman (eds) *Mediated Politics* (New York, Cambridge University Press, 2001), G. Murdock and P. Golding, 'Digital possibilities, market realities: the contradictions of communications convergence', in L. Panitch and C. Leys (eds) *A World of Contradictions: Socialist Register 2002* (London, Merlin Press, 2001), and numerous other analyses, all quoting significantly different figures (though mostly from the same ultimate source). The data cited by Castells have been used because these are the most recent available.
4. M. Castells, *The Internet Galaxy* (Oxford, Oxford University Press, 2001), p. 264.
5. *Ibid.*, p. 219.
6. C. Kramarae, 'The language and the nature of the Internet: the meaning of global', *New Media and Society*, 1 (1), 1999, p. 49.
7. Castells, *The Internet Galaxy*, p. 260.
8. J. Stratton, 'Cyberspace and the globalisation of culture', in D. Porter (ed.) *Internet Culture* (New York, Routledge, 1997).
9. D. Miller and D. Slater, *The Internet: An Ethnographic Approach* (Oxford, Berg, 2000), p. 86.
10. J. Tulloch, *Watching Television Audiences* (London, Arnold, 2000) and J. Curran, *Media and Power* (London, Routledge, 2002), among others, provide accounts of the development of this research.
11. For a fascinating insight into how frequent letter writing, and an efficient mail service, sustained interconnected middle-class networks in the mid-nineteenth century (in much the same way that email functions in contemporary Britain), see J. Uglow, *Elizabeth Gaskell* (London, Faber and Faber, 1994).
12. L. Gross, 'The gay global village in cyberspace', in N. Couldry and J. Curran (eds) *Contesting Media Power* (Boulder, CO, Rowman & Littlefield, 2003, forthcoming).

13. M. Mallapragada, 'The Indian diaspora in the USA and around the world', in D. Gauntlett (ed.) *Web Studies* (London, Arnold, 2000).

14. M. Poster, 'Cyberdemocracy: Internet and the public sphere', in D. Porter (ed.) *Internet Culture* (New York, Routledge, 1997). The best collection of essays, in this tradition, is D. Bell and B. Kennedy (eds) *The Cybercultures Reader* (London, Routledge, 2000).

15. For a useful critical review, see D. Slater, 'Social relationships and identity online and offline', in L. Lievrouw and S. Livingstone (eds) *The Handbook of New Media* (London, Sage, 2002).

16. N. Baym, 'Interpersonal life online' in L. Lievrouw and S. Livingstone (eds) *The Handbook of New Media* (London, Sage, 2002), p. 62.

17. M. Ito, 'Virtually embodied: the reality of fantasy in a multi-user dungeon', in D. Porter (ed.) *Internet Culture* (New York, Routledge, 1997).

18. S. K. Kent, *Gender and Power in Britain, 1640–1990* (London, Routledge, 1999).

19. H. Rheingold, *The Virtual Community* (Cambridge, MA, MIT Press, rev. edn, 2000).

20. National Election Studies (University of Michigan, Center for Political Studies), 'The NES guide to public opinion and electoral behaviour', www.umich.edu/-nes/nesguide/nesguide.htm (2002).

21. D. Butler and G. Butler, *Twentieth Century British Political Facts* (Basingstoke, Macmillan, 8th edn, 2000), pp. 141–2, 158–9.

22. *Ibid.*, pp. 233–9.

23. The International Institute for Democracy and Electoral Assistance (IDEA), 'Voter turnout', www.idea.int (2002).

24. K. Hill and J. Hughes, *Cyberpolitics* (Lanham, MA, Rowman & Littlefield, 1998).

25. S. Coleman, 'New media and democratic politics', *New Media and Society*, 1 (1), 1999.

26. J. Slevin, *The Internet and Society* (Cambridge, Polity Press, 2000); A. Willheim, *Democracy and the Digital Age* (New York, Routledge, 2000); S. Coleman, 'The new media and democratic politics', *New Media and Society*, 1 (1), 1999; C. Bellamy and J. Taylor, *Governing in the Information Age* (Milton Keynes, Open University Press, 1998).

27. M. Castells, *The Internet Galaxy* (Oxford, Oxford University Press, 2001), p. 249.

28. P. Evans and T. Wurster, *Blown to Bits* (Boston, MA, Harvard Business School Press, 2000), p. 228.

29. Wider issues in the 'information society debate', excluded here, are discussed in Chapter 19.

30. Interview with Crispin Jameson, Chief Executive of Outside.

31. P. Lovelock and J. Ure, 'The new economy: internet, telecommunications and electronic commerce?', in L. Lievrouw and S. Livingstone (eds) *The Handbook of New Media* (London, Sage, 2002).

32. D. Held, A. McGrew, D. Goldblatt and J. Perraton, *Global Transformations* (Cambridge, Polity Press, 1999).

33. M. Castells, *The Internet Galaxy* (Oxford, Oxford University Press, 2001), p. 66.

34. R. Mansell, 'New media and the power of networks' (London, London School of Economics and Political Science, Inaugural Professorial Lecture, 2001), p. 17.

35. L. Introna and H. Nissenbaum, 'Shaping the web: why the politics of search engines matters', *The Information Society*, 16, 2000.

36. M. Lim, 'The internet, social networks and reform in Indonesia', and S. Ling, 'The alternative media in Malaysia: their potential and limitations', both in N. Couldry and J. Curran (eds) *Contesting Media Power* (Boulder, CO, Rowman & Littlefield, 2003, forthcoming).
37. Y. Zhao, 'Falun Gong, identity, the struggle over meaning in and out of reformed China', in N. Couldry and J. Curran (eds) *Contesting Media Power* (Boulder, CO, Rowman & Littlefield, 2003, forthcoming).
38. S. Lax, 'The Internet and democracy', in D. Gauntlet (ed.) *Web Studies* (London, Arnold, 2000).
39. These arguments are developed further in J. Curran, *Media and Power* (London, Routledge, 2002).
40. J. Curran, 'Global journalism: a case study of the Internet', in N. Couldry and J. Curran (eds) *Contesting Media Power* (New York, Rowman & Littlefield, 2003, forthcoming).
41. J. Sinclair, E. Jacka and S. Cunningham (eds), *New Patterns in Global Television* (Oxford, Oxford University Press, 1996).
42. See Chapter 24.

18

New media in Britain

Introduction

The rhythm of change in the media does not resemble the regularity of the seasons. Thus the period 1900 to 1940 was a time of rapid transformation, when the hegemony of print, music-hall and piano was undermined by the rise of film, radio and gramophone (to say nothing of television, which first broadcast in Britain in 1936). By contrast, the following forty-year period was an era of relative stability, marked by a reshuffling of the media pack. Between 1940 and 1980, television became the principal mass medium, other media were demoted, and the transistor radio, Walkman and video recorder became popular media accessories. However, after 1980, the pace of change again quickened. The desktop computer became a mass medium; the internet and web came into their own; television channels – satellite, cable and digital terrestrial – mushroomed; production techniques changed across the media; and computer and video games won a mass following among the young. Still greater innovations, we are told, are waiting in the wings.

This acceleration of change was fuelled by new communications technology. The invention of microprocessors brought into being powerful, compact computers, and facilitated the creation of the internet. Satellites orbiting in space and relaying information between terminals on earth, and fibre optic cable systems transmitting coded impulses of light down hair-like strands of glass, transformed the carriage of communications. Above all, the digitization of communications (the conversion of words, numbers, sounds and images into electronic binary digits) initiated a chain reaction of innovation that still continues today. Digitization reduced production costs dramatically in many media industries. It offered enormous advantages in terms of compressing, storing, editing, copying and distributing communications. It enabled more digital television channels to be transmitted on the same spectrum. It also allowed new forms of interconnectivity to take place. For instance, it is now technically possible to email friends through an advanced television set, watch a video on a mobile phone, or view television on a computer. It is this potential for *convergence* – the coming together of different media technologies – that is giving rise to forecasts of imminent transformation.

New media, we are told, are remaking the world. According to the New Labour government, in 2000: 'The explosion of information has fuelled a democratic revolution of knowledge and active citizenship. If information is power, power can now be within the grasp of everyone'[1] Its cheerleading White Paper, *A New Future for Communications*, also descanted eloquently on the way in which new communications technology is expanding choice, extending media diversity (including the creation of over 250 new television channels in twenty years), and increasing pluralism of media ownership. Future developments, it concluded, will move us towards 'full and sustainable competition' in the broadcasting industry. The government's positive reading of technology-driven media expansion provided the main rationale for its decision to accelerate deregulation through its 2003 Communications Act.

However, while the media landscape is indeed changing, the current government's arguments have a suspiciously familiar ring. The Thatcher and Major governments (1979 to 1997) also unveiled a brave new world of media plenty when they travelled down the same deregulatory road; yet their forecasts of imminent media transformation proved to be risibly inaccurate. For example, Kenneth Baker, then Minister for Information and Technology, predicted in 1982 that: 'By the end of the decade multi-channel cable television will be commonplace countrywide . . . TV will be used for armchair shopping, banking, calling emergency services and many other services'.[2]

He was wrong on both counts. Far from becoming 'commonplace', cable television reached just 1 per cent of homes by the end of the 1980s.[3] Even in 1997, when the Conservatives left office, cable television had still not developed an interactive service.[4]

This and other failures of media forecasting by fallible ministers (and even more gullible city analysts) suggest that a greater critical distance is needed in the analysis of new media. For this reason, it is worth recalling what was anticipated when new media were launched, and documenting what happened afterwards.

Wonders of narrowcasting

In the 1980s, it was widely believed that 'new television' – delivered by cable and satellite – would be an immediate success. It embodied, we were told, an entirely new approach: 'narrowcasting' rather than broadcasting the customizing of programmes for specialist audiences and niche markets. It would also soon feature the ultimate seduction of interactivity, enabling viewers to shop, retrieve information and select new movies. It would be unstoppable.

Cable television got off the block first. It started as a fully commercial service in 1984 (after a series of community experiments initiated in 1972). No effort was spared to secure its success. From the outset, cable TV was exempted from the high-cost, public service requirements imposed on its competitors. In 1987, cable television operators were given permission to compete in the telephone market. In 1990, the prohibition on non-European ownership of cable television was lifted. Restrictions on the growth of cable TV oligopoly were also rescinded. By 1999, all but six of the country's 136 operational franchises were owned by just two companies, NTL and Telewest, both in turn controlled by American conglomerates.[5]

This unstinting regulatory hospitality had one desired effect. By 2000, an estimated £6 billion, most of which was inward investment, was spent on cabling Britain. But in every other way, cable television proved to be a failure. NTL and Telewest Communications failed to make any profit from their cable services in the UK. In 2002, only 13.7 per cent of homes in the UK sub-scribed to cable television – a miserable return on a massive investment incurred over a long period.[6] Even when there was a sustained growth of cable TV's households between 1993 and 1999 due to heavy investment in cable installation and promotion, the underlying participation rate – that is, the proportion of households passed by cable which subscribed to cable TV – remained almost static.[7] Cable TV was also disappointing in artistic and pro-fessional terms. Most of its programmes were recycled rather than new, and many were oriented ironically towards a mass market. Its future does not look bright. NTL and Telewest became so crippled by debt that, in 2000 to 2001, they cut back their ambitious investment plans, leaving half of UK house-holds in 2002 still without access to broadband cable.[8]

Satellite television began in Britain as a feed to cable television in 1984, but only really came into its own with the launch of a direct broadcasting service to homes in 1989. Murdoch's Sky TV gained 'first mover' advantage by launching fourteen months ahead of its rival, British Satellite Broadcasting. There was then an extended period of blood-letting, marked by heavy dis-counting and promotion, that resulted in the two companies making a combined estimated loss of £1.4 billion.[9] Murdoch emerged as the victor, in effective control of the merged company, BSkyB. Despite being based in Britain, and becoming in effect the British satellite monopoly broadcaster, BSkyB was exempted from burdensome public service obligations on the dubious grounds that it was a 'non-domestic' broadcaster. This combination of monopoly and exemption helped to make it profitable. However, BSkyB's main staple of films, cartoons, music channels and live sport persuaded only 18.4 per cent of households in the UK to subscribe to its services in 2002.[10]

Satellite and cable TV thus remain cadet members of the television system. In 2002, one-third of the country subscribed to their programmes. Yet satellite and cable television combined accounted for just 14 per cent of total prime time viewing in 2001.[11] Even in pay-TV, multi-channel households, people spend significantly more time watching 'free' channels than the ones they pay for.[12]

New dawn

Digital television was trumpeted in the late 1990s as the medium of the future. It would have better sound, picture quality and stability of reception than analogue television. It would inaugurate a new television experience – many more channels, near-video-on-demand, interactive empowerment. Between 2006 and 2010, all analogue TV sets would be switched off. This would create an all-win situation, in which the nation would have a better television service and the government would be able to make money by selling the additional spectrum released by the switch-off.

This new dawn began on 15 November 1998 when the two giants of ITV, Carlton and Granada, launched OnDigital, Britain's first digital terrestrial television channels. Yet, to general surprise, their picture and sound quality was sometimes greatly inferior to that of conventional television. Indeed, in some parts of the country the sound simply disappeared. This technical failure was caused by the fact that too many channels were packed into the available frequencies, causing transmission power to be curtailed in order to prevent interference with existing analogue signals. With the incompetence that characterized the entire history of OnDigital, the new venture was launched before its technology had been mastered.

OnDigital's conception was also flawed. It went head-to-head against BSkyB, a company with more money, more subscribers (built up over years), more channels and a smarter management. BSkyB did the obvious thing. It hit OnDigital as hard as it could before the new pretender found its feet. First, BSkyB's installation charges were cut, and then its set-top boxes were given away free. OnDigital's establishment funds drained away as it was forced to match this promotion. Only inspirational programming, at this stage, could have saved it. OnDigital's inspiration was Nationwide football, attracting fewer viewers (and smaller match crowds) than BSkyB's Premiership football. Observers watched with horrified fascination as ITV's finest presided over OnDigital's slow-motion death. Attempted mouth-to-mouth resuscitation, in the form of a belated relaunch as ITV Digital, failed. The company collapsed in 2002 with an estimated £1.2bn loss.[13]

The frequencies released by this débâcle were taken over by a consortium headed by the BBC, with junior partners BSkyB and the transmitter company, Crown Castle. The BBC offered a package of digital terrestrial TV channels that were free, once a £99 set-top adapter was paid for and installed. This new venture is still too recent to evaluate properly. In principle, it offers a way of reinvigorating public service broadcasting by enabling BBC television to cater more extensively for minority audiences (defined, so far, by age and interest). This time round, technical problems were minimized by opting for fewer channels in return for stronger transmission power. However, the BBC's resources are now being spread very thinly, and its new digital channels suffer from being underfinanced.

Yet, despite the digital conversion of cable and satellite television in 1998 to 1999, and the relaunch of digital terrestrial television in 2002, the digital TV project is still in trouble. The majority of households still relied on analogue TV in 2002.[14] The over-hyping of digital television has been followed by disenchantment. Digital picture quality seems no better than that of analogue TV, save to expert eyes. Near-video-on-demand turns out to mean a small selection of largely similar films, starting at staggered times. Interactivity takes a very restricted form offering only marginal gains, such as the choice of camera angles in football matches. The driving force of digital television – existing cable and satellite TV channels, supplemented by low budget, minority BBC television – seems unlikely to mobilize the British public to go digital.

This is an expensive option. It will require buying new digital television sets or upgrading existing analogue ones through the installation of set-tops, retuning and, in some cases, the purchase of new aerials. This upgrading will be made more onerous by the fact that many households now have more than one television set. It is not obvious who will be willing to pay for this huge investment, given that market research indicates that one-third of viewers show no interest in receiving digital television.[15]

What is becoming clear is that the government's proclaimed schedule of switching off all analogue television signals some time between 2006 and 2010 will have to be postponed. The question is now not when, but whether, this switch-off will take place.

True dawn

Like cable, satellite and digital television, the growth of internet use in Britain was slow and incremental. By January to March 1999, only 3.2 million households had internet access.

Then, in the summer of 1999, the internet craze took off. It persisted after the collapse of the dotcom bubble between 2000 and 2001. Between early 1999 and early 2002, the proportion of UK homes with net access soared from 13 to 42 per cent.[16] This was underpinned by a rapid acquisition of personal computers. By mid-2002, no less than 52 per cent of homes had a computer.[17]

The net thus overtook new TV in a three-year spurt of growth (which is still continuing at the time of writing). The net and the web offer a wider gateway to the world of information and entertainment than do satellite and cable television. Unlike new television, the internet enables largely unrestricted retrieval from a vast storehouse of information, as well as real time interactions with others. It also provides a means of self-expression and collective organization in the way that new television does not. The net is global in its reach, extending horizons potentially beyond the Anglo-American world of British cable and satellite television. It offers a variety of different pleasures from television, including that of 'sharing' music. Familiarity with the net has also become a work skill that is desired within the knowledge economy. Yet the considerable advantages conferred by net access are distributed very unevenly in Britain.

The strongest factors influencing entry into the online world are age and class (see Table 18.1). Thus net *use* is highest among 16- to 24-year-olds (89 per cent), and declines with age, dropping precipitately among those over 65 (12 per cent).[18] Home net *access* is greatest among the highest socio-economic grade (78 per cent), diminishes with each successive grade, and is least among the lowest (20 per cent).[19] This differentiation is linked to income. Among the highest income decile group, 78 per cent have home net access, compared with 11 per cent among the lowest decile group. Income differences also contribute to regional differences, with Ulster and the north-east lagging behind London and the south-east in terms of home net access.[20] By 2001 to 2002, the proportion of men going online was only slightly higher than that of women.[21]

Table 18.1 *Adult use of the internet in 2002*

	%
All adults	55
Age group	
16–24	89
25–34	74
45–54	60
55–64	40
65 and over	12
Gender	
Men	57
Women	54

Source: National Statistics Omnibus Survey (April 2002), Office for National Statistics. The figures relate to those who have accessed the internet at some time. Of these, 80 per cent had accessed the internet in the month prior to the survey.

Social differences in net access are likely to decline over time as home computers become more widely diffused. This said, lack of confidence and skills (given as a reason by 20 per cent in a recent survey), as well as limited disposable income, are likely to remain serious obstacles to net use, especially among the elderly and poor.[22] Their continuing exclusion from the offline world will reinforce other forms of social and economic marginalization.

The digital divide is also acquiring a new dimension. In 2002, only 6 to 8 per cent of people had broadband internet access at home.[23] This proportion will grow rapidly in the next few years. However, income disparities will give rise to a split between those with fast, broadband internet and those using a clunker, dial-up service.

Net consumption

Content on the web is still largely free. British users have been reluctant to pay a fee or subscription to website owners, and this has discouraged charging. Cautionary lessons abound. When FT.Com charged access to its special features in 2001, its user base of around three million yielded only 17,000 paying customers.[24]

But if the web is still a largely open space in which to roam, it is not the anarchic, decentralized cyberpolity of digerati legend. Nielsen ratings show that the top five 'web properties' attracting the largest unique audiences in the UK, and usually accounting also for the most time, are generally search engines: MSN, Google, Yahoo!, Microsoft and AOL Time Warner.[25]

What becomes more difficult to establish is the most visited content sites (partly because some of these have search engines). The best available data, based on audits of page impressions (the net equivalent of readership figures) during the period 1999–2001, is highly revealing (see Table 18.2).[26] It indicates the extent to which the commercialization of cyberspace has pushed civic discourse to the margins, and established a following for sport, entertainment and business (in particular, car, property and share information).

It also reveals that the most visited sites concerned with politics and news are without exception produced by established media organizations. The brand leaders are the websites of the *Guardian*, BBC Online News, *Financial Times*, *Times* Newspapers, *Telegraph* and *Sun*. In other words, the net replicates the dominance of established media organizations. Many people turn to cyberspace, it seems, mainly for mainstream rather than alternative sources of public affairs information.

The website league table also highlights the success of BBC Online General. This was initiated in 1994, and has since developed a distinctive public service definition of cyberspace. It offers a way of discovering more about the background of subjects covered by the BBC. It also mobilizes the resources of the different branches of the corporation to provide multimedia presentations on a wide range of topics. In addition, BBC Online provides a guide to the content of the web, uncorrupted by sponsorship – one of its principal attractions.

However, emailing is still more important than site visiting on the web. E-commerce, by contrast, has got off to a slow start at least as far as direct selling to the public is concerned. The main reasons given for not spending online are that people prefer to shop in person, and are worried about security.[27]

Table 18.2 *Popular internet websites*

Name	Page impressions (million)
Sports.Com	455.1
BBC Online General	321.1
Cricinfo.com (sport)	254.6
Faceparty (music and entertainment)	151.8
Autotrader	73.5
Rivals Digital Media (sport)	69
Guardian Unlimited	62.3
BBC Online News	58.2
FT.com	55.5
Rivals.net (sport)	47.8
Rightmove (property)	43.4
ADVFN (financial information)	36.3
TNL Online (Times Newspapers)	29.3
Interactive Investor International	27.7
Telegraph	26.2
Irish Times	25.5
Sun Online	24.7

Source: Audit Bureau of Circulation.

Convergence mythology

While the new media literature is preoccupied with technological convergence, the opposite of convergence is taking place. We are witnessing a proliferation of different communications technologies. The most widely adopted new medium (see Table 18.3) is the mobile phone, available to 79 per cent of households in the UK in 2002. A 1999 survey also found that 67 per cent of 6- to 17-year-olds had a TV-linked games machine in their home, and that two-thirds of this age group played video games on average for just under an hour and a half at least three days a week.[28] In addition to cable and satellite television, the internet, mobile phones and computer/video games, there are of course other 'new media' such as digital radio, the camcorder, video-phone (a long-term flop), view data (another flop in Britain), DVD, and personal video recorders (capable of recording fourteen to thirty hours of preselected programmes on a hard disk).

Communications technologies will converge in the future. Digitization paves the way for this because it converts different modes of communication – such as words and pictures – into a *common* code of 0s and 1s. However, before universal access to convergent technology becomes a reality, a number of obstacles need to be overcome. In particular a grand fusion of technologies, in whatever form, will utilize broadband digital networks. These are not fully developed in Britain (or elsewhere).

Table 18.3 *Diffusion of new media*

*Passed by Cable**	*Cable subscribers***	*Satellite subscribers***	*Home computers+*	*Online at home+*	*Broadband access +*	*Mobile phone++*
Households						
%	%	%	%	%	%	%
50	13.7	18.4	52	43	6–8[a]	79

Sources: *Independent Television Commission Annual Report* (London, ITC, 2001) p. 15.
***Social Trends 32* (London, Stationery Office, 2002), p. 211.
+*Consumers' Use of Internet* (London, Office of Telecommunications, Oftel Residential Survey, May 2002), Q9.[a]
++*Consumers' Use of Mobile Telephony* (London, Office of Telecommunications, (2002), Q9.[a]

Note:
[a]While the Oftel survey estimate is 8 per cent, industrial surveys offer slightly lower figures.

The communications infrastructure of Britain will be modernized through a combination of different technologies: fibre optic cable, standard telecommunications upgraded by digital subscriber line (DSL) technology, and wireless technologies such as third generation mobile and satellite services. This poses a number of technical problems. For example, DSL only works in some parts of the country because it has to be close to a local telephone exchange. Satellite can deliver broadband into the home, but most systems need a telephone line for transmissions out of the home.

Modernization also requires massive investment. Laying down fibre optic cable is extremely costly because it entails digging up and restoring roads. In 2000, British Telecommunications (BT) had only upgraded exchanges covering 38 per cent of the population for DSL (the cheaper option).[29] Many of the companies that will be involved in building 'high bandwidth Britain' participated, in the euphoric moment of the dotcom bubble, in the £22 billion bid for third generation mobile telephony spectrum. Some of this imprudent outlay will probably have to be written off, and this may slow down improvement of the country's communications infrastructure.

What happens will depend partly upon consumer reaction to the launch of advanced mobile phones. Whether these will mark a third false dawn – after cable and digital television – remains to be seen.

Sociological mythology

If technologists enthuse about media convergence, social democratic sociologists worry about media proliferation.[30] The growth in the number of TV channels (over 500 accessible in Britain), the rise of multi-TV-set households, the diffusion of time-shift video technology (with its capacity to facilitate specialized programme consumption), and the spread of minority media, have fuelled fears that social cohesion and democratic dialogue are being weakened. The fragmentation of the media system, it is argued, is eroding communication between social groups in a shared public space. It is allegedly subdividing the public sphere into 'sphericules'; encouraging individuals and sectional groups to assert their values and interests without regard to others; and more generally, undermining a shared sense of common purpose.

This argument raises a number of issues which cannot be explored here.[31] But perhaps the key point is that it fails to recognize how slowly the *core* media system is in fact changing in Britain. Despite the emergence of new media, television still eclipses all rivals in terms of the size of its audience and the time it absorbs. Its pre-eminence is only diminishing slowly by degrees. Thus, between 1985 and 1998, the average time spent watching television each day declined only marginally from 3.8 hours to 3.6 hours.[32]

The principal channels within this dominant medium are still remarkably popular. Of course, their ascendancy is less now than it was in the early 1960s when there were only two television channels to watch. Even so, BBC1 and ITV accounted for 63 per cent of prime-time television viewing in 2001. Still more striking, four terrestrial television channels were responsible for 80 per cent of prime-time consumption (see table 18.4). The national community still comes together on a regular basis, and is drawn into a debate about its common social processes, through mass television channels. These constitute the primary public sphere of contemporary society.

Table 18.4 *Share of television viewing in the United Kingdom, 2001*

	BBC 1	*BBC 2*	*ITV*	*C4*	*C5*	*Cable/ Satellite*
Daily (%)	27	11	27	10	6	20
Prime time (%) (18.00–22.30)	28	9	35	8	5	14

Source: *European Audiovisual Observatory Yearbook 2002*, Vol. 2, p. 82. All figures are rounded off to the nearest whole number.

The growth of new media has given rise to another elegiac sociological thesis. This points out that both satellite television and the internet transcend national boundaries. More generally, television is becoming integrated into the global economy and is showing increasingly, it is claimed, the same programmes around the world. The rise of transnational media and globalization are weakening, in this view, identification with the nation. They are also said to be eroding engagement in national politics since this derives ultimately from a sense of national belonging.[33]

While this thesis sounds plausible, it again makes the mistake of assuming that the core media system has undergone a fundamental change. In a British context, this is not correct. Although cable and satellite television transmit a large number of foreign (mostly American) programmes, it reaches – as we have seen – only a minority audience. While terrestrial channels buy more foreign programmes than before, their full integration into the global economy is prevented by protectionist regulation. Throughout the 1980s, commercial public service channels were required to fill 86 per cent or more of their time with programmes made in Europe. This figure was lowered by the Independent Television Commission in 1993 to 65 per cent in the case of ITV, and in 1998 to 60 per cent and 55 per cent respectively in the case of Channel 4 and 5.[34] The majority of programmes shown by BBC television throughout this period were made in Britain.

More generally, British terrestrial television promotes national identification by giving prominence to symbols of the nation, providing a shared social experience for the nation, and a news service strongly shaped by national news values (even down to its definition of the 'weather'). It also encourages involvement in national politics by keeping a spotlight continuously trained on Westminister, and by giving extensive coverage to general election campaigns.

Indeed, the argument that British television is weakening *national* identity and political engagement needs to be turned on its head. The problem is rather the other way round. British television journalism remains excessively parochial and nationalist, in a way that discourages engagement in European and global politics. British television reporting has failed also to respond adequately to the decline of the British state and the transfer of some of its sovereignty to global markets and agencies.

In short, two fashionable sociological theses make the false assumption that the media are being fundamentally transformed, with far-reaching consequences for how people connect to each other. In actual fact, the British media system is undergoing a process of evolutionary rather than revolutionary change. This limits, for good and also bad, changes in its wider influence.

Entrenched oligopoly

However, if new communications technology is not transforming society or revolutionizing the media, at least it might seem reasonable to suppose that it is changing the underlying *dynamics* of the media system. After all, we are told repeatedly that the technology-driven expansion of the media system is enabling new voices to be heard.

In a very limited sense, this is true. New technology has created new media sectors. It has also facilitated market entry and enabled new media enterprises to emerge. However, the market openings created by new technology, and attendant competition gains, have often proved short-lived. Time and again, market leaders have beaten off challenges to their ascendancy. The appearance of significant change conceals underlying continuity.

Thus the recent history of the newspaper industry illustrates the way in which leading groups continue to dominate. In the later 1980s, the introduction of digitized printing reduced costs, and led to the launch of new national newspapers. The dominant publishers responded by expanding their papers into multiple sections, and initiating a price war. They also bought new rivals, or launched new publications. This strategy broadly succeeded. After a brief period of market turbulence, entry costs rose and the threat of increased competition receded. The same few groups (some with new, dominant shareholders) remained firmly in control. Thus a comparison between 1985, the eve of the print revolution, and 2002 reveals only a modest reduction of market share. The top three groups' control of national circulation declined from 75 to 70 per cent in the case of dailies and from 83 to 79 per cent in the case of Sunday papers.[35] A similar pattern is revealed if a comparison is made between the respective market shares of the top four groups during the same period.

If long-term oligopoly was maintained in the national press, it grew in a spectacular way in the local press. Thus the leading five chains' share grew, between 1985 and 2002, from 55 to 69 per cent of total regional evening paper circulation, and from 74 to 85 per cent of total regional morning circulation.[36] The big five's share of the paid-for local weekly market soared from 27 to 70 per cent, and in the local freesheet market from 38 to 75 per cent between 1989 and 2002.[37]

New technology also assisted an assault on market hegemony in the music industry. The digitization of music production in the 1980s lowered costs, and made music recording easier. It became possible to assemble in the home the basic tools for music production – synthesizers, signal processors, mixer, a digital recorder and computer – without the need to go to expensive professional recording studios. This assisted the rise of independent music labels at a time when there was a growing fragmentation of music styles and tastes. However, the leading six music companies mobilized the enormous resources available to them as vertically integrated combines dominating the production, manufacture and distribution of music, not merely in Britain but also in the international market. Over time, they succeeded in incorporating many leading independent labels in network or partnership arrangements, in a form that was mutually advantageous. The majors provided development finance, distributional and promotional muscle, and a route into the international market, while independent companies furnished street credibility, low-cost production and a flexible strategy for coping with rapid changes of taste through the spreading of risk. Between 1990 and 1996, the six music majors actually increased their share of UK music product sales from 73 to 80 per cent.[38]

Just as home studio music production and computerized typesetting excited hopes in the 1980s about the popular take-over of the music and publishing industries, so similar fantasies were constructed around portable video equipment in the late 1970s. It was believed that the development of cheap and easy-to-use technology gave people access to the production of television programmes, and by extension to the control of television. This would lead, it was argued, to the democratization of society. However, what many in the community television movement failed to appreciate was that TV-making involves not only producing and editing programmes but also their funding, the assembling of talent, distribution and active promotion. A utopian approach, centred in this case on pre-digital technology, ended in disenchantment because it was divorced from a proper understanding of the economics of television.[39]

During the 1980s and 1990s, new technology further simplified TV production processes, reduced costs and multiplied the number of channels. This created new opportunities for programme-makers, which were extended by the introduction of a statutory independent production quota in 1990. However, this expansion of work took place within a more economically regulated environment. Monopolistic control was established over satellite television, duopolistic control over cable TV, and oligopolistic control over ITV companies. By 2002, Carlton and Granada owned eleven of the fifteen regional ITV companies, while the Scottish Media Group controlled both franchises in Scotland. The 2003 Communications Act opened the way for just one company to control all of ITV. It also permitted further increases in the concentration of ownership of commercial radio, which had greatly increased during the 1990s.

New technology brought into being a new media industry in the form of video games. However, it also facilitated the advance of three giants – Sony, Nintendo and Sega. They controlled, manufactured or licensed much of the video game technology. They also bought up – or developed partnership arrangements with – leading games producers around the world, including Britain. They used this global control over both hardware and software to maintain, despite occasional reverses, a remarkably enduring international domination of the video game market throughout the 1990s.

The creation of the internet has injected new pluralism into the media system because it is still not fully commercialized, and entry costs are lower than in most other media sectors. However, the cost of establishing, maintaining and promoting a 'high-profile' site are substantial.[40] The most visited news content sites, as we have seen, are controlled by leading news organizations. Their creation was inspired partly by a desire to limit competition. Broadsheets, in particular, were fearful that their lucrative classified advertising would be lost to net companies, and developed content sites partly in order to safeguard their control of this market. They also became persuaded that the development of an online presence would enhance the appeal of

their newspapers among young consumers. They therefore invested heavily in developing, maintaining, staffing – and subsidizing – their websites without having a clear idea of how to extract revenue from them.

Thus the conventional view that the rise of new media has greatly increased media pluralism needs to be heavily qualified. In many media sectors, leading companies have maintained or extended their position of dominance. Since this dominance tends to be confined to one media sector, it remains relatively unobtrusive. Britain does not have a massive media behemoth such as AOL Time Warner or the decomposing giant Vivendi (her nearest equivalent being the large British branch of Murdoch's News Corporation). Instead, there has developed a pattern of interlocking shareholdings and directorships across media sectors. There is also a number of mostly small-scale, joint ventures in which press, television or telecommunications companies have joined forces in high-risk new markets such as interactive television and net services. It only needs some oligopolies in different media sectors to build on existing ties and merge for an unprecedented degree of media concentration to develop at high speed in a deregulated environment.

Furthermore, the underlying dynamics weakening media pluralism have not disappeared but have actually strengthened. The media industries still have enormous economies of scale as a consequence of their very high 'first copy' costs and low reproduction costs. This gives a strong competitive advantage to large-scale, successful companies, and helps to explain why so many have retained their dominant market positions. To this advantage has now been added the growing benefits of economies of scope (reductions of cost or increases of revenue brought about by the bringing together of formerly separate economic activities), facilitated by digitization.[41] The speed and relatively low cost with which the same content resources could be 'repurposed' for both publishing and the net goes a long way to explaining, for example, why it was so easy for newspapers to colonize the online world. Indeed, the most significant way in which 'media convergence' may well occur in the next decade is in the form of ownership rather than of technology.

Diversity gains and losses

A distinction is sometimes made between media pluralism (referring to ownership) and diversity (referring to content). Cannot a compelling case be made that media expansion has greatly increased at least media diversity? After all, there has been a massive increase in media output. In December 1980, 300 hours of television programmes a week were available in Britain, yet by 2000 this had grown to over 40,000 hours a week.[42] This includes an enormous range of programmes – from art house movies to classic Hollywood, stand-up comedy to Bollywood, MTV music to continuous cartoons – that was either rationed or unavailable before.

However, calculations about increased diversity need to take account of

diversity losses as well as gains. While the add-on service of cable and satellite television introduced greater variety, this tended to be at the expense of the variety of the core television system. This can be illustrated, in a simple way, by television sport. The creation of new satellite sports channels greatly increased the volume and diversity of sports coverage, but it also led to the withdrawal of live coverage of key sporting events that were once available free on public service television. In effect, some people obtained a better sports service while the majority received a worse one.

In this case, the losses and gains involved were relatively transparent. A more general assessment is more difficult to make. However, the indications are that the emergence of new television channels weakened the core system by destabilizing the ecology on which it was based. Channel expansion also justified the deregulation of broadcasting, which made a deteriorating situation worse.

ITV emerged as the weak link in the public service system during the late 1980s and early 1990s. During its first thirty years, between 1955 and 1985, it had been a distinguished broadcaster. It had found no difficulty in supporting high-cost, low-audience programmes because it had been highly profitable as a consequence of its monopoly of television advertising. It had also been subject to an effective regulatory authority, especially after 1964. However, these two prerequisites of public service virtue – easy money and tough regulation – were subsequently eroded. ITV was exposed to advertising competition by the rise of cable and satellite TV in the late 1980s and early 1990s, the conversion of Channel 4 to the status of an independent advertising rival in 1993, and the launch of Channel 5 in 1997. In addition, the commercial television regulatory authority lost key powers as a consequence of the 1990 Broadcasting Act. This new legislation also replaced the traditional way of allocating ITV franchises, based on a programme and talent 'beauty contest', with an auction to the highest bidder (with some quality safeguards). As a consequence, ITV became subject to a less public service oriented management. This was typified by Paul Jackson, Carlton's Director of Programmes, who proclaimed in 1992:

If *World in Action* [ITV's flagship investigative journalism programme] were in 1993 to uncover three more serious miscarriages of justice while delivering an audience of three, four or five million, I would cut it. It isn't part of the ITV system to get people out of prison.[43]

During the same period, the BBC 's sense of élan was weakened by a new style of leadership, which seemed out of sympathy with its public service tradition.[44] When John Birt took over as Director General in 1992, he instituted for himself a tax arrangement that symbolized his market-oriented approach. Instead of being employed by the corporation he headed, Birt chose to be paid as a freelancer employed by his private company. He proceeded to convert the corporation into an internal market, constituted initially in 1993 by no less than 480 separate, self-sufficient accounting units. Intended to curb profligacy, it encouraged caution and tended to stifle creativity. It was followed by enervating 'efficiency gains', culminating in year-on-year budget cuts between 1996 and 2001.

The effect of all these changes was to lower the overall standard of broadcast journalism. Their impact was most noticeable in ITV where there was a cumulative shift towards tabloidization. Between 1987/8 and 1997/8, foreign coverage dropped from 15 per cent to a mere 7 per cent of ITV's current affairs programme content. This was part of a more general shift in which analysis of economic and political affairs gave ground to 'softer' crime and consumer features.[45] ITV also moved its main 10 o'clock news bulletin to a later slot in order to clear the evening for uninterrupted prime-time entertainment, until pressure forced the network to partly relent. Its new rival, Channel 5, joined this general drift away from public purpose. In the memorable phrase of its former programme director Dawn Airey, Channel 5 gave priority to 'films, fucking and football'.[46]

The quality of television drama also declined. Individual plays had been central to the golden era of television drama during the 1960s and 1970s. They provided the licensed space where new ideas and talent could be tried out, and demanding scripts could be presented. However, between 1978 and 1998, individual plays declined as a proportion of terrestrial television drama from 23 to 10 per cent. Their place was taken by an increasing emphasis on soaps and series because these provided a safer and more predictable form of television designed to deliver consistent ratings. This cumulative realignment was part of a more general pattern in which terrestrial television turned increasingly to tried and tested formulae, renewable series, recognized stars, and upbeat storylines.[47]

However, the partial decline of public service broadcasting was caused only partly by cable and satellite TV, and changes in policy that their rise justified. Furthermore, this decline was not monolithic. If some things got worse, others got better. New programme formats and styles broadened social access to television during the 1980s and 1990s. These ranged from brilliant, innovative reports in BBC2's prestigious *Newsnight* which sought to break free from its reliance on a political élite, to daytime talk shows which gave working-class women a greater voice.[48] During the Birt era (1992 to 2000), a greater attempt was made to employ more British Asian and Afro-Carribean programme-makers, and to address the distinctive concerns of ethnic minority audiences. The continuing popularity of British public service television programmes – and the continuing public support for the maintenance of the public service broadcasting system in Britain – attested to its underlying strength.

Some past damage has since been undone, and new improvements initiated. The BBC's internal market was swept away in 2000, in a wave of reform that gave increased power to programme-makers. The BBC's 2002 digital television initiative offers potentially a way of strengthening the diversity of publicly funded, free television. Nothing is set in stone. However, it is difficult to avoid the impression that we are perhaps moving into a new era when the extension of private choice in the form of pay-TV may be at the expense of public, collectively funded provision.

Conclusion

A stress on novelty and change has become part of the rhetoric of new media literature. This bears the unmistakable imprint of media hype designed to promote new media technology to consumers, and the 'liberalization' of official controls to policy-makers. However, the frequency with which expectations about new media have been disappointed should inject a new note of caution.

Of course, part of what is new is also exciting. The internet represents a historic advance; cable and satellite television has expanded choice; video games have become, at best, a new art-form; indie labels have tapped into rich and varied traditions of garageland music-making. But pleasure over what is new and different should not obscure the underlying continuity of the media's development during the last two decades.

Indeed, an emphasis on continuity is the central, unfashionable theme of this survey. Television is still the dominant popular medium – over half a century after it was first launched. Its main, terrestrial channels retain a mass following, and remain the primary public sphere of society. Television still supports national identity and national political participation in the era of globalization. Collectivist arrangements that allocate enormous resources to public service broadcasting, through the licence fee and free spectrum, continue to enjoy tacit public support. These are counterbalanced by market-based media sectors, such as the press, that are fundamentally the same as they always were. A small number of media companies remain firmly in control, and they are driven by the same logic of profit and power as before.

However, there now exists a widespread belief that new communications technology is transforming Britain's media. This conviction, shared by successive governments, is itself a powerful force for change. It has legitimated a process of deregulation that has damaged the media system when, with the benefit of new technology, it could have become so much better.

Notes

1. *A New Future for Communications* (London, Stationery Office, 2000), p. 8.
2. Cited in D. Goldberg, T. Prosser and S. Verhulst, *Regulating the Media* (Oxford, Clarendon Press, 1998), p. 10.

3. *Ibid.*, p. 101.
4. P. Goodwin, *Television Under the Tories* (London, British Film Institute, 1998), p. 68.
5. C. Leys, *Market-Driven Politics* (London, Verso, 2001), p. 127
6. *Social Trends 32* (London, Stationery Office, 2002), Table 13.2, p. 211.
7. S. Lax, 'The Internet and democracy', in D. Gauntlet (ed.) *Web Studies* (London, Arnold, 2000), p. 166.
8. *Independent Television Commission Annual Report* (London, ITC, 2001) p. 15.
9. N. Chenoweth, *Virtual Murdoch* (London, Secker & Warburg, 2001), p. 98.
10. *Social Trends 32* (London, Stationary Office, 2002), Table 13.2, p. 211.
11. *European Audiovisual Observatory Yearbook 2002* (Strasbourg, Council of Europe, 2002), Vol. 2, p. 82.
12. *Ibid.*, p. 83. Partly for this reason, the aggregated audience share of twenty 'Sky' TV channels (from Sky Premier to Sky Sports) in the country as a whole is tiny – a total of 6.2 per cent in the first six months of 2002. See *Television Audience Share Figures* (London, Independent Television Commission, 2002), p. 3.
13. T. Lennon, 'Digital TV: a phoenix risen from the ashes', *Free Press*, 129, 2002, p. 2.
14. The government's General Household Survey estimated that 42 per cent of households in 2001 had digital TV receivers. However, this included ITV Digital receivers that are now largely inactive.
15. D. Elstein, 'The politics of digital TV', www.OpenDemocracy.net/forum, 2002.
16. *Family Expenditure Survey* (1998 to 2001) and *Expenditure and Food Survey* (Office of National Statistics, 2001), www.statistics.gov.uk
17. *Ibid.*
18. *National Statistics Omnibus Survey* (Office of National Statistics, 2002), www.statistics.gov.uk. However, this does not entirely correspond to age differences in internet home access. See *Consumers' Use of the Internet*, Oftel Residential Survey, May 2002 (Office of Telecommunications, London, 2002).
19. *Expenditure and Food Survey* (2001 to 2002), Office of National Statistics, www.statistics.gov.uk
20. *Ibid.*
21. *National Statistics Omnibus Survey* (Office of National Statistics, 2002), www.statistics.gov.uk
22. *Ibid.*
23. Consumers' Use of the Internet: Oftel Residential Survey May, 2002 (Office of Telecommunications, London, 2002).
24. P. Preston, 'Somehow newspapers must make websites pay', *Observer*, 24 November 2002.
25. Nielsen Net Ratings (UK), November 2002.
26. Audit Bureau of Circulation (ABC) London. The figures are based on different audit periods between 2000 and 2002, and relate only to the self-selecting sites covered by ABC. The figures in the tables exclude Yahoo!, Ask Jeeves, Alta Vista and Bluewin Portal on the grounds that these are primarily search engines covered by Nielsen. A case could be made that BBC Online General should also be excluded.
27. *National Statistics Omnibus Survey* (Office of National Statistics, 2002), www.statistics.gov.uk

28. S. Livingstone and M. Bovill, *Young People: New Media* (London, London School of Economics and Political Science, 1999), pp. 5 and 12.

29. *A New Future for Communications* (London, Stationery Office, 2000), p. 31.

30. For example, T. Gitlin, 'Public sphere or sphericules?', in T. Liebes and J. Curran (eds) *Media, Ritual and Identity* (London, Routledge, 1998).

31. These are explored further in J. Curran, *Media and Power* (London, Routledge, 2002).

32. C. Leys, *Market-Driven Politics* (London, Verso, 2001), p. 110.

33. E. Katz, 'And deliver us from segmentation', *Annals of the American Academy of Political and Social Science*, 546, 1996.

34. Information derived from the Independent Television Commission. Some programmes are excluded from the quota requirements.

35. *Annual Report of the Press Council* (London, Press Council, 1985), Table 4, pp. 301–4: Audit Bureau of Circulation, 2002.

36. *Annual Report of the Press Council* (London, Press Council, 1985), Table 5, pp. 305–8; Audit Bureau of Circulation, 2002.

37. *Annual Report of the Press Council 1989* (London, Press Council, 1990), tables 4 and 5; Audit Bureau of Circulation, 2002.

38. P. McDonald, 'The music industry', in J. Stokes and A. Reading (eds) *The Media in Britain* (Basingstoke, Macmillan, 1999), p. 94. He warns that the reliability of these figures is 'open to debate'.

39. N. Garnham, *Communications and Capitalism* (London, Sage, 1990).

40. J. Cornford and K. Robins, 'New media', in J. Stokes and A. Reading (eds) *The Media in Britain* (Basingstoke, Macmillan, 1999), p. 113. They cite a consultancy estimate of $3.1 million per year for maintaining and managing a high-profile website.

41. However, there are also diseconomies of scale dramatized by the conflicts of interests and management cultures that beset AOL Time Warner in 2002 and 2003.

42. *A New Future for Communications* (London, Stationery Office, 2000), p. 7.

43. Cited in S. Barnett and A. Curry, *The Battle for the BBC* (London, Aurum Press, 1994), p. 249. *World in Action* was duly cut.

44. See Chapter 15.

45. S. Barnett and E. Seymour, '*A Shrinking Iceberg Travelling South*' (London, Campaign for Quality Television, 1999), p.16.

46. Cited in C. Leys, *Market-Driven Politics* (London, Verso, 2001), p. 127.

47. See n. 45.

48. J. Curran, 'Television journalism: theory and practice, the case of *Newsnight*', in P. Holland, *Television Handbook* (London, Routledge, 2nd edn, 2000).

Part IV

Theories of the media

19

Global futures, the information society, and broadcasting

When we talk about the future, we may reveal more about how we understand the present than make reliable predictions about what will happen. Thinking about the future can be enabling, offering us images and hopes worth working for, warnings worth heeding, or it can be disabling, obscuring what needs to be understood and tackled, urgently, now. J. G. Ballard, the great science fiction writer, much of whose work is catastrophically dystopic, and whose vision perhaps always stems from his own experience as a child in a Japanese prisoner-of-war camp, has written that now 'to some extent the future has been enclosed in the present, for most of us the notion of the future as an alternative scheme, as an alternative world to which we are moving no longer exists'.

Yet, recently, a series of words and ideas describing a new world order, a new economic regime, new politics, new social and community patterns, and even new psyches for a new industrial revolution (and of course a new millennium) have been gathering force. Just as the collapse of Marxism and Keynesianism in the late 1980s was heralded as the end of grand and overarching theories, paradoxically, another apparently indisputable iron law has emerged. The world, it seems, and everything in it has begun to be, and will be inexorably, 'globalized'. At the heart of this global revolution are a series of dramatic innovations, every one of which is dependent on developments in the media of communications. Sometimes, as agents of communication, they 'globalize' the world, sometimes as subjects they are 'globalized' But they are key – and like King Midas miraculously transform all they touch, if not exactly into gold, at least into something utterly new. Apparently we can see the future – and it is interactive and global.

Of course, like all successful ideas, globalization may have become so ubiquitous because it is right. On the other hand, it may have spread because it is particularly useful to some of those interest groups who trade in ideas. Certainly the term is very flexible, and it describes some things which are all too evidently changing. Nevertheless, for those on the political right, the rhetoric of globalization came in the nick of time. Just as the social and economic costs of the dominant liberal deregulatory, individualized, free market politics and policies of the 1970s and 1980s began to be counted, globalization emerged. A new term to describe an inevitable transformation, its most committed advocates agreed that the theory of globalization suggested that governments were in any case impotent, and that global economics and markets were beyond discipline. Globalization provided a new lease of life for a political project that might otherwise have begun to falter, and gave it a new, high-tech, modern appeal.

Simultaneously, the political left and self-consciously progressive social critics embraced globalization, first in a spirit of gloom as yet another capitalist conspiracy, and second, and more hopefully, as a new dawn – the revolution. It was convenient because despite the convulsions in the real world, the arch enemy remained comfortably familiar – a new, beefed-up version of the multinational corporation. Indeed, globalization theory had the additional attraction of demonstrating the illusory nature of conventional ameliorative politics and policies. Traditional democratic and representative politics were apparently dinosaurs, doomed to extinction in the face of new conditions. Moreover, something unimaginably different (and consequently unarguable) would develop. After the global information revolution had changed everything; interactive and direct democracy would emerge and consumers with necessarily technologically enhanced powers would be made more citizen-like.

Thus perhaps globalization became such a taken-for-granted idea because it perfectly captured and articulated conventional – and even comfortable – thoughts for such a wide variety of interests. Everywhere, from exotic foreign social theorists to domestic Anglo-Saxon professors, from politicians to television and telecommunications executives, it was agreed, wrote Anthony Giddens, that 'through the new technologies of computer and satellite, through the new media a new world will be made'.[1] Bright young gurus could argue 'We are now on the edge of another epochal shift towards human capital: the resources that communication will make matter are skill, ingenuity and creativity',[2] while commentators on communication, like Anthony Smith – always endearingly neophiliac – could claim 'If computers alter the nature of our groups, and our information, then most certainly the industries of the electronic media must be altering the pattern of society in general.' If you liked its consequences it resembled good old-fashioned progress. If you didn't – or had doubts – it was part of the same old conspiracy. But either way, there was not apparently all that much that could be done about it.

Indeed, the future of the convergence of communication technologies is often described in comfortingly familiar ways. It apparently offers interactive communication (like talking), information (like books), uncensorable, unlimited access of everyone to everything (like libraries, but better). In addition, it is said to offer interactive 'responsible' democracy, at a time when the rewards of being a citizen are increasingly restricted and there is the emergence of an excluded underclass, particularly so in the very wealthiest societies. Finally, it offers 'new ways of working' (when it is all too clear that 'old' ways of working – jobs – are in decline). These familiar virtuous capacities are to be linked and extended to make a new world; no one is in any doubt that this will be a new – global – order.

There is, of course, much evidence for extraordinary shifts in communication and huge increases in communicative patterns. Yet much of the abundant writing on globalization seems to assert general consequences on the basis of speculation rather than evidence. The distinguished French historian Robert Darnton, in an essay called 'The great cat massacre', which explains the sociological pressures which made the fourteenth-century Parisian printers find such pleasure in killing their masters' cats, argued that when we encounter a feeling, or an argument that is incomprehensible, 'When we cannot get a proverb, or a joke, or a ritual, or a poem – we know as historians we are on to something.'[3] Historical work is best started from how they, then, were different from us, and why. But perhaps in looking at contemporary thought our duty is related to Darnton's idea – but is an inversion of it. When everyone is so unanimous about a term and a process, then we need to stop and ask what it means (when everybody seems to know), what work it is doing, and for whom.

Technology

At the heart of the debate about globalization is an argument, hidden in a description, informed by a utopian projection. They are all ways of coming to terms with, and mastering, a series of undoubtedly dazzling new technological opportunities that may alter our very ideas about wants, needs, choice and social arrangements. What needs caution is the way in which unfounded projections into future patterns are then used to determine decisions and policy now.

In the past, broadcasting was a distinct technology – and the political and economic patterns of how it was distributed were greatly influenced by the scarcity of air waves to send it through. Telephones were another, separate technology and form of communication, governed by quite independent organizations and ways of thought. Finally, the storing and ordering of information, which had admittedly steadily increased in capacity over the century (and both the very best and the very worst action of states, in what Eric Hobsbawm has called *The Age of Extremes*, depended on the huge growth of this power), happened in different places using different technologies. The capacity to use information was influenced by other technologies (the telephone, the typewriter, the carbon copy, the photocopier), but information was manipulated in different places for different purposes from broadcasting or telephones.

These technologies have now converged. Limitless amounts of information can be gathered, grouped, carried, used, in new ways. Television and videos can come down the telephone lines, and cable and satellite offer breathtakingly increased capacity to carry communication. The evolution of the microchip at the centre of the revolution is so fast that it doubles in capacity every five years. At the heart of nearly all of these technological innovations – and indeed in the most abstract developments of the mathematical reasoning that underpins them – is the capacity to reduce complexity. This means that more and more information can be compressed and carried more quickly, more efficiently and more cheaply. With so much information capacity, individual consumers will be able to interact with any of the services they are offered, adjusting what they receive to what they want. We have hardly begun to understand how the telephone has changed our social habits, but interactive machines may change us more. Digital television, for example – the next big challenge for public service broadcasting – could offer not just a plethora of new channels, but also enhanced opportunities for people to explore what interests them.

Beyond these services there is the Wild West of the Internet. At the moment this is slow, and has exploding quantities of useless and trivial things cluttering it up. Yet its potential to provide a huge resource for learning and communication, and for developing novel kinds of understanding, is perhaps vast. In addition, there are the extraordinary combinations of these technologies that, for example, allow an expert consultant in a hospital to examine in detail the condition of a patient anywhere else. A combination of telecommunications, television and computers can produce a world of 'virtual reality' reproducing, ever more closely, either synthetic experience (as in games), or real experience (as in the medical example above). These developments have been a consequence of the spread of computers – of ever increasing power and ever decreasing cost – into homes and to every aspect of commerce and public life. The changes will be the result of exponential increase in the capacities of computing.

Such developments shrink distance and time. They are accompanied by a highly individualized image of knowledge. In this the emphasis is always on individuals 'creating', exploring, putting together what they need or want from the hugely increased choice and access provided by the new communication technologies. Together these changes have been said to herald the end of institutions as we have known them.

Nevertheless, these utopian scenarios (faintly reminiscent of the land of milk and honey where there is never scarcity) fail to account for, and indeed regard as an unimportant enquiry, how the question will be framed to put to the new services. People's wants, needs, questions and enquiries, their capacity to creatively interact will still be formed and made by their own education – or lack of it – and by the purposes they bring to addressing the system.

Second, there is the problem of who will provide what services, based on what principles. Indeed, we are seeing a whole new technology of communication emerging, perhaps for the very first time, determined by one principle, profit. But profit-driven services will have a pattern, just as clearly as any other. Indeed, one firm, Microsoft, owned by Bill Gates, already 'owns' the computer language that dominates worldwide computer use, and is seeking to gain monopoly control over access to the Internet. 'Choice' is thus already a chimera.

Many of the theories addressing the communication basis of globalization see technology as an uncontrollable natural force, a typhoon, relinking and remaking the world in new ways. In part they seek to explain what the communication revolution has done. Yet this approach sees other political, social and psychological arrangements as products of communication – but as having little consequence themselves. Technology in this account is the only free spirit abroad. It apparently produces globalization.

Evolutionists, pessimists and revolutionaries

Globalization is nevertheless hotly contested. Some say it is a good thing, others that it is damaging. However various the explanations of its effects, and despite their opposition to each other, the different proponents share more than they admit. They all seem to believe that nothing much can modify or change how it develops, they merely argue about the interpretations of consequences whose pattern they seem to assume is already determined by technology.

The first group, the evolutionists, claim that a new epoch has emerged, driven not by class antagonism, or the requirements of capitalism, but rather by information technologies. This is certainly not a new idea, and it was most clearly elaborated in the 1960s by Daniel Bell. Bell's quite elderly, though somewhat revamped, ideas have become fashionable again. Bell first suggested in 1963 that a new 'post-industrial' economy and society was developing. Making things – in factories – would become less important than knowing about how things were being made elsewhere. The service sector would supersede that of production, and 'workers' would be replaced by 'professionals' – the expert servants of knowledge. Just as machines had rationalized production, so the new technologies would rationalize the manipulation of information. Thus, for example, farming would become the calculable end product of greater knowledge and surveillance of the weather, grain genetics, soil monitoring, and so on.

Bell's vision was not only prescient, but also curiously cosy. This new age was going to emerge, apparently without nasty cataclysms, and indeed the world it would usher in was distinctly more pleasant than the one it replaced.

It offered less hard, dirty work, more cleaner, more interesting work and a more rational political and economic system. It offered an attractive prospect for the future, particularly to middle-class professionals who were apparently nice and steadily, and probably meritocratically, going to inherit the new epoch. It proposed an image of middle America, mildly and knowledgeably skilling the world. It suggested that knowledge, expertise, information and rational calculation would reign more powerfully. Indeed, as Krishnan Kumar has pointed out, 'The utopian tide of the 1960s flowed largely within a tide of technological optimism. The argument was not against technology, but against its abuse.'[4]

Perhaps not entirely surprisingly, entrepreneurs like Bill Gates, the pioneer of home computers, and by 1996 America's most wealthy businessman, talks, at least for public consumption, in firmly evolutionary tones. He argues that 'a fully developed information revolution will be affordable – almost by definition. An expensive system that connected a few big corporations and wealthy people simply would not be an information highway – it would be a private world. . . . The information revolution is a mass phenomenon or it is nothing.' The emergent social organization brought about by the information revolution will have inherently stable, socially desirable outcomes. 'We are all created equal in the virtual world,' Gates says. 'The information network will not eliminate barriers of prejudice or inequality but it will be a powerful force in that direction.'[5] The information revolution, according to this view, gently rationalizes and develops – it improves things.

In contrast there are pessimists, like Herbert Schiller, who argue that the communication revolution will merely reinforce existing inequalities in a world which is becoming perilously more divided. Such views emphasize the continuities that will determine the new technologies. They see the undoubted potential of the information revolution merely being squeezed through the economic and social relation of the 'old' power system – providing nothing more than new opportunities for old exploitation. Information poverty is just an additional and final burden to those already deprived in every other way.

Indeed, according to this view, the varied tastes, habits, cultures of the world are threatened, like the world's animal species, with extinction, by dominating, profit-driven, western culture. Thus, writes Schiller, Brazilian television, for example, 'is no more than the creolisation of U.S. Cultural products. It is the spiced up third world copy of western values, norms, and patterns of behavior.'[6]

There have also been even more flamboyant theorists like Michel Foucault, who identified surveillance and control, the arbitrary, but ever present, possibility of regulation, correction and domination as the intrinsic and essential feature of modern societies. The information revolution was the crowning extension of this. Following him, writers like Jean-François Lyotard not only suggested that 'information' was central to all contemporary institutions, but that everywhere beliefs in redemptive, 'meta-narratives' in the power of religion, science or democracy had collapsed, only to be replaced by an ever growing reliance on the computer's powers of ordering.

Finally, there are the revolutionaries. They are united in believing that something dramatically, recognizably novel must be occurring, or will soon occur, and they suggest that every conceivable aspect of life will be changed. Anthony Giddens, an early advocate of 'globalization', wrote, 'As different areas of the globe are drawn into interconnection with one another, waves of social transformation crash across virtually the whole earth's surface . . . the new modes of life will sweep us from all traditional types of social order in a quite unprecedented fashion.' What is now happening is 'a ruthless break with any and all preceding conditions'. The stable identities of cultures, economies, firms, work, needs and indeed personalities, are to be re-forged by globalization, says Brian Harvey, another theorist who claims much for global organization.

Within this the media and communication have a complicated role. They are seen as the most prominent example of the global economy. It is argued that as media products cost more to produce, as audiences expect ever higher production values, so are needed ever bigger markets to recoup their costs. Thus the same films and television programmes are to be seen worldwide. Moreover, the giant media conglomerates – always seeking attention unlike many international companies who prefer anonymity – are all too evidently prominent buyers and sellers of local media in many nations. Their empires, if not their owners, attract and court publicity. Further, media values are seen as the shock troops of global cultural revolution. Its generals are the giant companies whose logos bestride the world.

Global business giants

However, left-wing critics have been concerned about 'multi-national' corporations for many years. These powerful enterprises trading across the world were originally seen as the economic inheritors of political imperialism. From their home bases in the First World – America, Europe, Japan – they brought natural products from, and sold goods to, and indeed remodelled the economies of, the 'underdeveloped' world. Thus a Third World country would find itself giving up self-sufficient food production in order to produce a cash crop for export, only to find itself, as the 1980s and 1990s vividly showed, tragically over-dependent on the price the 'world' was prepared to pay for its coffee or sugar. The multi-national corporations according to these theories only saw the developing world in terms of potential markets, and the developing world's industries were swamped and annihilated by superior, cheaper products, sold to them from far away.

The role of the media was seen by many commentators to be critical to the process. However, in terms of the media industries themselves, the term 'multi-national' was something of a misnomer. Only America had a truly international market for its media goods, the essential form and style of some of which, for example, film, had originated in the United States. This had an apparently overwhelmingly dominating place in media markets all over the world for many years.

In the case of the media, the argument was that they were exporting western wants along with the programmes. In this way, it was thought that the media made people in poor countries want the things they saw. Sometimes what they saw and wanted were goods; sometimes, it was argued, what they saw and wanted were rights and freedoms.

This process had for a while been seen as having a potentially useful side. The media, it was believed, might work like Maynard Keynes' famous economic multiplier by magnifying and spreading ideas faster. It had been suggested in the early 1960s that the impediment which stood in the way of underdeveloped nations economies' progress was the inappropriate attitudes and habits of their peoples. The media, it was hoped, could help change those fast. It proved to be a far more difficult and fraught process than had been expected.

A more cautious interpretation was that the western media relentlessly bore values that advocated consumption. The media were the 'hidden' persuaders, whose images kept the whole developing, post-imperial world in thrall to the big corporations of the developed world – and through them at the mercy of the political whim of the imperial powers.

However, in the late 1980s, critics began to identify a new, bigger, badder, more authoritarian brother to the multi-national corporation: the transnational corporation. These even more huge businesses, made possible by exploitation of the new technologies of communication, were no longer the tools of any imperial political design other than their own. Enterprises based on 'home' nation states – and trading with its interests in mind – were said everywhere to be being replaced by autonomous, free-standing companies, as indifferent to the interests of the First as to those of the Third World. The transnational corporation, ruthless, uncontrollable, unfettered by responsibility or even habits, was world-dominating. Nation states no longer controlled them, but rather pathetically vied with each other to attract such companies' investments.

Using cheap, instantaneous, interactive communications, these corporations compose a production process out of a global base. Choosing cheap labour in one place, low taxes in another, good services elsewhere, these transnational corporations, it is argued, have broken free from the complex political ties and obligations of operating from one nation; of being national. Then, using the global media to sell their goods everywhere, they create new cultures. Such corporations owe allegiance only to profit. At the worst they become the only agents in the world capable of pursuing policy (even if that is profit); at the best they offer the promise of a new intra-corporate global world – which, somehow, may be better.

Indeed, the position of the media – which, unlike other commodities that also help shape politics, are peculiarly vulnerable – may make them become little more than pawns bought or sold to give companies a voice in national affairs. In fact, the great media empires, like Disney, provided the model for the theory of transnational corporations. The internationalization of the images of the products of these corporations displayed through the media provided powerful evidence of the nature of global markets – and, of course, stimulated their growth. Thus it is suggested that these corporations depended on the cheap, fast, interactive communications of complex data anywhere and that the information manipulation and processing capacities of the information revolutions produced a new industrial form. The imagery generated by the media produced new global markets and together they introduced a new epoch – the globalized world. The key characteristic of this world is that space and time are made irrelevant by communications. The strong theorists of globalization have thus produced a powerful reinterpretation of contemporary industrial developments.[7]

Yet, however recognizable this description is, there are some problems with it, not least that the world's markets have actually been globalized, in the sense of being open with growing international trade flows, for a very long time. Jevons, the great nineteenth-century economist, wrote in 1834 that 'the plains of North America and Russia are our cornfields, and the groves of Canada and the Baltic our timber groves. Peru sends us her silver, our coffee and sugar and spices come from India, and the Chinese grow tea for us.' Indeed, the most important shrinking of the world occurred perhaps in the 1860s when Reuters laid cables which immediately took news of ships, and markets, politics and rebellions, all over the world. In fact, the international economy has a complex history of relative openness and closure, but it is clear that the world has been shrunk for many years.

Furthermore, although the models of the transnational corporations are just what you would expect, in theory, to emerge from a globalized world, the actual evidence about their growth is more complex. Although nearly all modern businesses operate internationally, only very few are like the model of the transnational corporation. Most firms, and most compelling of all, most of the really successful firms that operate in multi-national situations, do so from an identifiable home national base. John Dunning, in a monumental study of multi-national corporations, concluded that throughout the world 'home' country sales still dominate multi-national corporation sales.[8] Even in industries where sales abroad were of overall importance, the basis of profit was clearly in one 'home market' first. In addition, some 'home' markets and indeed those that are seen as peculiarly advanced, for example, the Japanese and the German, remain remarkably closed to goods and services from other places.

Moreover, the companies which count as 'multi-national', as Hirst and Thompson point out, vary greatly in the kind and pattern of dependence they have on overseas sales. Some rely on a home market, some on a regional market, some on more diverse markets. For example, German firms (for strong historical reasons) are particularly heavily represented in South Africa. 'International businesses', Hirst and Thompson argue, 'are still largely confined to their home territories'; they remain heavily 'nationally embedded'.[9]

Moreover, investments, profits, exports, have different profiles in different nations. In many, regional markets are more important than global ones. There are transnational corporations, but not all firms are evolving towards being like them. Transnational firms are also changing, indeed, the world over; as *The Economist* pointed out, the most successful firms are getting smaller, not larger.

Moreover, world trade has not simply become more 'global' as the century has progressed – as the globalization orthodoxy implies. World trade was more open, more countries traded more of what they produced with other countries in 1914 than in 1995. France and Japan still, in 1997, export a smaller proportion of the goods they produce than they did before the First World War. Hirst and Thompson make a powerful case for at least looking at the evidence about what is happening to world trade, rather than, as they suggest the orthodox globalization theorists do, cavalierly marshalling complex data to support an over-simple, predetermined theory. The twentieth century has thus not seen a simple movement (impeded by a war or two) from closed national markets to open global ones.

One of the things that globalized media markets are supposed to be doing is producing a homogenized international global culture. 'Coca-Cola, Disney and McDonald's, from Moscow to New York, from Tiananmen Square to Papua, it is the same culture that is present everywhere: and thus it will be,' claims the strong globalizer, Rosenau. Most prominent, indeed most puzzling perhaps, is the spectacle of American-produced soap operas screened all over the world, or of British comedies watched and laughed at in places where their meanings can hardly be expected to resonate – for example, *Mr Bean* in Bosnia. This is such a strange development that it is often cited as definitive evidence of globalization's inevitable pattern. Orthodox globalization theorists cite it as demonstrating the existence of an already homogenized world 'taste'. Everybody, everywhere, likes the same things. The issue is further confused by the emphasis on viewers' choice. The public everywhere, they argue, must now be the same, for they choose the same programme to watch. Yet, in the case of television, what viewers choose between is what programme buyers have selected. It is not viewers but programme purchasers who dictate what is seen.

Indeed, buying cheap, imported programming, which is what American programmes are everywhere other than America, is not a sign of advanced, pioneer, 'global' tastes. On the contrary, it is evidence of impoverished media markets. Poor countries, poor entertainment systems, buy in relatively cheap (because not domestically produced) foreign programming. The more wealth an entertainment system has, the more it shows programmes made specifically for its own audiences. Indeed, there is evidence that many more sophisticated and wealthy entertainment markets (in contrast to the theoretical projections of globalization) are all beginning to show more 'upmarket' and more domestically produced programming. Showing 'world' culture may therefore be a transitional moment – not the highest or most developed point in entertainment markets.

Indeed, if we examine the attempts of the giant media corporations to globalize culture, it is evident that this is not as simple a process as the theorists argue. Attempts by Murdoch to run Asian satellite television stations failed. They did not do so because Murdoch's News International was obstinate about adhering to western cultural values – like objectivity, or impartiality; indeed, such expensive principles were quickly dispensed with if necessary. The satellite service to China, for example, was more than prepared to supply reporting conventionally doctored by the government. The station failed because audiences did not like the programmes it showed. 'Global' culture does not always sell well.

Thus, although world trade and the trade in media goods and communications have changed and there are profound problems involved with any simple assertion about culture internationally, the contemporary patterns of media markets are not, on closer examination, those so blithely agreed on by the more extreme global theorists. More tellingly, they are not likely to remain the same. Markets, the orthodox globalizers seem to have failed to notice, go on changing.

Nations, nationality and globalization

One of the things 'globalization' is widely agreed to have done, or to be doing, or soon will have done, is to kill off the nation state. As Daniel Bell argued, the territorial nation state was 'too small for the big problems of life, and too big for the small problems of life'.[10] Internationally, globalization is said to make the nation state increasingly irrelevant. John Gray, the right-wing political theorist, has, in this vein, recently argued that social democracy is similarly doomed.[11] There are many aspects of economic management that the nation has lost the power to control – financial speculation is now so swift and so huge that it could bring about the collapse of any economy. In addition, a state's internal policies increasingly can do little to modify international pressures. Paul Kennedy described the problem well: 'If a government is conscientiously attempting to provide better schools, better health care, housing and public utilities for its citizens, by what means can it raise the necessary funds without alarming investors who may be not at all interested in the well being of those citizens, but merely in their own profits?'[12] He indicates that even a well-intentioned government will now have greater problems in addressing the needs of its people – yet addressing such needs is the basis of government authority.

The nation state is historically still rather new and, as Eric Hobsbawm points out, what constitutes a nation is very flexible. Many 'nations' in Africa are the consequence of colonial politics, and are formed by arbitrary lines on maps that have no relationships to local territorial or cultural differences. Many others are the product of the collapse at the end of the First World War of 'multi-national empires'. 'A nation', wrote the communist dictator, Joseph Stalin, 'is a historically evolved stable community of language, territory, economic life and psychological make up, manifested in a community of culture.' The attractions of nationality resonate differently in different parts of the world. No one worries that California will declare separate national identity from American – even though its economy is larger than over four-fifths of the world's other nations. Ernest Gellner, the political philosopher, argued that nationality was 'in the end a principle which holds that the political and the national unit should be congruent.'[13] Gellner's idea was that urban industrialization led inevitably to nation-building. Moreover, many critics have disliked the nation state as a political form. 'As we shall see,' wrote Hobsbawm, that most Olympian of left-wing historians, 'the nation state is entirely irrelevant to the problems of the late twentieth century, for which it provides no general solutions. It merely complicates the task of addressing these problems'.[14] Indeed, the frailties of the nation state are now commonplaces of sociological theory and political journals. There is, writes John Dunn, a growing gap 'between the causal capabilities of even the most advanced nation state, and the effective demands placed on the powers'. Clearly, the issue of political responsibility in an internationalizing world is critical. The media, seeping images over national boundaries, and communications technologies undermining national self-determination, both contribute directly to this shift of power, and moreover are the carriers of other dissolving agents.

Globalization asserts the economic irrelevance of the nation state and claims that the same forces are dissipating cultural autonomy based on the nation for other, more temporary, allegiances. 'The threat to cultural identity comes variously from trade, from mobile capital, from the free flow of ideas and images. But it also comes from migrant labour', states a pamphlet produced by the radical (neither left- nor right-wing think-tank Demos), which both describes and indeed endorses the process.[15]

The communications revolution does mean that it is increasingly difficult for nations to protect their subjects from images, ideas, tastes even, of which they disapprove. The overthrow of the communist regimes in Eastern Europe was hastened by their domestic populations' finally unstoppable desire for the western media. In a rather different way, broadcasting certainly abetted more classic mass mobilization, both in China, and indeed in East Germany, where the sight on television of the huge immigration to the West finally brought down the Berlin Wall. States, of course, go on trying to prohibit what their subjects read and see, but new communications provide inventive mass samizdat alternatives. Thus the words of the Ayatollah Khomeini, the Iranian religious leader, exiled in Paris, rigorously banned from all public appearances, were nevertheless readily available throughout pre-revolutionary Iran: on tape.

In the recent past it was believed that the media would enhance the power of governments, but although the media are certainly important the effects are less simple than had been assumed; for example, one by-product of the telecommunications revolution may be that more angry 'have nots' can measure the privileges of the 'haves' with a more accurate eye. In a world marked, both within and between nations, by a steeply rising inequality, this may be dangerous.

Another aspect of the decline of nation states, it is argued – particularly vividly by politicians – is the usurping by the media of the nation state's right to formulate foreign policy. Thus, in America it has been suggested that 'real' time television, which shows events as they unfold, has begun to 'jump' governments into inappropriate action. Similarly, Douglas Hurd, when he was British Foreign Secretary, argued, 'There is nothing new in mass rape, in the shooting of civilians, in war crimes, in ethnic cleansing, in the burning of towns and cities. It has always happened. What is new is that a selection of these tragedies is now visible, within homes, to people around the world on television.'[16] On another occasion, a Foreign Office official added, 'It cannot be the object of foreign policy to wipe a tear from every eye – however much the cameras would like us to.' In America, a vigorous debate raged about the role of the media in compromising national defence and foreign policy. This evidence of media usurpation – dependent on the new technological capacity – is apparently an all too clear demonstration of the globalizers' analysis.

Something odd may be happening to how governments make policy, and the media may well be more influential. American foreign policy is increasingly governed by the 'body bag' factor; thus, while the American public can be made to back foreign intervention, they do not like to see on their television screens even one American harmed by fighting. Meanwhile, in Israel, when there was an Arab suicide bombing of an Israeli bus, the television cameras arrived with the police, before the ambulances, and the subsequent total coverage of the events certainly contributed to a drastic change in policy. The event was replayed, and its consequences became public, in a way which had a direct impact on government policy, and led to a rapid shift in Israeli politics. Yet even this process is by no means as clear as governments themselves claim. Nick Gowing, Channel 4's diplomatic editor, argued in a paper, based on extensive interviews, that governments were still well able to control news agendas. It is perhaps, at times, convenient for governments to be able to disclaim power.[17]

Yet, if the role of governments is changing, and the impact of the media is altering, does this mean that the nation state is dying? Eric Hobsbawm distinguishes between the 'epic' period of state-building at the end of the nineteenth century and the beginning of the twentieth, when states often attempted to subsume cultural and economic inequalities, and indeed reduce them by redistribution – from what he calls 'separatist' nationalism of the post-cold war period. Late twentieth-century politics, he argues sombrely, is marked by 'exclusitory identity politics'. This implies that group identity consists of some existential, supposedly primordial, unchangeable and therefore permanent personal characteristic shared with other members of the group and with absolutely no one else. It is this kind of nationalism that has led in part to the obscene resurgence of 'ethnic cleansing'. Yet, as the break-up of Bosnia showed, the media, so fêted as the agents of globalization, are nevertheless fundamental to any process of separation and demonization as well.

Some of the more extreme believers in globalization, like Kenichi Ohmae, in his book *The End of the Nation State*, argue that these developments are merely 'localism'. They argue that increasingly small areas secede from nations in order to relate independently to larger economic or indeed political blocks, like the EC.[18] There is evidence of several different kinds of such 'separation'. Some may be the logical outcome of the 1980s' elevation of self over collective interests – in which wealthy regions seek separate identity and separate in order to keep more of their wealth to themselves rather than subsidize poorer regions. Thus, rich middle-class Staten Island voted to cede from poor ghettoized New York in 1992. Rich Catalonia seeks independence from the poorer Southern Spain, and there has even been the suggestion that Northern industrial Italy might jettison the agrarian South. On the other hand, as Paul Bew, the Irish historian has pointed out, devolution and independence are also frequently sought despite the fact that the break has no such advantages – and may even have considerable disadvantages. Commentators have therefore pointed to this process of fragmentation and realignment of social and economic forces as evidence of the impact of globalization. Part of the shift is said to be in politics from political divisions based on economic difference, to what a Demos pamphlet called a 'more diffuse and shifting world of competing styles'.

Nevertheless, however obstructive, inflexible and old-fashioned, the nation state exists, and however much its demise might be regarded as desirable, nearly all these splinters and shifts take place in the name of nationalism. Indeed, 'nationalism' is a rhetoric which articulates an increasing, *not* a decreasing number of interests. Territorial disputes and wars have multiplied in the post-cold war new world order. Moreover, the recent increase in the migration of populations, which is also credited with breaking down national barriers (though it is still nowhere near as large as the vast diasporas created by the Second World War), is also leading to a new phenomenon, that of extreme nationalism – at a distance. Thus, groups who see their future as citizens of the states where they have settled nevertheless advocate the most virulent nationalism in their nations of origin – the American Irish, the English Sikhs, the Tamils in Holland, Zionists in America, the Turks in Germany, the Estonians in America, are all radically nationalistic. This new nationalism about issues in their distant 'homes' is made possible and articulated by a whole new range of satellite and press media. The media help make new and old nationalism.

Nationalism, as a very old, crude and powerful device for defining the community as innocent and identifying the guilty thus may well continue to flourish in a post-cold war settlement. Everywhere, media rituals accompany the process of splintering and reforming. Thus, the 'homogenizing' impact of American global culture, which is seen as such an important corollary of economic globalization, appears to have less impact on political identities than the orthodoxy requires. It is not that something is not happening, it is rather that the theory gets in the way of our capacity to examine the procedure.

Indeed, more than that, 'nationality' still remains a very robust way of categorizing systematic differences in the use and content of the media themselves. Viewing habits, computer preferences, film tastes, where and how the media are brought into homes, by whom they are used and for what purposes, are all remarkably different. A recent European Community report assessing the potential for the development of interactive services in European homes, concluded:

> Alongside increasingly shared habits, tastes, and routines, there exist very profound and deep national differences. We cannot say whether any of these separate patterns will, in time, come to dominate the technology, but we can say that homes in different European nations are innovating and consuming technologies for new purposes – but in very different ways.

It also needs to be noted that the idea that global communications are making national government irrelevant slips with deceptive ease from a description to a proscription. Indeed, as liberal free market ideas became dominant in government policies in the 1980s and 1990s, many prominent social analysts apparently happily clambered on board, speculating that nations were now increasingly irrelevant in part because governments could hardly be expected to do anything, because the tide of technological history was against them. How could mere national governments seek to control their own citizens' conditions of labour, or protect their broadcasting preferences when they faced what sociologists Scott Lasch and John Urry called 'disorganized capital'? A system unable even to understand its own self-interest, but blindly moving forward nevertheless.

'Policies', 'intentions', 'plans', let alone 'commitments', it was widely suggested, were misguided – as they would not be implementable in the face of overriding global forces, and their consequences would be increasingly unpredictable. Thus, the new social theorists elaborated a minimalist role for government, which was a remarkably comfortable fit with how governments wanted to describe their own redefined purpose. Many social scientists were unwittingly elaborating theories which did very little more than justify a specific neo-liberal ideology.

Indeed, some of the most enthusiastic advocates of globalization theory argue that as a corollary of the new epoch, 'government' in general will be little more than reactive and modestly palliative at most. Ulrich Beck, an important German social scientist, suggests that

> as political utopias have given away to discussions about side effects, it is noticeable that side effects risks fall under the responsibility of politics not business. That is to say business is not responsible for something over which it has control and politics is responsible for something over which it has no control.[19]

Beck says that we still look for politics 'on the wrong pages of newspapers' and he is contemptuously dismissive of the incompetence of 'traditional, national, rituals of political processes'. What really matters is happening outside, beyond, somewhere other than old-fashioned 'politics'.

Yet it is not only the case that nation states and nationality are still far more meaningful in media and political terms, as we have seen, than the strong globalizers have argued, but also nation states, however unsatisfactorily, are also still unavoidably the basis for global or regional regulation. Policies do get made, they have effects, and national governments make them. There has recently been a proliferation in international agencies, and while these may well represent important attempts to produce institutions that can come to terms with the internationalization of world affairs, of the 387 that have been developed in the period between 1990 and 1995, nearly 300 were the product of direct contact between national governments. There is a paradox here; the nation state may be part of the problem, but the development of institutions to address global problems still depends on nation states.

Part of the global theorists' orthodoxy is that 'policy' is irrelevant, because it is unsustainable, and its consequences unpredictable. Yet this is at odds with what we know about the most advanced economic products. These are now the result of increasingly sophisticated knowledge and expertise. This in turn is the product of policy. Thus, for example, creation of a new drug-mimicking gene in medical research represents a complex history of research. The role of the whole social and political environment, and indeed the consequences of policies, are highly significant in the production of such goods. Thus what Ozawa calls 'market enabling incentives' are actually more important than ever before. In turn, Denning argues that precisely because competition is so fierce, 'everything that governments do affects location decisions and outcomes'.[20] Thus policies are not made irrelevant by globalization, indeed economic development may be more sensitively dependent on them.

Indeed, the strong global theorists seem to have been listening to what governments have been saying they do – rather than watching how governments have been behaving. In many ways the rhetoric of 'minimalist' government of the 1980s served to mask a quite different reality, one in which governments increased their control over many areas of social life. All over the developed world, the process called 'privatization' has meant little more than hollowing out previously independent organizations by what was, in effect, state patronage. Governments are changing how and where they intervene, but they have not simply made themselves redundant.

Globalization thus points to the internationalization inherent in some aspects of media developments – but hardly accounts for the complexity of what has actually happened. Nations still exist, and indeed are needed. National preferences still exist, national patterns of media use and habit still exist. Policies about resources and distribution, though more difficult to get right and in some areas beyond the control of individual nation states, matter more, not less.

The media and the global personality

Globalization may be a big theory about the world, but such is its ambition that it is also said to have influenced – through the media – how we feel and how we relate to one another. We have, apparently, new characters and new human potentials for a new epoch.

Television is said to be the agent of this transformation. Ulrich Beck, in his best-selling book, wrote, 'Television isolates and standardizes. . . . On the one hand it removes people from conventional experiences. At the same time everyone is in a similar position, they all consume institutionally produced programmes. Television produces the standardized collective existence of isolated man – hermits the world over.' Anthony Giddens, in a similar vein, says that in 'personal life' there is a movement 'away from relationships symbolically or actually functional to "pure relationships"'. These are apparently 'entered into and sustained for their own sake and for no more than the rewards that associating with others can bring'. To go along with this suspiciously neat ideal type, Anthony Giddens describes a novel 'democracy of the emotions'. 'Emotional articulacy', or the capacity to describe feelings (though presumably even Giddens is not suggesting that those who do not describe them do not have them) is seen as a necessary product of a newly globalized world. Sexuality, feelings, relationships are to be chosen and need to be expressed because they can no longer be taken for granted. The mass media, agony aunts, soap operas, self-help manuals, the exploration of the self are remaking us into 'individuals in every sense'. So 'flexible' will be this modern self that you will be able, as it were, to shop around for a soul, and no doubt swap an inconvenient or old-fashioned one for something more up to date.

This is all little more than an oddly optimistic inversion of Marcuse's dystopic theories of the commodification of private life (or an opportunistic post-modernist philanderer's charter – relationships without responsibility). The argument is that these 'new' selves are both a product of and necessary for the further globalization of society. It is also, of course, the wholesale transcription and endorsement of neo-liberal emphasis on choice of identity – with the media now elevated to midwives of the self.

This suspiciously Weberian complicity of theory with progress – that personality formation now offers new opportunities for choice – hardly fits with the way in which most people in most societies experience personal choices. Indeed, that more marriages end in divorce is no more adequately explained by an increase in 'choice' than is a suicide rate. Even more strange is the basis of these ideas about 'emotional liberty' in assumptions about the impact of the media on our new flexible selves. There is overwhelming evidence about the impact of the media on institutional forms. There is very good reason to believe that the media influence some people in some circumstances in some ways. However, it is equally clearly known that there are no 'generalizable' media effects on individuals. The media do not simply 'make' people more violent or more loving. Moreover, theories about personal relationships have become more complex. In the past, theorists of economic development argued that marriages based on tradition and authority would, as societies 'modernized', be superseded by 'romantic' individualistic attachment. Yet we now know that the movement towards economic modernizations does not simply reproduce cultural values. Thus, fundamentalist religious movements frequently combine advanced economic practices with savagely reinforced traditional sexual moralities. Similarly, many sociologists claimed as a matter of self-evident development that the working-class extended family would inevitably be replaced by the nuclear middle-class version; yet in American and Europe, numerous studies have begun to reveal the re-emergence of the extended family across all classes as providers of acceptable child care for working mothers. There is simply no evidence that media have led to 'global' people with standardized global feelings. Some feelings they share, some they share less. Something interesting may well be happening to people's feelings and identities – but the strong globalization theories merely foreclose enquiry.

Choosing and meaning

Globalization is also seen as the agent of a whole series of shifts said to characterize a new era in the late twentieth century. 'Mass production, mass consumers, the big city, the big brother state, the sprawling housing estate, and the nation state are all in decline – flexibility, diversity, differentiation, mobility, decentralization, and internationalization, are in the ascendant. We are in transition to a new era', wrote one prophet in 1988 in an article called 'New times'.[21]

In the more extreme elaboration of these kinds of idea – in ideas derived from literary theory – it was also suggested that 'texts' (books written by authors, but also, of course, media products) were little more than an opportunity for different 'readers' to construct their own 'meanings'. All these theories had in common a scepticism about the existence of objective reality, let alone the possibility of arriving at an agreed understanding of it by rational means. They also elevated the cultural critic (or the consumer) at the expense of the producers (who, it was averred, did not know what they were doing, and whose intended, or even unintended, meanings were irrelevant to the more significant 'construction' of meanings by critics and readers). Of course, all this was very comforting and enhancing for critics, who according to their own account became far more important than the hapless 'authors'.

However, beneath this was another, perhaps more sinister compliance that the 'critics' themselves failed to recognize. The proliferation of media channels and opportunities had by no means been accompanied by investment in, or indeed a radical reappraisal of, how understandings and knowledge are produced. Indeed, all public, publicly owned, publicly accessible, available knowledge, research constructed around the pursuit of knowledge not profit, ways of manipulating data and understanding were, all over the world, in crisis. Ways of financing the production of media products – the software – were not rethought. This was not the product of some blind, inexorable technological force, globalization, but rather the pursuit of particular policies, based on particular ideologies, in particular places.

Plenitude and scarcity

Yet it is a key contention of the globalization theorists that the new communications technology means that there is a novel, positively orgiastic plenitude of information and 'meanings' available to everyone, so they suggest that to worry about production is absurd. We will be our own 'producers'.

Bill Gates, in his dismal utopian vision of a 'microsoft' world – *The Village* – has a vocabulary packed with images of plenty and excess. Admittedly, all this splendid novelty goes into 'the home of the future' (which he is building for himself) and it delivers such breathtaking expansions of human capacity as never having to open a window, and having the kettle ready boiling and your favourite television programme showing as you walk through the door (the home computer will do it for you). Quite why the technology of the future should share so many features with the housewife of the past is puzzling. However, the book is phrased in the familiar if, in this example, rather tired language of excess.

However, a more cheering aspect of Mr Gates' ideal home is that on the walls you could display 'any great picture from any great gallery the world over, in your home, at will'. What he doesn't mention is that his corporation has been steadily purchasing the reproduction rights from the great galleries. So what you could once see either freely, or via a charge to the gallery, will in the future inevitably enhance Mr Gates' own profits.

Information is seen as a new 'strategic resource', and writers from Alvin Toffler onwards have talked about the 'global information gladiators' or what Claud Baudrillard has called the 'information blizzard' or Lyotard 'message gluttony'. Television executives routinely now use the language of 'infinite capacity and infinite choice'. A kind of cerebral gargantuanism with a Rabelaisian panorama of novel exotic media delights is promised.

In some ways the plenitude argument is self-evidently right. Never has it been harder to avoid aesthetic experience. No doubt in the past, shepherds and peasants (especially those familiar with the poetry of Wordsworth or John Clare) derived intense pleasure from the familiar beauties of nature. They certainly had aesthetic experiences. But what is new is that streets and homes, public and private places, are now bombarded with images, purposively demanding response.

Indeed, in other areas the reformative capacity of the information revolution stretches everywhere; huge expanses of human government bureaucracy will soon be dispensed with, using new technology. Arming citizens with 'smart cards' from cradle to grave, insurance, tax, health, driving status, rights to benefits, and obligations, could all be encoded in the card's records. Government health and welfare bureaucracies could and probably will be replaced by systems better able to code and evaluate evidence more cheaply. It may release more resources for services, it may well reshape government.

However, 'plenitude' is in all these cases equated with 'better', or 'good'. Again, the reality will be more complex. There will, for example, be greater opportunities for surveillance. Yet nowhere is the contradiction between information or communication excess – and what it may actually mean – more stark than in the changes the communication revolution is bringing to news and news production.

Here the rhetoric is the now classic one of immensity and opportunity. New twenty-four-hour news services, new television channels, devoted to nothing but news, more news, from more places, faster, hotter news, with more pictures, national, local, international news on demand. If the global communication revolution started with Reuters cabling the world in the 1860s, then news surely represents the apogée of all that the globalizing theorists claim for the new epoch – and of course it is abundantly self-evident that there is a great deal 'more' news around than there used to be.

Yet, on closer examination, this turns out to be true only in a rather limited sense. News has always been a commodity, but recently newsgathering capacity has been savagely cut. Now, fewer journalists produce more stories more frequently. Increasingly, they have little time to understand the complex background of developing affairs. Understanding requires time, time costs, and reporters everywhere may be becoming more, not less, vulnerable to the well-packaged official lines produced, not only by governments, but by the armies of lobbyists employed by every conceivable interest to promote – and kill – stories.[22] Thus fewer journalists know less, cost less, are approached by ever more publicists, lobbyists and spin doctors, but they produce material that is disseminated more powerfully to more places.

New technologies of communication, satellite, cable, instantaneous transmission of pictures together with more stations, channels, and programmes, and the rise of the 'rolling newsday', and 'continuous news on demand', literally mean that deadlines occur so frequently that journalists have less time to collect – or order – news. Indeed, the 'news' room itself may be being displaced, as the editing is increasingly controlled by those with an interest in how they are presented. Presidential and parliamentary campaigns now work very hard indeed to produce media events that will unavoidably be chosen for television screens. That is what a 'photo-opportunity', at its crudest, represents. Martin Bell, the BBC's redoubtable war correspondent, writes, 'More news means worse. The multiplicity of deadlines takes us away from the real world and drives us back into our offices and edit suites. It is safer there.'[23] The man who was wounded on screen points out that, in nasty brutal wars where journalists are increasingly seen as key targets, 'we may find reasons to stay there'.

This process is made worse by the relentless competitive pressure on news organizations. Newspapers everywhere face slowly but steadily declining circulations; broadcasters everywhere face more stations competing for only slowly expanding audiences. Some suggest the effects of this will be benign; editorializing and the news room as the place where news is ordered and constructed (and, tacitly, it is suggested, biased) will decline. News will be, it is suggested, more like evidence and less like argument. However, at the moment, the clearest impact of the competition is not the abolition of news values, but rather a radical shift in them. News values are becoming more sensational, local and personal. They are becoming less about news – in the sense of things that citizens in a democracy need to know to exercise informed choices, and more about scandals and attracting audience attention. Indeed, a greater volume of news, on more channels, has not so far served to stretch news values. More has not meant different, in depth, more revealing, better informed news.

Moreover, news dies faster than ever before. We can, because of the global communications revolution, have an instantaneous 'real time' relationship to unfolding events. Yet this has come to mean that unless it is ingeniously managed, news is what is happening now, however trivial. It is not that there is no appetite for subtle, knowledgeable – even objective – news. The BBC's World Service has been increasingly popular with audiences, despite ever tighter constraints, precisely because of its generous, innovative, searching news values. Yet, the impact of the global communication revolution on news is so far producing quite the opposite to this kind of genre. At the moment, at least, issues which matter apparently die as fast as the trivial and absurd. In turn, this influences how we deal with wars and coups, famines and injustices abroad and at home. But the impact is not merely produced by 'volume'. More news is not the same as important news, indeed there is only in one rather limited sense more of it at all.[24]

The cornucopian imagery of global information plenitude is not merely unhelpful, it is misleading. More of anything is not necessarily benign, and globalization does not produce a land of milk and honey with no scarcity. We should address the emerging distributions of goods and services, not dream that no choices need be made. There may be hugely increased public 'access' to information made available by the new technology, but the information is not free. Indeed, so far we have hardly begun to increase public rights to this potential knowledge.

Indeed, one of the emerging crises in the new technology revolution is the financing of the production of knowledge. Piracy is endemic to many of the new technologies (though this is an issue the transnational corporations take seriously – it affects their profits – and will no doubt solve), the piracy of CDs and software is common everywhere. Unless we are, like many of the 'new' television channels, merely going to endlessly recycle our past in the brand new future, there are gathering problems about funding future culture. We listen to more CDs, but we go to fewer concerts, we consume more literature, but fewer authors make a living by writing.[25] Scientists are enjoined to raise research funds from private companies, who will then 'own' their results.[26] Universities are increasingly inadequately funded. Thus the potential for 'digital' television to offer extraordinary new services and opportunities is huge. However, if that unknown potential is to be liberating, novel, and to lead the public into thoughts and issues they had not expected, and needs that they did not know they had, it will need investment. Investment for purposes beyond that of short-term profit. In fact, scarcity is still here, the cornucopian imagery of the information explosion is a chimera – misleading us into believing that the only 'choices' to be made will be private ones.

Fin de siècle nihilism and globalization

The global communications revolution – and the future it is fast moulding – is often discussed as if it were too large and too inexorable for anything to be done about it. On the one hand, there is a resigned assertion of the paralysis of politics and irrelevancy of all that is past, and on the other a radiant faith in the inherent novelty of a technologically transformed world. The collapse of Eastern Europe and the end of the cold war gave added impetus to these ideas, because – whatever the reality – the conflict had provided the basis to support many ideas about the possibility of alternative social arrangements. The society we are now told we will get will apparently be constituted out of the myriad choices made by information and media consumers. It is as if we now believe that 'public good', indeed 'global good' will emerge (or may not emerge but nothing can be done about it) mysteriously out of the individual pursuit of self-interest and corporations' pursuit of profit. There is a powerful belief in the force of communications to reshape everything they touch. Nothing, as it were, can be done, but something new will emerge is the message.

Fin de siècle blues

Of course, a profoundly introverted sense of a propulsion towards the future has happened before – at the end of the nineteenth century. A strong sense of inevitable and meaningless change was then part of social understanding:

> Life no longer dwells in the whole. The word becomes sovereign and leaps out of the sentence, the sentence reaches out and obscures the meaning of the page, the page gains life at the expense of the whole – all, everywhere, is the anarchy of atoms, the disaggregation of the will, the hopelessness of intention facing the maelstrom.[27]

So wrote Nietzche – the great nineteenth-century philosopher – of the impossibility of action in modern conditions. Last time around, *fin de siècle* thinkers became increasingly obsessed with culture as the only worthwhile value. Moreover, it was seen as one divorced from any political or social consequences or meaning, 'Art for Art's Sake' alone. Part of this was a melancholic apathy about what could be done. But it was accompanied by a belief in the value of chaos. These were the dominant leitmotivs of the period.

At the end of the nineteenth century this was combined with an almost transcendence hope in the possibilities of scientific and technological solutions to the world's problems: 'all are awaiting the birth of a new order of things . . . industrial applications by a single electronic impulse will make the same thought vibrate between five continents. The axis is displaced and the world must crack that its equilibrium be restored', wrote a French socialist critic in the late 1880s.

In France, neo-impressionist painters believed that in the future painting could be based on what was 'real', not what people believed they saw. In the past they argued art had been based on intuitions about how things 'really' looked but, in the future, they said it would be based on scientific theory. The true identity of colour would be revealed by scientific research. In England,

Fabian reformers believed that the scrupulous scientific observation of social problems would by itself reveal what had to be done to eradicate them. Science, it was believed, would transform and improve human society. Thus a *'fin de siècle'* period is marked by a belief that something momentous is ending, and something epochal is about to happen. Pedestrian ideas about empirical observation, cautious policies, pragmatic views of change, are exchanged for far grander and more finite ideas.

So perhaps some aspect of orthodox 'globalization' theories are just an expression of *fin de siècle* fears and hopes? Certainly, as we have seen, they are far too wide to be able to describe many of the things that are actually happening. Huge changes are gathering speed, but in order to deal with these, we need evidence not speculation (let alone politically convenient speculation). It is not that the world is not changing, but that globalization – a useful rallying call to martial attention – is now more of a hindrance than a help in our increasingly important need to understand just what is happening. The convenient, melodramatic assertion that change is beyond control is lazy and absurd. None of the 'causes' of globalization, like Topsy, 'just grew', they happened because choices were being made. Nor will the 'new' millennium emerge out of the blue. Tastes in the media, uses for the media, ways of communication, have not reached some final state, they still go on developing and changing.

One of the more intriguing aspects of contemporary ideas is the extent to which watching television – apparently a humble enough activity – has become a resonant metaphor for many aspects of late twentieth-century life. Television watching is seen as private, symptomatic of pathology and opportunity. Robert Putnam, an American political scientist, concluded, in one work based on over twenty years' study of Italian politics, that 'the pattern is stark: one could have predicted the success or failure of government in Italy in the 1980s with extraordinary accuracy from the pattern of civic engagement nearly a century earlier'. Putnam then went on, in another work, to demonstrate that the 'cause' of civic disengagement, which he sees as spreading like a disease, disabling, depopulating civic institutions throughout American life, is television watching.[28] Women working, family break-up, urban dislocation, changes in work habits and hours, unemployment and over-employment, make no difference to whether Americans participate in the institutions of civic life, he claimed. However, being brought up in a television-watching democracy does. It is an extravagant claim – but a scrupulously researched one. That does not mean that it is right, but at least it prompts an argument.

Perhaps what we need, as we consider how communication and information may be reshaping how we live and our institutions, is a little more scepticism and a lot more evidence. It is not that things are not changing, nor that the future will not be radically different. But we need to know more about what is happening in governments and news rooms, in concerts, sitting rooms and in the recording studios. It might also be helpful if, rather than saying that we know what shape the future holds – and consequently abdicating any responsibility for it – we began to ask again what it might be possible to do to make it better.

Notes

1. Anthony Giddens, *Beyond Left and Right: The Future of Radical Politics* (Cambridge, Polity Press, 1994), p. 27.
2. Geoff Mulgan, *Politics in an Anti-Political Age* (Cambridge, Polity Press, 1995), p. 27.
3. Robert Darnton, *The Great Cat Massacre* (London, Allen Cave, 1985), p. 21.
4. K. Kumar, *Utopia and Anti-Utopianism in Modern Times* (Oxford, Blackwell, 1991), p. 402.
5. Bill Gates, *The Road Ahead* (London, Viking, 1995), pp. 226, 259.
6. Herbert Schiller, *Mass Communication and the American Empire* (Boulder, Westview Press, 1993), p. 13.
7. Paul Krugman, *Pop Internationalism* (New York, MIT Press, 1996), pp. 60–75.
8. John H. Dunning, *The Multinational Enterprises and the Global Economy* (Cambridge, Cambridge University Press, 1993).
9. Paul Hirst and Graham Thompson, *Globalization in Question* (Cambridge, Polity Press, 1996), pp. 97–8.
10. Daniel Bell, 'The world and the United States in 2013', *Daedelus*, 116 (3), p. 14.
11. John Gray, *After Social Democracy* (Demos, 1996).
12. Paul Kennedy, *Preparing for the 21st Century* (London, HarperCollins, 1993), p. 210.
13. E. Gellner, *Nations and Nationalists* (Cambridge, CUP, 1984), p. 2.
14. Eric Hobsbawm, *Nations and Nationalism Since 1780: Programme, Myth, Reality* (Cambridge, Cambridge University Press, 1992), p. 17.
15. Vincent Cable, *The World's New Fissures, Identities in Crisis* (Demos, 1994), p. 22.
16. Douglas Hurd, Speech to the Travellers' Club, reported in *The Times*, 17 June 1994.
17. Nick Gowing, 'Real time television and government policy', Shorenstein Centre Paper No. 13 (Cambridge, MA, Harvard University Press, 1994).
18. Ulrich Beck, *The Risk Society: Towards a New Modernity* (London, Sage, 1994), p. 224.
19. Ulrich Beck, *The Risk Society: Towards a New Modernity* (London, Sage, 1994), p. 227.
20. O. J. Denning, *The Multinational Corporation and the Global Economy* (Wokingham, Addison-Wesley, 1993), p. 143.
21. 'New times', *Marxism Today*, October 1988.
22. See, for example, Proceedings of the ESRC Whitehall Programme Conference, 'The Civil Service and the Media', 1996.
23. Martin Bell, *In Harm's Way: Reflections of a War Zone Thing* (London, Hamish Hamilton, 1995), p. 15.
24. For a further discussion see Jean Seaton, 'Misery and the media', in Jean Seaton and Tim Allen (eds) *The Media and Ethnic Violence* (London, UCL, 1996), pp. 12–31.

25. Royal Society of Literature Report, *Authors' Incomes* (1996), 'Research Funding in the Sciences', American National Foundation Report, 1995.
26. 'Nature research', *Nature* Vol. 3, 1996. France and America, 1995.
27. Frederick Nietzche, 'Prelude to plea for the future', in *The Birth of Tragedy*, trans. R. Hollingdale (Cambridge, CUP, 1990), p. 47.
28. See Robert Putnam, *Making Democracy Work: Civil Traditions in Modern Italy* (Princeton, Princeton University Press, 1989), and 'Bowling alone: television and civic disengagement in America' (*Daedalus*, 1995).

20

The sociology of the mass media

Do newspapers, broadcasting, and mass entertainment matter? Do they change society or merely reflect the changes created by others? This chapter will argue that the media do have an independent influence, but not in the sense that has often been assumed. The power of the press and broadcasting is not necessarily greatest when the political involvement in the media is most apparent.

One (determinist) tradition has stressed the relationship of the media with the governing class. It has argued that the media play an important part in modern society. Another (empirical or pluralist) school has looked at the response of audiences to the media, and has concluded that other social pressures overrule any independent effect. These two approaches have been regarded as opposed to one another. In fact, as we will show, they are not incompatible.

The Frankfurt School and the power of the press and broadcasting

'Propaganda, propaganda, propaganda,' Hitler said after the unsuccessful Munich *putsch* in 1923. 'All that matters is propaganda.' Although the Nazis emphasized the importance of oratory and public meetings, they were also fascinated by the emergence of the new technologies of mass communication in the USA and Britain. In particular they saw radio and film as a means of extending the influence of demagogy.

When Hitler came to power in 1933, a group of German intellectuals opposed to the new regime – and seeking to explain the fascist success – turned their attention to the role of the media. The so-called 'Frankfurt School' of writers argued that the roots of the fascist or 'authoritarian' personality were to be found in the nature of the family. However, in explaining what made a population potentially fascist, or why there was no revolt before the Nazi regime began to use widespread force, they also saw the press, radio, films, and even comics and popular music as reinforcing these early influences. The new mass media strengthened the habits and attitudes which made people susceptible to fascist arguments.

The USA, mass culture, and Europeans

Many members of the Frankfurt School became refugees and settled in the USA, for which they developed a profound distaste. Disorientated and home-sick they reacted against every aspect of the American way of life. They concluded that American mass culture was an irreversible force which was destroying superior European cultural traditions. What was worse, mass culture produced precisely the kinds of personality traits that made the population vulnerable to fascist domination. The Frankfurt writers believed, incorrectly, that the USA was also about to become fascist, as Germany had done before.

However, their reaction to mass culture is better understood as part of a more general European response to the USA. The Frankfurt analysis of the role of the press, films, and later television is very similar to that of the literary critic F. R. Leavis. Broadcasting, Leavis argued in 1932, was 'little more than a means of passive diversion but one that made active recreation, especially active use of the mind, more difficult'. And, in an essay called 'Mass civilization and minority culture', he concluded that 'The prospects of culture, then, are very dark. There is less room for hope, in that a standardized civilization is rapidly enveloping the world.' Many of Leavis's views on the USA during this period had been formed by reading a book by Robert and Helen Lynd called *Middletown*. This described the increasing isolation of individuals, social fragmentation, and the pervasiveness of the profit motive in a typical American town.

Thus the Frankfurt School writers shared with many other European social and literary critics a revulsion against American culture. Much of the work of writers like Marcuse and Adorno on the media was based on a rejection of that which was modern, mass, and American.

Liberalism and the individual, and the emergence of fascism

The Frankfurt critics, both in Germany and later in the USA, were concerned to explain the failure of liberalism, and of the liberal emphasis on freedom of speech, expression, and creativity. Writers like Adorno, Marcuse, and Arendt (although she can only loosely be described as a member of this group) pointed to what they saw as the weakness of these concepts in practice. These ideals, the Frankfurt writers believed, had degenerated into a corrupt and selfish individualism. The mass media had played a major part in this process: manipulating society by vulgarizing its culture. In an essay called 'The end of Utopia', Marcuse wrote, 'Today we have the capacity to turn the world into hell and we are well on the way to doing so.'

According to the Frankfurt School the unique individual personality was being destroyed by society. Adorno wrote in *Prisms* of the illusory importance and autonomy of private life which conceals the fact that it 'drags on only as an appendage of the social process'. The celebration of the home, family, and the individual which characterized liberal thought and bourgeois life in the nineteenth and twentieth centuries was already decayed. 'Nothing proved easier to destroy than the privacy and private morality of people who thought of nothing but safeguarding their private lives,' argued Arendt.[1] Totalitarianism was seen as both a cause of this process, and an effect of it.

The Frankfurt School saw the loss of individuality as the cause of dependence on great mass organizations. This analysis implied that society had returned to a more primitive form of association. The interdependence of highly specialized individuals, or what Durkheim called 'organic solidarity', had been succeeded by a new and barbarous homogeneity. Only a 'mechanical' cohesion was possible, dependent on similarity and standardization. Horkheimer argued that, paradoxically, individuality was impaired by the decline in the impulse for collective action. 'As the ordinary man withdraws from participating in political affairs, society tends to revert to the law of the jungle, which crushes all vestiges of individuality,' he wrote.[2] In this analysis the Frankfurt theorists were claiming that totalitarianism emerged as a result of corrupt social institutions and the decline of liberal principles.

There was also another explanation of the success of fascism, which might be characterized as a paranoid theory of change. In this a stealthy process of substitution occurs. This constitutes a Gresham's law of culture and personality, in which bad inexorably drives out good.

The mass media are the key agents of this process. They replace real cultural values with their 'look alikes'. This view that the media provide an ersatz inferior culture is an important element in the Frankfurt explanation of totalitarianism, which assumed that many of the changes brought about through the media would be fought if they were recognized. Horkheimer wrote in *The Eclipse of Reason* that

> Just as the slogans of rugged individualism are politically useful to large trusts in society seeking exemption from social control, so in mass culture the rhetoric of individuality, by imposing patterns for collective imitation, subverts the very principle to which it gives lip service.

Adorno, in a book called *The Jargon of Authenticity,* explains how the 'mass media can create an aura which makes the spectator seem to experience a non-existent actuality'. This subversion of values is a process which Hayek (a writer who came to rather different conclusions) also observed. 'To make a totalitarian system function effectively,' he wrote, 'it is not enough that everybody should be forced to work for the same ends. It is essential that people should come to regard them as their own ends.' The easiest way to do this, he argued, was to substitute new meanings for familiar and respected values, like liberty and freedom.

There is a third explanation of the success of totalitarianism in the work of the Frankfurt writers. In this totalitarianism emerges as the inevitable product of capitalism: the final subjugation of every aspect of life to commercial values. 'The individual now reproduces on the deepest level, in his instinctual structure, the values and behaviour patterns that serve to maintain domination,' wrote Marcuse.

Thus the School suggests three competing explanations of the emergence of fascism. The first sees totalitarian success as a consequence of the attrition of institutions. As Lasswell wrote, 'The Nazis came to power because of weak democracy.'[3] The second suggests that formerly vital values were hollowed out, and replaced with deluding substitutes. The third that fascism did not emerge by default but by evolution.[4] But whatever the explanation, the Frankfurt writers were agreed on one point: the new mass media were not merely a tool of totalitarianism, they were a major reason for its existence.

Entertainment

Above all else (according to the Frankfurt School) radio, film, popular music, and television share an overriding concern to entertain. This was the ultimate form of corruption. Indeed for these writers, 'entertainment' occupies much the same kind of role as self-abuse in pre-Freudian medical literature.

Entertainment promised relief and relaxation but, Rosenberg argued, 'Far from dispelling unrest, all the evidence on hand now suggests that mass culture exacerbates it.' Indeed the atomized individuals of mass society lose their souls to the phantom delights of the film, the soap opera, and the variety show. They fall into a stupor. This apathetic hypnosis Lazarsfeld was to call the 'narcotyzing dysfunction' of exposure to the mass media.

Entertainment thus led to blindness and lunacy. 'It is becoming increasingly plain', wrote Adorno in *The Authoritarian Personality*, 'that people do not behave in such a way as to further their interests, even when it is clear to them what these interests are.' People, it was argued, became insensitive to their own needs.

'The unreal delights and the frenzied fascination' of the mass media prevented them from acting collectively. They became the irrational victims of false wants. Marcuse argued that addiction to the media resulted in an absolute docility: the public had 'been enchanted and transformed into a clientèle by the suppliers of popular culture'. Reisman developed the analogy in *The Lonely Crowd:* 'Glamour in politics, the packaging of the leader, the treatment of the events by the mass media, substitutes for the self-interest of the inner directed man, the abandonment to society of the outer directed man.'

Industrialization and leisure

The Frankfurt School argued that leisure – empty time filled with entertainment – had been industrialized. The production of culture had become standardized and dominated by the profit motive as in other industries. In a mass society leisure was constantly used to induce the appropriate values and motives in the public. The modern media trained the young for consumption. '"The sphere of pleasure" has itself become a sphere of cares,' Reisman argued. Leisure had ceased to be the opposite of work, and had become a preparation for it.

The repetition of the forms of the mass media resembled the monotony of the assembly line: what Adorno called 'The ever-changing production of what is always the same'. In this process, it was argued, culture is consumed by the process of industrialization. Marcuse pointed at the practice of listening to serious music while doing other things (the phenomenon of 'Bach in the kitchen'). Music presented as 'classic', he suggested, 'comes to life as other than itself'. The fact that modern methods of reproduction have increased the quantity of music, art, and literature available to the public does not mean that culture spreads to the masses; rather that culture is destroyed in order to make entertainment.

'At its worst mass culture threatens not merely to cretinize our taste', argues Rosenberg, 'but to brutalize our senses while paving the way to totalitarianism.' Lazarsfeld and Merton put the case succinctly: 'Economic power seems to have reduced direct exploitation and to have turned to a subtler type of psychological exploitation,' they wrote of the USA in the 1950s. Overt totalitarian force was increasingly obsolescent. Radio, film, and television seemed even more effective than terror in producing compliance.

Complexity and mass culture

The Frankfurt School argued that although the messages of the media might be simple, explaining them was not. The overt content of any programme, film, or newspaper was merely the basis for interpretation. The mass media appeared to confirm the traditional values of British puritanical middle-class society. The real message they communicated, however, was one of 'adjustment and unreflecting obedience'. It was necessary to analyse not only the content, but also the form of the media and the way in which they were used. 'The trouble with the educated philistine', wrote Arendt, 'was not that he read the classics, but that he did so prompted by the ulterior motive of self-perfection.' Nothing, for the Frankfurt School, was what it seemed. It was always worse.

Their view of the illusion of apparent social relations was part of a developing analysis during the 1940s. Lasswell's *Psychopathology and Politics* had claimed 'that the significance of political opinions is not to be grasped apart from the private motives which they symbolized'. Political motives 'derive their vitality from the displacement of private effects upon public objects'. Later, in a bleak article written in 1941 on 'The garrison state', Lasswell also suggested that although 'instrumental democracy may be in abeyance the media will doubtless continue to purvey the symbols of mystic democracy'. Indeed capitalist culture was so powerful that it could even use opposition to further its own interests. As Benjamin wrote in *Illuminations,*

> We are confronted with the fact . . . that the bourgeois apparatus of pro-
> duction and publication is capable of assimilating, indeed of propagating
> an astonishing amount of revolutionary themes without ever seriously
> putting into question its own continued existence – or that of the class
> which owns it.

It follows from this that only that culture which was not assimilable and difficult to understand could be the source of genuine opposition.

Mass society theorists and the power of the media

The concern of Adorno, Arendt, and their colleagues with the direct psychological impact of the new media was in part a product of their experience
in Germany. The rise of Hitler encouraged the Frankfurt School to view all
mass audiences with suspicion, as though they were indistinguishable in
behaviour and malleability from the crowds at a Nazi rally.

These writers also, however, developed another more long-term concept of
the power of the media. Marcuse commented in *One Dimensional Man:*

> Objections are made that we greatly overrate the indoctrinating power of
> the media and that by themselves people would feel and satisfy the needs
> that are now superimposed upon them. This objection misses the point.
> The preconditioning does not start with the mass production of radio or
> TV. The people enter this stage as preconditioned receptacles of long
> standing. In this more complex view the public do not abdicate rational
> consideration of their interest blindly. More subtly, the whole basis of
> rational calculation is undermined.

Nevertheless, even this more complex explanation has a simple goal.
'Ideology for the Frankfurt School works one way,' Swingewood has commented, 'that is from above, seeping into working-class consciousness as an
alien and conservative force.' Even leisure had been reduced to an adjunct
of capitalism, its sole purpose 'the restoration of the human labour force
for labour',[5] while all human needs had been redirected into 'consumption' – the destructive exhaustion of resources rather than their creative use.
As a consequence the Frankfurt School saw the function of the media,
whether in the long run or more directly, as controlling the public in the
interests of capital.

It is here that the Frankfurt analysis is most vulnerable. What appears to be
a particular account of the media is actually a view of capitalist institutions

in general. Indeed the very strength of the Frankfurt analysis is dissipated in its generality.

Pluralism: the role of personal influence on the reaction of the audience to the media

The power of the media, and the pessimistic Frankfurt model of industrial society, were tested, challenged, and apparently refuted by American empirical researchers. A series of major surveys seemed to show that the media had very little influence on popular opinion.

In an odd way, the small town American gossip came to the rescue of democracy. Survey findings seemed to prove that people were not the isolated atomized automatons suggested by mass society theory. Thus the inhabitants of places which sounded like the locations for John Ford movies – Eerie County, Decatur, Elmira, and Rovere – appeared oblivious to, rather than hypnotized by, the blandishments of media propaganda. Far more important influences were provided by friends, neighbours, and drinking companions – whether people were deciding which presidential candidate to vote for or what brand of cornflakes to have for breakfast. It was personal contact, not media persuasiveness, that counted.

Market research methods were used to investigate whether the press and broadcasting had an effect on public attitudes. However, the concept of an 'effect' which was used in this research was very limited. Media messages were compared to 'bullets' and the only effects evaluated were immediate changes in audience attitudes.

Conceptualizing the power of the media

Nevertheless, empirical research as a whole has at least begun to question the way in which we understand the effects of the media. Thus writers on the press and broadcasting have credited the media with the power to 'influence' or 'persuade' their audience, to 'change attitudes', or even to 'affect behaviour'.

Yet these terms are imprecise and obscure. What is it to persuade or influence? All of the terms which are used to describe what the media do have a behaviourist basis, in which a single and external force – the media – has an impact on a single subject – the person. The empirical studies, in a very limited way, have re-examined these concepts. In a narrow attempt to measure effects they have at least dislodged terms which otherwise have been unquestioned.

The empirical work is inadequate. The theories which underlie our understanding of the media might be revealed more usefully than in an attempt to measure problematic phenomena. Indeed the early survey tradition of the 1940s and 1950s eventually abandoned interest in the media. However, it is possible to discuss the problem of how the power of the media might be conceptualized in examining the empirical work. For, as yet, there is no adequate vocabulary to describe the relationships between the media, individuals, and society.

Reinforcement

Early surveys seemed to show that the media did not change people's minds. 'Paradoxically campaign propaganda exerted one major effect – by producing no overt effect on voting behaviour at all – if by the latter "effect" we naïvely mean a change in vote,' wrote Lazarsfeld in 1944. In fact the media confirmed people in the opinions which they already held. Propaganda marshalled the faithful. It did not 'win over' the wavering or the opposed.

As election campaigns progressed, however, people became more interested in politics, but only because more of them had made up their minds. 'Thus they became both more likely to pay attention', wrote Schramm, 'and less likely to be converted as the campaign goes on.' Previously it had been

a[s]   ir attempt to arrive at a rational decision,
w   of information. But, because they were
u[n]   *ELLENE*   nterested. 'As a group', wrote Trenaman
a[n]   n't knows" were less well informed than
c[o]   per cent . . . showing a general lack of
in   ce of particular policies or the policies of
o[r]   n 'reinforcement' was insufficient on its
o[w]

Personal influence

The research showed that the audience was not homogeneous, and society was not a simple, centrally controlled hierarchy. There were strong defences against people being persuaded in spite of themselves. Further, some members of the audience had a role in the persuasion of others. Ideas, it was argued, 'flow from radio and print *to* the opinion leaders, and *from* them to the less active sections of the population'.[6]

The power which personal contact exercised over people's views was examined by Katz and Lazarsfeld in a study of women 'opinion leaders'. The study, done in the late 1940s, seemed to show that some individuals of high social status had little effect on other people's views, while some of low status were important opinion leaders. Personal influence 'intervened' between the message of the media and its reception by the public. Consequently it impeded any attempt at mass indoctrination by the media. What could be more satisfactory than to find that in a democracy wealth and power do not buy opinion?

It was also argued that opinion leaders were not a narrow élite. The same study showed that a high proportion of women were exercising influence over others in matters of marketing, fashion, movies, and politics. Moreover, the diffusion patterns of influence and the characteristics of opinion leadership were different for each area.

Thus it was concluded that the media had little or no independent effect on public opinion. Indeed rather than changing attitudes, behaviour, or the world it seemed that they merely confirmed the status quo.

Findings the researchers ignored

In fact it is possible to look at the findings of these surveys in another way and draw quite different conclusions. What appears insignificant when buried in a range of figures dealing with breakfast cereals and film stars becomes more interesting if taken on its own. Status and opinion leadership, for example, were not correlated in most areas, except public affairs. Here high-status women appeared to exercise considerably more influence than low-status women. The assumption that consumer behaviour and political behaviour obey the same rules is not supported in these findings. Hence it would be dangerous to take for granted that the media – as opposed to opinion leaders – shape opinions about consuming and opinions about voting in identical ways.

Election surveys of the 1940s and early 1950s are also open to reinterpretation. 'Not every public opinion change involved a personal contact,' Lazarsfeld, Berelson, and Gaudet admit in their study *The People's Choice*. 'Fifty-eight per cent [of the changes not the changers] were made without any remembered personal contact and were very often dependent upon the mass media' (these changes were widely distributed among those who changed their views at all). This effect was ignored.[7] It was concluded that the media had little influence. Becker and McCombs have also shown other contradictions in these studies. In the Eerie County survey a high proportion of electors who intended to vote Republican at the start of the campaign but who were exposed to Democrat propaganda switched to Democrat by polling day. Yet this finding was also ignored.

These studies did not show that the media had no effect, although this is what was concluded from them. They showed only that people did not necessarily change their minds because of direct media exposure. The media – as the studies empirically confirmed – raised interest, fixed opinions, and, crucially, informed the electorate. Most of what people knew about campaigns they had learnt from the media.

Understanding and information

Indeed during this same period, another approach to studying the effect of the media, that of experimental psychology, began to develop a rather different model of media influence from that of the surveys. 'The power of the media to persuade, at least where there is a democratic controversy,' wrote Poole, 'is very much less than is usually assessed, but their power to inform is enormous.' A series of psychological experiments carried out by Hovland during the 1940s examined the effects of films designed to inform American soldiers about the war in Europe. The films had little effect on 'morale' or 'motivation to serve'. Yet after they had seen the films the men talked significantly more about what was happening in Europe, and this knowledge persisted for weeks. 'The hammerlike blows of frenzied oratory', Hovland concluded, 'may produce acquiescence and later recrimination: autonomous decisions made under the cumulative pressure of facts do not exact this price.' The theory which lay behind this 'propaganda of facts', he points out, 'is not far removed from the logic of progressive education'.

These experiments also showed that people were particularly vulnerable to persuasion about subjects of which they had no direct experience. Moreover, the willingness of the public to believe what it is told is precisely related to the degree of trust it has in the source of the message. Since few people have first-hand experience of politics, and broadcasting is regarded as an especially authoritative source, these findings would suggest that the effects of the media on political opinion may be particularly strong.

Hovland later argued that the distinction drawn between his experimental results and those of survey research was misleading. His work showed that between one-third and one-half of the people he tested 'actually changed their views'. Yet the surveys had concluded that communications had little effect on attitudes. Hovland argued that some of these differences could be explained because laboratory studies examined immediate responses to media messages, while the surveys were typically conducted long after exposure. But also, he argued, the laboratory studies 'deliberately try to find some types of issue susceptive to change', while surveys attempted to assess the impact of the media on 'socially significant attitudes which are deeply rooted in prior experience and involving much personal commitment'.[8] That is to say, the surveys had investigated those attitudes least likely to be altered in the short term.

The active audience

Studies of the purposes for which members of the audience use the media, and the gratification they get from this use, have also emphasized that public response is varied and not homogeneous. Thus McQuail *et al.* have argued that people use the media for diversion (including escape from routine and unpleasant problems); for developing personal relationships (including substitute companionship); for confirming their personal identity; and for keeping themselves informed. It is implied that if people use the media to satisfy different needs they will also interpret and use the same media message in many different ways. Nevertheless, in the case of political communications, the most frequently expressed use of the media is that of surveillance, or using the media to acquire information.

Indeed the findings of the 'uses and gratifications' research are not incompatible with a stronger interpretation of the role of the media. Given the differences in education, work, and leisure opportunities it would be surprising if the audience response to the media was unitary. The problem is rather to integrate evidence about the differences in the quantity of people's media exposure; about variations in popular interpretations of the media; and about differences in the extent of recall, with other evidence about social divisions. Thus Katz asks, 'What needs, if any, are created by routine work on an assembly line and which forms of exposure will satisfy them?' It is also possible to ask whether the use of the media reinforces or ameliorates social differences. In either case, an explanation of variety in media use is an important part of any more adequate explanation of the power of broadcasting and the press.

Pluralism: the effects of what the audience knows

More recently attempts have been made to understand the effects of the media on knowledge as well as on opinion. Survey research had apparently shown that the media had little effect on attitudes; new evidence seems to show, by contrast, a dramatic impact on the range and depth of perceptions.

Changes in politics

Underlying these new approaches – and perhaps not unrelated to them – were changes in political behaviour. 'Party allegiance', wrote Blumler, 'which was once the rock of Gibraltar of the reinforcement doctrine of political communications effects has increasingly become its shifting sands.' The class basis of party support was apparently eroding in all the western democracies.

Consequently as the consistent voter became more rare, the nature of the 'floating' volatile voter changed. Previous research had shown floating voters to be an ignorant and apathetic section of the electorate. Recent research provides a different profile: undecided voters are seen, typically, as increasingly likely to be better informed than the majority.

Indeed if class continues to become a less accurate predictor of voting decisions, the media will play a more important role in political choice. By the 1980s television had become the dominating source of election information for nearly all voters. Yet this is the medium which might be expected to have the greatest effect on long-term political allegiances. For as class and social networks become less important as the determining source of political reinforcement, it has been suggested that voters will rely more heavily on information to make up their minds.

Views may become more strongly held because they are reinforced by the media. However views may also wither and die because they receive no public

reinforcement. Martin Harrop argues that this negative power of the media –
selectively to neglect some ideas – is a critical, and little recognized media
effect.[9]

Thus the media have an authoritative relationship with their audience.
This is one of dependence and trust and it provides the media with a potentially independent power base in society and one that may have become more
powerful recently.

Agenda setting

In addition attempts have been made to discover the effect of the media in
determining priorities: how far press, radio, and television coverage could
change a sense of which events were more important. On the basis of a study
of the emergence of issues during an American presidential campaign, Becker
and McCombs argued that such an influence was major, but gradual. There
was a distinction, however, between the effects of the press and television.
With newspaper influence there was a delayed reaction. 'The newspaper
agenda of political issues in June is a predictor of voters' agendas in October,'
they claimed. With television the impact was last minute, but immediate. By
the end of the campaign, television had become the most important determinant of voters' ideas.

The media's ordering of priorities particularly influenced voters without
strong views. Yet television's coverage of politics has now penetrated sections of the electorate who previously were little affected by political
communication because they were uninterested. Consequently the agenda
setting by the media seems to be becoming more significant to a larger proportion of the electorate.

The media's agenda of issues may be quite different from that of the political parties. As Seymour-Ure has shown, media coverage made a speech on
immigration delivered by Enoch Powell to a small audience in a church hall
familiar to 86 per cent of the population two days later. Before the speech
only 6 per cent of a Gallup Poll sample thought immigration an issue of
national importance; afterwards 27 per cent thought it was important, and
nearly 70 per cent of the public believed that the government would have to
take 'a harder line'. In effect, Seymour-Ure writes, Powell had 'won himself a
national constituency, a platform in the media from which to state his views
on most subjects with the certainty of having an audience'.

Neither Powell, nor the media, created the race issue in Britain. Nevertheless,
argues Seymour-Ure, the publicity surrounding his speech at a crucial moment
(during the debate on the controversial Race Relations Bill) pushed immigration to the front of the political stage, a position it has kept ever since.

The political effects of the media on public opinion are complex, and need
to be examined in their historical context. The media may exert great
influence over one group, but have little impact on the other members of a

society. Thus in many recent revolutions, the press and writing – despite close censorship – has been crucial in establishing cultures of opposition to authoritarian regimes among the educated classes. This was an essential condition of the success of the liberal revolution in Portugal in 1974. Yet, there, after the revolution, a dramatic change in the political direction of the media (from right to left), between the first and second democratic elections, had no effect on voting behaviour at all.[10] Similar patterns seem to be developing after the Eastern European revolutions of the late 1980s.

The first studies of the effects of the press and broadcasting had undermined earlier assumptions about the power of the media, suggesting that audiences were, after all, free. Anybody, it seemed, could make almost anything out of any message. Yet a re-examination of the evidence has thrown doubts on this view. It has been suggested that the media may not persuade the public directly; nevertheless they affect what people know, and what they think is important.

Media organizations

Of course, research into public responses to news and information is not the only way of considering the political role of the mass media. Another approach is to look at how news is produced: the processes of news-gathering, sifting, and editing, and the administration of news and entertainment organizations. The virtue of this method is that it helps us to understand what pressures shape the commodity presented to the public. Its limitation is that in considering how rival interests balance one another, there has been a tendency to ignore the broader problem of those important but powerless interests which have no influence at all.

Making news

News-rooms are always under pressure: the unexpected is always about to happen, the scoop is only a telephone call away. This is the professional self-image. However, for journalists (as for politicians, doctors, and firemen) crises that are frequent enough develop a pattern: the unexpected becomes the predictable.

Journalists solve these pressures by developing a set of rules. Tuchman argues that 'the routinely non-routine is constituted in practical tasks: in work'. Tuchman, however, also suggests that objectivity is little more than a protective 'strategic ritual', a set of conventions about the origins and presentation of facts that allows journalists to defend their selection of newsworthy events and interpretations. In an extreme form, Tuchman's definition of news precludes any distinction between relatively good or bad journalistic practices. Nevertheless, this interpretation highlights the way in which accuracy is by no means the same thing as objectivity.

The events that are honoured by being made news are those that are easy to obtain. They are by no means necessarily the most significant events which have occurred. In order to get made into news, events have to happen in places convenient for the newsgathering agencies, to be of a recognized and acceptable kind, come from a reliable and predictable source, and fit into journalists' framework of news values. These rules and habits have become worldwide and, as Golding and Elliot argue, 'News changes very little when the individuals that produce it are changed.' Even the international flow of news is determined not by the importance of events but by the organization of the news-processing industries.

The popular image of journalists (elaborated in many movies) as intrepid hunters after hidden truths is hardly realistic. Specialist reporters in particular are closely involved with, and indeed dependent upon, their sources. Thus crime reporters identify with the police, defence correspondents with the services, and industrial relations experts with the trade unions.[11] But, in addition, journalists, who are better seen as bureaucrats than as buccaneers, begin their work from a stock of plausible, well-defined, and largely unconscious assumptions. Part of their job is to translate untidy reality into neat stories with beginnings, middles, and denouements.

The values which inform the selection of news items usually serve to reinforce conventional opinions and established authority. At the same time, a process of simplification filters out the disturbing or the unexpected. The need of the media to secure instant attention creates a strong prejudice in favour of familiar stories and themes, and a slowness of response when reality breaks the conventions.

Pseudo-events

Many items of news are not 'events' at all, that is in the sense of occurrences in the real world which take place independently of the media. An important development alongside the mass media has been the growth of organizations, professions, and skills aimed at manipulating the media.

In a pioneering study (*Public Relations and American Democracy*, 1951) J. A. R. Pimlott reviewed attempts to control news and public opinion in the USA. Prompted by his own experience as a civil servant closely involved with the implementation of Labour's post-war programme in Britain, he was concerned with the use of public relations to win support for central planning and social reform – in particular the New Deal. He also considered the dangers which public relations presented. The book takes issue with the '*laissez-faire* school' argument that free competition ensures a fair hearing for both sides of every major issue. In many cases, the author pointed out, it is 'nobody's business to put the other side'. In the early 1930s American unions had complained that because of inadequate resources, they were unable to compete with the publicity of employers. Pimlott felt that there was some justice in the trade union case during the Depression, that 'more than ever before strikes are being won or lost in the newspapers'. His conclusions were pessimistic. It was impossible to control the growth of public relations by government intervention. Nevertheless, newspapers could help 'by transferring some of the energy which they devote to attacks upon government propaganda to attacking the misuse of public relations by private industry'.

Indeed the notion that 'events' compete for attention in the press and broadcasting is misleading. Often the media are desperately anxious to secure enough content (of the kind they want) to fill their space or time.

In this way, much of what is perceived as 'news' is little more than free advertising. 'Not for nothing does the trainee journalist have to sit as part of his qualifying exams a test in how to write a press handout,' writes McBarnett. The local press is particularly vulnerable to pre-digested news. Much of what appears as 'political news' is in fact written by councillors, candidates, and MPs. The same process also determines much of what appears nationally, leading to what Boorstin has called 'pseudo-events' – activities whose only real purpose is to secure and control media coverage.

Entertainment

What is entertainment? All media industries compete to create it. Even with news and documentaries, the pressure to be 'entertaining' – to hold audiences by being immediately accessible and stimulating – overrides other considerations. A high proportion of media content has no other aim but to amuse, flatter, excite, mystify, or titillate the public and so keep its attention.

Thus Michael Tracey has argued that the most prominent anxiety of producers of political television was not the sensitivity of their relationships with the political élite, but rather the development of an entertainment formula. Discussion programmes were composed as much for dramatic excitement as for political balance. 'Did you see her on women's lib?' he quotes a producer enquiring. 'Marvellous woman. Never stops talking. Liable to throw something.'

Yet just as little 'serious' material is presented without a sugar coating, so too there is nothing – or almost nothing – that can be deemed 'pure' entertainment. Soap opera, comedy, variety, and pop may not be intended to have any effect on the views of their audiences. But, it can be argued, there is scarcely a joke or a lyric that does not reflect a social attitude, and one with political consequences .

Some writers have suggested that entertainment encourages political passivity. Gitlin has argued that it often 'provides a legitimation of depoliticized forms of deviance, usually ethnic or sexual, and a delegitimation of the dangerous, the out of bounds, the violent'.[12] The resolution of social problems typically presented in fictional programmes may influence how they come to be seen in the real world.

It is not only the content of the media which may have implications for attitudes but also the form of programmes. Dyer has argued, in his discussion of light entertainment, that the way in which stars are presented, pictures shot, and the studio audience used, may all affect the meaning communicated by programmes. In so far as 'leisure' is seen by programme-makers as being opposed to work, then entertainment 'has to do something about the reality of work, it has to have an attitude towards it'.

Audiences

It is often argued that the mass media 'reflect' society because they are obliged to please their audiences. Yet many researchers have commented on the apparent remoteness of producers from their potential viewers. 'It is not so much that people don't know what the audience wants,' Alvarado and Buscombe write, 'as that in the actual process of production people were working more to please themselves.'

However, while writers on political broadcasting have seen this ignorance of the audience as a problem – 'the vital missing link', as Tracey calls it – writers on creative and fictional broadcasting have seen it as a safeguard. 'A model of popular television', write Alvarado and Buscombe, 'which sees it either as a cynical manipulation, or a straightforward identity of tastes between producers and audience, would be an over-simplification.'

The demands of the audience do not, then, exert any direct pressure on producers. Producers have only a vague image of those whom watch their programmes. Yet they have a clear, if unconscious, notion of whom they are actually addressing: well-informed, critical, professional people like themselves.

Institutional pluralists

One argument has been that television in particular is not so much a player in the political game as the referee: setting the rules and arbitrating between contending forces.

This view of the political role of the media has been expressed most clearly by Anthony Smith. 'Television', he argues,

> has become the Theatre of Politics in both senses of the term. Like the theatre of classical times its structures combine into a memory system. Its disciplines incorporate the moral norms of politics as these apply at a given moment of history.

Thus the nature of the rules and their application reflect the politics of the time. The decision about whether to interview a terrorist on television, or the choice of 'controversial' topics for discussion, precisely indicates the political mood as it is perceived by producers and editors. Changes in the relationship between 'current affairs', 'comment', and 'news', or what is seen as 'hard fact' determine the manner in which information is presented to the public. In this way the limits of the permissible, the acceptable, and the appropriate constitute a series of snapshots of prevailing attitudes.

These pressures, however, are always seen by these writers as emerging from a free market of influence. Reviewing research into media organization, Blumler has argued that 'Researchers may be near the heart of competition through communication that is waged in a democratic pluralist society.' Burns has suggested that the politics of broadcasting are the politics of accommodation, while Smith, in his book *The Shadow in the Cave,* argued that 'If broadcasting is to be used as a tool for the intelligent exchange of cultural products, political information and controversial disquisition, it needs to be left flexible and left alone.'

Yet 'negotiation' and 'amplification' are inadequate metaphors for a process in which so much power has come to be invested in the message carrier itself. Hirsch and Gordon have argued that commercial pressure has limited the range of opinion expressed in the quality press. 'The picture we suggest of the quality press is a band of opinion occupying the broad centre of British politics from about half way into the moderate left through to the edges of the extreme right.' But broadcasting has usurped the role of the popular press as a supplier of political information to the mass audience, while preserving the same 'consensus band' of opinion as the quality newspapers. Thus the audience of BBC or ITV news includes most readers of the *Mirror* and the *People*, but these programmes' political values (not just their concern with information) are closer to those of *The Times* and the *Observer.*

That the media order events, and discriminate between them, is not in itself evidence of their systematic effect on public understanding. But while some groups can bring powerful pressures to bear on the work that the media do, others can bring none. The market for information is no more free than any other.

The new determinists: class and market

Another view of the press and broadcasting is that they reinforce and legitimize the present structure. The media, it is argued, distract public attention from real problems by manufacturing events and inflating trivial issues. However, the press and broadcasting, the new British cultural critics have suggested, do not merely express the interests of the dominant class. This is not only because this class does not always have one simple unitary interest, but also because the media at times reflect other interpretations of society.

However, it should be noted that these writers – many of whom have been associated with the Centre for Contemporary Cultural Studies at Birmingham – rarely question the concepts of 'lived experience', culture, struggle, resistance, or social control in their work. These ideas are accepted as self-evident and unproblematic, and used as the basis for explaining other phenomena. This inadequacy limits the work of these writers.[13]

Ideology

Ideology, writes Stuart Hall, 'entails the proposition that ideas are not self-sufficient, that their roots lie elsewhere'. Indeed while the audience for the media contains most members of society, only a few groups have any control over what the media produce. Hall concludes that they 'reproduce the definition of the powerful, without being in a simple sense in their pay'.

Hall argues that the media do not simply trick their audience: to some extent they must meet its needs. The independence of the media is at times quite genuine. For instance Hall suggests that broadcasting organizations have 'a wide measure of autonomy in their programming'.[14] However, this independence, though not a device, is actually serving a highly sophisticated function within a complex system. Precisely because the media produce material which is good, impartial, and serious, they are accorded a high degree of respect and authority. Since, in practice, the ethic of the press and television is closely associated with a homogeneous establishment this provides a vital support for the existing order. In this way, the apparent autonomy of organizations like the BBC 'veils and mystifies the structure of constraints'. Independence, Hall argues, is not 'a mere cover, it is central to the way power and ideology are mediated in societies like ours'. Thus we seem to have a more sophisticated instance of 'false consciousness'. The public are bribed with good radio, television, and newspapers into an acceptance of the biased, the misleading, and the status quo.

Hall emphasizes that the media change the world. They do not passively reflect class interests that have already been well developed. The media often articulate interests not previously expressed. That they do so is not because of the intentions of those who produce them. Rather it is a consequence of the situation and function of the press and broadcasting. The media, Hall suggests in a 1977 essay, help us 'not simply to *know more* about "the world", but to make sense of it'.

The mass media are not, according to this approach, crude agents of propaganda. They organize public understanding. However, the overall interpretations they provide in the long run are those which are most preferred by, and least challenging to, those with economic power.

Class, culture, and experience

Part of this approach to the power of the media has been a concern with the way in which different classes experience their position. The work of E. P. Thompson and that of Raymond Williams has been an important influence here. Both of these writers have been concerned with the nineteenth-century reaction to industrialization (although this has often been mistaken for a reaction to capitalism). Thus Thompson has written about working-class movements which opposed industrial developments, and Williams has examined the social criticism implied in the aesthetic reaction to industrialization of the Romantic movement. Barnett has argued that Williams puts too much faith in the political force of cultural opposition. 'Where economistic strategies rely upon the spontaneous momentum of industrial struggles to accomplish the overthrow of capitalism,' he suggests, 'Williams's book contains a cultural argument that is logically similar.'[15] In this way the independence of working-class culture has come to be seen not only as a source of opposition to capitalism, but also as leading to a socialist rejection of it.

This tradition has led the cultural critics to focus on working-class response to, and use of, the media. Thus Finn and Grant argue that people are 'not merely on "the receiving end" of their objective class position'. Classes take over, interpret, and use ideologies which are presented to them: they make them their own. This is particularly true of the ideas transmitted by the media.

According to this view, the working class is imprisoned by an ideology it often rejects. Many workers are not taken in by the view of society handed down to them. This can be seen from 'oppositional' behaviour which is generally not overtly political. Thus Willis has considered the division in a boys' comprehensive between those who are subservient to the imposed system and take exams, and those who regard the examination system as a confidence trick that will not help them. Willis argues that the second group of disrespectful layabouts actually have a better understanding of the world and their place in it. He suggests that 'Oppressed, subordinate and minority groups can have a hand in constructing their own vibrant cultures and are not merely dupes.'

Yet the relationship between working-class culture and political action is hardly inevitable. The relationship between lifestyle and class is also more difficult to explain than these writers have implied. In addition, those who have written about the sociology of art, literature, or film have found no simple correlation between the social origins of artists, writers, and film-makers and the political implications of their work. Indeed, as Garnham has pointed out, just because cultural goods are made within the capitalist system it 'does not follow that these commodities will necessarily support the dominant ideology'. This is not to argue that there is no relationship between class, cultural products, and experience; only that a direct relationship cannot be taken for granted. At the same time, even if it is true that experience of the media has become an intrinsic part of working-class culture, it cannot therefore be automatically assumed to be good.

The market

The pluralists largely ignore market pressures. The new determinist writers, in contrast, give them a crucial role. However, the determinist analysis of working-class culture leads to a contradiction. Goods – including the products of the media industries – are produced, it is argued, not to meet needs but to earn profits. Hence the goods are often worthless or inappropriate in themselves. However, workers are not necessarily enslaved by the distortions of the market. By appropriating what the system throws up, the working class preserves its cultural autonomy. Thus claims Willis, 'from the rubbish available within a preconstituted market', working-class groups 'generate viable cultures, and through their work on received commodities actually formulate a living and lived out concretized critique'.

The work of Willis, Hebdige, and others provides an analysis of particular groups within the working class. Yet on the one hand, any attempt to generalize these conclusions to 'working-class culture' has to be treated with caution because of the narrow base of the research; on the other, the new critics seem to want to have their cake and eat it. Is television a subtle form of exploitation, the more sinister for being good? Is it 'rubbish available within a preconstituted market', to use Willis's phrase for consumer goods in general? If the former, then it is hard to see how – or why – the working class should adopt oppositional 'concretized critiques' of it in their lifestyles. If the latter, and working-class culture manages to incorporate or appropriate the media product and remain 'viable' and 'lived out', then how thorough is the exploitation?

Pop music produces an interesting example. Is rock 'n' roll an expression of youth culture? Or is it a prime instance of capital discovering a new market and exploiting it? Few people would want to say that rock is intrinsically bad, or that it is not an important element in working-class life. No industry is more brazenly oriented towards quick, easy profits; in few are market pressures more immediate. Yet it is hard to sustain the argument that rock is handed down 'rubbish'.

Pop or rock fans are hardly an oppositional body taken *en masse*. As Frith points out, they are well aware that the product they buy is made and sold primarily to make profits. The reality is that rock is not simply a market-oriented concoction of the recording studios of Decca or EMI. Nor is it authentic folk music living an independent life in the community. Nor, for that matter, is it a distortion of a musical tradition plucked out of its native environment. Rather it is the product of a complex set of relationships in which music, fans, the media, profit takers, and distribution systems all play a part.

News values and power

The new cultural critics are most interesting when they deal with the content of the media and its relationships to power. *Policing the Crisis: Mugging, the*

State, and Law and Order by Hall *et al.,* for example, both describes the career of a category of news story, cases of 'mugging', and also analyses its influence on the judiciary, the police, and the public.

The authors show how the media created anxiety by giving a new name to an old offence. This in turn precipitated an aggressive sentencing policy which was seen as a necessary response to an earlier mistakenly 'soft' attitude towards offenders. Yet as Hall and others show, not only had the rate of increase in crimes of violence actually declined in the period before the emergence of the mugging story, but also far from becoming more lenient, sentences had steadily become longer. The curious inversion of facts, the authors argue, can be explained only in terms of the media's most general function of reworking ideology and maintaining the status quo.

The new cultural critics emphasize that their explanation of this process does not imply any deliberate conspiracy. 'Within its limits', Hall has written, broadcasting, for example, 'shows little evidence of intentional bias, but the trouble is the matter of unwitting bias'. Rather the coincidence of interests between the media and those with economic power is secured by professional and organizational values, and a shared perspective of the way in which society is organized. Thus Murdoch, writing about the reporting of an anti-Vietnam rally in 1968, argued that 'despite this element of autonomy, the basic definition of the situation which underlies the news reporting of political events very largely coincides with the definitions provided by the legitimate power holders'.

Social control

Thus the media are seen by the determinists as one powerful agency of social control – as a means of inhibiting opposition to the social order. In a similar argument, Bourdieu has described the function of the education system, which he sees as justifying the established order, by

> using the overt connection between qualifications and jobs as a smoke-screen for the connection – which it records surreptitiously under the cover of a formal equality – between the qualifications people obtain and the cultural capital they have inherited – in other words through the legitimation it confers on the framework of this form of heritage.

Differences in the use of the media, the distribution of tastes and preferences, are thus more than a mere expression of class. They are a vital means of making people accept different class opportunities, and those interpretations of events which are the least challenging to existing social arrangements.

Indeed in the analysis of the cultural critics, the media perform a special role in addition: they maintain and repair consensus as the nature of the status quo changes. Thus the crime of 'mugging', launched and amplified by the press, did not emerge accidentally. Rather it arose 'in the middle of a general moral panic about the rising rate of crime. Far from triggering into existence what did not previously exist, it clearly focuses what is widespread and free floating.'

The concept of social control seems to imply an imminent crisis, one that will eventually erupt but which is at present controlled. The emergence of the 'mugging' story is therefore interpreted merely as a symptom of a more fundamental crisis, one in which there has been a collapse in the willingness of the public to accept the authority of the state. The individual discrete 'moral panics' of the 1960s are seen as having been superseded by a more general breakdown. The only rationale, it is argued, for

> entrusting the management of the corporate capitalist state to a social democracy is either (1) that in a tight squeeze it can better win the collaboration of the working-class organization for the state, or (2) that if there is going to be a crisis Labour might as well have it!

In this way there is a danger that social structure is anthropomorphized: it becomes an active agent in pursuit of its own persistence.

However, despite the limitations of the concepts of social control, the determinist explanation of the role of the media is revealing. The media do not merely express the interests of the ruling class, rather they have an independent function in ordering the world. The media do not merely 'reflect' social reality: they increasingly help to make it.

Conclusion

As we have seen, the pluralist analysis of the effects of the media contains an apparent contradiction. On the one hand, it seems to show that the media do have an influence, both on what people know and on the political system. On the other hand it seems to suggest that, so far from having an independent power, the media merely reflect the balance of forces within society. Thus the pluralists are left saying that the press and broadcasting function as an ideological marketplace, a focus for competing pressures without an impact of their own. At the same time in taking a favourable view of 'pluralist' balance, this position tends to ignore the extent to which the weaker and unorganized groups are excluded from the process altogether.

Is the determinist approach any better? The cultural critics share the pluralists' view that the media have a key political role, stressing the way in which press and broadcasting shape public understanding. They differ from the pluralists in their preoccupation with the real or supposed role of the media as an instrument of class domination.

Thus the determinists have pointed to a major weakness in the pluralist case: the model of a freely competitive marketplace of ideas breaks down because some groups are unable to compete. At the same time the empirical evidence of the pluralists gives powerful backing to the determinists' conviction that the media exert an important and uncontrolled influence. Yet the determinist explanation in terms of class manipulation and exploitation is too mechanistic, obscuring a series of complex relationships which have yet to be explained.

Notes

1. H. Arendt, *The Burden of Our Time* (London, Secker & Warburg, 1950), p. 331.
2. M. Horkheimer, *The Eclipse of Reason* (London, Oxford University Press, 1947), p. 135.
3. H. D. Lasswell, 'The garrison state', *American Journal of Sociology*, 46 (1941), p. 462.
4. This 'strong' interpretation they share with F. Hayek, *The Road to Serfdom* (London, Routledge & Kegan Paul, 1944). He indicts socialism, they blame fascism.
5. H. Arendt, *The Life of the Mind,* Vol. 2, *Thinking* (London, Secker & Warburg, 1978), p. 93.
6. E. Katz and P. Lazarsfeld, *Personal Influence: The Part Played by People in the Flow of Mass Communication* (New York, Free Press, 1955).
7. P. Becker and M. McCombs point this out in 'The development of political cognition' in S. H. Chaffee (ed.), *Political Communication: Issues and Strategies* (Beverly Hills, CA, Sage, 1975).
8. C. I. Hovland, 'Reconciling conflicting results derived from experimental and survey studies of attitude change', *American Psychologist*, 14 (1959), p. 11.
9. M. Harrop and A. Sharp, *Can Labour Win?* (Harlow, Fabian Research Bureau/ Longman, 1989).
10. For a further development of this case, and a consideration of its more general implications, see J. Seaton and B. Pimlott, 'The role of the media in the Portuguese revolution' in A. Smith (ed.), *Newspapers and Democracy: International Essays in a Changing Medium* (Cambridge, MA, MIT Press, 1980); J. Seaton and B. Pimlott, 'Political power and the Portuguese media' in L. Graham and D. Wheeler (eds), *In Search of Modern Portugal: The Revolution and its Consequences* (Wisconsin, University of Wisconsin Press, 1983); B. Pimlott and J. Seaton, 'The Portuguese media in transition' in K. Maxwell (ed.), *The Press and the Rebirth of Iberian Democracy* (Westwood, CT, Greenwood, 1983).
11. See J. Seaton, 'Trade unions and the media' in B. Pimlott and C. Cook (eds), *Trade Unions in British Politics* (Harlow, Longman, 1983).
12. T. Gitlin, 'Prime time ideology: the hegemonic process in television entertainment', *Social Problems*, 26, 3 (1979), p. 111.
13. James Curran does not share some of Jean Seaton's reservations about the writers discussed in this part of the chapter.
14. S. Hall, 'The external/internal dialectic on broadcasting', *4th Symposium on British Broadcasting Policy* (February 1972).
15. A. Barnett in R. Williams (ed.), *Politics and Letters: Interviews with the New Left Review* (London, New Left Books, 1979), p. 98.

21

The liberal theory of press freedom

According to classical liberal theory, the freedom to publish in the free market ensures that the press reflects a wide range of opinions and interests in society. If a viewpoint is missing in the press, this is only because it lacks a sufficient following to sustain it in the marketplace. As the heroine puts it in Tom Stoppard's play, *Night and Day,* 'The *Flat Earth News* is free to sell a million copies. What it lacks is the ability to find a million people with . . . a conviction that the earth is flat. Freedom is neutral.'

The free market supposedly makes the press a representative institution. 'The broad shape and nature of the press', argues John Whale, 'is ultimately determined by no one but its readers.' This is because newspapers and magazines must respond to the concerns of their readers if they are to stay in business.

Some liberal theorists even liken the operation of the market to that of electoral democracy. Their claim is that newspapers submit themselves to public judgement every time they go on sale, whereas politicians stand for election at infrequent intervals. Consequently newspapers are closer to the people than elected representatives. This leads traditional liberal theorists to argue that the constitutional role of the press is to supervise government on behalf of the people. As the 'fourth estate', the press scrutinizes the actions of the executive, and relays public opinion to lawmakers. The press also keeps people informed about what is happening in the world, and provides a forum of public debate. It thus lubricates the workings of democracy by facilitating the formation of public opinion.

To sum up, the press has four key functions in liberal theory: informing the public; scrutinizing government; staging a public debate; and expressing public opinion. To this are sometimes added other lesser or ancillary functions such as expressing the shared values of the public, assisting society to adapt to change, and exposing wrongdoing.

Concealed beneath the fold of these arguments, often well out of sight, is a contentious premise. Liberal theory assumes tacitly that press freedom is a property right exercised by publishers on behalf of society. According to this approach, publishers should be free to direct personally their newspapers, or delegate authority to others, as they see fit. What they do is consistent, ultimately, with the public interest since their actions are regulated by the free market. This ensures, in liberal theory, that the press is free, diverse and representative.

Threadbare legacy

These arguments are derived mostly from the mid-Victorian era, and in some cases even earlier. They date from a time when publishing costs were low, most newspapers were mainly concerned with public affairs, and the state was dominated by a landed élite. Much has changed since then. This should compel a critical rethinking of liberal theory.

Take, for example, the argument that the processes of market democracy make the press a representative institution. This ignores the privileged position of capital in the seemingly open contest of the free market, and overlooks evidence that the press has long been more right-wing than the public it is supposed to represent.[1] The traditional liberal approach often also views the press as the principal intermediary between the state and public within an archaic conception of polity. This disregards the organizations of civil society which are the main agencies through which public concerns are represented. It also ignores the development of opinion polls and focus groups, which are more useful guides to public thinking than press editorials. Indeed, one of the consequences of the growth of survey research is that it has revealed how unrepresentative newspapers can be. The *Sun*, for example, was widely thought to be the authentic voice of popular Thatcherism. However, survey research reveals that only a minority of its readers actually voted Conservative during the four general elections of the Conservative ascendancy (1979 to 1997).

The liberal conception of the press as an agency of information is also in need of a critical overhaul. The press is now primarily part of the entertainment industry: less than 20 per cent of the content of the national popular press is allocated to political, economic and social issues. Admittedly, gossip about TV stars in the tabloid press may be said, in a circuitous way, to contribute to a normative debate about changing social relations. But this is not what is meant by liberal theorists when they repeat age-old phrases about the press being a vital source of public information and life-blood of democracy.

Even the honourable liberal conception of the press as an independent watch-dog is beginning to look time-worn. The press is now organized into large corporations, whose profitability is affected by the policy outcomes of a greatly enlarged government. The government, in turn, is affected by the editorial positions of the press, not least because ministers operate in a turbulent environment, no longer stabilized by strong class loyalties, corporatist conciliation and mass party machines. This produces a situation in which press scrutiny of government, and official policy on the press, can be significantly influenced by calculations of mutual advantage. This is a far cry from the simple liberal image of the press as a 'public sentinel', whose critical independence is secured through the freedom of the market.

This chapter will concentrate on exposing the frailties of *conventional* liberal theory by comparing the reports of the last three Royal Commissions of the Press, published in 1949, 1962 and 1977. The latter two reports represent staging posts in a cumulative process of disenchantment with traditional liberal thought. Yet manifestly flawed – indeed frock-coated – versions of liberal press theory continue to be advanced in highly intelligent contemporary analyses of the press.[2] It is still necessary, it seems, to make the case that traditional liberal argument is in need of revision, and to rub in the point that this implies a shift in public policy.[3]

Freedom to publish

'Free enterprise,' declared the first Royal Commission on the Press, 'is a prerequisite of a free press.' Underlying this belief was a relatively untroubled conviction that the unrestricted freedom to publish produces a diverse and representative press. The Commission expected to find that 'the press as a whole gives an opportunity for all important points of view to be effectively presented in terms of the varying standards of taste, political opinion, and education among the principal groups of the population'. Wartime regulation was blamed for preventing new publications from springing up to meet changes in public demand. Anticipating deregulation, the Commission rejected proposals for assisting the launch of new papers as unnecessary. The natural creativity of the market, it assumed, would again make the press representative.

The 1977 Commission was forced to make a different assessment. Its blunt conclusion was that 'anyone is free to start a daily national newspaper, but few can afford even to contemplate the prospect'. It also noted that the national press was overwhelmingly right-wing and manifestly unrepresentative. Indeed, 'in February 1974 . . . the share of newspaper (national daily) circulation held by papers supporting the Conservative Party was 71% greater than Conservative votes as a percentage of the votes cast'.

High entry costs were found to curtail the freedom to publish in other sectors of the press. Even establishing a new local evening paper in a town with no direct competition would cost in 1977, according to the Commission, between £2 million and £3 million. The cost of launching a new magazine in the main consumer sectors was also found to be high. As for new paid-for weeklies, there are 'not many places left with the right conditions to provide a permanent market'.

The assumption that 'anyone' is free to start a new paper has been an illusion ever since the industrialization of the press. That it is an illusion was exposed in unsparing detail by the last Commission. In effect, it dislodged a key foundation stone of liberal theory.

Diversity and chain ownership

The 1949 Commission argued that proprietors should be free to conduct their publications as they wished. This was justified partly on the grounds that proprietors had the right to safeguard their financial investments in a high-risk industry. The Commission also believed that publishers' freedom from restraint underpinned the diversity of the press.

This hands-off approach assumed that chain ownership would not develop into a major problem. 'There is no reason to expect,' declared the Commission, 'that the aggressive expansion of chain undertakings [in the daily and Sunday press] which characterised the early period will be resumed. Neither in the local nor in the periodical press nor in the news agencies do we expect a significant trend towards further concentration of ownership.'

The 1962 Commission was obliged to revise this assessment. It found that the share of circulation controlled by the major chains had 'substantially increased' in all parts of the press. The leading three proprietors' share of the national daily press had soared to 89 per cent. There were, it added, 'spectacular movements towards concentration of ownership' in the periodical press. Only among local weeklies was concentration 'negligible'.

This latter conclusion had to be discarded. Acceleration of chain ownership since 1962 had been greatest, concluded the 1977 Commission, in the local weekly press. Unlike before, new acquisitions had also resulted in the same three proprietors dominating both the national daily and the Sunday markets. In addition, the Commission highlighted a phenomenon which had previously received little attention – the emergence of subregional monopolies in which all or nearly all 'competing' local morning, evening and weekly papers were owned by the same group.

These changes in press ownership led to a shift in perspective. Whereas the first two Commissions had taken for granted the right of proprietors to determine editorial policy, the third Commission talked of the need to 'protect editors and journalists from owners'. The exercise of proprietorial power no longer appeared to be legitimate as a basis for securing press diversity, at a time when only three men controlled over half of total daily and Sunday newspaper sales in Britain.

Loss of independence

This shift in attitude was also influenced by other changes. The first Commission had advanced as a subsidiary justification for proprietorship the claim that it safeguarded the independent integrity of the press. 'It is undoubtedly a great merit of the British press,' declared the Commission, 'that it is completely independent of outside financial interests and that its policy is the policy of those who own and control it.' The Commission thus invoked the classical liberal view of the press as an independent fourth estate, uncompromised by vested interest.

However, most of the British press was bought up by, or diversified into, interests outside publishing during the 1960s and 1970s. By 1977, all but one of the leading publishing groups in both the national and regional press were part of larger conglomerates with holdings in fields as diverse as oil, transport, mining, construction, engineering, finance or the leisure industries. 'Rather than saying that the press has other business interests,' concluded the last Commission, 'it would be truer to argue that the press has become a subsidiary of other industries.'

This clearly undermined the case for proprietorial control as a guarantee of the press's independence to which the first Commission had paid such fulsome tribute. It also cast in a new light the Commission's contention, cited above, that proprietors had the right to exercise control over their investments in the high-risk press industry. If investigative journalists discover wrongdoing by a parent or sister company, should their employers have the legitimate right to suppress what they found? More generally, can the freedom of the press be equated with the freedom of conglomerates, owning much of the press, to promote its business interests? These were questions which clearly troubled the 1977 Commission, and partly explains why it was much less enthusiastic about 'the rights' of proprietors than its predecessors.[4]

Since the Commission's report, most large press groups have refocused their activities on communications, though many still retain some non-media interests. However, this shift has compromised in a new way rather than restored the press's independence. National papers are mostly owned by multi-media conglomerates, with a strong vested interest in promoting the deregulation of the media industries. Indeed, they are active lobbyists of government: hardly the credentials of a disinterested fourth estate.

Competition, choice, and new technology

The first Commission attached great importance to the role of competition in making the press accountable. Due to competitive pressures, argued the Commission, 'whatever a paper's purpose and however it is owned, it cannot escape the necessity of offering the public what some at least of the public will buy'.

Although the Commission was troubled by the large number of newspaper closures during the inter-war period, it viewed this as a temporary lapse caused mainly by publishers' extravagance and lack of adaptability. 'In the provincial press as a whole,' it concluded, 'there is nothing approaching monopoly and we can see no strong tendency towards monopoly.'

The Commission's optimism was confounded by events. The total number of newspaper titles continued to decline (see Table 21.1). The cities in the UK with a choice of directly competing local morning or evening papers were reduced by 1974 to only London, Edinburgh and Belfast (see Table 21.2). By 1975 only 18 per cent of towns with a local paper had a choice of weeklies under separate ownership, a proportion that was little over half of what it had been in 1961. In short, competition – the *deus ex machina* of liberal theory which makes the consumer 'sovereign' and proprietors accountable – had been seriously eroded in much of the regional press.

The last Commission found some solace in the emergence of freesheets, a development which became more salient in the period after it reported. However, the rise of freesheets reduced the number of paid-for weeklies (see Table 21.1). It further eroded local press autonomy by generating papers totally reliant on advertising. Freesheets also became organized increasingly into chains, many of them the same chains that dominated the local press. By 1988 the five largest publishers of freesheets were responsible between them for 338 free newspapers, and a further 243 paid-for papers.

Table 21.1 *The number of newspaper titles, 1921 to 2002*

	1921	1937	1948	1961	1976	1988	2002	% reduction 1921–2002
National press								
National daily	14	11	11	10	9	12	12	14.3
National Sunday	14	10	10	8	7	9	11	21.4
Regional/local press								
Morning	41	27	27	22	20	18	19	53.6
Morning freesheets	–	–	–	–	–	–	6	–
Evening	93	83	80	77	79	74	74	20.4
Sunday	7	7	6	5	6	8	11	(57)
Sunday freesheets	–	–	–	–	–	–	10	–
Weekly and bi-weekly	1485	1303	1307	1219	1072	801	509	65.7
Freesheets	–	–	–	–	185[a]	896[b]	640	–
Total[c]	1654	1441	1441	1341	1193	922	646	61.6

Sources: Royal Commission on the Press 1947–9 Report, Appendix 2, tables 2–3; *Royal Commission on the Press 1961–2 Report*, Appendix 3, tables 3 and 5; *Royal Commission on the Press 1974–7 Final Report*, Annex 3, table 4; *Press Council Annual Report 1988*, Table 1 and Table A.

Notes
[a]This relates to 1975.
[b]In addition, there was one local daily and one Sunday freesheet.
[c]Excluding freesheets.

The sustained contraction in the number of newspaper titles troubled both the 1962 and 1977 Commissions. What also disturbed them was evidence that there was an inbuilt impetus towards contraction since this suggested that the trend would continue. 'The natural tendency,' concluded the 1962 Commission, 'of the economic factors affecting [newspaper] production and sale is to diminish the number of papers where competition is close.' This pessimistic conclusion was based on its analysis of the unequal competitive relationship that often developed between strong and weak papers. Successful papers, the Commission found, enjoyed a double advantage over weaker competitors: they had generally lower unit costs due to greater economies of scale, and more revenue. This enabled them to outspend their rivals; win more circulation through higher spending; and drive their weaker rivals into debt by making them incur additional expenditure in an attempt to stay competitive. Despite drawing attention to 'countervailing forces' offsetting scale economies, the 1977 Commission broadly endorsed this view. It also pointed to further ways in which powerful press groups were increasing their market dominance. Economies of consolidation were enabling them to buy out rivals, in the local press, at above the market rate. The large financial resources and accumulated expertise of leading press groups also equipped them to be successful innovators. The 1977 Commission found that only two out of a sample of twenty-four local weeklies launched between 1961 and 1976 had originated from independent publishers. It also discovered that more than half of the consumer magazines with a circulation of over 30,000 set up between 1966 and 1974 had come from just four publishing groups. 'The larger companies,' the Commission's research team concluded, 'are better placed to incur the considerable costs that are required to enter some markets.'[5]

Table 21.2 *The number of urban centres with competing local dailies, 1921 to 2002*[a]

| | Urban centres with a choice of: | |
	Local morning paper[b]	Local evening paper
1921[c]	15	27
1937[c]	6	10
1948	4	11
1961	2	9
1974	2	1
1988	2	–
2002	2	–

Sources: *Royal Commission on the Press 1947–9 Report*, Appendix 2, table 1; *Royal Commission on the Press 1961–2 Report*, Appendix 3, table 4; N. Hartley, P. Gudgeon and R. Crafts, *Concentration of Ownership in the Provincial Press*, Royal Commission on the Press 1974–7, Research Series 5 (London, HMSO, 1977), table 6.1; *Press Council Annual Report 1988*, table 1; Newspaper Society database as at 1 January 2002.

Notes
[a]Excluding freesheets.
[b]Excluding London.
[c]Excluding Ulster.

The last two Commissions also came to the uncomfortable conclusion that there was no free market solution to the long-term problem they identified: namely that competition tends to erode competition. The 1962 Commission reluctantly concluded that increased efficiency in the press – although desirable in itself – offered no panacea. Cost saving, it argued, might offer a weak publication temporary respite, 'but the important point,' it stressed, 'is that reduction in costs, however desirable in itself, will not, if equally applied to all newspapers, improve the relative position of the weaker publication.' Similarly the 1977 Commission emphasized that potential savings could be achieved through the introduction of new technology, but also concluded that this would not neutralize the dynamic inequalities inherent in competition between weak and strong papers.

The introduction of new technology in the national press during the 1980s seemed for a time to refute this pessimism since it led to the launch of new national titles. However, the majority of these new papers folded, and it is now clear that little was permanently changed. Contrary to what was predicted at the time, new technology did not substantially reduce the market share of leading publishers; it did not extend the ideological range of the newspaper press; it did not reinvigorate popular publishing through the proliferation of new, minority papers; and its impact in refuelling competition in the national press was short-lived.[6] The last new (general interest) national daily to be launched was Shah's ephemeral *Post* in 1988; and the last new national Sunday (save for a new daily stablemate, *Star Sunday,* in 2002) was the *Sunday Correspondent* (1989 to 1990). Due to multiplying supplements, national press costs rose, shielding publishers from new competition.

Indecision

The last two Commissions' reports reveal the gradual weakening of beliefs that have legitimated the market-based press system for over a century. In particular, they point to four problems. High entry costs make the press unrepresentative; the growth of chain ownership erodes its diversity; wider business entanglements weaken the press's claims to disinterest; and, above all, the recurrence of market failure undermines those processes which are said, in liberal theory, to make the press accountable.

These long-term problems are not specific to Britain, but are manifested all over the world. One response to them has been to promote the ideals of social responsibility and objective journalism by fostering the commitment of journalists to professional norms that transcend the demands of their employing organizations. It is a strategy that has been pursued vigorously in the United States, primarily as a way of mitigating the consequences of the growth of press chains and local monopoly in the American press. It has also become, in practice, a way of relegitimating the market system. However, in a British context it has radical implications, since it upholds impartial journalism and professional autonomy in a way that challenges the partisan, hierarchical character of the national tabloid press.

The alternative route is the social market strategy pursued particularly in northern Europe. This has taken various forms: general press subsidies, selective grants to minority papers, aid for the launch of new publications, and press-specific anti-monopoly measures.[7] This approach seeks to sustain diversity and competition through public intervention, and is also a way of relegitimating the market system. However, even this option has radical implications in Britain because it means deviating from the traditional British press policy of having no policy.

In the event, the last two Royal Commissions dithered between these two strategies without fully backing either. Their indecision was the root cause of their ineffectiveness.

Social market flirtation

Perhaps the closest the Press Commissions came to following a social market strategy was to advocate special anti-monopoly measures for the press. This was tentatively initiated by the 1949 Commission which proposed that the Monopolies Commission should monitor changes in press ownership with increased vigilance. This proposal had no discernible effect.

In 1961 its successor recommended the setting up of a Press Amalgamations Court. A variant of this proposal was adopted in 1965. It required all large press groups to obtain the permission of the Secretary of State before they were allowed to purchase a newspaper. The 1977 Commission demonstrated that this approach had failed: all fifty press acquisitions between 1965 and 1977, falling within the terms of anti-monopoly controls, had been allowed. The Commission argued that anti-monopoly legislation needed to be strengthened in five ways. Its advice was ignored.

Since its report, nothing has happened to suggest that feeble anti-monopoly legislation has had any significant influence on the press. Out of 172 transfers of newspaper ownership to major press groups between 1980 and 2000, only three applications (all involving minor papers) were refused, and a further five were approved subject to conditions.[8] All major acquisitions – including Murdoch's purchase of *The Times* and *Sunday Times* in 1981[9] and the Guardian Group's acquisition of the *Observer* in 1993 – were allowed.

The last two Commissions placed enormous faith in the power of legislation to restrain the growth of press concentration. They rejected proposals for divesting the major press groups – originating from the centre as well as from the left of the political spectrum.[10] They also opposed the introduction of selective press subsidy systems now operating in a number of Britain's neighbouring countries. In effect they put most of their weight behind one particular strategy. It failed.

Restriction on joint media ownership

The Press Commissions had slightly more success in seeking to keep the press and broadcasting industries separate in the interests of maintaining media pluralism. However, this success came late, and proved to be short-lived.

Against the prescient advice of the first Press Commission, newspaper owners were allowed to be investors in commercial television when it was launched in 1955. The second Press Commission was critical of this involvement, but was prevented from making an explicit recommendation by its terms of reference. Contrary to the spirit of its report, press groups continued to retain shareholdings in commercial television. Indeed, they were even given a prescriptive right to participate in setting up local commercial radio stations in their circulation areas when independent radio was introduced in 1972.

This prescriptive right was ended by the 1981 Broadcasting Act on the recommendation of the 1977 Press Commission. The IBA also adopted a policy of reducing substantial press interests in commercial television and radio in response to the urging of both the 1977 Press Commission and the 1977 Annan Committee on Broadcasting. This was codified in the 1990 Broadcasting Act which prevented any press group from having a controlling stake in a television franchise.

However, the tide turned during the deregulatory 1990s. The 1996 Broadcasting Act partly reversed previous policy by allowing most newspaper groups (with less than a 20 per cent share of the national market) to expand into terrestrial television, and by relaxing the rules about cross-ownership of local press and local radio. The New Labour administration indicated its willingness to go further down this path in 2001, after protracted public soundings dominated by self-interested media lobbying. The Communications Act (2003) opens the door to Murdoch's acquisition of Channel 5, if it becomes available for sale.

This was preceded by the adoption of more liberal rules governing the development of satellite and cable television (and later digital multiplexes), allowing extensive cross-ownership to develop. The key turning-point was 1990 when Rupert Murdoch, controller of the largest press group in Britain, was allowed to dominate British satellite television by retaining control of the merged satellite broadcaster BSkyB.

Self-regulation

If the Press Commissions' flirtation with social market policies was a relative failure, the tentative steps they took to promote the professionalization of the press was scarcely more successful. The most concrete reform to emerge from their efforts was the establishment of a self-regulatory agency. This was conceived by the 1949 Commission as a well-funded and widely respected public body concerned not only with investigating complaints against the press but also with such matters as the recruitment and education of journalists and the promotion of substantial research into the press. The 'General Council of the Press', envisaged by the Commission, was to be similar to the General Medical Council. It would embody and promote a professional culture among journalists.

The Press Council was set up reluctantly by the industry in 1953, in an enfeebled form, following the threat of statutory regulation. The Press Council's shortcomings were roundly condemned by the 1962 Commission, which urged government legislation if there was no improvement. This produced some reforms – notably, the appointment of an independent chairman and the annual publication of press concentration statistics. However, these reforms failed to impress the third Commission. 'We hope,' concluded its scathing report, 'that in future the Press Council will be more vigilant in demonstrating the independence and impartiality to which it lays claim.'

The 1977 Commission made twelve recommendations for a complete overhaul of the Press Council's organization and procedures. Nine of these (including most of the important ones) were rejected. However, the fresh threat of legislation, with all-party support, led to another round of reluctant reforms in 1989 to 1990. This included, after twenty-seven years of foot-dragging, the formulation of a code of conduct for journalists. However, these reforms were judged to be too little and too late by the Calcutt Committee which recommended that the Press Council be disbanded and replaced by a more effective agency.

The Press Complaints Commission (PCC) was established in 1991. When it was investigated by Sir David Calcutt in 1993, it was found to be failing the public:

> The Press Complaints Commission is not . . . an effective regulator of the press. It has not been set up in a way, and is not operating a code of conduct, which enables it to command not only press but also public confidence. . . . It is not the truly independent body that it should be.

This indictment led eventually to the appointment of a new chairman, Lord Wakeham, in 1995. Once again, the cycle of public scrutiny and condemnation, followed by contrition and the promise of reform, was resumed. Once again, minor improvements were made. The PCC became a more user-friendly, efficient, publicity-conscious organization. The backing of key figures in the industry ensured that it carried more clout than the 1980s Press Council had done. Wakeham proved to be adept at courting the powerful, until he resigned his PCC chairmanship in 2002 in order to spend more time with his lawyers in relation to his involvement with the Enron bankruptcy scandal.

However, despite some improvements, two fundamental problems besetting press self-regulation were not solved. The PCC was not fully independent of the industry which funded it. It was also not very effective. It had no power to command evidence, award fines or order the payment of compensation. It also lacked moral authority because it did not enjoy the whole-hearted consent of the press industry, and was only accepted as a 'lesser evil' to statutory regulation. Its main function was to assist informal conciliation between outraged members of the public and the press. The PCC made much of the publication of its adjudications, and claimed that this was a powerful deterrent against abuse. It did not broadcast how few cases it actually adjudicated – a policy dictated by the fact that adjudications upset its paymasters (and establishing the truth with limited powers and budget is no easy matter). In 2002, the PCC upheld only 0.6 per cent of the complaints it received.

However, the principal deficiency of press self-regulation was not its lack of independence nor its ineffectiveness, but its dearth of ambition. The Press Council and PCC did not commission and publish substantial research, stage formative debates, honour leading journalists or restructure journalism education. Indeed, it never really embodied a professionalizing project. Unwanted by the press, it settled for being a customer complaints service, and discreet lobbyist for the industry.

Yet, the first Commission had hoped that the reform of journalism education would instil a spirit of public service among journalists. It wanted the content of journalism education to be broadened, and its organization streamlined nationally – objectives ardently sought also by the third Commission. In the event, journalism training continued to impart a narrow range of skills and knowledge, and to foster an unquestioning attitude. Its organization, always piecemeal, became more fragmented in the 1990s. The National Training of Journalists (NCTJ) qualification never became, as the third Commission hoped, a respected yardstick of professional competence. It is possessed, according to the latest available survey, by only a minority of journalists.[11]

While narrow vocational training was overtaken by the student-led expansion of media studies in British universities during the 1980s and 1990s, this was neither anticipated nor desired by the first and third Commissions, which echoed the industry's hostility towards undergraduate media degrees. This hostility turned into angry denunciation, when the press experienced the novelty of being subject to watch-dog scrutiny. 'This paper regards a degree in media studies as a disqualification for the career of journalism', thundered one respected daily (*Independent*, 31 October 1996), a view echoed by other papers. A major investment was thus made in media education without British universities acquiring an accepted role in supporting and interpreting the ideals of professional journalism, in the way that it did in the United States and elsewhere.

The Commissions' professionalizing project failed also because it was overwhelmed by stronger forces than it was able to command. Powerful commercial pressures were unleashed in the national press after 1956 when newsprint rationing was lifted, and again in the 1980s with the introduction of new technology. In the national press, this led for a time to a decline in standards of accuracy, notorious cases of chequebook journalism, more prurient intrusions into private grief not justified by the public interest, the parading of imaginary folk devils, and outbreaks of nasty, almost sadistic bullying of sad people. In the regional press, a tendency towards lazy, public relations-led journalism was reinforced by editorial cost-cutting, falling sales and the consolidation of the freesheets.

However, it was tabloid excess which most outraged public opinion. By 1993, only 10 per cent of the public believed that journalists could generally be trusted to tell the truth. This was a drop of almost half by comparison with ten years earlier, and placed journalists at the bottom of fifteen groups in terms of public credibility, below even politicians.[12] In 2002, a reformulated question elicited another damning response: 75 per cent in the UK said that they 'tended not to trust' the printed press. This was enormously higher than any other country in the European Union.[13] There could scarcely have been a more telling indictment of the Press Commissions' professionalizing strategy for reforming the press.

Uneasy ambivalence

Press Commissions have also advocated other reforms – that newspapers should display prominently the name of their owner, that they should declare an interest when reporting on topics in which their parent or associated companies are financially involved, and that the press should abide by a Charter of good practice drawn up by the last Commission, which would be policed by a reformed Press Council and, if it proved necessary, by statute. All these proposals were ignored.

However, the last of these is worth examining briefly because it highlights the uneasiness, borne of misgivings about the liberal inheritance, that informed the work of the last Commission. At first glance, its Charter reflected a completely traditionalist position. It had been inspired by the publisher's campaign against the union 'closed shop', and contained detailed prohibitions against union influence. The Charter was prefaced by acceptance of the newspaper publishers' argument that 'in reality editorial and managerial decisions were inseparable'. The publisher's pregogative was also justified by an idealized image of the free market as a guarantor of 'the right of a man to express what he believes'.

However, another part of the Commission's report had questioned whether the market really functioned in the freedom-enhancing way that it was supposed to. The Commission was in fact more ambivalent than it appeared to be at first sight. Press freedom, it suggested, should not only be equated with publishers' freedom from restraint; it also had something to do with the freedom of people who edit and work in newspapers. This approach was reflected in the clauses of its proposed Charter which upheld the freedom of conscience of individual journalists, and the right of the editor to accept any contribution 'notwithstanding the views of his proprietor'. However, the Commission then found itself in deep waters because the strengthening of staff rights is advocated by some as a way of securing the independence of the press. Internal democracy, it declared hastily, is 'a complex and disputed subject' about which it was unable to 'express a view'.

This dalliance with reformism ensured that the proposed Charter was quietly buried at the behest of publishers. The same kind of reformist ambivalence is to be found elsewhere in the Commission's report. Newspapers, it declared, should behave 'with proper restraint'; the press should recruit, like broadcasting, more graduates; young journalists should attend improving courses and 'learn about society'. Indeed, the Commission seemed intent, at times, on transplanting the public service rationale of broadcasting to the press, but its moves in this direction were hesitant and contradictory. It wanted a public service orientation, but not the framework of public regulation underpinning it. It favoured a more balanced, responsible approach, but saw merit in the free market tradition of outspoken comment. Unable to define precisely what it meant by professionalism, the Commission was not very successful at promoting it. But its flirtation with the idea of public service was nevertheless revealing: it was an attempt to co-opt a different theoretical tradition in a bid to bolster the increasingly threadbare classical theory of press freedom.

Weak reformism

The three Commissions were sharply critical of the press, yet failed to come up with solutions to the problems they identified.[14] The sum total of their efforts was failed anti-monopoly legislation and ineffectual self-regulation. No major reform of the press was attempted after their appointment.

Publishers were the main cause of this cumulative failure. They opposed at every turn any statutory reform of the press. Apart from the *Guardian* management's brief apostasy in the 1960s when it lobbied privately for a press subsidy system, and differences over legal protection of privacy (with senior executives in the Guardian Group again stepping out of line), publishers on both left and right made common cause in resisting any public intervention in the press. Their opposition was fired by a righteous libertarianism which equated their freedom from restraint with public liberty. This became the central idea shaping the regulatory environment of the press.

This was partly because the press was an important disseminator of ideas about itself. Publishers draped the mantle of freedom around their shoulders, and created doubt and uncertainty about the desirability of reform. However, the main reason why reformism failed was that the press intimidated the political class. The political cost of 'doing something' about the shortcomings of the press was judged to be too high. For example, Clement Atlee, the astute prime minister of the first majority Labour governments (1945 to 1951), was opposed to appointing the first Royal Commission on the Press on the grounds that this would upset the press.[15] The Callaghan Labour government (1976 to 1979) quietly buried the third Commission's proposals for tougher press monopoly legislation because it did not want to add to its political problems.

Politicians' loss of nerve was cumulative, and now seems unlikely to be reversed at least in the short term. In 1931, Stanley Baldwin, leader of the Conservative Party, spearheaded a campaign against the 'power without responsibility' of the press barons. It was inspired by revulsion against the abuses of the press, outrage at the pretensions of a newly independent power, and above all a desire to save his career and strike back at his principal critics.[16] However, this campaign was followed shortly afterwards by the forging of an uneasy *rapprochement* between the Conservative Party and the predominantly right-wing press, which persisted for much of the subsequent period.

The case of the Labour Party was more complex. It was traditionally critical of the 'millionaire press' but its antagonism mellowed a little in the 1930s when it became a publisher of a mass circulation daily. However, the labour movement ceased to be a major stakeholder in the press system when its newspapers closed down in the 1960s. Its alienation turned into mounting hostility when the trade union movement became the target of sustained press attack during the 1970s. The first sign of a political shift occurred in 1974, with the publication of the Labour Party Study Group report, *People and the Media*, most of whose proposals became official policy. Reworked versions of these, committing the party to curbing press concentration and promoting press pluralism, were incorporated into its 1983 and 1987 general election manifestos. However, by the 1990s, the Labour leadership became increasingly mute on the subject of press reform. Greater priority was given to winning press support, symbolized by Tony Blair's 1995 trip to Hayman Island, Australia, to speak to News Corporation executives about the need for an 'open and competitive media market'. This was followed by a sustained courting of right-wing newspapers after New Labour was elected in 1997, and re-elected in 2001. Legislative reform of the press dropped off the agenda because it threatened New Labour's successful but precarious bonding with right-wing press tycoons.

The voices calling for change were thus marginalized. The Campaign for Press and Broadcasting Freedom (CPBF), established in 1979, continued to be an eloquent and idealistic exponent of reform. However, its principal sponsors, the press unions, were crushed. The CPBF's representations went largely unheeded by government, regardless of which party was in power, and its arguments tended not to get a hearing in the press it wanted to reform.

Public dissatisfaction with the press, registered periodically in opinion polls, continued to be high. However, this dissatisfaction was channelled by backbench MPs in the direction of limited proposals – in particular, private members' bills for privacy protection or right of reply – partly in response to their own concerns about shielding their private lives from critical scrutiny. There was thus no powerful force subjecting the press to sustained criticism, and building support for major reform.[17]

However, the politics of radio and television proved to be different from that of the press. If reformers failed in the press, they had more success in broadcasting. This produced, as we shall see, a fundamental inconsistency at the heart of media policy.

Notes

1. This is a central theme of Part I of this book.
2. Thus, Richard Shannon claims, without qualification, that 'anyone can start up a newspaper' – something that has not been true for over a century. This (and other liberal assumptions) is advanced in his scholarly and thought-provoking defence of the Press Complaints Commission: *A Press Free and Responsible* (London, John Murray, 2001), p. 5.
3. For a recent attempt to rethink liberal theory and policy in a radical democratic form, see the final chapter in J. Curran, *Media and Power* (London, Routledge, 2002).
4. Among other things, Colin Seymour-Ure wrote a powerful paper for the Commission arguing that the transfer of control of the press from political parties to unaccountable business conglomerates weakened the legitimacy of the press (see his 'National daily papers and the party system' in *Studies on the Press,* Royal Commission on the Press Working Paper 3, London, HMSO, 1977).
5. N. Hartley, P. Gudgeon and R. Crafts, *Concentration of Ownership in the Provincial Press,* Royal Commission on the Press 1974–7, Research Series 5 (London, HMSO, 1977); *Periodicals and the Alternative Press*, Royal Commission on the Press, Research Series 6 (London, HMSO, 1977).
6. See Chapter 7.
7. P. Murschetz, 'State support for the daily press in Europe: a critical appraisal', *European Journal of Communication*, 1998, 13 (3); E. Skogerbo, 'The press subsidy system in Norway', *European Journal of Communication*, 1997 12 (1); P. Humphreys, *Mass Media and Media Policy in Western Europe* (Manchester, Manchester University Press, 1996).
8. Department for Culture, Media and Sport (DCMS), *Consultation on Media Ownership Rules* (London, DCMS, 2001), p. 25.
9. The government failed to refer Murdoch's purchase of Times Newspapers to the Monopolies Commission on the grounds that the newspaper group was in such financial difficulty that its immediate future was in doubt. This was not the case.
10. Proposals for divestment came from, among others, Sir Geoffrey Crowther (Royal Commission on the Press, Oral Evidence, Vol. 1, p. 5, London, HMSO, 1962), and Professor Jeremy Tunstall (Royal Commission on the Press 1974–7, unpublished evidence), both from the centre left of the political spectrum.

11. A. Delano and J. Henningham, *The News Breed: British Journalists in the 1990s* (London, London Institute, 1996).
12. R. Worcester, 'Demographics and values: what the British public reads and what it thinks about its newspapers', in H. Stephenson and M. Bromley (eds) *Sex, Lies and Democracy* (London, Longman, 1998).
13. Eurobarometer Survey, 2002, cited in the *Guardian*, 24 April 2002.
14. The 1977 Commission contained a minority report, signed by two members, proposing a National Printing Corporation and a Launch Fund to assist the establishment of new publications. These recommendations were ignored.
15. Its appointment was secured through a private member's bill.
16. For a brief description of the context of this campaign, see Chapter 5.
17. For different interpretations of the politics of press regulation, see J. Curran, 'Press reformism 1918–98: a study of failure', in H. Tumber (ed.) *Media Power, Professionals and Policies* (London, Routlege, 2000), and the more optimistic T. O'Malley and C. Soley, *Regulating the Press* (London, Pluto, 2000).

22

Broadcasting and the theory of public service

· British broadcasting was started as a public service, and this proved as creative commercially as it was innovative culturally. Indeed, until recently every stage of its development, from the emergence of the BBC, through the introduction of commercial television, to the founding of Channel 4, depended on a set of linked and radical expansions. First, at each stage a novel source of finance was discovered. In turn the growth of broadcasting was financed by the licence fee, advertising revenue, and then a tax on the profits of the commercial companies (but one devoted to making programmes). These sources of finance did not compete with each other, and were key to the possibility of political independence. Each stage produced new audiences for broadcasting – the BBC creating an image of its audience as 'participants' in the great affairs of the nation, commercial television popularizing the medium, and Channel 4 decisively registering and enhancing the interests of minority audiences. Finally of course, at each stage new kinds of programmes and styles of addressing audiences were evolving. Until the 1980s, broadcasting in Britain was not fettered but liberated for cultural and political expansion by the requirements of public service.

The principle of public service – which has always been fought over and continually reinterpreted – was not the paternalistic and abstract rule which critics have suggested. Nor has it been damaging to entrepreneurial initiative. Indeed, public service regulation has secured the survival of a successful broadcasting industry, one which has become more significant economically and which has become an important exporter of programmes while continuing to discuss and mould national issues. It has of course also never been perfect. Broadcasters have often failed to perceive the public interest and, even more frequently, have been too acquiescent to political pressure. Broadcasting has often been used by dominant political actors. Nevertheless, it has provided a flexible means of managing and developing an important utility which has been commercially successful and also served the public.

In the 1980s 'public service' became unfashionable. Yet those who derided it often had a financial interest in weakening it, or, alternatively, disliked the political autonomy of broadcasting. However, public service is not a static or dated ideal, it is one we need to redefine and develop. What were the origins of the principle and how did it come to be undermined?

Broadcasting in Britain – monopoly or duopoly – always depended on an assumption of commitment to an undivided public good. This lay beneath all official thinking on radio and television until the 1970s. In 1977 the Annan Report abandoned this assumption, and replaced it with a new principle of liberal pluralism. The ideal ceased to be the broad consensus – the middle ground upon which all men of good sense could agree. Rather it became, for Annan and those who supported and inspired him, a free marketplace in which balance could be achieved through the competition of multiplicity of independent voices. The result has been confusion and crisis, from which no new received doctrine has yet emerged.

So, by 1982, the Hunt Report on the introduction of cable television could begin to modify the principles of balance and quality even further. These were relegated to a part of the national service in the BBC and ITV. Although both the Hunt Report and the subsequent White Paper advocated some safe-guards to protect the British system from the damaging effects of foreign satellite transmissions, and to guarantee the rights of the networks to televise events of national interest, the basis of public service broadcasting was aban-doned. Thus cable television, free from constraining ideals, was left to produce programmes that 'were sufficiently attractive for the public to buy'.[1] The 1990 Broadcasting Act suggested that contenders for broadcasting fran-chises should produce 'sufficient amounts of quality programmes', but not only was this undefined, it only occupied two paragraphs in the Act. By con-trast, conditions governing the financial arrangements for the auction of franchises took up fifteen pages.

However, the most obvious long-term symptom of the change in the status of the concept has been a shift in terminology. The concept of public service is elaborated in all broadcasting reports before that of the Annan Committee. As early as 1923 the Sykes Report argued that broadcasting was 'of great national importance as a medium for the performance of a valuable public service'.[2] The next report – that of the Crawford Committee in 1926 – sug-gested that in view of the scale, significance, and potentialities of broadcasting, the duties and status of the Corporation which it had just cre-ated 'should correspond with those of a public service, and the directorate should be appointed with the sole object of promoting the utmost utility and development of the enterprise'.[3]

Later reports developed the consequences of this view. 'The influence of broadcasting upon the mind and speech of the nation', commented the Ullswater Report, made it an 'urgent necessity in the national interest that the broadcasting service should at all times be conducted in the best possible manner and to the best possible advantage of the people'.[4] In 1950 the Beveridge Report on broadcasting characterized the ideal of public service more actively. 'Like the work of the universities,' Beveridge suggested, 'the work of broadcasting should be regarded as a public service for a social purpose.'[5] The Pilkington Report, which considered both the BBC and the commercial service in 1962, added to this definition: 'The concept of broadcasting has always been of a service, comprehensive in character, with the duty of a public corporation of bringing to public awareness the whole range of ... activity and expression developed in society.'[6] Indeed the organization of commercial television was as much a product of the ideal of public service broadcasting as the BBC's had been originally. Thus successive reports developed the idea of broadcasting as a public service – catering for all sections of the community, reaching all parts of the country regardless of cost, seeking to educate, inform, and improve, and prepared to lead public opinion rather than follow it.

The Annan Report in many respects broke with this tradition for the first time. This change was noticeable, both in the evidence which was presented to the committee, as well as in the conclusion of the report. Even the reformers, whether of the left or right, disregarded the public service principle entirely. The BBC referred to it in only the most apologetic tone. The Annan Committee itself took a pluralist view: broadcasting should cater for the full range of groups and interests in society, rather than seek to offer moral leadership. 'For the individual life is a gamble, he is entitled to stake everything, if he desires, on one interpretation of life,' it argued. 'But broadcasting organizations have to back the field, and put their money on all the leading horses which line up at the starting gate.'[7] In one elegant metaphor, much of the basis of public service broadcasting had been dismissed, despite the fact that Channel 4 was, in many ways, in practice an extension of it.

Indeed the Annan Report's reinterpretation of public service unintentionally left British broadcasters defenceless against the threats posed by recent technological developments. By so transforming public service it left no grounds on which to manage or control the impact of the inevitable introduction of cable, video, or satellite broadcasting. Since 1977, reports and White Papers on the future of these very technologies have not even attempted to assess the impact of unregulated competition for audiences, revenues, and programmes on the television system as a whole. Thus it was possible for the Hunt Report to suggest that viewers' willingness to pay for cable television simply constituted a new source of revenue. It was claimed that this would not divert resources from existing channels. (However, it was not apparently thought necessary to support this assertion by either evidence or argument.)

By contrast there was a radical development in the 1986 Peacock Report, which reinterpreted the role of the market in broadcasting.[8] While advocating what Samuel Brittan, a leading monetarist journalist and theorist and member of the Peacock Committee, called 'the goal that British Broadcasting should move towards a sophisticated market system based on consumer sovereignty', the report perceived public service commitments as actually protecting consumer sovereignty. Brittan commented that 'The existence of a tax-financed BBC and the IBA regulation of commercial television were justified by Peacock as a second best, but very successful, attempt to replicate artificially the programme structure of a true broadcasting market.' More than that, the committee took up the elaboration of the public service ideal developed in Channel 4 provision, and suggested that a mature broadcasting service would operate like the publishing industry. 'Pre-publication censorship, whether of printed material, plays, films, broadcasting or other creative activities or expressions of opinion, has no place in a free society', the report argued, and recommended that the government 'embark forthwith on a phased programme for ending it'. Brittan went on to point out not only that the report widened the scope of its enquiries far beyond its original brief of considering the introduction of advertising on to the BBC (which it rejected), by assessing the future of broadcasting and how that could be best managed in the context of technological developments, but also that the report demonstrated the fundamental social significance of broadcasting. As Brittan commented:

> Peacock exposed many of the contradictions in the Thatcherite espousal of market forces. In principle, Mrs Thatcher and her supporters are in favour of de-regulation, competition, and choice. But they are distrustful . . . of plans to allow people to listen to and watch what they like, subject only to the law of the land. They espouse the market system but dislike the libertarian value judgements involved in its operation: value judgements which underlie the Peacock Report.[9]

The Peacock Report put public service back on the agenda at just the point when the broadcasting organizations seemed to have abandoned it.

In fact, this abandonment by the broadcasting organizations is a problem, for the authority of British broadcasting has always depended on the pursuit of public service. Indeed by relinquishing any claim to this, the broadcasting institutions have put into jeopardy a whole set of complex relationships between themselves, the state, their audiences, and their programme policy. What caused this crisis? What are its consequences?

The state and broadcasting

One cause of the collapse of the principle of public service broadcasting has been the deterioration in the relationship between the state and broadcasting institutions. In the Sykes Report, Charles Trevelyan argued that 'We consider such a potential power over public opinion and the life of the nation ought to remain with the state.' Because broadcasting was so important it was seen as 'essential that permission to transmit, and the matter to be transmitted should be subject to public authority'.

Air waves were a scarce resource which did not obey national boundaries. Consequently the state was obliged to control the right to broadcast in all societies. In the early British broadcasting reports, however, there is a consensus that state regulation is the best guarantee of broadcasting independence and accountability. As the Crawford Report put it, only the state could license the BBC to be 'a public corporation acting as trustee for the national interest'.

In the 1920s the problem of the relationship of government with broadcasting was dealt with by making new rules and creating new machinery. It was taken for granted that the control over the administration of an organization could be kept quite separate from whatever the organization did. Hence it was possible for broadcasting to be politically accountable, and yet remain independent of any political influence. The Sykes Report noted that any detailed control of the work of the Corporation would make a government 'constantly open to suspicion that it was using an opportunity to its own advantage'. It was therefore decided that the minister responsible for the service would be able to answer questions in the House on matters of principle and finance, but he should not be held responsible for the programmes themselves. Later the problem seemed to disappear. Complaints about government intervention were rare, and the issue of excessive interference no longer seemed to exist.

In 1936 the Ullswater Report commented, 'We have no reason to suppose that, in practice, divergent views of public interest have been held by the Corporation and government departments.' Pilkington argued in 1962 that 'The practical resolution of the problem was made easier because the first priority of the department concerned with exercising the government's responsibility (the GPO) is with technical matters.' No conflict had arisen between broadcasters and governments over the definition of public interest.

However, by the 1970s this pragmatic argument was felt to be inadequate. Imperceptibly the problem had become one of defending broadcasters against the state. The relationship was increasingly characterized as one of vigilant and stealthy hostility. A cold war had been declared between them.

This was partly a consequence of the changing nature of politics in Britain. In a world of increasingly sophisticated news reporting this posed problems for both the BBC and the IBA. 'Politics' and political balance could be treated simply in two- or three-party terms in the 1950s. By the 1970s this was no longer the case. The emergence of centre parties made the work of 'striking a balance' far more difficult for broadcasters. In addition many fields which had previously been regarded as non-controversial and administrative had moved into the political arena. But also because of a proliferation of parties, interests, and pressure groups, because of a widening gap between the

major parties and, most of all, because of the rise of issues – of which
Northern Ireland was the most critical – for which the gentlemanly and con-
stitutionalist assumptions of the early rule-makers could not cater. The
problem of providing 'balance' in dealing with treasonable activities in
Ulster – when, whether, and under what conditions to interview terrorists or
members of illegal organizations, how to discuss the issue at all – forced the
broadcasting directorates to make new rules and, in effect, to add to the
corpus of Britain's unwritten constitution.

The questions which the public asked about broadcasting, the Annan
Report claimed, were becoming 'more critical, more hostile and more political'. At the same time, there was a new public mood, 'at once inflationary in
the expectation of what political power could achieve, and deflationary
towards those in power who failed to give effect to these expectations'.

The interests of governments had come, by the late 1970s, to be seen as
inimical to those of broadcasting. The distinction between the broadcasting
bureaucracies and what they produced had been challenged. Previously the
quality and balance of a company's programmes were believed to be guaranteed by the good order of the administration. This view was now replaced by
one of increasingly detailed suspicion. More than that, broadcasters' institutionalized caution about the power of governments had developed into a
rejection of all kinds of intervention by the state.

This has had profound consequences for the legitimacy of the public service broadcasting organizations. The Annan Report argued that the
authorities have a dual role: on the one hand they exist to ensure that broadcasters operate in the public interest and are responsive to public opinion,
particularly as expressed in parliament. On the other hand, they exist 'also to
defend broadcasters from undue pressure from whatever quarter'. But these
are not complementary obligations; rather they are contradictory. The
authorities are supposed both to reflect political pressure and to resist it. It
used to be possible for the authorities to perform these two functions when
the interests of the state and the broadcasting organization were seen as similar, if not identical. However, once their interests are opposed, the two
aspects of the authorities' role are increasingly difficult to reconcile.

Accountability and broadcasting

This situation would matter less if other mechanisms designed to relate
broadcasting institutions to society seemed less perfunctory. Since 1926 they
have all suffered from attrition.

Reith rapidly turned the Governors, supposedly 'the trustees of the
national interest', into creatures of the Director General. In both commercial
television and the BBC, the Boards of Governors depend for their information upon the organizations they were designed to supervise, and they have no
independent secretariat or research function. The Governors have remained

relatively powerless, and do not see their job as one of representing external interests or views. Similarly the role of the advisory committees was ingeniously reinterpreted. Reith ensured that these acted as specialists (whether in music, speech, or religion) who merely offered their advice over particular policy issues to the Corporation, rather than experts in broadcasting as such.

Indeed the only independent source of power left within these supposedly governing bodies is that of the Chairman of the Board. This power derives from the Chairman's close personal association with the Director General – or the administrative head of the independent service. Yet this intimacy leads to what Heller has called 'the tendency of broadcasting authorities to identify their interests, and by implication the national interest very closely with the survival of the organization they supervise'.[10]

However, in the 1980s a series of political crises in which the role of broadcasting was crucial – the Falklands War, continuing trouble in Ireland, disputes about the interpretation of foreign events, and profound disagreements about the management of the economy – all exposed the potential vulnerability of the governing body and the Chairman to political influence. Indeed, the Conservative government sought to dominate the governors more directly than any previous administration, by swamping the board with its own supporters. In the 1980s, the problem was not so much the identification of the Chairman with the institution, but rather the identification of the Chairman with the government in power.

Yet the broadcasting organizations had given up so much of the ground themselves. By the 1980s the IBA was to claim that accountability was only a minority interest. The Annan Report had endorsed a system which was little more than a pious rhetoric. 'On balance', the report concluded '. . . while some improvements could be made, the relations between government and parliament and the broadcasting authorities do not require much adjustment: the chain of accountability is adequate.' Annan apparently believed that accountability was a purely abstract idea – one which includes no reference to the public. But the paragraph nevertheless ends, 'We do not consider, however, that the relations between the broadcasters and the public are satisfactory.' If, as Annan suggested, broadcasting is to abandon the independence of public service, and be based, rather, on a principle of representative pluralism, then the inadequacy of the Governors, and advisory committees, becomes even more serious. By the 1990s accountability had almost been dispensed with as a value. It had, up to a point, been replaced by that of market success.

Independent professionals or men with an interest?

The independence of broadcasting from the state has recently been seen as the most important condition of the service's accountability. This independence has in turn been reduced to the freedom of programme-makers. Yet as

Beveridge once commented, 'To whom is a broadcaster responsible? If it is only to his own conscience the decision might better be described as irresponsible.'

This emphasis on broadcasters' rights is a consequence of focusing the assessment of broadcasting on individual programmes. Pilkington was the last report to elaborate the tradition of public service, and it also argued that 'A service of broadcasting should be judged, not by the stated aims of the broadcasters, but by its achievements.' The Annan Report endorsed this approach.

Nevertheless, broadcasting and broadcasting institutions cannot be understood merely as a collection of separate programme 'texts'. As an ACCT Report commented, judging broadcasting organizations by their product 'was like being asked to evaluate the Milk Marketing Board by drinking milk – relevant, but not adequate'.[11]

Broadcasting is a process which cannot be entirely understood from its products. Few would claim that the whole nature of the industrial enterprise can be understood from the shop floor of one factory. Neither can all the pressures which condition broadcasting institutions be revealed by an examination of what Tracey has called 'the world of determination of a television programme'[12] – however important that study might be. The emphasis on programmes as the most important criterion for judging broadcasting reinforces the arbitrary role of professionals at the expense of more general considerations of public service.

The Annan Report claimed that 'Good broadcasting would reflect the competing demands of a society which was increasingly multi-racial and pluralist.' In turn, this variety could be secured only by giving the 'talented broadcasters' greater freedom of expression.

However, broadcasters are not necessarily influenced by a wide variety of interests. Much research has shown how little producers and directors consider their audience. The only information about viewers which seriously affects producers is knowledge of the size of the audience. This is not because audience research is incapable of providing more complex detail, but because to know more would put producers under even greater stress. 'For a sociologist', commented Burns, 'it was rather like watching the whole practice of medicine being reduced to the use of a thermometer.'[13] Producers value the opinion of their colleagues most, but they see very little even of them.

The public interest cannot simply rely on the quality of broadcasters, because to do so is to ignore the pressures which determine broadcasting choices. 'When one stresses the role of individuals manning the system,' Garnham argues, 'one is tempted to await a Messiah who will come over – and help transform the system.'[14]

However, the relationship of broadcasters to their organization has also altered. Burns argued that there had been a considerable change in attitude since the 1960s. Then staff expressed a devotion to public service 'and a belief in the BBC's normative role in the cultural, moral and political life of the country'. By the 1970s this had been replaced by a commitment to professional values. Indeed as Kumar points out, the emergence of professionalism as the dominating ideology is the product of a particular moment in the evolution of broadcasting organizations. Even the notion of 'lively broadcasting' which determines the professionals' judgements 'expresses a particular stance towards the audience, a judgement of what the audience can and cannot take, which reflects a particular conception of the purposes of broadcasting'.[15]

Indeed the new 'scientific management' of broadcasting organizations has greater power than earlier administrations, whose main concern had been to protect and assist programme-makers who had far higher status within the organization. 'Because of the need to allocate time and resources economically,' Burns argued, 'working relations became impersonally functional.' The steady march of rational managerialism had led to a withering of institutional ardour.

Indeed, professionalism is now being superseded in many broadcasting organizations by crude financial managerialism. The pursuit of profit rather than excellence is more likely to dominate decisions in the next decade. Government reforms, culminating in the 1989 Broadcasting Bill,[16] and the auctioning of Channels 3 and 5 to the 'highest bidders' (who in order to bid have to pass a programme quality 'threshold', but who were awarded franchises solely on their ability to raise the largest amounts of capital)[17] will inevitably reduce the power of programme-makers. These pressures are already evident: in the past broadcasting administrators had often been programme-makers first; in a survey of appointments to top posts in television the majority of posts were given to 'accountants, bankers, and financial managers'.[18] Consequently not only were the talented programme-makers upon whom Annan, for instance, rested the future of broadcasting less committed to public service than before, but also they had become less important within broadcasting organizations.

Independence and the theory of broadcasting

The significance of broadcasting independence is also disputed. One side suggests that the independence is functional and must be extended to guarantee accountable broadcasting. The other argues that this same independence poses a serious threat to political institutions, whose control over broadcasting should be strengthened. Working from the same assumptions about the role of the media, Anthony Smith and Colin Seymour-Ure arrived at diametrically opposed diagnoses and solutions.

According to classic liberal theory the independence of a journalist depended on his ability to follow the uninhibited dictates of his conscience. According to Smith, this is an illusory ideal. In discussing the 1968 crisis in

French broadcasting he argues that, 'The ORTF strikers had stumbled across the central dilemmas of broadcasting and were demanding in the name of freedom . . . a right which no broadcaster has ever really achieved – the right to be an individual member of a Fourth Estate.' In its place Smith put forward a far more sophisticated and powerful version of the theory, in which the independence of broadcasters is not an individual right – but rather a functional necessity.

Broadcasters are not free, but are 'brokers and megaphones, impresarios and mediators', he suggested. The 'independence' of broadcasting institutions from political control was one solution to a dilemma all broadcasting systems had to solve: namely the necessity not only of regulating the right to broadcast but also of ensuring that broadcasting served the interests of all sections of society. For, Smith suggested, 'The institutions of broadcasting inaugurated a special problem of unlegitimized and unselective power.' Broadcasters are obliged to negotiate political conflict and not take sides in it – precisely because of the immense and dangerous nature of their power. In stable systems countervailing interests would always be able to enforce damaging sanctions if broadcasters became partisan.

This model implies that all political interests in society can, in practice, be reconciled. It is a logical extension of broadcasting institutions' own view of their role as arbiters that they come to see conflict and opposition as the products of failures in communication. Nevertheless, if there are real differences in interest, incompatible policies, and irreconcilable principles, then the role of the broker becomes untenable.

However, the functional independence of broadcasting institutions has many of the same policy consequences as the older liberal individualism. For, Smith argued, the way to meet recent criticisms is to give broadcasters more independence. The more perfectly broadcasters can do anything they want, the more adequate the service will be. As he is reported as commenting to the Annan Committee:

> If I am free to say anything I want to say except the one thing I want to say then I am not free. . . . In broadcasting . . . a single prohibition imposed on a national broadcasting authority or within it tends to corrode the whole output.

Colin Seymour-Ure views the 'independence' of broadcasters rather differently. The independence of the press – no longer the client of political parties – and 'now part of vast corporations who may have very direct interests in the outcomes of policy decisions' is vulnerable because it is compromised by ownership. Broadcasters, moreover, having abandoned the protection of 'public service' ideology are also susceptible to accusations of bias. Seymour-Ure argues that:

Some Labour politicians used to take comfort in the fact that although the press might be disproportionately conservative, at least broadcasting was balanced. This is no longer true. No doubt broadcasters are not wilfully biased. But the simple fact of deciding their own programme content may in the extreme case lead to a projection of party politicians and leaders that might run entirely counter to the parties' own views.

He suggests that the current interpretation of broadcasting independence has seriously damaged the political system.

The ideal of broadcasting independence – unlimited by any obligation to public service – has become increasingly inadequate. It has contributed to a growing anti-government ethos. It is hostile to many forms of political partisanship. It may inhibit political change and development. It may be that, as Seymour-Ure comments, the period of mass-based party organization is ending, for one effect of television in many countries seems to be 'the erosion of intervening structures between representatives and electors'. Nevertheless, any increase in the autonomy of broadcasting institutions may have more serious political consequences than had been expected. Rather it is the democratic processes which need support: not because broadcasters are malign but because of the inexorable pressure of broadcasting independence on the handling of politics. And the devotion of increasing amounts of political energy to managing the media – rather than managing politics.

Choice versus public service?

Double think, according to George Orwell, is the 'power of holding two contradictory beliefs in one's mind simultaneously and accepting both of them'. Through successive regimes, *double think* has nevertheless precisely defined the attitude of politicians towards broadcasting. On the one hand there are people (government ministers, for instance) who tend to believe that the worse excesses of broadcasting, as of the trade unions, should be curbed. There are others (shadow ministers, for instance) who look to broadcasting as a means to correct political bias.

Never, however, have the contradictions been so glaring as in the recent past. The politics of the 1980s and 1990s were orchestrated in a language of freedom, choice, non-intervention, withdrawal of the state: yet they were deformed with successive governmental limitations on the public right to be informed. Where individuals have sought to challenge state manipulation of the news the government showed neither mercy nor moderation in making an example of offenders. Indeed, the effective range of discussion and investigation is probably narrower here than in most modern democracies – including France, Sweden, West Germany, and possibly even the USA. It may not be long before the former Eastern bloc leaves us behind in the matter of broadcasting freedom. Who can imagine the Home Office giving a foreign

Annan nt implemented ..

camera crew *carte blanche* to film what they liked in the Maze Prison – in the way that the Soviet authorities recently provided open access to a western team in one of the USSR's remaining political gaols?

In addition to this, during the 1980s the Conservative government blatantly used television for government propaganda – with a massive increase in public sector advertising. Between 1980 and 1989, commercial television revenues doubled in real terms, and the proportion of advertising revenue generated by the public sector over that period quadrupled, indeed by 1989 it had become the largest single buyer of television advertising. The privatizations of public utilities were the single largest source of television advertising finance between 1990 and 1995.[19] If the ostensible purpose of the advertising was the sale of shares in the shortly to be privatized public sector industries, it also furthered the ideology of privatization.

Throughout the period, public service broadcasting was compared unfavourably with 'the real choice offered to consumers by a more effective market'.[20] Successive reports, government green papers, and bills proposed to 'set free broadcasters from the narrow constraints of control' and it was repeatedly argued that satellite, cable, and a deregulated broadcasting system would offer the public a greater choice of programmes more sensitively tailored to their wants by the competitive pressures of the market. In part, of course, government policy was attempting to adapt to a new situation in which cable and satellite would deliver such a multitude of channels and services that the previous regime of regulation would become practically impossible. But more than this, policy was driven by a profound hostility to the principles of public service broadcasting.

Yet the ideology of 'choice' was absurd. Commercial broadcasting is based not on the sale of programmes to audiences, but on the sale of audiences to advertisers. Thus the introduction of more competitors will reduce advertising revenues both by spreading them between a greater number of channels and by splitting potential audiences into even smaller groups. As the main incentive will remain the attraction of the largest possible audience, the competing channels, less constrained by regulation to produce a variety of programmes, will tend to show more of the same or similar programmes.

Indeed, if one contradiction of Thatcherism was that free market rhetoric was accompanied by interventionist practice, another was that talk of the marketplace was accompanied by its virtual eradication. Technological change – with its requirement for long-term investment and large-scale capitalization – has produced a bureaucratic jungle of profit-taking conglomerates, which own shares in all the media which the public consumes. The small number of corporate owners are not competitive in a sense that could conceivably be expected to produce an improved product; but their financial rivalry will undoubtedly impose pressure to produce a cheaper one. That means an almost inevitable lowering of standards, since it is cheaper to buy in internationalized soap opera than to make your own drama, and so on. The result is likely to be a lesser variety of the kind of programmes that many of us watch some of the time, and some of us watch most of the time, but which do not attract top audience ratings. We are all, on occasions, members of minorities. Thus the victims of media concentration are variety, creativity, and quality, while the proliferation of broadcasting channels in the hands of a small band of operators, 'liberated' by government policy from the obligations of public service variety, is likely to make matters worse. 'Choice', without positive direction, is a myth, for all too often the market will deliver more – but only more of the same.

Conclusion

Broadcasters have come to see the state as their enemy. Yet broadcasting institutions ultimately depend on the state for their legitimation. This authority cannot be replaced by a pluralist ideal of reflecting social and cultural variety. Indeed the adoption of this principle has left broadcasters peculiarly vulnerable to the more general attack on public service broadcasting.

Moreover, arguments with quite different aims from those of the broadcasters, but apparently related, are being used to undermine broadcasting responsibility and independence. Thus neither the emphasis on the authority of the viewers' right to choose from a greater variety of programmes, nor the elaboration of some aspects of the local and regional role of the media, let alone the distinction between a 'service' the public will pay for and a public service, are intended to strengthen the creative autonomy of broadcasters. On the contrary, they are arguments which enhance the power of commercial interests in determining the patterns of broadcasting provision.

Thus without a commitment to public service, broadcasters are increasingly vulnerable to detailed political interference in the content of programmes. Broadcasting in Britain has in the past had a considerable degree of autonomy from other institutions: it has not in any simple sense been biased. This autonomy is now threatened, partly because the consensus about what constitutes the 'middle ground' of agreed opinion has broken down, partly because the reliance on the skill of professional broadcasters which has replaced it is unjustified, and partly because of the erosion of public service broadcasting. Broadcasting needs to find a new relationship to the state – and a new form of commitment to public service, and indeed a new definition of public service that will work in the conditions of increased competition.

Notes

1. *Report of the Enquiry into Cable Expansion and Broadcasting Policy* (Hunt Report, 1982) [Cmnd 8697].
2. *Broadcasting Committee: Report* (Sykes Report, 1923) [Cmnd 1951], X, 13, para. 21.

3. *Report of the Broadcasting Committee* (Crawford Report, 1926) [Cmnd 2599], VIII, 327, para. 49.
4. *Report of the Broadcasting Committee* (Ullswater Report, 1936) [Cmnd 5091], VII, 617, para. 7.
5. *Report of the Broadcasting Committee* (Beveridge Report, 1951) [Cmnd 8116], IX, 1, para. 217.
6. *Report of the Committee on Broadcasting* (Pilkington Report, 1962) [Cmnd 1755], IV, 259, para. 23.
7. *Report of the Committee on the Future of Broadcasting* (Annan Report, 1977) [Cmnd 6753], XVI, para. 311.
8. *Report of the Committee on Financing the BBC* (Peacock Report, 1986) [Cmnd 9824], II, para. 636.
9. S. Brittan, 'The fight for freedom in broadcasting', *Political Quarterly*, 58, 1 (March 1987).
10. C. Heller, *Broadcasters and Accountability*, BFI Television Monograph 3 (London, British Film Institute, 1978), p. 39.
11. ACCT report, quoted in C. Heller, *Broadcasters and Accountability*, BFI Television Monograph 3 (London, British Film Institute, 1978), p. 50.
12. M. Tracey, *The Production of Political Television* (London, Routledge & Kegan Paul, 1978), p. 13.
13. T. Burns, *The BBC: Public Institution and Private World* (London, Macmillan, 1977), p. 137.
14. N. Garnham, *Structures of Television*, BFI Television Monograph 1 (London, British Film Institute, 1973), p. 21.
15. K. Kumar, 'Holding the middle ground: The BBC, the public and the professional broadcaster' in J. Curran, M. Gurevitch, and J. Woollacott (eds), *Mass Communication and Society* (London, Edward Arnold/Open University, 1977), p. 232.
16. Broadcasting Bill, Bill No. 9, December 1989 (London, HMSO, 300906).
17. See Martin Cave, 'The conduct of auctions for broadcasting franchises', *Fiscal Studies* 10, 1 (Feb. 1989), pp. 17–31.
18. 'New managers, new talents', *Vision* (Dec. 1989), pp. 15–31.
19. 'Television advertising by sector', *Campaign* (July 1989); 'Public utilities flotation advertising spend 1990–95', Hargreaves & Whitticker, Spencer Report, *Adcam*, 1996.
20. S. Velachesky, 'Broadcasting choice', *Hobbart Papers on Liberal Economics* (June 1989), p. 7.

Part V

Politics of the media

23

Contradictions in media policy

Introduction

To inform, to discuss, to mirror, to bind, to campaign, to challenge, to entertain and to judge – these are the important functions of the media in any free
country. The purpose of public policy should be to enable the media to perform them more effectively. Yet historically, very different traditions of
promoting these ideals or indeed pursuing no ideals at all have developed in
relation to different media. Traditionally, press policy has taken the form of
having no policy, and the functioning of newspapers has been left largely to
market forces. By contrast, television and radio have been required to pursue
objectives set by Parliament, and have been subject to extensive regulation.

However, during the Conservative ascendancy of the 1980s and early 1990s,
there appeared to be a revolution in official thinking about the media. It was
argued that broadcasting should be shaped more by the market, and less by
public bureaucracy. The state was portrayed as a threat to media freedom,
and regulation was attacked as an obstacle to satisfying the consumer. These
themes were invoked, for example, by supporters of the deregulatory
Broadcasting Acts of 1990 and 1996. The clear implication was that the gap
between press and broadcasting policy should diminish, and the market
should be allowed to reign.

A new version of policy consistency was pursued under New Labour,
elected in 1997 and again in 2001. The formerly separate worlds of broadcasting, telephones, computers and print were coming together, it was
proclaimed, as a consequence of technological convergence, and this neces-
sitated the development of a common approach for all communications.
'Sectoral policies' for separate media, of a kind pursued by previous administrations, needed to be replaced by a single, coherent vision for the
communications industry as a whole.

A new, unifying theme was also advanced by New Labour.
'Communications industries,' declared a 2001 government consultation document, 'constitute a large and growing part of our national income.' Their

continued growth will promote investment, employment, innovation, choice, diversity and lower consumer prices. However, Britain's communications industry is also faced with intensified competition in a more globally integrated market. Consequently, a key objective of communication policy must be, in the words of the government's 1998 Green Paper, 'not only to defend the domestic position, but also to attract a share of global revenues and jobs to the UK'.

A new ministry was also created to brush away the cobwebs of the past, and impose a new sense of direction and purpose. In 1992, the John Major government established the Department of National Heritage (the nearest synonym to 'culture' that conservative sensibilities would allow). It was renamed the Ministry of Culture, Media and Sport (CMS) by the incoming New Labour government in 1997, and was rededicated to the task of developing an 'integrated' communications policy.

Yet six years later, New Labour had still failed to fulfil its promise of 'coherent regulation in a converging environment'. Like the New Right Conservative administrations that preceded it, the Blair government merely added another layer of piecemeal reform. Indeed it added to, rather than detracted from, the confusion at the heart of British media policy.

Efficiency

This confusion has survived repeated attempts to inject order and clarity. Indeed, superficially, official reports on media industries over the past sixty years appear to have much in common. One recurrent theme has been the emphasis on greater efficiency. Thus in 1949 the Gater Report on the British Film Industry called for more effective financial planning, while the second (1962) Press Commission urged that better machinery for negotiation should be established, a point also stressed by the Prices and Incomes Board Report on the press in 1967. In the same way the Annan Report (1977) concluded that 'clear lines of decision making, fewer chieftains, better communications' were needed, and the Peacock Report on the BBC (1986) argued that 'the assessment of efficiency is one of our Committee's chief aims'. Such comments, few of which have ever had any significant effect, have become part of the ritual of investigation.

Most official reports have also taken an optimistic view of the independence of journalists and programme-makers, and their capacity for autonomous reform. Thus two Royal Commissions on the press stressed in identical words that 'on the quality of the individual journalist depends not only the status of the whole profession of journalism but the possibility of bridging the gap between what society needs from the press and what the press is at present giving it'. Similarly, the Annan Report argued that 'the strength of British broadcasting lies in the creativity of people who make programmes'.

Hence successive reports have suggested better recruitment policies, improved training and education, greater integrity and responsibility among communicators, and new opportunities for independent producers. Annan (1977) proposed an Open Broadcasting Authority which would show minority programmes made by 'small independent production groups', a term which is reminiscent of the 'small independent producer' which film policy has been trying unsuccessfully to help since the Moyne Report in 1936, and which Peacock (1986) championed for mainstream television. In the same way, three Royal Commissions put their faith in individual entrepreneurs as the best way of sustaining a varied press. Even the Calcutt Report (1990) on privacy suggested that newspaper ethics depended 'on the calibre of the individual conscience' – an engagingly innocent view of the solution to tabloid exploitation.

This emphasis on individuals as the mainspring of improvement has resulted in economic and institutional constraints being neglected. Repeated attempts to boost film production have foundered because they have not been combined with reform of film distribution and exhibition. Public funding of films swelled the profits of large production companies when there was a buoyant film industry, and is now leading to a significant number of films being made that are never shown in commercial cinemas. Similarly, the Annan Committee proposed an Open Broadcasting Authority (Channel 4, as it became known) to introduce more adventurous minority programmes, yet failed to suggest how its finance could be arranged to protect it from the economic pressures which inhibited experimental programming on the other channels. In the event, an ingenious cross-subsidy scheme was introduced initially in a form which insulated Channel 4 from conformist market pressure, but this owed nothing to Annan's vague advice on funding. In much the same way, the Peacock Committee hoped that by forcing the BBC and ITV to take a fixed quota of programmes from production companies, a new legion of fearless, independent programme-makers would spring up to create more diverse, popular programmes. What the Committee did not anticipate was that the independent production quota (first introduced in 1986 and extended in 1990) would expand a vulnerable, casualized, low-paid sector of the television workforce that lacked either the power or the autonomous resources to fulfil what was expected of it. Yet the Peacock Committee (chaired by a noted neo-liberal economist) was in fact more alert to economic structures than most such committees. Although appointed by a government hostile to the BBC, it nevertheless protected the BBC because for the first time its main object was to consider the financial structures that underlay cultural considerations. If the BBC was funded by advertising, Peacock warned, the result would be reduced choice and worse programmes.

However, this inattention to economic constraints occasionally had positive outcomes, though more by accident than by design. When the Annan Committee recommended a minority television channel, it did not anticipate that this would provide a shot in the arm of the ailing film industry. By giving individual one-off, British art movies a secure, predictable audience on television, Channel 4 improved film-makers' capacity to raise film finance. By offering an additional distribution system, Channel 4 also gave new opportunities for people to see the work of a network of creative and important film-makers. However, this failed to solve the financial crisis of British film-making. In France, where the film industry was relatively more successful, state finance was more readily and consistently available – a crucial factor in artistic and commercial success.

Government and lame ducks

Government intervention has sometimes been justified as an exceptional measure that will make subsequent interference unnecessary and restore a stable and competitive market. This has been particularly true of British film policy which has been shaped by a combination of crisis-driven expediency and unfulfilled optimism. Thus in 1927 a Board of Trade inquiry into the film industry advocated special measures to deal with 'unfair, devious and improper trading' by American competitors. This report resulted in the Cinematograph Act, 1927, which obliged distributors and exhibitors to purchase and show quotas of British films. But this was intended to be only a short-term measure, to promote 'free and equitable trade'. In 1949 the National Film Finance Corporation was set up to provide loans for film production. It was seen as a response to a temporary inability of British film producers to obtain private investment capital. The Eady Levy, introduced during the same period, was designed to promote national film production through a tax on box-office takings which was supposed to fall most heavily on successful foreign imports. Similarly, the last Royal Commission on the press also recommended that newspapers should be offered cheap loans in order to pay for the introduction of new printing technology during a period of financial crisis. Its advice was sensibly ignored.

Most of these measures, though advocated as temporary expedients, became settled features of public policy. The 'temporary' import quota introduced in 1927 was strengthened in 1938, supplemented during the 1940s, and abandoned only in 1983. The National Film Finance Corporation, set up as a self-financing agency, was forced to write off many loans and so became a continuing source of state finance for the film industry. It was closed in 1986, subsequently replaced by the anorexic British Screen Finance (with some public money), and then revived, with infusions of lottery funds, as the Film Council in 2000. The Eady Levy survived until 1984 even though it reinforced American domination of the British film industry by subsidizing American-backed films which were only nominally British. The rationale for the levy had changed, and it came to be seen as a way of maintaining employment rather than supporting national culture. All these one-off interventions proved more long-lasting or served different purposes than were originally intended. They might all have been more successful if they had been designed to address long-term problems rather than short-term crises.

Thus official media reports display over the years many of the same short-comings and engage in the same ritual responses, while glossing over problems which their recommendations failed to solve. Yet the essential conservatism of official policy is less important than its contradictions. Good policy is not necessarily consistent policy, but one of the most curious features of government relations with the media has been the way in which reports on the press, broadcasting and film industries have often conflicted sharply with one another.

Variety in policy goals

Thus broadcasting regulation has long sought to preserve a space for national collective expression. As late as the 1970s, no more than 14 per cent of television programmes on BBC or ITV was allowed to be foreign (excluding Commonwealth countries). 'Foreign' was changed to mean non-EEC countries in the 1981 Broadcasting Act, but strict rationing of foreign programmes continued. The foreign allowance was raised to 35 per cent of commercial, terrestrial TV programmes in 1993, and to slightly higher quotas for Channels 4 and 5 in 1998. This protectionist policy was backed up by limitations on foreign ownership of broadcasting. Until 2003, non-EU corporations were not allowed to acquire Channel 3 and 5 companies, though the restriction on majority holding of cable TV companies was lifted in 1990, and that on new multiplex, digital enterprises was waived in 1996.

However, what was thought desirable in television and radio was not deemed important in the press. There has never been any restriction on foreign ownership of British newspapers. Official enquiries into the press, unlike those into broadcasting, have never seen this as an issue. In film policy, by contrast, cultural autonomy has been believed to be important but it has been eclipsed as an objective by the need to sustain a film industry underwritten by American money. This was acknowledged tacitly by the 1968 review of film legislation when it argued that the National Film Finance Corporation should be maintained not to defend British cultural production but because 'it constitutes a real attraction for foreign investment'.

The competing claims of the economy, 'culture' and the political system are negotiated in media policy, and resolved in divergent ways in different industries. In film policy, priority has come to be given to maintaining jobs; in television, more attention has been given to cultural concerns. This has resulted in films being conceived and regulated in quite different ways, depending upon whether they are watched in the cinema, on video or on 'live' television.

In the case of television, resources have been redistributed in order to promote quality and diversity. The obligation imposed by the Independent Television Commission (ITC) on ITV companies to provide a mixed schedule ensures that some of the revenue generated by programmes (including films) reaching large audiences is invested in more demanding or more minority-oriented programmes watched by smaller audiences. Yet the same principle was never applied to the allocation of film funds through the Eady Levy. This tax on cinema takings was paid to production companies in proportion to the box-office revenue for their films. It constituted a bounty distributed according to market demand. 'The levy,' concluded the 1968 Board of Trade review, 'should not be used to breed indifference to economic reality.' Underlying this argument was a concern that cultural or qualitative concerns should not encroach upon market efficiency and the survival of British film-making. By contrast, there has never been a policy in relation to videos apart from a prohibition against objectionable sex and violence.

State as threat

One reason for these underlying tensions and contradictions is that media policy has been shaped by different philosophies. A common feature of much official thinking about the working of the media has been a liberal suspicion of the state. However, this suspicion assumed such evangelical proportions in the case of successive Royal Commissions on the press that it led them into an implicit confrontation with other media enquiries.

Thus the last Royal Commission on the Press (1977) advanced a sweeping definition of what was acceptable:

> We are strongly against any scheme which would make the press, or any section of it, dependent on government through reliance on continuing subsidies from public funds. We are also opposed absolutely to the establishment of any body which could, or might have to, discriminate among publications in such a way as to amount to censorship in the sense of preferring to support some publications and not others.

This view was echoed explicitly by the second Press Commission (1962), and implicitly by the first (1949). Subsidies targeted towards weak publications were rejected on the grounds that they could lead to government manipulation. Yet non-selective subsidies were repudiated because they failed to offer special help to the vulnerable. The first approach was found wanting because it might lead to censorship, the second because it was ineffectual. This catch-22 formulation in effect ruled out most forms of market intervention.

Yet the dangers that successive public enquiries into the press detected in allocating public resources seemed less of a problem in other sectors of the media. 'No public body,' thundered the third Press Commission, 'should ever be put in a position of discriminating like a censor between one applicant and another.' This is exactly what the Independent Broadcasting Authority, among other public agencies, did when this advice was given. It is what the Independent Television Commission, Radio Authority, Film Council and Arts Council (whose grants include small publications) does now, and what the Office of Communications will do in the future. The processes of public selection that press enquiries, steeped in a tradition of anti-statism, found so alarming are in fact common practice.

The Press Commissions' objection to all policies that can lead potentially to state dependence is equally maverick. If this precept is introduced into the broadcasting sector, it would lead to the immediate privatization of the BBC and Channel 4, the deregulation of all channels, and the free trading of their shares on the open market. Yet not even the most right-wing broadcasting enquiry – chaired by Sir Alan Peacock – has been willing to go this far.

Press Commissions' negative view of the state contrasts with their positive view of the market. This is seen as the sheet-anchor of press independence, a view that coloured their opinion of market processes in general. Having rejected public subsidies that induce economic dependence or involve a process of choice, they perceived no difficulty in another kind of subsidy – advertising – that induces economic dependence, involves a process of choice and indeed tends to favour Conservative papers because of their affluent readerships. In the Commissions' view, public subsidies are fraught with dangers; private ones are not. Similarly, successive Press Commissions failed to make an explicit connection between the high costs of market entry and the predominantly right-wing character of the national press. To have done so would have meant questioning their idealized view of the market as neutral, in contrast to the partiality they perceived to be lurking in the actions of state-linked agencies.

Benign state

By contrast, public reports on broadcasting generally view the state in a more positive light. Conservative paternalism and an Arnoldian concern with moral and cultural values originally contributed to this view. A liberal corporatist tradition also played a part, equating central planning with the rational and scientific use of resources, as did a radical commitment to redistribution through the state. Broadcasting was also viewed as being so powerful an influence that it needed to be harnessed to the general good.

All nine major reports on British broadcasting argued that a publicly appointed agency could act in the public interest, if it was established by the state for this purpose. As the Crawford Committee (1926) put it, 'The actual commission should be persons of judgement and independence, free of commitments, and . . . they will inspire confidence by having no other interests to promote than those of public service.'

Broadcasting has been repeatedly presented in reports as serving the public interest as a consequence of being subject to regulations framed for the public good and controlled by people committed to the best interests of the entire community. The BBC was financed from licence revenue and was therefore, in the words of the Pilkington Report (1962), under 'no obligation, express or implied, to pursue any other objective other than that of public service'. Public regulation was seen as both necessary and desirable even after the introduction of commercial television.

This conception of state-sponsored public service has depended on a number of principles. First, that broadcasting services should be made available to everyone in the UK, and not merely developed in areas where it was easy or cheap to do so, or restricted to those who could pay for them. Second, public service broadcasting should produce a wide variety of high-quality programmes because it is not controlled by the forces that make for low standards and uniformity. Finally, that public regulation should ensure broadcasters' accountability through the relationship of the broadcasting authority with Parliament.

Whereas press enquiries are in general pro-market, the opposite is generally the case with broadcasting enquiries. Indeed, public service is deemed necessary in order to make up for the deficiencies of free enterprise. The Crawford Committee (1926) argued that 'no company or body constituted on trade lines for profit . . . can be regarded as adequate . . . in view of the broader considerations which now begin to emerge.' The Ullswater Committee (1936) regarded commercial advertising as incompatible with 'the intellectual and ethical integrity which the broadcasting system in this country has attained'. Much of this opposition has been based on the belief that what the Beveridge Committee (1951) called 'competition for numbers' results in standardized programming. This view has been justified by references to the deplorable condition of commercial broadcasting in the USA. 'Experience in other countries,' concluded the Pilkington Report in 1962, 'is that this kind of competition, so far from promoting the purposes of broadcasting, or extending the range of programmes, or helping to realise the potential of the medium, serves rather to restrict them.'

The necessity of extensive public regulation was never questioned in official reports on television or radio until the Thatcherite era. There were signs of unease before that, most notably a concern about the relationship between government (and in particular party politicians) and broadcasting. But this gave rise to reform, not repudiation, of the public service system. There was also a gradual weakening of the sense of cultural purpose associated with Lord Reith. As the Annan Report commented, 'the ideals of middle-class culture, so felicitously expressed by Matthew Arnold a century ago . . . found it ever more difficult to accommodate . . . the variety of expression of what is good'. The Annan Committee found it harder to define what 'good' broadcasting was than did Pilkington. Nevertheless, Annan did make qualitative judgements, finding the BBC's output, on balance, superior to that of ITV. Annan was opposed to the unrestricted commercial control of broadcasting, and saw the fact that ITV made 'some programmes which both stimulate and entertain, and are not concocted in order to drug their audience into an uncritical stupor' as a product of public regulation. Even the Peacock Committee, which in certain important respects broke with the broadcasting consensus, nevertheless clung to a conception of public service broadcasting as 'a commitment to produce a wide range of high quality programmes to maximise consumer appreciation'. The current system of collective provision and commercial controls was producing in its judgement a 'mixed diet' of programmes 'at a low cost' that 'has broadened the horizon of a great number of viewers'. While it favoured long-term deregulation, it still made the case for a residual public service system which would secure 'programmes of merit which would not survive in a market where audience ratings was the sole criterion'. These were, it added, not just minority programmes but included ones that attract 'medium sized audiences of which virtually all the population at some stage form a part'.

Broadcasting and press reports do not each constitute a single unity. The second Press Commission was more critical of the market than other Press Commissions, while the Peacock Committee was more anti-statist than the broadcasting enquiries that had preceded it. But in general broadcasting policy has been framed within a pro-state, anti-market framework, while press policy has been formulated within a framework that is anti-state and pro-market. This has produced recurrent inconsistencies that cannot be explained away in terms of technological differences between the two media. For example, the idea that government should give money to a publishing corporation, even one with a publicly appointed managing authority, would have been anathema to all Press Commissions which could not countenance even selective subsidies. Yet this is what the Annan Committee proposed when it suggested that a government grant could be given to start an Open Broadcasting Authority, and what the Peacock Committee recommended when it suggested that its proposed Public Service Broadcasting Council could be financed by the taxpayer.

Divergent histories

Differences of perspective are rooted partly in different histories. The press began as an agency of news and political comment. It was also organized as a free market system from 1695 onwards. Traditionally, it has been viewed within a taken-for-granted market framework, and evaluated primarily in terms of its functioning within the democratic system. A neo-liberal, 'politics of information' approach has coloured the work of all major public enquiries into the press.

By contrast, during the 1920s radio was not allowed to compete fully with the news service of the press, and was organized as a public service monopoly. It was evaluated primarily in terms of its contribution to culture, education and entertainment, defined by formative Victorian debates. This legacy had an enduring influence on how broadcasting was viewed by subsequent public enquiries.

From the outset, it was also accepted that broadcasting had to be regulated by the state because spectrum frequency was a scarce public resource which needed to be managed in the public interest. This was always an ideological argument, masquerading as a technical one, since it presupposed that public interest management of spectrum scarcity was best entrusted to the state rather than to the marketplace. But it powerfully influenced the approach of all public investigations into broadcasting, even that of the Peacock Committee which sought to challenge and renegotiate this statist legacy.

Consequently, press and broadcasting reports have tended to approach their work in different ways. While Royal Commissions on the press have focused generally on the quality of news and political comment, and formulated their conclusions within a free market system of thought, broadcasting enquiries have concerned themselves generally with the full range of programmes, and promoted reform from a public service viewpoint. This has regularly produced divergent or incommensurate conclusions. Thus in 1960 the Pilkington Committee recommended a ban on television advertisements 'appealing to human weakness'; yet two years later the second Royal Commission on the press did not even consider the content of newspaper and magazine advertising, let alone recommend its reform. Similarly, the Annan Committee recommended that the joint ownership of commercial broadcasting companies and record or music publishing companies be banned, on the grounds that there was bound to be a conflict of interest between them. The third Royal Commission on the press, also reporting in 1977, did not propose (or even discuss) a similar measure in relation to the music press and record production.

These discrepancies merely illustrate the different intellectual frameworks in which press and broadcasting policy are conceived. However, these frameworks no longer make sense. Popular newspapers devote less than a quarter of their editiorial content to news and analysis of public affairs. Indeed, television has usurped the role of the press as the principal source of news. The distinction between media of 'information' and those of 'culture and entertainment' have completely broken down. The spectrum scarcity justification for public service broadcasting has also been undermined by the development of cable, satellite and digital television. Hence the different policy approaches which have been developed to deal with broadcasting and the press are completely inadequate.

Pressure groups and policy

Another source of inconsistency in media policy derives from the fact that it is shaped by public enquiries confined to one media industry. These have not been given common terms of reference, and they have not been set to work within an integrated framework of communications policy.

The inevitable consequence has been that public enquiries have responded to the divergent pressure groups and economic interests at work in different media industries. Broadcasting enquiries have been powerfully influenced by the BBC, and for this reason have tended to uphold the principles of public service. Press enquiries have been shaped by publishers – who have invested large resources to influence them – and have tended to champion their *laissez-faire* approach.

This sectoral narrowness has also tended to nurture self-interested inconsistency. To take but one example, the 1977 Press Commission favoured limited press holdings in profitable television and radio franchises because, following press lobbying, it came around to the view that these were a valuable, potential source of cross-subsidy for vulnerable newspapers. Similarly the Prime Minister's Working Party on the Film Industry (1977), influenced closely by the views of the industry, proposed that television should finance film-making. On the other hand, the Annan Committee (1977) was exposed to broadcasters who were hostile to the idea that broadcasting should subsidize less profitable media. It consequently opposed the view that 'like an aged parent, the film industry has a right to look to television to support it in its old age'. It rejected the proposal (already endorsed by the Working Party on the Film Industry) for money for film investment to come out of the television levy. It was also much more hostile than the 1977 Press Commission to cross-ownership between press and broadcasting.

A second consequence of the uncoordinated way in which communications policy has evolved is that reforms, proposed and implemented for one industry, have had unforeseen consequences for other media. For example, the decision to establish commercial television in 1955 to 1956, in the wake of Selwyn Lloyd's minority report, contributed almost certainly to the epidemic of newspaper and magazine closures that the second Press Commission was then appointed to investigate in 1961.

This source of inconsistency has yet to be rectified. New Labour (like the Major government that preceded it) has produced policy proposals covering more than one medium, and invited comment. But it has yet to initiate a full-blown public enquiry into the communications industry which critically scrutinizes divergent media policy and proposes a coherent alternative.

Continuing confusion

Of course, a degree of variation in approach to different media could reasonably be justified in terms of their contrasting characteristics. However, in practice, policy differences are rooted in the histories of different media, and the polarized politics of communication that these have produced. Policy difference is not the product of rational differentiation between media, nor is it presented in these terms.

However, during the 1980s and 1990s, the rise of the New Right held out the promise of greater policy consistency, at least on its impoverished terms. It sought to reorganize broadcasting on the free market lines of the press. However, while it made policy inroads, and while market values were strengthened within the broadcasting system, its project failed ultimately through lack of political and public support. The BBC and Channel 4 were not privatized. Although a 'light touch' regulator of commercial TV (ITC) was established in 1990, it had a much heavier hand than its press counterpart, the Press Council/Complaints Commission. The ITC licensed the right to 'publish' on domestic airwaves; it excluded television companies which failed to submit adequate public service programme plans; and it was able to impose fines – a power that it used. Unlike the supine Press Complaints Commission, the ITC exerted a significant and positive influence on the industry it regulated.

Indeed, the New Right phase of media reform introduced new contradictions. The ostensible purpose behind rolling back public bureaucracy was to enlarge freedom. However, the Conservative government did not approve of the uses to which this freedom was put. In 1984, it introduced legislation to outlaw video 'nasties'. In 1988, it established the Broadcasting Standards Council (BSC) to monitor levels of sex and violence on television. In 1990, it required broadcasting bodies to reflect BSC codes in relation to sex and violence. During the later 1980s, the Conservative government also lobbied unsuccessfully other European governments to take a tough stand against television sex in the Television without Frontiers Directive (1989). Although committed ostensibly to increasing freedom of expression, the Thatcher government also introduced in 1988 a ban on broadcasting the voices of supporters of terrorist organizations (including democratically elected Sinn Fein politicians). This conflict between the pursuit of market freedom and the increase of state censorship reflected an underlying tension, at the heart of modern conservatism, between market liberalism and moral authoritarianism.

However, New Labour proved to be no more successful than its predecessors in rationalizing media policy. One reason for this was that, under New Labour, the Department of Trade and Industry in effect continued to be a second 'media ministry', and promoted a market brief, while the Ministry of Culture, Media and Sport was more oriented towards public service policies. A second reason was that New Labour's promotion of global media competitiveness as a central objective tended to clash with its aims of promoting media quality, diversity and access. A third reason is that its reappraisal focused on telecommunications, broadcasting and print, but sidelined film (even though film is now funded and distributed partly by televison, and the two media are inextricably linked).

New Labour's rethinking led to some bureaucratic tidying: the Broadcasting Standards Commission (formerly Council), Independent Television Commission, Radio Authority and Radio Communications Agency were merged in 2003 to become the Office of Communications. However, its central objective, announced in 1998, of ending 'inconsistent regulation' of the communications industries seems to be no nearer realization. Major inconsistencies remain. Television and radio, but not the press, are required to be impartial. Leading television organizations must strive for quality – not something that newspapers need to consider. 'Unfairness' and unwarranted intrusions into privacy can be redressed by a regulator, with legal powers, in television and radio but not in the press. While a public corporation (BBC) and state-appointed public trust (Channel 4) are deemed to improve the quality of broadcasting, similar organizations are unthinkable for the press.

While an opportunistic rationalization of this inconsistency could be formulated, no Minister has yet attempted this. In New Labour's Green, White and Consultation Papers, public service broadcasting is defended but no equivalent defence is offered for a free market approach to the press. The latter is just assumed to be right, without any argument or reason being given. In this way, the contradiction at the heart of media policy persists – unacknowledged, unexplained and unjustified – as it has done for the past eighty years. All that New Labour's rhetoric about the need for an integrated communications policy has achieved is to expose how incoherent it remains.

24

Central debates in media politics

Introduction

The media are major sources of pleasure, absorbing over thirty hours a week in the average person's life. They are central to the democratic life of Britain. They are also a way in which different social groups connect to each other, and join in the shared conversation of society. How the media are organized and regulated therefore matters.

Yet public policy about the media is often presented as an arcane subject concerned with regulators, markets and 'externalities'. It seems to belong to a rarefied world where only experts are qualified to speak, and where the issues involved are susceptible solely to technocratic solutions.

But in essence the debate about how best to organize and manage the mass media is exceedingly simple. It also involves choices that affect everyone. It is not something that can be left to specialists to determine.

What follows is a summary of public discussion about mass communications policy. It reports not only the principal policy options but crucially the thinking behind them. The aim is to provide a map that marks clearly the main points of entry into the democratic politics of the media. It also seeks to highlight the way in which media politics is no longer purely national – the exclusive concern of national government and of those to which it is account-able – but is acquiring a significant European and international regulatory dimension.

Free market

Free market ideas have been the main driving force shaping media policy for the past twenty years. They have encouraged the adoption of deregulatory policies under successive Conservative administrations during the 1980s and 1990s, and under New Labour since 1997.

The starting-point of the free market approach is that consumers are the best judges of what is in their own best interests. Media policy should be geared therefore to creating the conditions of greatest possible competition in which consumers exercise sovereign control. This produces a system that gives people what they want; a diverse range of media goods to choose from; and fearless media that are independent of government. There is no conflict between the needs of society and the functioning of the market system. 'All provision for the consumer on a competitive basis in a non-distorted market,' writes the *Financial Times* journalist, Samuel Brittan, 'is a *public service*' (emphasis added).[1]

The market empowers the consumer, fosters freedom and makes for efficiency. It follows from this that there is very little need to reform the press since it is organized along free market lines. The main media target drawing the firepower of neo-liberals is public service broadcasting. It is indicted on three main counts. The BBC and other public service broadcasting bodies are said to be controlled by an unrepresentative élite who foist their cultural values on the public. Public service broadcasting organizations are vulnerable to government pressure because they are dependent on state-sponsored privileges. They are run by bureaucracies prone to waste and profligacy. According to some critics, the BBC is also an unaccountable haven for radicals. This is in marked contrast to the competitive environment of the press where the consumer is in control and where, consequently, unpopular radical views get short shrift.

The case for deregulation, argue neo-liberals, has been further reinforced by technological innovation. It used to be maintained plausibly that broadcasting channels had to be managed in the public interest because the scarcity of airwave frequencies produced a natural oligopoly, but fibre-optic cable, satellite and digital broadcasting has multiplied the number of television channels. These are supplemented by video, the internet, and – in the pipeline – a new generation of convergent, digital media. The traditional consensual justification for public service broadcasting, based on spectrum scarcity, no longer applies in the era of media plenty.

The world is also changing, it is argued, in a way that makes media competitiveness a key objective of communications policy. The media are part of the rapidly growing information and knowledge economy, which increasingly is significant as a source of wealth and employment. However, home-grown media are also exposed to fierce international competition as a consequence of the globalization of the media economy. It is therefore imperative in the neo-liberal view that the burden of bureaucracy be lifted in order to promote market efficiency. Regulation designed to foster media diversity has also been rendered unnecessary by media expansion. It should be discarded immediately since it impedes new investment that will increase consumer choice. Traditional misgivings about media concentration also need to be reappraised in the light of new priorities. 'Some concentration of [media] ownership,' suggests New Labour's Green Paper on *Regulating Communications,* 'has been regarded as inevitable, and possibly desirable, since it confers advantage in terms of global competitiveness.'[2]

These different arguments contributed, at different stages, to a cumulative policy of broadcasting deregulation. The 1990 Broadcasting Act inaugurated the sale of ITV franchises to the highest bidder, subject to some quality safeguards. It also established a 'light touch' regulator (Independent Television Commission) which lowered quotas on the import of television programmes. The 1996 Broadcasting Act relaxed restrictions on ITV and commercial radio mergers.

The 2003 Communications Act is the latest staging post in broadcast deregulation. It sanctions an increase of commercial radio and ITV concentration. It opens the door to large press groups gaining control of Channel 5. It also allows British terrestrial television to be bought by an owner outside the EU, reflecting a shift of New Labour thought away from defending national capitalism to championing the interests of the consumer. It also establishes a new regulator, the Office of Communications (OFCOM), with a brief to 'roll back regulation promptly when regulation becomes unnecessary'.[3] The assumption is that the expansion of the media system, supported by the digital revolution, will lessen the need for formal regulation.

Yet the pace of deregulation is still not fast enough for committed neo-liberals. For example, the Adam Smith Institute argues that the BBC should be broken up into 'an association of independent and separately financed stations' funded partly by advertising. It believes that the market should prevail since 'the only fair criterion of judging a programme is by how many people like it'.[4] Similarly, Rupert Murdoch believes that increased cross-media ownership should be positively welcomed since it increases investment and is therefore 'a force for diversity'.[5] In the past two years, a number of conservative commentators have also called for the lifting of the requirement on broadcasters to display due impartiality on controversial issues. They argue that this limits free speech in support of an ideal of objectivity that is unobtainable and illusory (echoing ironically a standard left argument of the 1970s).

Pressure for deregulation comes not only from the right in Britain, but also from neo-liberals entrenched within part of the European Commission. The deregulation of telephone services in EU countries, completed in 1998, was acclaimed by the Deputy Director General of the Commission's Competition Directorate as a welcome step towards 'open and competitive structures in telecoms and media sectors' that would unlock 'high growth potential'.[6] In 1998, the Competition Directorate also proposed unsuccessfully that public service broadcasters should be prevented from making programmes of a kind made by commercial broadcasters – a policy that, if pursued, would have confined the public service tradition to the Himalayan mountain range of high culture provision.[7]

The wind of deregulation blows not only from Brussels but also from Geneva. In 2000, the UK began new negotiations to liberalize world trade in services – including media services – under the auspices of the World Trade

Organization (WTO). The aim is to extend the scope of free trade in services that was agreed in principle (General Agreement on Trade in Services (GATS)). During the last (Uruguay) round of negotiations completed in 1993, there was a stand-off between the European Union and the United States in which the two sides agreed, in effect, to disagree over media regulation. Since then, the climate of opinion in Europe has shifted in favour of a more neo-liberal agenda. The stakes involved in the current negotiations are high. Multilateral agreements arising from it will establish legally enforceable rights, with the aim of preventing, in the words of the WTO Secretariat, future 'reversals and slippages'.

At issue is the full range of limitations on the free trade of media works. This includes national public funding of broadcasting (in principle, a distorting subsidy); EU subsidies in support of European film and television production; restrictions on the import of television programmes in Europe; national film quotas (no longer operating in Britain); lottery funding and tax relief for British film production; and prohibitions on non-EU ownership of media. The position of the British government is that it supports the extension of media free trade, and will seek to have removed US restrictions on foreign ownership of American television. At the same time, it will aim to 'avoid the undesirable outcomes that some have referred to'.[8] In short, cultural horse-trading has begun in earnest, with the US government (and American media industries) leading the charge in favour of opening up the public sector and regulated private sectors of the media to the 'liberating' blast of the free market.

Social market

The pressure to deregulate is restrained by the social market tradition. While this tradition is committed in principle to the market as the best way of organizing the media, it is inclined to be critical of the way in which the market operates in practice. This leads to demands for media regulation as a way of protecting the public from corporate abuse or market failure.

The social market tradition is the wild card in the media pack because it draws support from both New Labour and the right. It has a way of undermining or weakening the position of its natural constituency. Within the right it has caused havoc by making the case for controls, and within the left it has caused consternation by arguing in favour of market solutions. Its wayward unpredictability is perhaps best illustrated first by two policy documents produced during the Conservative era.

The key social market text of the 1980s is the Peacock Report (1986). The Peacock committee was set up to investigate whether the BBC should take advertising. It widened its brief to consider the development of the entire broadcasting system. Dominated by clever neo-liberals, the committee recommended – as expected – that 'British broadcasting should move towards a

sophisticated market system based on consumer sovereignty'.[9] It also advocated a transitional strategy of cumulative deregulation that significantly
influenced the 1990 Broadcasting Act.

Yet, instead of pressing for rapid liberalization, the Peacock Committee
surprised everybody by making a right-wing case for public service broadcasting as a necessary, short-term response to market failure. There was
insufficient advertising, it argued, to fund good programmes on both the
BBC and ITV. A ratings war between the two would reduce programme diversity and consumer choice. Subscription television was too underdeveloped to
sustain adequate minority provision. The best way of securing the benefits of
a free market, it argued, in a situation where the market was underdeveloped,
was public service policy. This is because 'collective provision or regulation of
programmes does provide [now] a better simulation of a market designed to
reflect consumer preferences than a policy of laissez-faire' because it generates a real choice of programmes.

The significance of this report, published during the height of
Thatcherism, was that it took the wind out of the growing political campaign
to fast-track deregulation. The report made in effect a short-term market
case for the BBC and regulation of commercial broadcasting. In the event,
many of its longer term proposals – to be phased in over fifteen years – for
nurturing a competitive market were ignored. New television sets were not
required to be manufactured in a form suitable for pay-TV systems; the
BBC's licence fee was not abolished; a new fall-back agency, that would channel grants towards 'programmes of a more demanding kind', was not put in
place in order to make acceptable a lurch towards deregulation. In the event,
the Peacock Report was drawn upon selectively in order to defend rather
than to destroy public service broadcasting.

The key social market document of the 1990s was the Conservative government's White Paper on *Media Ownership* (1995). The government's policy
review had been prompted by a powerful media lobby pressing for a major
liberalization of anti-monopoly controls, in the context of the rise of cable
and satellite television. There was also growing internal pressure within the
Conservative Party in favour of a media-friendly initiative, as a way of mend-
ing fences with estranged media allies. This pressure was increased by the
shifting position of the New Labour opposition, which eventually outflanked
the Conservative government from the right by urging still fewer restraints on
media concentration. It thus required social market nerves of iron to hold the
line in favour of significant anti-monopoly regulation. What resulted was an
eloquent case, marshalled by a now forgotten radical Conservative, Stephen
Dorell (then National Heritage Minister), in a notable White Paper:

A free and diverse media are an indispensable part of the democratic
process. They provide the multiplicity of voices and opinions that informs
the public, influences opinion and engenders political debate. They

promote the culture of dissent which any democracy must have. In so doing, they contribute to the cultural fabric of the nation and help define our sense of identity and purpose. If one voice becomes too powerful, this process is placed in jeopardy and democracy is damaged. Special media ownership rules . . . are needed therefore to provide safeguards necessary to maintain diversity and plurality.[10]

While the fostering of a successful and competitive media industry was an 'important objective' of public policy, 'the main objective must . . . be to secure a plurality of sources of information and opinion, and a plurality of editorial control over them'. The needs of democracy must come first.

General competition legislation, the White Paper argued, is not an adequate basis for regulating the media; it is framed primarily with economic objectives in mind, and would allow levels of media concentration that would be inappropriate given the media's strategic role in the democratic process. While the expansion in the number of media outlets makes possible some liberalization of controls on a cumulative basis, significant limits still need to be placed on the expansion of large media corporations. In the event, the White Paper's proposed limits were relaxed in response to intensive industrial lobbying when a new Heritage Minister, Virginia Bottomley, framed the 1996 Broadcasting Act, and were eased a great deal more in 2003. Even so, the 1995 White Paper remains a monument of social market thought.

A dexterous argument has since surfaced that seeks to undermine its stand. This claims that there should be a shift from structural to behavioural regulation.[11] In plain language, this means that a much greater degree of media concentration is acceptable, providing steps are taken to prevent the abuse of market power. The focus should be not on policing structures of ownership, but on preventing damaging forms of market behaviour. Thus it is entirely acceptable for a major corporation to monopolize a 'gateway technology', such as set-top boxes or electronic programme guides, providing regulatory steps are taken to ensure that competitors have access to this technology at fair prices. However, this argument ignores the still telling central point of the 1995 White Paper – namely that anti-monopoly media regulation is needed not only to maintain fair competition but also to prevent the distortion of democracy.

The most recent social market texts of importance are written by two Keynsian economists, Andrew Graham and Gavyn Davies (now Chairman of the BBC). They attempt to justify the existence of public service broadcasting in terms of market theory. Their first argument is that television has 'public good' characteristics: its programmes can be consumed – unlike a Mars bar – by an infinite number of people without incurring additional costs. A public licence fee is therefore a good way of paying for the fixed costs of broadcasting, and sharing in the cheap supply of programmes. It is, in other words, a good package deal that takes advantage of the distinctive

nature of television and radio technology. Second, extensive regulation is
needed, they argue, to cope with a built-in tendency for a small number of
companies to dominate the broadcasting market. This arises from the economic advantages of size. 'Thus, while one source of monopoly, spectrum
scarcity, has gone, it has been replaced by another – the natural monopoly of
economies of scale and of scope.'[12] Public intervention is needed more than
ever, therefore, to sustain real choice. Regulation alone is not sufficient
because regulators tend to be influenced unduly by the industries they oversee. A publicly owned organization such as the BBC is needed because it
offers 'merit goods' that set standards, and influence both the wider broadcasting industry and public demand.

These arguments clearly influenced New Labour's White Paper on communications policy (2000).[13] However, the White Paper's overt thrust was
that there should be, over time, a movement away from onerous regulation of
broadcasting in favour of self-regulation and the setting of general objectives.
But this explicitly pro-market message was wrapped in social market terms
that made clear a continuing commitment to public control of broadcasting.
Creative programme quality, impartial briefing of the electorate, maintaining
diversity of content and pluralism of voices were all seen as things that were
desirable, and not something that could be safely left to the market to achieve.
The entire document – and indeed New Labour's broadcasting policy – may
be viewed as an attempt to square a circle: a strong commitment to the
market, combined with a highly developed sense of its limitations. It is a
typical social market position that justifies – and indeed elevates – the regulator as champion of the public interest.

Media development

There is another market-oriented approach which views the state as a pro-
moter of media enterprise. Especially prominent in sections of the European
Commission, it emphasizes, as does New Labour, the importance of the communications industries as generators of wealth and employment. It also tends
to stress the significance of the media as agencies of collective self-expression
and, potentially, of European identity. Adherents of the media industrial
development approach often point to the growing deficit in audio-visual
trade between Europe and the United States, arguing that this is a measure
both of the declining competitiveness of Europe's audio-visual industries, and
of growing 'coca-colanisation' of European culture.

The underlying problem, it is argued, is that the American film and television industries have an enormous competitive advantage. Whereas European
film and television enterprise is fragmented into national industries catering
for different language publics, its American rival caters for one vast domestic
market. This enables the American majors to achieve large economies of
scale, outspend their European rivals and undercut them by price. Indeed,

after recouping their costs from their home market, American television companies can sell the overseas transmission rights of their programmes for as little as one-twentieth of the cost of making new programmes in Europe. This creates a very strong incentive to import programmes from the USA even if market research indicates a strong preference in most European countries for home-grown TV products.

The solution, in the view of this developmental approach, is for the European state to offer a helping hand to Europe's beleaguered communications industries. It should provide a co-ordinating role by facilitating the standardization of new technology. It should also subsidize indigenous film and television production, and facilitate distribution of their products.

Financial support was concentrated initially on the film industry, and took the form mainly of soft loans administered through the European Film Distribution Office. This broadened into the Media Programme, introduced in 1991, which sought to promote European co-production and improved distribution within the EU through modest subsidies. This was augmented by the Media 2 Programme, started in 1996, which attempted to encourage private investment in film and programme production. This gave way, in turn, to the Media Plus Programme, started in 2001, with a focus on training, improving transnational circulation of European audio-visual works, both inside and outside the EU, and the support of new projects arising from the development of digital technologies. The budget for the Media Plus Programme is 400 million euros for the period 2001 to 2005.[14] It operates in conjunction with the 'e-Europe' initiative designed to assist start-ups in the audio-visual sector. However, this long-term financial support has been relatively ineffectual primarily because it has given priority to supporting an integrated *European* media industry rather than developing successful media enterprise in Europe. During the period of its functioning, the American film industry greatly increased, ironically, its share of the European film market.

The second part of this approach is openly protectionist. The Television Without Frontiers Directive, introduced in 1989, required EU states to ensure where possible that over half of transmission time in television channels is given over to television programmes made in Europe. Audits conducted by the European Commission in 1996 and 1998 revealed that in most countries this quota was supported by national legislation and enforced successfully (though no attempt has been made by the British government to enforce it on BSkyB). Other, indirect forms of protectionism are also widespread. The television licence fee system, operating in most European countries, in effect channels vast sums of money into domestic television production. Britain introduced through the Independent Television Commission a little known requirement on commercial terrestrial television companies in 1993, and revised in 1998, that they 'originate' (make or commission) the majority of their television programmes in Europe. This has helped to protect Britain's position as a major programme producer, and the second biggest programme exporter in the world (after the USA).

Tensions have developed between media industrial developmental and social market approaches. This is best illustrated by conflicts, during the early 1990s, over anti-monopoly controls. In 1990 and 1992, the European Parliament called upon the European Commission to curb growing media concentration through the introduction of a new Directive that would impose a common limit on media consolidation. It was a classic social market initiative designed to impose 'best national practice' – the toughest anti-monopoly controls – as a legally enforced norm throughout the EU. The media industries counter-lobbied, seeking to turn the MEPS' initiative to their advantage by advocating permissive monopoly policy as the European norm, with the aim of undermining strong monopoly controls imposed in some nation states. They won the support of the European Commission which argued, with caveats, that increased media concentration in Europe was desirable because it made for greater international competiveness – a classic market development position.[15] Different nation states within the EU then took opposing positions, which caused the European Parliament initiative to run into the ground in the mid-1990s.

Market pluralism

Another 'market engineering' approach takes the form of assisting minority media. Its overriding objective is to promote media diversity and pluralism within the market as a way of extending consumer choice and democratic debate. Within liberal market theory, it is usually justified as a way of sustaining competition, and restoring market equilibrium, in the context of market failure.

The best known example of this approach is the press subsidies system developed in Sweden and Norway, with less ambitious versions in Austria, the Netherlands and elsewhere.[16] At the centre of the Nordic experiment is a selective subsidy extended to non-market leaders. This subsidy is allocated in relation to circulation and newsprint volume, without reference to editorial content, and is administered by a public body with all-party representation. While this approach is now running into difficulties, it has been successful over the long term in sustaining a minority political press – on both left and right – that would have been eliminated by market forces. This has helped to extend and enrich Scandinavian democracy.

What makes the Scandinavian press subsidies approach notable is that it is an attempt to restructure the terms of market competition in an entire industry in order to sustain minority voices. However, the more common version of this approach entails ad hoc interventions that try to do one of three things: to help new media to start, to assist their distribution, or to enable them to survive through the drip-feed of subsidy.

Thus the high costs of market entry are the justification for a number of schemes designed to assist new start-ups. This is typified by the subsidy available for the setting up of new newspapers in Austria. The principal way this approach is manifested in Britain is the provision of seed money for selected film projects allocated through the newly established Film Council.

Distribution exclusions are the rationale for various producer access proposals, such as giving publishers the legal right to have their lawful newspapers and magazines stocked and displayed by newsagents (as in France, Germany and Greece); and establishing new regional arts cinemas as a way of increasing the independent film sector's access to the market (inspired by municipal ownership of cinemas in Norway). The most significant form in which this approach has been developed in Britain is the requirement (consolidated by the 1990 Broadcasting Act) that terrestrial television organizations take 25 per cent of their programming from independent production companies.

In addition, there are a number of proposals for ongoing subsidies for media judged to be a public good. A recent unexpected convert to this approach is the Radio Authority, in the twilight of its life. Surveying the failure of community radio to take off in a permanent form, it concluded with the suggestion that financial support should be made available for small-scale, radio broadcasting. Possible sources of finance, it suggested, could be revenue from the cash payments made by national commercial radio licensees or a levy on radio advertising.[17] The principal current beneficiaries of this type of subsidy in Britain are theatres supported by the Arts Council.

In general, this approach usually involves piecemeal interventions within particular industries. What has not yet been attempted is an integrated approach that surveys all communications industries, and considers how best to support, with limited funds, media pluralism. This would lead almost certainly to the identification of low-cost media sectors where public money would go a long way in supporting clearly identified objectives. It is perhaps a task that the newly established Office of Communications should undertake.

Public service approach

While the traditional market approach is concerned with satisfying the wants of the individual consumer, the public service approach is concerned with serving the needs of society. In essence, this comes down to three things: serving the needs of democracy, generating content that has cultural value, and promoting social inclusion.

The locus of public service loyalty used to be exclusively the BBC. But as the public service system has developed over time, so it has come to mean not only the BBC but also regulated commercial broadcasting and Channel 4 (a public trust). It comprises that part of the broadcasting system which has a legal obligation to serve the welfare of society.

While the general justification for public service broadcasting has been referred to in different places in this book, it may be helpful to summarize here its main themes.

First, public service broadcasting is committed to reporting the news impartially, and to giving due prominence to coverage of public affairs. It thus ensures that people are briefed properly to exercise their rights and obligations as citizens, and contributes to the healthy functioning of the democratic system. In contrast, market-driven media tend to shrink news in favour of entertainment, offer 'infotainment' instead of informative analysis, and follow private and partisan agendas. Compare, argue public service advocates, the quality of BBC's or ITN's news service with that of the 'bingo-jingo' tabloids.

Second, public service broadcasting maintains high programme standards and contributes to the cultural resources of society, rather than merely offering what is profitable. It seeks to democratize culture by making widely available the best works of literature, drama, art and music. It aims to renew and develop cultural tradition by supporting innovation and experiment. Above all, it is committed to catering for the diversity of the public, the enthusiasms of minorities, as well as of the majority. It responds to the breadth of public taste rather than its lowest common denominator.

Third, public service broadcasting is preferable because it is best at binding together and integrating an increasingly privatized society. It ensures that everyone has access to a shared, unifying experience, because it does not discriminate against outlying areas or low income groups on the grounds of cost or profitability. Its approach is inclusive, seeking to draw together society in its diversity and to frame public discussion in terms of what serves the general good. In addition, because it invests in making programmes rather than relying, like BSkyB, on cheap imports, it maintains a cultural space through which society can express itself and define its collective identity.

Supporters of the public service system have felt increasingly beleaguered as they have watched the advancing tide of market liberalism penetrate the institutions of public service broadcasting, and weaken its functioning. However, the public service sector of British broadcasting still enjoys widespread public and political support. The public service tradition also enjoys strong support in Europe, a key form of protection. This was manifested when public broadcasters combined in the 1990s to persuade Europe's political leadership to amend explicitly the EU's free trade rules. In 1997, a Protocol was annexed to the EU Treaty of Amsterdam endorsing the public funding of broadcasting for public service objectives. This was secured with two purposes in mind – to contain the alliance of neo-liberals within the European Commission and the private media industry lobby, and to define Europe's negotiating position in the post-Uruguay development of international trade regulation.

Political manoeuvres now need to be accompanied, argue public service radicals, by reforms that enhance the actual performance of public service broadcasting. In Britain, one key issue is how best to defend the political independence of the BBC. All those appointed to chair the BBC during the Conservative ascendancy were government supporters. Indeed, Marmaduke Hussey, a long-standing chairman of the BBC (1986 to 1996) was a brother-in-law of a Cabinet minister; Stuart Young, his predecessor (1983 to 1986), was a brother of a Cabinet minister. The new chairman of the BBC, Gavyn Davies, appointed by New Labour, is predictably a New Labour insider.

The appointments system has become corrupted, and needs to be reformed. The best way to achieve this is to remove control of broadcasting appointments (including the boards of OFCOM as well as the BBC) from government, and to establish an independent appointments committee, with elected representatives from broadcasting staff and nominees from leading civic and social organizations. A further way of shoring up the independence of the BBC is to replace its royal charter – subject to periodic renewal, usually accompanied by pre-renewal, government intimidation – with its formal establishment through an Act of Parliament. After over eighty years of distinguished service, the BBC should no longer be considered a probationer on a temporary contract.

A second issue is how best to insulate programme-makers working in commercial television organizations from increasingly overwhelming commercial pressures. Here, the best strategy is to extend positive programme regulation – a commitment to quality, information, innovation, origination and diversity – to the entire television system, including cable and satellite television. Pressure should also be exerted to discourage the Office of Communications from moving from formal regulation towards self-regulation. Formal regulation creates spaces in which programme-makers can achieve some freedom from the market; self-regulation in a commercial, ratings-dominated context will cause these spaces to contract.

The third issue has to do with revising the public purpose and legacy of British broadcasting. Traditionally, the British public service approach has delegated considerable decision-making power to programme-makers at the level of producer. This is because the British model is more independent of the market than the US broadcasting system and more independent of civil society than the representative-ridden structures of mainstream European broadcasting. There is much to be said for this British approach since it makes for programme quality.

However, this distinctive British approach also has weaknesses, which its more complacent champions overlook. British television is very insular – much more so than, say, Norwegian or Swedish television. It tends to under-represent the diversity of British society as a consequence of being excessively metropolitan and linked too closely to Britain's political élite.

Yet there are reformist tendencies within the broadcasting community which are seeking to improve the system from within. Their agenda of reform includes: cultivating a more international orientation suitable for a globalized world; developing innovative forms of journalism that involve greater audience participation or a wider net of news sources; making programmes that connect to a greater diversity of ethnic, subcultural and ideological communities; and exploiting digital television to extend minority provision. The wider community should strengthen the position of reformers by reformulating the public purpose of broadcasting. This should take the form of adopting a new objective, to be adopted in the next broadcasing bill to go before Parliament: a commitment to give adequate expression to the different viewpoints and concerns of the public. In other words, representative pluralism should become a statutory aim of the British public service tradition. Broadcasters' existing public duty to inform should also be amended to make explicit reference to events and trends outside Britain.

Radical visions

Over the years, a number of radical visions have been advanced for the root-and-branch reform of the media system. While these have no chance of being implemented in the prevailing political climate, they are worth alluding to in order to keep in play alternative ways of thinking about the organization of the media. Socialist and liberal versions of this visionary tradition are best represented, respectively, by Raymond Williams and John Keane.[18]

The late Raymond Williams argued that collective control over the means of mass communication was needed to further a 'cultural revolution', based on a universal right to transmit and receive information. This would enable people to grow in the power to direct their own lives, extend collective understanding through the exchange of experience, and develop 'the capacity for personal and independent response and choice'.

Broadcasting, according to Williams, has been stunted by authoritarian, commercial and paternal forms of organization. The untried alternative is a 'democratic' one. The BBC and commercial broadcasting should be replaced by public trusts which would own production and transmission facilities on behalf of society and lease these, on long-term contracts, to independent companies which would control programme-making. These companies would be run by broadcasters in a democratic way, not by administrators who would be required to work within the framework of 'elected policy'.

Similarly, newspapers should be acquired by newspaper trusts and leased to their editors and journalists. Newsprint companies should be in separate public ownership, and provide supplies at a 'fair and open price'. Within this system, working journalists should determine editorial policy.

The underlying principle behind this proposed reorganization is that 'the active contributors [should] have control over their own means of expression'. When the means of expression are so costly that they are beyond their means to own, society should step in to enable them to exercise control over their own work. This form of public intervention is enabling, since it secures the freedom of journalists and creative staff and protects them 'alike from the bureaucrat and the speculator'.

By contrast, John Keane approaches the task of restructuring the media from the perspective of a radical liberal who, in his own words, 'acknowledges the facts of complexity, diversity and difference, and – in plain English – harbours doubts about whether any one person, group, committee, party or organisation can be trusted to make superior choices on matters of concern to citizens'. What is needed, in his view, is a pluralistic media system which involves different people in different ways in overseeing the exercise of power in society. Only some media, he suggests, should be subject to what he calls 'the time-consuming and unwieldy procedures of direct democracy', the strategy favoured by Williams.

Yet despite their differences of approach, both Williams and Keane tread rather similar paths. They both mount a critique of market and state-linked media. They both seek to create media that are independent – what Keane calls in a Germanic formulation 'non-market-non-state media institutions'. In both cases, this results in the search for self-effacing forms of public intervention that are positively enabling. In Keane's case, this means 'a wide range of different regulated markets for different audiences and services'. These could include, among other things, time-share and common carrier arrangements with private media corporations; the funding of local independent cinemas, recording studios, and lease-back broadcasting facilities; subsidized political newspapers; co-operatively run publishers and distributors; and even a reformed BBC.

However, the 'third route' rhetoric of both Williams and Keane raises almost as many questions as it answers. One unresolved issue is how state involvement is to be reined back in the way they both want. The intricate cat's-cradle of subsidies, allocations, interventions, regulations and market suspensions outlined by Keane would lead, in fact, to a very extensive exercise of authority over the media by agencies that are part of the state. The same is true, to a lesser extent, of Williams's scheme. He assumes mistakenly that leasing the technical means of communication, on long-term contracts, to communicator-controlled consortia will enable 'public trusts' to take a back seat. In fact these trusts or some other public agency would have to fund these consortia initially, and decide whether to support them if they ran into financial trouble. By default, public authorities would exercise some of the power exercised formerly by what Williams calls revealingly 'functionless financial groups' within the market system. This is not to imply that public agency involvement necessarily leads to state editorial control, since checks and balances can be introduced in order to avoid this. But the radical public service approach often invokes an anti-statist rhetoric that sits uneasily with what it actually proposes. It also pays too little detailed attention to ways of preventing the abuse of state power, by conveniently excising this danger through the use of emollient words such as 'enabling' and 'facilitating'.

The second key issue is who should be entrusted with control over the media. Raymond Williams argued that control should lie with professional communicators since 'any restriction of the freedom of individual contribution' is a restriction on the freedom of society. But why should professional communicators, who are unrepresentative of society and often surprisingly uninformed about their audiences even within market systems, be established as a communications élite with exclusive rights of control over the media? Indeed, why should they be elevated above others in the same organization, rather in the manner of the Master and Fellows of Oxbridge Colleges (a mandarin élite to which Williams himself belonged)? Different people within the radical tradition give different answers to these questions. Some syndicalists favour workers' control in different spheres of operation, with media staff controlling the editorial process, and production workers controlling the production process. In Tom Baistow's view, editors or their equivalent should function as trustees of the public interest, and their autonomy should be legally protected from private employers and trade unions alike. Others, still, argue for consumer, party, social group, professional or local community representation in the organization of the media. For example, the Militant Tendency, a Trotskyist organization, proposes that broadcasting and newspaper organizations should be allocated to political parties in accordance with the votes cast in the previous general election, while magazines should be handed over to scientific, technical and professional organizations – a scheme that leaves little scope for the voice of the consumer, and excludes organizations that the Militant Tendency regards as 'undemocratic'. By contrast, John Keane beguilingly argues, as we have seen, that different media should be controlled by different people in different ways.

The dominant view is that media workers' power should be balanced in some way by the rights of the public. This still leaves open how much influence media workers should have, and in what form. The basic options in ascending order of significance are: staff entitlement to information; the right to be consulted about major decisions; participation in senior appointments; representation on decision-making committees (editorial committees, boards of management, supervisory boards and so on); regular staff elections to senior management posts; and full workers' control.

These blue-sky debates seem completely removed from the reality of pragmatic, market-oriented media politics steered by governments with an overdeveloped sensitivity to what powerful media organizations want; yet wider debate can open up new avenues of thought and action. In the 1970s, a growing volume of criticism directed against the comfortable (small 'c') conservative duopoly of the BBC and ITV gave rise to a search for a new way of doing public service broadcasting. This open debate – involving people from different ideological and political homes – led to an informed consensus in favour of creating a new form of public service organization: a 'publishing house' which would commission rather than make programmes. It would be innovative, serve minorities, and extend the ideological spectrum (though this latter idea was largely missing from the 'official' literature). The concept won the backing of the Annan Committee, the support of the outgoing Labour (Callaghan) government, and of the first Thatcher administration, with the result that Channel 4 was born in 1982. The public service tradition became richer as a consequence of this addition.

Perhaps the time has now come to concentrate on how the internet may be developed further in a public service form. The internet offers certain technological capabilites that can be used to public advantage; it is global; it is interactive, enabling potentially many-to-many dialogue, instead of a one-way flow of communication; and it operates at relatively low cost. It is ideally suited as a way of developing an international debate about matters – from the global environment to religious conflict – that concern us all. Because it is interactive, it is also plainly a key tool in building an international public sphere that can monitor, and seek to hold to account, the new system of international power and regulation that has taken shape.

The Ford Foundation committed, in 2002 to 2003, over a million dollars to a modest, British-based website, openDemocracy, started by Anthony Barnett (founder of Charter 88, arguably the most influential pressure group in Britain in the 1990s). The Foundation recognized the potential of the internet to host an international debate, and wanted to facilitate a greater dialogue between Americans and people outside the USA, after 11 September. The resulting, exciting project indicates what can be achieved.[19]

Where one charitable organization initiated, other organizations with more resources and a wider agenda should follow. Developing and maintaining a website, commissioning new contributions on a regular basis, organizing translations, moderating interactive debates, making these debates known through promotion, takes time and money. The international organization, with the status and resources best able to achieve this, is the United Nations. It should be encouraged to initiate a global public service internet magazine, though on an arms-length basis free from the stifling control of its bureaucracy. There could also be a second tier of continent-based, public service internet media. The European state has the resources – and the incentive of a Europe-building agenda – to make this a reality.

Basis of legal debate

So far, we have focused mainly on policy discussion concerned with media organization. Overlaying this discussion is another, related debate concerned with media law. Libertarians in this legal debate stress the importance of freedom of expression, and the public's right to know the basis on which all decisions affecting the common good are made. Paternalists tend to emphasize other concerns such as the right to a fair trial, national security, a good reputation, privacy and freedom from crime. The main dispute between them is about where the balance should be struck between these competing rights. Their debate is often informed by different perceptions of the public. Paternalists tend to emphasize the susceptibility of vulnerable members of the public to media control, while libertarians tend to stress the critical independence of media audiences.

There is also another axis of contention. Some paternalists argue that the media should be prevented from violating the norms and moral values of society. This goes beyond the standard case for limited censorship, based on preventing serious harm from being done to others, and potentially constitutes a rationale for a broad measure of control directed against anything that is deemed offensive. Libertarians respond to this challenge in different ways. Some reject the argument outright: liberty, argued George Orwell, means letting people say things you do not want to hear. Others demur by saying that a communication has to be offensive to *reasonable* people. Others, still, negotiate by making a distinction between media that are ubiquitous and those that are less intrusive, and between media that reach a general audience and those that are seen only by adults. In general, they suggest, it is better to restrict access to a communication than to suppress it entirely.

Legal paternalism

During the 1980s and early 1990s, the tide generally flowed in favour of greater legal and moral controls. The Video Recordings Act (1984) introduced a far-reaching system of censorship directed at 'video nasties'. The Broadcasting Standards Council was established in 1988 to provide a focus of public concern about sex, violence, and standards of taste and decency in broadcasting. It was strengthened by being given the power to compel transmission of its indictments in 1990, and was merged with the Broadcasting Complaints Council in 1996. Broadcasters were required by the 1990 Broadcasting Act not to transmit programmes offensive to public feeling. However, an attempt by the British government to secure moral regulation of broadcasting through concerted European action met with only limited success due to the resistance of some of Britain's partners. The most significant moral injunction in the 1989 Television Without Frontiers Directive is that directed against 'programmes which might seriously impair the . . . development of minors'. Conservative administrations also exerted strong pressure, both through private channels and through public flak, for broadcasters to censor themselves, most notably in relation to Northern Ireland. When this encountered some resistance, a gagging prohibition was imposed in 1988 on direct transmissions of speech from

Sinn Fein and other 'terrorist' organizations until public policy changed with the establishment of a ceasefire in Northern Ireland.

This growth of prohibition and moral regulation did not go far enough in the view of some. Obscenity and indecency laws should be strengthened in order to outlaw widely available pornographic images of women and gratuitous media displays of violence. The rationale for this is not necessarily that violence shown on television leads in a stimulus–response fashion to imitative acts. The more sophisticated argument is that routine exposure to violence on television strengthens already existing dispositions towards violence, both in particular individuals and in the culture of society; and that pornography reinforces mysogenistic attitudes, and consequently encourages harmful actions against women. But if some of these arguments appear plausible, they are also difficult to verify empirically. There is still, in Cumberbatch and Howitt's phrase, 'a measure of uncertainty' about the consequences of media pornography and violence.[20]

The second argument for taking tougher action against pornogaphy is that it is offensive; it is experienced as oppressive; it demeans with its constant suggestion of women's availability; and it encourages scorn and contempt. The counter-arguments are that safeguards already exist against the most offensive forms of pornography; suppressing freedom of speech is objectionable; and over-zealous puritanism may also be viewed as repressive.

Calls for stronger controls against sexism are paralleled by demands for greater protection against racism. Legislation against incitement to racial hatred was introduced in 1965 in the wake of Labour's loss of the safe seat, Smethwick, with the help of the slogan, 'If you want a nigger for a neighbour, vote Labour'. However, prosecutions are usually only successful if it can be shown that racist statements are likely to lead to actual violence or a breakdown of public order. The Tabachnik Report from the Board of Deputies of British Jews (1992) argued that legislation should be strengthened by extending to social groups the same protection against defamation that is currently available to individuals. The counter-argument to this is that it would lead to a substantial extension of censorship, and could be counterproductive in fanning rather than subduing the flames of hatred and intolerance.

An area where curbs are most often pressed is privacy. Until recently, the right to privacy was legally protected only indirectly through copyright, property and confidentiality law. The second Calcutt enquiry (1992) recommended the establishment of a statutory press complaints tribunal with the power to impose prior restraint (i.e. pre-publication censorship) against unwarranted press intrusions into privacy – a proposal rejected both by the Major government and the then Labour opposition. However, in 1998, the European Convention of Human Rights was passed into British law as the Human Rights Act. It contains a clause that 'everyone has the right to respect for his private and family life, his home and his correspondence',[21] balanced by the right of freedom of expression. This countervailing right was accentuated in an amendment to the Human Rights Bill, framed in response to press pressure, that directs the courts to pay special attention to freedom of expression. What is now likely to happen is that a privacy right against the media will emerge in a weak form through cumulative judicial judgement.

Legal libertarianism

Those who press for more censorship are answered by those who argue for less. Heading the libertarian agenda is a proposal that freedom of expression should be given special protection by being embodied in a written constitution. Free speech, it is argued, is under increasing attack and needs to be entrenched as a constitutional right. This would mean, for example, that the BBC could turn to the lawcourts for protection if it felt that its freedom was being curtailed improperly by government. Opponents argue that this reform would be alien to the legal and political tradition of this country. Its effect would be to force judges to make 'political' decisions, a task to which they are unsuited.

In general, the tide flowed during the late 1990s and early 2000s towards cautious libertarianism. A major objective of the libertarian movement – a Freedom of Information Act – was passed in 2000, but will not become fully operational until January 2005. It establishes the right to any official information unless the government or public authority can show that disclosure would cause real harm to essential interests such as defence, security, law enforcement or privacy. The continuing concern of campaigners is that exclusions should not be unduly restrictive in practice. They are also pressing for more disclosure in the private sector, if the information is of public interest.

A second target is reform of the 1989 Official Secrets Act. This replaced the blunderbuss of the discredited 1911 Official Secrets Act with an armalite rifle designed to deter, it is claimed, legitimate whistle-blowers and proper investigation. It leaves informants such as Sarah Tisdall (gaoled in 1984 for leaking information to the *Guardian* about how the government proposed to manage public opinion when the first US cruise missile was sited in Britain) liable to prosecution, even though their offence was to embarrass the government rather than undermine security. Libertarian critics argue that the Act should be replaced with a narrower measure applying only where disclosure would cause serious damage to defence, security, international relations, law enforcement or safety, and that crucially it should contain a full public interest defence for breaches of official secrets. The counter-argument to this is that public servants should be deterred from breaching their position of trust, and the weakening of official security would hamper the war against terrorism.

In the general battle over media law, legal libertarians have the best tunes. They have developed an eloquent rhetoric in which media freedom is equated with the freedom of society. On the one side, there is the cause of freedom and the people; on the other, there is repression by authority supported by secrecy and censorship. But what is generally concealed in this rhetorical presentation is that media freedom is usually defined in practice as the free speech rights of media property owners, and those they appoint. What is being argued for, in reality, is an enlargement of their rights at the expense of other rights, on the grounds that this is in the general interest.

This case is often powerful because the cause of freedom is compelling. But the limitations of this case are also highlighted when the issue at stake is *whose* free speech should be upheld. In the late 1970s and early 1980s, Fleet Street workers took industrial action on several occasions to secure the right of reply for targets of press attacks. From 1981 onward, a number of MPs proposed private members' bills, with cross-party support, that would give to victims of press distortion or factual misrepresentation a legal right to secure published corrections, broadly in line with right-of-reply laws in a number of northern European countries. Both of these initiatives sought to enlarge rather than restrict freedom of communication through the press. In both cases, they were strongly resisted as an attack on the free speech rights of press controllers to determine what goes into their newspapers. This under-lined the sometimes exclusive nature of the freedom which uncritical libertarians present as universal.

A quizzical response also seems appropriate in the wake of attempts to strengthen the rights of media staff. These have defined implicitly the freedom *of* the media as including freedom *within* the media. Generally, they have taken a modest form such as the proposal that journalists should have a right of conscience recognized in their contracts of employment. Yet these pro-posals have been consistently opposed by the National Publishers Association. The freedom of the press remains the freedom of the people who own it, however it is presented.

Map of media politics

Policy discussion about media organization is dominated by the debate between advocates of the free market and public service. One side calls for the media to be free of regulation other than the law of the land. The other side sings the praises of the British broadcasting system, and declares it to be the best in the world. Between these two polarities of market radicalism and public service complacency are a number of intermediate positions that we have explored. They tend to be associated, however, with either a market or public service tradition.

There is also another discussion concerned specifically with media law. Here, the main split is between paternalists who want society to be protected from irresponsible media, and libertarians who emphasize the need to uphold freedom of expression. This second division cuts across the first. This produces four clearly identifiable groups occupying different quadrants, set out below in ideal-typical terms.

The authoritarian right generally want the media to be deregulated in the economic sphere but to be subject to stronger legal restraint. They are responding to what they see as a basic problem: the tendency of the free market to promote ever more media violence, increased pornography, individualistic values weakening moral order, and in some contexts dangerously subversive views. Their response to this dilemma is to press ahead in advancing market freedom but to take tough steps in curbing its 'ill effects'; for example, they favour selling TV channels to the highest bidder, but introducing stronger moral censorship.

Those on the libertarian-inclined left reverse this logic. They favour greater public service regulation of the media, while seeking to minimize direct legal controls. Market censorship is, in their view, an important way in which the media are restricted. They seek therefore to lift market restriction through public service regulation that opens up channels of free self-expression and democratic debate. Their desire also to reduce political and moral censorship imposed through the courts is not, in their view, inconsistent. They are advancing twin ways of building a more pluralistic media system.

The libertarian right – represented by some in the 'modernizing tendency' of the Conservative Party – follow a different route. They are 'joined-up' libertarians, committed to minimizing the role of the state in all aspects of the media. Indeed, they subscribe to the classic republican view that the role of the state should be confined to that of 'nightwatchman'. They are thus consistent in arguing against both 'bureaucratic' regulation of the media, and also heavy-handed moral and political censorship.

In the final quadrant, the paternalist left – represented by some feminists and some activist members of the 'new municipal left' – favour a strong state in both private and public spheres. They support public ownership and regulation of broadcasting. However, they also favour a stronger legal stand against pornography and racial hatred, and expect institutions of the state, both nationally and locally, to promote a moral order based on mutuality and social respect.

In short, the simple dichotomy of left and right no longer describes adequately the politics of the media. To add to this complexity, the sphere of media politics now operates at three levels: the nation state (still the most important), the European Union, and the global politics of international trade regulation. Indeed, because the world of media politics is increasingly complex and shifting, it is possible to hope that we can build a better media system – one that combines power *with* responsibility to the people.

Notes

1. Samuel Brittan, 'The case for the consumer market', in C. Veljanovski (ed.) *Freedom in Broadcasting* (London, Institute of Economic Affairs, 1989), p. 35.

2. *Regulating Communications* (London, Stationery Office, 1998), p. 16.

3. *A New Future for Communications* (London, Stationery Office, 2000), p. 95.

4. Adam Smith Institute, *Omega Report: Communications Policy* (London, Adam Smith Institute, 1984); Adam Smith Institute, *Funding the BBC* (London, Adam Smith Institute, 1985).

5. Rupert Murdoch, *Freedom in Broadcasting* (London, News International, 1989), p. 9.

6. Cited in Graham Murdock and Peter Golding, 'Digital possibilities, market realities: the contradictions of communications convergence', in Leo Panitch and Colin Leys (eds) *A World of Contradictions* [Socialist Register 2002] (London, Merlin, 2001),p. 116.

7. Colin Leys, *Market-Driven Politics* (London, Verso, 2001), p. 148.

8. *Liberalising Trade in Services: A New Consultation on the World Trade Organisation GATS Negotiations* (London, Department of Trade and Industry, 2002).

9. *Report of the Committee on Financing the BBC* (London, HMSO, 1986).

10. *Media Ownership* (London, HMSO, 1995), p. 3.

11. For a useful exposition of behavioural regulation arguments, see David Goldberg, Tony Prosser and Stefaan Verhulst, *Regulating the Changing Media* (Oxford, Clarendon Press, 1998).

12. Andrew Graham and Gavyn Davies, *Broadcasting, Society and Policy in the Multimedia Age* (Luton, University of Luton Press, 1997), p.1.

13. *A New Future for Communications* (London, Stationery Office, 2000), p. 50.

14. Stylianos Papathanassopoulos, *European Television in the Digital Age* (London, Sage, 2002), p.18.

15. *Pluralism and Media Concentration in the Internal Market: Commission Green Paper* (Brussels, Commission of the European Communities Green Paper, 1992); *Follow-Up to the Consultative Process Relating to the Green Paper on 'Pluralism and Media Concentration in the Internal Market'* (Brussels, Commission of the European Communities, 1994); cf. S*trategy Options to Strengthen the European Programme Industry in the Context of the Audiovisual Policy of the European Union* (Brussels, European Commission Green Paper, 1994).

16. P. Murschetz, 'State support for the daily press in Europe: a critical appraisal', *European Journal of Communication*, 13 (3), 1998; E. Skogerbo, 'The press subsidy system in Norway', *European Journal of Communication*, 12 (1), 1997.

17. *A New Future for Communications* (London, Stationery Office, 2000), p. 40.

18. Raymond Williams, *Communications* (London, Chatto & Windus, rev. edn, 1966); John Keane, *Media and Democracy* (Cambridge, Polity Press, 1991). For an alternative version of this tradition, not summarized here, see James Curran, *Media and Power* (London, Routledge, 2002), Chapter 8.

19. I should declare an interest as someone involved, peripherally, in its initial development. An assessment of its significance is provided in James Curran, 'Global journalism: a case study of the internet', in Nick Couldry and James Curran (eds) *Contesting Media Power* (Boulder, CO, Rowman & Littlefield, 2003).

20. Guy Cumberbatch and Denis Howitt, *A Measure of Uncertainty* (London, Libbey, 1989); cf. Brian McNair, *Mediated Sex* (London, Arnold, 1996).
21. Cited in Eric Barendt and Lesley Hitchens, *Media Law: Cases and Materials* (Harlow, Longman, 2000), p. 248.

Bibliography

Public reports and papers

Broadcasting

Broadcasting Committee: Report (Sykes Report, 1923) [Cmd 1951].
Report of the Broadcasting Committee (Crawford Report, 1926) [Cmd 2599].
Report of the Television Committee (Selsdon Report, 1935) [Cmd 3703].
Report of the Broadcasting Committee (Ullswater Report, 1936) [Cmd 5091].
Report of the Television Committee (Hankey Report, 1944) (Privy Council Office).
Broadcasting Policy (1946) [Cmd 6852].
Report of the Broadcasting Committee (Beveridge Report, 1951) [Cmd 8116].
Report of the Broadcasting Committee 1949 (1951/2) [Cmd 8117].
Broadcasting, Memorandum on the Report of the Broadcasting Committee (1951) [Cmd 8291].
Broadcasting, Memorandum on the Report of the Broadcasting Committee, 1949 (1952) [Cmd 8550].
The Television Act 1954, 2 & 3 Eliz. II, c. 55.
Report of the Committee on Broadcasting (Pilkington Report, 1962) [Cmnd 1753].
The Television Act 1964, 12 & 13 Eliz. II, c. 21.
The University of the Air (1966) [Cmnd 2992].
An Alternative Service of Radio Broadcasting (1971) [Cmnd 4636].
Sound Broadcasting Act 1972, 19 & 20 Eliz. II, c. 31.
Session 1971–2 Independent Broadcasting Authority, Sub-Committee B, House of Commons Paper 465 (1972).
Observations on the Second Report of the Select Committee of the Nationalized Industries (1973) [Cmnd 5244].
Report of the Committee on the Future of Broadcasting (Annan Report, 1977) [Cmnd 6753].
Radio Choices and Opportunities (1982) [Cm 92].
Broadcasting without Frontiers, EEC paper, No. 9 (1984).
Report of the Committee on Financing the BBC (Peacock Report, 1986) [Cmnd 9824].
Subscription Television: A Study for the Home Office (London, HMSO, 1987).
Radio: Choices and Opportunities (1987) [Cm 92].
Broadcasting in the '90s: Competition, Choice and Quality (1987) [Cm 517].
The Future of Broadcasting, Home Affairs Committee (1988).

Broadcasting Bill, House of Commons (1989).

The Future of Broadcasting, House of Commons Home Affairs Committee 1987–8 (London, HMSO, 1988).

Broadcasting Act 1990 (London, HMSO, 1990).

The Future of the BBC (Department of National Heritage, London, HMSO, 1992) [Cm 2098].

Broadcasting Act 1996 (London, HMSO, 1996).

Independent Television Commission Annual Report (London, ITC, 2001).

European Audiovisual Observatory Yearbook 2002 (Strasbourg, Council of Europe, 2002), Vol. 2.

Television Audience Share Figures (London, Independent Television Commission, 2002).

The press

Annual Report of the Press Council (London, Press Council, 1985).

Competition Commission, *Johnson Press plc and Trinity Mirror plc: A Report into the Proposed Merger* (London, Stationery Office, 2002) [Cm 5495].

Department for Culture, Media and Sport (DCMS), *Consultation on Media Ownership Rules* (London, DCMS, 2001).

Monopolies Commission (1965–6), *The Times Newspaper and Sunday Times* (London, HMSO, 1966).

Monopolies Commission (1967–8), *Thomson Newspapers and Crusha and Son Ltd,* House of Commons Paper 66 (London, HMSO, 1968).

Monopolies Commission (1969–70), *George Outram and Company Ltd and Hamilton Advertiser Ltd and Baird and Hamilton Ltd,* House of Commons Paper 76 (London, HMSO, 1970).

Monopolies Commission (1971–2), *The Berrows Organisation Ltd and the County Express Group,* House of Commons Paper 224 (London, HMSO, 1972).

Monopolies Commission (1972–3), *Westminster Press Ltd and Kentish Times Ltd, Gravesend and Dartford Reporter Ltd and F. J. Parsons Ltd, Subsidiaries of Morgan-Grampian Ltd,* House of Commons Paper 460 (London, HMSO, 1973).

Monopolies Commission (1973–4), *Courier Printing and Publishing Company Ltd and Associated Newspapers Group Ltd,* House of Commons Paper 108 (London, HMSO, 1974).

Monopolies Commission (1974–5), *G. and A. N. Scott Ltd and The Guardian and Manchester Evening News Ltd,* House of Commons Paper 349 (London, HMSO, 1975).

Monopolies and Mergers Commission, *The Supply of National Newspapers* (London, HMSO, 1993).

Monopolies and Mergers Commission, *Daily Mail and General Trust Plc. and T. Bailey Forman Limited* (London, HMSO, 1994).

Monopolies and Mergers Commission, *Northcliffe Newspapers and Aberdeen Journals Ltd* (London, HMSO, 1996).

Monopolies and Mergers Commission, *The Observer and George Outram* (London, HMSO, 1981).

Monopolies and Mergers Commission, *Wholesaling of Newspapers and Periodicals* (London, HMSO, 1978).

National Board for Prices and Incomes, *Wages, Costs and Prices in the Printing Industry* (1965) [Cmnd 2750].

National Board for Prices and Incomes, *Costs and Revenue of National Daily Newspapers* (1967) [Cmnd 3435].

National Board for Prices and Incomes, *Journalists' Pay* (1969) [Cmnd 4077].

National Board for Prices and Incomes, *Costs and Revenue of National Newspapers* (1970) [Cmnd 4277].

Privacy and Media Intrusion (National Heritage Committee, House of Commons, 1992–3, HMSO, 1993).

Privacy and Media Intrusion: The Government's Response (London, HMSO, 1995).

Report of the Committee on Contempt of Court (1975) [Cmnd 5794].

Report of the Committee on Data Protection (Lindop Committee, 1978) [Cmnd 7341].

Report of the Committee on Defamation (Faulks Committee, 1975) [Cmnd 5571].

Report of the Committee on the Official Secrets Act (1972) [Cmnd 7140].

Report of the Committee on Privacy and Related Matters (Calcutt Committee, 1990) [Cm 1102].

Report of a Court of Inquiry into the Problems Caused by the Introduction of Web-offset Machines (1967) [Cmnd 3184].

Review of Press Self-Regulation (1993) [Cm 2135].

Royal Commission on the Press 1947–9 Report (1949) [Cmnd 7700].

Royal Commission on the Press 1961–2 Report (1962) [Cmnd 1811].

Royal Commission on the Press Interim Report (1976) [Cmnd 6553].

Royal Commission on the Press 1974–7 Final Report (1977) [Cmnd 6810].

Royal Commission on the Press Final Report Appendices (1977) [Cmnd 6810–1–6].

Select Committee of the House of Commons on Newspaper Stamps, *Parliamentary Papers*, xvii (1851).

Film

Cinematograph Films Act (1927) [Cmnd 2053].

Report of the Committee appointed by the Board of Trade (Moyne Report, 1936) [Cmnd 2053].

Report on Tendencies to Monopoly in the Cinematograph Film Industry (Palache Report, 1944) [Cmnd 4059].

Report of the Working Party on Film Production Costs (Gater Report, 1949) [Cmnd 7837].

Report of the Committee on the Distribution and Exhibition of Cinematograph Films (Plant Report, 1949) [Cmnd 7837].

Cinematograph Films Council, Distribution and Exhibition of Cinematograph Films (London, HMSO, Board of Trade, 1950).

Cinematograph Films Bill 1960, 8 & 9 Eliz. II.

The Films Act, House of Commons Paper 206 (1960).

Board of Trade Review of Films Legislation (1968) [Cmnd 3584].

The Prime Minister's Working Party on the Future of the Film Industry (Wilson Report, 1976) [Cmnd 6372].

Report of the Committee on Film Finance (1985) [Cmnd 7610].

Monopolies and Mergers Commission, *Report on the Supply of Films for Exhibition* (London, HMSO, 1994).

The British Film Industry (National Heritage Select Committee, House of Commons, 1995) (London, HMSO, 1995).

Media and information

A New Future for Communications (London, Stationery Office, 2000) [Cm 5010].

Commission of the European Communities (1994) *The EU and the Globalisation of Technology* (Forecasting in Science and Technology Report) (EUR 15150, Brussels).

Commission of the European Communities (1996) *Culture, Homes and the use of Information Technology* (EC EUR 174011, Brussels).

Europe and the Global Information Society (Bangemann Report) (Brussels, European Council, 1994).

Consumers' Use of the Internet, Oftel Residential Survey, May (Office of Telecommunications, London, 2002).

Follow-up to the Consultative Process Relating to the Green Paper on 'Pluralism and Media Concentration in the Internal Market' (Brussels, Commission of the European Communities, 1994).

Globalization of the Mass Media (Washington, United States Department of Commerce, 1993).

Liberalising Trade in Services: A New Consultation on the World Trade Organisation GATS Negotiations (London, Department of Trade and Industry, 2002).

Media Ownership: The Government's Proposals (Department of National Heritage, London, HMSO, 1995).

Pluralism and Media Concentration in the Internal Market (Brussels, Commission of the European Communities Green Paper, 1992).

Regulating Communications: Approaching Convergence in the Information Age (London, Stationery Office, 1998) [Cm 4022].

Report by the Think-Tank on the Audiovisual Policy in the European Union (Vasconcelos Report) (Luxembourg, Commission of the European Communities, 1994).

Strategy Options to Strengthen the European Programme Industry in the Context of the Audiovisual Policy of the European Union (Brussels, European Commission Green Paper, 1994).

Miscellaneous public reports referred to in the book

Parliamentary Debates (1918–60; 1940–43) (London, Hansard).

Machinery of Government Report (1918) [Cmnd 9230].

Board of Education, *Inspectors' Report* (1932) [Cmnd 4068].

Board of Education Consultative Committee on Secondary Education (Spens Report, 1938), 10/119.

Report of the Department Committee on Curriculum and Examinations in Secondary Schools (Norwood Report, 1943).

The Nation's Schools: Their Plans and Purposes, Ministry of Education Pamphlet 1 (London, HMSO, 1945).

Royal Commission on Local Government (1969) (Redcliffe Maud Report), Research Paper 9, *Community Attitudes Survey* [Cmnd 3409].

Civil Service Department, Computers in Central Government: The Year Ahead (London, HMSO, 1971).

Report of the Committee on Privacy (1972) [Cmnd 5012].

Royal Commission on the Distribution of Income and Wealth, Report 4 (1976) [Cmnd 6626].

Report of the Committee on Standards in Public Life (1996) (Nolan Report) [Cmnd 1028].

Family Expenditure Survey (1998–2001) *Office of National Statistics*, www.statistics.gov.uk

Expenditure and Food Survey (2001), *Office of National Statistics*, www.statistics.gov.uk

Social Trends 32 (London, Stationery Office, 2002).

National Statistics Omnibus Survey, April 2002, www.statistics.gov.uk

The press

General historical perspectives

R. D. Altick, *The English Common Reader* (Chicago, Ill., University of Chicago Press, 1957; London, Phoenix, 1963).

A. Andrews, *The History of British Journalism*, 2 vols (London, Richard Bentley, 1859).

G. Boyce, 'The fourth estate: the reappraisal of a concept' in G. Boyce, J. Curran and P. Wingate (eds), *Newspaper History* (London, Constable, 1978).

P. Brendon, *The Life and Death of the Press Barons* (London, Secker & Warburg, 1982).

C. J. Bundock, *The National Union of Journalists: A Jubilee History, 1907–1957* (London, Oxford University Press, 1957).

J. Chalaby, *The Invention of Journalism* (London, Macmillan, 1998).

D. Chaney, *Processes of Mass Communication* (London, Macmillan, 1972).

M. Conboy, *The Press and Popular Culture* (London, Sage, 2002).

G. A. Cranfield, *The Press and Society* (Harlow, Longman, 1978).

J. Curran, 'Capitalism and control of the press 1800–1975' in J. Curran, M. Gurevitch and J. Woollacott (eds), *Mass Communication and Society* (London, Edward Arnold/Open University, 1977).

——'The press as an agency of social control: an historical perspective' in G. Boyce, J. Curran and P. Wingate (eds), *Newspaper History* (London, Constable, 1978).

——'Communications, power and social order' in T. Bennett, J. Curran, M. Gurevitch and J. Woollacott (eds), *Culture, Media and Society* (London, Methuen, 1981).

K. Drotner, *English Children and their Magazines, 1751–1945* (New Haven, Yale University Press, 1989).

M. Engel, *Tickle the Public* (London, Gollancz, 1996).

H. R. Fox Bourne, *English Newspapers* (London, Chatto & Windus, 1887; London, Russell & Russell, 1966).

J. Grant, *The Newspaper Press*, 3 vols (London, Tinsley Brothers, 1871–2).

D. Griffiths (ed.), *The Encyclopedia of the British Press, 1422–1992* (London, Macmillan, 1992).

M. Harris and A. Lee (eds), *The Press in English Society from the Seventeenth to Nineteenth Centuries* (London and Toronto, Associated University Presses, 1986).

R. Harrison, G. Woolven and R. Duncan, *The Warwick Guide to British Labour Periodicals 1790–1970* (Brighton, Harvester Press, 1977).

S. Harrison, *Poor Men's Guardians: A Record of the Struggles for a Democratic Newspaper Press 1763–1973* (London, Lawrence & Wishart, 1974).

P. Hennessy, *Whitehall* (London, HarperCollins, 1989).

——*Never Again* (London, HarperCollins, 1992).

H. Herd, *The March of Journalism* (London, Allen & Unwin, 1952).

F. Knight Hunt, *The Fourth Estate* (London, David Bogue, 1850).

P. Knightley, *The First Casualty: The War Correspondent as Hero, Propagandist and Myth Maker from the Crimea to Vietnam* (London, Deutsch, 1975).

S. Koss, *The Rise and Fall of the Political Press in Britain,* vols 1–2 (London, Hamish Hamilton, 1981 and 1984).

A. Marshall, *Changing the Word: The Printing Industry in Transition* (London, Comedia, 1983).

M. Milne, *Newspapers of Northumberland and Durham* (Newcastle, Frank Graham, 1972).

S. Morison, *The English Newspaper* (Cambridge, Cambridge University Press, 1932).

A. E. Musson, *The Typographical Association: Origins and History up to 1949* (London, Oxford University Press, 1954).

C. Pebody, *English Journalism* (London, Cassell, Petter & Galpin, 1882).

D. Read, *The Power of News: The History of Reuters* (Oxford, Oxford University Press, 1992).

G. Scott, *Reporters Anonymous: The Story of the Press Association* (London, Hutchinson, 1968).

F. S. Siebert, T. Peterson and W. Schramm, *Four Theories of the Press* (Urbana, Ill., University of Illinois Press, 1956; New York, Books for Libraries Press, 1973).

A. Smith, *The Newspaper: An International History* (London, Thames & Hudson, 1979).

——'Technology and control: the interactive dimensions of journalism' in J. Curran, M. Gurevitch and J. Woollacott (eds), *Mass Communication and Society* (London, Edward Arnold/Open University Press, 1977).

G. Storey, *Reuter's Century 1851–1951* (London, Parrish, 1951).

K. von Stutterheim, *The Press in England* (London, Allen & Unwin, 1934).

H. A. Taylor, *The British Press* (London, Arthur Barker, 1961).

J. Tunstall, 'Editorial sovereignty in the British press: its past and present' in *Studies on the Press,* Royal Commission on the Press 1974–7 Working Paper 3 (London, HMSO, 1977).

A. P. Wadsworth, 'Newspaper circulations 1800–1954', *Transactions of the Manchester Statistical Society*, iv (1955).

C. White, *Women's Magazines, 1693–1968* (London, Michael Joseph, 1970).

F. Williams, *Dangerous Estate* (Harlow, Longman Green, 1959; London, Arrow, 1959).

R. Williams, *The Long Revolution* (London, Chatto & Windus, 1961).

——'The press and popular culture: an historical perspective' in G. Boyce, J. Curran and P. Wingate (eds), *Newspaper History* (London, Constable, 1978).

C. Wilson, *First with the News: The History of W. H. Smith 1792–1972* (London, Cape, 1985).

Newspaper histories

Anon, *The History of the Times*, vols 1–5 (1935–58).

D. Ayerst, *The Guardian: Biography of a Newspaper* (London, Collins, 1971).

Lord Burnham, *Peterborough Court: Story of the Daily Telegraph* (London, Cassell, 1955).

P. Chippendale and C. Horrie, *Disaster! The Rise and Fall of the News on Sunday* (London, Sphere, 1988).

——*Stick it Up Your Punter! The Rise and Fall of the Sun* (London, Heinemann, 1990).

A. Christiansen, *Headlines All My Life* (London, Heinemann, 1961).

P. Cockburn, *The Years of the Week* (Harmondsworth, Penguin, 1971).

H. Cudlipp, *Publish and be Damned* (London, Andrew Dakers, 1953).

M. Edelman, *The Mirror – A Political History* (London, Hamish Hamilton, 1966).

W. Fienburgh, *25 Momentous Years: A 25th Anniversary in the History of the Daily Herald* (London, Odhams Press, 1955).

G. Fraser and K. Peters, *The Northern Lights* (London, Hamish Hamilton, 1978).

M. A. Gibb and F. Beckwith, *The Yorkshire Post: Two Centuries* (Leeds, Yorkshire Conservative Newspaper Co, 1954).

S. Glover, *Paper Dreams* (Harmondsworth, Penguin, 1994).

P. M. Handover, *History of the London Gazette, 1665–1965* (London, HMSO, 1965).

D. Hart-Davis, *The House the Berrys Built* (London, Coronet, 1991).

A. Hetherington, *Guardian Years* (London, Chatto & Windus, 1981).

D. Hill, *Tribune 40* (London, Quartet, 1977).

W. Hindle, *The Morning Post, 1772–1937* (London, Routledge & Kegan Paul, 1937).

H. Hobson, P. Knightley and L. Russell, *The Pearl of Days: An Intimate Memoir of the Sunday Times, 1822–1972* (London, Hamish Hamilton, 1972).

D. Kynaston, *The Financial Times* (London, Viking, 1988).

L. Lamb, *Sunrise* (London, Macmillan, 1989).

R. J. Lucas, *Lord Glenesk and the Morning Post* (London, Alston Rivers, 1910).

I. McDonald, *History of the Times 1939–66*, Vol. 5 (London, Times Books, 1984).

R. McKay and B. Barr, *The Story of the Scottish Daily News* (Edinburgh, Canongate, 1976).

H. Richards, *The Bloody Circus: The Daily Herald and the Left* (London, Pluto, 1997).

J. W. Robertson Scott, *The Story of the Pall Mall Gazette* (London, Oxford University Press, 1950).

H. R. G. Whates, *The Birmingham Post, 1857–1957* (Birmingham Post and Mail, 1957).

O. Woods and J. Bishop, *The Story of the Times* (London, Michael Joseph, 1983).

Nineteenth-century press history

W. E. Adams, *Memoirs of a Social Atom,* 2 vols (London, Hutchinson, 1903).

Anon, *Guide to Advertisers* (London, 1851).

A. Aspinall, 'Statistical accounts of London newspapers 1800–36', *English Historical Review,* lxv (1950).

——*Politics and the Press, 1780–1850* (London, Home & Van Thal, 1949; Brighton, Harvester Press, 1973).

I. Asquith, 'Advertising and the press in the late eighteenth and early nineteenth centuries: James Perry and the *Morning Chronicle,* 1790–1821', *Historical Journal,* xvii (1975).

P. Bailey, *Leisure and Class in Victorian England* (London, Routledge & Kegan Paul, 1978).

V. Berridge, 'Popular Sunday papers and mid-Victorian society' in G. Boyce, J. Curran and P. Wingate (eds), *Newspaper History* (London, Constable, 1978).

T. Boyle, *Black Swine in the Sewers of Hampstead* (London, Hodder & Stoughton, 1989).

L. Brake, A. Jones and L. Madden (eds), *Investigating Victorian Journalism* (London, Macmillan, 1990).

L. Brown, *Victorian News and Newspapers* (Oxford, Clarendon, 1985).

T. Catling, *My Life's Pilgrimage* (London, John Murray, 1911).

P. Catterall, C. Seymour-Ure and A. Smith (eds), *Northcliffe's Legacy* (Basingstoke, Macmillan, 2000).

I. R. Christie, 'British newspapers in the late Georgian age' in *Myth and Reality in Late 18th Century British Politics* (London, Macmillan, 1970).

C. D. Collet, *History of the Taxes on Knowledge* (London, T. Fisher Unwin, 1899).

S. Coltham, 'The *Bee-Hive* newspaper: its origins and early struggle' in A. Briggs and J. Saville (eds), *Essays in Labour History* (London, Macmillan, 1960).

——'The British working-class press in 1867', *Bulletin for the Society for the Study of Labour History* (autumn 1967).

F. Dilnot, *Adventures of a Newspaper Man* (London, Smith, Elder, 1913).

J. A. Epstein, 'Feargus O'Connor and the *Northern Star*', *International Review of Social History*, xxi (1976).

T. H. S. Escott, *Masters of English Journalism* (London, T. Fisher Unwin, 1911).

K. Flint, *The Woman Reader 1836–1914* (Oxford, Clarendon Press, 1993).

J. Foster, *Class Struggle and the Industrial Revolution: Early Industrial Capitalism in Three English Towns* (London, Weidenfeld & Nicolson, 1974).

M. D. George, *English Political Caricature, 1792–1832* (London, Oxford University Press, 1959).

E. Glasgow, 'The establishment of the *Northern Star* newspaper', *History*, xxxix (1954).

B. Harrison, 'A world of which we had no conception: liberalism and the temperance press, 1830–1872', *Victorian Studies*, xiii (December 1969).

J. Hatton, *Journalistic London* (London, Sampson Low, 1882).

A. F. Havighurst, *Radical Journalist: H. W. Massingham* (Cambridge, Cambridge University Press, 1974).

P. Hollis, *The Pauper Press* (London, Oxford University Press, 1970).

D. Hopkin, 'The socialist press in Britain 1890–1910' in G. Boyce, J. Curran and P. Wingate (eds), *Newspaper History* (London, Constable, 1978).

D. Hudson, *Thomas Barnes of the Times* (Cambridge, Cambridge University Press, 1943).

L. James (ed.), *Print and the People, 1819–1851* (London, Allen Lane, 1976).

E. E. Kellett, 'The press' in G. M. Young (ed.), *Early Victorian England* (London, Oxford University Press, 1934).

C. Kent, 'Higher journalism and the mid-Victorian clerisy', *Victorian Studies*, xiii (December 1969).

S. Koss, *Fleet Street Radical: A. G. Gardiner and the Daily News* (London, Allen Lane, 1973).

A. J. Lee, 'The management of a Victorian local newspaper: the *Manchester City News*, 1864–1900', *Business History*, xv (1973).

——'The radical press' in A. Morris (ed.), *Edwardian Radicalism, 1900–1914* (London, Routledge & Kegan Paul, 1974).

——*The Origins of the Popular Press, 1855–1914* (London, Croom Helm, 1976).

J. R. McCulloch, *Dictionary of Commerce and Commercial Navigation* (London, Longman, Brown & Green, 1854).

Mitchell's Newspaper Press Directory (Mitchell).

P. Mountjoy, 'The working-class press and working-class conservatism' in G. Boyce, J. Curran and P. Wingate (eds), *Newspaper History* (London, Constable, 1978).

A. E. Musson, 'Newspaper printing in the Industrial Revolution', *Economic History Review*, x, 2nd series (1957–8).

V. Neuberg, 'The literature of the streets' in H. J. Dyos and M. Wolff (eds), *The Victorian City* (London, Routledge & Kegan Paul, 1973).

T. Nevett, 'Advertising and editorial integrity in the nineteenth century' in M. Harris and A. Lee, *The Press in English Society from the Seventeenth to Nineteenth Centuries* (London and Toronto, Associated University Presses, 1986).

L. O'Boyle, 'The image of the journalist in England, France and Germany, 1815–1848', *Comparative Studies in Society and History*, x (1968).

P. O'Malley, 'Capital accumulation and press freedom, 1800–1850', *Media, Culture and Society*, 3, 1 (1981).

H. J. Perkin, 'The origins of the popular press', *History Today*, vii (1957).

R. Pound and G. Harmsworth, *Northcliffe* (London, Cassell, 1959).

R. Price, *An Imperial War and the British Working Class: Working-class Attitudes and Reactions to the Boer War 1899–1902* (London, Routledge & Kegan Paul, 1972).

D. Read, *Press and People 1790–1850* (London, Edward Arnold, 1961).

J. Roach, 'Education and public opinion' in C. Crawley (ed.), *War and Peace in an Age of Upheaval* (Cambridge, Cambridge University Press, 1965).

F. G. Salmon, 'What the working class read', *Nineteenth Century*, cxiii (1886).

M. Sanderson, 'Literacy and social mobility in the Industrial Revolution', *Past and Present*, 5, 6 (1972).

A. R. Schoyen, *The Chartist Challenge: A Portrait of George Julian Harney* (London, Heinemann, 1956).

J. Shattock and M. Wolff (eds), *The Victorian Periodical Press: Samplings and Soundings* (Leicester, University of Leicester Press, 1982).

H. Simonis, *The Street of Ink* (London, Cassell, 1917).

J. A. Spender, *Life, Journalism and Politics,* 2 vols (London, Cassell, 1927).

J. F. Stephen, 'Journalism', *Cornhill Magazine*, 6 (1862).

L. Stone, 'Literacy and education in England 1640–1900', *Past and Present*, 42 (1969).

J. D. Symon, *The Press and its Story* (London, Seeley Service, 1914).

T. Tholfsen, *Working-Class Radicalism in Mid-Victorian Britain* (London, Croom Helm, 1976).

D. Thompson, *The Chartists* (London, Maurice Temple Smith, 1984).

E. P. Thompson, *The Making of the English Working Class* (London, Gollancz, 1963).

R. K. Webb, *The British Working-Class Reader, 1790–1848* (London, Allen & Unwin, 1955).

W. H. Wickwar, *The Struggle for the Freedom of the Press, 1819–1832* (London, Allen & Unwin, 1928).

J. Wiener (ed.), *Millions for the Millions* (New York, Greenwood, 1992).

J. H. Wiener, *The War of the Unstamped* (New York, Cornell University Press, 1969).

Twentieth-century press history

J. R. Adams, *Media Planning* (London, Business Books, 1971).

A. Angell, *The Press and the Organisation of Society* (London, Labour Publishing Co, 1922).

D. Ayerst, *Garvin of the Observer* (London, Croom Helm, 1985).

Lord Beaverbrook, *Men and Power* (London, Hutchinson, 1956).

W. Belson, *The British Press* (London, London Press Exchange, 1959).

T. Bower, *Maxwell: The Outsider* (London, Aurum, 1989).

O. Boyd-Barrett, C. Seymour-Ure and J. Tunstall, *Studies on the Press*, Royal Commission on the Press, Working Paper 3 (London, HMSO, 1977).

R. Braddon, *Roy Thomson* (London, Fontana, 1968).

P. Brendon, *Eminent Edwardians* (London, Secker & Warburg, 1979).

T. B. Browne, *Advertisers' ABC* (London, Browne, 1927).

A. Calder, *The People's War* (London, Panther, 1971).

S. Chibnall, *Law-and-Order News* (London, Tavistock, 1977).

C. Chisholm, *Marketing and Merchandising* (London, Modern Business Institute, 1924).

A. Chisolm and M. Davie, *Beaverbrook* (London, Hutchinson, 1992).

H. Christian (ed.), *The Sociology of Journalism and the Press*, Sociological Review Monograph 29 (Keele, University of Keele, 1980).

A. Christiansen, *Headlines All My Life* (London, Heinemann, 1961).

T. Clarke, *My Northcliffe Diary* (London, Gollancz, 1931).

——*Northcliffe in History* (London, Hutchinson, 1950).

G. Cleverley, *The Fleet Street Disaster* (London, Constable, 1976).

C. Cockburn, *Brothers: Male Dominance and Technological Change* (London, Pluto, 1983).

M. Cockerell, P. Hennessy and D. Walker, *Sources Close to the Prime Minister* (London, Macmillan, 1984).

R. Cockett, *Twilight of Truth* (London, Weidenfeld & Nicolson, 1989).

S. Cohen and J. Young, *The Manufacture of News* (London, Constable, 1973).

H. Cox and D. Morgan, *City Politics and the Press* (Cambridge, Cambridge University Press, 1973).

R. A. Critchley, *UK Advertising Statistics* (London, Advertising Association, n.d.).

H. Cudlipp, *At Your Peril* (London, Weidenfeld & Nicolson, 1962).

——*Walking on the Water* (London, Bodley Head, 1976).

J. Curran, 'The impact of TV on the audience for national newspapers, 1945–68' in J. Tunstall (ed.), *Media Sociology* (London, Constable, 1970).

——(ed.), *The British Press: A Manifesto* (London, Macmillan, 1978).

——'Advertising and the press' in J. Curran (ed.), *The British Press: A Manifesto* (London, Macmillan, 1978).

T. Driberg, *Beaverbrook* (London, Weidenfeld & Nicolson, 1956).

H. W. Eley, *Advertising Media* (London, Butterworth, 1932).

H. Evans, *Good Times, Bad Times* (London, Weidenfeld & Nicolson, 1983).

B. Falk, *He Laughed in Fleet Street* (London, Hutchinson, 1933).

M. Ferguson, *Forever Feminine* (London, Heinemann Educational, 1983).

P. Ferris, *The House of Northcliffe* (London, Weidenfeld & Nicolson, 1971).

C. Freer, *The Inner Side of Advertising: A Practical Handbook for Advertisers* (London, Library Press, 1921).

H. Fyfe, *Sixty Years of Fleet Street* (London, W. H. Allen, 1949).

F. R. Gannon, *The British Press and Germany, 1936–1939* (London, Oxford University Press, 1971).

N. Garland, *Not Many Dead* (London, Hutchinson, 1990).

J. E. Gerald, *The British Press under Government Economic Controls* (Minneapolis, University of Minnesota Press, 1956).

P. Gibbs, *Adventures in Journalism* (London, Harper, 1923).

F. Giles, *Sundry Times* (London, Murray, 1986).

G. Glenton and William Pattinson, *The Last Chronicle of Bouverie Street* (London, Allen & Unwin, 1963).

P. Golding and S. Middleton, *Images of Welfare* (Oxford, Martin Robertson, 1982).

D. Goodhart and P. Wintour, *Eddie Shah and the Newspaper Revolution* (London, Coronet, 1986).

J. Haines, *Maxwell* (London, Macdonald, 1989).

S. Hall, 'The social eye of *Picture Post*', *Cultural Studies*, ii (1971).

——'Deviancy, politics and the media' in M. McIntosh and P. Rock (eds), *Deviancy and Social Control* (London, Tavistock, 1973).

S. Hall, C. Critcher, T. Jefferson, J. Clarke and B. Roberts, *Policing the Crisis: Mugging, the State, and Law and Order* (London, Macmillan, 1978).

J. Halloran, P. Elliott and G. Murdock (eds), *Demonstrations and Communication* (Harmondsworth, Penguin, 1970).

D. Hamilton, *Who is to Own the British Press?* (London, Birkbeck College, 1976).

R. Harris, *Gotcha: The Media, The Government and The Falklands War* (London, Faber, 1983).

W. Harris, *J. A. Spender* (London, Cassell, 1946).

G. Harrison and F. C. Mitchell, *The Home Market: A Handbook of Statistics* (London, Allen & Unwin, 1936).

N. Hartley, P. Gudgeon and R. Crafts, *Concentration of Ownership in the Provincial Press,* Royal Commission on the Press 1974–7, Research Series 5 (London, HMSO, 1977).

P. Hartmann, 'Industrial relations in the news media', *Industrial Relations Journal*, 6, 4 (London, HMSO, 1977).

——'News and public perceptions of industrial relations', *Media, Culture and Society*, 1, 3 (1979).

P. Hartmann and C. Husband, *Racism and the Mass Media* (London, Davis-Poynter, 1974).

Lord Hartwell, *William Camrose* (London, Weidenfeld & Nicolson, 1992).

J. Harvey (ed.), *The War Diaries of Oliver Harvey 1941–5* (London, Collins, 1978).

M. Hastings, *Editor* (Basingstoke, Macmillan, 2002).

H. Henry (ed.), *Behind the Headlines* (London, Associated Business Press, 1978).

——*The Dynamics of the British Press 1961–1984* (London, Advertising Association, 1986).

A. Hetherington, *News, Newspapers and Television* (London, Macmillan, 1985).

C. Higham, *Advertising* (London, Williams & Norgate, 1925).

F. Hirsch and D. Gordon, *Newspaper Money: Fleet Street and the Search for the Affluent Reader* (London, Hutchinson, 1975).

P. Hoch, *The Newspaper Game* (London, Calder & Boyars, 1974).

R. Hoggart (ed.), *Your Sunday Paper* (London, University of London Press, 1967).

M. Hollingsworth, *The Press and Political Dissent* (London, Pluto Press, 1986).

D. Hubback, *No Ordinary Press Baron* (London, Weidenfeld & Nicolson, 1985).

Hulton Readership Surveys (London, Hulton, 1947–55).

N. Hunter, *Advertising Through the Press* (London, Pitman, 1925).

Institute of Incorporated Practitioners in Advertising, *An Analysis of Press Circulations 1934* (London, IIPA, 1934).

——*Survey of Press Readership* (London, IIPA, 1939).

——*National Readership Surveys* (London, IIPA, 1956–67).

——*Joint Industry Committee for National Readership Surveys* (London, IIPA, 1968–84).

S. Inwood, 'The press in the First World War, 1914–1916', unpublished Ph.D. thesis (University of Oxford, 1971).

I. Jackson, *The Provincial Press and the Community* (Manchester, Manchester University Press, 1971).

S. Jenkins, *Market for Glory* (London, Faber, 1986).

N. Kaldor and R. Silverman, *A Statistical Analysis of Advertising Expenditure and of the Revenue of the Press* (Cambridge, Cambridge University Press, 1948).

P. Kimble, *Newspaper Reading in the Third Year of the War* (London, Allen & Unwin, 1942).

C. King, *The Future of the Press* (London, MacGibbon & Kee, 1967).

——*Strictly Personal* (London, Weidenfeld & Nicolson, 1969).

——*With Malice Towards None: A War Diary* (ed. W. Armstrong) (London, Sidgwick & Jackson, 1970).

——*Without Fear or Favour* (London, Sidgwick & Jackson, 1971).

——*The Cecil King Diary 1965–70* (London, Cape, 1972).

S. Koss, *Fleet Street Radical: A. G. Gardiner and the Daily News* (London, Allen Lane, 1973).

G. Lansbury, *The Miracle of Fleet Street* (London, Victoria House, 1925).

M. Leapman, *Barefaced Cheek* (London, Hodder & Stoughton, 1983).

H. P. Levy, *The Press Council* (London, Macmillan, 1967).

L. London, *Whitehall and the Jews, 1933–48* (Cambridge, Cambridge University Press, 2000).

London Research Bureau, *Press Circulations Analysed 1928* (London Research Bureau, 1928).

A. G. Lyall, *Market Research: A Practical Handbook* (London Research Bureau 1933).

D. McLachlan, *In the Chair, Barrington-Ward of The Times, 1927–48* (London, Weidenfeld & Nicolson, 1971).

S. McLachlan and P. Golding, 'Tabloidization in the British press: a quantitative investigation into changes in British newspapers, 1952–1997' in C. Sparks and J. Tulloch, *Tabloid Tales* (Lanham, Rowman & Littlefield, 2000).

I. McLaine, *Ministry of Morale* (London, Allen & Unwin, 1979).

D. McQuail, *Analysis of Newspaper Content,* Royal Commission on the Press 1974–7, Research Series 4 (London, HMSO, 1977).

Mass Observation, *The Press and its Readers* (London, Art & Technics, 1949).

T. S. Mathews, *The Sugar Pill: An Essay on Newspapers* (London, Gollancz, 1957).

R. J. Minney, *Viscount Southwood* (London, Odhams Press, 1954).

S. Mulvern, *The End of the Street* (London, Methuen, 1986).

G. Munster, *Rupert Murdoch* (Victoria, Viking Press, 1985).

G. Murdock, 'Class, power and the press: problems of conceptualisation and evidence' in H. Christian (ed.), *The Sociology of Journalism and the Press*, Sociological Review Monograph 29 (Keele, University of Keele, 1981).

D. Murphy, *The Silent Watchdog: The Press in Local Politics* (London, Constable, 1976).

——*The Stalker Affair and the Press* (London, Unwin Hyman, 1991).

A. Neil, *Full Disclosure* (London, Macmillan, 1996).

News Chronicle, A Survey of Reader Interest (1934).

H. Nicolson, *Diaries and Letters* (London, Collins, 1967).

Lord Northcliffe, *Newspapers and their Millionaires* (London, Associated Newspapers, 1922).

L. Owen, *Northcliffe: The Facts* (privately published, 1931).

W. Parsons, *The Power of the Financial Press* (Aldershot, Elgar, 1989).

Periodicals and the Alternative Press, Royal Commission on the Press 1974–7, Research Series 6 (London, HMSO, 1977).

F. Pethick-Lawrence, *Fate Has Been Kind* (London, Hutchinson, 1943).

H. Porter, *Lies, Damned Lies and Some Exclusives* (London, Chatto & Windus, 1984).

R. Pound and G. Harmsworth, *Northcliffe* (London, Cassell, 1959).

A. Rappaport, *The British Press and Wilsonian Neutrality* (London, Oxford University Press, 1951).

Report on the British Press (London, Political & Economic Planning, 1938).

G. Robertson, *People Against the Press* (London, Quartet, 1983).

D. Rooney, 'Thirty years of competition in the British tabloid press: the *Mirror* and the *Sun* 1968–1998' in C. Sparks and J. Tulloch, *Tabloid Tales* (Lanham, Rowman & Littlefield, 2000).

T. Russell, *Commercial Advertising* (London, Putnam, 1919).

A. P. Ryan, *Lord Northcliffe* (London, Collins, 1953).

C. Seymour-Ure, *The Press, Politics and the Public* (London, Methuen, 1968).

——'Policy-making in the press', *Government and Opposition*, iv, 4 (1969).

——*The Political Impact of the Mass Media* (London, Constable, 1974).

——'The press and the party system between the wars' in G. Peele and C. Cook (eds), *The Politics of Reappraisal, 1918–1939* (London, Macmillan, 1976).

——*The British Press and Broadcasting Since 1945* (2nd edn) (Oxford, Blackwell, 1996).

R. Shannon, *A Press Free and Responsible* (London, John Murray, 2001).

A. Sharf, *The British Press and Jews Under Nazi Rule* (London, Oxford University Press, 1964).

W. Shawcross, *Rupert Murdoch* (London, Chatto & Windus, 1992).

K. Sisson, *Industrial Relations in Fleet Street* (Oxford, Blackwell, 1975).

A. Smith, *The British Press Since the War* (Newton Abbot, David & Charles, 1974).

A. C. H. Smith, E. Immirzi and T. Blackwell, *Paper Voices: The Popular Press and Social Change, 1933–1965* (London, Chatto & Windus, 1975).

Social and Community Planning, *Attitudes to the Press,* Royal Commission on the Press 1974–7, Research Series 3 (London, HMSO, 1977).

J. A. Spender, *Life, Journalism and Politics* (London, Cassell, 1927).

R. Stannard, *With the Dictators of Fleet Street* (London, Hutchinson, 1934).

Survey of the National Newspaper Industry (London, Economist Intelligence Unit, 1965).

A. J. P. Taylor, *English History 1914–1945* (Harmondsworth, Pelican, 1970).
——*Beaverbrook* (London, Hamish Hamilton, 1972).
——(ed.), *Off the Record: W. P. Crozier, Political Interviews 1933–1943* (London, Hutchinson, 1973).
S. J. Taylor, *Shock! Horror! The Tabloids in Action* (London, Bantam, 1991).
Lord Thomson of Fleet, *After I Was Sixty* (London, Hamish Hamilton, 1975).
The Times, The History of The Times, iv: The 150th Anniversary and Beyond, 1912–1948, 2 vols (London, The Times Publishing Co, 1952).
J. Tunstall, *The Westminster Lobby Correspondents* (London, Routledge & Kegan Paul, 1970).
——*Journalists at Work* (London, Constable, 1971).
——'The problem of industrial relations news in the press' in *Studies on the Press,* Royal Commission on the Press 1974–7, Working Paper 3 (London, HMSO, 1977).
——*The Media in Britain* (London, Constable, 1983).
——*Newspaper Power* (Oxford, Oxford University Press, 1996).
J. Whale, *Journalism and Government* (London, Macmillan, 1972).
C. White, *The Women's Periodical Press in Britain 1946–1976,* Royal Commission on the Press, Working Paper 4 (London, HMSO, 1977).
H. Wickham Steed, *The Press* (Harmondsworth, Penguin, 1938).
T. Wilson (ed.), *The Political Diaries of C. P. Scott* (London, Collins, 1970).
R. Winsbury, *New Technology and the Press*, Royal Commission on the Press and Acton Society Press Group (London, HMSO, 1975).
C. Wintour, *Pressures on the Press: An Editor looks at Fleet Street* (London, Deutsch, 1972).
J. E. Wrench, *Geoffrey Dawson and our Times* (London, Hutchinson, 1955).

Broadcasting

Memoirs and biographies

R. Baker, *Here is the News* (London, Leslie Frewin, 1966).
G. Beadle, *Television, A Critical Review* (London, Allen & Unwin, 1963).
M. Bell, *In Harm's Way: Reflection of a War Zone* (London, Hamish Hamilton, 1994).
M. Bhose, *Michael Grade: Screening the Image* (London, Virgin, 1992).
J. Birt, *John Birt the Autobiography* (London, Little, Brown, 2002).
A. Boyle, *Only the Wind Will Listen: Reith of the BBC* (London, Hutchinson, 1972).
C. Brewer, *The Spice of Variety* (London, Muller, 1948).
D. G. Bridson, *Prospero and Ariel: The Rise and Fall of Radio* (London, Gollancz, 1971).
H. Brittain, *The ABC of the BBC* (London, Pearson, 1932).
J. C. Cassell, *In Town Tonight* (London, Harrap, 1935).
S. Chesmore, *Behind the Microphone* (London, Nelson, 1935).
Sir Kenneth Clark, *The Other Half: A Self-Portrait* (London, Murray, 1977).
Sir Alfred D. Cooper, *Old Men Forget* (London, Hart-Davis, 1953).
N. Davenport, *Memoirs of a City Radical* (London, Methuen, 1959).
R. Day, *Television – A Personal Report* (London, Hutchinson, 1961).
——*Day by Day* (London, William Kimber, 1975).
B. Deane, *Seven Ages, An Autobiography, 1927–72* (London, Hutchinson, 1973).

J. Dimbleby, *Richard Dimbleby: A Biography* (London, Hodder & Stoughton, 1975).

R. Dimbleby, *The Waiting Year* (London, Hodder & Stoughton, 1944).

P. P. Eckersley, *The Power Behind the Microphone* (London, Cape, 1941).

R. Eckersley, *The BBC and All That* (London, Sampson, Low, Marston, 1946).

L. Fielden, *The Natural Bent* (London, Deutsch, 1960).

V. Gielgud, *Years of the Locust* (London, Nicholson & Watson, 1947).

G. W. Goldie, *Facing the Nation: Television and Politics, 1936–76* (London, Bodley Head, 1977).

M. Gorham, *Sound and Fury* (London, Percival-Maskell, 1948).

F. Grisewood, *The World Goes By* (London, Secker & Warburg, 1952).

——*Years in the Mirror* (London, Gollancz, 1967).

H. Grisewood, *One Thing at a Time* (London, Hutchinson, 1968).

H. Hall, *Here's to the Next Time* (London, Deutsch, 1935).

L. Henry, *My Laugh Story* (Edinburgh, Simon Paul, 1937).

A. S. Hibberd, *This is London* (Plymouth, Macdonald & Evans, 1950).

Lord Hill of Luton (C. Hill), *Both Sides of the Hill* (London, Heinemann, 1967).

——*Behind the Screen* (London, Sidgwick & Jackson, 1974).

J. Hilton, *This and That* (London, Allen & Unwin, 1938).

J. Isaacs, *Storm over Four: A Personal Account* (London, Weidenfeld & Nicolson, 1989).

P. J. Kavanagh, *The Itma Years* (London, Heinemann, 1974).

T. Kavanagh, *Tommy Handley* (London, Hodder & Stoughton, 1949).

F. Keane, *Rivers of Blood; Reporting Rwanda* (London, Hamish Hamilton, 1995).

L. Kennedy, *Ludo: A Life* (London, Macmillan, 1989).

R. S. Lambert, *Ariel and All His Quality* (London, Gollancz, 1940).

C. A. Lewis, *Broadcasting from Within* (London, George Newnes, 1924).

E. Maschwitz, *No Chip on My Shoulder* (London, Jenkins, 1957).

A. Milne, *D. G. The Memoirs of a British Broadcaster* (London, Hodder & Stoughton, 1988).

S. A. Mosely, *Broadcasting in my Time* (London, Rich & Cowan, 1935).

——*Private Diaries* (London, Parrish, 1960).

E. Nixon, *John Hilton* (London, Allen & Unwin, 1946).

J. Payne, *This is Jack Payne* (London, Marston, 1932).

——*Signature Tune* (Edinburgh, Simon Paul, 1947).

W. Pickles, *Between You and Me* (London, Heinemann, 1949).

J. B. Priestley, *Margin Released* (London, Mercury, 1966).

J. C. W. Reith, *Into the Wind* (London, Hodder & Stoughton, 1949).

R. Silvey, *Who's Listening?* (London, Allen & Unwin, 1974).

C. Stuart, *The Reith Diaries* (London, Collins, 1975).

Sir Stephen Tallents, *Man and Boy* (London, Faber, 1943).

H. Thomas, *With an Independent Air* (London, Weidenfeld & Nicolson, 1977).

M. Tracey, *A Variety of Lives: A Biography of Sir Hugh Greene* (London, Bodley Head, 1982).

M. Whitehouse, *Who Does She Think She Is?* (London, New English Library, 1971).

The history of broadcasting

M. Abrams, *Granada Viewership Survey* (1959).

R. Alston, *Taking the Air* (London, Hodder & Stoughton, 1951).

G. L. Archer, *A History of Broadcasting to 1926* (London, Allen & Unwin, 1938).

J. Bakewell and N. Garnham, *The New Priesthood: British Television Today* (Harmondsworth, Allen Lane, 1970).

S. Barnett (ed.), *Funding the BBC's Future* (London, BFI, 1988).

S. Barnett and A. Curry, *The Battle for the BBC* (London, Aurum Press, 1993).

S. Barnett and E. Seymour, *'A Shrinking Iceberg Travelling South'* (London, Campaign for Quality Television, 1999).

E. Barnouw, *A Tower in Babel: The History of Broadcasting in the United States* (London, Oxford University Press, 1966).

BBC Handbook (London, BBC, annually).

BBC, 'Comparative European programming', *BBC Handbook* (London, BBC, 1934).

——*The Third Programme: Plans for October–December 1944* (London, BBC, 1944).

——*The Public and their Programmes* (London, BBC, 1959).

J. Bennett, *British Broadcasting and the Danish Resistance Movement 1940–1945* (Cambridge, Cambridge University Press, 1965).

P. Black, *The Biggest Aspidistra in the World* (London, BBC, 1972).

——*The Mirror in the Corner* (London, Hutchinson, 1972).

P. Bloomfield, *BBC* (London, Eyre & Spottiswoode, 1941).

G. Brandt (ed.), *Television Drama* (Cambridge, Cambridge University Press, 1981).

A. Briggs, *The History of Broadcasting in the United Kingdom*: Vol. I, *The Birth of Broadcasting*; Vol. II, *The Golden Age of Wireless*; Vol. III, *The War of Words*; Vol. IV, *Sound and Vision* (London, Oxford University Press, 1961, 1965, 1970 and 1979).

——'The rise of the mass entertainment industry' (Fisher Lecture, 1961).

——*The BBC Governors* (London, BBC, 1979).

——*The BBC: The First Fifty Years* (Oxford, Oxford University Press, 1985).

P. J. Brown, 'Broadcasting in Britain', *London Quarterly Review,* 145, 1 (January 1926).

A. R. Burrows, *The Story of Broadcasting* (London, Cassell, 1924).

Sir Cyril Burt, 'The psychology of listeners', *BBC Quarterly*, 4, 2 (April 1949).

H. L. Childs and J. B. Whitton (eds), *Propaganda by Shortwave* (London, Oxford University Press, 1943).

J. A Cole, *Lord Haw Haw – and William Joyce* (London, Collins, 1964).

C. A. R. Crosland, 'The mass media', *Encounter* (November 1962).

R. H. S. Crossman, 'The politics of viewing', *New Statesman* (25 October 1968).

——'The BBC, Labour and the public', *New Statesman* (17 July 1971).

C. Curran, *Code or Conscience* (London, BBC, 1970).

——*A Maturing Democracy* (London, BBC, 1973).

——*The Seamless Robe* (London, Bodley Head, 1979).

—— 'Television journalism: theory and practice, the case of *Newsnight*' in P. Holland, *Television Handbook* (London, Routledge, 2nd edn, 2000).

R. Day, 'Troubled reflections of a TV journalist', *Encounter* (May 1970).

B. Deane, *The Theatre At War* (London, Harrap, 1956).

S. Delmer, *Black Boomerang* (London, Secker & Warburg, 1962).

D. Docherty, D. E. Morrison and M. Tracey, *Keeping Faith? Channel Four and its Audience* (London, Libbey, 1988).

L. W. Doob, 'Goebbels' principles of propaganda', *Public Opinion Quarterly,* 21, 2 (1950).

P. P. Eckersley, *Captain Eckersley Explains* (London, Hodder & Stoughton, 1924).

——*All About your Microphone* (London, BBC Broadcast Library, 1925).

——*The Power Behind the Microphone* (London, Cape, 1941).

H. Fairlie, 'TV, idiot box', *Encounter* (August 1959).

——'The BBC' in H. S. Thomas (ed.), *The Establishment: A Symposium* (London, New English Library, 1962).

Sir Robert Fraser, *The Coming of Independent Television* (London, Hutchinson, 1955).

——*ITA Notes* (October 1970).

V. Gielgud, *British Radio Drama 1922–1956* (London, Harrap, 1957).

P. Goodwin, *Television Under the Tories* (London, British Film Institute, 1998).

G. W. Goldie, 'The new attraction', *Listener* (26 December 1940).

——'TV report', *Listener* (23 October 1968).

——*Facing the Nation: Television and Politics 1936–1976* (London, The Bodley Head, 1977).

M. Gorham, *Broadcasting and Television Since 1900* (London, Collins, 1952).

T. Green, *The Universal Eye: World Television in the Seventies* (London, The Bodley Head, 1972).

——'The future of broadcasting in Britain', Granada Guildhall Lecture (1972).

H. C. Greene, 'The BBC since 1958', *BBC Handbook* (1969).

——*The Third Floor Front: A View of Broadcasting in the Sixties* (London, The Bodley Head, 1969).

T. Harrisson, 'War books', *Horizon* (December 1941).

D. Hawkins and D. Boyd (eds), *BBC War Report* (London, Oxford University Press, 1946).

Sir William Hayley, *The Central Problem of Broadcasting* (London, BBC, 1948).

C. Horrie and S. Clarke, *Fear and Loathing at the BBC* (London, Heinemann, 1993).

IBA, *Annual Reports.*

ITV, *The Annan Report: An ITV View* (London, ITV, 1977).

E. T. Lean, *Voices in the Darkness* (London, Allen & Unwin, 1943).

M. Leapman, *The Last Days of the Beeb* (London, Coronet, 1987).

D. McLachlan, *Room 39* (London, Weidenfeld & Nicolson, 1968).

Mass Observation, *The War Begins at Home* (London, Chatto & Windus, 1940).

H. Matheson, *Broadcasting* (London, Butterworth, 1933).

——'Listener research in broadcasting', *Sociological Review*, 27, 3 (1935).

A. Mitchell, 'The decline of current affairs television', *Political Quarterly*, 44, 1 (1973).

S. Nicholas, *The Echo of War: Home Front Propaganda 1939–45* (Manchester, Manchester University Press, 1995).

H. Nicolson, *The Third Programme: A Symposium of Opinions and Plans* (London, BBC, 1947).

S. Orwell and I. Angus (eds), *The Collected Essays, Letters and Journalism of George Orwell* (Harmondsworth, Penguin, 1971).

B. Paulu, *British Broadcasting: Radio and Television in the United Kingdom* (Oxford, Oxford University Press, 1957).

G. Pedrich, *Battledress Broadcasters* (London, Marston, 1964).

R. Postgate, *What to Do with the BBC?* (London, Hogarth, 1935).

J. B. Priestley, *Postscripts* (London, Heinemann, 1940).

J. C. W. Reith, *Broadcast over Britain* (London, Hodder & Stoughton, 1924).

N. Riley, *999* (London, Gollancz, 1943).

C. J. Rolo, *Radio Goes to War* (London, Hutchinson, 1943).

G. Ross, *T. V. Jubilee* (London, W. H. Allen, 1961).

P. Rotha (ed.), *Television in the Making* (London, The Bodley Head, 1956).

P. Scannell, 'The social eye of television, 1946–1955', *Media, Culture, and Society*, 1, 1 (1979).

——*Radio, Television and Modern Life* (Oxford, Blackwell, 1996).

P. Scannell and D. Cardiff, 'The social foundations of British broadcasting' in J. Curran, M. Gurevitch and J. Woollacott (eds), *Mass Communication and Society* (London, Edward Arnold/Open University Press, 1977).

J. Seaton, 'The BBC and the Holocaust', *European Journal of Communication*, 2, 1 (1987).

——'Reporting atrocities' in J. Seaton and B. Pimlott, *The Media in British Politics* (Aldershot, Gower, 1987).

——*The Media and the Constitution* (London, Charter 88, 1993).

——'Broadcasting in the 1980s: is it possible to under-estimate public taste?', *Political Quarterly*, Special issue on broadcasting, 47, 1 (1993), pp. 50–76.

——'Yesterday's men: deception or mistake?', together with edited transcript of 1994 ICBH Witness Seminar, *Contemporary British History*, 10, 3 (1996).

——'Misery and the media: the media and ethnic violence', *Contemporary Politics*, 2, 2 (1996), pp. 59–79.

G. Seldes, *The Great Audience* (London, Oxford University Press, 1950).

T. Shaw, *Eden, Suez and the Mass Media* (Birmingham, I.B. Tauris, 1995).

R. Silvey, 'Some recent trends in listening', *BBC Handbook* (London, BBC, 1946).

——'TV viewing in Britain', *Public Opinion Quarterly*, 25, 2 (1950).

——*Whose Listening?* (London, The Bodley Head, 1974).

Lord Simon of Wythenshawe, *The BBC from Within* (London, Gollancz, 1953).

A. Smith, *The Shadow in the Cave* (London, Allen & Unwin, 1973).

——*British Broadcasting* (Newton Abbot, David & Charles, 1974).

S. W. Smithers, *Broadcasting from Within* (London, Pitmans, 1938).

N. Swallow, *Factual Television* (London, Focal Press, 1966).

J. Swift, *Adventures in Vision* (London, Lehmann, 1950).

I. Thomas, *Warfare By Words* (London, Gollancz, 1942).

The Times, special broadcasting number (14 August 1934).

P. Todd, 'Scarcity of TV time', *Campaign* (26 January 1979).

M. Tracey, *Whitehouse* (London, Constable, 1979).

R. West, *The Meaning of Treason* (London, Macmillan, 1948).

H. Wheldon, 'Competition in television', Address to the Royal Society of Arts (1971).

——*Tastes and Standards in BBC Programmes* (London, BBC, 1973).

H. H. Wilson, *Pressure Group* (London, Secker & Warburg, 1961).

F. Worsley, *ITMA* (London, Collins, 1948).

The background to broadcasting

M. Abrams, 'Advertising', *Listener* (15 December 1956).

——'Motivation research', *Advertising Quarterly* (November 1959).

P. Addison, *The Road to 1945* (London, Cape, 1975).

K. Allsop, *The Angry Decade* (London, Owen, 1958).

N. Annan, 'Love among the moralists', *Encounter* (February 1960).

E. Barendt and L. Hitchens, *Media Law* (Harlow, Longman, 2000).

D. Bell, 'Advertising: is it worth it?', *Listener* (13 December 1956).

W. H. Beveridge, *Unemployment: A Problem of Industry* (London, Longman Green, 1910).

——*Public Service in War and Peace* (London, Constable, 1920).

——*Constructive Democracy* (London, Allen & Unwin, 1937).

——*Power and Influence* (London, Hodder & Stoughton, 1953).

V. Bogdanor and R. Skidelsky, *The Age of Affluence* (Harmondsworth, Penguin, 1970).

E. Bowen, *The Heart of the Matter* (London, Faber, 1944).

V. Brittain, *Testament of Friendship* (London, Macmillan, 1940).

G. Bruntz, *Allied Propaganda and the Collapse of the German Empire in 1918* (Stanford, Calif., Stanford University Press, 1938).

Sir Cyril Burt, *The Distribution and Relations of Educational Abilities* (London, London County Council, 1917).

——'The measurement of mental capacities', Henderson Trust Lecture 7, Edinburgh (1927).

——(ed.), *How The Mind Works* (London, Allen & Unwin, 1933).

——*Intelligence and Fertility* (London, Cassell, 1952).

D. Butler and R. Rose, *The British General Election of 1959* (London, Macmillan, 1960).

Lord Butler, *The Education Act of 1944 and After*, First Noel Buxton Lecture, University of Essex (Harlow, Longman, 1965).

——*The Art of the Possible* (London, Hamish Hamilton, 1971).

A. Calder, *The People's War: Britain 1939–45* (London, Cape, 1969).

H. Cantril, *Public Opinion 1935–46* (Princeton, NJ, Princeton University Press, 1951).

C. Cockburn, *I Claud* (Harmondsworth, Penguin, 1967).

C. A. R. Crosland, *The Future of Socialism* (London, Cape, 1956).

R. H. S. Crossman, 'Psychological warfare', *Journal of the Royal United Services Institution* (August 1952).

——'The lessons of 1945' in P. Anderson and R. Blackburn (eds), *Towards Socialism* (London, Fontana, 1965).

H. Dalton, 'The "popular front"', *Political Quarterly*, 4, 7 (1936).

M. E. Dimmock, *British Public Utilities and National Development* (London, Allen & Unwin, 1933).

C. H. Dobinson (ed.), *Education in a Changing World* (Oxford, Oxford University Press, 1951).

T. Driberg, *The Best of Both Worlds* (Phoenix House, 1958).

M. R. D. Foot, *Resistance: An Analysis of European Resistance to Fascism* (London, Methuen, 1976).

P. Foot, *The Politics of Harold Wilson* (Harmondsworth, Penguin, 1968).

Fougasse (pseud. C. K. Bird), *The Changing Face of Britain* (London, Methuen, 1950).

B. Gates, *The Road Ahead* (Boston, Viking, 1995).

M. Gilbert, *Churchill*, Vol. 5 (London, Heinemann, 1976).

M. Gilbert and R. Gott, *The Appeasers* (London, Weidenfeld & Nicolson, 1963).

D. Gordan, 'Ten points about the crisis in the British film industry', *Sight and Sound*, 43, 2 (1974).

L. Gorden, *The Public Corporation in Great Britain* (Oxford, Oxford University Press, 1938).

P. H. J. H. Gosden, *Education in the Second World War* (London, Methuen, 1972).

C. Handy, *The Age of Unreason* (Boston, Mass., Harvard University Press, 1989).

——'The New Federalist Papers', *Harvard University Business Review*, 3 (Autumn 1992).

——*The Empty Raincoat* (London, HarperCollins, 1993).

J. Harris, *William Beveridge* (Oxford, Clarendon Press, 1977).

N. Harris, *Competition and the Corporate State* (London, Methuen, 1972).

R. Harris, *Politics Without Prejudice* (Tonbridge, Staples, 1956).

T. Harrisson, 'Who'll win?', *Political Quarterly*, 15, 4 (1944).

——*Living Through the Blitz* (Harmondsworth, Penguin, 1978).

J. Harvey-Jones, *Making it Happen* (London, BBC Books, 1994).

E. Hobsbawm, *Nations and Nationalism since 1780* (Cambridge, Cambridge University Press, 1992).

——*The Age of Extremities* (London, Allen Lane, 1994).

J. A. Hodson, *Somewhere in France . . . B.E.F.* (London, Whithey Grove, 1940).

——*War Diary* (London, Gollancz, 1941).

——*The Home Front* (London, Gollancz, 1944).

W. Hutton, *The State We Are In* (London, Cape, 1996).

L. J. Kamin, *The Science and Politics of IQ* (Harmondsworth, Penguin, 1977).

P. Kennedy, *Preparing for the 21st Century* (London, HarperCollins, 1993).

Labour Party, *Twelve Wasted Years* (London, Labour Party, 1963).

D. Low, *Low's Autobiography* (London, Michael Joseph, 1956).

R. Low, *The History of the British Film*, Vol. 1 (London, Allen & Unwin, 1948).

I. McLaine, 'The Ministry of Information', unpublished D.Phil. thesis (University of Oxford, 1976).

——*The Ministry of Morale* (London, Allen & Unwin, 1978).

F. Marquis (ed.), *The Memoirs of the Rt Hon. the Earl of Woolton* (London, Cassell, 1959).

A. Marr, *Ruling Britannia* (London, Penguin, 1996).

A. Marwick, 'Middle opinion in the thirties', *English Historical Review*, 79, 2 (1964).

Mass Observation, *The War Begins at Home* (London, Chatto & Windus, 1940).

——*Home Propaganda* (London, Chatto & Windus, 1941).

——*War Factory* (London, Gollancz, 1943).

——*The Journey Home* (London, Murray, 1944).

——*The Press and Its Readers* (London, Art & Technics, 1949).

Ministry of Pensions, *Neuroses in War Time* (London, HMSO, 1940).

J. Montgomery, *The Fifties* (London, Collins, 1965).

H. Morrison, *Socialization and Transport* (London, Constable, 1933).

G. Mulgan, *Politics in an Anti-Political Age* (Cambridge, Polity Press, 1995).

H. Nicolson, *Diaries and Letters 1930–45* (London, Collins, 1967).

T. H. O'Brien, *British Experiments in Public Ownership and Control* (London, Allen & Unwin, 1937).

F. Owen, 'This war', *Horizon* (February 1940).

V. Packard, *The Hidden Persuaders* (London, Longman, 1957).

S. Papathanassopoulos, *European Television in the Digital Age* (London, Sage, 2002).

H. Pelling, *Britain and the Second World War* (London, Collins, 1970).

B. Pimlott, *Labour and the Left in the 1930s* (Cambridge, Cambridge University Press, 1977).

——*Hugh Dalton* (London, Cape, 1985).

——*Harold Wilson* (London, HarperCollins, 1993).

——*The Queen: A Biography of Queen Elizabeth II* (London, HarperCollins, 1996).

J. W. C. Reith, *Personality and Career* (London, George Newnes, 1925).

——*Winning Spurs* (London, Hutchinson, 1966).

P. Renshaw, *The General Strike* (London, Methuen, 1975).

W. A. Robson, *Public Enterprise* (London, New Fabian Research Bureau, 1937).

——*Nationalized Industry and Public Ownership* (London, Allen & Unwin, 1960).

R. J. W. Selleck, 'The scientific educationalist', *British Journal of Educational Studies*, 15, 3 (June 1967).

B. Simon, *Education and the Labour Movement, 1870–1920* (London, Lawrence & Wishart, 1965).

——*The Politics of Educational Reform, 1920–1940* (London, Lawrence & Wishart, 1971).

——*Intelligence, Psychology and Education* (London, Lawrence & Wishart, 1978).

P. Sissons and R. French (eds), *The Age of Austerity* (Harmondsworth, Penguin, 1962).

R. Skidelsky, *Politicians and the Slump* (London, Macmillan, 1967).

——'Keynes and the reconstruction of liberalism', *Encounter* (April 1979).

——*Maynard Keynes: A Biography – The World After Communism* (London, Macmillan, 1995).

J. Strachey, *Post D* (London, Gollancz, 1940).

B. Sweet–Escott, *Baker Street Irregular* (London, Collins, 1966).

J. Symons, *The General Strike* (London, Cressett, 1957).

S. Tallents, *The Projection of England* (London, Empire Marketing Board, 1932).

A. J. P. Taylor, *English History 1914–1945* (London, Allen & Unwin, 1965).

——*Beaverbrook* (London, Hamish Hamilton, 1972).

M. Thatcher, *The Downing Street Years* (London, HarperCollins, 1995).

R. Titmuss, *Problems of Social Policy* (London, Longman/HMSO, 1950).

Sir Robert Vansittart, *Black Record: Germans Past and Present* (London, Hamish Hamilton, 1941).

P. E. Vernon and J. B. Barry, *Personnel Selection in the British Forces* (London, University of London Press, 1949).

Beatrice Webb's Diaries, 1924–32, ed. M. Cole (London, Longman Green, 1956).

W. Whitelaw, *The Whitelaw Memoirs* (London, Aurum Press, 1989).

N. S. Wilson, *Education in the Forces, 1939–1946: The Civilian Contribution* (London, Allen & Unwin, 1949).

S. W. L. Woodward, *British Foreign Policy in the Second World War* (London, HMSO, 1970/1).

H. Young, *One of Us: A Biography of Margaret Thatcher* (London, Cape, 1993).

Sociology

T. W. Adorno, *Prisms* (Sudbury, Spearman, 1967).

——*The Jargon of Authenticity* (London, Routledge & Kegan Paul, 1973).

T. W. Adorno, E. F. Brunswick, D. J. Levinson and R. N. Sandford, *The Authoritarian Personality* (London, Harper & Row, 1950).

M. Alvarado and E. Buscombe, *Hazell: The Making of a Television Series* (London, British Film Institute, 1978).

H. Arendt, *The Burden of Our Time* (London, Secker & Warburg, 1950).

——*The Life of the Mind,* Vol. 2, *Thinking* (London, Secker & Warburg, 1978).

U. Beck, *The Risk Society* (London, Sage, 1995).

P. Becker and M. McCombs, 'The development of political cognition' in S. H. Chaffee (ed.), *Political Communication: Issues and Strategies* (Beverly Hills, Calif., Sage, 1975).

B. Berelson, 'The state of communication research', *Public Opinion Quarterly*, 31, 2 (1959).

S. Blanchard, *What's This Channel Four?* (London, Comedia, 1983).

J. G. Blumler, 'The audience', in *The Political Effects of Mass Communication* (Milton Keynes, Open University Press, DE 353, 1977).

——'The intervention of television in British politics', *Report of the Committee on the Future of Broadcasting* (Annan Report) (1977) [Cmnd 6753, Appendix E].

——'An overview of recent research into the impact of broadcasting in democratic politics' in M. J. Clark (ed.), *Politics and the Media* (Oxford, Pergamon Press, 1979).

J. G. Blumler and M. Gurevitch, 'Towards a comparative framework for political communication' in S. H. Chaffee (ed.), *Political Communication: Issues and Strategies* (London, Sage, 1975).

J. G. Blumler and D. McQuail, *Television in Politics: Its Uses and Influences* (London, Faber, 1968).

J. G. Blumler and J. Madge, *Citizenship and Television* (London, Political & Economic Planning, 1965).

D. Boorstin, *The Image, Or What Happened to the American Dream* (Harmondsworth, Penguin, 1963).

P. Bourdieu, *Outline of a Theory of Practice* (Cambridge, Cambridge University Press, 1977).

O. Boyd-Barrett, D. Seymour-Ure and J. Tunstall, *Studies on the Press,* Royal Commission on the Press 1974–7, Working Paper 3 (London, HMSO, 1977).

B. Brown, 'An interview with the film censor', *Screen*, 23, 5 (1982).

——'Pornography: some modest proposals', *M/F* (January 1982).

S. Bryant, *The Television Heritage* (London, British Film Institute, 1990).

M. Bulmer, *Working-Class Images of Society* (London, Routledge & Kegan Paul, 1975).

T. Burns, *The BBC, Public Institutions and Private World* (London, Macmillan, 1977).

H. Cantril, *The Invasion From Mars: A Study in the Psychology of Panic* (Princeton, NJ, Princeton University Press, 1940).

D. Chaney, *Processes of Mass Communication* (London, Macmillan, 1972).

M. Cockerell, P. Hennessy and D. Walker, *Sources Close to the Prime Minister* (London, Macmillan, 1984).

S. Cohen, *Images of Deviance* (Harmondsworth, Penguin, 1971).

S. Cohen and J. Young (eds), *The Manufacture of News* (London, Constable, 1973).

Conference of Socialist Economics Microelectronics Group, *Microelectronics: Capitalist Technology and the Working Class* (CSE Books, 1980).

I. Connell, 'Commercial broadcasting and the British left', *Screen*, 24, 6 (1983).

G. Cumberbatch and D. Howitt, *A Measure of Uncertainty: The Effects of the Mass Media* (London, Libbey, 1989).

J. Curran, 'The boomerang effect: the press and the battle for London 1981–6' in J. Curran and A. Smith (eds), *Impacts and Influences* (London, Methuen, 1986).

——'Culturalist perspectives of news organizations: a reappraisal and a case study' in M. Ferguson (ed.), *Public Communication* (London, Sage, 1990).

——'The new revisionism in mass communication research: a reappraisal', *European Journal of Communications*, 5, 2–3 (1990).

J. H. Dunning, *Multinational Corporations and the Global Economy* (Wokingham, Addison-Wesley, 1993).

R. Dyer, *Light Entertainment,* BFI Television Monograph 2 (London, British Film Institute, 1973).

M. Edelmann, *The Symbolic Uses of Politics* (Urbana, Ill., University of Illinois Press, 1964).

P. Elliot, *The Making of a Television Series* (London, Constable, 1972)

——'Intellectuals and "The information society" and the disappearance of the public sphere', *Media, Culture and Society*, 6, 4 (1982).

P. Elliot, G. Murdoch and P. Schlesinger, 'Terrorism and the state: a case study in the discourse of television', *Media, Culture and Society*, 5, 2 (1983).

——*Televising Terrorism* (London, Comedia, 1984).

J. Ellis, *Visible Fiction: Cinema, TV, Video* (London, Routledge & Kegan Paul, 1982).

E. J. Epstein, *News from Nowhere* (New York, Random House, 1973).

R. Ericson, P. Baranec and J. Chan, *Visualizing Deviance* (Milton Keynes, Open University Press, 1987).

J. Fiske, *Television Culture* (London, Methuen, 1987).

S. Frith, *The Sociology of Rock* (London, Constable, 1979).

——*The Aesthetics of Rock* (London, Macmillan, 1997).

P. Fussell, *The Great War in Modern Memory* (London, Oxford University Press, 1975).

N. Garnham, *Structures of Television*, BFI Television Monograph 1 (London, British Film Institute, 1973).

——'Contribution to a political economy of mass communications', *Media, Culture and Society*, 1, 2 (April 1979).

——'Public service versus the market', *Screen*, 24, 1 (1983).

E. Gellner, *Nations and Nation Building* (Cambridge, Cambridge University Press, 1984).

A. Giddens, *The Transformations of Intimacy: Sexuality, Love and Eroticism in Modern Societies* (Cambridge, Polity Press, 1992).

——*Post-Modernity* (Cambridge, Polity Press, 1994).

——*Beyond Left and Right* (Cambridge, Polity Press, 1995).

T. Gitlin, 'Prime time ideology: the hegemonic process in television entertainment', *Social Problems*, 25, 3 (1979).

——*The Whole World is Watching* (Berkeley, Calif., University of California Press, 1982).

Glasgow University Media Group, *Bad News* (London, Routledge & Kegan Paul, 1976).

——*More Bad News* (London, Routledge & Kegan Paul, 1980).

P. Golding, *The Mass Media* (Harlow, Longman, 1974).

P. Golding and P. Elliot, *Making the News* (Harlow, Longman, 1979).

P. Golding and S. Middleton, *Images of Welfare* (London, Macmillan, 1980).

J. H. Goldthorpe and D. Lockwood, *The Affluent Worker: Political Attitudes and Behaviour* (Cambridge, Cambridge University Press, 1968).

S. Hall, 'The external/internal dialectic on broadcasting', *4th Symposium on British Broadcasting Policy*, February 1972.

——'The determination of news photographs' in S. Cohen and J. Young (eds), *The Manufacture of News* (London, Constable, 1973).

——'The hinterland of science: ideology' in Centre for Contemporary Cultural Studies, *On Ideology* (London, Hutchinson, 1977).

——'Culture, the media and the ideological effect' in J. Curran, M. Gurevitch and J. Woollacott (eds), *Mass Communication and Society* (London, Edward Arnold/Open University, 1977).

——'Newspapers, parties and classes', in J. Curran (ed.), *The British Press: A Manifesto* (London, Macmillan, 1978).

S. Hall, C. Critcher, T. Jefferson, J. Clarke and B. Roberts, *Policing the Crisis: Mugging, the State, and Law and Order* (London, Macmillan, 1978).

S. Hall, C. Curtis and I. Connell, 'The unity of current events TV' in Centre for Contemporary Cultural Studies, *Working Papers in Cultural Studies*, 9 (spring 1976).

J. D. Halloran and G. Murdoch, *Demonstrations and Communications* (Harmondsworth, Penguin, 1970).

P. Halmos (ed.), *Sociology of Mass Media Communicators*, Sociological Review Monograph 13 (Keele, University of Keele, 1969).

R. Harris, *Gotcha! The Media and the Falklands War* (London, Faber, 1983).

M. Harrop, 'Voters and the media' in J. Seaton and B. Pimlott (eds), *The Media in British Politics* (Aldershot, Gower, 1987).

M. Harrop and R. Worcester (eds), *Political Communication: The 1979 General Election* (London, Macmillan, 1981).

P. Hartmann and C. Husband, *Racism and the Mass Media* (London, Davis-Poynter, 1973).

B. Harvey, *The Condition of Post-Modernity* (Oxford, Oxford University Press, 1992).

F. Hayek, *The Road to Serfdom* (London, Routledge & Kegan Paul, 1944).

D. Held, *Democracy and the New International Order* (Cambridge, Polity Press, 1993).

——(ed.), *Prospects for Democracy* (Cambridge, Polity Press, 1994).

C. Heller, *Broadcasters and Accountability*, BFI Television Monograph 3 (London, British Film Institute, 1978).

E. Herman and N. Chomsky, *Manufacturing Consent* (New York, Pantheon, 1988).

P. M. Hirsch, 'Processing fads and fashions', *American Journal of Sociology*, 46, 1 (1977).

P. Hirst, *After Thatcher* (London, Hutchinson, 1991).

P. Hirst and S. Khilnani, *Re-Inventing Democracy* (London, Political Quarterly, 1996).

P. Hirst and G. Thompson, *Globalisation in Question* (Cambridge, Polity Press, 1996).

D. Hobson, *Crossroads* (London, Methuen, 1983).

P. Hoch, *The Newspaper Game* (London, Calder & Boyars, 1974).

R. Hoggart, *The Uses of Literacy* (London, Chatto & Windus, 1957).

A. Hooper, *The Military and the Media* (London, Routledge & Kegan Paul, 1981).

M. Horkheimer, *The Eclipse of Reason* (Oxford, Oxford University Press, 1947).

C. I. Hovland, *Experiments in Mass Communication* (Princeton, NJ, Princeton University Press, 1949).

——'Reconciling conflicting results derived from experimental and survey studies of attitude change', *American Psychologist*, 14, 3 (1959).

J. Howkins, *New Technologies, New Policies* (London, British Film Institute, 1982).

G. A. Huaco, *The Sociology of Film Art* (New York, Basic Books, 1965).

C. Husband (ed.), *White Media and Black Britain* (London, Routledge & Kegan Paul, 1962).

B. Jackson and D. Marsden, *Education and the Working Class* (London, Routledge & Kegan Paul, 1962).

M. Jay, *The Dialectical Imagination* (London, Heinemann, 1973).

E. Katz and P. Lazarsfeld, *Personal Influence: The Part Played by People in the Flow of Mass Communication* (West Drayton, Free Press, 1955).

T. Klapper, *The Effects of Mass Communication* (West Drayton, Free Press, 1960).

F. G. Kline and P. J. Tichenor, *Current Perspectives in Mass Communications Research* (London, Sage, 1972).

W. Kornhauser, *The Politics of Mass Society* (London, Routledge & Kegan Paul, 1959).

R. Kuhn, 'Government broadcasting in the 1980s: cross channel perspective', *Political Quarterly*, 53, 4 (1982).

——'Ballot box', *Stills* (May–June 1983).

K. Kumar, 'Holding the middle ground: the BBC, the public and the professional broadcaster' in J. Curran, M. Gurevitch and J. Woollacott (eds), *Mass Communication and Society* (London, Edward Arnold/Open University Press, 1977).

——*Policy and Progress* (Harmondsworth, Penguin, 1978).

——*Utopia and Anti-Utopianism in Modern Times* (Oxford, Blackwell, 1991).

S. Lambert, *Channel 4* (London, British Film Institute, 1982).

K. Lang, 'Images of society, media research in Germany', *Public Opinion Quarterly*, 22, 3 (1974).

K. Lang and G. Lang, *Politics and Television* (New York, Quadrangle, 1968).

——*The Battle For Public Opinion: Watergate and the Media* (Westport, Conn., Greenwood Press, 1982).

S. Lasch and J. Urry, *The End of Organised Capital* (Cambridge, Polity Press, 1990).

H. D. Lasswell, *Psychopathology and Politics* (Chicago, Ill., University of Chicago Press, 1930).

——'The garrison state', *American Journal of Sociology*, 46, 2 (1941).

P. Lazarsfeld and R. Merton, 'Mass communication, popular taste and organised social action' in B. Rosenberg and D. White (eds), *Mass Culture* (West Drayton, Free Press, 1957).

P. Lazarsfeld and F. Stanton, *Radio Research 1942–3* (Boston, Mass., Duell Sloan Pearce, 1944).

P. Lazarsfeld, B. Berelson and H. Gaudet, *The People's Choice* (New York, Columbia University Press, 1944).

M. Leapman, *Treachery? The Power Struggle at TVAM* (London, Allen & Unwin, 1984).

F. R. Leavis, *Mass Civilisation and Minority Culture* (London, Minority Press, 1930).

——*The Common Pursuit* (London, Chatto & Windus, 1952).

——*Scrutiny: A Retrospect* (Cambridge, Cambridge University Press, 1962).

——*A Selection From Scrutiny*, 2 vols (Cambridge, Cambridge University Press, 1968).

F. R. Leavis and D. Thompson, *Culture and Environment* (London, Chatto & Windus, 1933).

Q. D. Leavis, *Fiction and the Reading Public* (London, Chatto & Windus, 1932).

T. Lovell, 'Sociology of aesthetic structures' in D. McQuail (ed.), *Sociology of Mass Communications* (Harmondsworth, Penguin, 1972).

L. Lowenthal, *Prophets of Deceit* (New York, Harper & Row, 1949).

R. S. Lynd and H. M. Lynd, *Middletown: A Study on Contemporary American Culture* (London, Constable, 1929).

——*Middletown: In Transition* (London, Constable, 1935).

A. McBarnett, 'The North Sea oil story', *Scottish Journal of Sociology*, 3, 1 (1977).

D. McQuail, *Towards a Sociology of Mass Communication* (West Drayton, Collier Macmillan, 1969).

——*Sociology of Mass Communications* (Harmondsworth, Penguin, 1972).

——'Review of sociological writings on the press', Royal Commission on the Press 1974–7, Working Paper 2 (London, HMSO, 1977).

——*Mass Communication Theory: An Introduction* (2nd edn) (London, Sage, 1987).

H. Marcuse, *'The End of Utopia', Five Lectures* (Harmondsworth, Allen Lane, 1970).

——*One Dimensional Man* (London, Routledge & Kegan Paul, 1974).

M. Mendelsohn and I. Crespi, *Polls, Television and the New Politics* (New York, Harper & Row, 1970).

R. K. Merton, *Social Theory and Social Structure* (West Drayton, Free Press, 1957).

F. Mulhearn, *The Moment of Scrutiny* (London, New Left Books, 1979).

K. Ohmae, *The Borderless World* (London, Collins, 1993).

——*The End of the Nation State* (London, HarperCollins, 1996).

E. Ostrom, *Governing the Commons* (Oxford, Oxford University Press, 1994).

T. Pateman, *Language, Truth and Politics* (Brighton, Southern Books, 1974).

——*Television and the February 1974 General Election* (London, British Film Institute, 1976).

J. A. R. Pimlott, *Public Relations and American Democracy* (Princeton, NJ, Princeton University Press, 1951; repr. 1974).

A. Ray and K. Rowan (eds), *Inside Information: British Government and the Media* (London, Constable, 1982).

D. Reisman, *The Lonely Crowd* (New Haven, Conn., Yale University Press, 1950).

J. P. Robinson, 'The press as king-maker', *Journalism Quarterly*, 41, 4 (1974).

B. Rosenberg and D. White (eds), *Mass Culture* (West Drayton, Free Press, 1957).

P. Schlesinger, *Putting 'Reality' Together* (London, Constable, 1974).

——'Rethinking the sociology of journalism: source strategies and the limits of media-centrism' in M. Ferguson (ed.), *Public Communication* (London, Sage, 1990).

J. Seaton, 'The image of trade unions in the media' in B. Pimlott and C. Cook (eds), *Trade Unions in British Politics* (Harlow, Longman, 1982).

——'The media and the politics of unemployment' in S. Allen, S. Waton and S. Wood (eds), *Unemployment* (London, Macmillan, 1985).

——'Politics and the media in Britain', *Journal of Western European Politics*, special broadcasting issue (London, summer 1985).

J. Seaton and B. Pimlott, 'The role of the media in the Portuguese Revolution' in A. Smith (ed.), *Newspapers and Democracy* (Cambridge, Mass, MIT Press, 1980).

——'The Portuguese media in transition' in K. Maxwell (ed.), *The Press and the Rebirth of Iberian Democracy* (Westport, Conn., Greenwood Press, 1983).

——'Political power and the Portuguese media' in L. Graham (ed.), *In Search of*

Modern Portugal: The Revolution and its Consequences (Madison, University of Wisconsin Press, 1983).

C. Seymour-Ure, *The Press, Politics and Public* (London, Methuen, 1968).

——*The Political Impact of the Mass Media* (London, Constable, 1974).

——*The American President: Power and Communication* (London, Macmillan, 1982).

——'The SDP and the media', *Political Quarterly*, 53, 4 (1982).

E. Shils, *The Intellectuals and the Powers* (Chicago, Ill., University of Chicago Press, 1972).

E. Shils and M. Janowitz, 'Cohesion and disintegration in the Wehrmacht in World War II', *Public Opinion Quarterly*, 12, 3 (London, 1948).

P. Siegelhart (ed.), *Chips with Everything* (London, Comedia, 1982).

P. Slater, *The Origin and Significance of the Frankfurt School* (London, Routledge & Kegan Paul, 1977).

A. Smith, *The Politics of Information* (London, Macmillan, 1968).

——*The Shadow in the Cave* (London, Allen & Unwin, 1973).

——(ed.), *Television and Political Life* (London, Macmillan, 1979).

——'The fading of the industrial age', *Political Quarterly*, 53, 3 (June 1983).

——*From Books to Bytes* (London, BFI, 1993).

B. L. Smith, H. D. Lasswell and R. Casey, *Propaganda Communication and Public Opinion* (Princeton, NJ, Princeton University Press, 1946).

A. Swingewood, *The Myth of Mass Culture* (London, Macmillan, 1977).

M. Tracey, *The Production of Political Television* (London, Routledge & Kegan Paul, 1978).

J. Trenaman, *Communications and Comprehension* (London, Collins, 1967).

J. Trenaman and D. McQuail, *Television and the Political Image* (London, Methuen, 1961).

G. Tuchman, 'Making news by doing work', *American Journal of Sociology*, 79, 1 (1973).

——(ed.), *The TV Establishment* (New York, Random House, 1975).

J. Tulloch, *Watching Television Audiences* (London, Arnold, 2000).

J. Tunstall, *Advertising Man* (London, Constable, 1969).

——*The Westminster Lobby Correspondents* (London, Routledge & Kegan Paul, 1970).

——*Journalists at Work* (London, Constable, 1971).

——*The Media in Britain* (London, Constable, 1983).

F. Webster, *The Information Society* (Cambridge, Polity Press, 1996).

E. G. Wedell, *Broadcasting and Public Policy* (London, Michael Joseph, 1968).

——*Structures of Broadcasting* (Manchester, Manchester University Press, 1970).

J. Whale, *The Half Shut Eye* (London, Macmillan, 1969).

——*The Politics of the Media* (London, Fontana, 1977).

R. Williams, *The Long Revolution* (Harmondsworth, Pelican, 1965).

——*Communications* (London, Chatto & Windus, 1966).

——*Television: Technology and Cultural Form* (London, Fontana, 1974).

——*Drama from Ibsen to Brecht* (Harmondsworth, Penguin, 1976).

——*Keywords* (London, Fontana, 1976).

——*Marxism and Literature* (Oxford, Oxford University Press, 1977).

——*Politics and Letters: Interviews with the New Left Review* (London, New Left Books, 1979).

J. Willis and T. Wollen (eds), *The Neglected Audience* (London, British Film Institute, 1990).

P. Willis, *Learning to Labour* (Farnborough, Saxon House, 1977).

——*Sacred and Profane Culture* (London, Routledge & Kegan Paul, 1978).

P. Willmott and M. D. Young, *Family and Class in a London Suburb* (London, Routledge & Kegan Paul, 1960).

——*The Symmetrical Family* (London, Routledge & Kegan Paul, 1973).

Mass communications readers

O. Boyd Barrett and C. Newbold (eds), *Approaches to Media* (London, Arnold, 1995).

R. Collins, J. Curran, N. Garnham, P. Scannell, P. Schlesinger and C. Sparks (eds), *Media, Culture and Society: A Critical Reader* (London, Sage, 1986).

J. Curran and M. Gurevitch (eds), *Mass Media and Society* (2nd edn) (London, Arnold, 1996).

J. Curran and A. Smith (eds), *Impacts and Influences* (London, Methuen, 1987).

J. Curran, M. Gurevitch and J. Woollacott (eds), *Mass Communication and Society* (London, Edward Arnold/Open University, 1977).

J. Curran, D. Morley and V. Walkerdine (eds), *Cultural Studies and Communications* (London, Arnold, 1996).

J. Downing, A. Mohammadi and A. Sreberny-Mohammadi (eds), *Questioning the Media* (2nd edn) (London, Sage, 1995).

J. Eldridge (ed.), *Getting the Message* (London, Routledge, 1993).

M. Ferguson (ed.), *Public Communication* (London, Sage, 1990).

M. Gurevitch, T. Bennett, J. Curran and J. Woollacott (eds), *Culture, Society and the Media* (London, Methuen, 1982).

M. Levy and M. Gurevitch (eds), *Defining Media Studies* (New York, Oxford University Press, 1994).

D. McQuail (ed.), *Sociology of Mass Communication: Selected Reading* (Harmondsworth, Penguin, 1972).

R. Manoff and M. Schudson (ed.), *Reading the News* (New York, Pantheon, 1987).

P. Marris and S. Thornham (eds), *Media Studies* (Edinburgh, Edinburgh University Press, 1996).

J. Munns, *A Cultural Studies Reader* (London, Longman, 1996).

E. Seiter, H. Borchers, G. Kreutzner and E.-M. Warth (eds), *Remote Control* (London, Routledge, 1989).

Economic approaches to the media

T. P. Barwise, A. S. C. Ehrenberg and G. J. Goodhart, 'Audience appreciation and audience size', *Journal of the Market Research Society*, 21, 4 (October 1979).

L. Brown, *Television: The Business Behind the Box* (New York, Harcourt Brace Jovanovich, 1971).

M. Cave, 'The conduct of auctions for broadcasting franchises', *Fiscal Studies*, 10, 1 (February 1989).

R. H. Coase, *British Broadcasting: A Study in Monopoly* (London, Longman Green, 1950).

——'The market for goods and the market for ideas', *American Economic Review* (1974), p. 384.

R. Collins, N. Garnham and G. Locksley, *The Economics of Television: The UK Case* (London, Sage, 1987).

——*The Economics of Television* (London, Sage, 1988).

T. Congdon, B. Sturgess, NERA, W. Shaw, A. Graham and G. Davies, *Paying for Broadcasting* (London, Routledge, 1992).

J. Curran, 'Advertising and the press' in J. Curran (ed.), *The British Press: A Manifesto* (London, Macmillan, 1978).

——'Press freedom as a property right', *Media, Culture and Society*, 1, 1 (1979).

——'Advertising as a patronage system', *Sociological Review Monograph*, 29 (1980).

——'The impact of advertising on the British mass media' in R. Collins *et al.* (eds), *Media Culture and Society: A Critical Reader* (London, Sage, 1986).

J. Curran, A. Douglas and G. Whannel, 'The political economy of the human interest story' in A. Smith (ed.), *Newspapers and Democracy* (Cambridge, Mass., MIT Press, 1981).

R. Darlington, 'Telecoms: the broadband revolution', *Information Technology and Public Policy*, 8, 1 (winter 1989).

E. Epstein, *Broadcast Journalism. The Ratings Game* (London and New York, Vintage, 1975).

J. E. Gerald, *The British Press under Government Economic Controls* (Minneapolis, University of Minnesota Press, 1956).

T. Gitlin, *Inside Prime Time* (New York, Pantheon, 1983).

P. Golding and G. Murdoch, 'Culture, communications and political economy', in J. Curran and M. Gurevitch (eds), *Mass Media and Society* (2nd edn) (London, Arnold, 1996).

G. J. Goodhart, A. S. C. Ehrenberg and M. A. Collins, *The Television Audience: Patterns of Viewing* (Farnborough, Saxon House, 1975)

N. Gowing, 'Real time television and political crises' (Shorenstein Centre Paper, Kennedy School of Government, 1994).

T. H. Gubach, *The International Film Industry* (Indiana, University of Indiana Press, 1971).

A. Henney, 'Regulating public and privatized monopolies: a radical approach', *Policy Journal for the Public Finance Corporation* (February 1986).

F. Hirsch and D. Gordan, *Newspaper Money* (London, Hutchinson, 1975).

P. M. Hirsch, 'Processing fads and fashions', *American Journal of Sociology*, 77 (1972).

S. Hoyer, S. Hadenius and I. Weibull, *The Politics and Economics of the Press: A Developmental Perspective* (Beverly Hills, Calif., Sage, 1975).

R. E. Jackson, 'Satellite business systems and the concept of the dispersed enterprise', *Media, Culture and Society*, 1, 3 (1979).

F. D. Klingender and S. Legg, *Money Behind the Screen* (London, Lawrence & Wishart, 1937).

M. Matson, 'Telecoms: the broadband revolution', Parliamentary Information Technology Committee 2 (22 November 1989).

A. Mattelart (trans. M. Chanan), *Multinational Corporations and the Control of Culture* (Brighton, Harvester Press, 1979).

K. Morgan and A. Sayer, *Microcircuits of Capital: Sunrise Industry and Uneven Development* (London, Polity Press, 1987).

V. Mosco, *The Political Economy of Information* (Madison, Wisconsin University Press, 1988).

G. Mulgan, *Communication and Control* (London, Polity Press, 1990).

G. Murdock, 'Redrawing the map of the communications industries: concentration and ownership in the era of privatization' in M. Ferguson (ed.), *Public Communication* (London, Sage, 1990).

G. Murdock and P. Golding, 'For a political economy of mass communication' in J. Saville and R. Miliband (eds), *The Socialist Register 1973* (London, Merlin, 1974).

——'Capitalism, communication and class relations' in J. Curran, M. Gurevitch and J. Woollacott (eds), *Mass Communication and Society* (London, Edward Arnold/Open University Press, 1977).

Political and Economic Planning, *The British Press* (London, PEP, 1938).

——*The Factual Film* (London, Arts Enquiry, PEP, 1947).

——*The British Film Industry* (London, PEP, 1952).

R. Putnam, *Hanging Together: Cooperation and Conflict in Seven Power Summits* (Cambridge, Mass., Harvard University Press, 1987).

K. Robins and F. Webster, 'Mass communications and information technology' in R. Miliband and J. Saville (eds), *The Socialist Register 1979* (London, Merlin, 1979).

H. Schiller, *Who Knows: Information in the Age of Fortune 500* (New Jersey, Ablex, 1981).

——*Mass Communications and the American Empire* (Boulder, Col., Westview Press, 1993).

M. Sharp (ed.), *Europe and New Technologies* (London, Pinter, 1989).

A. Smith, 'Subsidies and the press in Europe', *Political and Economic Planning*, 43, 569 (1977).

——*The Geopolitics of Information* (London, Faber, 1980).

——*Goodbye Gutenburg: The Newspaper Revolution of the 1980s* (London, Oxford University Press, 1980).

S. G. Sturmey, *The Economic Development of Radio* (London, Duckworth, 1958).

J. Taylor, 'The broadband revolution: implications for major networks', *Information Technology and Public Policy*, 8, 1 (winter 1990).

J. Tunstall, *The Media are American* (London, Constable, 1977).

T. Varis, 'The international flow of television programmes', *Journal of Communication*, 34 (1984).

F. Wolf, *Television Programming for News and Current Affairs* (New York, Praeger, 1972).

Politics of British mass media

Adam Smith Institute, *Omega Report: Communications Policy* (London, Adam Smith Institute, 1984).

——*Funding the BBC* (London, Adam Smith Institute, 1985).

M. Aldridge and N. Hewitt (eds), *Controlling Broadcasting* (Manchester, Manchester University Press, 1994).

N. Ascherson, 'Newspapers and internal democracy' in J. Curran (ed.), *The British Press: A Manifesto* (London, Macmillan, 1978).

T. Austin and T. Haines (eds), *The Times Guide to the House of Commons June 2001* (London, Times Books, 2001).

R. Avery (ed.), *Public Service Broadcasting in a Multichannel Environment* (New York, Longman, 1993).

T. Baistow, *Fourth-Rate Estate* (London, Comedia, 1985).

E. Barendt, *Broadcasting Law* (Oxford, Oxford University Press, 1993).

J. Barron, *Freedom of the Press for Whom?* (Ontario, Midland, 1975).

D. Berry, L. Cooper and C. Landry, *Where is the Other News?* (London, Comedia, 1980).

J. Blumler and M. Gurevitch, *The Crisis of Public Communication* (London, Routledge, 1995).

S. Brittan, 'The fight for freedom in broadcasting', *Political Quarterly*, 58 (1987).

——'The case for the consumer market' in C. Veljanovski (ed.), *Freedom in Broadcasting* (London, Institute of Economic Affairs, 1989).

Broadcasting Research Unit, *The Public Service Idea* (London, Broadcasting Research Unit, 1985).

D. Butler and G. Butler, *Twentieth-Century British Political Facts, 1900–2000* (8th edn) (Basingstoke, Macmillan, 2000).

V. Cable, *The World's New Fissure* (London, Demos, 1994).

M. Cockerell, *Live from No. 10* (London, Faber and Faber, 1988).

R. Collins, *Television: Culture and Policy* (London, Unwin Hyman, 1990).

——*Satellite Television in Western Europe* (revised edn) (London, Libbey, 1992).

——*Broadcasting and Audio-visual Policy in the European Single Market* (London, Libbey, 1994).

R. Collins and C. Murroni, *New Media, New Policies* (Cambridge, Polity Press, 1996).

L. Cooper, C. Landry and D. Berry, *The Other Secret Service* (London, Comedia, 1980).

G. Cumberbatch and D. Howitt, *A Measure of Uncertainty* (London, Libbey, 1989).

J. Curran (ed.), *The British Press: A Manifesto* (London, Macmillan, 1978).

——'Rethinking the media as a public sphere' in P. Dahlgren and C. Sparks (eds), *Communication and Citizenship* (London, Routledge, 1991).

——'Regulation and deregulation of the British media', in K. E. Gustafsson (ed.) *Media Structure and the State* (Gothenburg, University of Gothenburg, 1995).

——'Mass media and democracy revisited' in J. Curran and M. Gurevitch (eds), *Mass Media and Democracy* (2nd edn) (London, Arnold, 1996).

——'Media and democracy: the third route' in M. Andersen (ed.), *Media and Democracy* (Oslo, University of Oslo, 1996).

——'Television journalism: theory and practice. The case of *Newsnight*' in P. Holland, *Television Handbook* (London, Routledge, 1997).

—— 'Press reformism 1918–98: a study of failure' in H. Tumber (ed.), *Media Power, Professionals and Policies* (London, Routlege, 2000).

—— *Media and Power* (London, Routledge, 2002).

—— 'Global journalism: a case study of the internet' in Nick Couldry and James Curran (eds), *Contesting Media Power* (Boulder, Col., Rowman & Littlefield, 2003).

J. Curran, J. Ecclestone, G. Oakley and A. Richardson (eds), *Bending Reality: The State of the Media* (London, Pluto Press, 1986).

P. Dahlgren, *Television and the Public Sphere* (London, Sage, 1995).

—— (eds), *Communication and Citizenship* (London, Routledge, 1991).

P. Dahlgren and C. Sparks (eds), *Journalism and Popular Culture* (London, Sage, 1992).

M. Dickinson and S. Street (eds), *Cinema and the State* (London, British Film Institute, 1985).

B. Franklin, *Packaging Politics* (London, Arnold, 1994).

C. Gardiner and J. Sheppard, 'Transforming TV: the limits of left policy', *Screen*, 25, 2 (1984).

N. Garnham, 'Public service versus the market', *Screen*, 24, 1 (1983).

——'Telecommunications policy in the United Kingdom', *Media, Culture and Society*, 7, 1 (1985).

——*Communications and Capitalism* (London, Sage, 1990).

T. Gitlin, 'Public sphere or sphericules?' in T. Liebes and J. Curran (eds), *Media, Ritual and Identity* (London, Routledge, 1998).

Glasgow University Media Group, *Really Bad News* (London, Writers & Readers, 1982).

D. Goldberg, T. Prosser and S. Verhulst, *Regulating the Changing Media* (Oxford, Clarendon Press, 1998).

P. Golding and G. Murdock, 'Confronting the market: public intervention and press diversity' in J. Curran (ed.), *The British Press: A Manifesto* (London, Macmillan, 1978).

——'The new communications revolution' in J. Curran, J. Ecclestone, G. Oakley and A. Richardson (eds), *Bending Reality: The State of the Media* (London, Pluto Press, 1986).

A. Graham and G. Davies, *Broadcasting, Society and Policy in the Multimedia Age* (Luton, University of Luton Press, 1997).

J. Gray, *After Social Democracy* (London, Demos, 1996).

K. E. Gustafsson, 'Government policies to reduce newspaper entry barriers', *Journal of Economics*, 6, 1 (1993).

I. Hargreaves, *A Sharper Vision: The BBC and the Communication Revolution* (London, Demos, 1993).

S. Harvey (ed.), *The Regions, the Nation, the BBC* (London, BFI, 1993).

S. Harvey and K. Robins, 'Voices and places: the BBC and regional policy', *Political Quarterly*, 65, 1 (1994).

S. Hearst, 'The development of cable systems and services', *Political Quarterly*, 54, 3 (1983).

P. Hennessy, D. Walker and M. Cockerell, *Sources Close to the Prime Minister* (London, Macmillan, 1985).

D. Hesmondhaulgh, *The Cultural Industries* (London, Sage, 2002).

S. Holland, 'Countervailing press power' in J. Curran (ed.), *The British Press: A Manifesto* (London, Macmillan, 1978).

S. Hood (ed.), *Behind the Scenes* (London, Lawrence & Wishart, 1994).

S. Hood and G. O'Leary, *Questions of Broadcasting* (London, Methuen, 1990).

R. Horwitz, 'The First Amendment meets some new technologies: broadcasting, common carriers and free speech in the 1990s', *Theory and Society* (1990).

P. Humphreys, *Mass Media and Media Policy in Western Europe* (Manchester, Manchester University Press, 1996).

N. Jones, *Soundbites and Spin Doctors* (London, Cassell, 1995).

E. Katz, 'And deliver us from segmentation', *Annals of the American Academy of Political and Social Science*, 546 (1996).

J. Keane, *The Media and Democracy* (Cambridge, Polity Press, 1991).

S. K. Kent, *Gender and Power in Britain, 1640–1990* (London, Routledge, 1999).

A. Knight, *A British Success Story* (London, News International, 1993).

Labour Party, *People and the Media* (London, Labour Party, 1974).

C. Landry, D. Morley, R. Southwood and P. Write, *What a Way to Run a Railroad* (London, Comedia, 1985).

Colin Leys, *Market-Driven Politics* (London, Verso, 2001).

L. Lichtenberg, 'The Dutch model of press policy', in K. E. Gustafsson (ed.), *Media Structure and the State* (Gothenberg, University of Gothenberg, 1995).

S. Livingstone and P. Lunt, *Talk on Television* (London, Routledge, 1994).

C. MacCabe and Olivia Stewart (eds), *The BBC and Public Service Broadcasting* (Manchester, Manchester University Press, 1986).

P. McDonald, 'The music industry' in J. Stokes and A. Reading (eds), *The Media in Britain* (Basingstoke, Macmillan, 1999).

B. McNair, *Mediated Sex* (London, Arnold, 1996).

——*News and Journalism in the UK* (2nd edn) (London, Routledge, 1996)

D. McQuail and K. Siane (eds), *New Media Politics* (London, Sage, 1986).

T. Madge, *Beyond the BBC* (London, Macmillan, 1989).

W. Melody, 'Communication policy in the global information economy: whither the public interest' in M. Ferguson (ed.), *Public Communication* (London, Sage, 1990).

Militant, *What We Stand For* (London, Militant, 1985).

E. Moonman (ed.), *The Press: A Case for Commitment* (London, Fabian Society Trust, 391, 1969).

G. Mulgan and K. Worpole, *Saturday Night or Sunday Morning* (London, Comedia, 1986).

P. Murschetz, 'State support for the daily press in Europe: a critical appraisal', *European Journal of Communication*, 13, 3 (1998).

R. Murdoch, 'Freedom in broadcasting', *MacTaggart Lecture 1989* (London, News International, 1989).

R. Negrine, *Politics and the Mass Media in Britain* (2nd edn) (London, Routledge, 1994).

T. O'Malley and C. Soley, *Regulating the Press* (London, Pluto Press, 2000).

R. Picard, *Ravens of Odin* (Ames, Iowa State University Press, 1988).

V. Porter, 'The Janus character of television' in G. Locksley (ed.), *Integration: The Single European Market and the Information Communication Technologies* (London, Pinter, 1990).

G. Robertson, *People Against the Press* (London, Quartet, 1983).

G. Robertson and A. Nicol, *Media Law* (3rd edn) (Harmondsworth, Penguin, 1992).

L. Sabato, *Feeding Frenzy: Attack Journalism and Politics* (New York, Free Press, 1995).

Paddy Scannell, 'Public service broadcasting and modern public life' in P. Scannell, P. Schlesinger and C. Sparks (eds), *Culture and Power* (London, Sage, 1992).

P. Schlesinger, 'From public service to commodity: the political economy of teletext in the UK', *Media, Culture and Society*, 7, 4 (1984).

J. Seaton, 'Government policy and the mass media' in J. Curran (ed.), *The British Press: A Manifesto* (London, Macmillan, 1978).

——'Broadcasting and politics in Britain' in R. Kuhn (ed.), *Broadcasting and Politics in Western Europe* (London, Sage, 1985).

——'The media and politics in Britain', *Journal of Western European Politics*, 6, 3 (June 1985).

——'Pornography annoys' in J. Curran (ed.), *Bending Reality: The State of the Media* (London, Pluto Press, 1986).

——'The media and the politics of unemployment' in S. Allen (ed.), *The Experience of Unemployment* (London, Macmillan, 1986).

——'Atrocities and the media', *European Journal of Communications*, 2, 1 (January 1987).

——'The Holocaust: a case study of atrocities and the media' in J. Seaton and B. Pimlott (eds), *The Media in British Politics* (Aldershot, Gower, 1987).

——'Down with Aunt Tabitha: a modest media proposal' in B. Pimlott and T. Wright (eds), *The Alternative: Politics for a Change* (London, W. H. Allen, 1990).

——(ed.) *The Media of Conflict* (London, Zed Books, 1998).

——*Politics & the Media in the New Milennium* (Blackwell, 1998).

J. Seaton and B. Pimlott, 'The struggle for balance: the BBC and the politicians 1926–1945' in J. Seaton and B. Pimlott (eds), *The Media in British Politics* (Aldershot, Gower, 1987).

C. Seymour-Ure, 'Leaders and the media' in J. Seaton and B. Pimlott (eds), *The Media in British Politics* (Aldershot, Gower, 1987).

J. Sinclair, E. Jacka and S. Cunningham (eds), *New Patterns in Global Television* (Oxford, Oxford University Press, 1996).

E. Skogerbo, 'The press subsidy system in Norway', *European Journal of Communication*, 12, 1, (1997).

A. Smith, *Subsidies and the Press in Europe* (London, Political & Economic Planning, 1977).

R. Sparks and I. Taylor, 'Mass communications' in P. Brown and R. Sparks (eds), *Beyond Thatcherism* (Milton Keynes, Open University Press, 1989).

W. Stevenson (ed.), *All our Futures* (London, BFI, 1993).

C. Veljanovski (ed.), *Freedom in Broadcasting* (London, Institute of Economic Affairs, 1989).

J. Whale, *The Politics of the Media* (London, Fontana, 1980).

P. Whitehead, 'Reconstructing broadcasting' in J. Curran, J. Ecclestone, G. Oakley and A. Richardson (eds), *Bending Reality: The State of the Media* (London, Pluto Press, 1986).

R. Worcester, 'Demographics and values: what the British public reads and what it thinks about its newspapers' in H. Stephenson and M. Bromley (eds), *Sex, Lies and Democracy* (London, Longman, 1998).

New media

J. Abbate, *Inventing the Internet* (Cambridge, MA, MIT Press, 2000).

Advertising Statistics Yearbook 2002 (London, Advertising Association, 2002).

N. Baym, 'Interpersonal life online' in L. Lievrouw and S. Livingstone (eds), *The Handbook of New Media* (London, Sage, 2002).

D. Bell and B. Kennedy (eds), *The Cybercultures Reader* (London, Routledge, 2000).

C. Bellamy and J. Taylor, *Governing in the Information Age* (Milton Keynes, Open University Press, 1998).

T. Berners-Lee, *Weaving the Web* (London, Orion, 2000), p. 56.

A. Briggs and P. Burke, *A Social History of the Media* (Cambridge, Polity Press, 2002).

M. Cassells, *The Internet Galaxy* (Oxford, Oxford University Press, 2001).

N. Chenoweth, *Virtual Murdoch* (London, Secker Warburg, 2001).

S. Coleman, 'New media and democratic politics', *New Media and Society*, 1, 1 (1999).

J. Cornford and K. Robins, 'New media' in J. Stokes and A. Reading (eds), *The Media in Britain* (Basingstoke, Macmillan, 1999).

J. Curran, 'Global journalism: a case study of the internet' in N. Couldry and J. Curran (eds), *Contesting Media Power* (New York, Rowman & Littlefield, 2003, forthcoming).

D. Elstein, 'The politics of digital TV', www.openDemocracy.net/forum, 2002.

P. Evans and T. Wurster, *Blown to Bits* (Boston, Mass., Harvard Business School Press, 2000).

P. Flichy, 'New media history' in L. Lievrouw and S. Livingstone (eds), *The Handbook of New Media* (London, Sage, 2002).

J. Gillies and R.Cailliau, *How the Web Was Born* (Oxford, Oxford University Press, 2000).

G. Goggin, 'Pay per browse? The Web's commercial future' in D. Gauntlett (ed.), *Web Studies* (London, Arnold, 2000).

L. Gross, 'The gay global village in cyberspace' in N. Couldry and J. Curran (eds), *Contesting Media Power* (Boulder, Col., Rowman & Littlefield, 2003, forthcoming).

D. Held, A. McGrew, D. Goldblatt and J. Perraton, *Global Transformations* (Cambridge, Polity Press, 1999).

K. Hill and J. Hughes, *Cyberpolitics* (Lanham, Mass., Rowman & Littlefield, 1998).

M. Ito, 'Virtually embodied: the reality of fantasy in a multi-user dungeon' in D. Porter (ed.), *Internet Culture* (New York, Routledge, 1997).

N. Klein, *No Logo* (London, Flamingo, 2001).

C. Kramarae, 'The language and the nature of the Internet: the meaning of global', *New Media and Society*, 1, 1 (1999).

S. Lax, 'The Internet and democracy' in D. Gauntlet (ed.), *Web Studies* (London, Arnold, 2000).

T. Lennon, 'Digital TV: a phoenix risen from the ashes', *Free Press*, 129, 2002.

L. Lessig, *Code and Other Laws of Cyberspace* (New York, Basic Books, 1999).

—— *The Future of Ideas* (New York, Random House, 2001).

S. Levy, *Hackers* (London, Penguin, 1994).

M. Lim, 'The internet, social networks and reform in Indonesia' in N. Couldry and J. Curran (eds), *Contesting Media Power* (Boulder, Col., Rowman & Littlefield, 2003, forthcoming).

S. Ling, 'The alternative media in Malaysia: their potential and limitations' in N. Couldry and J. Curran (eds), *Contesting Media Power* (Boulder, Col., Rowman & Littlefield, 2003, forthcoming).

S. Livingstone and M. Bovill, *Young People: New Media* (London, London School of Economics and Political Science, 1999).

P. Lovelock and J. Ure, 'The new economy: internet, telecommunications and electronic commerce?' in L. Lievrouw and S. Livingstone (eds), *The Handbook of New Media* (London, Sage, 2002).

R. McChesney, *Rich Media, Poor Democracy* (Urbana, University of Illinois Press, 1999).

M. Mallapragada, 'The Indian diaspora in the USA and around the world' in D. Gauntlett (ed.), *Web Studies* (London, Arnold, 2000).

R. Mansell, 'New Media and the Power of Networks' (London, London School of Economics and Political Science, Inaugural Professorial Lecture, 2001).

D. Miller and D. Slater, *The Internet: An Ethnographic Approach* (Oxford, Berg, 2000).

V. Miller, 'Search engines, portals and global capitalism' in D. Gauntlett (ed.), *Web Studies* (London, Arnold, 2000).

G. Murdock and P. Golding, 'Digital possibilities, market realities: the contradictions of communications convergence' in L. Panitch and C. Leys (eds), *A World of Contradictions: Socialist Register 2002* (London, Merlin Press, 2001).

J. Naughton, *A Brief History of the Future* (London, Phoenix, 2000)

N. Negroponte, *Being Digital* (London, Hodder & Stoughton, 1996 [1995]).

K. Patelis, 'The political economy of the Internet' in J. Curran (ed.), *Media Organisations in Society* (London, Arnold, 2000).

M. Poster, 'Cyberdemocracy: Internet and the public sphere' in D. Porter (ed.), *Internet Culture* (New York, Routledge, 1997).

——*The Second Media Age* (Cambridge, Polity Press, 1995).

M. Price, *Media and Sovereignty* (Cambridge, MIT Press, 2002).

H. Rheingold, *The Virtual Community* (rev. edn) (Cambridge, MA, MIT Press, 2000).

D. Schiller, *Digital Capitalism* (Cambridge, MA, MIT Press, 2000).

D. Slater, 'Social relationships and identity online and offline' in L. Lievrouw and S. Livingstone (eds), *The Handbook of New Media* (London, Sage, 2002).

J. Slevin, *The Internet and Society* (Cambridge, Polity Press, 2000).

C. Sparks, 'From dead trees to live wires: the Internet's challenge to the traditional newspaper' in J. Curran and M. Gurevitch (eds), *Mass Media and Society* (3rd edn) (London, Arnold, 2000).

—— 'The internet and the global public sphere' in W. Lance Bennett and R. Entman (eds), *Mediated Politics* (New York, Cambridge University Press, 2001).

L. Stein and N. Sinha, 'New global media and communication policy: the role of the state in the twenty-first century' in L. Lievrouw and S. Livingstone (eds), *The Handbook of New Media* (London, Sage, 2001).

J. Stratton, 'Cyberspace and the globalisation of culture' in D. Porter (ed.), *Internet Culture* (New York, Routledge, 1997).

T. Streeter, 'Romanticism in business culture: the Internet, the 1990s, and the origins of irrational exuberance' in A. Calabrese and C. Sparks (eds), *Toward a Political Economy of Culture* (Boulder, Col., Rowman & Littlefield, 2003, forthcoming).

A. Willheim, *Democracy and the Digital Age* (New York, Routledge, 2000)

S. Williams, *Free as in Freedom* (Sebastopol, Calif., O'Reilly, 2002).

B. Winston, *Media Technology and Society* (London, Routledge, 1998).

Y. Zhao, 'Falun Gong, identity, the struggle over meaning in and out of reformed China' in N. Couldry and J. Curran (eds), *Contesting Media Power* (Boulder, Col., Rowman & Littlefield, 2003, forthcoming).

Index

Long, Gerald 70
Lonrho 82
Lord Haw Haw 130
Lynn, Vera 134
Lytton, Bulwer 19

MacDonald, Ramsay 118
McIntyre, Donald 83
MacIntyre, Ian 218
MacKenzie, Kelvin 73
Macleod, Joseph 143
McQuail, Denis 102, 203
Major, John 74, 222
Mallapragada, Madhavi 262
management 218–27, 371
Manchester Guardian 43
Marcuse, 324, 326, 327, 328
market forces 29, 86, 202, 342
market pluralism 400–1
market research 31, 45, 51, 88, 92,
    187–8, 329
marketing strategies 190
Martin, Kingsley 127
mass culture 26, 198, 324, 327–8
mass entertainment 173
mass media 325
Mass Observation 131, 139, 146
Matheson, Hilda 111, 117, 123, 150
Matthews, Victor 71
Maxwell, Robert 72
Mayhew, Christopher 161
media: audience relationships 333;
    consumption 248; control 406;
    corporations 250; crime 343;
    development 398–400; dominant
    class 339; empirical research 329;
    globalization 304, 309–10, 313–14;
    independence 340; influence 174–5;
    internet 287; law 408, 411; modern
    society 323; organizations 335–9;
    ownership 393; pluralism 287–8;
    policy 379–91; politics 392–412;
    proliferation 283–5; regulation 397–8;
    voting 333; websites 281
Microsoft 250, 301
Militant Tendency 406
Miller, Daniel 261
Milne, Alisdair 215
minority programmes 190, 191, 381
mobile phones 282, 283
Morrison, Herbert 112, 116, 117
Mosaic 254
Mosley, Sir Oswald 119

Moyne Report (1936) 381
Mrs Mopp 133–4
mugging 343
multi-national corporations 303
Murdoch, Rupert 67, 69–71, 74–5, 77,
    81, 99, 201, 209, 212, 307, 354, 355,
    394
music 286, 291, 342

narrowcasting 276
nation states 308, 309, 310, 312
national identity 308
national press 33, 101, 350
National Television Council 161
National Union of Journalists 98
National Union of the Working Classes
    11, 14
nationalism 311
nationalization 116
Negroponte, Nicholas 248
Neil, Andrew 70–1, 83
Nelson, Ted 240
neo-liberalism 393
neophiliacs 197
net advertising 250, 255
net marketing 267
net sociology 259, 262
Netscape 248, 254
network enterprise 269
New Labour 74, 75, 276, 355, 379, 389,
    390, 396
news 128, 139–40, 168, 316–17, 332,
    335–6, 342, 388
news groups 265
News International 212, 307
News on Sunday 100
News of the World 26, 70
newspapers: advertising 4, 6–7, 29–34;
    broadsheets 26, 93–7; circulations
    9–10, 33; competition 44, 317; ethics
    381; as information source 140, 347;
    liberal theory 346; ownership 39,
    76–7, 102; personal proprietorship
    69–73; policy 383; politics 35, 47–9;
    production 98, 286; running costs 27,
    45, 49, 80, 352; taxes 7–8; values 85,
    317
Newspapers Proprietors Association
    (NPA) 57
newsprint rationing 64
Nicolson, Harold 138, 143, 147, 156
Nolan Committee on Standards in
    Public Life (1994) 215